THE
HUMAN
RIGHTS
READER

Second Edition

THE
HUMAN
RIGHTS
READER

Second Edition

Major Political Essays,
Speeches, and Documents from
Ancient Times to the Present

EDITED BY

MICHELINE R. ISHAY

Routledge
Taylor & Francis Group
New York   London

This edition published in 2012 by Routledge
2 Park Square, Milton Park, Abingdon, Oxon OX14 4RN
711 Third Avenue, New York, NY 10017, USA

Routledge is an imprint of the Taylor & Francis Group, an informa business

International Standard Book Number-10: 0-415-95160-7 (Softcover) 0-415-95159-3 (Hardcover)
International Standard Book Number-13: 978-0-415-95160-9 (Softcover) 978-0-415-95159-3 (Hardcover)

Library of Congress Cataloging-in-Publication Data

The human rights reader : major political essays, speeches, and documents from ancient times to the present / edited by Micheline R. Ishay. -- 2nd ed.
   p. cm.
  ISBN-13: 978-0-415-95159-3
  ISBN-13: 978-0-415-95160-9
  1. Human rights--History--Sources. I. Ishay, Micheline.

JC571.H7699 2007
323.09--dc22   2006033032

Visit the Taylor & Francis Web site at
http://www.taylorandfrancis.com

and the Routledge Web site at
http://www.routledge.com

Printed and bound in the United States of America by Edwards Brothers Malloy on sustainably sourced paper.

Pour mon père, Edmond Ishay

BRIEF CONTENTS

DETAILED CONTENTS

PREFACE

Until the first edition of *The Human Rights Reader: Major Speeches, Essays, and Documents from the Bible to the Present* came out in 1997, there was no comprehensive canon on the history of human rights, and that publication represented my first effort to convey that history. I spent much of the next seven years researching and writing *The History of Human Rights: From Ancient Times to the Era of Globalization* (published by University of California Press in 2004). As I worked on that book, it became clear that the original reader needed to be revised and expanded.

The new *Human Rights Reader* draws its conceptual organization from my *History of Human Rights*. Like *The History*, each of the first five parts, which correspond to five historical phases in the history of human rights, is subdivided into three sections. The first presents the arguments on behalf of human rights (or human rights in the making) associated with the historical phase under consideration; the second conveys the corresponding debate over acceptable ways to promote those human rights; and the third shows the views of contributors from that period on the question of the inclusiveness of human rights. Finally, Part VI of the reader gathers major historical legal documents, organized to represent the major themes of the modern legal history of human rights.

As potential selections were divided into the five historical phases and the concluding set of legal documents, an important criterion for inclusion was their contribution to informing fundamental questions that retain contemporary relevance. These include: What are the origins of human rights? Why did Europeans so strongly influence the modern notion of human rights? Has socialism made a lasting contribution to the legacy of human rights? Is self-determination promoting or undermining a universal notion of human rights? Is globalization eroding or advancing human rights? Are human rights universal or culturally bound? Must human rights be sacrificed for the demands of national security?

To ensure a full representation of the controversies over such critical questions, the new *Human Rights Reader* was expanded substantially. The parts corresponding to the original reader contain additional selections (particularly Part I on the pre-Enlightenment era), and a new part, on the globalization era, has been added. To provide historical and theoretical context, each of the six parts is preceded by an editorial introduction and, in four of the parts, a selection was chosen to provide the reader with a general background on the history and themes represented in the readings that follow.

In addition, where the titles of selections were absent (or too far removed from the chosen excerpts to identify the content), I added titles that will help readers quickly find topics of particular interest. Titles without quotes and usually preceded by the word "on" are mine. Also, I changed all British spelling to American for the sake of consistency and the ease of the reader. Finally, I removed archaic or cumbersome references, while adding editorial notes where needed for clarification. Original references are annotated to help scholars (and other curious readers) to retrieve the unedited source.

Undoubtedly, one can always challenge the choice of one selection over another, and some readers will no doubt conclude that one set of ideas, or a region of the world, is favored. (Based on reactions to my first reader, however, there will be sharp differences over which viewpoints are favored.) The principal criteria guiding the selections of this new *Human Rights Reader*, beyond the manifest historical importance of some of the readings, were their value in illustrating the main clusters of rights that comprise the U.N. Universal Declaration of Human Rights (1948) and the illumination they provide to critical human rights debates. For readers who wish to deepen their knowledge, more complete depictions and analyses of each historical phase, and more material on the complexity of particular debates, can be found in my *History of Human Rights*, the scholarly companion of this book.

My own historical journey through the creation of *The New Human Rights Reader* benefited from many helpers, who were at times unfortunate victims of my drive to finish this project. I thank Steve Bronner for remaining an unconditional supporter over the years; Ginni Ishimatsu for her friendship and expertise on Asian religions and traditions; Steve Roach, Matt Dickhoff, Sasha Breger, and Rebecca Otis, and particularly Joel Pruce, for their industrious research help with the final proof. I owe a special thanks to David Michael Gillespie, for showing exemplary diligence, uncomplaining devotion, and enthusiasm throughout this project, and in general for being such a great research assistant.

At Taylor & Francis, I would like to express my gratitude for the excellent work of the project editor Gerry Jaffe, the copy editor Sheyanne Armstrong, and my very capable acquiring editors Robert Tempio and Michael Kerns.

My deepest thanks, and apologies for the time this project consumed, go to my shining stars, Adam and Elise, who feed me with joy and hope during the best of times and worst of times, and to their father, David Goldfischer, who lends to this and my other intellectual endeavors the power of his mind and the strength of his heart. Beyond this fountain of strength, I remain grateful to my loving mother, Rachele Bazini, and for the human rights courage of my father, Edmond Ishay. They showed me, through the determination and decency they carried with them as refugees and immigrants across three continents, the path that made all the difference. This book is dedicated to my father and to the generations of fighters for human rights that preceded and will follow him.

INTRODUCTION

HUMAN RIGHTS: HISTORICAL AND CONTEMPORARY CONTROVERSIES[1]

BY MICHELINE R. ISHAY

We stand today at the threshold of a great event both in the life of the United Nations and in the life of mankind, that is, the approval by the General Assembly of the Universal Declaration of Human Rights. This declaration may well become the international Magna Carta of all men everywhere. We hope its proclamation by the General Assembly will be an event comparable to the proclamation of the Declaration of the Rights of Man by the French people in 1789, the adoption of the Bill of Rights by the people of the United States, and the adoption of comparable declarations at different times in other countries.

Eleanor Roosevelt, 1948

The spirit of human rights has been transmitted consciously and unconsciously from one generation to another, carrying the scars of its tumultuous past. Today, invoking the United Nations (U.N.) Universal Declaration of Human Rights, adopted by the United Nations General Assembly in 1948, one may think of human rights as universal, inalienable, and indivisible, as rights shared equally by everyone regardless of sex, race, nationality, and economic background. Yet conflicting political traditions across centuries have elaborated different visions of human rights rooted in past social struggles.

Eleanor Roosevelt, however, was resolute in her efforts to overcome ideological and philosophical tensions among the eighteen delegates who composed the first U.N. human rights commission, over which she presided. Indefatigable, she mediated many disputes that ultimately led to the drafters' agreement on the central tenets of human rights. Comparing those rights to the portico of a temple, René Cassin, one of the most influential drafters, divided the twenty-seven articles of the Declaration among four pillars. The four pillars supported the roof of the portico (articles 28 to 30), which stipulated the conditions under which the rights of individuals could be realized within society and the state. The first two articles of the declaration are represented by the courtyard steps of the portico and stand for human dignity, shared by all individuals regardless of their religion, creed, ethnicity, or sex. The first pillar represents articles 3 to 11 and covers the rights of individuals, notably the right to life, liberty, and security. The second pillar, encompassing articles 12 to 17 of the Declaration, invokes civil and property rights; the third, delineated in articles 18 to 21, stands for political and social rights; and the fourth (articles 22 to 27) focuses on economic, social, and cultural rights.[2]

Drawing from the rallying cry of the French Revolution, Cassin identified these four pillars as "dignity, liberty, equality, and fraternity," corresponding to the successive generations of rights. It is worth noting that while these four clusters of rights do not correspond precisely to the historical chronology of emergent visions (or generations) of human rights, they serve as a useful historical reference for this reader. For instance, with some thematic adjustment consistent with history, one can associate the concept of dignity with monotheistic and nonmonotheistic religions; the preponderance of (civil) liberty arguments can be identified primarily with the Enlightenment legacy; the fight for greater economic and political equality with the socialist and labor movements of the industrial revolution; and fraternity with the notions of group and cultural rights identified with anti-imperialist movements in nineteenth-century Europe and within the twentieth-century colonized world.

Inspired by Cassin, what follows is a brief consideration of these five periods, each of which can be associated with critical controversies regarding human rights. These controversies are of more than merely historical interest; they underlie and animate contemporary political battles over human rights and help structure this reader. The first controversy concerns the debate over the origins of human rights (Part I). Did they emerge out of humanity's great religions and ancient secular traditions? Or did human rights arise from a fundamental challenge to the narrow worldviews embraced by those traditions? The second controversy is over the validity of the claim that our modern conception of rights, wherever in the world it may be voiced, is predominantly European in origin (Part II). The third controversy concerns the often-overlooked socialist contribution to human rights — a contribution obscured by Stalinism and Maoism (Part III). The fourth controversy, over the right to self-determination, originally invoked against imperialism, continues to provoke conflicts between opposed groups fighting for sovereignty over the same territories (Part IV). Finally, the fifth controversy considers whether globalization in its multifaceted economic and cultural forms is a boon or a threat from a human rights perspective (Part V). This part also considers whether the new security regime consolidated after September 11 is serving to promote or undermine human rights in our age of globalization.

PART I: THE CONTROVERSY OVER THE ORIGINS OF HUMAN RIGHTS

When embarking on a historical investigation of the origins of human rights, the first question one confronts is: Where does that history begin? It is a politically charged question, as difficult to answer as the one addressing the end of history. The question of the end of history has always implied the triumph of one particular worldview over another. Thus, Friederich Hegel's vision of history ending with the birth of the Prussian state celebrated the superiority of German liberal and cultural views of his time over other beliefs; Karl Marx's prediction that history would end with the withering away of the state and the birth of a classless society emerged from a deepening struggle against the abuses of early industrialization; and Francis Fukuyama's declaration of the end of history exemplified liberal euphoria in the immediate aftermath of the Soviet collapse.

Similarly, where one locates the beginning of a history tends to privilege a particular worldview; a history of human rights can be perceived as a way either to defend a specific status quo or value system against possible challengers, or to legitimize the claims of neglected agents of history. It is in this context that one can understand the fight between religious creationists and evolutionary Darwinists in American schools, and the clash between some defenders of the Western canon, on the one hand, and some advocates of African and Third World studies, on the other. Identifying the origins of human rights will inescapably invite a similar debate. For example, skeptics over the achievements of Western civilization are correct to point out that current notions of morality cannot be associated solely with European history.

Modern ethics is in fact indebted to a worldwide spectrum of both secular and religious traditions. Thus, the concept of proportionate punishment and justice was first professed by the Hammurabi Code of ancient Babylon. The Hebrew Bible celebrates the sanctity of life and reciprocal entitlements. The Hindu and Buddhist religions offered the earliest defense of the ecosystem. Confucianism promoted widespread education. The ancient Greeks and Romans endorsed natural laws and the capacity of every individual to reason. Christianity and Islam encouraged human solidarity, just as both considered the problem of moral conduct in wartime.

Yet the idea that religion is a source of our current human rights tradition remains contested by some scholars, who regard religious edicts and commandments as the very antithesis of rights. Often presented as injunctions against proscribed behaviors, many religious invocations of moral duties would correspond closely to later secular conceptions of rights. For example, the Biblical injunction "thou shall not kill" implies the right to secure one's life, just as "thou shall not steal" implies a right to property.

At the same time, while all religions and secular traditions prior to the Enlightenment may have shared basic views of a common good, no ancient religious or secular belief system regarded all individuals as equal. From Hammurabi's Code to the New Testament to the Koran, one can identify a common disdain toward indentured servants (or slaves), women, and homosexuals — as all were excluded from equal social benefits. While emphasizing a universal moral embrace, all great civilizations have thus tended to rationalize unequal entitlements for the weak or the "inferior." Yet, while such commonalities are noteworthy, they should not overshadow one of history's most consequential realities: it has been the influence of the West that has prevailed, including Western conceptions of universal rights.

PART II: THE CONTROVERSY OVER THE LIBERAL LEGACY AND THE ENLIGHTENMENT

If the civilizations and ethical contributions of China, India, and the Muslim world towered over those of medieval Europe, is it equally true that the legacy of the European Enlightenment supersedes other influences on our current understanding of human rights? The necessary conditions for the Enlightenment, which combined to bring an end to the Middle Ages of Europe, included the scientific revolution, the rise of mercantilism, the launching of maritime explorations of the globe, the consolidation of the nation-state, and the emergence of a middle class. These developments stimulated the expansion of Western power, even as they created propitious circumstances for the development of modern conceptions of human rights. They ultimately shattered feudalism and delegitimized appeals by kings to divine rights.

As Europe was plagued by religious wars pitting Catholics and Protestants in a struggle to redefine religious and political structures, human rights visionaries like Hugo Grotius, Samuel Pufendorf, Emmerich de Vattel, and René Descartes constructed a new secular language, affirming a common humanity that transcended religious sectarianism. Over the next two centuries, revolutionaries in England, America, and France would use a similar discourse to fight aristocratic privileges or colonial authority, and to reorganize their societies based on human rights principles. Armed with the scientific confidence of their era, they struggled for the right to life, for freedom of religion and opinion, and for property rights, and ultimately broke the grip of monarchical regimes.

Notwithstanding the incontestable debt of modern conceptions of human rights to the European Enlightenment, the positive legacy of that era remains widely contested. Many rightly argue that the Enlightenment did not fulfill its universal human rights promises. In the early nineteenth century, slavery continued in the European colonies and in America. Throughout the European-dominated world (with the brief exception of revolutionary France), women failed to achieve equal rights with men, propertyless men were denied the right to vote and other political rights, children's rights continued to be usurped, and the right to sexual preference was not even considered. Given those shortcomings, critics have argued that the Enlightenment legacy of human rights represented little more than an imperialist masquerade, designed to bend the rest of the world to its will under the pretense of universality.

While the development of capitalism in Europe contributed to the circumstances necessary for the development of a secular and universal language of human rights, the early European liberal agenda inadvertently taught that very language to its challengers. Thus, the international languages of power and resistance were simultaneously born in the cradle of the European Enlightenment. Not only did the Enlightenment thinkers invent the language of human rights discourse, but they launched arguments over the nature of human rights that continue to preoccupy us today.

Now as then, we find ourselves pondering the role of the state — as both the guardian of basic rights and the behemoth against which one's rights need to be defended. During the Enlightenment and still today, this dual allegiance to one's state and to universal human rights has contributed to the perpetuation of a double standard of moral behavior, in which various appeals to human rights obligations remain subordinated to the "the national interest." Just as the celebrated Declaration of the Rights of Man and the Citizen (1789) was followed by Napoleon's realpolitik during his reign over the European continental system, Fukuyama's end-of-history vision predicated on liberal rights has confronted post–September 11 claims that civil liberties must yield to the need for national security.

In addition, we are still embroiled in Enlightenment debates over whether a laissez-faire approach to economic activity is the best way to promote democratic institutions and global peace, as such early advocates as Immanuel Kant and Thomas Paine are echoed more than two centuries later by thinkers such as the political theorist Michael Doyle and the economist Milton Friedman. Further, we remained engaged in the Enlightenment argument over when and how one may justly wage war (see Hugo Grotius, Part II, Chapter 6). The current forms of these debates, one should add, are not merely a contemporary variant of the early liberal tradition, but have been modified and enriched by the socialist contribution.

PART III: THE CONTROVERSY OVER THE SOCIALIST CONTRIBUTION AND THE INDUSTRIAL AGE

The nineteenth-century industrial revolution and the growth of the labor movement opened the gates of freedom to previously marginalized individuals, who challenged the classical liberal economic conception of social justice. Yet, despite the important socialist contribution to the human rights discourse, the human rights legacy of the socialist — and especially the Marxist — tradition is today widely dismissed. Bearing in mind the atrocities that have been committed by communist regimes in the name of human rights, the historical record still needs to show that the struggle for universal suffrage, social justice, and worker's rights — principles endorsed in the Universal Declaration of Human Rights (articles 18 to 21) and by the two main 1966 International Covenants on Human Rights (see Part VI, Chapter 15) — was strongly influenced by socialist thought.

Indeed, the Chartists in England — early socialist precursors — and later the European labor parties, played a large role in the campaign for voting and social rights. Disenfranchised from the political process, propertyless workers realized that without a political voice, they would not be able to address the widening economic gap between themselves and the rising industrial capitalists. In other words, the historical struggle for universal suffrage was launched and largely waged by the socialist movement. As Marx put it in the *New York Daily Tribune* of 1850: "The carrying of universal suffrage in England … [is] a far more socialistic measure than anything which has been honored with that name on the Continent" (Karl Marx, on universal suffrage, Part III, Chapter 8).

While liberals retained their preoccupation with liberty, Chartists and socialists focused on the troubling possibility that economic inequity could make liberty a hollow concept — a belief that resonated powerfully with the bourgeoning class of urban workingmen and women. Highlighting this inconsistency, French socialist Louis Blanc declared (on the material basis of rights, Part III, Chapter 8):

> But the poor man, you say, has the *right* to better his position? So! And what difference does it make, if he has not the power to do so? What does the right to be cured matter to a sick man whom no one is curing? Right considered abstractly is the mirage that has kept the people in abused condition since 1789. … Let us say it then for once and for all: freedom consists, not only in the RIGHTS that have been accorded, but also in the power given men to develop and exercise their faculties, under the reign of justice and the safeguard of law.

In this sense, socialists became legitimate heirs of the Enlightenment, applying the universal promises of "liberté, égalité, fraternité" to the political realities of the nineteenth century.

From the nineteenth century onward, radical and reformist socialists alike called for redefining the liberal agenda, to include increased economic equity, the right to trade unions, child welfare, universal suffrage, the restriction of the workday, the right to education, and other social welfare rights. Most of these principles were encapsulated in the U.N. Covenant on Social, Cultural, and Economic Rights. By then, these key elements of the original socialist platform had long since been embraced as mainstream tenets of liberalism. So long as arguments are framed in terms of universal rights, liberals and socialists have thus shared a key premise, i.e., universalism, that could provide a basis for reasoned debate. In that sense, both visions of rights have often been allied in opposition to the recurrent challenge posed by adherents of cultural and national relativism.

PART IV: THE CONTROVERSY OVER THE RIGHT TO SELF-DETERMINATION AND THE IMPERIAL AGE

The liberal nationalist writings of Jonathan Gottlieb Fichte, Giuseppe Mazzini, John Stuart Mill, and Theodore Herzl, among other social thinkers of the nineteenth century, foreshadowed the twentieth century's quest to codify the right to self-determination. If generally invoked throughout nineteenth-century Europe against imperial domination or ethnic oppression, the right to a homeland would become a central issue of twentieth-century international affairs. Yet the intensifying assertion of self-determination as an inalienable human right, throughout the twentieth century, was imbued with contradictions from the outset.

At the time of the ratification of the Covenant of the League of Nations (1919), advocates, such as President Woodrow Wilson, failed to foresee that imperialist and fascist leaders would invoke the notion of national rights to justify their expansionist policies, contributing to the horrors of World War II. Few recognized, despite the warnings of Rosa Luxemburg, that such rights would be left far too vague in international legal documents. Indeed, Article 1 of the two main human rights covenants, adopted by the U.N. in 1966, stipulated that "all peoples have the right of self-determination. By virtue of that right they freely determine their political status and freely pursue their economic and cultural development."

Written in such sweeping terms, that legal codification of self-determination never specified which type of political regime a newly independent state would establish. It never addressed the possibility that legitimizing one group's national aspirations would be invoked at the expense of others and possibly create conflicts; it never resolved to what extent a prospective independent state was economically viable, and thereby at least potentially a truly sovereign state; and it never considered how an economically nonviable new state might be doomed to permanent economic dependency and neocolonial political subordination.

The search for appropriate standards for implementing self-determination rights started before World War I, as a nationalist tide swept Central and Eastern Europe, fragmenting the Ottoman and Austro-Hungarian Empires. With the ever more defiant ascendance of nationalism and the threat of war on the eve of World War I, puncturing the universalist hopes of the second Socialist International, socialists such as Rosa Luxemburg and Vladimir Lenin reflected on how to resolve the question of self-determination, addressing the need to establish standards for legitimizing this otherwise vacuous claim. With the anticolonial struggle spreading through Asia and Africa to overthrow European imperial domination in the mid-twentieth century, a new set of leaders and thinkers including Mahatma Gandhi, Sati' al-Husri, Kwame Nrkuma, and Frantz Fanon, emerged from the colonized world, building their claims on previous rationales and quests for self-determination. Because the right to self-determination can result in contending claims to the same disputed territory, the meaning of this right remains far from obvious and needs to be elaborated in light of historical and political precedents.

PART V: THE CONTROVERSY OVER GLOBALIZATION'S IMPACT ON HUMAN RIGHTS

There is clear evidence that globalization coincides with a widening gap between the rich and poor within and between societies, an association that has propelled anti-Western sentiments, nationalist backlashes, and war. At the same time, one can make the case that the plight of the poorest countries can be attributed not to globalization but to their exclusion from the global marketplace. More inclusive globalization — from this point of view — would not only reduce ethnic sectarianism, but also generate new opportunities for human rights movements.

However one judges its overall benefits and adverse effects, globalization has affected people in different ways, creating a plethora of ever more specific and conflicting human rights demands. For instance, if the fight for labor rights has been reenergized in recent years, organized labor continues to be divided internationally between workers from rich and poor countries, and domestically between the interests of those who are unionized and those who are not. Similarly, while the unprecedented ravaging of the global environment has prompted the emergence of a global ecological movement, that movement is animated by different social and economic priorities in the developed and the developing world. The abuses of a growing illegal immigrant labor force and the hardships suffered by refugees fleeing from poverty, repression, or war have led to calls for fairer immigration and refugee laws. At the same time, low-skilled immigrants to richer countries conflict with the interests of unemployed and low-wage workers in the developed world, pitting two needy communities against each other.

Undoubtedly, these conflicts over rights have intensified cultural and regional differences. Indeed, if globalization erodes national distinctions, creating a more integrated world, as internationalists from liberal or socialist persuasions have hoped (in different ways), efforts to protect national patrimonies against waves of immigrants, foreign imports, or the overall homogenization of the world into universal consumerism have revived the appeal of cultural rights. Whereas staunch internationalists fear a world of competing cultures, which would favor the triumph of the most belligerent fundamentalists at the expense of women and other disenfranchised groups, cultural rights proponents worry that tendentious "universal" moral perspectives of the most powerful players will prevail over the cultural values of subordinated nations.

That fight between internationalists and cultural relativists has intensified and has taken a tragic turn since September 11. In many resentful, economically or culturally aggrieved areas of the world, the Western maestros of globalization are seen as responsible for overlooking oppression and creeping poverty and must now face the inevitable "blowback." These sentiments in turn have unleashed Western fear of the Muslim world, strengthened demagogic assertions of American Western superiority, and made it politically viable to insist on adopting whatever means are necessary for security. Torn between their internationalist aspirations and the immediate dangers of the post–September 11 world, human rights advocates have been debating the extent to which security rights can override civil and other human rights, the legitimacy of humanitarian intervention to overthrow tyrants by force, and whether globalization represents desirable interdependence or a mask for empire.

The various schisms within the human rights community remind us why the main drafters of the Universal Declaration of Human Rights argued with such fervor for the indivisibility of human rights. By doing so, they were challenging assertions that security rights prevail over civil rights, as has been claimed in the "age of terror," or that development rights justify civil and political repression, as argued by some Asian political elites. In short, they were trying to reduce the prospect that specific rights could be opportunistically elaborated to advance the political agenda of this or that leader or this or that movement, thereby undermining an all-encompassing and universal perspective on human rights.

To help regain clarity of purpose amidst these divisions, this book invites its readers to acquaint themselves with the original sources of human rights discourse and the historical debates that have shaped our current understandings of human rights. The central themes developed in the Universal Declaration of Human Rights provide a useful path for navigating through the major historical speeches, polemical writings, and legal documents. Each of the first five parts of this reader corresponds to critical historical junctures in the development of human rights: The Origins, Secular, Asian, and Monotheistic Traditions; The Legacy of Liberalism and the Enlightenment; The Socialist Contribution and the Industrial Age; The Right to Self-Determination and the Imperial Age; and Human Rights in the Era of Globalization. Each of these parts is in turn divided into three sections. The first presents the human rights of the period under consideration, the second reviews debates over acceptable ways to promote human rights, and the third addresses views on the inclusiveness of human rights. Finally, Part VI of the reader gathers major historical legal documents, organized to represent the major themes of the modern legal history of human rights. This new *Human Rights Reader: Major Political Essays, Speeches, and Documents from the Bible to the Present* is also designed as a companion to my *History of Human Rights: From Ancient*

Times to the Era of Globalization (University of California Press, 2004). There one can encounter the historical context in which the contending visions of human rights — illuminated by this reader — have emerged.

ENDNOTES

1 This introduction is a broader and altered version of my previous article, "What Are Human Rights? Six Historical Controversies," *Journal of Human Rights,* Vol. 3, No. 3 (September 2004), 359–371.
2 For further elaboration, see Mary Ann Glendon, *A World Made New* (New York: Random House, 2001), 173–192.

PART I

The Origins: Secular, Asian, and Monotheistic Traditions

INTRODUCTION

With Jacques Maritain (1882–1973), Part I introduces readers to the preliminary work on human rights undertaken by the United Nations Educational, Scientific, and Cultural Organization (UNESCO) in 1947. To assist the Human Rights Commission drafting committee, UNESCO commissioned a questionnaire, designed by Maritain, to study the Chinese, Islamic, Hindu, American, and European peoples on human rights traditions and legal perspectives. Seventy responses came back from notable leaders and social thinkers, including the pacifist leader of the Indian independence movement, Mahatma Gandhi, Italian philosopher and historian Benedetto Croce, Indian Muslim poet and philosopher Hamayun Kabir, Indian social scientist S. V. Puntambekar, Chinese philosopher Chung-Shul Lo, and British historian and journalist E. H. Carr.

Maritain was a well-noted political thinker and well suited to manage this ambitious project. He had written extensively on religion and culture, the philosophy of science, epistemology, and political theory. His moral philosophy, inspired by Aristotelian and Thomist principles of justice, maintained that everyone could recognize that certain basic universal rights were like natural rights, fundamental and inalienable. The challenge he posed to various political leaders and social thinkers around the world was "to imagine an agreement of minds between men who come from the four corners of the globe and belong to different cultures and civilizations." The responses to the UNESCO questionnaires revealed a conception of universal ethics beyond the "narrow limits of the Western tradition and [that] its beginning in the West as well as in the East coincides with the beginning of Philosophy."

The selections in Part I begin with some of the findings gathered by Maritain from responses to the UNESCO survey, then build on those important observations by documenting the nature and scope of traditional sources of ethical thought. Drawn from critical themes developed in the Universal Declaration of Human Rights, these traditional contributions are divided into four chapters: "Liberty, Tolerance, and Codes of Justice," "Social and Economic Justice," "Just War and Peace," and "Justice for Whom?" Each chapter contains selections from the perspectives of secular, Asian, and monotheist traditions. Chapter 4 illuminates the extent to which those ethical traditions were universal in scope as well as the ways in which they favored some groups over others. To assist the reader, titles have been provided for most of the selections.

I.1 JACQUES MARITAIN: THE GROUNDS FOR AN INTERNATIONAL DECLARATION OF HUMAN RIGHTS (1947)

Of the tasks assigned to the United Nations Organization, one of those which could and should most nearly affect the conscience of the peoples, is the drawing up of an *International Declaration of Human Rights*. The task was committed to the Economic and Social Council of the United Nations. UNESCO's part was to consult philosophers and assemble their replies. This volume is a collection of the most significant texts thus gathered in the course of UNESCO's inquiry into the philosophic bases of human rights....

"How," I asked, "can we imagine an agreement of minds between men who are gathered together precisely in order to accomplish a common intellectual task, men who come from the four corners of the globe and who not only belong to different cultures and civilizations, but are of antagonistic spiritual associations and schools of thought ... ?" Because, the goal of UNESCO is a practical goal, agreement between minds can be reached spontaneously, not on the basis of common speculative ideas, but on common practical ideas, not on the affirmation of one and the same conception of the world, of man and of knowledge, but upon the affirmation of a single body of beliefs for guidance in action. No doubt, this is little enough, but it is the last resort to intellectual agreement. It is, nevertheless, enough to enable a great task to be undertaken, and it would do much to crystallize this body of common practical convictions.

The Grounds of an International Declaration of Human Rights[1]

An international declaration of human rights must be the expression of a faith to be maintained no less than a program of actions to be carried out. It is a foundation for convictions universally shared by men however great the differences of their circumstances and their manner of formulating human rights: it is an essential element in the constitutional structure of the United Nations. In order that all peoples and all governments shall be made aware that the authority and goodwill of the United Nations will be exercised with ever increasing power to apply these means for the advancement of human happiness in the great society, it is fitting that its members solemnly proclaim a declaration of rights to the civilized world. Such a declaration depends, however, not only on the authority by which rights are safeguarded and advanced, but also on the common understanding which makes the proclamation feasible and the faith practicable.

The preparation of a Declaration of Human Rights faces fundamental problems concerning principles and interpretations as well as political and diplomatic problems concerning agreement and drafting. For this reason the UNESCO Committee on the Philosophic Principles of the Rights of Man has undertaken, on the basis of a survey of the opinion of scholars in the various parts of the world, an examination of the intellectual bases of a modern bill of rights, in the hope that such a study may prove useful to the Commission on Human Rights of the Economic and Social Council both in suggesting common grounds for agreement and in explaining possible sources of differences. The UNESCO Committee is convinced that the members of the United Nations share common convictions on which human rights depend, but it is further convinced that those common convictions are stated in terms of different philosophic principles and on the background of divergent political and economic systems. An examination of the grounds of a bill of rights should therefore serve to reveal, on the one hand, the common principles on which the declaration rests and to anticipate, on the other hand, some of the difficulties and differences of interpretation which might otherwise delay or impede agreement concerning the fundamental rights which enter into the declaration.

The United Nations stands as the symbol to all of victory over those who sought to achieve tyranny through aggressive war. Since it was created to maintain the peace of mankind and, as it maintains peace, to make ever more full the lives of men and women everywhere, it is fitting that it should record its faith in freedom and democracy and its determination to safeguard their power to expand. That faith in freedom and democracy is founded on the faith in the inherent dignity of men and women. The United Nations cannot succeed in the great purposes to which it is committed unless it so acts that this dignity is given increasing recognition, and unless steps are taken to create the conditions under which this dignity may be achieved more fully and at constantly higher levels. Varied in cultures and built upon different institutions, the members of the United Nations have, nevertheless, certain great principles in common. They believe that men and women, all over the world, have the right to live a life that is free from the haunting fear of poverty and insecurity. They believe that they should have a more complete access to the heritage, in all its aspects and dimensions, of the civilization so painfully built by human effort. They believe that science and the arts should combine to serve alike peace and the well-being, spiritual as well as material, of all men and women without discrimination of any kind. They believe that, given goodwill between nations, the power is in their hands to advance the achievement of this well-being more swiftly than in any previous age.

It is this faith, in the opinion of the UNESCO Committee, which underlies the solemn obligation of the United Nations to declare, not only to all governments, but also to their peoples, the rights which have now become the vital ends of human effort everywhere. These rights must no longer be confined to a few. They are claims which all men and women may legitimately make, in their search, not only to fulfill themselves at their best, but to be so placed in life that they are capable, at their best, of becoming in the highest sense citizens of the various communities to which they belong and of the world community, and in those communities of seeking to respect the rights of others, just as they are resolute to protect their own.

Despite the antiquity and the broad acceptance of the conception of the rights of man,

and despite the long evolution of devices to protect some human rights by legal systems, the systematic proclamation of declarations of human rights is recent. The history of the philosophic discussion of human rights, of the dignity and brotherhood of man, and of his common citizenship in the great society is long: it extends beyond the narrow limits of the Western tradition and its beginnings in the West as well as in the East coincide with the beginnings of philosophy. The history of declarations of human rights, on the other hand, is short and its beginnings are to be found in the West in the British Bill of Rights and the American and French Declarations of Rights formulated in the seventeenth and eighteenth centuries, although the right of the people to revolt against political oppression was very early recognized and established in China. The relation of philosophic considerations to the declarations of human rights is suggested by the differences of these two histories. The philosophic temper of the times was an indispensable background and preparation for each statement of human rights, but despite the broad agreements among the resulting statements there was no more agreement among philosophers in the eighteenth than in the twentieth century. Moreover, despite the faith in human dignity and the formula for human happiness prepared by philosophers, an implementation was needed in social and political institutions to secure human rights for men. An international declaration of human rights is involved in precisely the same problems. The philosophies of our times, notwithstanding their divergencies, have deepened the faith in the dignity of man and have vastly expanded the formula for his happiness; but the differences of philosophies have led to varied and even opposed interpretations of fundamental rights and the practical import of philosophies has become more marked.

The civil and political rights which were formulated in the eighteenth century[2] have since that time been incorporated into the constitution or the laws of almost every nation in the world. During the same period, the developments of technology and industrial advances have led to the formation of a conception of economic and social rights.

The older civil and political rights have sometimes been extended to embrace these new rights. In such applications and other contexts of the newer rights, the meanings have frequently undergone modification, and indeed the two have sometimes been thought to be in conflict. Finally, as science and technology have given men greater control over nature, rights which were in the past reserved for the few have gradually been extended to the many and are now potentially open to all. This addition of new rights and the changes in the significance of old rights in the context of developing knowledge and technology presents problems as well as opportunities. Perhaps the greatest problem involved in the basic ideas which underlie a declaration of human rights is found in the conflict of ideas which have been used to relate the social responsibilities entailed in the material and social developments of the nineteenth century to the civil and political rights earlier enunciated. This conflict has even shaken the simple form of the faith in the dignity of man which was based on the confidence in progress and the advance of knowledge, for it is the source of complexities in the interpretation of liberty and equality and of their interrelations, as well as of apparent contradictions among the fundamental human rights. In like fashion, the problem of the implementation of human rights, new and old, depends on the tacit or explicit resolution of basic philosophic problems, for the rights involve assumptions concerning the relations not only of men to governments, but also of the relations of groups of men to the State and of States to one another, and in the complex of these interrelations the interdependence of rights and duties has been redefined.

Notwithstanding these difficulties, the UNESCO Committee on the Philosophic Principles of the Rights of Man is convinced that the perspectives open to men, both on the planes of history and of philosophy, are wider and richer than before. The deeper the re-examination of the bases of human rights that is made, the greater are the hopes that emerge as possible. The Committee has therefore circulated to a select list of the scholars of the world a series of questions concerning the changes of intellectual and historical circumstances between the classical declarations of human rights which stem from the eighteenth century and the bill of rights made possible by the state of ideas and the economic potentials of the present. On the basis of that inquiry, it has set down briefly, first, what seem to it some of the significant consequences of the evolution of human rights and, second, a schematic formulation of basic rights which in its opinion can and should be vindicated for all men. The history and the schematism grew out of the discussions of the Committee during its meetings in Paris from June 26th to July 2nd, but although they are based on a study of the replies received to the questionnaire, they do not represent the options of all the scholars who contributed to the symposium.

The fundamental human rights which were specified first and proclaimed widely at the beginnings of the modern period were rights which regulated man's relations to political and social groups and which are therefore usually referred to as *Civil and Political Rights*. They had as purpose to protect man in actions which do not derogate from the freedom or well-being of others and to assign to him the exercise of functions by which he might exert a proper influence on the institutions and laws of the State. As a result of religious movements and the development of national states, a series of freedoms were formulated more and more precisely and insistently from the Renaissance to the eighteenth century: to free man from unwarranted interference in his thought and expression, the freedom of conscience, worship, speech, assembly, association and the press. During the seventeenth century, each of these freedoms received eloquent defense on the grounds not only that they may be granted without danger to the peace of the State, but also that they may not be withheld without danger. Legal implementation for their protection was step by step provided by the institution of courts or the extension of the jurisdiction of existing courts, and these rights may, therefore, be associated with respect to the means of securing them, with other personal rights and with the right to justice, by which it was recognized that all men have an equal right to seek justice by appeal to law and in that appeal to be protected from summary arrest, cruel treatment and unjust punishment. As civil rights, moreover, they are closely related to the right to political action by which the function of citizens in States is defined, and the growth of democratic institutions during this period is largely an expression of the conviction men can achieve justice and the defense of their rights only by participation direct or indirect in the governments by which they are ruled. Political rights were therefore written into instruments and institutions of government, whereas civil rights, protected from interference by governments by recourse to courts, were written into bills of rights. The right to political action within a State discussed during this period, moreover, in close conjunction with the right to rebellion or revolution by which men might set up a government in conformity with justice if the fundamental principles of justice and the basic human rights are violated in such fashion as to permit no redress by recourse to peaceful means, and also in conjunction with the right to citizenship by which men may abandon their existing citizenships and assume the citizenship of any country which is prepared to accept them as citizens. Finally, during the nineteenth century, the discussion of the right to political action made increasingly clear that it is a right which can be exercised wisely only in conjunction with the right to information by which the citizen may equip himself for the proper exercise of his political functions.

During the nineteenth century there were added to these rights another set of fundamental human rights which grew out of the recognition that to live well and freely man must have at least the means requisite for living and which was made increasingly practicable by the advances in technology and industrialization in making the means of livelihood potentially accessible to all men. These have come to be called *Economic and Social Rights*. They were first treated as subdivisions or extensions of civil and political rights, but in the course of the last hundred years it has become apparent that they are different in kind from the older

rights and that they therefore require difference in implementation. In their earliest form they are associated with the right to property, which in the eighteenth century was conceived by many philosophers to be the basic human right from which the others are derived, in such a fashion that even liberty and the pursuit of happiness are often treated as property rights of man. The evolution of social and economic rights depended on the discussion of the relation of the ownership and the use of property, of private and common ownership, and of private rights and public responsibility. Similarly, the right to education was early conceived to belong to all men, and the institution of public systems of education was designed to effect the realization of that right. Likewise, the right to work was treated first as a freedom consequent on the right to property and was only later implemented with legal provisions for bargaining and arbitration concerning the conditions and the rewards of work. The right to protection of health usually started in the various States from modest beginnings in pure food and drugs legislation under the provisions of police power, and slowly extended to the provision of minimum medical and dietetic services, while the end of the nineteenth century and the beginning of the twentieth century saw the growth of various forms of social security designed to embody the right to maintenance during infancy, old age, sickness and other forms of incapacity, and involuntary unemployment. Finally, there are few to deny, in the retrospect of technological advances, today, the right of all to share in the advancing gains of civilization and to have full access to the enjoyment of cultural opportunities and material improvements.

Since the increased accessibility of economic and social rights was achieved as a consequence of the advances of science and since the ideals and accomplishments of an age find their expression in art and literature, a new emphasis has been placed on rights of the mind: on the right to inquiry, expression and communication. Whether the purpose of communication be the expression of an idea or an emotion, the furthering of an individual or social purpose, or the formulation of an objective and scientific truth, the right is grounded both in the purpose of developing to the full the potentialities of men and in the social consequences of such communications.

[1] Final result of the UNESCO inquiry on the theoretical bases of human rights, drafted by the committee of experts on the basis of the various contributions to the inquiry.

[2] Editor: It is often forgotten that universal suffrage without property franchise was advocated in the nineteenth century.

CHAPTER 1

Liberty, Tolerance, and Codes of Justice

As one considers early texts, it becomes very clear that the ideas of dignity, religious tolerance, fair ruling, legal transparency, and progressive punishment, among other liberties, did not emerge *tabula rasa* during the Enlightenment. Instead, these notions have deep roots in ancient religions and secular traditions. It is equally clear, however, that the Enlightenment represented an enormous advance in the development of human rights.

1.1 UNITED NATIONS UNIVERSAL DECLARATION OF HUMAN RIGHTS (1948): ARTICLES 1, 3, 5–12, 18–20, AND 27

Article 1

All human beings are born free and equal in dignity and rights. They are endowed with reason and conscience and should act toward one another in a spirit of brotherhood.

Article 3

Everyone has the right to life, liberty and the security of person.

Article 5

No one shall be subjected to torture or to cruel, inhuman or degrading treatment or punishment.

Article 6

Everyone has the right to recognition everywhere as a person before the law.

Article 7

All are equal before the law and are entitled without any discrimination to equal protection of the law. All are entitled to equal protection against any discrimination in violation of this Declaration and against any incitement to such discrimination.

Article 8

Everyone has the right to an effective remedy by the competent national tribunals for acts violating the fundamental rights granted him by the constitution or by law.

Article 9

No one shall be subjected to arbitrary arrest, detention or exile.

Article 10

Everyone is entitled to full equality to a fair and public hearing by an independent and impartial tribunal, in the determination of his rights and obligations and of any criminal charge against him.

Article 11

1. Everyone charged with a penal offense has the right to be presumed innocent until proved guilty according to law in a public trial at which he has had all the guarantees necessary for his defense.

2. No one shall be held guilty of any penal offense on account of any act or omission which did not constitute a penal offense, under national or international law, at the time when it was committed. Nor shall a heavier penalty be imposed than the one that was applicable at the time the penal offense was committed.

Article 12

No one shall be subjected to arbitrary interference with his privacy, family, home or correspondence, nor to attacks upon his honor and reputation. Everyone has the right to the protection of the law against such interference or attacks.

Article 18

Everyone has the right to freedom of thought, conscience and religion; this right includes freedom to change his religion or belief, and freedom, either alone or in community with others and in public or private, to manifest his religion or belief in teaching, practice, worship and observance.

Article 19

Everyone has the right to freedom of opinion and expression; this right includes freedom to hold opinions without interference and to seek, receive and impart information and ideas through any media and regardless of frontiers.

Article 20

1.   Everyone has the right to freedom of peaceful assembly and association.

2.   No one may be compelled to belong to an association.

Article 27

1.   Everyone has the right freely to participate in the cultural life of the community, to enjoy the arts and to share in scientific advancement and its benefits.

2.   Everyone has the right to the protection of the moral and material interests resulting from any scientific, literary or artistic production of which he is the author.

THE SECULAR TRADITION

From Babylon to the Greeks to the Roman Empire, one cannot overlook the influential contributions of Hammurabi, Plato, Aristotle, Cicero, and Epictetus when considering the early origins of human rights. The 282 laws drafted by Hammurabi, king of Babylonia (1728–1686 B.C.E.) marked the inception of the conviction that some laws are so basic as to be beyond the reach of even the king to alter them. This concept of the law as a check against the abuse of power is a feature of most modern legal systems. The Hammurabi Code (1700 B.C.E.) focused on various liberties and the overall integrity and transparency of the judiciary system. Yet the most important contribution was illustrated by the Talion principle, "eye for an eye, tooth for a tooth," or the idea that the nature of the punishment would be determined by the security of the offense (see Section 1.2).

Later, in ancient Greece, the search for justice would be associated with the philosopher Plato (427/428–348/347 B.C.E.). Plato's *Republic* (c. 360 B.C.E.) rests on the foundation of eternal ideas of Truth or Forms that represent universals or absolutes. For Socrates, as reported by Plato, absolute justice can be achieved only when individuals fulfill the tasks to which each is suited, in harmony with the common good. Going about one's own business cannot create harmonious cooperation and mutual care, which are fundamental to the sound functioning of a just polity. Rousseau's notion of the "General Will," and contemporary defenders of group rights, would later echo Socrates' teaching. (See Section 1.3 On Justice in the State and the Individual.)

Like Plato, Aristotle (384–322 B.C.E.) had a profound impact on the development of the notion of justice and human rights. Aristotle's *Politics* (c. 350 B.C.E.) shows how the concepts of justice, virtue, and rights change in accordance with different kinds of constitutions and circumstances. Evaluating the strengths and weaknesses of various democracies, oligarchies, and tyrannies, Aristotle concluded that mixed constitutions — backed by a strong middle class — represent the fairest and most stable forms of governance. In other words, he maintained that virtue and justice blossom better between extremes. Aristotle sought to discuss the condition of a perfect state within the bounds of possibility, so long as "virtue has external goods enough for the performance of good actions." (See Section 1.4 On Justice and Political Constitutions.)

In a similar tradition, Roman statesman, lawyer, and scholar Marcus Tullius Cicero (106–43 B.C.E.) was also a believer in the common good and republican principles. Indeed, his *De Legibus* (*The Laws*, 52 B.C.E.) laid out the foundations of natural law, a concept closely related to modern conceptions of human rights. The gods, he argued, entrusted individuals with the capacity to reason, to derive subsistence from nature, and to unite peacefully with other fellow citizens. Despite distinctions of race, religion, and opinion, individuals are bound together in unity through an understanding that "the principle of right living is what makes men better." The notion that everything is just by virtue of customs or the laws of a nation is a foolish idea. "Would that be true," asked Cicero, "even if these laws had been enacted by tyrants?" Cicero appealed to universal laws that transcended unfair customs, and to the idea that one should be "a citizen of the whole universe, as it were of a single city."

Following in the footsteps of Cicero, the Greek Stoic philosopher Epictectus of Hierapolis (135–55 B.C.E.) advanced the idea of "universal brotherhood." Though he later became a freeman, his *Discourses* (compiled by his student Arian after his death) were shaped by his original status as a slave. Epictectus challenged the common conception of freedom: If neither kings, nor one's friends, nor slaves are truly free, then who is really free? The answer is one who is not enslaved by one's body, one's desires, one's passions and emotions, but who through reason can control his appetites and at the same time does not fear death. Diogenes and Socrates are Epictectus' stoic heroes, for they were driven not by their passions, but by a detached love for the common good, the gods, and their "real country": the universe (see Section 1.6).

1.2 HAMMURABI CODE: ON FREEDOM OF SPEECH AND CIVIL RIGHTS (C. 1700 B.C.E.)

Freedom of Speech and Its Limitations

§ 1

If a man has accused a man and has charged him with man-slaughter and has not substantiated his charge, his accuser shall be put to death.

§ 2

If a man has charged a man with sorcery and then has not proved [it against] him, he who is charged with the sorcery shall go to the holy river; he shall leap into the holy river and, if the holy river overwhelms him, his accuser shall take and keep his house; if the holy river and he come back safe, he who has charged him with sorcery shall be put to death; he who leapt into the holy river shall take and keep the house of his accuser.

§ 127

If a man has caused a finger to be pointed at a high-priestess or a married lady and does not substantiate his slanderous comments, they shall flog that man before the judges and shave half his head.

If a man has come forward in a case to bear witness to a felony and then has not proved the statement that he has made; if that case is a capital one, that man shall be put to death.

If he has come forward to bear witness to [a claim for] corn or money, he shall remain liable for the penalty for that suit.

Civil Rights and Codes of Justice

§ 5

If a judge has tried a suit, caused a sealed tablet to be executed, [and having made a judgment] thereafter varies his judgment, they shall convict that judge of varying [his] judgment and he shall pay twelve-fold the claim in that suit; then they shall remove him from his place on the bench of judges in the assembly, and he shall not [again] sit in judgment with the judges.

Limitations on Punishment

Talion Law: "An Eye for an Eye"

§ 195

If a son strikes his father, they shall cut off his fore-hand.

§§ 196–205

If a man has put out the eye of a free man, they shall put out his eye.

If he breaks the bone of a [free] man, they shall break his bone.

If he puts out the eye of a servant or breaks the bone of a servant he shall pay 1 maneh of silver.

If he puts out the eye of a [free] man's slave or breaks the bone of a [free] man's slave, he shall pay half his price.

If a man knocks out the tooth of a [free] man equal [in rank] to him [self], they shall knock out his tooth.

If he knocks out the tooth of a servant he shall pay 1/3 maneh of silver.

If a man strikes the cheek of a [free] man who is superior [in rank], he shall be beaten with 60 stripes with a whip of ox-hide in the assembly.

If the man strikes the cheek of a free man equal to him [self in rank], he shall pay 1 maneh of silver.

If a servant strikes the cheek of a servant, he shall pay 10 shekels of silver.

If the slave of a [free] man strikes the cheek of a free man, they shall cut off his ear.

§§ 206–208

If a man strikes a [free] man in an affray and inflicts a wound on him, that man may swear "Surely I did not strike [him] wittingly," and he shall pay the surgeon.

If he dies of the striking, he may swear likewise; if [the victim is] a [free] man, he shall pay ½ maneh of silver.

If [he is] a [servant], he shall pay 1/3 maneh of silver.

§ 215

If a surgeon has made a deep incision in [the body of] a [free] man with a lancet of bronze and saves the man's life or has opened the caruncle(?) in [the eye of] a man with a lancet of bronze and saves his eye, he shall take 10 shekels of silver.

1.3   PLATO: JUSTICE IN STATE AND INDIVIDUAL (*THE REPUBLIC*, 360 B.C.E.)

Book 4

... "At any rate, wisdom, discipline, courage, and the ability to mind one's own business are all comparable in this respect; and we can regard justice as making a contribution to the goodness of our city comparable with that of the rest." ...

"Suppose a builder and a shoemaker tried to exchange jobs, each taking on the tools and the prestige of the other's trade, or suppose alternatively the same man tried to do both jobs, would this and other exchanges of the kind do great harm to the state?"

"Not much."

"But if someone who belongs by nature to the class of artisans and business men is puffed up by wealth or popular support or physical strength or any similar quality, and tries to do an Auxiliary's job; or if an Auxiliary who is not up to it tries to take on the functions and decisions of a Ruler and exchanges tools and prestige with him; or if a single individual tries to do all these jobs at the same time — well, I think you'll agree that this sort of mutual interchange and interference spells destruction to our state."

"Certainly."

"Interference by the three classes with each other's jobs, and interchange of jobs between them, therefore, does the greatest harm to our state, and we are entirely justified in calling it the worst of evils."

"Absolutely justified."

"But will you not agree that the worst of evils for a state is injustice?"

"Of course."

"Then that gives us a definition of injustice. And conversely, when each of our three classes (businessmen, Auxiliaries, and Guardians) does its own job and minds its own business, that, by contrast, is justice and makes our city just."

"I entirely agree with what you say," he said.

"Don't let's be too emphatic about it yet," I replied. "If we find that the same definition of justice applies to the individual, we can finally agree to it — there will be nothing to prevent us; if not, we shall have to think again. For the moment let us finish our investigation." ...

"In fact the provision that the man naturally fitted to be a shoemaker, or carpenter, or anything else, should stick to his own trade has turned out to be a kind of image of justice — hence its usefulness."

"Justice, therefore, we may say, is a principle of this kind; but its real concern is not with external actions, but with a man's inward self. The just man will not allow the three elements which make up his inward self to trespass on each other's functions or interfere with each other, but, by keeping all there in tune, like the notes of a scale (high, middle, and low, or whatever they be), will in the truest sense set his house in order, and be his own lord and master and at peace with himself. When he has bound these elements into a single controlled and orderly whole, and so unified himself, he will be ready for action of any kind, whether personal, financial, political or commercial; and whenever he calls any course of action just and fair, he will mean that it contributes to and helps to maintain this disposition of mind, and will call the knowledge which controls such action wisdom. Similarly, by injustice he will mean any action destructive of this disposition, and by ignorance the ideas which control such action."

"That is all absolutely true, Socrates."

"Good," I said, "so we shan't be very far wrong if we claim to have discerned what the just man and the just state are, and in what their justice consists."

"Certainly not."

"Shall we make the claim, then?"

"Yes."

"So much for that," I said. "And next, I suppose, we ought to consider injustice."

"Obviously."

"It must be some kind of internal quarrel between these same three elements, when they interfere with each other and trespass on each other's functions, or when one of them sets itself up to control the whole when it has no business to do so, because its natural role is one of subordination to the control of its superior. This sort of situation, when the elements of the mind are in confusion, is what produces injustice, indiscipline, cowardice, ignorance and vice of all kinds."

"Yes, that's so."

"And if we know what injustice and justice are, it's clear enough, isn't it, what is meant by acting unjustly and doing wrong or, again, by acting justly?"

"How do you mean?"

"Well," I said, "there is an analogy here with physical health and sickness."

"How?"

"Healthy activities produce health, and unhealthy activities produce sickness."

"True."

"Well, then, don't just actions produce justice, and unjust actions injustice?"

"They must."

"And as health is produced by establishing a natural order of control and subordination among the constituents of the body, disease by the opposite process, so justice is by establishing in the mind a similar order of control and subordination among its constituents, and injustice by opposite process."

"Certainly."

"It seems, then, that virtue is a kind of mental health or beauty or fitness, and vice a kind of illness or deformity or weakness."

"That is so."

"And virtue and vice are in turn the result of one's practice, good or bad."

"They must be." ...

"We are sticking obstinately to the verbal debating point that different natures should not be given the same occupations; but we haven't considered what we mean by natures being the same or different, and what our intention was when we laid down the principle that different natures should have different jobs, similar natures similar jobs."

"No, we've not taken that into consideration."

"Yet we might just as well, on this principle, ask ourselves whether bald men and longhaired men are not naturally opposite types, and having agreed that they are, allow bald men to be cobblers and forbid long-haired men to be, or vice versa."

"That would be absurd."

"But the reason why it is absurd," I pointed out, "is simply that we were not assuming that natures are the same or different in an unqualified sense, but only with reference to their suitability for the same or different kinds of employment."

1.4 ARISTOTLE: ON JUSTICE AND POLITICAL CONSTITUTIONS (*THE POLITICS*, C. 350 B.C.E.)

Book IV, Chapter II

We have now to inquire what is the best constitution for most states, and the best life for most men, neither assuming a standard of virtue which is above ordinary persons, nor an education which is exceptionally favored by nature and circumstances, nor yet an ideal state which is an aspiration only, but having regard to the life in which the majority are able to share, and to the form of government which states in general can attain. As to those aristocracies, as they are called, of which we were just now speaking, they either lie beyond the possibilities of the greater number of states, or they approximate to the so-called constitutional government, and therefore need no separate discussion. And in fact the conclusion at which we arrive respecting all these forms rests upon the same grounds. For if what was said in the *Ethics*[1] is true, that the happy life is the life according to virtue lived without impediment, and that virtue is a mean, then the life which is in a mean, and in a mean attainable by every one, must be the best. And the same principles of virtue and vice are characteristic of cities and of constitutions; for the constitution is in a figure the life of the city.

Now in all states there are three elements: one class is very rich, another very poor, and a third in a mean. It is admitted that moderation and the mean are best, and therefore it will clearly be best to possess the gifts of fortune in moderation; for in that condition of life men are most ready to follow ratio-

nal principle. But he who greatly excels in beauty, strength, birth, or wealth, or on the other hand who is very poor, or very weak, or very much disgraced, finds it difficult to follow rational principle. Of these two the one sort grows into violent and great criminals, the others into rogues and petty rascals. And two sorts of offenses correspond to them, the one committed from violence, the other from roguery. Again, the middle class is least likely to shrink from rule, or to be over-ambitious for it; both of which are injuries to the state. Again, those who have too much of the goods of fortune, strength, wealth, friends, and the like, are neither willing nor able to submit to authority. The evil begins at home; for when they are boys, by reason of the luxury in which they are brought up, they never learn, even at school, the habit of obedience. On the other hand, the very poor, who are in the opposite extreme, are too degraded. So that the one class cannot obey, and can only rule despotically; the other knows not how to command and must be ruled like slaves. Thus arises a city, not of freemen, but of masters and slaves, the one despising, the other envying; and nothing can be more fatal to friendship and good fellowship in states than this: for good fellowship springs from friendship; when men are at enmity with one another, they would rather not even share the same path. But a city ought to be composed, as far as possible, of equals and similars; and these are generally the middle classes. Wherefore the city which is composed of middle-class citizens is necessarily best constituted in respect of the elements of which we say the fabric of the state naturally consists. And this is the class of citizens which is most secure in a state, for they do not, like the poor, covet their neighbors' goods; nor do others covet theirs, as the poor covet the goods of the rich; and as they neither plot against others, nor are themselves plotted against, they pass through life safely. Wisely then did Phocylides pray, "Many things are best in the mean; I desire to be of a middle condition in my city."

Then it is manifest that the best political community is formed by citizens of the middle class, and that those states are likely to be well-administered, in which the middle class is large, and stronger if possible than both the other classes, or at any rate than either singly; for the addition of the middle class turns the scale, and prevents either of the extremes from being dominant. Great then is the good fortune of a state in which the citizens have a moderate and sufficient property; for where some possess much, and the others nothing, there may arise an extreme democracy, of a pure oligarchy; or a tyranny may grow out of either extreme — either out of the most rampant democracy, or out of an oligarchy; but it is not so likely to arise out of the middle constitutions and those akin to them. I will explain the reason of this hereafter, when I speak of the revolutions of states. The mean condition of state is clearly best, for no other is free from faction; and where the middle class is large, there are least likely to be factions and dissensions. For a similar reason large states are less liable to faction than small ones, because in them the middle class is large; whereas in small states it is easy to divide all the citizens into two classes who are either rich or poor, and to leave nothing in the middle. And democracies are safer and more permanent than oligarchies, because they have a middle class which is more numerous and has a greater share in the government for when there is no middle class, and the poor greatly exceed in number, troubles arise, and the state soon comes to an end. A proof of the superiority of the middle class is that the best legislators have been of a middle condition; for example, Solon, as his own verses testify; and Lycurgus, for he was not a king; and Charondas, and almost all legislators.

These considerations will help us to understand why most governments are either democratical or oligarchical. The reason is that the middle class is seldom numerous in them, and whichever party, whether the rich or the common people, transgresses the mean and predominates, draws the constitution its own way, and thus arises either oligarchy or democracy. There is another reason — the poor and the rich quarrel with one another, and whichever side gets the better, instead of establishing a just or popular government, regards political supremacy as the prize of victory, and the one party sets up a democracy and the other an oligarchy. Further, both the parties which had the supremacy in Hellas looked only to the interest of their own form of government, and established in states, the one, democracies, and the other, oligarchies; they thought of their own advantage, of the public not at all. For these reasons the middle form of government has rarely, if ever, existed, and among a very few only. One man alone of all who ever ruled in Hellas was induced to give this middle constitution to states. But it has now become a habit among the citizens of states, not even to care about equality; all men are seeking for dominion, or, if conquered, are willing to submit.

What then is the best form of government, and what makes it the best, is evident; and of other constitutions, since we say that there are many kinds of democracy and many of oligarchy, it is not difficult to see which has the first and which the second or any other place in the order of excellence, now that we have determined which is the best. For that which is nearest to the best must of necessity be better, and that which is furthest from it worse, if we are judging absolutely and not relatively to given conditions: I say "relatively to given conditions," since a particular government may be preferable, but another form may be better for some people.

Book VII, Chapter I

He who would duly inquire about the best form of a state ought first to determine which is the most eligible life; while this remains uncertain the best form of the state must also be uncertain; for, in the natural order of things, those may be expected to lead the best life who are governed in the best manner of which their circumstances admit. We ought therefore to ascertain, first of all, which is the most generally eligible life, and then whether the same life is or is not best for the state and for individuals.

Assuming that enough has been already said in discussions outside the school concerning the best life, we will now only repeat what is contained in them. Certainly no one will dispute the propriety of that partition of goods which separates them into three classes, viz. external goods, goods of the body, and goods of the soul, or deny that the happy man must have all three. For no one would maintain that he is happy who has not in him a particle of courage or temperance or justice or prudence, who is afraid of every insect which flutters past him, and will commit any crime, however great, in order to gratify his lust of meat or drink, who will sacrifice his dearest friend for the sake of half-a-farthing, and is as feeble and false in mind as a child or a madman. These propositions are almost universally acknowledged as soon as they are uttered, but men differ about the degree or relative superiority of this or that good. Some think that a very moderate amount of virtue is enough, but set no limit to their desires of wealth, property, power, reputation, and the like. To whom we reply by an appeal to facts, which easily prove that mankind do not acquire or preserve virtue by the help of external goods, but external goods by the help of virtue, and that happiness, whether consisting in pleasure or virtue, or both, is more often found with those who are most highly cultivated in their mind and in their character, and have only a moderate share of external goods, than among those who possess external goods to a useless extent but are deficient in higher qualities; and this is not only matter of experience, but, if reflected upon, will easily appear to be in accordance with reason. For, whereas external goods have a limit, like any other instrument, and all things useful are of such a nature that where there is too much of them they must either do harm, or at any rate be of no use, to their possessors, every good of the soul, the greater it is, is also of greater use, if the epithet useful as well as noble is appropriate to such subjects. No proof is required to show that the best state of one thing in relation to another corresponds in degree of excellence to the interval between the natures of which we say that these very states are states: so that, if the soul is more noble than our possessions or our bodies, both absolutely and in relation to us, it must be admitted that the best state of either has a similar ratio to the other. Again, it is for the sake of the soul

that goods external and goods of the body are eligible at all, and all wise men ought to choose them for the sake of the soul, and not the soul for the sake of them.

Let us acknowledge then that each one has just so much of happiness as he has of virtue and wisdom, and of virtuous and wise action. God is a witness to us of this truth, for he is happy and blessed, not by reason of any external good, but in himself and by reason of his own nature. And herein of necessity lies the difference between good fortune and happiness; for external goods come of themselves, and chance is the author of them, but no one is just or temperate by or through chance. In like manner, and by a similar train of argument, the happy state may be shown to be that which is best and which acts rightly; and rightly it cannot act without doing right actions, and neither individual nor state can do right actions without virtue and wisdom. Thus the courage, justice, and wisdom of a state have the same form and nature as the qualities which give the individual who possesses them the name of just, wise, or temperate.

Thus much may suffice by way of preface: for I could not avoid touching upon these questions, neither could I go through all the arguments affecting them; these are the business of another science.

Let us assume then that the best life, both for individuals and states, is the life of virtue, when virtue has external goods enough for the performance of good actions. If there are any who controvert our assertion, we will in this treatise pass them over, and consider their objections hereafter....

Now the soul of man is divided into two parts, one of which has a rational principle in itself, and the other, not having a rational principle in itself, is able to obey such a principle. And we call a man in any way good because he has the virtues of these two parts. In which of them the end is more likely to be found is no matter of doubt to those who adopt our division; for in the world both of nature and of art the inferior always exists for the sake of the better or superior, and the better or superior is that which has a rational principle. This principle, too, in our ordinary way of speaking, is divided into two kinds, for there is a practical and a speculative principle. This part, then, must evidently be similarly divided. And there must be a corresponding division of actions; the actions of the naturally better part are to be preferred by those who have it in their power to attain to two out of the three or to all, for that is always to every one the most eligible which is the highest attainable by him. The whole of life is further divided into two parts, business and leisure, war and peace, and of actions some aim at what is necessary and useful, and some at what is honorable. And the preference given to one or the other class of actions must necessarily be like the preference given to one or other part of the soul and its actions over the other; there must be war for the sake of peace, business for the sake of leisure, things useful necessary for the sake of things honorable. All these points the statesman should keep in view when he frames his laws; he should consider the parts of the soul and their functions, and above all the better and the end; he should also remember the diversities of human lives and actions. For men must be able to engage in business and go to war, but leisure and peace are better; they must do what is necessary and indeed what is useful, but what is honorable is better. On such principles children and persons of every age which requires education should be trained.

[1] *Nic. Eth.* i 1098ᵃ 16, *vii* 1153ᵇ 10, *x* 1177ᵃ 12.

1.5 CICERO (*THE LAWS*, 52 B.C.E.)

Book I

... In our present investigation we intend to cover the whole range of universal Justice and Law in such a way that our own civil law, as it is called, will be confined to a small and narrow corner....

Law is the highest reason, implanted in Nature, which commands what ought to be done and forbids the opposite. This reason, when firmly fixed and fully developed in the human mind, is Law. And so they believe that Law is intelligence, whose natural function it is to command right conduct and forbid wrongdoing....

... Animal which we call man, endowed with foresight and quick intelligence, complex, keen, possessing memory, full of reason and prudence, has been given a certain distinguished status by the supreme God who created him; for he is the only one among so many different kinds and varieties of living beings who has a share in reason and thought, while all the rest are deprived of it. But what is more divine, I will not say in man only, but in all heaven and earth, than reason? And reason, when it is full grown and perfected, is rightly called wisdom. Therefore, since there is nothing better than reason, and since it exists both in man and God, the first common possession of man and God is reason. But those who have reason in common must also have right reason in common. And since right reason is Law, we must believe that men have Law also in common with the gods. Further, those who share Law must also share Justice; and those who share these are to be regarded as members of the same commonwealth. If indeed they obey the same authorities and powers, this is true in a far greater degree; but as a matter of fact they do obey this celestial system, the divine mind, and the God of transcendent power. Hence we must now conceive of this whole universe as one commonwealth of which both gods and men are members.

And just as in States distinctions in legal status are made on account of the blood relationships of families, according to a system which I shall take up in its proper place, so in the universe the same thing holds true, but on a scale much vaster and more splendid, so that men are grouped with Gods on the basis of blood relationship and descent....

Therefore among all the varieties of living beings, there is no creature except man which has any knowledge of God, and among men themselves there is no race either so highly civilized or so savage as not to know that it must believe in a god, even if it does not know in what sort of god it ought to believe. Thus it is clear that man recognizes God because, in a way, he remembers and recognizes the source from which he sprang.

Moreover, virtue exists in man and God alike, but in no other creature besides; virtue, however, is nothing else than Nature perfected and developed to its highest point; therefore there is a likeness between man and God. As this is true, what relationship could be closer or clearer than this one? For this reason, Nature has lavishly yielded such a wealth of things adapted to man's convenience and use that what she produces seems intended as a gift to us, and not brought forth by chance; and this is true, not only of what the fertile earth bountifully bestows in the form of grain and fruit, but also of the animals; for it is clear that some of them have been created to be man's slaves, some to supply him with their products, and others to serve as his food. Moreover innumerable arts have been discovered through the teachings of Nature; for it is by a skillful imitation of her that reason has acquired the necessities of life....

But out of all the material of the philosophers' discussions, surely there comes nothing more valuable than the full realization that we are born for Justice, and that right is based, not upon men's opinions, but upon Nature. This fact will immediately be plain if you once get a clear conception of man's fellowship and union with his fellowmen. For no single thing is so like another, so exactly its counterpart, as all of us are to one another. Nay, if bad habits and false beliefs did not twist the weaker minds and turn them in whatever direction they are inclined, no one would be so like his own self as all men would be like all others. And so, however we may define man, a single definition will apply to all. This is a sufficient proof that there is no difference in kind between man and man; for if there were, one definition could not be applicable to all men; and indeed reason, which alone raises us above the level of the beasts and enables us to draw inferences, to prove and disprove, to discuss and solve problems, and to come to conclusions, is certainly common to us all, and, though varying in what it learns, at least in the capacity to learn it is invariable. For the same things are invariably perceived by the senses, and those things which stimulate the senses, stimulate them in the same way in all men; and those rudimentary troubles, joys, desires, and fears haunt the minds of all men without distinction, and even if different men have different beliefs, that does not prove, for example, that it is not the same quality of superstition that besets those races which worship dogs and cats as gods, as that which torments other races. But what nation does not love courtesy, kindliness, gratitude, and remembrance of favors bestowed? What people does not hate and despise the haughty, the wicked, the cruel, and the ungrateful? Inasmuch as these considerations prove to us that the whole human race is bound together in unity, it follows, finally, that knowledge of the principles of right living is what makes men better....

Socrates was right when he cursed, as he often did, the man who first separated utility from justice; for this separation, he complained, is the source of all mischief....

Those of us who are not influenced by virtue itself to be good men, but by some consideration of utility and profit, are merely shrewd, not good. For to what lengths will that man go in the dark who fears nothing but a witness and a judge? What will he do if, in some desolate spot, he meets a helpless man, unattended, whom he can rob of a fortune? Our virtuous man, who is just and good by nature, will talk with such a person, help him, and guide him on his way; but the other, who does nothing for another's sake, and measures every act by the standard of his own advantage — it is clear enough, I think, what he will do!...

But the most foolish notion of all is the belief that everything is just which is found in the customs or laws of nations. Would that be true, even if these laws had been enacted by tyrants? If the well-known Thirty had desired to enact a set of laws at Athens, or if the Athenians without exception were delighted by the tyrants' laws, that would not entitle such laws to be regarded as just, would it? No more, in my opinion, should that law be considered just which a Roman interrex[1] proposed, to the effect that a dictator might put to death with impunity any citizen he wished, even without a trial.

For Justice is one; it binds all human society, and is based on one Law, which is right reason applied to command and prohibition. Whoever knows not this Law, whether it has been recorded in writing anywhere or not, is without Justice.

But if Justice is conformity to written laws and national customs, and if, as the same persons claim, everything is to be tested by the standard of utility, then anyone who thinks it will be profitable to him will, if he is able, disregard and violate the laws. It follows that Justice does not exist at all, if it does not exist in Nature, and if that form of it which is sidered the foundation of Justice, that will mean the destruction of which human society depends. For these virtues originate in our natural inclination to love our fellow-men, and this is the foundation of Justice. Otherwise not merely consideration for men but also rites and pious observances in honor of the gods are done away with; for I think that these ought to be maintained, not through fear, but on account of the close relationship which exists between man and God. But if the principles of Justice were founded on the decrees of peoples, the edicts of princes, or decisions of judges, then Justice would sanction robbery and adultery and forgery of wills, in case these acts were approved by the votes or decrees of the populace. But if so great a power belongs to the decisions and decrees of fools that the laws of Nature can be changed by their votes, then why do they not ordain that what is bad and baneful shall be changed by their votes, then why do they not ordain that what is bad and baneful shall be considered good and salutary? Or, if a law can make Justice out of Injustice, can it not also make good out of bad? But in fact we can perceive the difference between good laws and bad by referring them to no other standard than Nature; indeed, it is not merely Justice and Injustice which are distinguished by Nature, but also and without exception things which are honorable and dishonorable. For since an intelligence common to us all makes things known to us and formulates them in our minds, honorable actions are ascribed by us to virtue, and dishonorable actions to vice; and only a madman would conclude

that these judgments are matters of opinion, and not fixed by Nature. For even what we, by a misuse of the term, call the virtue of a tree or of a horse, is not a matter of opinion, but is based on Nature. And if that is true, honorable and dishonorable actions must also be distinguished by Nature. For if virtue in general is to be tested by opinion, then its several parts must also be so tested; who, therefore, would judge a man of prudence and, if I may say so, hard common sense, not by his own character but by some external circumstance? For virtue is reason completely developed; and this certainly is natural; therefore everything honorable is likewise natural. For just as truth and falsehood, the logical and illogical, are judged by themselves, and not by anything else, so the steadfast and continuous use of reason in the conduct of life, which is virtue, and also inconstancy, which is vice [are judged] by their own nature.

[Or, when a farmer judges the quality of a tree by Nature,] shall we not use the same standard in regard to the characters of young men? Then shall we judge character by Nature, and judge virtue and vice, which result from character, by some other standard? But if we adopt the same standard for them, must we not refer the honorable and the base to Nature also? Whatever good thing is praiseworthy must have within itself something which deserves praise, for goodness itself is good by reason not of opinion but of Nature. For, if this were not true, men would also be happy by reason of opinion; and what statement could be more absurd than that? Wherefore since both good and evil are judged by Nature and are natural principles, surely honorable and base actions must also be distinguished in a similar way and referred to the standard of Nature. But we are confused by the variety of men's beliefs and by their disagreements, and because this same variation is not found in the senses, we think that Nature has made these accurate, and say that those things about which different people have different opinions and the same people not always identical opinions are unreal. However, this is far from being the case. For our senses are not perverted by parent, nurse, teacher, poet, or the stage, nor led astray by popular feeling; but against our minds all sorts of plots are constantly being laid, either by those whom I have just mentioned, who, taking possession of them while still tender and unformed, color and bend them as they wish, or else by that enemy which lurks deep within us, entwined in our every sense — that counterfeit of good, which is, however, the mother of all evils — pleasure. Corrupted by her allurements, we fail to discern clearly what things are by Nature good, because the same seductiveness and itching does not attend them....

In addition, if it be true that virtue is sought for the sake of other benefits and not for its own sake, there will be only one virtue, which will most properly be called a vice. For in proportion as anyone makes his own advantage absolutely the sole standard of all his actions, to that extent he is absolutely not a good man; therefore those who measure virtue by the reward it brings believe in the existence of no virtue except vice. For where shall we find a kindly man, if no one does a kindness for the sake of anyone else than himself? Who can be considered grateful, if even those who repay favors have no real consideration for those to whom they repay them? What becomes of that sacred thing, friendship, if even the friend himself is not loved for his own sake, "with the whole heart," as people say? Why, according to this theory, a friend should even be deserted and cast aside as soon as there is no longer hope of benefit and profit from his friendship! But what could be more inhuman than that? If, on the other hand, friendship is to be sought for its own sake, then the society of our fellow-men, fairness, and Justice, are also to be sought for their own sake. If this is not the case then there is no such thing as Justice at all for the very height of injustice is to seek pay for Justice. But what shall we say of sobriety, moderation, and self-restraint; of modesty, self-respect, and chastity? Is it for fear of disgrace that we should not be wanton, or for fear of the laws and the courts? In that case men are innocent and modest in order to be well spoken of, and they blush in order to gain a good reputation! I am ashamed even to mention chastity!...

For when the mind, having attained to a knowledge and perception of the virtues, has abandoned its subservience to the body and its indulgence of it, has put down pleasure as if it were a taint of dishonor, has escaped from all fear of death or pain, has entered into a partnership of love with its own, recognizing as its own all who are joined to it by Nature; when it has taken up the worship of the gods and pure religion, has sharpened the vision both of the eye and of the mind so that they can choose the good and reject the opposite — a virtue which is called prudence because it foresees — then what greater degree of happiness can be described or imagined? And further, when it has examined the heavens, the earth, the seas, the nature of the universe, and understands whence all these things came and whither they must return, when and how they are destined to perish, what part of them is mortal and transient and what is divine and eternal; and when it almost lays hold of the ruler and governor of the universe, and when it realizes that it is not shut in by [narrow] walls as a resident or some fixed spot, but is a citizen of the whole universe, as it were or a single city — then in the midst of this universal grandeur, and with such a view and comprehension of nature, ye immortal gods, how well it will know itself], according to the precept of the Pythian Apollo! How it will scorn and despise and count as naught those things which the crowd calls splendid! And in defense of all this, it will erect battlements of dialectic, of the science of distinguishing the true from the false, and of the art, so to speak, of understanding the consequences and opposites of every statement. And when it realizes that it is born to take part in the life of a State, it will think that it must employ not merely the customary subtle method of debate, but also the more copious continuous style, considering, for example, how to rule nations, establish laws, punish the wicked, protect the good, honor those who excel, publish to fellow-citizens precepts conducive to their well-being and credit, so designed as to win their acceptance; how to arouse them to honorable actions, recall them from wrongdoing, console the afflicted, and hand down to everlasting memory the deeds and counsels of brave and wise men, and the infamy of the wicked. So many and so great are the powers which are perceived to exist in man by those who desire to know themselves: and their parent and their nurse is wisdom....

[1] This evidently refers to a law proposed by L. Valerius Flaccus in 82 B.C. with reference to Sulla's dictatorship. Cf. Cicero, *De Lege Agraria* III, 4; Act II in *Verrem* III, 82.

1.6 EPICTECTUS, "OF FREEDOM" ("THE DISCOURSES OF FREEDOM," 135 B.C.E.)

Book I, Chapter 7

He is free who lives as he likes; who is not subject to compulsion, to restraint, or to violence; whose pursuits are unhindered, his desires successful, his aversions unincurred. Who, then, would wish to live in error? "No one." Who would live deceived, erring, unjust, dissolute, discontented, dejected? "No one." No wicked man, then, lives as he likes; therefore no such man is free. And who would live in sorrow, fear, envy, pity, with disappointed desires and doing that which he would avoid? "No one." Do we then find any of the wicked exempt from these evils? "Not one." Consequently, then, they are not free....

Consider what is our idea of freedom in animals. Some keep tame lions, and feed them and even lead them about; and who will say that any such lion is free? Nay, does he not live the more slavishly the more he lives at ease? And who that had sense and reason would wish to be one of those lions? Again, how much will caged birds suffer in trying to escape? Nay, some of them starve themselves rather than undergo such a life; others are saved only with difficulty and in a pining condition; and the moment they find any opening, out they go. Such a desire have they for their natural freedom, and to be at their own disposal, and unrestrained. And what harm can this confinement do you? "What say you? I was born to fly where I please, to live in the open air, to sing when I please. You deprive me of all this, and then ask what harm I suffer?"

Hence we will allow those only to be free who will not endure captivity, but, so soon as they are taken, die and so escape. Thus Diogenes somewhere says that the only way to freedom is to die with ease. And he writes to the Persian king, "You can no more enslave the Athenians than you can enslave the fish." "How? Can I not get possession of them?" "If you do," said he, "they will leave you, and be gone like fish. For catch a fish, and it dies. And if the Athenians, too, die as soon as you have caught them, of what use are your warlike preparations?" This is the voice of a free man who had examined the matter in earnest, and, as it might be expected, found it all out....

Since, then, neither they who are called kings nor the friends of kings live as they like, who, then, after all, is free? Seek, and you will find; for you are furnished by nature with means for discovering the truth. But if you are not able by these alone to find the consequence, hear them who have sought it. What do they say? Do you think freedom a good? "The greatest." Can anyone, then, who attains the greatest good be unhappy or unsuccessful in his affairs? "No." As many, therefore, as you see unhappy, lamenting, unprosperous — confidently pronounce them not free. "I do." Henceforth, then, we have done with buying and selling, and such like stated conditions of becoming slaves. For if these propositions hold, then, whether the unhappy man be a great or a little king — of consular or bi-consular dignity — he is not free. "Agreed."

Further, then, answer me this: do you think freedom to be something great and noble and valuable? "How should I not?" Is it possible, then, that he who acquires anything so great and valuable and noble should be of an abject spirit? "It is not." Whenever, then, you see anyone subject to another, and flattering him contrary to his own opinion, confidently say that he too is not free; and not only when he does this for a supper, but even if it be for a government, nay, a consulship. Call those indeed little slaves who act thus for the sake of little things; and call the others, as they deserve, great slaves. "Be this, too, agreed." Well, do you think freedom to be something independent and self-determined? "How can it be otherwise?" When, therefore, it is in the power of another to restrain or to compel, say confidently that this man is not free. And do not pay any attention to his grandfathers or great-grandfathers, or inquire whether he has been bought or sold; but if you hear him say from his heart and with emotion, "my master," though twelve lictors should march before him,[1] call him a slave. And if you should hear him say, "Wretch that I am! What I must suffer!" call him a slave. In short, if you see him wailing, complaining, unprosperous, call him a slave, even in purple....

What is it, then, that makes a man free and independent? For neither riches, nor consulship, nor the command of provinces nor of kingdoms, can make him so; but something else must be found. What is it that keeps anyone from being hindered and restrained in penmanship, for instance? "The science of penmanship." In music? "The science of music." Therefore in life too, it must be the science of living. As you have heard it in general, then, consider it likewise in particulars. Is it possible for him to be unrestrained who desires any of those things that are within the power of others? "No." Can he avoid being hindered? "No." Therefore neither can he be free. Consider, then, whether we have nothing or everything in our own sole power — or whether some things are in our own power and some in that of others. "What do you mean?" When you would have your body perfect, is it in your own power, or is it not? "It is not." When you would be healthy? "It is not." When you would be handsome? "It is not." When you would live or die? "It is not." Body then is not our own; but is subject to everything that proves stronger than itself. "Agreed." Well, is it in your own power to have an estate when you please, and such a one as you please? "No." Slaves? "No." Clothes? "No." A house? "No." Horses? "Indeed, none of these." Well, if you desire ever so earnestly to have your children live, or your wife, or your brother, or your friends, is it in your own power? "No, it is not."

Will you then say that there is nothing independent, which is in your own power alone, and unalienable? See if you have anything of this sort. "I do not know." But consider it thus: can anyone make you assent to a falsehood? "No one." In the matter of assent then, you are unrestrained and unhindered. "Agreed." Well, and can anyone compel you to exert your aims towards what you do not like? "He can; for when he threatens me with death, or fetters, he thus compels me." If, then, you were to despise dying or being fettered, would you any longer regard him? "No." Is despising death, then, an action in our power, or is it not? "It is." Is it therefore in your power also to exert your aims towards anything, or is it not? "Agreed that it is. But in whose power is my avoiding anything?" This, too, is in your own. "What then if, when I am exerting myself to walk, anyone should restrain me?" What part of you can he restrain? Can he restrain your assent? "No, but my body.".…

And when you are thus prepared and trained to distinguish what belongs to others from your own; what is liable to restraint from what is not; to esteem the one your own property, but not the other; to keep your desire, to keep your aversion, carefully regulated by this point — whom have you any longer to fear? "No one." For about what should you be afraid — about what is your own, in which consists the essence of good and evil? And who has any power over this? Who can take it away? Who can hinder you, any more than God can be hindered? But are you afraid for body, for possessions, for what belongs to others, for what is nothing to you? And what have you been studying all this while, but to distinguish between your own and that which is not your own; what is in your power and what is not in your power; what is liable to restraint and what is not? And for what purpose have you applied to the philosophers — that you might nevertheless be disappointed and unfortunate? No doubt you will be exempt from fear and perturbation! And what is grief to you? For whatsoever we anticipate with fear, we endure with grief. And for what will you any longer passionately wish? For you have acquired a temperate and steady desire of things dependent on will, since they are accessible and desirable; and you have no desire of things uncontrollable by will so as to leave room for that irrational, and impetuous, and precipitate passion.

Since then you are thus affected with regard to things, what man can any longer be formidable to you? What has man that he can be formidable to man, either in appearance, or speech, or mutual intercourse? No more than horse to horse, or dog to dog, or bee to bee. But things are formidable to everyone, and whenever any person can either give these to another, or take them away, he becomes formidable too. "How, then, is this citadel to be destroyed?" Not by sword or fire, but by principle. For if we should demolish the visible citadel, shall we have demolished also that of some fever, of some fair woman — in short, the citadel [of temptation] within ourselves; and have turned out the tyrants to whom we are subject upon all occasions and every day, sometimes the same tyrants, sometimes others? But here is where we must begin; hence demolish the citadel, and turn out the tyrants — give up body, members, riches, power, fame, magistracies, honors, children, brothers, friends; esteem all these as belonging to others. And if the tyrants be turned but, why should I also demolish the external citadel, at least on my own account? For what harm does it do *me* from its standing? Why should I turn out the guards? For in what point do they affect me? It is against others that they direct their fasces, their staves, and their swords. Have I ever been restrained from what I willed, or compelled against my will? Indeed, how is this possible? I have placed my pursuits under the direction of God. Is it his will that I should have a fever? It is my will too. Is it his will that I should pursue anything? It is my will too. Is it his will that I should desire? It is my will too. Is it his will that I should obtain anything? It is mine too. Is it not his will? It is not mine. Is it his will that I should be tortured? Then it is my will to be tortured. Is it his will that I should die? Then it is my will to die....

A person who reasons thus, understands and considers that if he joins himself to God, he shall go safely through his journey.

"How do you mean, join himself?" That whatever is the will of God may be his will too; that whatever is not the will of God may not be his. "How, then, can this be done?" Why, how otherwise than by considering the workings of God's power and his administration? What has he given me to be my own, and independent? What has he reserved to himself? He has given me whatever depends on will. The things within my power he has made incapable of hindrance or restraint. But how could he make a body of clay incapable of hindrance? Therefore he has subjected possessions, furniture, house, children, wife, to the revolutions of the universe. Why, then do I fight against God? Why do I will to retain that which depends not on will; that which is not granted absolutely, but how — in such a manner and for such a time as was thought proper? But he who gave takes away. Why, then, do I resist? Besides being a fool, in contending with a stronger than myself, I shall be unjust, which is a more important consideration. For from where did I get these things when I came into the world? My father gave them to me. And who gave them him? And who made the sun; who the fruits; who the seasons; who their connection and relations with each other?

And after you have received all, and even your very self, from God, are you angry with the giver, and do you complain, if he takes anything away from you? Who are you; and for what purpose did you come? Was it not he who brought you here? Was it not he who showed you the light? Has not he given you companions? Has not he given you senses? Has not he given you reason? And as whom did he bring you here — was it not as a mortal? Was it not as one to live with a little portion of flesh upon earth, and to see his administration; to behold the spectacle with him, and partake of the festival for a short time? After having beheld the spectacle and the solemnity, then, as long as it is permitted you, will you not depart when he leads you out, adoring and thankful for what you have heard and seen? "No; but I would enjoy the feast still longer." So would the initiated in the mysteries, too, be longer in their initiation; so, perhaps, would the spectators at Olympia see more athletes. But the solemnity is over. Go away. Depart like a grateful and modest person; make room for others. Others, too, must be born as you were; and when they are born must have a place, and habitations, and necessaries. But if the first do not give way, what room is there left? Why are you insatiable, never satisfied? Why do you crowd the world?...

The man who is unrestrained, who has all things in his power as he wills, is free; but he who may be restrained or compelled or hindered, or thrown into any condition against his will, is a slave. "And who is unrestrained?" He who desires none of those things that belong to others. "And what are those things which belong to others?" Those which are not in our power, either to have or not to have; or to have them thus or so. Body, therefore, belongs to another; its parts to another; property to another. If, then, you attach yourself to any of these as your own, you will be punished as he deserves who desires what belongs to others. This is the way that leads to freedom, this the only deliverance from slavery, to be able at length to say, from the bottom of one's soul,

Conduct me, Zeus, and thou, O Destiny,
Wherever your item, have fixed my lot.

Diogenes was free. "How so?" Not because he was of free parents, for he was not; but because he was so in himself; because he had cast away all which gives a handle to slavery; nor was there any way of getting at him, nor anywhere to lay hold on him, to enslave him. Everything sat loose upon him; everything was merely tied on. If you laid hold on his possessions, he would rather let them go than follow you for them; if on his leg, he let go his leg; if his body, he let go his body; acquaintance, friends, country, just the same. For he knew the source from which he had received them, and from whom, and upon what conditions he received them. But he would never have forsaken his true parents, the gods, and his real country [the universe]; nor have suffered anyone to be more dutiful and obedient to them than he; nor would anyone have died more readily for his country than he.

He never had to inquire whether he should act for the good of the whole universe; for he remembered that everything that exists has its source in its administration, and is commanded by its ruler.

Accordingly, see what he himself says and writes. "Upon this account," said he, "O Diogenes, it is in your power to converse as you will with the Persian monarch and with Archidamus, king of the Lacedemonians." Was it because he was born of free parents? Or was it because they were descended from slaves, that all the Athenians, and all the Lacedemonians, and Corinthians, could not converse with them as they pleased; but feared and paid court to them? Why then is it in your power, Diogenes? "Because I do not esteem this poor body as my own. Because I want nothing. Because this and nothing else is a law to me." These were the things that enabled him to be free.

And that you may not think I am showing you the example of a man dear of incumbrances, without a wife or children or country or friends or relations, to bend and draw him aside, take Socrates, and consider him, who had a wife and children, but held them not as his own; had a country, friends, relations, but held them only so long as it was proper, and in the manner that was proper; submitting all these to the law and to the obedience due to it. Hence, when it was proper to fight, he was the first to go out, and exposed himself to danger without the least reserve. But when he was sent by the thirty tyrants to apprehend Leon, because he esteemed it a base action, he did not even deliberate about it; though he knew that, perhaps, he might die for it. But what did that signify to him? For it was something else that he wanted to preserve, not his mere flesh; but his fidelity, his honor, free from attack or subjection. And afterwards, when he was to make a defense for his life, does he behave like one having children, or a wife? No, but like a man alone in the world. And how does he behave, when required to drink the poison? When he might escape, and Crito would have him escape from prison for the sake of his children, what did he say? Does he think it a fortunate opportunity? How should he? But he considers what is becoming, and neither sees nor regards anything else. "For I am not desirous," he says, "to preserve this pitiful body; but that part which is improved and preserved by justice, and impaired and destroyed by injustice." Socrates is not to be basely preserved. He who refused to vote for what the Athenians commanded; he who despised the thirty tyrants; he who held such discourses on virtue and mortal beauty — such a man is not to be preserved by a base action, but is preserved by dying, instead of running away. For a good actor is saved when he stops when he should stop, rather than acting beyond his time....

[1]Socrates, with four other persons, was commanded by the Thirty Tyrants of Athens to fetch Leon, a leader of the opposition, from the isle of Salamis, in order to be put to death. His companions executed their commission, but Socrates remained at home and chose rather to expose his life to the fury of the tyrants than be accessory to the death of an innocent person. He would most probably have become a sacrifice to their vengeance if the oligarchy had not shortly after been dissolved.

ASIAN RELIGIONS AND TRADITIONS

Epictectus' notion of a fearless attachment to liberty and detached love for the universe reminds us of the wisdom found in many Buddhist and Asian texts. Skeptics regarding claims of an Asian contribution to human rights will find pause for reflection in the writings of Confucius, Kautilya, Asoka, and various Buddhist texts.

Confucius (551–479 B.C.E.) was one of the most influential thinkers and social philosophers of China, whose teachings have deeply influenced East Asia across the centuries. His *Analects* is a short collection of discussions with his disciples over a period of thirty to forty years, sometime during the Warring States period (479–221 B.C.E.), and compiled after his death. There, Confucius considered how a virtuous ruler should be chosen based on his own merits, including his moral conduct and devotion to his people. A ruler, Confucius taught, should exhort his people to extol his example, showing respect, tolerance, trustworthiness, quickness, and generosity toward others (see Section 1.7).

Inspired by a similar vision, the Indian political thinker, economist, and king maker during the Mauryan Empire, Kautilya (also known as Chanakaya, c. 350–275 B.C.E.), wrote *The Arthashastra* (c. 300 B.C.E.). This classic almanac explored how statecraft and strategy could be wedded to the moral teachings of the important Indian scriptures, the Vedas. A precursor to Machiavelli's *The Prince*, Kautilya's *Arthashastra* argued for a benevolent autocratic king with obligations to rule his subjects fairly, to manage a transparent judiciary and penal system, and to regulate an efficient and solid economy (see Section 1.8).

Kautilya's legacy undoubtedly influenced Asoka, the ruler of the Mauryan Empire of India. The early part of Asoka's reign was filled with bloody battles. Yet after his conquest of Kalinga, along the east coast of India, where 100,000 people were reportedly killed and thousands of men and women deported, Asoka renounced violence and converted to Buddhism. From that point onward, he based his kingdom on the dharma principles of nonviolence, tolerance for all religious sects and different opinions, obedience to parents, magnanimity toward friends, humane treatment of servants, and generosity toward all (see Section 1.9).

After the death of the historical Buddha, Siddhartha Gautama, Buddhism spread beyond northern India. It arrived in China during the first century from Central Asia by way of the Silk Road, the main trade route linking China to India and the Middle East. Drawn from a cosmological love for all living and nonliving beings, there are certain moral codes shared by all Buddhists, such as a strict renunciation of killing, stealing, lying, ingesting intoxicants, and partaking in harmful sex. Consistent with these moral codes, Chinese verses from the Mahaparinirvana Sutra (early fourth century) suggest that to have access to the Buddha Aksobhya's Pure Land (a paradisiacal realm in which devotees may be reborn after death) requires selfless performance of good deeds, along with a commitment not to injure living beings, to slander, to steal, or to ravish other men's wives, and so forth (see Section 1.10).

1.7 CONFUCIUS: "ON RIGHTFUL CONDUCT OF RULERS AND SUBJECTS" (*THE ANALECTS*, 479–221 B.C.E.)

Book I

2. Yu Tzu said, "It is rare for a man whose character is such that he is good as a son and obedient as a young man to have the inclination to transgress against his superiors; it is unheard of for one who has no such inclination to be inclined to start a rebellion. The gentleman devotes his efforts to the roots, for once the roots are established, the Way will grow therefrom. Being good as a son and obedient as a young man is, perhaps, the root of a man's character."

5. The Master said, "In guiding a state of a thousand chariots, approach your duties with reverence and be trustworthy in what you say; avoid excesses in expenditure and love your fellow men; employ the labor of the common people only in the right seasons."

6. The Master said, "A young man should be a good son at home and an obedient young man abroad, sparing of speech but trustworthy in what he says, and should love the multitude at large but cultivate the friendship of his fellow men. If he has any energy to spare from such action, let him devote it to making himself cultivated."

8. The Master said, "A gentleman who lacks gravity does not inspire awe. A gentleman who studies is unlikely to be inflexible.

   "Make it your guiding principle to do your best for others and to be trustworthy in what you say. Do not accept as friend anyone who is not as good as you.

   "When you make a mistake, do not be afraid of mending your ways."

12. Yu Tzu said, "Of the things brought about by the rites, harmony is the most valuable. Of the ways of the Former Kings, this is the most beautiful, and is followed alike in matters great and small, yet this will not always work: to aim always at harmony without regulating it by the rites simply because one knows only about harmony will not, in fact, work."

14. The Master said, "The gentleman seeks neither a full belly nor a comfortable home. He is quick in action but cautious in speech. He goes to men possessed of the Way to be put right. Such a man can be described as eager to learn."

Book IV

1. The Master said, "Of neighborhoods benevolence is the most beautiful. How can the man be considered wise who, when he has the choice, does not settle in benevolence?"

2. The Master said, "One who is not benevolent cannot remain long in straitened circumstances, nor can he remain long in easy circumstances.

   "The benevolent man is attracted to benevolence because he feels at home in it. The wise man is attracted to benevolence because he finds it to his advantage."

4. The Master said, "If a man sets his heart on benevolence, he will be free from evil."

6. The Master said, "I have never met a man who finds benevolence attractive or a man who finds unbenevolence repulsive. A man who finds benevolence attractive cannot be surpassed. A man who finds unbenevolence repulsive can, perhaps, be counted as benevolent, for he would not allow what is not benevolent to contaminate his person.

   "Is there a man who, for the space of a single day, is able to devote all his strength to benevolence? I have not come across such a man whose strength proves insufficient for the task. There must be such cases of insufficient strength, only I have not come across them."

7. The Master said, "In his errors a man is true to type. Observe the errors and you will know the man."

8. The Master said, "He has not lived in vain who dies the day he is told about the Way."

BOOK XII

5. Ssu-ma Niu appeared worried, saying, "All men have brothers. I alone have none." Tzu-hsia said, "I have heard it said: life and death are a matter of Destiny; wealth and honor depend on Heaven. The gentleman is reverent and does nothing amiss, is respectful towards others and observant of the rites, and all within the Four Seas are his brothers. What need is there for the gentleman to worry about not having any brothers?"

6. Tzu-chang asked about perspicacity. The Master said, "When a man is not influenced by standers which are assiduously repeated or by complaints for which he feels a direct sympathy, he can be said to be perspicacious. He can at the same time be said to be farsighted."

22. Fan Ch'ih asked about benevolence. The Master said, "Love your fellow men."

He asked about wisdom. The Master said, "Know your fellow men."

Fan Ch'ih failed to grasp his meaning. The Master said, "Raise the straight and set them over the crooked. This can make the crooked straight."

Fan Ch'ih withdrew and went to see Tzu-hsia, saying, "Just now, I went to see the Master and asked about wisdom. The Master said, 'Raise the straight and set them over the crooked. This can make the crooked straight' What did he mean?"

Tzu-hsia said, "Rich, indeed, is the meaning of these words. When Shun possessed the Empire, he raised Kao Yao from the multitude and by so doing put those who were not benevolent at a great distance. When T'ang possessed the Empire, he raised Yi Yin from the multitude and by so doing put those who were not benevolent at a great distance."

24. Tseng Tzu said, "A gentleman makes friends through being cultivated, but looks to friends for support in benevolence."

BOOK XV

10. Tzu-kung asked about the practice of benevolence. The Master said, "A craftsman who wishes to practice his craft well must first sharpen his tools. You should, therefore, seek the patronage of the most distinguished Counsellors and make friends with the most benevolent Gentlemen in the state where you happen to be staying."

BOOK XVIII

6. Tzu-chang asked Confucius about benevolence. Confucius said, "There are five things and whoever is capable of putting them into practice in the Empire is certainly 'benevolent.'"

"May I ask what they are?"

"They are respectfulness, tolerance, trustworthiness in word, quickness and generosity. If a man is respectful he will not be treated with insolence. If he is tolerant he will win the multitude. If he is trustworthy in word his fellow men will entrust him with responsibility. If he is quick he will achieve results. If he is generous he will be good enough to be put in a position over his fellow men."

8. The Master said, "Yu, have you heard about the six qualities and the six attendant faults?"

"No."

"Be seated and I shall tell you. To love benevolence without loving learning is liable to lead to foolishness. To love cleverness without loving learning is liable to lead to deviation from the right path. To love trustworthiness in word without loving learning is liable to lead to harmful behavior. To love forthrightness without loving learning is liable to lead to intolerance. To love courage without loving learning is liable to lead to indiscipline."

BOOK XX

1. Decide on standard weights and measures after careful consideration, and re-establish official posts fallen into disuse, and government measures will be enforced

everywhere. Restore states that have been annexed, revive lines that have become extinct, raise men who have withdrawn from society and the hearts of all the common people in the Empire will turn to you.

What was considered of importance: the common people, food, mourning and sacrifice.

If a man is tolerant, he will win the multitude. If he is trustworthy in word, the common people will entrust him with responsibility. If he is quick he will achieve results. If he is impartial the common people will be pleased.

The distinction here between "the gentleman" and "the small man" is not, as is often the case, drawn between the ruler and the ruled but within the class of the ruled.

1.8 KAUTILYA: ON THE PENAL SYSTEM (*THE ARTHASHASTRA*, C. 200 B.C.E.)

Principles of the Penal Code

Only the Rule of Law can guarantee security of life and the welfare of the people. {i.5.2}

The maintenance of law and order by the use of punishment is the science of government (*dandaniti*). {from 1.4.3}

It is the power of punishment alone which, when exercised impartially in proportion to guilt and irrespective of whether the person punished is the king's son or the enemy, that protects this world and the next. {3.1.42}

A severe king [meting out unjust punishment] is hated by the people he terrorizes, while one who is too lenient is held in contempt by his own people. Whoever imposes just and deserved punishment is respected and honored. {1.4.8–10}

An innocent man who does not deserve to be penalized shall not be punished, for the sin of inflicting unjust punishment is visited on the king. He shall be freed of the sin only if he offers thirty times the unjust fine to *Varuna* (the god who chas-

tizes unjust behavior of kings) and then distributes it to Brahmins. {4.13.42,43}

The special circumstances of the person convicted and of the particular offense shall be taken into account in determining the actual penalty to be imposed. {3.20.20}

Fines shall be fixed taking into account the customs (of the region and the community) and the nature of the offense. {2.22.15}

In all cases, the punishment prescribed shall be imposed for the first offense; it shall be doubled for the second and trebled for the third. If the offense is repeated a fourth time, any punishment, as the king pleases, may be awarded.[1] {2.27.18}

Leniency shall be shown in imposing punishments on the following: a pilgrim, an ascetic, anyone suffering from illness, hunger, thirst, poverty, fatigue from a journey, suffering from an earlier punishment, a foreigner or one from the countryside. {3.20.21}

Whenever *brahmacharis*, *vanaprasthas* or *sanyasins* have to pay fines, they may instead perform rituals and penances for the benefit of the King, for as many days as the amount of the fine (in panas). Likewise, heretics without money shall observe a fast for the number of days equivalent to the fine. This rule does not apply to [serious crimes such as] defamation, theft, assault and abduction; in such cases, the prescribed punishment shall be implemented. {3.1638–1641}

Thus, the king shall first reform [the administration], by punishing appropriately those officers who deal in wealth; they, duly corrected, shall use the right punishments to ensure the good conduct of the people of the towns and the countryside. {4.9.28}

Either due to the increase in criminality of the population or due to the misguided [greedy?] nature of kings, it has become customary to levy a surcharge of eight per cent on fines below one hundred panas and five per cent on fines above that; this is illegal. Only the basic fine [as prescribed in this text] is legal. {3.17.15.16}

Death Penalty

The cruel punishments listed below are prescribed by great sages in the *shastras*. [However,] for crimes which are not cruel, the simple death penalty [without torture] is equally just. {4.11.26}

	Theft	
Of cattle herds (more than 10 heads)	Death without torture	{4.11.15,16}
Stealing or killing a royal elephant or royal horse; stealing a royal chariot	Impalement	{4.11.7}
Theft of weapons or armor by anyone who is not a soldier	Death by a firing squad of archers	{4.11.22}
Damage to water works		
Breaking the dam of a reservoir	Death by drowning in the same place	{4.11.17}
	Death as a result of scuffle or a fray	
(No capital punishment if death occurs after seven days)		
On the spot	Death with torture	{4.11.1}
Within seven days	Death without torture	{4.11.2}
	Manslaughter	
With a weapon	Death without torture	{4.11.5}
	Murder	
With cruelty	Impalement	{4.11.7}
Murder during highway robbery		
Murder during housebreaking		
	Poisoning	
Poisoner — man or woman not pregnant (special provision of delayed implementation of punishment for pregnant women)	Death by drowning	{4.11.18}
	Sale of Human Flesh	
Treason	Death	{4.10.15}
Anyone who tries to usurp the throne, attacks the royal residence, encourages enemies or jungle tribes to rebel, incites a revolt in the city, countryside or army	Death by burning from head to foot (Does not apply to Brahmins, who shall be blinded.)	{4.11.11,12}
	Parricide, fratricide, etc.	
Killing mother, father, son, brother, teacher, or ascetic	Death by burning the shaved head	{4.11.13}
Accidental death	Death without torture	{4.11.15}
	Crimes by women	
Murdering husband, guru, child or children, by a weapon, poisoning, or setting fire to the house	Death by being torn apart by bullocks	{4.11.19}
Prostitute murdering a client	Death by being burnt alive or by drowning	{2.27.22}
	Arson	
Setting fire to a pasture, a field, a threshing ground, a house, a productive forest or an elephant forest	Death by burning	{4.11.20}

Mutilation

Monetary Fines In Lieu

Mutilation	Equivalent Fine (in panas)
Thumb and forefinger	54
Tip of nose	54
All fingers of the [right] hand	100
Sinews of the feet	200
Middle and index fingers	200
A foot	300
A hand [usually right hand?]	400
An ear and the nose	500
Both feet	600
A hand and a foot	700
Blinding both eyes	800
Left hand and both feet	900
Both ears and nose	1000

{From 4.10.1,2,7–14; 4.12.1,3,7}

[For those who remove or cremate criminals executed by impaling them on a stake, the prescribed punishment is also death by impaling; the monetary equivalent in this case is the Highest SP {4.11.8}. There is no monetary equivalent to the cutting off of penis and testicles {4.13.30}.]

Miscellaneous Punishments

Brahmins

[The punishment for a Brahmin guilty of a serious offense is branding and exile.]

The guilt of a Brahmin shall be displayed publicly and permanently so that he may be excluded from all activities of Brahmins. The brand shall indicate the nature of the offense as follows:

Crime	Brand
Theft	A dog
Drinking alcoholic liquor	The vintner's flag
Murder	A headless torso
Rape of a teacher's wife	The female sexual organ

After publicly proclaiming a Brahmin's guilt and branding him, he shall be exiled or sent to [work in] the mines. {4.8.28,29}

Food and Drink Taboos

Eating or drinking prohibited things		
If done voluntarily	Exile	{4.13.2}
Making someone eat or drink a prohibited thing depending on the varna of the person made to do so		
Brahmin	Highest SP	{4.13.1}
Kshatriya	Middle SP	
Vaishya	Lowest SP	
Sudra	54 panas	

Death by Being Gored by an Elephant

Being gored to death by an elephant is as meritorious as having the sacred bath at the end of the *Asvamedha* [horse] sacrifice. Hence, anyone who seeks such a death [voluntarily] shall make oblatory gifts of the following: a *drona* of rice, a jar of wine, garlands and a piece of cloth to clean the tusks. {4.13.15,16}

Witchcraft and Black Magic

Performing magic or witchcraft is a punishable offense except when it is done in order to arouse love in a wife towards her husband, in a husband towards his wife or in a suitor towards his beloved. {4.13.28}

Punishments

Mahout of an elephant which gores to death someone who did not volunteer	Highest SP	{4.13.17}
Anyone who practices witchcraft	Same results to be meted out	{4.13.27}
Causing injury by black magic	Middle SP	{4.13.29}

1.9 ASOKA: "AGAINST RELIGIOUS INTOLERANCE AND DISCRIMINATION WITHIN THE COMMUNITY" (*THE EDICTS*, 272–231 B.C.E.)

Rock Edict VII

King Priyadarśi wishes members of all faiths to live everywhere in his kingdom.

For they all seek mastery of the senses and purity of mind. Men are different in their inclinations and passions, however, and they may perform the whole of their duties or only part.

Even if one is not able to make lavish gifts, mastery of the senses, purity of mind, gratitude, and steadfast devotion are commendable and essential.

Rock Edict XII

King Priyadarśi honors men of all faiths, members of religious orders and laymen alike, with gifts and various marks of esteem. Yet he does not value either gifts or honors as much as growth in the qualities essential to religion in men of all faiths.

This growth may take many forms, but its root is in guarding one's speech to avoid extolling one's own faith and disparaging the faith of others improperly or, when the occasion is appropriate, immoderately.

The faiths of others all deserve to be honored for one reason or another. By honoring them, one exalts one's own faith and at the same time performs a service to the faith of others. By acting otherwise, one injures one's own faith and also does disservice to that of others. For if a man extols his own faith and disparages another because of devotion to his own and because he wants to glorify it, he seriously injures his own faith.

Therefore concord alone is commendable, for through concord men may learn and respect the conception of Dharma accepted by others.

King Priyadarśi desires men of all faiths to know each other's doctrines and to acquire sound doctrines. Those who are attached to their particular faiths should be told that King Priyadarśi does not value gifts or honors as much as growth in the qualities essential to religion in men of all faiths.

Many officials are assigned to tasks bearing on this purpose the officers in charge of spreading Dharma, the superintendents of women in the royal household, the inspectors of cattle and pasture lands, and other officials.

The objective of these measures is the promotion of each man's particular faith and the glorification of Dharma.

1.10 CHINESE BUDDHIST VERSES: ON MORAL CONDUCT (MAHAPARINIRVANA SUTRA, EARLY 4TH CENTURY)

Do no injury to living beings,
Hold firmly to all the
  rules of restraint,
Accept the Buddha's
  exquisite teaching,
And you will be born in
  Aksobhya's Land.
Do not steal other
  people's property,
Always be kind and
  generous to all,
Everywhere build
  habitations for monks,
And you will be born in
  Aksobhya's Land.
Do not ravish others'
  wives and daughters,
Do not take your own wife
  at the wrong time,
Have your bed in keeping
  with the precepts,
And you will be born in
  Aksobhya's Land.
Keep watch on your mouth
  and avoid false speech
Either for your own
  sake or for others,
In search of advantage
  or out of fear,
And you will be born in
  Aksobhya's Land.
Do not slander any good
  acquaintance,
Keep far away from evil company,
Let your mouth always
  speak agreeably,

And you will be born in
  Aksobhya's Land.
Be the same as all the
  bodhisattvas,
Always free from evil utterances,
So that men will gladly
  hear what you say,
And you will be born in
  Aksobhya's Land.
Even when you are
  playing and laughing
Do not utter inappropriate words,
Be careful always to
  speak timely words,
And you will be born in
  Aksobhya's Land.
Seeing others receive
  gain and service,
Let your thoughts be always
  those of gladness,
Never let knots of
  jealousy be tied,
And you will be born in
  Aksobhya's Land.
Cause no affliction to
  living beings,
Let your thoughts always
  be those of kindness,
Do not employ evil expedients,
And you will be born in
  Aksobhya's Land.
Perverted views say
  there is no giving
To one's parents, no past
  and no future.
If you do not entertain
  such notions,
Then you will be born in
  Aksobhya's Land.
Dig good wells beside
  roads in the desert,
Plant and cultivate orchards
  of fruit trees,
Always give nourishment
  to mendicants,
And you will be born in
  Aksobhya's Land.

MONOTHEISM

One can only marvel at how the same precepts as one encounters in Buddhism are also found in monotheism. The Ten Commandments of the Hebrew Bible (see Section 1.11) represented a code of morality, justice, and mutual respect shared by the three monotheistic religions. Indeed, "thou shall not kill," "thou shall not steal," "thou shall not give false evidence against your neighbor," and "thou shall not covet your neighbor's wife," among other tenets, find their equivalents in both the New Testament (see Section 1.12) and the Koran (see Section 1.13). Some of these injunctions directly translate into later formulations of rights, e.g., the right to life, the right to property, and protection against calumny.

Like the secular and Asian traditions, these three religions preached universalism. Under one God, the creator of all that exists, all humankind is viewed as a unity (e.g., Micah's vision in the Hebrew Bible), with no race existing for itself alone. The New Testament (c. 50) professes a similar universal ethics through the word of Jesus and his apostles. In Acts 17–19, Paul reminds the Athenians that God created all humankind, and that individuals of all races were equal under God's tutelage. The Koran, like Judaism and Christianity, also provides universal moral guidance for all believers. The Koran, it should be noted, consists of 114 chapters (Surahs) that according to the Muslim tradition were revealed to Mohamed prior to his death in 632 — with commentaries compiled at a later stage.

1.11 THE HEBREW BIBLE: ON UNIVERSALISM AND THE TEN COMMANDMENTS

Exodus 20:1–5

God spoke, and these were his words:

I am the Lord your God who brought you out of Egypt, out of the land of slavery.

You shall have no other God to set against me.

You shall not make a carved image for yourself nor the likeness of anything in the heavens above, or on the earth below, or in the waters under the earth.

You shall not bow down to them or worship them; for I, the Lord your God, am a jealous god. I punish the children for the sins of the fathers to the third and fourth generations of those who hate me. But I keep faith with thousands, with those who love me and keep my commandments.

You shall not make wrong use of the name of the Lord your God; the Lord will not leave unpunished the man who misuses his name.

Remember to keep the sabbath day holy. You have six days to labor and do all your work. But the seventh day is a sabbath of the Lord your God; that day you shall not do any work, you, your son or your daughter, your slave or your slave-girl, your cattle or the alien within your gates; for in six days the Lord made heaven and earth, the sea, and all that is in them, and on the seventh day he rested. Therefore the Lord blessed the sabbath day and declared it holy.

Honor your father and your mother, that you may live long in the land which the Lord your God is giving you.

You shall not commit murder.

You shall not commit adultery.

You shall not steal.

You shall not give false evidence against your neighbor.

You shall not covet your neighbor's house; you shall not covet your neighbor's wife, his slave, his slave-girl, his ox, his ass, or anything that belongs to him.

When all the people saw how it thundered and the lightning flashed, when they heard the trumpet sound and saw the mountain smoking, they trembled and stood at a distance. "Speak to us yourself," they said to Moses, "and we will listen; but if God speaks to us we shall die." Moses answered, "Do not be afraid. God has come only to test you, so that the fear of him may remain with you and keep you from sin." So the people stood at a distance, while Moses approached the dark cloud where God was.

Exodus 21:22–25

When, in the course of a brawl, a man knocks against a pregnant woman so that she has a miscarriage but suffers no further hurt, then the offender must pay whatever fine the woman's husband demands after assessment.

Wherever hurt is done, you shall give life for life, eye for eye, tooth for tooth, hand for hand, foot for foot, burn for burn, bruise for bruise, wound for wound.

Exodus 23:1–3

You shall not spread a baseless rumor. You shall not make common cause with a wicked man by giving malicious evidence.

You shall not be led into wrongdoing by the majority, nor, when you give evidence in a lawsuit, shall you side with the majority to pervert justice; nor shall you favor the poor man in his suit.

Amos 9:7–15

"Are not you Israelites like Cushites to me?"
says the Lord.
"Did I not bring Israel up from Egypt,
the Philistines from Caphtor, the Aramaeans from Kir?
"Behold, I, the Lord God,
have my eyes on this sinful kingdom,
and I will wipe it off the face of the earth."
A Remnant Spared and Restored
"Yet I will not wipe out the family of Jacob root and branch,"
says the Lord.
"No, I will give my orders,
I will shake Israel to and fro through all the nations
as a sieve is shaken to and fro
and not one pebble falls to the ground.
They shall die by the sword, all the sinners of my people,

who say, 'Thou wilt not let disaster come near us
or overtake us.'
On that day I will restore
David's fallen house;
I will repair its gaping walls and restore its ruins;
I will rebuild it as it was long ago,
that they may possess what is left of Edom
and all the nations who were once named mine."
This is the very word of the Lord, who will do this.
"A time is coming," says the Lord,
"when the ploughman shall follow hard on the vintager,
and he who treads the grapes after him who sows the seed.
The mountains shall run with fresh wine,
and every hill shall wave with corn.
I will restore the fortunes of my people Israel;
they shall rebuild deserted cities and live in them,
they shall plant vineyards and drink their wine,
make gardens and eat the fruit.
Once more I will plant them on their own soil,
and they shall never again be uprooted
from the soil I have given them."
It is the word of the Lord your God.

Psalm 118:18–22

The Lord did indeed chasten me,
but he did not surrender me to Death.
Open to me the gates of victory;
I will enter by them and praise the Lord.
This is the gate of the Lord;
the victors shall make their entry through it.
I will praise thee, for thou hast answered me
and hast become my deliverer.
The stone which the builders rejected
has become the chief corner-stone.

1.12 THE NEW TESTAMENT: ON FAITH AND THE LAW (C. 50)

Matthew 22:34–40

Hearing that he had silenced the Sadducees, the Pharisees met together; and one of their number tested him with this question: "Master, which is the greatest commandment in the Law?" He answered, "'Love the Lord your God with all your heart, with all your soul, with all your mind.'" That is the greatest commandment. It comes first. The second is like it: 'Love your neighbor as yourself.' Everything in the Law and the prophets hangs on these two commandments."

Galatians 3:1–29

YOU STUPID GALATIANS! You must have been bewitched — you before whose eyes Jesus Christ was openly displayed upon his cross! Answer me one question: did you receive the Spirit by keeping the law or by believing the gospel message? Can it be that you are so stupid? You started with the spiritual; do you now look to the material to make you perfect? Have all your great experiences been in vain — if vain indeed they should be? I ask then: when God gives you the Spirit and works miracles among you, why is this? Is it because you keep the law, or is it because you have faith in the gospel message?

Look at Abraham: he put his faith in God, and that faith was counted to him as righteousness. You may take it, then, that it is the men of faith who are Abraham's sons. And Scripture, foreseeing that God would justify the Gentiles through faith, declared the Gospel to Abraham beforehand: "In you all nations shall find blessing."

Thus it is the men of faith who share the blessing with faithful Abraham.

On the other hand those who rely on obedience to the law are under a curse; for Scripture says, "A curse is on all who do not persevere in doing everything that is written in the Book of the Law." It is evident that no one is ever justified before God in terms of law; because we read, "he shall gain life who is justified through faith."

Now law is not at all a matter of having faith: we read, "he who does this shall gain life by what he does." Christ bought us freedom from the curse of the law by becoming for our sake an accursed thing; for Scripture says, "A curse is on everyone who is hanged on a gibbet." And the purpose of it all was that the blessing of Abraham should in Jesus Christ be extended to the Gentiles, so that we might receive the promised Spirit through faith.

My brothers, let me give you an illustration. Even in ordinary life, when a man's will and testament has been duly executed, no one else can set it aside or add a codicil. Now the promises were pronounced to Abraham and to his issue. It does not say "issues" in the plural, but in the singular, "and to your issue"; and the issue intended is Christ. What I am saying is this: a testament, or covenant, had already been validated by God; it cannot be invalidated, and its promises rendered ineffective, by a law made four hundred and thirty years later. If the inheritance is by legal right, then it is not by promise; but it was by promise that God bestowed it as a free gift on Abraham.

Then what of the law? It was added to make wrongdoing a legal offense. It was temporary measure pending the arrival of the issue to whom the promise was made. It was promulgated through angels, and there was an intermediary; but an intermediary is not needed for one party acting alone, and God is one.

Does the law, then, contradict the promises? No, never! If a law had been given which had power to bestow life, then indeed righteousness would have come from keeping the law. But Scripture has declared the whole world to be prisoners in subjection to sin, so that faith in Jesus Christ may be the ground on which the promised blessing is given, and given to those who have such faith.

Before this faith came, we were close prisoners in the custody of law, pending the revelation of faith. Thus the law was a kind of tutor in charge of us until Christ should come, when we should be justified through faith; and now that faith has come, the tutor's charge is at an end.

For through faith you are all sons of God in union with Christ Jesus. Baptized into union with him, you have all put on Christ as a garment.

There is no such thing as Jew and Greek, slave and freeman, male and female; for you are all one person in Christ Jesus.

But if you thus belong to Christ, you are the issue of Abraham, and so heirs by promise.

Matthew 5:1–48 —
The Sermon on the Mount

When he saw the crowds he went up the hill. There he took his seat, and when his disciples had gathered round him he began to address them. And this is the teaching he gave:

"How blest are those who know their need of God; the kingdom of Heaven is theirs.

How blest are the sorrowful; they shall find consolation.

How blest are those of a gentle spirit; they shall have the earth for their possession.

How blest are those who hunger and thirst to see right prevail; they shall be satisfied.

How blest are those who show mercy; mercy shall be shown to them.

How blest are those whose hearts are pure; they shall see God.

How blest are the peacemakers; God shall call them his sons.

How blest are those who have suffered persecution for the cause of right; the kingdom of Heaven is theirs.

"How blest you are, when you suffer insults and persecution and every kind of calumny for my sake. Accept it with gladness and exultation, for you have a rich reward in heaven; in the same way they persecuted the prophets before you.

"You are salt to the world. And if salt becomes tasteless, how is its saltness to be restored? It is now good for nothing but to be thrown away and trodden underfoot.

You are light for all the world. A town that stands on a hill cannot be hidden. When a lamp is lit, it is not put under the meal-tub, but on the lamp-stand, where it gives light to everyone in the house. And you, like the lamp, must shed light among your fellows, so that, when they see the good you do, they may give praise to your Father in heaven.

"Do not suppose that I have come to abolish the Law and the prophets; I did not come to abolish, but to complete. I tell you this: so long as heaven and earth endure, not a letter, not a stroke, will disappear from the Law until all that must happen has happened. If any man therefore sets aside even the least of the Law's demands, and teaches others to do the same, he will have the lowest place in the kingdom of Heaven, whereas anyone who keeps the Law, and teaches others so, will stand high in the kingdom of Heaven. I tell you, unless you show yourselves far better men than the Pharisees and the doctors of the law, you can never enter the kingdom of Heaven.

"You have learned that our forefathers were told, 'Do not commit murder; anyone who commits murder must be brought to judgment.' But what I tell you is this: Anyone who nurses anger against his brother must be brought to judgment. If he abuses his brother he must answer for it to the court; if he sneers at him he will have to answer for it in the fires of hell.

"If, when you are bringing your gift to the, altar, you suddenly remember that your brother has a grievance against you, leave your gift where it is before the altar. First go and make your peace with your brother, and only then come back and offer your gift.

"If someone sues you, come to terms with him promptly while you are both on your way to court; otherwise he may hand you over to the judge, and the judge to the constable, and you will be put in jail. I tell you, once you are there you will not be let out till you have paid the last farthing.

"You have learned that they were told, 'Do not commit adultery.' But what I tell you is this: If a man looks on a woman with a lustful eye, he has already committed adultery with her in his heart. If your right eye is your undoing, tear it out and fling it away; it is better for you to lose one part of your body than for the whole of it to be thrown into hell. And if your right hand is your undoing, cut it off and fling it away; it is better for you to lose one part of your body than for the whole of it to go to hell.

"They were told, 'A man who divorces his wife must give her a note of dismissal.' But what I tell you is this: If a man divorces his wife for any cause other than unchastity he involves her in adultery; and anyone who marries a divorced woman commits adultery.

"Again, you have learned that our fore-fathers were told, 'Do not break your oath,' and, 'Oaths sworn to the Lord must be kept.' But what I tell you is this: You are not to swear at all — not by heaven, for it is God's throne, nor by earth, for it is his footstool, nor by Jerusalem, for it is the city of the great King, nor by your own head, because you cannot turn one hair of it white or black. Plain 'Yes' or 'No' is all you need to say; anything beyond that comes from the devil.

"You have learned that they were told, 'Eye for eye, tooth for tooth.' But what I tell you is this: Do not set yourself against the man who wrongs you. If someone slaps you on the right cheek, turn and offer him your left. If a man wants to sue you for your shirt, let him have your coat as well. If a man in authority makes you go one mile, go with him two. Give when you are asked to give; and do not turn your back on a man who wants to borrow.

"You have learned that they were told, 'Love your neighbor, hate your enemy.' But what I tell you is this: Love your enemies and pray for your persecutors; only so can you be children of your heavenly Father, who makes his sun rise on good and bad alike, and sends the rain on the honest and the dishonest. If you love only those who love you, what reward can you expect? Surely the tax gatherers do as much as that. And if you greet only your brothers, what is there extraordinary about that? Even the heathen do as much. There must be no limit to your goodness, as your heavenly Father's goodness knows no bounds."

1.13 THE KORAN: ON TOLERANCE AND JUST SOCIETY (C. 632)

Surah 49

9. If two parties among
The Believers fall into
A quarrel, make ye peace
Between them: but if
One of them transgresses
Beyond bounds against the other,
Then fight ye (all) against
The one that transgresses
Until it complies with
The command of Allah;
But if it complies, then
Make peace between them
With justice, and be fair:
For Allah loves those
Who are fair (and just).

10. The Believers are but
A single Brotherhood:
So make peace and
Reconciliation between your
Two (contending) brothers;
And fear Allah, that ye
May receive Mercy.

11. Ye who believe!
Let not some men
Among you laugh at others.
It may be that
The (latter) are better
Than the (former)
Nor let some women
Laugh at others:
It may be that
The (latter) are better,
Than the (former):
Nor defame, nor be
Sarcastic to each other,
Nor call each other
By (offensive) nicknames:
Ill-seeming is a name
Connoting wickedness,
(To be used of one)
After he has believed:
And those who
Do not desist are
(Indeed) doing wrong.

12. Ye who believe!
Avoid suspicion as much
(As possible): for suspicion
In some cases is a sin:
And spy not on each other.
Nor speak ill of each other
Behind-their backs.
Would any
Of you like to eat
The flesh of his dead
Brother? Nay, ye would
Abhor it ... But fear Allah:
For Allah is Oft-Returning,
Most Merciful.

13. Mankind! We created
You from a single (pair)
Of a male and a female,
And made you into
Nations and tribes, that
Ye may know each other (Not that ye may
       despise
Each other). Verily
The most honored of you
In the sight of Allah
Is (he who is) the most Righteous of you.
And Allah has full knowledge
And is well-acquainted
(With all things).

16. Say: "What! Will ye
Instruct Allah about your Religion?"
But Allah knows
All that is in the heavens
And on earth: He has
Full knowledge of all things.

17. They impress on thee
As a favor that they
Have embraced Islam.
Say, "Count not your Islam
As a favor upon me":
Nay, Allah has conferred
A favor upon you
That He has guided you
To the Faith, if ye
Be true and sincere.

18. "Verily Allah Knows
The secrets of the heavens

And the earth: and Allah
Sees well all
That ye do."

Surah 50

1. Qaf:
By the Glorious Qur'an (Thou art Allah's
       Messenger).

2. But they wonder that
There has come to them
A Warner from among
Themselves.
So the Unbelievers say:
"This is a wonderful thing!"

4. We already know
How much of them
The earth takes away:
With Us is a Record Guarding (the full
       account).
So they are in a confused state.

Surah 2

C.50. The Society thus organized
Must live under laws
That would guide their everyday life —
Based on eternal principles
Of righteousness and fair dealing.
Cleanliness and sobriety,
Honesty and helpfulness,
One to another — yet shaped
Into concrete forms, to suit
Times and circumstances,
And the varying needs
Of average men and women:
The food to be clean and wholesome;
Blood feuds to be abolished;
The rights and duties of heirs
To be recognized after death,
Not in a spirit of Formalism,
But to help the weak and the needy
And check all selfish wrongdoing;
Self-denial to be learnt by fasting;
The courage to fight in defense
Of right, to be defined;
The Pilgrimage to be sanctified
As a symbol of unity;

Charity and help to the poor
To be organized; unseemly riot
And drink and gambling
To be banished; orphans to be protected;
Marriage, divorce, and widowhood
To be regulated; and the rights of women,
Apt to be trampled under foot;
Now clearly affirmed.

168. O ye people!
Eat of what is on earth,
Lawful and good;
And do not follow
The footsteps of the
Evil One,
For he is to you

An avowed enemy.

169. For he commands you
What is evil
And shameful,
And that ye should say
Of Allah that of which
Ye have no knowledge.

170. When it is said to them:
"Follow what Allah hath revealed,"
They say: "Nay! We shall follow
The ways of our fathers."
What! Even though their fathers
Were void of wisdom and guidance?

CHAPTER 2

Social and Economic Justice

Traditions from the Hammurabi Code to early Islamic thought also contained perspectives that emphasize both the right to property and the harmony and peace that result from communal ownership. As for the question of social and economic justice or equality, Article 22 of the Universal Declaration of Human Rights stipulates that each human possesses "economic, social, and cultural rights, [as] indispensable for his dignity and the free development of his personality." While the modern struggle over social and economic rights grew out of the industrial revolution and the subsequent working class movement, it is also true that calls for economic justice originated in ancient times.

2.1 UNITED NATIONS UNIVERSAL DECLARATION OF HUMAN RIGHTS (1948): ARTICLES 17 AND 22–26

Article 17

1.   Everyone has the right to own property alone as well as in association with others.

2.   No one shall be arbitrarily deprived of his property.

Article 22

Everyone, as a member of society, has the right to social security and is entitled to realization, through national effort and international cooperation and in accordance with the organization and resources of each State, of the economic, social and cultural rights indispensable for his dignity and the free development of his personality.

Article 23

1.   Everyone has the right to work, to free choice of employment, to just and favorable conditions of work and to protection against unemployment.

2.   Everyone, without any discrimination, has the right to equal pay for equal work.

3.   Everyone who works has the right to just and favorable remuneration insuring for himself and his family an existence worthy of

human dignity, and supplemented, if necessary, by other means of social protection.

4.   Everyone has the right to form and to join trade unions for the protection of his interests.

Article 24

Everyone has the right to rest and leisure, including reasonable limitation of working hours and periodic holidays with pay.

Article 25

1.   Everyone has the right to a standard of living adequate for the health and well-being of himself and of his family, including food, clothing, housing and medical care and necessary social services, and the right to security in the event of unemployment, sickness, disability, widowhood, old age or other lack of livelihood in circumstances beyond his control.

2.   Motherhood and childhood are entitled to special care and assistance. All children, whether born in or out of wedlock shall enjoy the same social protection.

Article 26

1.   Everyone has the right to education. Education shall be free, at least in the elementary and fundamental stages. Elementary education shall be compulsory. Technical and professional education shall be made gener-

ally available and higher education shall be equally accessible to all on the basis of merit.

2. Education shall be directed to the full development of the human personality and to the strengthening of respect for human rights and fundamental freedoms. It shall promote understanding, tolerance and friendship among all nations, racial or religious groups, and shall further the activities of the United Nations for the maintenance of peace.

3. Parents have a prior right to choose the kind of education that shall be given to their children.

THE SECULAR TRADITION

As early as in the period of King Hammurabi (1728–1686 B.C.E.), one can find laws securing both creditors' and employees' rights and regulating work relationships (see Section 2.2). In the premodern era, the question of property rights had already divided Socrates and Aristotle, setting the stage for the tempestuous conflicts over property rights characterizing the past three centuries. Favoring communal ownership of property, Socrates, as reported by Plato, warned in *The Republic* (c. 360 B.C.E.) that property rights could fragment the polity and tear "the city in pieces by differing about 'mine' and 'not mine,'" thereby undermining the common end (see Section 2.3). Opposing Socrates, Aristotle would defend the importance of property rights, pointing out: "When everyone has his own separate sphere of interest, there will not be the same ground for quarrels" (see Section 2.2).

2.2 HAMMURABI CODE: ON PROPERTY (C. 1700 B.C.E)

§ 6

If a man has stolen property belonging to a god or a palace, that man shall be put to death, and he who has received the stolen property from his hand shall be put to death.

§ 7

If a man buys silver or gold or slave or slave-girl or ox or sheep or ass or anything else whatsoever from a [free] man's son or a [free] man's slave or has received [them] for safe custody without witnesses or contract that man is a thief; he shall be put to death.

§ 8

If a man has stolen an ox or a sheep or an ass or swine or a boat, if [it is the property] of a god [or] if [it is the property] of a palace, he shall pay 30-fold; if [it is the property] of a servant, he shall replace [it] 10-fold. If the thief has not the means of payment he shall be put to death.

§ 21

If a man has broken into a house, they shall put him to death and hang him before the breach which he has made.

§§ 22–24

If a man has committed robbery and is caught, that man shall be put to death.

If the robber is not caught, the man who has been robbed shall formally declare whatever he has lost before a god, and the city and the mayor in whose territory or district the robbery has been committed shall replace whatever he has lost for him.

If [it is] the life [of the owner that is lost], the city or the mayor shall pay one maneh of silver to his kinsfolk.

§ 25

If a fire has broken out in a man's house and a man who has gone to extinguish [it] has coveted an article of the owner of the house and takes the article of the owner of the house, that man shall be cast into that fire.

2.3 PLATO: ON THE COMMUNITY OF PROPERTY (*THE REPUBLIC*, C. 360 B.C.E.)

"In our city the language of harmony and concord will be more often heard than in any other. As I was describing before, when any one is well or ill, the universal word will be 'with me it is well' or 'it is ill.'"

"Most true."

"And agreeably to this mode of thinking and speaking, were we not saying that they will have their pleasures and pains in common?"

"Yes, and so they will."

"And they will have a common interest in the same thing which they will alike call 'my own,' and having this common interest they will have a common feeling of pleasure and pain? Yes, far more so than in other States. And the reason of this, over and above the general constitution of the State, will be that the guardians will have a community of women and children?"

"That will be the chief reason."

"And this unity of feeling we admitted to be the greatest good, as was implied in our own comparison of a well-ordered State to the relation of the body and the members, when affected by pleasure or pain?"

"That we acknowledge, and very rightly."

"Then the community of wives and children among our citizens is clearly the source of the greatest good to the State?"

"Certainly."

"And this agrees with the other principle which we were affirming — that the guardians were not to have houses or lands or any other property; their pay was to be their food, which they were to receive from the other citizens, and they were to have no private expenses; for we intended them to preserve their true character of guardians."

"Right, he replied."

"Both the community of property and the community of families, as I am saying, tend to make them, more truly guardians; they will not tear the city in pieces by differing about 'mine' and 'not mine'; each man dragging any acquisition which he has made into a separate house of his own, where he has a separate wife and children and private pleasures and pains; but all will be affected as far as may be by the same pleasures and pains because they are all of one opinion about what is near and dear to them, and therefore they all tend towards a common end."

"Certainly, he replied."

"And as they have nothing but their persons which they can call their own, suits and complaints will have no existence among them; they will be delivered from all those quarrels of which money or children or relations are the occasion."

"Of course they will."

"Neither will trials for assault or insult ever be likely to occur among them. For that equals should defend themselves against equals we shall maintain to be honorable and right; we shall make the protection of the person a matter of necessity."

"That is good, he said."

"Yes; and there is a further good in the law, viz. that if a man has a quarrel with another he will satisfy his resentment then and there, and not proceed to more dangerous lengths."

"Certainly."

"To the elder shall be assigned the duty of ruling and chastising the younger."

"Clearly."

"Nor can there be a doubt that the younger will not strike or do any other violence to an elder, unless the magistrates command him; nor will he slight him in any way. For there are two guardians, shame and fear, mighty to prevent him: shame, which makes men refrain from laying hands on those who are to them in the relation of parents; fear, that the injured one will be succored by the others who are his brothers, sons, fathers."

"That is true, he replied."

"Then in every way the laws will help the citizens to keep the peace with one another?"

"Yes, there will be no want of peace."

"And as the guardians will never quarrel among themselves there will be no danger of the rest of the city being divided either against them or against one another."

"None whatever."

"I hardly like even to mention the little meannesses of which they will be rid, for they are beneath notice: such, for example, as the flattery of the rich by the poor, and all the pains and pangs which men experience in bringing up a family, and in finding money to buy necessaries for their household, borrowing and then repudiating, getting how they can, and giving the money into the hands of women and slaves to keep — the many evils of so many kinds which people suffer in this way are mean enough and obvious enough, and not worth speaking of."

"Yes, he said, a man has no need of eyes in order to perceive that."

"And from all these evils they will be delivered, and their life will be blessed as the life of Olympic victors and yet more blessed."

"How so?"

"The Olympic victor, I said, is deemed happy in receiving a part only of the blessedness which is secured to our citizens, who have won a more glorious victory and have a more complete maintenance at the public cost. For the victory which they have won is the salvation of the whole State; and the crown with which they and their children are crowned is the fullness of all that life needs; they receive rewards from the hands of their country while living, and after death have an honorable burial."

"Yes, he said, and glorious rewards they are."

"Do you remember, I said, how in the course of the previous discussion some one who shall be nameless accused us of making our guardians unhappy — they had nothing and might have possessed all things — to whom we replied that, if an occasion offered, we might perhaps hereafter consider this question, but that, as at present advised, we would make our guardians truly guardians, and that we were fashioning the State with a view to the greatest happiness, not of any particular class, but of the whole?"

"Yes, I remember."

"And what do you say, now that the life of our protectors is made out to be far better and nobler than that of Olympic victors — is the life of shoemakers, or any other artisans, or of husbandmen, to be compared with it?"

"Certainly not."

"At the same time I ought here to repeat what I have said elsewhere, that if any of our guardians shall try to be happy in such a manner that he will cease to be a guardian, and is not content with this safe and harmonious life, which, in our judgment, is of all lives the best, but infatuated by some youthful conceit of happiness which gets up into his head shall seek to appropriate the whole state to himself, then he will have to learn how wisely Hesiod spoke, when he said, 'half is more than the whole'."

2.4 ARISTOTLE: ON PROPERTY (THE POLITICS, C. 350 B.C.E.)

Book II, Chapter 5

1262^b39 The next subject for consideration is property. What is the proper system of property for citizens who are to live under the best form of constitution? Should property be held in common or not? This is an issue which may be considered in itself, and apart from any proposals for community of women and children. Even if women and children are held separately, as is now universally the case, questions relating to property still remain for discussion. Should use and ownership both be common? For example, there may be a system under which plots of land are owned separately, but the crops (as actually happens among some tribal peoples) are brought into a common stock for the purpose of consumption. Secondly, and conversely, the land may be held in common ownership, and may also be cultivated in common, but the crops may be divided among individuals for their private use; some of the barbarian peoples are also said to practice this second method of sharing. Thirdly, the plots and the crops may both be common.

1263^a8 When the cultivators of the soil are a different body from the citizens who own it, the position will be different and easier to handle; but when the citizens who own the soil do the work themselves, the problems of property will cause a good deal of trouble. If they do not share equally in the work and in the enjoyment of the produce, those who do more work and get less of the produce will be bound to raise complaints against those who get a large reward and do little work. In general it is a difficult business to live together and to share in any form of human activity, but it is specially difficult in such matters. Fellow-travelers who merely share in a journey furnish an illustration: they generally quarrel about ordinary matters and take offense on petty occasions So, again, the servants with whom we are most prone to take offense are those who are particularly employed in ordinary everyday services.

1263ª21 Difficulties such as these, and many others are involved in a system of community of property. The present system would be far preferable, if it were embellished with social customs and the enactment of proper laws. It would possess the advantages of both systems, and would combine the merits of a system of community of property with those of the system of private property. For, although there is a sense in which property *ought* to be common, it should in general be private. When everyone has his own separate sphere of interest, there will not be the same ground for quarrels; and they will make more effort, because each man will feel that he is applying himself to what is his own.

1263ª30 On such a scheme, too, moral goodness will ensure that the property of each is made to serve the use of all, in the spirit of the proverb, which says Friends' goods are goods in Common. Even now there are some cities in which the outlines of such a scheme are so far apparent, as to suggest that it is not impossible; in well-ordered cities, more particularly, there are some elements of it already existing, and others which might be added: [In these cities] each citizen has his own property; part of which he makes available to his friends, and part of which he uses as though it was common property.

In Sparta, for example, men use one another's slaves, and one another's horses and dogs, as if they were their own; and they take provisions on a journey, if they happen to be in need, from the farms in the countryside. It is clear from what has been said that the better system is that under which property is privately owned but is put to common use and the function proper to the legislator is to make men so disposed that they will treat property in this way.

1263ª40 In addition, to think of a thing as your own makes an inexpressible difference, so far as pleasure is concerned. It may well be that regard for oneself is a feeling implanted by nature, and not a mere random impulse. Self-love is rightly censured, but that is not so much loving oneself as loving oneself in excess. It is the same with one who loves money; after all, virtually everyone loves things of this kind. We may add that a very great pleasure is to be found in doing a kindness and giving some help to friends, or guests, or comrades; and such kindness and help become possible only when property is privately owned. But not only are these pleasures impossible under a system in which the city is excessively unified; the activities of two forms of goodness are also obviously destroyed. The first of these is temperance in the matter of sexual relations (it is an act of moral value to keep away from the wife of another through temperance): the second is generosity in the use of property. In a city which is excessively unified no man can show himself generous, or indeed do a generous act; for the function of generosity consists in the proper use which is made of property.

1263ᵇ15 This kind of legislation may appear to wear an attractive face and to demonstrate benevolence. The hearer receives it gladly, thinking that everybody will feel towards everybody else some marvellous sense of friendship — all the more as the evils now existing under ordinary forms of government (lawsuits about contracts, convictions for perjury, and obsequious flatteries of the rich) are denounced as due to the absence of a system of common property. None of these, however, is due to property not being held in common. They all arise from wickedness. Indeed it is a fact of observation that those who own common property, and share in its management, are far more often at variance with one another than those who have property separately — though those who are at variance in consequence of sharing in property look to us few in number when we compare them with the mass of those who own their property privately.

1263ᵇ27 What is more, justice demands that we should take into account not only the evils which people will be spared when they have begun to hold their property in common, but also the benefits of which they will be deprived. Their life can be seen to be utterly impossible.

1263ᵇ29 The cause of the fallacy into which Socrates falls must be held to be his incorrect premises. It is true that unity in some respects is necessary both for the household and for the city, but unity in all respects is not. There is a point at which a city, by advancing in unity, will cease to be a city: there is another point at which it will still be a city but a worse one because it has come close to ceasing altogether to be a city. It is as if you were to turn harmony into mere unison, or to reduce a theme to a single beat. The truth is that the city, as has already been said, is a plurality; and education is therefore the means of making it a community and giving it unity. It is therefore surprising that one who intends to introduce a system of education, and who believes that the city can achieve goodness by means of this system, should none the less think that he is setting it on the right track by such methods as he actually proposes, rather than by the method of social customs, of mental culture, and of legislation. An example of such legislation may be found in Sparta and Crete, where the legislator has made the institution of property serve a common use by the system of common meals.

1264ᵃ1 There is another matter which must not be ignored: we are bound to pay some regard to the long past and the passage of the years, in which these things would not have gone unnoticed if they had been really good. Almost everything has been discovered already; though some things have not been combined with one another, and others are not put into practice. It would shed a great deal of light on these matters, if we could watch the actual construction of such a constitution. The foundation of any city will always involve the division and distribution of its members into classes, partly in the form of associations for common meals, and partly in that of clans and tribes. It follows that the only peculiar feature of the legislation is the rule that the guardians are not to farm the land; and even that is a rule which the Spartans are already attempting to follow.

1264ᵃ1 Socrates does not explain the character of the whole constitution so far as concerns those who share in it, nor indeed is it easy to explain. The mass of the citizens who are not guardians will be, in effect, nearly the whole of the citizen body. But their position is left undefined. We are not told whether the farmers are also to have property in common, or to own it individually; nor do we learn whether their women and children are to be common to them all, or to belong to each separately.

1264ᵃ17 The first alternative is that all things should belong to them all in common. In that case, what will be the difference between them and the guardians? What advantage will they gain by accepting the government of the guardians? What convinces them actually to accept it? — unless it be some device such as is used in Crete, where the serfs are allowed to enjoy the same general privileges as their masters, and are excluded only from athletic exercises and the possession of arms.

1264ᵃ22 The second alternative is that these institutions should be the same for the farmers as they are in most cities today. In that case, we may inquire, what the character of their association will be? There will inevitably be two cities in one, and those cities will be opposed to one another — the guardians being made into something of the nature of an army of occupation, and the farmers, artisans, and others being given the position of ordinary civilians. Again, legal complaints, and actions at law, and all the other evils which he describes as existing in cities as they are, will equally exist among them. Certainly Socrates says that, in virtue of their education, they will not need a number of regulations (such as city ordinances, market by-laws, and the like); but it is also true that he provides education only for the guardians. A further difficulty is that he has the farmers control their holdings on condition that they pay a quota of their produce to the guardians. This is likely to make them far more difficult to handle, and much more filled with high ideas of their own importance, than other people's helots, penestae, or serfs.

ASIAN RELIGIONS AND TRADITIONS

While entitlements to property were recognized in many Asian societies, visionaries such as Confucius, Kautilya, Manu, and Buddha considered the limitation of wealth as essential to the achievement of peaceful and just societies. In *The Annalects* (c. 551–479 B.C.E.), Confucius taught his disciples how a benevolent leader needed to enhance the economic well-being of his people, because "where there is even distribution there is no such a thing as poverty, where there is harmony there is no such a thing as underpopulation and where there is stability, there is no such a thing as overturning" a ruler (see Section 2.5).

Driven by similar concerns, Kautilya's *Arthashastra* (c. 300 B.C.E.) outlined rules that both guaranteed individual ownership over property and protected labor rights, such as a worker's right to a salary for work done, even if he is subsequently fired for negligence (see Section 2.6). *The Laws of Manu* is a foundational work of Hindu law and ancient Indian society (c. 200 B.C.E.). Having elaborated different rules for different castes, Manu argued that certain laws, such as the ones pertaining to property, were to be considered fundamental. "The king," Manu maintained in *The Laws*, "must give back to men of all classes property taken by thieves; a king who uses it for himself commits the offense of a thief." The notion of restitution of stolen property was also invoked in many Buddhist texts (see Section 2.7). Overall, Buddhist writings praised donations to the needy as spiritually more enriching than property accumulation (see Section 2.8).

2.5 CONFUCIUS: ON FAIR DISTRIBUTION AND EDUCATION (*THE ANNALECTS*, C. 551–479 B.C.E.)

BOOK XVI

Confucius said: "Ch'iu, the gentleman detests those who, rather than saying outright that they want something, can be counted on to gloss over their remarks. What I have heard is that the head of a state or a noble family worries not about underpopulation but about uneven distribution, not about poverty but about instability.[1] For where there is even distribution there is no such thing as poverty, where there is harmony there is no such thing as underpopulation and where there is stability there is no such thing as overturning. It is for this reason that when distant subjects are unsubmissive one cultivates one's moral quality in order to attract them, and once they have come one makes them content. But you and Yu have not been able either to help your master to attract the distant subjects when they are unsubmissive or to preserve the state when it is disintegrating. Instead, you propose to resort to the use of arms within the state itself. I am afraid that Chi-sun's worries lie not in Chuan Yi but within the walls of his palace."

BOOK XX

2. Tzu-chang asked Confucius, "What must a man be like before he can take part in government?"

The Master said, "If he exalts the five excellent practices and eschews the four wicked practices he can take part in government."

Tzu-chang said, "What is meant by the five excellent practices?"

The Master said, "The gentleman is generous without its costing him anything, works others hard without their complaining, has desires without being greedy, is casual without being arrogant, and is awe-inspiring without appearing fierce."

Tzu-chang said, "What is meant by 'being generous without its costing him anything'?"

The Master said, "If a man benefits the common people by taking advantage of the things around them that they find beneficial, is this not being generous without its costing him anything? If a man, in working others hard, chooses burdens they can support, who will complain? If, desiring benevolence, a man obtains it, where is the greed? The gentleman never dare neglect his manners whether he be dealing with the many or the few, the young or the old. Is this not being casual without being arrogant? The gentleman, with his robe and cap adjusted properly and dignified in his gaze, has a presence which inspires people who see him with awe. Is this not being awe-inspiring without appearing fierce?"

BOOK VII

2. The Master said, "Quietly to store up knowledge in my mind, to learn without flagging, to teach without growing weary, these present me with no difficulties."

3. The Master said, "It is these things that cause me concern: failure to cultivate virtue, failure to go more deeply into what I have learned, inability, when I am told what is right, to move to where it is, and inability to reform myself when I have defects."

7. The Master said, "I have never denied instruction to anyone who, of his own accord, has given me so much as a bundle of dried meat as a present."

8. The Master said, "I never enlighten anyone who has not been driven to distraction by trying to understand a difficulty or who has not got into a frenzy trying to put his ideas into words.

"When I have pointed out one corner of a square to anyone and he does not come back with the other three, I will not point it out to him a second time."

BOOK XV

8. The Master said, "To fail to speak to a man who is capable of benefiting is to let a man go to waste. To speak to a man who is incapable of benefiting is to let one's words go to waste. A wise man lets neither men nor words go to waste."

36. The Master said, "When faced with the opportunity to practice benevolence do not give precedence even to your teacher."

37. The Master said, "The gentleman is devoted to principle but not inflexible in small matters."

39. The Master said, "In instruction there is no separation into categories."

40. The Master said, "There is no point in people taking counsel together who follow different ways."

[1]The text is corrupt here. In the light of what follows, this passage should, probably, read: "... worries not about poverty but about uneven distribution, not about underpopulation but about disharmony, not about overturning but about instability."

2.6 KAUTILYA: ON LABOR AND PROPERTY RIGHTS
(*ARTHASHASTRA*, C. 300 B.C.E.)

Chapter XIV

Rules Regarding Laborers; and Co-operative Undertaking

A servant neglecting or unreasonably putting off work for which he has received wages shall be fined 12 panas and be caught hold of till the work is done. He who is incapable to turn out work, or is engaged to do a mean job, or is suffering from disease, or is involved in calamites shall be shown some concession or he shall allow his master to get the work done by a substitute. The loss incurred by his master or employer owing to such delay shall be made good by extra work.

§185

An employer may be at liberty to get the work done by another provided there is no such adverse condition that the former shall not employ another servant to execute the work, nor shall the latter go elsewhere for work. My preceptor holds that not taking work on the part of an employer from his employee when the latter is ready, shall be regarded as work done by the laborer. But Kautilya objects to it; for wages are to be paid for work done, but not for work that is not done. If an employer, having caused his laborer to do a part of work, will not cause him to do the rest for which the latter may certainly be ready, then the unfinished portion of the work has to be regarded as finished. But owing to consideration of changes that have occurred in time and place or owing to bad workmanship of the laborer, the employer may not be pleased with what has already been turned out by the laborer. Also the workman may, if unrestrained, do more than agreed upon and thereby cause loss to the employer.[2]

The same rules shall apply to guilds of workmen (sangha-bhrtāh). Guilds of workmen shall have a grace of seven nights over and above the period agreed upon for fulfilling their engagement. Beyond that time they shall find substitutes and get the work completed. Without taking permission from their employers, they shall neither leave out anything undone

nor carry away anything with them from the place of work. They shall be fined 24 panas for taking away anything and 12 panas for leaving out anything undone. Thus the rules regarding laborers. Guilds of workmen (sanghbhrtah, workmen employed by companies) as well as those who carry on any co-operative work (sambhūya samutthāthārah) shall divide their earnings (vetanam wages) either equally or as agreed upon among themselves.

Cultivators or merchants shall, either at the end or in the middle of their cultivation or manufacture, pay to their laborers as much of the latter's share as is proportional to the work done. If the laborers, giving up work in the middle, supply substitutes, they shall be paid their wages in full.

But when commodities are being manufactured, wages shall be paid out according to the amount of work turned out; for such payment does not affect the favorable or unfavorable results on the way (i.e. in the sale of merchandise by pedlars).

§186

A healthy person who deserts his company after work has been begun shall be fined 12 panas; for none shall, of his own accord, leave his company. Any person who is found to have neglected his share of work by stealth shall be shown mercy (abhayam) for the first time, and given a proportional quality of work anew with promise of proportional share of earnings as well. In case of negligence for a second time or of going elsewhere, he shall be thrown out of the company (pravāsanam). If he is guilty of a glaring offense (mahāparādhe), he shall be treated as the condemned.

Chapter XVI

§190

Whatever of the property of his own subjects the king brings back from the forests and countries of enemies, shall be handed over to its owner. Whatever of the property of citizens robbed by thieves the king cannot recover, shall be made good from his own pocket. If the king is unable to recover such things, he shall either allow any self-elected person (svayamgraāha) to fetch them, or pay an equivalent ransom to the sufferer. An adventurer may enjoy whatever the king graciously gives him out of the booty he has plundered from an enemy's country excepting the life of an ārya and the property belonging to gods, Brāhmanas or ascetics. Thus sale without ownership is dealt with.

As to the title of an owner to his property: The owners who have quitted their country where their property lies shall continue to have their title to it. When the owners other than, minors, the aged, those that are afflicted with disease or calamities, those that are sojourning abroad, or those that have deserted their country during national disturbances, neglect for ten years their property which is under the enjoyment of others, they shall forfeit their title to it....

2.7 MANU: ON PROPERTY RIGHTS
(*THE LAWS*, C. 200 B.C.E.)

[27] The king should protect the estate and other inherited property of a boy until he has come home (after his studies) or passed beyond his childhood. [28] In the same way, he should protect women who are barren or have no sons, who have no families, who are faithful wives, widows, or ill. [29] But if, while these women are alive, their own relatives take away this (property), a just king should punish them with the punishment for theft.

[30] If the owner of any property has disappeared, the king should keep it in trust for three years; within three years the owner may take it, and after that the king may take it. [31] If someone says, "This is mine," he should be questioned in accordance with the rules; if he describes the shape, the number, and so forth, he deserves that property as the owner. [32] But if he does not accurately declare the time and place (of the loss) and the color, shape, and measurements of the lost property, then he deserves a fine equal to its value. [33] Now, the king may take a sixth part of property (thus) lost and found, or a tenth, or a twelfth, bearing in mind the laws of good men. [34] Property that has been lost and then found should be placed in the keeping of the appropriate people; if the king catches thieves trying to steal it he should have them killed by an elephant.

[35] If a man says truthfully of a treasure-trove, "This is mine," the king should take a sixth part of it, or a twelfth. [36] But if he lies, he should be fined an eighth of his own property, or a smaller, fraction of the treasure, when its value has been calculated. [37] And when a learned priest finds a treasure that was previously hidden, he may take it even without leaving anything, for he is the overlord of everything. [38] But when the king finds ancient treasure hidden in the earth, he should give half to the twice-born and put half in his treasury. [39] The king gets half of ancient treasures and minerals in the ground because he protects (it) and because he is the overlord of the earth.

[40] The king must give back to men of all classes property taken by thieves; a king who uses it for himself commits the offense of a thief. [41] Taking into consideration the laws of the castes, districts, guilds, and families, a king who knows justice should establish the particular law of each. [42] Men who carry out their own innate activities and engage each in his own particular innate activity become dear to people even when they are far away...

[47] When a creditor urges (the king) for the recovery of a debt from a debtor, he should make the debtor give the creditor the money that he has proven due him. [48] He should make the debtor pay by forcing him through whatever means the creditor can use to obtain his own money. [49] By law, by legal action, by a trick, by the usual custom and, fifth, by force, he may recover money that has been lent. [50] If a creditor recovers his money from a debtor by himself, the king should not prosecute him for recovering his own property. [51] But if a man denies a debt that has been proven by a legal instrument, (the king) should make him pay the money to the creditor, as well as a small fine, according to his ability.

[52] When a debtor has been told in court, "Pay," and he denies the debt, the plaintiff must call (a witness who was) at the place (where the debt was contracted), or adduce some other legal instrument. [53] If he calls someone who was not at the place or if he takes back what he has stated or does not realize that his earlier and subsequent state-

ments of fact do not harmonize; [54] or if he states what he means to prove and then afterwards departs from it, or when questioned about a properly acknowledged statement of fact does not uphold it; [55] or if he converses with witnesses in a place where they should not converse, or does not wish to answer a question put to him, or rushes out; [56] or if he is told, "Speak," and does not speak, or does not prove what he has said, or does not know what comes first and what comes last, then he loses his case...

[59] If (a debtor) falsely denies a certain sum of money, or (a creditor) falsely claims it, the king should make both of them pay a fine of double the amount, for they do not understand justice. [60] If (a debtor) is brought to court by a creditor and, when questioned, denies (the debt), he must be proven (guilty) by at least three witnesses, in the presence of the king and the priests.

2.8 BUDDHISM: ON THE LIMITATION OF PROPERTY AND ALTRUISM (*BODHICARYĀVATĀRA OF SĀNTIDEVA*, C. 8TH CENTURY)

Hungry Ghost (Preta) Realm

People who steal food become katapūtana pretas, who are deprived of energy and who feed on corpses.

Those who harm children and out of desire lead them astray are reborn as katapūtanas, feeding on fetal matter.

People who are vile and utterly wretched, selfish and ever-lusting, are reborn after death as pretas with goiters.

The person who hinders the practice of dāna and who gives nothing himself will become an emaciated preta with a big belly and a mouth the size of a needle.

The person who hoards his wealth for the sake of his family, without enjoying it or giving it away, is reborn as a preta who receives only what is given as funeral offerings made to the dead.

The person who wishes to deprive others of their wealth and who gives only to regret it immediately becomes a preta consuming excrement, phlegm, and vomit.

The person who, out of anger, speaks unkind words that cut to the quick will, as a result of that act, be for a long time a preta with a flaming mouth.

And the person who causes strife, who has a fierce disposition and no pity, will become a preta agitated by fear, feeding on worms and various kinds of insects....

Human Realm

Among gods, asuras, and humans, nonviolence leads to a long life; violence gives rise to a short life. Thus, one should abstain from violence.

Leprosy, consumption, fever, madness, and other human diseases are due to killing, tying up, and whipping creatures.

People who steal others' property and give out nothing whatsoever will never themselves become wealthy, strive as they may.

One who takes goods that were not given but who also gives gifts will, after death, first become wealthy but then exceedingly poor.

One who neither steals nor gives nor is excessively niggardly will, with great effort, obtain a lasting fortune in the next life.

People who do not steal others' property, who are generous and free from greed, obtain what they wish: great wealth that cannot be taken away.

One who, in this world, makes donations of alms food will be reborn ever-happy: endowed with long life, good complexion, strength, good fortune, and good health.

One who makes offerings of clothes will become modest, good looking, and well dressed, enjoying life and cutting a handsome figure.

People who happily, without regret, make a donation of a dwelling, will, in a future life, be endowed with palaces and everything they want.

By virtue of a gift of a lamp, a person will come to have good eyes; by the gift of a musical instrument, a good voice; by the gift of beds and seats, ease and comfort....

He who abstains from the wives of others will obtain the wives he desires; and he who stays away from his own wives, when the place and time are not right, will again be reborn as a man....

Altruistic Intent

May I too, through whatever good I have accomplished by doing all this, become one who works for the complete alleviation of the sufferings of all beings.

May I be medicine for the sick; may I also be their physician and attend to them until their disease no longer recurs.

With showers of food and water, may I eliminate the pain of hunger and thirst, and during the intermediate periods of great famine between eons, may I be food and drink.

And may I be an inexhaustible storehouse for the poor, and may I always be first in being ready to serve them in various ways.

So that all beings may achieve their aims, may I sacrifice, without regret, the bodies, as well as the pleasures that I have had, and the merit of all the good that I have accomplished and will accomplish in the past, present, and future.

Nirvāna means to renounce everything. My mind is set on nirvāna, so because I am to renounce everything, it is best for me to give it to others.

MONOTHEISM

The avoidance of excessive wealth and selfless charity were similarly encouraged by the three monotheist religions. The Hebrew Bible urged people to help secure both work and rest for the laborer, the poor, and the foreigner (see Section 2.9). In a similar vein, the New Testament condemned the greed and abuses of the rich and stipulated that those who live a frugal and altruistic life would have better prospects for a blissful afterlife in heaven (see Section 2.10). Charity is also a central injunction of the Koran, which reminds believers not to waste property vainly or show off, but to help the poor and the needy (see Section 2.11).

2.9 THE HEBREW BIBLE: ON THE WELFARE OF THE POOR, THE LABORER, AND THE STRANGER

Exodus 20:8–11

Remember to keep the sabbath day holy. You have six days to labor and do all your work. But the seventh day is a sabbath of the Lord your God; that day you shall not do any work, you, your son or your daughter, your slave or your slave-girl, your cattle or the alien within your gates; for in six days the Lord made heaven and earth, the sea, and all that is in them, and on the seventh day he rested. Therefore the Lord blessed the sabbath day and declared it holy.

Exodus 22:21–27

You shall not wrong an alien, or be hard upon him; you were yourselves aliens in Egypt. You shall not ill-treat any widow or fatherless child. If you do, be sure that I will listen if they appeal to me; my anger will be roused and I will kill you with the sword; your own wives shall become widows and your children fatherless.

If you advance money to any poor man amongst my people, you shall not act like a money-lender: you must not exact interest in advance from him.

If you take your neighbor's cloak in pawn, you shall return it to him by sunset, because it is his only covering. It is the cloak in which he wraps his body; in what else can he sleep? If he appeals to me, I will listen, for I am full of compassion.

Exodus 23:6–11

You shall not deprive the poor man of justice in his suit. Avoid all lies, and do not cause the death of the innocent and the guiltless; for I the Lord will never acquit the guilty. You shall not accept a bribe, for bribery makes the discerning man blind and the just man give a crooked answer.

You shall not oppress the alien, for you know how it feels to be an alien; you were aliens yourselves in Egypt.

For six years you may sow your land and gather its produce; but in the seventh year you shall let it lie fallow and leave it alone. It shall provide food for the poor of your people, and what they leave the wild animals may eat. You shall do likewise with your vineyard and your olive-grove.

Deuteronomy 15:1–11

At the end of every seventh year you shall make a remission of debts. This is how the remission shall be made: everyone who holds a pledge shall remit the pledge of anyone indebted to him. He shall not press a fellow-countryman for repayment, for the Lord's year of remission has been declared. You may press foreigners; but if it is a fellow-countryman that holds anything of yours, you must remit all claim upon it. There will never be any poor among you if only you obey the Lord your God by carefully keeping these commandments which I lay upon you this day; for the Lord your God will bless you with great prosperity in the land which he is giving you to occupy as your patrimony. When the Lord your God blesses you, as he promised, you will lend to men of many nations, but you yourselves will not borrow; you will rule many nations, but they will not rule you.

When one of your fellow-countrymen in any of your settlements in the land which the Lord your God is giving you becomes poor, do not be hard-hearted or close-fisted with your countryman in his need. Be open-handed towards him and lend him on pledge as much as he needs. See that you do not harbor iniquitous thoughts when you find that the seventh year, the year of remission, is near, and look askance at your needy countryman and give him nothing. If you do, he will appeal to the Lord against you, and you will be found guilty of sin. Give freely to him and do not begrudge him your bounty, because it is for this very bounty that the Lord your God will bless you in everything that you do or undertake. The poor will always be with you in the land, and for that reason I command you to be open-handed with your countrymen, both poor and distressed, in your own land.

Deuteronomy 24:10–15

When you make a loan to another man, do not enter his house to take a pledge from him. Wait outside, and the man whose creditor you are shall bring the pledge out to you. If he is a poor man, you shall not sleep in the cloak he has pledged. Give it back to him at sunset so that he may sleep in it and bless you; then it will be counted to your credit in the sight of the Lord your God.

You shall not keep back the wages of a man who is poor and needy, whether a fellow-countryman or an alien living in your country in one of your settlements. Pay him his wages on the same day before sunset, for he is poor and his heart is set on them: he may appeal to the Lord against you, and you will be guilty of sin.

Proverbs 14:31–34

He who oppresses the poor insults his Maker; he who is generous to the needy honors him.

An evil man is brought down by his wickedness; the upright man is secure in his own honesty.

Wisdom is at home in a discerning mind, but is ill at ease in the heart of a fool.

Righteousness raises a people to honor; to do wrong is a disgrace to any nation.

2.10 THE NEW TESTAMENT: ON GREED AND CHARITY (C. 50)

Mark 10:20–31

"But, Master," he replied, "I have kept all these since I was a boy." Jesus looked straight at him; his heart warmed to him, and he said, "One thing you lack: go, sell everything you have, and give to the poor, and you will have riches in heaven; and come, follow me." At these words his face fell and he went away with a heavy heart; for he was a man of great wealth.

Jesus looked round at his disciples and said to them, 'How hard it will be for the wealthy to enter the kingdom of God!" They were amazed that he should say this, but Jesus insisted, "Children, how hard it is to enter the kingdom of God! It is easier for a camel to pass through the eye of a needle than for a rich man to enter the kingdom of God." They were more astonished than ever, and said to one another, "Then who can be saved?" Jesus looked at them and said, "For men it is impossible, but not for God; everything is possible for God."

At this Peter spoke. "We here," he said, "have left everything to become your followers." Jesus said, "I tell you this: there is no one who has given up home, brothers or sisters, mother, father or children, or land, for my sake and for the Gospel, who will not receive in this age a hundred times as much — houses, brothers and sisters, mothers and children, and land — and persecutions besides; and in the age to come eternal life. But many who are first will be last and the last first."

2 Corinthians 8:7–15

You are so rich in everything — in faith, speech, knowledge, and zeal of every kind, as well as in the loving regard you have for us — surely you should show yourselves equally lavish in this generous service! This is not meant as an order; by telling you how keen others are I am putting your love to the test. For you know how generous our Lord Jesus Christ has been: he was rich, yet for your sake he became poor, so that through his poverty you might become rich.

Here is my considered opinion on the matter. What I ask you to do is in your own interests. You made a good beginning last year both in the work you did and in your willingness to undertake it. Now I want you to go on and finish it: be as eager to complete the scheme as you were to adopt it, and give according to your means. Provided there is an eager desire to give, God accepts what a man has; he does not ask for what he has not. There is no question of relieving others at the cost of hardship to yourselves; it is a question of equality. At the moment your surplus meets their need, but one day your need may be met from their surplus. The aim is equality; as Scripture has it, "The man who got much had no more than enough, and the man who got little did not go short."

2 Corinthians 9:6–12

Remember: sparse sowing, sparse reaping; sow bountifully, and you will reap bountifully. Each person should give as he has decided for himself; there should be no reluctance, no sense of compulsion; God loves a cheerful giver. Thus you will have ample means in yourselves to meet each and every situation, with enough and to spare for every good cause. Scripture says of such a man: "He has lavished his gifts on the needy, his benevolence stands fast for ever." Now he who provides seed for sowing and bread for food will provide the seed for you now; he will multiply it and swell the harvest of your benevolence, and you will always be rich enough to be generous. Through our action such generosity will issue in thanksgiving to God, for as a piece for willing services this is not only a contribution towards the needs of God's people; more than that, it overflows in flood of thanksgiving to God.

James 5:1–7

Next a word to you who have great possessions. Weep and wail over the miserable fate descending on you. Your riches have rotted; your fine clothes are moth-eaten; your silver and gold have rusted away, and their very rust will be evidence against you and consume your flesh like fire. You have piled up wealth in an age that is near its close. The wages you never paid to the men who mowed your fields are loud against you, and the outcry of the reapers has reached the ears of the Lord of Hosts. You have lived on earth in wanton luxury, fattening yourselves like cattle — and the day for slaughter has come. You have condemned the innocent and murdered him; he offers no resistance.

Be patient, my brothers, until the Lord comes. The farmer looking for the precious crop his land may yield can only wait in patience, unit the autumn and spring rains have fallen.

2.11 THE KORAN: ON SOCIAL AND ECONOMIC AID (C. 632)

Surah 2 Section 34

254. Ye who believe!
Spend out of (the bounties)
We have provided for you,
Before the Day comes
When no bargaining
(Will avail), nor friendship
Nor intercession.
Those who reject Faith — they
Are the wrongdoers.

Surah 2 Section 37

268. The Evil One threatens
You with poverty
And bids you to conduct
Unseemly Allah promiseth
You his forgiveness
And bounties.
And Allah careth for all
And He knoweth all things.

269. He granteth wisdom
To whom He pleaseth;
And he to whom wisdom
Is granted receiveth
Indeed a benefit overflowing;
But none will grasp the Message
But men of understanding.

270. And whatever ye spend
In charity or devotion,
Be sure Allah knows it all.
But the wrongdoers
Have no helpers.

271. If ye disclose (act
Of) charity, even so
It is well,
But if ye conceal them,
And make them reach
Those (really) in need,
That is best for you:
It will remove from you
Some of your (stains
Of) evil. And Allah
Is well-acquainted
With what ye do.

273. (Charity is) for those
In need, who, in Allah's cause
Are restricted (from travel)
And cannot move about
In the land, seeking
(For trade or work):
The ignorant man thinks,
Because of their modesty,
That they are free from want.
Thou shalt know them
By their (unfailing) mark:
They beg not importunately
From all and sundry,
And whatever of good
Ye give, be assured
Allah knoweth it well.

Surah 3 Section 2

14.   Fair in the eyes of men
Is the love of things they covet:
Women and sons;
Heaped-up hoards
Of gold and silver; horses
Branded (for blood and
Excellence
And (wealth of) cattle
And well-tilled land.
Such are the possessions
Of this world's life;
But in nearness to Allah
Is the best of the goals
(To return to).

Surah 4 Section 5

29.   O ye who believe
Eat not up your property
Among yourselves in vanities;
But let there be amongst you
Traffic and trade
By mutual good will:
Nor kill (or destroy)
Yourselves: for verily
Allah hath been to you
Most Merciful!

Surah 4 Section 33

To (benefit) every one,
We have appointed
Sharers and heirs.

To property left
By parents and relatives.
To those, also, to whom
Your right hand was pledged,
Give their due portion.
For truly Allah is witness
To all things.

When the emigration took place from Makkah to Madīnah, bonds and links of brotherhood were established between the "Emigrants" and the "helpers," and they share in each other's inheritance. Later, when the community was solidly established, and relations with those left behind in Makkah were resumed, the rights of blood-relations in Makkah, and the Helper-brethren in Madīnah were both safeguarded ...

Surah 12 Section 24

215. They ask thee
What they should spend
(In charity). Say: Whatever
Ye spend that is good,
Is for parents and kindred
And orphans
And those in want
And for wayfarers.
And whatever ye do
That is good — Allah
Knoweth it well.

CHAPTER 3

Justice, War, and Peace

If excessive wealth was a source of misery and war, what rules should guide decisions on war and peace? Some traditions invoked the right to rebel against tyranny, others developed guidelines to ensure that wars were waged justly and conducted with restraint, and still others insisted on passive resistance no matter what the provocation. In the contemporary era, the Geneva Convention of 1949, the United Nations Charter of 1945, and the Preamble of the Universal Declaration of Human Rights of 1948 address similar concerns.

3.1 UNITED NATIONS UNIVERSAL DECLARATION OF HUMAN RIGHTS (1948): ARTICLES 28–30

Article 28

Everyone is entitled to a social and international order in which the rights and freedoms set forth in this Declaration can be fully realized.

Article 29

1.   Everyone has duties to the community in which alone the free and full development of his personality is possible.

2.   In the exercise of his rights and freedoms, everyone shall be subject only to such limitations as are determined by law solely for the purpose of securing due recognition and respect for the rights and freedoms of others and of meeting the just requirements of morality, public order and the general welfare in a democratic society.

3.   These rights and freedoms may in no case be exercised contrary to the purposes and principles of the United Nations.

Article 30

Nothing in this Declaration may be interpreted as implying for any State, group or person any right to engage in any activity or to perform any act aimed at the destruction of any of the rights and freedoms set forth herein.

THE SECULAR TRADITION

The secular tradition owes greatly to the moral lessons drawn from *The History of the Peloponnesian War*. Its author, Greek historian Thucydides (c. 460/455–400 B.C.E.), recounts the war waged between Sparta and Athens during the fifth century. His Melian dialogue, showing the failure of the Melians to avert destruction through appeals to justice, famously dramatizes the confrontation between naked power and morality (see Section 3.2). Horrified by the loss of lives during the Greek wars, Socrates in Plato's *Republic* (c. 360 B.C.E.) implored the Greeks not to enslave their enemies (whether Greeks or others), not to ravage their lands, not to burn their houses, and not to kill innocents (see Section 3.2).

3.2 THUCYDIDES: ON JUSTICE VERSUS POWER: "THE MELIAN DIALOGUE" (*THE HISTORY OF THE PELOPONNESIAN WAR*, C. 411 B.C.E.)

... The Melians are colonists of the Lacedaemonians who would not submit to Athens like the other islanders. At first they were neutral and took no part. But when the Athenians tried to coerce them by ravaging their lands, they were driven into open hostilities. The generals, Cleomedes the son of Lycomedes and Tisias the son of Tisimachus, encamped with the Athenian forces on the island. But before they did the country any harm they sent envoys to negotiate with the Melians. Instead of bringing these envoys before the people, the Melians desired them to explain their errand to the magistrates and to the dominant class. They spoke as follows:

85   "Since we are not allowed to speak to the people, lest, forsooth, a multitude should be deceived by seductive and unanswerable arguments which they would hear set forth in a single uninterrupted oration(for we are perfectly aware that this is what you mean in bringing us before a select few), you who are sitting here may as well make assurance yet surer. Let us have no set speeches at all, but do you reply to each several statement of which you disapprove, and criticize it at once. Say first of all how you like this mode of proceeding."

86   The Melian representatives answered: "The quiet interchange of explanations is a reasonable thing, and we do not object to that. But your warlike movements, which are present not only to our fears but to our eyes, seem to belie your words. We see that, although you may reason with us, you mean to be our judges; and that at the end of the discussion, if the justice of our cause prevail and we therefore refuse to yield, we may expect war; if we are convinced by you, slavery."

87   Ath.: "Nay, but if you are only going to argue from fancies about the future, or if you meet us with any other purpose than that of looking your circumstances in the face and saving your city, we have done; but if this is your intention we will proceed."

88   Mel.: "It is an excusable and natural thing that men in our position should neglect no argument and no view which may avail. But we admit that this conference has met to consider the question of our preservation; and therefore let the argument proceed in the manner which you propose."

89   Ath.: ... "You and we should say what we really think, and aim only at what is possible, for we both alike know that into the discussion of human affairs the question of justice only enters where there is equal power to enforce it, and that the powerful exact what they can, and the weak grant what they must."

90   Mel.: "Well, then, since you set aside justice and invite us to speak of expediency, in our judgment it is certainly expedient that you should respect a principle which is for the common good; that to every man when in peril a reasonable claim should be accounted a claim of right, and that any plea which he is disposed to urge, even if failing of the point a little, should help his cause. Your interest in this principle is quite as great as ours inasmuch as you, if you fall, will incur the heaviest vengeance, and will be the most terrible example to mankind."

91   Ath.: "The fall of our empire, if it should fall, is not an event to which we look forward with dismay; for ruling states such as Lacedaemon are not cruel to their vanquished enemies. With the Lacedaemonians, however, we are not now contending; the real danger is from our many subject states, who may of their own motion rise up and overcome their masters. But this is a danger which you may leave to us. And we will now endeavor to show that we have come in the interests of our empire, and that in what we are about to say we are only seeking the preservation of your city. For we want to make you ours with the least trouble to ourselves, and it is for

the interests of us both that you should not be destroyed."

92 Mel.: "It may be your interest to be our masters, but how can it be ours to be your slaves?"

93 Ath.: "To you the gain will be that by submission you will avert the worst; and we shall be all the richer for your preservation."

94 Mel.: "But must we be your enemies? Will you not receive us as friends if we are neutral and remain at peace with you?"

95 Ath.: "No, your enmity is not half so mischievous to us as your friendship; for the one is in the eyes of our subjects an argument of our power, the other of our weakness."

96 Mel.: "But are your subjects really unable to distinguish between states in which you have no concern, and those which are chiefly your own colonies, and in some cases have revolted and been subdued by you?"

97 Ath.: "Why, they do not doubt that both of them have a good deal to say for themselves on the score of justice, but they think that states like yours are left free because they are able to defend themselves, and that we do not attack them because we dare not. So that your subjection will give us an increase of security, as well as an extension of empire. For we are masters of the sea, and you who are islanders, and insignificant islanders too, must not be allowed to escape us."

98 Mel.: "But do you not recognize another danger? For, once more, since you drive us from the plea of justice press upon us your doctrine of expediency, we must show you what is for our interest, and, if it be for yours also, may hope to convince you: — Will you not be making enemies of all who are now neutrals? When they see how you are treating us they will expect you some day to turn against them; and if so, are you not strengthening the enemies whom you already have, and bringing upon you others who, if they could help, would

never dream of being your enemies at all?"

99 Ath.: "We do not consider our really dangerous enemies to be any of the peoples inhabiting the mainland who, secure in their freedom, may defer indefinitely any measures of precaution which they take us, but islanders who, like you, happen to be under no control, and all who may be already irritated by the necessity of submission to our empire — these are our real enemies, for they are the most reckless and most likely to bring themselves as well as us into a danger which they cannot but foresee."

100 Mel.: "Surely then, if you and your subjects will brave all this risk, you to preserve your empire and they to be quit of it, how base and cowardly would it be in us, who retain our freedom, not to do and suffer anything rather than be your slaves."

101 Ath.: "Not so, if you calmly reflect: for you are not fighting against equals to whom you cannot yield without disgrace, but you are taking counsel whether or not you resist an overwhelming force. The question is not one of honor but of prudence."

102 Mel.: "But we know that the fortune of war is sometimes and not always on the side of numbers. If we yield now, all is over; but if we fight there is yet a hope that we may stand upright."

103 Ath.: "Hope is a good comforter in the hour of danger, and when men have something else to depend upon, although hurtful, she is not ruinous. But when her spend-thrift nature has induced them to stake their all, they see her as she is in the moment of their fall, and not till then. While the knowledge of her might enable them to be ware of her, she never fails. You are weak and a single turn of the scale might be your ruin. Do not you be thus deluded; avoid the error of which so many are guilty, who, although they might still be saved if they would take the natural means, when visible grounds of confidence forsake them, have recourse to the invis-

ible, to prophecies and oracles and the like, which ruin men by the hopes which they inspire in them."

104 Mel.: "We know only too well how hard the struggle must be against you and against fortune, if she does not mean to be impartial. Nevertheless we do not despair of fortune; for we hope to stand as high as you in the favor of heaven, because we are righteous and you against whom we contend are righteous; and we are satisfied that our deficiency in power will be compensated by the aid of our allies the Lacedaemonians; they cannot refuse to help us, if only because we are their kinsmen, and for the sake of their own honor. And therefore our confidence is not so utterly blind as you suppose."

105 Ath.: "As for the Gods, we expect to have quite as much of their favor as you: for we are not doing or claiming anything which goes beyond common opinion, about divine or men's desires about human things...."And then as to the Lacedaemonians — when you imagine that out of very shame they will assist you, we admire the innocence of your idea, but we do not envy you the folly of it. The Lacedaemonians are exceedingly virtuous among themselves, and according to their national standard of morality. But, in respect of their dealings with others, although many things might be said, they can be described in few words — of all men whom we know they are the most notorious for identifying what is pleasant with what is honorable, and what is expedient with what is just. But how inconsistent is such a character with your present blind hope of deliverance!"

106 Mel.: "That is the very reason why we trust them; they will look to their interest, and therefore will not be willing to betray the Melians, who are their own colonist lest they should be distrusted by their friends in Hellas and play into the hands of their enemies.

107 Ath.: "But do you not see that the path of expediency is safe, whereas justice and honor involve danger in practice, and such dangers the Lacedaemonians seldom care to face."

108 Mel.: "On the other hand, we think that whatever perils there may be, they will be ready to face them for our sakes, and will consider danger less dangerous where we are concerned. For if they need our aid we are close at hand, and they can better trust our loyal feeling because we are their kinsmen....

111 Ath.: Your strongest grounds are hopes deferred, and what power you have is not to be compared with that which is already arrayed against you. Unless after we have withdrawn you mean to come, as even now you may, to a wiser conclusion, you are showing a great want of sense. For surely you cannot dream of flying to that false sense of honor which has been the ruin of so many when danger and dishonor were staring them in the face. Many men with their eyes still open to the consequences have found the word 'honor' too much for them, and have suffered a mere name to lure them on, until it has drawn down upon them real and irretrievable calamities; through their own folly they have incurred a worse dishonor than fortune would have inflicted upon them. If you are wise you will not run this risk; you ought to see that there can be no disgrace in yielding to a great city which invites you to become her ally on reasonable terms, keeping your own land, and merely paying tribute; and that you will certainly gain no honor if, having to choose between two alternatives, safety and war, you obstinately prefer the worse. To maintain our rights against equals, to be politic with superiors, and to be moderate towards inferiors is the path of safety. Reflect once more when we have withdrawn, and say to yourselves over and over again that you are deliberating about your one and only country, which may be saved or may be destroyed by a single decision."

112 The Athenians left the conference: the Melians, after consulting among themselves, resolved to persevere in their refusal.

113 The Athenian envoys returned to the army; and the generals, when they found that the Melians would not yield, immediately commenced hostilities. They surrounded the town of Melos with a wall, dividing the work among the several contingents. They then left troops of their own and of their allies to keep guard both by land and by sea, and retired with the greater part of their army; the remainder carried on the blockade....

115 Later the Athenians put to death all who were of military age, and made slaves of the women and children. They then colonized the island, sending thither five hundred settlers of their own.

3.3 PLATO: ON HOW TO TREAT ONE'S ENEMY (*THE REPUBLIC*, C. 360 B.C.E.)

"[H]ow will our soldiers treat their enemies? First, over slavery. Do you think it is right for Greeks to sell Greeks into slavery, or to allow others to do so, so far as they can prevent it? Ought they not rather to make it their custom to spare their fellows, for fear of failing under barbarian domination?"

"It would be infinitely better to spare them."

"There will then be no Greek slave in our sate, and it will advise other Greek states to follow suit."

"Certainly. That would encourage them to let each other alone and turn against the barbarian."

"Then is it a good thing to strip the dead, after a victory, of anything but their arms? It gives the cowards an excuse not to pursue the enemy who are still capable of fight, if they can pretend they are doing their duty by poking about among the dead. Indeed, many an army has been lost before now by this habit of plunder. And don't you think there's something low and mean about plundering a corpse, and a kind of feminine small-mindedness in treating the body as an enemy when the fighting spirit which fought in it has flown? It's rather like the dog's habit of snarling at the stones thrown at it, but

keeping clear of the person who's throwing them."

"Yes, it's very like that."

"So we'll have no stripping of corpses and no refusal to allow burial."

"I entirely agree," he said.

"Nor shall we dedicate the arms of our enemies in our temples, particularly if they are the arms of fellow-Greeks and we have any feeling of loyalty towards them. On the contrary, we shall be afraid that we should desecrate a temple by offering them the arms of our own people, unless indeed Apollo rules otherwise."

"Quite right."

"Then what about devastating the lands and burning the houses of Greek enemies? What will your soldiers do about that?"

"I'd like to know what you think about it."

"I don't think they ought to do either, but confine themselves to carrying off the year's harvest. Shall I tell you why?"

"Yes."

"I think that the two words 'war' and 'civil strife' refer to two different realities. They are used of disputes which arise in two different spheres, the one internal and domestic, the other external and foreign; and we call a domestic quarrel 'civil strife,' and an external one 'war.'"

"Quite a suitable definition."

"Then do you think it equally suitable if I say that all relations between Greek and Greek are internal and domestic, and all relations between Greek and barbarian foreign and external?"

"Yes."

"Then when Greek fights barbarian or barbarian Greek we shall say they are at war and are natural enemies, and that their quarrel is properly called a 'war'; but when Greek fights Greek we shall say that they are naturally friends, but that Greece is torn by faction, and that the quarrel should be called 'civil strife.'"

"I agree with your view."

"Consider, then," I went on, "what happens in civil strife in its normal sense, that is to say, when there is civil war in a single state. If the two sides ravage each other's land and burn each other's houses, we think it an outrage, and regard two parties who dare to lay waste the country which bore and bred them as lacking in all patriotism. But we think it reasonable, if the victors merely carry off their opponents' crops and remember that they can't go on fighting forever but must come to terms some time."

"Yes, because the last frame of mind is the more civilized."

"Well, then," I said, "your city will be Greek, won't it?"

"It must be."

"And its people brave and civilized?"

"Certainly."

"Then they will love their fellow-Greeks, and think of Greece as their own land, in whose common religion they share."

"Yes, certainly."

"And any quarrel with Greeks they will regard as civil strife, because it is with their own people, and so won't call it 'war.'"

"That's true."

"They will fight in the hope of coming to terms. And their object will be to correct a friend and bring him to his senses, rather than to enslave and destroy an enemy. It follows that they will not, as Greeks, devastate Greek lands or burn Greek dwellings; nor will they admit that the whole people of a state — men, women, and children — are their enemies, but only the minority who are responsible for the quarrel. They will not therefore devastate the land or destroy the houses of the friendly majority, but press their quarrel only until the guilty minority are brought to justice by the innocent victims."

"For myself?" he said, "I agree that our citizens ought to behave in this way to their enemies; though when they are fighting barbarians they should treat them as the Greeks now treat each other."

"Then let us lay it down as a law for our Guardians, that they are neither to ravage land nor burn houses."

"We will do so," he agreed; "it is a good rule, like all our others."

ASIAN RELIGIONS AND TRADITIONS

Averting, even abolishing, warfare was also an issue of concern on the Asian continent. Living during a period of war among feudal states, Chinese scholar Confucius (551–479 B.C.E.) urged rulers to ensure that, above all, people have enough food to eat, maintaining that this was the best way to ward off wars (see Section 3.3). If a ruler fails to provide for his people, he "endanger[s] the altars to the gods of earth and grain" (the symbol of independence of the state) and should be replaced, claimed Mencius, 372 to 289 B.C.E. (see Section 3.4). A disciple of Confucius and a Chinese official, Mencius wrote during the Warring State Period (319–312 B.C.E.). By Confucius' and Mencius' accounts, the Indian ruler Asoka would have undoubtedly been praised for following the Kaliṅga war, having renounced all forms of violence and informed his people and neighboring countries of his unshakable resolution to live by his decision until the end of his reign (see Section 3.5).

3.4 CONFUCIUS: ON PEACE AND ECONOMIC JUSTICE (*THE ANALECTS*, C. 551–479 B.C.E.)

Book XII

7. Tzu-kung asked about government. The Master said, "Give them enough food, give them enough arms, and the common people will have trust in you."

Tzu-kung said, "If one had to give up one of these three, which should one give up first?"

"Give up arms."

Tzu-kung said, "If one had to give up one of the remaining two, which should one give up first?"

"Give up food. Death has always been with us since the beginning of time, but when there is no trust, the common people will have nothing to stand on."

42. Tzu-lu asked about the gentleman. The Master said, "He cultivates himself and thereby achieves reverence."

"Is that all?"

"He cultivates himself and thereby brings peace and security to his fellow men."

"Is that all?"

"He cultivates himself and thereby brings peace and security to the people. Even Yao and Shun would have found the task of bringing peace and security to the people taxing."

3.5 MENCIUS: ON THE RIGHT TO OVERTHROW A TYRANT (C.372–289 B.C.E.)

Book VII, Part B

1. Mencius said, "How ruthless was King Hui of Liang! A benevolent man extends his love from those he loves to those he does not love. A ruthless man extends his ruthlessness from those he does not love to those he loves."

"What do you mean?" asked Kung-sun Ch'ou.

"King Hui of Liang sent his people to war, making pulp of them, for the sake of gaining further territory. He suffered a grave defeat and when he wanted to go to war a second time he was afraid he would not be able to win, so he herded the young men he loved to their death as well. This is what I meant when I said he extended his ruthlessness from those he did not love to those he loved."

2. Mencius said, "In the Spring and Autumn period there were no just wars. There were only cases of one war not being quite as bad as another. A punitive expedition is a war waged by one in authority against his subordinates. It is not for peers to punish one another by war."

4. Mencius said, "There are people who say, 'I am expert at military formations; I am expert at waging war.' This is a grave crime. If the ruler of a state is drawn to benevolence he will have no match in the Empire. When he marched on the south, the northern barbarians complained; when he marched on the east, the western barbarians complained. They all said, 'Why does he not come to us first?'"

"When King Wu marched on Yin, he had three hundred war chariots and three thousand brave warriors. He said, 'Do not be afraid. I come to bring you peace, not to wage war on the people.' And the sound of the people knocking their heads on the ground was like the toppling of a mountain. To wage a punitive war is to rectify. There is no one who does not wish himself rectified. What need is there for war?"

5. Mencius said, "A carpenter or a carriage-maker can pass on to another the rules of his craft, but he cannot make him skillful." — *Ramen*

6. Mencius said, "When Shun lived on dried rice and wild vegetables, it was as though he was going to do this for the rest of his life. But when he became Emperor, clad in precious robes, playing on his lute, with the two daughters [of Yao] in attendance, it was as though this was what he had been used to all his life."

7. Mencius said, "Only now do I realize how serious it is to kill a member of the family of another man. If you killed his father, he would kill your father; if you killed his elder brother, he would kill your elder brother. This being the case, though you may not have killed your father and brother with your own hands, it is but one step removed." *Eye for an eye, Hammurabi*

8. Mencius said, "In antiquity, a border station was set up as a precaution against violence. Today it is set up to perpetrate violence."

9. Mencius said, "If you do not practice the Way yourself, you cannot expect it to be practiced even by your own wife and children."

13. Mencius said, "There are cases of a ruthless man gaining possession of a state, but it has never happened that such a man gained possession of the Empire."

14. Mencius said, ["The people are of supreme importance; the altars to the gods of earth and grain come next; last comes the ruler.] That is why he who gains the confidence of the multitudinous people will be Emperor; he who gains the confidence of the Emperor will be a feudal lord; he who gains the confidence of a feudal lord will be a Counsellor. When a [feudal lord endangers the altars to the gods of earth and grain[1] he should be replaced.] When the sacrificial animals are sleek, the offerings are clean and the sacrifices are observed at due times, and yet floods and droughts come, then the altars should be replaced."

[1]The symbol of independence of the state.

3.6 ASOKA: ON PEACE AND JUSTICE (*THE EDICTS*, C. 272–231 B.C.E.)

The Occasion and the Purpose of the Edicts: The Kaliṅga War, Asoka's Change of Heart, and the Ideal of Conquest by Dharma

Rock Edict XIII

The Kaliṅga country was conquered by King Priyadarśi, Beloved of the Gods, in the eighth year of his reign. One hundred and fifty thousand persons were carried away captive, one hundred thousand were slain, and many times that number died.

Immediately after the Kaliṅgas had been conquered, King Priyadarśi became intensely devoted to the study of Dharma, to the love of Dharma, and to the inculcation of Dharma.

The Beloved of the Gods, conqueror of the Kaliṅgas, is moved to remorse now. For he has felt profound sorrow and regret because the conquest of a people previously unconquered induces slaughter, death, and deportation.

But there is a more important reason for the king's remorse. The Brāhamanas and Sramanas [the priestly and ascetic orders] as well as the followers of other religions and the householders — who all practiced obedience to superiors, parents, and teachers, and proper courtesy and firm devotion to friends, acquaintances, companions, relatives, slaves, and servants — all suffer from the injury, slaughter, and deportation inflicted on their loved ones. Even those who escaped calamity themselves are deeply afflicted by the misfortunes suffered by those friends, acquaintances, companions, and relatives for whom they feel an undiminished affection. Thus all men share in the misfortune, and this weighs on King Priyadarśi's mind....

AGAINST AGGRESSION AND TENSION BETWEEN STATES

Kaliṅga Edict II

King Priyadarśi says:

I command that the following instructions be communicated to my officials at Samāpā. Whenever something right comes to my attention, I want it put into practice and I want effective means devised to achieve it. My principal means to do this is to transmit my instructions to you.

All men are my children. Just as I seek the welfare and happiness of my own children in this world and the next, I seek the same things for all men.

Unconquered peoples along the borders of my dominions may wonder what my disposition is toward them. My only wish with respect to them is that they should not fear me, but trust me; that they should expect only happiness from me, not misery; that they should understand further that I will forgive them for offenses which can be forgiven; that they should be induced by my example to practice Dharma; and that they should attain happiness in this world and the next.

I transmit these instructions to you in order to discharge my debt [to them] by instructing you and making known to you my will and my unshakable resolution and commitment. You must perform your duties in this way and establish their confidence in the King, assuring them that he is like a father to them, that he loves them as he loves himself, and that they are like his own children.

Having instructed you and informed you of my will and my unshakable resolution and commitment, I will appoint officials to carry out this program in all the provinces. You are able to inspire the border peoples with confidence in me and to advance their welfare and happiness in this world and the next. By doing so, you will also attain heaven and help me discharge my debts to the people.

This edict has been inscribed here so that my officials will work at all times to inspire the peoples of neighboring countries with confidence in me and to induce them to practice Dharma.

This edict must be proclaimed every four months [at the beginning of the three seasons — hot, rainy, and cold] on Tissya days [i.e., when the moon is in the constellation containing Tigsa, Sirius]; it may also be proclaimed in the intervals between those days; and on appropriate occasions it may be read to individuals.

By doing this, you will be carrying out my commands.

MONOTHEISM

That pacifist conviction also found expression in the Hebrew Bible, when Micah demanded that a "nation shall not lift a sword against nation, nor shall they learn war anymore" (Micah 4:3). Yet if a war was unavoidable, despite all efforts to avert it, the Hebrews, the Bible stipulated, would have to treat their prisoners humanely (see Section 3.4). The same positions were originally adopted among early Christians. By urging followers "never to pay back evil for evil," the New Testament reflected a view similar to that of the Buddhist leader Asoka. Yet once the Roman emperor Constantine (c. 280–337) adopted Christianity as the religion of the state, this pacifist belief was gradually altered.

The notion of requiring a just cause to embark on war, along with specific limits, also became part of Islamic teaching. In the Koran (c. 632), a war is just when waged for self-defense to protect against internal or external aggression by non-Islamic populations, and against those who violate their oaths by breaking a treaty. Despite some radical interpretations of Islam today, one should note that the Koran calls for temperance during wartime and urges soldiers of faith "to protect the lives of non-combatants, the elderly, children, and women, as well as the lives of imprisoned soldiers" (see Section 3.8).

Medieval Catholic thinkers would further develop the notion of just war. Saint Augustine (350–430), bishop of Hippo in Roman Africa, a dominant figure of the Western Roman Church, wrote *City of God* (413–426), a work that was prompted by the sacking of Rome by the Goths and other barbarians. Augustine recognized that the expansion of Rome and the imposition of its language on conquered nations inevitably bred wars — both outside and within its imperial frontiers. If there is such a thing as just war, maintained Augustine, then just war is a "cruel necessity" even if the aggressor must meet his due. Augustine's goal, however, was a society freed from trouble and misfortune. He believed that individuals have the ability to draw on their best natural qualities and to seek peace with others. Christianizing Plato's view of justice in *The Republic* (c. 360 B.C.E.), he asserted that peace could not be maintained without an organic and orderly concept of justice and faith (see Section 3.9).

The Crusades prompted Italian Dominican theologian Saint Thomas of Aquinas (1224/5–1274) to argue for additional just war guidelines. In his *Summa Theologica* (1265–1273), Aquinas drew his understanding of rationality and rights from the influx of Arabian science and Aristotelian ethics. Echoing Aristotle, he argued that natural rights, which he carefully distinguished from divine rights, should be the basis for justice, peace, and unity. Under what circumstances, he then asked, can wars be considered just? Refuting various objections claiming the inherently sinful objectives of war, Aquinas argued that wars were just if waged with self-restraint by sovereign authority for self-defense, for the sake of the common good, and with the intention of a peaceful end. Provided that the ends are just, he continued, wars can be undertaken either openly or by means of ambushes. Wars were unjust, on the other hand, if they were motivated by self-aggrandizement, the lust for power, or conducted with cruelty. He also viewed as unlawful the taking up of arms by clerics and bishops, who should only have recourse to spiritual arms. Private wars were sinful for Aquinas, for they derived from private passions and could not yield rational and peaceful ends (see Section 3.10).

3.7 HEBREW BIBLE: ON TEMPERANCE IN WAR AND PEACE AMONG NATIONS

Exodus 23:2–5

You shall not be led into wrongdoing by the majority, nor, when you give evidence in a lawsuit, shall you side with the majority to pervert justice; nor shall you favor the poor man in his suit.

When you come upon your enemy's ox or ass straying, you shall take it back to him.

When you see the ass of someone who hates you lying helpless under its load, however unwilling you may be to help it, you must give him a hand with it.

Proverbs 25:21–23

If your enemy is hungry, give him bread to
    eat;
if he is thirsty, give him water to drink;
so you will heap glowing coals on his head,
and the Lord will reward you.
As the north wind holds back the rain
so an angry glance holds back slander.

Micah 4:1–5

In days to come
the mountain of the Lord's house
shall be set over all other mountains,
lifted high above the hills.
People shall come streaming to it,
and many nations shall come and say,
"Come, let us climb up on to the mountain
    of the Lord,
to the house of the God of Jacob,
that he may teach us his ways
and we may walk in his paths."
For instruction issues from Zion,

and out of Jerusalem comes the word of the
    Lord;
he will be judge between many peoples
and arbiter among mighty nations afar.
They shall best their swords into mattocks
and their spears into pruning knives;
nation shall not lift sword against nation
nor ever again be trained for war,
and each man shall dwell under his own
    vine,
under his own fig-tree, undisturbed.
For the Lord of hosts himself has spoken.
All peoples may in the name of their gods,
but we will walk in the name of the Lord
    our God
for ever and ever.

3.8 NEW TESTAMENT: "NEVER PAY BACK EVIL FOR EVIL" (C. 50)

Romans 12:17—13:6

Never pay back evil for evil. Let your aims be such as all men count honorable. If possible, so far as it lies with you, live at peace with all men. My dear friends, do not seek revenge, but leave a place for divine retribution for there is a text which reads, "Justice is mine," says the Lord, "I will repay." But there is another text: "If your enemy is hungry, feed him; if he is thirsty, give him a drink; by doing this you will heap live coals on his head." Do not let evil conquer you, but use good to defeat evil.

Every person must submit to the supreme authorities. There is no authority but by act of God, and the existing authorities are instituted by him; consequently anyone who rebels against authority is resisting a divine institution, and those who so resist have themselves to thank for the punishment they will receive. For government, a terror to crime, has no terrors for good behavior. You wish to have no fear of the authorities? Then continue to do right and you will have their approval, for they are God's agents working for your good. But if you are doing wrong, then you will have cause to fear them; it is not for nothing that they hold the power of the sword, for they are God's agents of punishment, for retribution on the offender. That is why you are obliged to submit. It is an obligation imposed not merely by fear of retribution but by conscience. That is also why you pay taxes. The authorities are in God's service and to these duties they devote their energies.

3.9 KORAN: ON JUST WAR (C. 632)

Surah 2

C.51. *Fighting in defense of Truth and Right*

Is not to be undertaken lightheartedly,
Nor to be evaded as a duty.
Life and Death are in the hands of Allah.
Not all can be chosen to fight
For Allah. It requires constancy,
Firmness, and faith. Given these,
Large armies can be routed
By those who battle for Allah,
As shown by the courage of David,
Whose prowess single-handedly
Disposed of the Philistines,
The mission of some of the messengers,
Like Jesus, was different —
Less wide in scope than that
Of Mustafa, and He carries it out
As He wills.

Section 24

190. Fight in the cause of Allah
Those who fight you,[1]
But do not transgress limits;
For Allah loveth not transgressors.
191. And slay them
Wherever ye catch them,
And turn them out
From where they have
Turned you out;

For tumult and oppression;
Are worse than slaughter;
But fight them not
At the sacred Mosque,
Unless they (first)
Fight you there;
But if they fight you,
Slay them.
Such is the reward of those who suppress
    faith.

216. Fighting is prescribed
Upon you, and ye dislike it[2]
But it is possible
That ye dislike a thing
Which is good for you,
And that ye love a thing
Which is bad for you.
But Allah knoweth,
And ye know not.

Surah 3

157. And if ye are slain, or die,
In the way of Allah,
Forgiveness and mercy
From Allah are far better
Than all they could amass.

158. And if ye die, or are slain,
Lo! It is unto Allah
That ye are brought together.

Surah 5

45. We ordained therein for them:
"Life for life, eye for eye,
Nose for nose, ear for ear,
Tooth for tooth, and wounds
Equal for equal." But if
Anyone remits the retaliation
By way of charity, it is
An act of atonement for himself.
And if any fail to judge
By (the light of) what Allah
Hath revealed, they are
(No better than) wrongdoers.[3]

Surah 9

12. But if they violate their oaths
After their covenant,
And taunt you for your Faith[4]
Fight ye the chiefs of Unfaith:
For their oaths are nothing to
them:
That thus they may be restrained.

13. Will ye not fight people
Who violated their oaths,
Plotted to expel the Messenger
And took the aggressive
By being the first (to assault) you?
Do ye fear them? Nay,
It is Allah Whom ye should
More justly fear, if ye believe!

14. Fight them, and Allah will,
Punish them by your hands,
Cover them with shame,
Help you (to victory) over them,
Heal the breasts of Believers.[5]

15. And still the indignation of their hearts
For Allah will turn (in mercy)
To whom He will; and Allah
Is All-Knowing, All-Wise.

Surah 42

39. And those who, when
An oppressive wrong is inflicted
On them, (are not cowed
But) help and defend
themselves.[6]

40. The recompense for an injury is an injury equal thereto.

41. (In degree): but if a person
Forgives and makes reconciliation,
His reward is due
From Allah: for (Allah)
Loveth not those who
Do wrong.

42. The blame is only
Against those who oppress
Men with wrongdoing
And insolently transgress

Beyond bounds through the land,
Defying right and justice:
For such there will be
A Penalty grievous.

43. But indeed if any
Show patience and forgive,
That would truly be
An exercise of courageous will
And resolution in the conduct
Of affairs.

Surah 49

13. O mankind! We created
You From a Single (pair)
Of a male and a female,
and made you into
Nations and tribes, that
Ye may know each other
(Not that ye may despise
Each other). Verily
The most honored of you
In the sight of Allah
Is (he who is) the most
Righteous of you.
And Allah has full knowledge
And is well-acquainted
(With all things).

[1]War is permissible in self-defense, and under well-defined limits. When undertaken, it must be pushed with vigor (but not relentlessly), but only to restore peace and freedom for the worship of Allah. In any case strict limits must not be transgressed: women, children, old and infirm men should not be molested, nor trees and crops cut down, nor peace withheld when the enemy comes to terms.

[2]To fight in the cause of Truth is one of the highest forms of charity. What can you offer that is more precious than your own life? But here again the limitations come in. If you are a mere brawler or a selfish aggressive person, or a vainglorious but you deserve the highest censure. Allah knows the value of things better than you do.

[3]The significant words in the three cases are *unbelievers*, *wrongdoers*, and *rebellious*, and each fits the context. If the Jews tamper with their books, they are unbelievers; if they give false judgments, they are wrongdoers. If the Christians follow not their light, they are rebellious.

[4] Not only did the enemies break their oaths shamelessly, but they even taunted the Muslims on their faith and the "simple minded" way in which they continued to respect their part of the treaty, as if they were afraid to fight!

[5] Heal the breasts of believers, i.e., of wounds that they may have sustained from the assaults, taunts, and cruelty of the enemy.

[6] We have the following further qualities in those who wish to serve Allah. (5) They are ready at all times to hearken to Allah's Signs, or to listen to the admonitions of prophets of Allah, and to follow the true Path, as they understand it; (6) they keep personal contact with Allah, by habits of Prayer and Praise; (7) their conduct in life is open and determined by mutual Consultation between those who are entitled to a voice, e.g., in private domestic affairs, as between husband and wife, or other responsible members of the household; in affairs of business, as between partners or parties interested; and in State affairs, as between rulers and ruled, or as between different departments of administration, to reserve the unity of administration; (8) they do not forget Charity, or the help due to their weaker brethren, out of the wealth or gifts or talents or opportunities, which Allah had provided for themselves; and (9) when other people use them despitefully, they are not cowed down or terrorized into submission and acceptance of evil, but stand up for their rights within the limits mentioned in verse 40.

3.10 SAINT AUGUSTINE: ON WAR, PEACE, AND HARMONY (*THE CITY OF GOD*, 413–426)

7. *Of the diversity of languages, by which the intercourse of men is prevented; and of the misery of wars, even of those called just*

After the state or city comes the world, the third circle of human society — the first being the house, and the second the city. And the world, as it is larger, so it is fuller of dangers, as the greater sea is the more dangerous. And here, in the first place, man is separated from man by the difference of languages. For if two men, each ignorant of the other's language, meet, and are not compelled to pass, but, on the contrary, to remain in company, dumb animals, though of different species, would more easily hold intercourse than they, human beings though they be. For their common nature is no help to friendliness when they are prevented by diversity of language from conveying their sentiments to one another; so that a man would more readily hold intercourse with his dog than with a foreigner. But the imperial city has endeavored to impose on subject nations not only her yoke, but her language, as a bond of peace, so that interpreters, far from being scarce, are numberless. This is true; but how many great wars, how much slaughter and bloodshed, have provided this unity! And though these are past, the end of these miseries has not yet come. For though there have never been wanting, nor are yet wanting, hostile nations beyond the empire, against whom wars have been and are waged, yet, supposing there were no such nations, the very extent of the empire itself has produced wars of a more obnoxious description — social and civil wars — and with these the whole race has been agitated, either by the actual conflict or the fear of a renewed outbreak. If I attempted to give an adequate description of these manifold disasters, these stern and lasting necessities, though I am quite unequal to the task, what limit could I set? But, say they, the wise man will wage just wars. As if he would not all the rather lament the necessity of just wars, if he remembers that he is a man; for if they were not just he would not wage them, and would therefore be delivered from all wars. For it is the wrong-doing of the opposing party which compels the wise man to wage just wars; and this wrong-doing, even though it gave rise to no war, would still be matter of grief to man because it is man's wrongdoing. Let every one, then, who thinks with pain on all these great evils, so horrible, so ruthless, acknowledge that this is misery. And if any one either endures or thinks of them without mental pain, this is a more miserable plight still, for he thinks himself happy because he has lost human feeling....

12. *That even the fierceness of war and all the disquietude of men make towards this one end of peace, which every nature desires*

Whoever gives even moderate attention to human affairs and to our common nature, will recognize that if there is no man who does not wish to be joyful, neither is there any one who does not wish to have peace. For even they who make war desire nothing but victory — desire, that is to say, to attain to peace with glory. For what else is victory than the conquest of those who resist us? And when this is done there is peace. It is therefore with the desire for peace that wars are waged, even by those who take pleasure in exercising their warlike nature in command and battle. And hence it is obvious that peace is the end sought for by war. For every man seeks peace by waging war, but no man seeks war by making peace. For even they who intentionally interrupt the peace in which they are living have no hatred of peace, but only wish it changed into a peace that suits them better: They do not, therefore, wish to have no peace, but only one more to their mind. And in the case of sedition, when men have separated themselves from the community, they yet do not effect what they wish, unless they maintain some kind of peace with their fellow-conspirators. And therefore even robbers take care to maintain peace with their comrades, that they may with greater effect and greater safety invade the peace of other men. And if an individual happens to be of such unrivaled strength, and to be so jealous of partnership, that he trusts himself with no comrades, but makes his own plots, and commits depredations and murders on his own account, yet he maintains some shadow of peace with such persons as he is unable to kill, and from whom he wishes to conceal his deeds. In his own home, too, he makes it his aim to be at peace with his wife and children, and any other members of his household; for unquestionably their prompt obedience to his every look is a source of pleasure to him. And if this be not rendered, he is angry, he chides and punishes; and even by this storm he secures the calm peace of his own home, as occasion demands. For he sees that peace cannot be maintained unless all the members of the same domestic circle be subject to one head, such as he himself is in his own house. And therefore if a city or nation offered to submit itself to him, to serve him in the same style as he had made his household serve him, he would no longer lurk in a brigand's hiding-places, but lift his head in open day as a king, though the same covetousness and wickedness should remain in him. And thus all men desire to have peace with their own circle whom they wish to govern as suits themselves. For even those whom they make war against they wish to make their own, and impose on them the laws of their own peace....

He, then, who prefers what is right to what is wong, and what is well-ordered to what is perverted, sees that the peace of unjust men is not worthy to be called peace in comparison with the peace of the just. And yet even what is perverted must of necessity be in harmony with, and in dependence on, and in some part of the order of things, for otherwise it would have no existence at all. Suppose a man hangs with his head downwards, this is certainly a perverted attitude of body and arrangement of its members; for that which nature requires to be above is beneath, and vice versa. This perversity disturbs the peace of the body, and is therefore painful. Nevertheless the spirit is at peace with its body, and labors for its preservation, and hence the suffering; but if it is banished from the body by its pains, then, so long as the bodily framework holds together, there is in the remains a kind of peace among the members, and hence the body remains suspended. And inasmuch as the earthy body tends towards the earth, and rests on the bond by which it is suspended, it tends thus to its natural peace, and the voice of its own weight demands a place for it to rest; and though now lifeless and without feeling, it does not fall from the peace that is natural to its place in creation, whether it already has it, or is tending towards it. For if you apply embalming preparations to prevent the bodily frame from moldering and dissolving, a kind of peace still unites part to part, and keeps the whole body in a suitable place on the earth — in other words, in a place that is at peace with the body. If, on the other hand, the body receive no such care, but be left to the natural course, it is disturbed by exhalations that do not harmonize with one another, and that offend our senses; for it is this which is perceived in putrefaction until it is assimilated to the elements of the world, and particle by particle enters into peace with them. Yet throughout this process the laws of the most high Creator and Governor are strictly observed, for it is by Him the peace of the universe is administered. For although minute animals are produced from the carcass of a larger animal, all these little atoms, by the law of the same Creator, serve the animals they belong to in peace. And although the flesh of dead animals be eaten by others, no matter where it be carried, nor what it be brought into contact with, nor what it be converted and changed into, it still is ruled by the same laws which pervade all things for the conservation of every mortal race, and which bring things that fit one another into harmony.

13. *Of the universal peace which the law of nature preserves through all disturbances, and by which every one reaches his desert in a way regulated by the just Judge*
The peace of the body then consists in the duly proportioned arrangement of its parts. The peace of the irrational soul is the harmonious repose of the appetites, and that of the rational soul the harmony of knowledge and action. The peace of body and soul is the well-ordered and harmonious life and health of the living creature. Peace between man and God is the well-ordered obedience of faith to eternal law. Peace between man and man is well-ordered concord. Domestic peace is the well-ordered concord between those of the family who rule and those who obey. Civil peace is a similar concord among the citizens. The peace of the celestial city is the perfectly ordered and harmonious enjoyment of God, and of one another in God. The peace of all things is the tranquillity of order. Order is the distribution which allots things equal and unequal each to its own place. And hence, though the miserable, in so far as they are such, do certainly not enjoy peace, but are severed from that tranquillity of order in which there is no disturbance, nevertheless, inasmuch as they are deservedly and justly miserable, they are by their very misery connected with order. They are not, indeed, conjoined with the blessed, but they are disjoined from them by the law of order. And though they are disquieted, their circumstances are notwithstanding adjusted to them, and consequently they have some tranquillity of order, and therefore some peace. But they are wretched because, although not wholly miserable, they are not in that place where any mixture of misery is impossible. They would, however, be more wretched if they had not that peace which arises from being in harmony with the natural order of things. When they suffer, their peace is in so far disturbed; but their peace continues in so far as they do not suffer, and in so far as their nature continues to exist. As, then, there may be life without pain, while there cannot be pain without some kind of life, so there may be peace without war, but there cannot be war without some kind of peace, because war supposes the existence of some natures to wage it, and these natures cannot exist without peace of one kind or other.
And therefore there is a nature in which evil does not or even cannot exist; but there cannot be a nature in which there

is no good. Hence not even the nature of the devil himself is evil, in so far as it is nature, but it was made evil by being perverted. Thus he did not abide in the truth, but could not escape the judgment of the Truth; he did not abide in the tranquillity of order, but did not therefore escape the power of the Ordainer. The good imparted by God to his nature did not screen him from the justice of God by which order was preserved in his punishment; neither did God punish the good which He had created, but the evil which the devil had committed. God did not take back all He had imparted to his nature, but something He took and something He left, that there might remain enough to be sensible of the loss of what was taken. And this very sensibility to pain is evidence of the good which has been taken away and the good which has been left. For, were nothing good left, there could be no pain on account of the good which had been lost. For he who sins is still worse if he rejoices in his loss of righteousness. But he who is in pain, if he derives no benefit from it, mourns at least the loss of health. And as righteousness and health are both good things, and as the loss of any good thing is matter of grief, not of joy — if, at least, there is no compensation, as spiritual righteousness may compensate for the loss of bodily health — certainly it is more suitable for a wicked man to grieve in punishment than to rejoice in his fault. As, then, the joy of a sinner who has abandoned what is good is evidence of a bad will, so his grief for the good he has lost when he is punished is evidence of a good nature. For he who laments the peace his nature has lost is stirred to do so by some relics of peace which make his nature friendly to itself. And it is very just that in the final punishment the wicked and godless should in anguish bewail the loss of the natural advantages they enjoyed, and should perceive that they were most justly taken from them by that God whose benign liberality they had despised. God, then,

the most wise Creator and most just Ordainer of all natures, who placed the human race upon earth as its greatest ornament, imparted to men some good things adapted to this life, to wit, temporal peace, such as we can enjoy in this life from health and safety and human fellowship, and all things needful for the preservation and recovery of this peace, such as the objects which are accommodated to our outward senses, light, night, the air, and waters suitable for us, and everything the body requires to sustain, shelter, heal, or beautify it and all under this most equitable condition, that every man who made a good use of these advantages suited to the peace of his mortal condition, should receive ampler and better blessings, namely, the peace of immortality, accompanied by glory and honor in an endless life made fit for the enjoyment of God and of one another in God; but that he who used the present blessings badly should both lose them and should not receive the others....

3.11 SAINT THOMAS AQUINAS: ON JUST WAR (*SUMMA THEOLOGICA*, 1265–1273)

Question 40 of War
(In Four Articles)[1]

We must now consider war, under which head there are four points of inquiry: (1) Whether some kind of war is lawful? (2) Whether it is lawful for clerics to fight? (3) Whether it is lawful for belligerents to lay ambushes? (4) Whether it is lawful to fight on holy days?

First Article

Whether It Is Always Sinful to Wage War?

We proceed thus to the First Article:

Obj. 1. It would seem that it is always sinful to wage war. Because punishment is not inflicted except for sin. Now those who wage war are threatened by Our Lord with punishment; according to Matth. xxvi. 52: *All that take the sword shall perish with the sword.* Therefore all wars are unlawful.

Obj. 2. Further, whatever is contrary to a Divine precept is a sin. But war is contrary to a Divine precept, for it is written (Matth. v. 39): *But I say to you not to resist evil*; and (Rom. xii. 19): *Not revenging yourselves, my dearly beloved, but give place unto wrath.* Therefore war is always sinful.

Obj. 3. Further, nothing, except sin, is contrary to an act of virtue. But war is contrary to peace. Therefore war is always a sin.

Obj. 4. Further, the exercise of a lawful thing is itself lawful, as is evident in scientific exercises. But warlike exercises which take place in tournaments are forbidden by the Church, since those who are slain in these trials are deprived of ecclesiastical burial. Therefore it seems that war is a sin in itself.

On the contrary, Augustine says in a sermon on the son of the centurion: *If the Christian Religion forbade war altogether, those who sought salutary advice in the Gospel would rather have been counseled to cast aside their arms, and to give up soldiering altogether. On the contrary, they were told: "Do violence to no man; ... and be content with your pay."* If he commanded them to be content with their pay, he did not forbid soldiering.

I answer that, In order for a war to be just, three things are necessary. First, the authority of the sovereign by whose command the war is to be waged. For it is not the business of a private individual to declare war, because he can seek for redress of his rights from the tribunal of his superior. Moreover it is not the business of a private individual to summon together the people, which has to be done in wartime. And as the care of the common weal is committed to those who are in authority, it is their business to watch over the common weal of the city, kingdom or province subject to them. And just as it is lawful for them to have recourse to the sword in defending that common weal against internal disturbances, when they punish evil-doers, according to the words of the Apostle (Rom. xiii. 4): *He beareth not the sword in vain: for he is God's minister, an avenger to execute wrath upon him that doth evil*; so too, it is their business to have recourse to the sword of war in defending the common weal against external enemies. Hence it is said to those who are in authority (Ps. lxxxi. 4): *Rescue the poor and deliver the needy out of the hand of the sinner*; and for this reason Augustine says (*Contra Faust* xxii. 75): *The natural order conducive to peace among mortals demands that the power to declare and counsel war should be in the hands of those who hold the supreme authority.*

Secondly, a just cause is required, namely that those who are attacked, should be attacked because they deserve it on account of some fault Wherefore Augustine says (*QQ in Hept.*, qu. *x, super Jos*): *A just war is wont to be descried as one that avenges wrongs, when a nation or state has to be punished, for refusing to make amends for the wrongs inflicted by its subjects, or to restore what it has seized unjustly.*

Thirdly, it is necessary that the belligerents should have a rightful intention, so that they intend the advancement of good, or the avoidance of evil. Hence Augustine says (*De Verb Dom.*): *True religion looks upon as peaceful those wars that are waged not for motives of aggrandizement, or cruelty, but with the object of securing peace, of punishing evil-doers, and of uplifting the good.* For it may happen that the war is declared by the legitimate authority, and for a just cause, and yet be rendered unlawful through a wicked intention. Hence Augustine says (*Contra Faust.* xxii. 74): *The passion for inflicting harm, the cruel thirst for vengeance, a pacific and relentless spirit, the fever of revolt, the lust of power, and such like things, all these are rightly condemned in war.*

Reply Obj. 1. As Augustine says (*Contra Faust.* xxii. 70): *To take the sword is to arm oneself in order to take the life of anyone, without the command or permission of superior or lawful authority.* On the other hand, to have recourse to the sword (as a private person) by the authority of the sovereign or judge, or [as a public person] through zeal for justice, and by the authority, so to speak, of God, is not to take the sword, but to use it as commissioned by another, wherefore it does not deserve punishment. And yet even those who make sinful use of the sword are not always slain with the sword, yet they always perish with their own sword, because, unless they repent, they are punished eternally for their sinful use of the sword.

Reply Obj. 2. Such like precepts, as Augustine observes (*De Serm. Don in Monte* L 19), should always be borne in readiness of mind, so that we be ready to obey them, and, if necessary, to refrain from resistance or self-defense. Nevertheless it is necessary sometimes for a man to act otherwise for the common good, or for the good of those with whom he is fighting. Hence Augustine says (*Ep. ad Marcellin.* cxxxviii): *Those whom we have to punish with a kindly severity, it is necessary to handle in many ways against their will. For when we are stripping a man of the lawlessness of sin, it is good for him to be vanquished, since nothing is more hopeless than the happiness of sinners, whence arises a guilty impunity, and an evil will, like an internal enemy.*

Reply Obj. 3. Those who wage war justly aim at peace, and so they are not opposed to peace, except to the evil peace, which Our Lord *came not to send upon earth* (Matth. x. 34). Hence Augustine says (*Ep. ad Benif.* clxxxix): *We do not seek peace in order to be at war, but we go to war that we may have peace. Be peaceful therefore, in warring, so that you may vanquish those whom you war against, and bring them to the prosperity of peace.*

Reply Obj. 4. Manly exercises in warlike feats of arms are not all forbidden, but those which are inordinate and perilous, and end in slaying or plundering. In olden times warlike exercises presented no such danger, and hence they were called *exercises of arms or bloodless wars*, as Jerome states in an epistle.

[1] Editor selected the first question for this excerpt.

CHAPTER 4

Justice for Whom?

If brotherly compassion or humanity in war and elsewhere were mandated in all major religions and secular traditions, the notion of cosmopolitanism would carry far narrower meanings from Hammurabi's to Mohamed's time than today. Slaves, women, foreigners, and homosexuals, among others, were rarely considered full-fledged members of early universal projects. While exclusive in a modern sense, the ancients scripted the fundamental notions of universal ethics that their modern descendants would broaden and encode in national and international laws.

4.1 UNITED NATIONS UNIVERSAL DECLARATION OF HUMAN RIGHTS (1948): ARTICLES 1–2, 4, 13–14, 16, AND 24

Article 1

All human beings are born free and equal in dignity and rights. They are endowed with reason and conscience and should act toward one another in a spirit of brotherhood.

Article 2

Everyone is entitled to all the rights and freedoms set forth in this Declaration, without distinction of any kind, such as race, color, sex, language, religion, political or other opinion, national or social origin, property, birth or other status.

Furthermore, no distinction shall be made on the basis of political, jurisdictional or international status of the country or territory to which a person belongs, whether it be independent, non-self-governing or under any other limitation of sovereignty.

Article 4

No one shall be held in slavery or servitude; slavery and the slave trade shall be prohibited in all their forms.

Article 13

1.   Everyone has the right to freedom of movement and residence within the borders of each state.

2.   Everyone has the right to leave any country, including his own, and to return to his country.

Article 14

1.   Everyone has the right to seek and to enjoy in other countries asylum from persecution.

2.   This right may not be invoked in the case of prosecutions genuinely arising, from non-political crimes or from acts contrary to the purposes and principles of the United Nations.

Article 16

1.   Men and women of full age, without any limitation due to race, nationality, or religion, have the right to marry and to found a family. They are entitled to equal rights as to marriage, during marriage and at its dissolution.

2.   Marriage shall be entered into only with the free and full consent of the intending spouses.

3.   The family is the natural and fundamental group unit of society and is entitled to protection by society and the State.

Article 24

2.   Motherhood and childhood are entitled to special care and assistance. All children, whether born in or out of wedlock shall enjoy the same social protection.

THE SECULAR TRADITION

If the Hammurabi Code (c. 1700 B.C.E.) included legal protection for widows, sick wives, and daughters, women were not granted the same rights as men, and their rights varied depending upon their social status. For instance, an adulterous wife — and her lover — was subject to death at her husband's discretion, but a betrayed wife did not enjoy a similar prerogative. Similarly, slaves were endowed with far fewer rights than patricians or freemen. While Mesopotamian slaves were acquired in war or purchased in markets at home and abroad, their fate was slightly better than that of Roman slaves: they were able to marry and their masters did not have the power to take their lives (see Section 4.2).

Socrates, as expressed through the voice of Plato, was unique among the ancients for his position on women. Not only did he encourage the fair treatment of women, who had few rights in ancient Greece, but Plato was among the first Western thinkers to assert, in *The Republic* (c. 360 B.C.E.), that women had abilities similar to those of men and that, depending upon their individual capacities, they should receive the same kind of education, be entrusted to similar offices, and fulfill the same tasks as their male counterparts (see Section 4.3). Reflecting homosexual mores in Greek society, Socrates praised homosexual friendship as admirable. "If two males came together," he said in *The Symposium* (c. 360 B.C.E.), "they would have the satisfaction of sexual intercourse, and then relax, turn to their work and think about the other things in their life" (see Section 4.4).

Sympathetic to homosexuality, like his predecessor, Aristotle disagreed with Plato over the role of women and slaves in society. In contrast to Plato, Aristotle argued in *The Politics* (c. 350 B.C.E.) in defense of slavery. Because barbarians were less rational than Greeks, he maintained they were by nature suited to be enslaved as a "living tool." Aristotle also departed from Plato's view of women by asserting male superiority over women, and that this difference may "hold good for mankind in general."

4.2 HAMMURABI CODE: ON WOMEN AND SLAVES (C. 1700 B.C.E.)

Marriage requires a contract

§ 128

If a man has taken a (woman to) wife and has not drawn up a contract for her, that woman is not a wife.

§ 129

If a married lady is caught lying with another man they shall bind them and cast them into the water; if her husband wishes to let his wife live, then the king shall let his servant live.

Woman is servant

§ 130

If a man has raped a married lady, who is dwelling in her father's house, that man shall be put to death; that woman then goes free.

Woman must take oath if suspected of cheating

§§ 131–132

If the husband of a married lady has accused her but she is not caught lying with another man, she shall take an oath by the life of a god and return to her house.

If a finger has been pointed at the married lady with regard to another man and she is not caught lying with the other man, she shall leap into the holy river for her husband.

§§ 148–149

If a man has married a wife who falls ill [and] he sets his face to marry another woman, he may marry (her). He shall not divorce his wife, she shall dwell in the house which he has built, and he shall continue to maintain her so long as she lives.

If that woman does not consent to dwell in the house of her husband, he shall make good to her dowry which she brought from the house of her father and so she shall go [away].

§ 150

If a man has bestowed a field, a plantation, a house, or chattels on his wife (and) has executed a sealed tablet for her, after [the death of] her husband her sons shall not bring a claim (for it) against her; the mother shall give (the charge of) her estate to her son whom she loves. She shall not give (it) to another person.

§ 153

If a woman has procured the death of her husband on account of another man, they shall impale that woman.

§ 154

If a man commits incest with daughter, they shall banish that man from the city.

§§ 175–176

If either a slave of a palace or a slave of a servant has married a lady and she bears sons, the owner of the slave shall make no claim to the sons of the lady for slavery.

(sons of slaves can't be slaves?

§§ 209–214

If a man strikes the daughter of a (free) man (and) causes her to lose the fruit of her womb, he shall pay shekels of silver for the fruit of her womb. — Pay for the baby, not the woman

If that woman dies, they shall put his daughter to death. — Death of his daughter. value sons or eye for eye

If he causes the daughter of a servant to lose the fruit of her womb by striking her, he shall pay 5 shekels of silver.

If that woman dies, he shall pay 1/2 maneh of silver.

If he has struck the slave-girl of a (free) man and causes her to lose the fruit of her womb, he shall pay 2 shekels of silver.

If that slave-girl dies, he shall pay 1/3 maneh of silver.

— Man is never killed for killing women or their children

§ 279

If a man will buy a slave (or) a slave-girl and he or she becomes liable to a claim, he who has sold him shall meet the claims.

§§ 280–282

If a man buys a man's slave (or) slave-girl in a foreign country and then, whenever they come (back) into the country, the owner of the slave or of the slave-girl discovers either his slave or his slave-girl, if that slave and slave-girl are natives of the country, their release shall be then granted without (any payment of) money.

If (they are) natives of another country, the buyer indeed shall state before a god (the amount of) the money which he has paid and the owner of the slave or the slave-girl shall give the money which he has paid to the merchant and shall redeem his slave or his slave-girl.

If the slave states to his master "Thou art not my master" his master shall convict him as his slave and cut off his ear. Suppressing speech

4.3 PLATO: ON WOMEN'S ABILITIES (*THE REPUBLIC*, C. 360 B.C.E.)

… "For men born and educated like our citizens, the only way, in my opinion, of arriving at a right conclusion about the possession and use of women and children is to follow the path on which we originally started, when we said that the men were to be the guardians and watchdogs of the herd."

"True."

"Let us further suppose the birth and education of our women to be subject to [similar or nearly similar regulations] then we shall see whether the result accords with our design." — Experimenting

"What do you mean?"

"What I mean may be put into the form of a question, I said: Are dogs divided into hes and shes, or do they both share equally in hunting and in keeping watch and in the other duties of dogs? Or do we entrust to the males the entire and exclusive care of the flocks, while we leave the females at home,

[handwritten: Women can pursue everything a man can, but they will be inferior]

under the idea that the bearing and suckling their puppies is labor enough for them?"

"No, he said, they share alike; the only difference between them is that the males are stronger and the females weaker."

"But can you use different animals for the same purpose, unless they are bred and fed in the same way?"

"You can not."

"Then, if women are to have the same duties as men, they must have the same nurture and education?"

"Yes."

"The education which was assigned to the men was music and gymnastic."

"Yes."

"Then women must be taught music and gymnastic and also the art of war, which they must practice like the men?"

"That is the inference, I suppose."

[handwritten: It'll be weird]

"I should rather expect, I said, that several of our proposals, if they are carried out, being unusual, may appear ridiculous."

"No doubt of it."

"Yes, and the most ridiculous thing of all will be the sight of women naked in the palaestra, exercising with the men, especially when they are no longer young; they certainly will not be a vision of beauty, any more than the enthusiastic old men who in spite of wrinkles and ugliness continue to frequent the gymnasia."

[handwritten: Women working out alongside men?]

[handwritten: Old men will frequent men to see the ladies]

"Yes, indeed, he said: according to present notions the proposal would be thought ridiculous."

"But then, I said, as we have determined to speak our minds, we must not fear the jests of the wits which will be directed against this sort of innovation; how they will talk of women's attainments both in music and gymnastic, and above all about their wearing armor and riding upon horseback! ..."

[handwritten: odd to think women could not engage in music]

"You are quite right, he replied, in maintaining the general inferiority of the female sex: although many women are in many things superior to many men, yet on the whole what you say is true."

"And if so, my friend, I said, there is no special faculty of administration in a state which a woman has because she is a woman, or which a man has by virtue of his sex, but the gifts of nature are alike diffused in both;

all the pursuits of men are the pursuits of women also, but in all of them a woman is inferior to a man."

"Very true."

"Then are we to impose all our enactments on men and none of them on women?"

"That will never do."

"One woman has a gift of healing, another not; one is a musician, and another has no music in her nature?"

"Very true."

"And one woman has a turn for gymnastic and military exercises, and another is unwarlike and hates gymnastics?"

"Certainly."

"And one woman is a philosopher, and another is an enemy of philosophy; one has spirit, and another is without spirit?"

"That is also true."

"Then one woman will have the temper of a guardian, and another not. Was not the selection of the male guardians determined by differences of this sort?"

"Yes."

"Men and women alike possess the qualities which make a guardian; they differ only in their comparative strength or weakness."

"Obviously."

"And those women who have such qualities are to be selected as the companions and colleagues of men who have similar qualities and whom they resemble in capacity and in character?"

"Very true."

"And ought not the same natures to have the same pursuits?"

"They ought."

"Then, as we were saying before, there is nothing unnatural in assigning music and gymnastic to the wives of the guardians — to that point we come round again."

"Certainly not."

"The law which we then enacted was agreeable to nature, and therefore not an impossibility or mere aspiration; and the contrary practice, which prevails at present, is in reality a violation of nature."

"That appears to be true."

"We had to consider, first, whether our proposals were possible, and secondly whether they were the most beneficial?"

"Yes."

"And the possibility has been acknowledged?"

"Yes."

"The very great benefit has next to be established?"

"Quite so."

"You will admit that the same education which makes a man a good guardian will make a woman a good guardian; for their original nature is the same?..."

4.4 PLATO: ON HOMOSEXUALS (*THE SYMPOSIUM*, C. 360 B.C.E.)

Pasanius: "Every activity in itself is neither right nor wrong. Take our present activity: we could be drinking or singing or discussing. None of these is right in itself; the character of the activity depends on the way it is done. If it is done rightly and properly, it is right; if it is not done properly, it is wrong. So not every type of loving and Love is right and deserves to be praised, but only the type that motivates us to love rightly.

Common Love is genuinely 'common' and undiscriminating in its effects; this is the kind of love that inferior people feel. People like this are attracted to women as much as boys, and to bodies rather than minds. They are attracted to partners with the least possible intelligence, because their sole aim is to get what they want, and they don't care whether they do this rightly or not. So the effect of love on them is that they act without discrimination: it is all the same to them whether they behave well or not. The reason is that their love derives from the goddess who is much younger than the other, and who, because of her origin, is partly female and partly male in character.

The other love derives from the Heavenly goddess, who has nothing of the female in her but only maleness; so this love is directed at boys. This goddess is also older, and so avoids abusive violence. That's why those inspired with this love are drawn towards the male, feeling affection for what is naturally more vigorous and intelligent. You can also distinguish, within the general class of those attracted to boys, the ones who are motivated purely by the heavenly type of love.

These are attracted to boys only when they start to have developed intelligence, and this happens around the time that they begin to grow a beard. I think that those who begin love-affairs at this point show their readiness to spend their whole lives together and to lead a fully shared life. They do not plan to trick the boy, catching him while he is still young and foolish, and then leaving with a laugh, running off to someone else.

There should even be a law against affairs with young boys, to prevent great effort being spent on something whose outcome is unclear. In the case of young boys, it is unclear whether they will end up good or bad in mind or body. Good men make this rule for themselves and are glad to do so...."

Aristophanes: "Zeus cut humans into two, as people cut sorb-apples in half before they preserve them or as they cut hard-boiled eggs with hairs.... [Then, Zeus] moved their genitals round to the front; until then, they had genitals on the back of their bodies, and sexual reproduction occurred not with each other but on the earth, as in the case of cicadas. So Zeus moved the genitals round to the front and in this way made them reproduce in each other, by means of the male acting inside the female. The aim of this was that, if a man met with a woman and entwined himself with her, they would reproduce and the human race would be continued. Also, if two males came together, they would at least have the satisfaction of sexual intercourse, and then relax, turn to their work, and think about the other things in their life.]

That's how, long ago, the innate desire of human beings for each other started. It draws the two halves of our original nature back together and tries to make one out of two and to heal the wound in human nature. Each of us is a matching half of a human being, because we've been cut in half like flatfish, making two out of one, and each of us is looking for his own matching half. Those men who are cut from the combined gender (the androgynous, as it was called then) are attracted to women, and many adulterers are from this group. Similarly, the women who are attracted to men and become adulteresses come from this group. Those women who are cut from the female gender are not at all interested in men, but are drawn much more towards women: female homosexuals come from this group.

Those who are cut from the male gender go for males. While they are boys, because they are slices of the male gender, they are attracted to men and enjoy sleeping with men and being embraced by them. These are the best of their generation, both as boys and young men, because they are naturally the bravest. Some people say that they are shameless, but that isn't true. It's not out of shamelessness that they do this but because they are bold, brave and masculine, and welcome the same qualities in others. Here is clear evidence of this: men like this are the only ones who, when grown up, end up as politicians. When they become men, they're sexually attracted to boys; they have no natural interest in getting married and having children, although they are forced to do this by convention. They are quite satisfied by spending their lives together and not getting married. In short, such people become lovers of boys and boys who love their male lovers, always welcoming their shared natural character."

4.5 ARISTOTLE: ON THE JUSTIFICATION OF SLAVERY (*THE POLITICS*, 350 B.C.E.)

Chapter 5

There is a principle of rule and subordination in nature at large: it appears especially in the realm of animate creation. By virtue of that principle, the soul rules the body; and by virtue of it the master, who possesses the rational faculty of the soul, rules the slave, who possesses only bodily powers and the faculty of understanding the directions given by another's reason. But nature, though she intends, does not always succeed in achieving a clear distinction between men born to be masters and men born to be slaves.

1254ª17 We have next to consider whether there are, or are not, some people who are by nature such as are here defined; whether, in other words, there are some people for whom slavery is the better and just condition, or whether the reverse is the case and all slavery is contrary to nature. The issue is not difficult; whether we study it philosophically in the light of reason, or consider it empirically on the basis of the actual facts. The relation of ruler and ruled is one of those things which are not only necessary, but also beneficial; and there are species in which a distinction is already marked, immediately at birth, between those of its members who are intended for being ruled and those who are intended to rule. There are also many kinds both of ruling and ruled elements. (Moreover the rule which is exercised over the better sort of subjects is a better sort of rule — as, for example, rule exercised over a man is better than rule over an animal. The reason is that the value of something which is produced increases with the value of those contributing to it; and where one element rules and the other is ruled, there is something which they jointly produce.) In all cases where there is a compound, constituted of more than one part but forming one common entity, whether the parts be continuous or discrete, a ruling element and a ruled can always be traced. This characteristic is present in animate beings by virtue of the whole constitution of nature; for even in things which are inanimate there is a sort of ruling principle, such as is to be found, for example, in a musical harmony. But such considerations perhaps belong to a more popular method of inquiry; and we may content ourselves here with saying that animate beings are composed, in the first place, of soul and body, with the former naturally ruling and the latter naturally ruled. When investigating the natural state of things; we must fix our attention, not on those which are in a corrupt, but on those which are in a natural condition. It follows that we must consider the man who is in the best state both of body and soul, and in whom the rule of soul over body is accordingly evident; for with vicious people or those in a vicious condition, the reverse would often appear to be true — the body ruling the soul as the result of their evil and unnatural condition....

1254ᵇ27 It is nature's intention also to erect a physical difference between the bodies of freemen and those of the slaves, giving the latter strength for the menial duties of life, but making the former upright in carriage and (though useless for physical labor) useful for the various purposes of civic life — a life which tends, as it develops, to be divided into military service and the occupations of peace. The contrary of nature's intention, however, often happens: there are some slaves who have the bodies of freemen, as there are others who have a freeman's soul. But, if there were men who were as distinguished in their bodies alone as are the statues of the gods, all would agree that the others should be their slaves. And if this is true when the difference is one of the body, it may be affirmed with still greater justice when the difference is one of the soul; though it is not as easy to see the beauty of the soul as it is to see that of the body.

1254ᵇ39 It is thus clear that, just as some are by nature free, so others are by nature slaves, and for these latter the condition of slavery is both beneficial and just....

1255ᵃ21 There are some who, clinging, as they think, to a sort of justice (for law is a sort of justice), assume that slavery in war is just. Simultaneously, however, they contradict that assumption; for in the first place it is possible that the original cause of a war may not be just, and in the second place no one would ever say that someone who does not deserve to be in a condition of slavery is really a slave. If such a view were accepted, the result would be that men reputed to be of the highest rank would be turned into slaves or the children of slaves, if

they [or their parents] happened to be captured and sold into slavery. This is the reason why they do not like to call such people slaves, but prefer the term to barbarians. But by this use of terms they are, in reality, only seeking to express that same idea of the natural slave which we began by mentioning. They are driven, in effect, to admit that there are some who are everywhere slaves, and others who are everywhere free. The same line of thought is followed in regard to good birth. Greeks regard themselves as well born not only in their own country, but absolutely and in all places; but they regard barbarians as well born only in their own country — thus assuming that there is one sort of good birth and freedom which is absolute, and another which is only relative....

Chapter 7

The training of slaves, and the art of using them properly. How they be justly acquired.

1255ᵇ1 The argument makes it clear that the rule of the master and that of the statesman are different from one another, and that it is not the case that all kinds of rule are, as some thinkers hold, identical. One kind of rule is exercised over those who are naturally free; the other over slaves; and again the rule exercised over a household by its head is that of a monarch (for all households are monarchically governed), while the rule of the statesman is rule over freemen and equals. Now masters are not so termed in virtue of any knowledge which they have acquired, but in virtue of their own endowment; and the same is true of slaves and freemen generally. But there may be a kind of knowledge which belongs to masters, and another which belongs to slaves; and the latter would be of the nature of the knowledge taught by the man of Syracuse, who instructed servants for pay in the discharge of their ordinary duties.

Instruction in such subjects might be extended further: it might include, for example, the art of cookery and other similar forms of skilled domestic service. The reason why this might be done is that the duties differ; some are of a higher standing, even if others are needed more. As the proverb says:

Slave may go before slave, and master may go before master.

All such forms of knowledge are necessarily of a servile character. But there is also a form of knowledge belonging to the master, which consists in the use of slaves: a master is such in virtue not of acquiring, but of using slaves. This knowledge belonging to the master is

something which has no great or majestic character: the master must simply know how to command what the slave must know how to do. This is why those who are in a position to escape from being troubled, by it delegate, the management of slaves to a steward, and spend on politics or philosophy the time they are thus able to save. The art of acquiring slaves for ownership differs both from the art of being a master and from that of being a slave — that is to say, when it is justly practiced; for in that case it is a particular form of the art of war, or of the art of hunting.

1255ᵇ39 This should be an adequate account of the distinction between master and slave.

ASIAN RELIGIONS AND TRADITIONS

While the Hinduism of Kautilya's *Arthashastra* (c. 300 B.C.E.) also viewed women as inferior beings, a woman should nevertheless expect to receive protection from her husband, divorce by mutual consent, or be taken care of by her husband's family (if she becomes a widow). Punishment for adultery or rape varied, depending upon the caste of the victim and perpetrator. While slavery was recognized, Kautilya offered some protection to slaves by punishing masters who enslaved children younger than eight years old and masters who impregnated female slaves without freeing them (see Section 4.6).

Caste regulations in India were further legislated in the *Laws of Manu* (c. 200 B.C.E.). A woman's subjugation to a man, whom she "should serve as a god," was absolute. "In childhood a woman should be under her father's control, in youth under her husband's, and when her husband is dead under her sons'." She should never have independence. One should note the Buddhist repudiation of the caste system, and its relatively kinder view of women's plight, recognizing their "hundreds of disadvantages" on earth. Yet even under Buddhism, women were not granted the same privileges as men (see Section 4.8).

4.6 KAUTILYA: ON WOMEN, SLAVERY, AND HOMOSEXUALITY (*THE ARTHASHASTRA*, C. 300 B.C.E.)

Chapter II

If a woman after re-marriage attempts to take possession of her own property under the plea of maintaining her sons by her former husband, she shall be made to endow it

in their name. If a woman has many male children by many husbands, then she shall conserve her property in the same condition as she had received from her husbands. Even that property which has been given her with full powers of enjoyment and disposal, a remarried woman shall endow in the name of her sons.

A barren widow who is faithful to the bed for her dead husband may, under the protection of her teacher, enjoy her property as long as she lives: for it is to ward off calamities that women are endowed with property. On her death, her property shall pass into the hands of kinsmen. If the husband is alive and the wife is dead, then her sons and daughters shall divide her property among themselves. If there are no sons, her daughters shall divide her property among themselves. If there are no sons, her daughters shall have it. In their absence her husband shall take that amount of money (sulka) which he had given her, and her relatives shall re-take whatever in the shape of gift or dowry they had presented her. Thus the determination of the property of a woman is dealt with.

Remarriage of Males

If a woman either brings forth no (live) children, or has no male issue, or is barren, her husband shall wait for eight years before marrying another. If she bears only a dead child, he has to wait for ten years. If she brings forth only females, he has to wait for twelve years. Then if he is desirous to have sons, he may marry another. In case of violating this rule, he shall be made to pay her not only sulka, her property (stridhana) and an adequate monetary compensation (adhivedanikamartham), but also a fine of 24 panas to the government. Having given the necessary amount of sulka and property (stridhana) even to those women who have not received such things on the occasion of their marriage with him, and also having given his wives the proportionate compensation and an adequate subsistence (vrtti), he may marry any number of women; for women are created for the sake of sons. If many or all of them are at the same time in menses, he shall lie with felt woman among them whom he married earlier or who has a living son.

If a husband is of bad character, or is long gone abroad, or has become traitor to his king, or is likely to endanger the life of his wife, or has fallen from his caste, or has lost virility, he may be abandoned by his wife.

Chapter III

Maintenance of Woman

A woman who has a right to claim maintenance for an unlimited period of time shall be given as much food and clothing as is necessary for her, or more than is necessary in proportion to the income of the maintainer. If the period (for which such things are to be given to her, with one-tenth of the amount in addition) is limited, then a certain amount of money, fixed proportion to the income of the maintainer, shall be given to her; so also if she has not been given her sulka, property, and compensation (due to her for allowing her husband to remarry). If she places herself under the protection of anyone belonging to her father-in-law's family or if she begins to live independently, then her husband shall not be sued (for her maintenance). Thus the determination of maintenance is dealt with....

Enmity between Husband and Wife

A woman, who hates her husband, who has passed the period of seven turns of her menses, and who loves another, shall immediately return to her husband both the endowment and jewelry she has received from him, and allow him to lie down with another woman. A man, hating his wife, shall allow her to take shelter in the house of a mendicant woman, or of her lawful guardians or of her kinsmen. If a man falsely denies his intercourse with his wife, though it be proved by eyewitness or through a spy, he shall pay a fine of 12 pana. A woman, hating her husband, cannot dissolve her marriage with him against his will. Nor can a man dissolve his marriage with his wife against her will. But from mutual enmity, divorce may be obtained.

Chapter IV

In the case of husbands who have long gone abroad, who have become ascetics; or who have been dead, their wives, having no issue, shall wait for them for the period of seven menses; but if they have given birth to children, they shall wait for a year. Then (each of these women) may marry the brother of her husband. If there are a number of brothers to her last husband, she shall marry such a one of them who is next in age to her former husband, or as is virtuous and capable of protecting her, or one who is the youngest and unmarried. If there are no brothers to her lost husband, she may marry one who belongs to the same gotra as her husband's or a relative, *i.e.*, of the same family. But if there are many such persons as can be selected in marriage, she shall choose one who is a near relation of her lost husband....

Chapter XII

[...]If a slave who is less than eight years old and has no relatives, no matter whether he is born a slave in his master's house, or fallen to his master's share of inheritance, or has been purchased or obtained by his master in any other way, is employed in mean avocations against his will or is sold or mortgaged in a foreign land; or if a pregnant female slave is sold, or pledged without any provision for her confinement, her master shall be punished with the first amercement. The purchaser and abettors shall likewise be punished.

Failure to set a slave at liberty on the receipt of a required amount of ransom shall be punished with a fine of 12 panas; putting a slave under confinement for no reason (samrodhaschākaranāt) shall likewise be punished.

The property of a slave shall pass into the hands of his kinsmen; in the absence of any kinsmen, his master shall take it.

When a child is begotten on a female slave by her master, both the child and its mother shall at once be recognized as free. If, for the sake of subsistence, the mother has to remain in her bondage, her brother and sister shall be liberated.

Selling or mortgaging the life of a male or a female slave once liberated shall be punished with a fine of 12 panas, with the exception of those who enslave themselves. Thus the rules regarding slaves.

Power of Masters over
Their Hired Servants

Neighbors shall know the nature of agreement between a master and his servant. The servant shall get the promised wages. As to wages not previously settled, the amount shall be fixed in proportion to the work done and the time spent in doing it (karmakālānurūpam = at the rate prevailing at the time). Wages being previously unsettled, a cultivator shall obtain 1/10th of the crops grown, a herdsman 1/10th of the butter clarified, a trader 1/10th of the sale proceeds. Wages previously settled shall be paid and received as agreed upon.

Artisans, musicians, physicians, buffoons, cooks and other workmen, serving of their own accord, shall obtain as much wages as similar persons employed elsewhere usually get or as much as experts (kuśalāh) shall fix....

No man shall have sexual intercourse with any woman against her will.

When a woman, being desirous of intercourse, yields herself to a man of the same caste and rank, she shall be fined 12 panas, while any other woman who is an abettor in the case shall be fined twice as much. Any woman who abets a man in having intercourse with a maiden against her will shall not only pay a fine of 100 panas, but also please the maiden, providing her with an adequate nuptial fee.

A woman who, of her own accord, yields herself to a man, shall be slave to the king.

For committing intercourse with a woman outside a village or for spreading false report regarding such things, double the usual fines shall be imposed....

When a man rescues a woman from enemies, forests, or floods, or saves the life of a woman who has been abandoned in forests, forsaken in famine, or thrown out as if dead, he may enjoy her as agreed upon during the rescue.

A woman of high caste, with children and having desire for sexual enjoyment, may be let off after receiving an adequate amount of ransom.

Those women who have been rescued from the hands of thieves, from floods, in famine; or in national calamities, or who, having been abandoned, missed, or thrown out as if dead in forests, have been taken home, may be enjoyed by the rescuer as agreed upon....

When a man performs witchcraft to win the sister of his own father or mother, the wife of a maternal uncle or of a preceptor, his own daughter-in-law, daughter, or sister, he shall have his limb cut off and also be put to death, while any woman who yields herself to such an offender shall also receive similar punishment. Any woman who yields herself to a slave, a servant, or a hired laborer shall be similarly punished.

A Kshatriya who commits adultery with an unguarded Brāhman woman shall be punished with the highest amercement; a Vaiśya doing the same shall be deprived of the whole of his property; and a Śūdra shall be burnt alive wound round in mats.

Whoever commits adultery with the queen of the land shall be burnt alive in a vessel. *Caste hierarchy still applies*

[A man who commits adultery with a woman of low caste shall be banished, with prescribed mark branded on his forehead, or shall be degraded to the same caste.]

A Śūdra or a śvapāka who commits adultery with a woman of low caste shall be put to death, while the woman shall have her ears and nose cut off.

Adultery with a nun (pravrajitā) shall be punishable with a fine of 24 panas, while the nun who submits herself shall also pay a similar fine.

A man who forces his connection with a harlot shall be fined 12 panas....

[A man having sexual intercourse with another man shall also pay the first amercement.]

When a senseless man has sexual intercourse with beasts, he shall be fined 12 panas; when he commits the same act with idols (representatives) of goddesses (daivatapratim), he shall be fined twice as much....

Nuns are given leeway (*) — They are respected

Men shall only be fined for having sex with other men.

4.7 MANU: ON WOMEN AND THE CASTE SYSTEM (*THE LAWS*, C. 200 B.C.E.)

Chapter 3

[8] A man should not marry a girl who is a redhead or has an extra limb or is sickly or has no body hair or too much body hair or talks too much or is sallow; [9] or who is named after a constellation, a tree, or a river, or who has a low-caste name, or is named after a mountain, a bird, a snake, or has a menial or frightening name. [10] He should marry a woman who does not lack any part of her body and who has a pleasant name, who walks like a goose or an elephant, whose body hair and hair on the head is fine, whose teeth are not big, and who has delicate limbs. [11] A wise man will not marry a woman who has no brother or whose father is unknown, for fear that she may be an appointed daughter or that he may act wrongly.

[12] A woman of the same class is recommended to twice-born men for the first marriage; but for men who are driven by desire, these are the women, in progressively descending order: [13] According to tradition, only a servant woman can be the wife of a servant; she and one of his own class can be the wife of a commoner; these two and one of his own class for a king; and these three and one of his own class for a priest. [14] Not a single story mentions a servant woman as the wife of a priest or a ruler, even in extremity. [15] Twice-born men who are so infatuated as to marry women of lower caste quickly reduce their families, including the descendants, to the status of servants. [16] A man falls when he weds a servant woman, according to Atri and to (Gautama) the son of Utathya, or when he has a son by her, according to Śaunaka, or when he has any children by her, according to Bhrgu. [17] A priest who climbs into bed with a servant woman goes to hell; if he begets a son in her, he loses the status of priest.

[18] The ancestors and the gods do not eat the offerings to the gods, to the ances-

tors, and to guests that such a man makes with her, and so he does not go to heaven. [19] No redemption is prescribed for a man who drinks the saliva from the lips of a servant woman or is tainted by her breath or begets a son in her....

Chapter 5

[147] A girl, a young woman, or even an old woman should not do anything independently, even in (her own) house. [148] In childhood a woman should be under her father's control, in youth under her husband's, and when her husband is dead, under her sons'. She should not have independence. [149] A woman should not try to separate herself from her father, her husband, or her sons, for her separation from them would make both (her own and her husband's) families contemptible. [150] She should always be cheerful, and clever at household affairs; she should keep her utensils well polished and not have too free a hand in spending. [151] When her father, or her brother with her father's permission, gives her to someone, she should obey that man while he is alive and not violate her vow to him when he is dead....

[153]A husband who performs the transformative ritual (of marriage) with Vedic verses always makes his woman happy, both when she is in her fertile season and when she is not, both here on earth and in the world beyond. [154] A virtuous wife should constantly serve her husband like a god, even if he behaves badly, freely indulges his lust, and is devoid of any good qualities. [155] Apart (from their husbands), women cannot sacrifice or undertake a vow or fast; it is because a wife obeys her husband that she is exalted in heaven....

Chapter 8

[299] If a wife, a son, a slave, a menial servant, or a full brother has committed an offense, they may be beaten with a rope with a split bamboo cane, [300] but only on the back of the body, and never on the head;

anyone who beats them anywhere else will incur the guilt of a thief....

Chapter 10

[51] The dwellings of "Fierce" Untouchables and "Dog-cookers" should be outside the village; they must use discarded bowls, and dogs and donkeys should be their wealth. [52] Their clothing should be the clothes of the dead, and their food should be in broken dishes; their ornaments should be made of black iron, and they should wander constantly. [53] A man who carries out his duties should not seek contact with them; they should do business with one another and marry with those who are like them. [54] Their food, dependent upon others, should be given to them in a broken dish, and they should not walk about in villages and cities at night. [55] They may move about by day to do their work, recognizable by distinctive marks in accordance with the king's decrees; and they should carry out the corpses of people who have no relatives; this is a fixed rule. [56] By the king's command, they should execute those condemned to death, always in accordance with the teachings, and they should take for themselves the clothing, beds, and ornaments of those condemned to death....

[62] Giving up the body instinctively for the sake of a priest or cow or in the defense of women and children is the way for even the excluded (castes) to achieve success. [63] Manu has said that non-violence, truth, not stealing, purification, and the suppression of the sensory powers is the duty of the four classes, in a nutshell. [64] If someone born from a priest in a servant woman produces a child with someone of the higher (caste), the lower (caste) reaches the status of birth of the higher caste after the seventh generation. [63] (Thus) a servant attains the rank of priest, and a priest sinks to the rank of servant; and you should know that this can happen to someone born of a ruler, too, or of a commoner. [66] But if this (question) should arise: "Which is higher, someone born by chance from a priest father in a non-Aryan[1] mother, or from a non-Aryan

father in a mother of the priestly class?" [67] This is the decision: "Someone born from an Aryan father in a non-Aryan woman may become an Aryan in high qualities; but someone born from a non-Aryan father in an Aryan mother is a non-Aryan."

[1] Editor: Aryan means noble.

4.8 MAHAYANA BUDDHISM: ON THE AFFLICTION OF WOMANHOOD (*THE TWELVE VOWS OF BHAISAJYAGURU,* EARLY 4TH CENTURY)

8. "When I have attained enlightenment, any woman who is afflicted by the hundreds of various disadvantages of womanhood and who wishes to be liberated from being reborn as a loathsome female should bear my name in mind, and she will no longer be reborn in the female state, right up until enlightenment."

12. "When I have attained enlightenment, any beings who have no clothes, who are poor, who are plagued by cold and heat and mosquito bites and suffering day and night — if they bear my name in their minds, I will clothe them in wonderful garments, dyed various colors; and I will bring them pleasures in various ways by means of jewels, ornaments, perfumes, garlands, unguents, and the sounds of song and musical instruments; in these ways I will fulfill all the wishes of all beings."

MONOTHEISM

The universalist stance of the three monotheist religions — Judaism, Christianity, and Islam — was also undermined by the religions' attitudes toward slaves, women, and homosexuals. Slave owners did not have absolute power over their slaves. Masters were urged to treat their slaves in a just and humane way and enable them to earn their freedom after a seven-year limit or for a certain sum of money. Yet none of the three monotheist religions called for an ending to slavery.

Despite encouragement to take care of women and admonitions not to inflict pain on widows or pregnant women, women were always subordinate to men, and at times were regarded as the property of their husbands. An Israelite woman could not divorce her husband unless her husband agreed — even if he had committed adultery. The Christian wife was condemned to learn in silence under the authority of her husband. Muslim women were subjected to the loss of child custody once divorced and entitled to only half the inheritance of a comparable male heir.

Concerning homosexuality, the three religions were even less charitable. Drawing from Leviticus 18:22 and 20:13, Paul warned: "No fornicators or idolaters, none who are guilty of adultery or homosexual perversion … will possess the kingdom of God." Along with Judaism and Christianity, Islam condemned same-sex intimate behavior, and the Islamic Shaaria religious laws even consider it a crime. One may question, given the severity of some punishments and the lesser rights enjoyed by women, slaves, and homosexuals, the extent to which the ancient traditions contributed to the development of human rights. However, as the forces of history unveiled conflicting power relations and created conjectural opportunities for the inclusion of new social participants, these previously overlooked historical agents would eventually become visible, forcefully asserting their liberty and equality, contributing to the pursuit of justice and peace with visions rooted in, but broader and deeper than, those advanced in ancient times (see Sections 4.9 to 4.11).

4.9 THE HEBREW BIBLE: ON ADULTERY AND HOMOSEXUALITY, THE STRANGER AND THE SLAVE

Exodus 22:16–18

When a man seduces a virgin who is not yet betrothed, he shall pay the bride-price for her to be his wife. If her father refuses to give her to him, the seducer shall pay in silver a sum equal to the bride-price for virgins.

You shall not allow a witch to live.

Leviticus 18:23

You shall not lie with a man as with a woman: that is an abomination.

Leviticus 19:33–37

When an alien settles with you in your land, you shall not oppress him. He shall be treated as a native born among you, and you shall love him as a man like yourself, because you were aliens in Egypt. I am the LORD your God.

You shall not pervert justice in measurement of length, weight, or quantity. You shall have true scales, true weights, true measures dry and liquid. I am the LORD your God who brought you out of Egypt. You shall observe all my rules and laws and carry them out. I am the LORD.

Leviticus 20:10–21

If a man commits adultery with his neighbor's wife both adulterer and adulteress shall be put to death. The man who has intercourse with his father's wife has brought shame on his father. They shall both be put to death; their blood shall be on their own heads. [1]If a man has intercourse with his daughter-in-law, they shall both be put to death. Their deed is a violation of nature; their blood shall be on their own heads. If a man has intercourse with a man as with a woman, they both commit an abomination. They shall be put to death and their blood shall be on their own heads. [If man takes both a woman and her mother, that is lewdness.] Both he and they

\# The Graduate

shall be burnt; thus there shall be no lewdness in your midst. A man who has sexual intercourse with any beast shall be put to death, and you shall kill the beast. If a woman approaches any animal to have intercourse with it, you shall kill both woman and beast. They shall be put to death; their blood shall be on their own heads. If a man takes his sister, his father's daughter or his mother's daughter, and they see one another naked, it is a scandalous disgrace. They shall be cut off in the presence of their people.

The man has had intercourse with his sister and he shall accept responsibility. If a man lies with a woman during her monthly period and brings shame upon her, he has exposed her discharge and she has uncovered the source of her discharge; they shall both be cut off from their people. You shall not have intercourse with your mother's sister or your father's sister: it is the exposure of a blood-relation. They shall accept responsibility. A man who has intercourse with his uncle's wife has brought shame upon his uncle. They shall accept responsibility for their sin and shall be proscribed and put to death. If a man takes his brother's wife, it is impurity. He has brought shame upon his brother; they shall be proscribed.

Deuteronomy 15:12–17

When a fellow-Hebrew, man or woman, sells himself to you as a slave, he shall serve you for six years and in the seventh year you shall set him free. But when you set him free, do not let him go empty-handed. Give to him lavishly from your flock, from your threshing-floor and your winepress. Be generous to him, because the LORD your God has blessed you. Do not take it amiss when you have to set him free, for his six years' service to you has been worth twice the wage of a hired man. Then the LORD your God will bless you in everything you do. Remember that you were slaves in Egypt and the LORD your God redeemed you; that is why I am giving you this command today.

If, however, a slave is content to be with you and says, "I will not leave you, I love you and your family," then you shall take an awl and pierce through his ear to the door, and he will be your slave for life. You shall treat slave-girl in the same way.

4.10   THE NEW TESTAMENT: ON WOMEN, HOMOSEXUALS, AND SLAVES (C. 50)

John 7:53- 8:1-11

AND THEY WENT each to his home, and Jesus to the Mount of Olives. At daybreak he appeared again in the temple, and all the people gathered round him. He had taken his seat and was engaged in teaching them when the doctors of the law and the Pharisees brought in a woman caught committing adultery. Making her stand out in the middle they said to him, "Master, this woman was caught in the very act of adultery. In the Law Moses has laid down that such women are to be stoned. What do you say about it?" They put the question as a test, hoping to frame a charge against him. Jesus bent down and wrote with his finger on the ground. When they continued to press their question he sat up straight and said, "That one of you who is faultless shall throw the first stone." Then once again he bent down and wrote on the ground. When they heard what he said, one by one they went away, the eldest first; and Jesus was left alone, with the woman still standing there. Jesus again sat up and said to the woman, "Where are they? Has no one condemned you?" She answered, "No one, sir." Jesus said, "Nor do I condemn you. You may go; do not sin again."

1 Corinthians 6:9-10

Surely you know that the unjust will never come to the possession of the kingdom of God. Make no mistake: no fornicator or idolater, none who are guilty either of adultery or of homosexual perversion, no thieves or grabbers or drunkards or slanderers or swindlers, will possess the kingdom of God.

1 Corinthians 6:13–20

But it is not true that the body is for lust; it is for the Lord — and the Lord for the body. God not only raised our Lord from the dead; he will also raise us by his power. Do you not know that your bodies are limbs and organs of Christ? Shall I then take from Christ his bodily parts and make them over to a harlot? Never! You surely know that anyone who links himself with a harlot becomes physically one with her (for Scripture says, "The pair shall become one flesh"); but he who links himself with Christ is one with him, spiritually. Shun fornication. Every other sin that a man can commit is outside the body; but the fornicator sins against his own body. Do you not know that your body is a shrine of the indwelling Holy Spirit, and the Spirit is God's gift to you? You do not belong to yourselves; you were bought at a price. Then honor God in your body.

1 Corinthians 7:1–17

And now for the matters you wrote about. It is a good thing for a man to have nothing to do with women; but because there is so much immorality, let each man have his own wife and each woman her own husband. The husband must give the wife what is due to her, and the wife equally must give the husband his due. The wife cannot claim her body as her own; it is her husband's. Equally, the husband cannot claim his body as his own; it is his wife's. Do not deny yourselves to one another, except when you agree upon a temporary abstinence in order to devote yourselves to prayer; afterwards you may come together again; otherwise, for lack of self-control, you may be tempted by Satan.

All this I say by way of concession, not command. I should like you all to be as I am myself; but everyone has the gift God has granted him, one this gift and another that.

To the unmarried and to widows I say this: it is a good thing if they stay as I am myself; but if they cannot control themselves, they should marry. Better be married than burn with vain desire.

To the married I give this ruling, which is not mine but the Lord's: a wife must not separate herself from her husband; if she does, she must either remain unmarried or be reconciled to her husband; and the husband must not divorce his wife.

To the rest I say this, as my own word, not as the Lord's: if a Christian has a heathen wife, and she is willing to live with him, he must not divorce her; and a woman who has a heathen husband willing to live with her must not divorce her husband. For the heathen husband now belongs to God through his Christian wife, and the heathen wife through her Christian husband. Otherwise your children would not belong to God, whereas in fact they do. If on the other hand the heathen partner wishes for a separation, let him have it. In such cases the Christian husband or wife is under no compulsion; but God's call is a call to live in peace. Think of it: as a wife you may be your husband's salvation; as a husband you may be your wife's salvation.

However that may be, each one must order his life according to the gift the Lord has granted him and his condition when God called him. That is what I teach in all our congregations.

Galatians 3:28–29

There is no such thing as Jew and Greek, slave and freeman, male and female; for you are all one person in Christ Jesus. But if you thus belong to Christ, you are the "issue" of Abraham, and so heirs by promise.

Ephesians 5:22–27

Wives, be subject to your husbands as to the Lord; for the man is the head of the woman, just as Christ also is the head of the church. Christ is, indeed, the Saviour of the body; but just as the church is subject to Christ, so must women be to their husbands in everything.

Husbands, love your wives, as Christ also loved the church and gave himself up for it, to consecrate it, cleansing it by water and word, so that he might present the church to himself all glorious, with no stain or wrinkle or any thing of the sort, but holy and without blemish.

Colossians 3:20–23

Children, obey your parents in everything, for that is pleasing to God and is the Christian way. Fathers, do not exasperate your children, for fear they grow disheartened. Slaves, give entire obedience to your earthly masters, not merely with an outward show of service, to curry favor with men, but with single-mindedness, out of reverence for the Lord. Whatever you are doing, put your whole heart into it, as if you were doing it for the Lord and not for men, knowing that there is a Master who will give you your heritage as a reward for your service.

1 Timothy 2:11–15

A woman must be a learner, listening quietly and with due submission. I do not permit a woman to be a teacher, nor must woman domineer over man; she should be quiet. For Adam was created first, and Eve afterwards; and it was not Adam who was deceived; it was the woman who, yielding to deception, fell into sin. Yet she will be saved through motherhood — if only women continue in faith, love, and holiness, with a sober mind.

Philemon 1–25

From Paul, a prisoner of Christ Jesus, and our colleague Timothy, to Philemon our dear friend and fellow-worker, and Apphia our sister, and Archippus our comrade-in-arms, and the congregation at your house.

Grace to you and peace from God our Father and the Lord Jesus Christ.

I thank my God always when I mention you in my prayers, for I hear of your love and faith towards the Lord Jesus and towards all God's people. My prayer is that your fellowship with us in our common faith may deepen the understanding of all the blessings that our union with Christ brings us. For I am delighted and encouraged by your love; through you, my brother, God's people have been much refreshed.

Accordingly, although in Christ I might make bold to point out your duty, yet, because of that same love, I would rather appeal to you. Yes, I, Paul, ambassador as

I am of Christ Jesus — and now his prisoner — appeal to you about my child, whose father I have become in this prison.

I mean Onesimus, once so little use to you, but now useful indeed, both to you and to me. I am sending him back to you, and in doing so I am sending a part of myself. I should have liked to keep him with me, to look after me as you would wish, here in prison for the Gospel. But I would rather do nothing without your consent, so that your kindness may be a matter not of compulsion, but of your own free will. For perhaps this is why you lost him for a time, that you might have him back for good, no longer as a slave, but as more than a slave — as a dear brother, very dear indeed to me and how much dearer to you, both as man and as Christian.

If, then, you count me partner in the faith, welcome him as you would welcome me. And if he has done you any wrong or is in your debt, put that down to my account. Here is my signature, Paul; I undertake to repay — not to mention that you owe your very self to me as well. Now brother, as a Christian, be generous with me, and relieve my anxiety; we are both in Christ!

I write to you confident that you will meet my wishes; I know that you will in fact do better than I ask. And one thing more: have a room ready for me, for I hope that, in answer to your prayers, God will grant me to you.

Epaphras, Christ's captive like myself, sends you greetings. So do Mark, Aristarchus, Demas, and Luke, my fellow-workers.

The grace of the Lord Jesus Christ be with your spirit!

4.11 THE KORAN: ON WOMEN, HOMOSEXUALS, SLAVES AND NONBELIEVERS (C. 632)

Surah 2

Section 23

… Your wives,
Are your garments
And ye are their garments.
Allah knoweth what ye
Used to do secretly among yourselves;
But He turned to you
And forgave you;
So now associate with them,
And seek what Allah
Hath ordained for you,
And eat and drink,
Until the white thread
Of dawn appear to you
Distinct from its black thread;
Then complete your fast
Till the night appears,
But do not associate
With your wives
While ye are in retreat
In the mosques. Those are
Limits (set by) Allah:
Approach not nigh thereto.
Thus doth Allah make clear
His signs to men: that
They may learn self-restraint.

Section 29

When ye divorce
Women and they fulfill
The term of their ('Iddah)[1],
Either take them back
On equitable terms
Or set them free
On equitable terms;
But do not take them back
To injure them, (or) to take
Undue advantage,
If any one does that,
He wrongs his own soul.
Do not treat Allah's Signs
As a jest,
But solemnly rehearse
Allah's favors on you,
And the fact that He
Sent down to you
The Book
And Wisdom,
For your instruction.
And fear Allah,
And know that Allah
Is well-acquainted
With all things.

Section 30

When ye divorce
Women and they fulfill
The term of their ('Iddah),
Do not prevent them
From marrying
Their (former) husbands,
If they mutually agree
On equitable terms.
This instruction
Is for all amongst you,
Who believe in Allah
And the Last Day.
That is (the course
Making for) most virtue
And purity amongst you.
And Allah knows,
And ye know not.
The mothers shall give suck
To their offspring
For two whole years,
If the father desires
To complete the term.
But he shall bear the cost
Of their food and clothing
On equitable terms.
No mother shall be
Treated unfairly
On account of her child.
Nor father
On account of his child,
An heir shall be chargeable
In the same way.

Surah 4

Section 1

O mankind! Reverence
Your Guardian-Lord,
Who created you
From a single Person,
Created, of like nature,
His mate, and from them twain
Scattered (like seeds)
Countless men and women —
Fear Allah, through whom
Ye demand your mutual (rights)
And (reverence) the wombs
(That bore you): for Allah
Ever watches over you....

From what is left by parents
And those nearest related
There is a share for men
And a share for women,
Whether the property be small
Or large — a determinate share.
But if at the time of division
Other relatives, or orphans,
Or poor, are present,
Feed them out of the (property)
And speak to them
Words of kindness and justice.
O ye who believe!
Ye are forbidden to inherit
Women against their will. Nor should ye
     treat them
With harshness, that ye may
Take away part of the dower
Ye have given them — except
Where they have been guilty
Of open lewdness;
On the contrary live with them
On a footing of kindness and equity.
If ye take a dislike to them
It may be that ye dislike
A thing, and Allah brings about
Through it a great deal of good.
But if ye decide to take
One wife in place of another,
Even if ye had given the latter
A whole treasure for dower,
Take not the least bit of it back;
Would ye take it by slander
And a manifest wrong?
And how could ye take it
When ye have gone in
Unto each other, and they have
Taken from you a solemn covenant?

Section 13

Never should a Believer
Kill a Believer; but
(If it so happens) by mistake,
(Compensation is due);
If one (so) kills a Believer,
It is ordained that he
Should free a believing slave,
And pay compensation
To the deceased's family, unless
They remit it freely.
If the deceased belonged

To a people at war with you,
And he was a Believer,
The freeing of a believing slave
(Is enough). If he belonged
To a people with whom
Ye have a treaty of mutual
Alliance, compensation should
Be paid to his family,
And a believing slave be freed.
For those who find this
Beyond their means, (is prescribed)
A fast for two months running:
By way of repentance
To Allah; for Allah hath
All knowledge and all wisdom.
If a man kills a Believer
Intentionally, his recompense
Is Hell, to abide therein
(Forever): and the wrath
And the curse of Allah
Are upon him, and
A dreadful penalty
Is prepared for him.

Surah 12

O ye who believe!
The law of equality²
Is prescribed to you
In cases of murder:
The free for the free,
The slave for the slave,
The woman for the woman.
But if any remission
Is made by the brother³
Of the slain, then grant
Any reasonable demand,
And compensate him
With handsome gratitude.
This is a concession
And a Mercy
From your Lord.

Surah 16

Section 10

Allah sets forth the Parable
(Of two men: one) a slave
Under the dominion of
another;
He has no power of any sort;

And (the other) a man
On whom We have bestowed
Goodly favors from Oursleves.
And he spends thereof (freely),
Privately and publicly:
Are the two equal? (By no means;)
Praise be to Allah. But
Most of them understand not.

Surah 26

Section 9

"Of all the creatures
In the world, will ye
Approach males,

"And leave those whom Allah
Has created for you
To be your mates?
Nay, ye are a people
Transgressing (all limits)!"

¹ Islam tries to maintain the married stateas far as possible, especially where children are concerned, but it is against the restriction of the liberty of men and women in such vitally important matters as love and family life. It will check hasty action as far as possible, and leave the door to reconciliation open at many stages. Even after divorce a suggestion of reconciliation is made, subject to certain precautions (mentioned in the following verses) against thoughtless action. A period of waiting (iddah) for three monthly courses is prescribed, in order to see if the marriage conditionally dissolved is likely to result in issue. But this is not necessary where the divorced woman is a virgin (Q. 33:49). It is definitely declared that men and women shall have similar rights against each other.

² ... Our law of equality only takes account of three conditions in civil society; free for free, slave for slave, woman for woman. Among free men or women, all are equal: you cannot ask that because a wealthy, or highly born, or influential man is killed, his life is equal to two or three lives among the poor or the lowly. Not in cases of murder, can you go into the value or abilities of a slave. A woman is mentioned separately because her position as a mother or an economic worker is different. She does not form a third class, but a division in the other two classes. One life having been lost, do not waste many lives in retaliation: at most, let the Law take one life under strictly prescribed conditions, and shut the door to private vengeance or tribal retaliation. But if the aggrieved party consents (and this condition of consent is laid down to prevent worse evils), forgiveness and brotherly love is better, and the door

of Mercy is kept open. In Western law, no felony can be compounded.

[3] The brother: The term is perfectly general; all men are brothers in Islam. In this, and in all questions of inheritance, females have similar rights to males, and therefore the masculine gender imports both sexes. Here we are considering the rights of the heirs in light of the larger brotherhood. In 2:178–179 we have the rights of the heirs to life as it were in 2:180–182 we proceed to the heirs to property.

PART II

The Legacy of Liberalism and the Enlightenment

INTRODUCTION

The Enlightenment represented the formative age of our modern conception of human rights. It was a period in which the Catholic Christendom of the Middle Ages yielded to the modern concept of the nation-state; in which political thinkers and leaders guided by natural law contested divine right; and in which alternative political allegiances and new economic interactions were gradually encapsulated in the English Bill of Rights (1689), the U.S. Declaration of Independence (1776), and the French Declaration of the Rights of Man and Citizen (see all three documents in Part VI). The rights to life, civil liberty, and property became the credo of the new age. To promote these liberties, Enlightenment thinkers envisioned the spread of commercial enterprises and republican institutions, whose advance could also usher in an age of enduring peace. If war was not altogether condemned, its pursuit was greatly restricted under new guidelines of just war.

II.1   UNITED NATIONS UNIVERSAL DECLARATION OF HUMAN RIGHTS (1948): ARTICLE 3

Article 3
Everyone has the right to life, liberty and the security of person.

CHAPTER 5

Liberal Visions of Human Rights

Freedom of expression and religion was central to the new liberal state imagined by the intellectual architects of the Enlightenment. The Church and its dogmatic monopoly over earthly affairs had so far protected the divine rights of kings, as well as the political and economic privileges of the nobility and the clergy. A revolution in thought, calling for the end of Catholic censorship, for the separation of church and state, and for the rights to life and property, was now under way.

THE FIGHT FOR FREEDOM OF EXPRESSION AND AGAINST RELIGIOUS OPPRESSION

Famous for poems like *Paradise Lost* (1667) and *Paradise Regained* (1671), English poet John Milton (1608–1674) gained early notoriety for his eloquent fight for freedom of the press. Written in response to a censorship act of the parliament and inspired by Isocrates' oration to the Aeropagus (the high court of Athens), Milton's *Areopagitica: A Speech for the Liberty of Unlicensed Printing* (1644) became a powerful reminder for future generations of the "liberty to know, to utter, and to argue freely according to conscience." (see Section 5.2).

In the spirit of Milton, British political thinker John Locke (1632–1704) wrote *A Letter Concerning Toleration* (1763) amidst fear that Catholicism might take over England. To ward off civil unrest, Locke argued for the toleration of different religions rather their suppression. Because forced conversion was not the path to salvation, he argued, religion should remain separate from the state. To what degree that separation should exist continues to be widely debated in liberal democracies (see Section 5.3).

Across the Channel, French writer and philosopher Voltaire (1694–1778) carried Locke's torch of tolerance throughout the last bitter decade of the French Ancient Regime. Those who suffered persecution because of their religious beliefs would find in Voltaire one of their most eloquent defenders. A deist at heart, Voltaire authored a number of publications — *The Lisbon Disaster* (1756), *Candide* (1759), *The Tragedy of Tancrède* (1760), and the *Philosophical Dictionary* (1764) — denouncing any form of religious fanaticism that persecutes so-called heretics; he also decried the power of the clergy, which perpetuated evil and suppressed the individual's capacity to think for herself (see Section 5.4).

5.1 UNITED NATIONS UNIVERSAL DECLARATION OF HUMAN RIGHTS (1948): ARTICLES 18–19

Article 18

Everyone has the right to freedom of thought, conscience and religion; this right includes freedom to change his religion or belief, and freedom, either alone or in community with others and in public or private, to manifest his religion or belief in teaching, practice, worship and observance.

Article 19

Everyone has the right to freedom of opinion and expression; this right includes freedom to hold opinions without interference and to seek, receive and impart information and ideas through any media and regardless of frontiers.

5.2 JOHN MILTON: ON CENSORSHIP (*AREOPAGITICA*, 1644)

... I deny not, but that it is of greatest concernment in the Church and Commonwealth, to have a vigilant eye how books demean themselves as well as men; and thereafter to confine, imprison, and do sharpest justice on them as malefactors. For books are not absolutely dead things, but do contain a potency of life in them to be as active as that soul was whose progeny they are; nay, they do preserve as in a vial the purest efficacy and extraction of that living intellect that bred them. I know they are as lively, and as vigorously productive, as those fabulous dragon's teeth; and being sown up and down, may chance to spring up armed men. And yet, on the other hand, unless wariness be used, as good almost kill a man as kill a good book. Who kills a man kills a reasonable creature, God's image; but he who destroys a good book kills reason itself, kills the image of God, as it were in the eye. Many a man lives a burden to the earth; but a good book is the precious life-blood of a master spirit, embalmed and treasured up on purpose to a life beyond life. 'Tis true, no age can restore a life, whereof perhaps there is no great loss; and revolutions of ages do not oft recover the loss of a rejected truth, for the want of which whole nations fare the worse.

We should be wary therefore what persecution we raise against the living labors of public men, how we spill that seasoned life of man, preserved and stored up in books; since we see a kind of homicide may be thus committed, sometimes a martyrdom, and if it extend to the whole impression, a kind of massacre; whereof the execution ends not in the slaying of an elemental life, but strikes at that ethereal and fifth essence, the breath of reason itself, slays an immortality rather than a life....

Many there be that complain of Divine providence suffering Adam to transgress; foolish tongues! When God gave him reason, He gave him freedom to choose, for reason is but choosing; he had been else a mere artificial Adam, such an Adam as he is in the motions. We ourselves esteem not of that obedience, or love, or gift, which is of force: God therefore left him free, set before him a provoking object, ever almost in his eyes; herein consisted his merit, herein the right of his reward, the praise of his abstinence. Wherefore did He create passions within us, pleasures round about us, but that these rightly tempered are the very ingredients of virtue? ...

This justifies the high providence of God, who, though He commands us temperance, justice, continence, yet pours out before us, even to a profuseness, all desirable things, and gives us minds that can wander beyond all limit and satiety. Why should we then affect a rigor contrary to the manner of God and of nature, by abridging or scanting those means, which books freely permitted are, both to the trial of virtue and the exercise of truth? It would be better done, to learn that the law must needs be frivolous, which goes to restrain things, uncertainly and yet equally working to good and to evil. And were the chooser, a dram of well-doing should be preferred before many times as much the forcible hindrance of evil-doing. For God sure esteems the growth and completing of one virtuous person more than the restraint of ten vicious....

Another reason, whereby to make it plain that this Order will miss the end it seeks, consider by the censoring quality which ought to be in every licenser. It cannot be denied but that he who is made judge to sit upon the birth or death of books, whether they may be wafted into this world or not, had need to be a man above the common measure, both studious, learned, and judicious; there may be else no mean mistakes in the censure of what is passable or not; which is also no mean injury. If he be of such worth as behaves him, there cannot be a more tedious and unpleasing journeywork, a greater loss of time levied upon his head, than to be made the perpetual reader of un-chosen books and pamphlets, of times huge volumes....

I never found cause to think that the tenth part of learning stood or fell with the clergy: nor could I ever but hold it for a sordid and unworthy speech of any churchman who had a competency left him. If therefore ye be loath to dishearten utterly and discontent, not the mercenary crew of false pretenders to learning, but the free and ingenuous sort of such as evidently were born to study, and love learning for itself, not for lucre or any other end but the service of God and of truth, and perhaps that lasting fame and perpetuity of praise which God and good men have consented shall be the reward of those whose published labors advance the good of mankind, then know that, so far to distrust the judgment and the honesty of one who hath but a common repute in learning, and never yet offended, as not to count him fit to print his mind without a tutor and examiner, lest he should drop a schism, or something of corruption, is the greatest displeasure and indignity to a free and knowing spirit that can be put upon him....

Lords and Commons cannot make us now less capable, less knowing, less eagerly pursuing of the truth, unless ye first make yourselves, that made us so, less the lovers, less the founders of our true liberty. We can grow ignorant again, brutish, formal and slavish, as ye found us; but you then must first become that which ye cannot be, oppressive, arbitrary and tyrannous, as they were from whom ye have freed us. That our hearts are now more capacious, our thoughts more erected to the search and

expectation of greatest and exactest things, is the issue of your own virtue propagated in us; ye cannot suppress that, unless ye reinforce an abrogated and merciless law, that fathers may dispatch at will their own children. And who shall then stick closest to ye, and excite others? Not he who takes up arms for coat and conduct, and his four nobles of Danegelt. Although I dispraise not the defense of just immunities, yet love my peace better, if that were all. Give me the liberty to know, to utter, and to argue freely according to conscience, above all liberties....

5.3 JOHN LOCKE: ON THE SEPARATION OF RELIGION AND STATE (*A LETTER CONCERNING TOLERATION*, 1689)

... No man can, if he would conform his faith to the dictates of another. All the life and power of true religion consist in the inward and full persuasion of the mind; and faith is not faith without believing. Whatever profession we make, to whatever outward worship we conform, if we are not fully satisfied in our own mind that the one is true, and the other well pleasing unto God, such profession and such practice, far from being any furtherance, are indeed great obstacles to our salvation. For in this manner, instead of expiating other sins by the exercise of religion, I say, in offering thus unto God Almighty such a worship as we esteem to be displeasing unto Him, we add unto the number of our other sins those also of hypocrisy, and contempt of His Divine Majesty.

In the second place, the care of souls cannot belong to the civil magistrate, because his power consists only in outward force; but true and saving religion consists in the inward persuasion of the mind, without which nothing can be acceptable to God. And such is the nature of the understanding, that it cannot be compelled to the belief of anything by outward force. Confiscation of estate, imprisonment, torments, nothing of that nature can have any such efficacy as to make men change the inward judgment that they have framed of things. It may indeed be alleged that the magistrate may make use of arguments, and thereby draw the hetero-dox into the way of truth, and procure their salvation. I grant it; but this is common to him with other men. In teaching, instruct-ing, and redressing the erroneous by reason, he may certainly do what becomes any good man to do. Magistracy does not oblige him to pat off either humanity or Christianity; but it is one thing to persuade, another to command; one thing to press with argu-ments, another with penalties. This civil power alone has a right to do; to the other goodwill is authority enough. Every man has commission to admonish, exhort, convince another of error, and, by reasoning, to draw him into truth; but to give laws, receive obe-dience, and compel with the sword, belongs to none but the magistrate. And upon this ground, I affirm that the magistrate's power extends not to the establishing of any articles of faith, or forms of worship, by the force of his laws. For laws are of no force at all without penalties, and penalties in this case are absolutely impertinent, because they are not proper to convince the mind. Neither the profession of any articles of faith, nor the conformity to any outward form of worship (as has been already said), can be available to the salvation of souls, unless the truth of the one, and the acceptableness of the other unto God, be thoroughly believed by those that so profess and practice. But penalties are no way capable to produce such belief. It is only light and evidence that can work a change in men's opinions; which light can in no manner proceed from corporal suffer-ings, or any other outward penalties.

In the third place, the care of the salvation of men's souls cannot belong to the magis-trate; because, though the rigor of laws and the force of penalties were capable to con-vince and change men's minds, yet would not that help at all to the salvation of their souls. For there being but one truth, one way to heaven, what hope is there that more men would be led into it if they had no rule but the religion of the court, and were put under the necessity to quit the light of their own reason, and oppose the dictates of their own consciences, and blindly to resign themselves up to the will of their governors, and to the religion which either ignorance, ambition,

or superstition had chanced to establish in the countries where they were born? In the variety and contradiction of opinions in reli-gion, wherein the princes of the world are as much divided as in their secular interests, the narrow way would be much straitened; one country alone would be in the right, and all the rest of the world put under an obliga-tion of following their princes in the ways that lead to destruction; and that which heightens the absurdity, and very ill suits the notion of a Deity, men would owe their eternal happiness or misery to the places of their nativity.

These considerations, to omit many oth-ers that might have been urged to the same purpose, seem unto me sufficient to conclude that all the power of civil government relates only to men's civil interests, is confined to the care of the things of this world, and hath nothing to do with the world to come.

Let us now consider what a church is. A church, then, I take to be a voluntary society of men, joining themselves together of their own accord in order to the public worshipping of God in such manner as they judge accept-able to Him, and effectual to the salvation of their souls.

I say it is a free and voluntary society.... No man by nature is bound unto any par-ticular church or sect, but everyone joins himself voluntarily to that society in which he believes he has found that profession and worship which is truly acceptable to God....

The end of a religious society (as has already been said) is the public worship of God, and, by means thereof, the acquisition of eternal life. All discipline ought therefore to tend to that end, and all ecclesiastical laws to be thereunto confined. Nothing ought nor can be transacted in this society relating to the possession of civil and worldly goods. No force is here to be made use of upon any occasion whatsoever. For force belongs wholly to the civil magistrate, and the pos-session of all outward goods is subject to his jurisdiction....

[W]hencesover their authority be sprung, since it is ecclesiastical, it ought to be con-fined within the bounds of the Church, nor can it in any manner be extended to civil affairs, because the Church itself is a thing absolutely separate and distinct from the commonwealth. The boundaries on both sides are fixed and immovable. He jumbles heaven and earth together, the things most remote and opposite, who mixes these two societies, which are in their original, end, business, and in everything perfectly distinct and infinitely different from each other. No man, therefore, with whatsoever ecclesiastical office he be dignified, can deprive another man that is not of his church and faith either of liberty or of any part of his worldly goods upon the account of that difference between them in religion. For whatsoever is not lawful to the whole Church cannot by any ecclesiastical right become lawful to any of its members.

5.4   VOLTAIRE: "RELIGION"
(*PHILOSOPHICAL DICTIONARY,* 1764)

I MEDITATED last night; I was absorbed in the contemplation of nature; I admired the immensity, the course, the harmony of these infinite globes which the vulgar do not know how to admire.

I admired still more the intelligence which directs these vast forces. I said to myself: "One must be blind not to be dazzled by this spectacle; one must be stupid not to recognize the author of it; one must be mad not to worship Him. What tribute of worship should I render Him? Should not this tribute be the same in the whole of space, since it is the same supreme power which reigns equally in all space? Should not a thinking being who dwells in a star in the Milky Way offer Him the same homage as the thinking being on this little globe where we are? Light is uniform for the star Sirius and for us; moral philosophy must be uniform. If a sentient, thinking animal in Sirius is born of a tender father and mother who have been occupied with his happiness, he owes them as much love and care as we owe to our parents. If someone in the Milky Way sees a needy cripple, if he can relieve him and if he does not do it, he is guilty toward all globes. Everywhere the heart has the same duties: on the steps of the throne of God, if He has

a throne; and in the depth of the abyss, if He is an abyss."

I was plunged in these ideas when one of those genii who fill the intermundane spaces came down to me. I recognized this same aerial creature who had appeared to me on another occasion to teach me how different God's judgments were from our own, and how a good action is preferable to a controversy.

He transported me into a desert all covered with piled up bones; and between these heaps of dead men there were walks of evergreen trees and at the end of each walk a tall man of august mien, who regarded these sad remains with pity.

"Alas! my archangel," said I, "where have you brought me?"

"To desolation," he answered.

"And who are these fine patriarchs whom I see sad and motionless at the end of these green walks? They seem to be weeping over this countless crowd of dead."

"You shall know, poor human creature," answered the genius from the intermundane spaces; "but first of all you must weep."

He began with the first pile. "These," he said, "are the twenty-three thousand Jews who danced before a calf, with the twenty-four thousand who were killed while lying with Midianitish women. The number of those massacred for such errors and offenses amounts to nearly three hundred thousand.

"In the other walks are the bones of the Christians slaughtered by each other for metaphysical disputes. They are divided into several heaps of four centuries each. One heap would have mounted right to the sky; they had to be divided."

"What!" I cried, "Brothers have treated their brothers like this, and I have the misfortune to be of this brotherhood!"

"Here," said the spirit, "are the twelve million Americans killed in their fatherland because they had not been baptized."

"My God! Why did you not leave these frightful bones to dry in the hemisphere where their bodies were born, and where they were consigned to so many different deaths? Why assemble here all these abominable monuments to barbarism and fanaticism?"

"To instruct you."

"Since you wish to instruct me," I said to the genius, "tell me if there have been peoples other than the Christians and the Jews in whom zeal and religion wretchedly transformed into fanaticism, have inspired so many horrible cruelties."

"Yes," he said. "The Mohammedans were sullied with the same inhumanities, but rarely; and when one asked *amman*, pity, of them and offered them tribute, they pardoned. As for the other nations there has not been one right from the existence of the world which has ever made a purely religious war. Follow me now." I followed him.

A little beyond these piles of dead men we found other piles; they were composed of sacks of gold and silver, and each had its label: *Substance of the heretics massacred in the eighteenth century, the seventeenth and the sixteenth.* And so on in going back: *Gold and silver of Americans slaughtered*, etc., etc. And all these piles were surmounted with crosses, miters, croziers, triple crowns studded with precious stones.

"What, my genius! It was then to have these riches that these dead were piled up?"

"Yes, my son."

I wept; and when by my grief I had merited to be led to the end of the green walks, he led me there.

"Contemplate," he said, "the heroes of humanity who were the world's benefactors, and who were all united in banishing from the world, as far as they were able, violence and rapine. Question them."

I ran to the first of the band; he had a crown on his head, and a little censer in his hand; I humbly asked him his name. "I am Numa Pompilius," he said to me. "I succeeded a brigand, and I had brigands to govern: I taught them virtue and the worship of God; after me they forgot both more than once; I forbade that in the temples there should be any image, because the Deity which animates nature cannot be represented. During my reign the Romans had neither wars nor seditions, and my religion did nothing but good. All the neighboring peoples came to honor me at my funeral: that happened to no one but me."

I kissed his hand, and I went to the second. He was a fine old man about a hundred years old, clad in a white robe. He put his middle-finger on his mouth, and with the other hand he cast some beans behind him. I recognized Pythagoras. He assured me he had never had a golden thigh, and that he had never been a cock; but that he had governed the Crotoniates with as much justice as Numa governed the Romans, almost at the same time; and that this justice was the rarest and most necessary thing in the world. I learned that the Pythagoreans examined their consciences twice a day. The honest people! How far we are from them! But we who have been nothing but assassins for thirteen hundred years, we say that these wise men were arrogant.

In order to please Pythagoras, I did not say a word to him and I passed to Zarathustra, who was occupied in concentrating the celestial fire in the focus of a concave mirror, in the middle of a hall with a hundred doors which all led to wisdom. (Zarathustra's precepts are called *doors*, and are a hundred in number.) Over the principal door I read these words which are the précis of all moral philosophy and which cut short all the disputes of the casuists: "When in doubt if an action is good or bad, refrain."

"Certainly," I said to my genius, "the barbarians who immolated all these victims had never read these beautiful words."

We then saw the Zaleucus, the Thales, the Aniximanders, and all the sages who had sought truth and practiced virtue.

When we came to Socrates, I recognized him very quickly by his flat nose. "Well," I said to him, "here you are then among the number of the Almighty's confidants! All the inhabitants of Europe, except the Turks and the Tartars of the Crimea, who know nothing, pronounce your name with respect. It is revered, loved, this great name, to the point that people have wanted to know those of your persecutors. Melitus and Anitus are known because of you, just as Ravaillac is known because of Henry IV; but I know only this name of Anitus. I do not know precisely who was the scoundrel who calumniated you, and who succeeded in having you condemned to take hemlock."

"Since my adventure," replied Socrates, "I have never thought about that man; but seeing that you make me remember it, I have much pity for him. He was a wicked priest who secretly conducted a business in hides, a trade reputed shameful among us. He sent his two children to my school. The other disciples taunted them with having a father who was a currier; they were obliged to leave. The irritated father had no rest until he had stirred up all the priests and all the sophists against me. They persuaded the counsel of the five hundred that I was an impious fellow who did not believe that the Moon, Mercury and Mars were gods. Indeed, I used to think, as I think now, that there is only one God, master of all nature. The judges handed me over to the poisoner of the republic; he cut short my life by a few days: I died peacefully at the age of seventy; and since that time I pass a happy life with all these great men whom you see, and of whom I am the least."

After enjoying some time in conversation with Socrates, I went forward with my guide into a grove situated above the thickets where all the sages of antiquity seemed to be tasting sweet repose.

I saw a man of gentle, simple countenance, who seemed to me to be about thirty-five years old. From afar he cast compassionate glances on these piles of whitened bones, across which I had had to pass to reach the sages' abode. I was astonished to find his feet swollen and bleeding, his hands likewise, his side pierced, and his ribs flayed with whip cuts. "Good Heavens!" I said to him, "Is it possible for a just man, a sage, to be in this state? I have just seen one who was treated in a very hateful way, but there is no comparison between his torture and yours. Wicked priests and wicked judges poisoned him; is it by priests and judges that you have been so cruelly assassinated?"

He answered with much courtesy — "Yes."

"And who were these monsters?"

"*They were hypocrites.*"

"Ah! That says everything; I understand by this single word that they must have condemned you to death. Had you then proved to them, as Socrates did, that the Moon was not a goddess, and that Mercury was not a god?"

"*No, these planets were not in question. My compatriots did not know at all what a planet is; they were all arrant ignoramuses. Their superstitions were quite different from those of the Greeks.*"

"You wanted to teach them a new religion, then?"

"*Not at all; I said to them simply — 'Love God with all your heart and your fellow-creature as yourself, for that is man's whole duty.' Judge if this precept is not as old as the universe; judge if I brought them a new religion. I did not stop telling them that I had come not to destroy the law but to fulfill it; I had observed all their rites; circumcised as they all were, baptized as were the most zealous among them, like them I paid the Corban; I observed the Passover as they did, eating standing up a lamb cooked with lettuces. I and my friends went to pray in the temple; my friends even frequented this temple after my death; in a word, I fulfilled all their laws without a single exception.*"

"What! These wretches could not even reproach you with swerving from their laws?"

"*No, without a doubt.*"

"Why then did they put you in the condition in which I now see you?"

"*What do you expect me to say! They were very arrogant and selfish. They saw that I knew them; they knew that I was making the citizens acquainted with them; they were the stronger; they took away my life: and people like them will always do as much, if they can, to whoever does them too much justice.*"

"But did you say nothing, do nothing that could serve them as a pretext?"

"*To the wicked everything serves as pretext.*"

"Did you not say once that you were come not to send peace, but a sword?"

"*It is a copyist's error; I told them that I sent peace and not a sword. I have never written anything; what I said can have been changed without evil intention.*"

"You therefore contributed in no way by your speeches, badly reported, badly interpreted, to these frightful piles of bones which I saw on my road in coming to consult you?"

"*It is with horror only that I have seen those who have made themselves guilty of these murders.*"

"And these monuments of power and wealth, of pride and avarice, these treasures, these ornaments, these signs of grandeur, which I have seen piled up on the road while I was seeking wisdom, do they come from you?"

"*That is impossible; I and my people lived in poverty and meanness: my grandeur was in virtue only.*"

I was about to beg him to be so good as to tell me just who he was. My guide warned me to do nothing of the sort. He told me that I was not made to understand these sublime mysteries. Only did I conjure him to tell me in what true religion consisted.

"*Have I not already told you? Love God and your fellow-creature as yourself.*"

"What! If one loves God, one can eat meat on Friday?"

"*I always ate what was given me; for I was too poor to give anyone food.*"

"In loving God, in being just, should one not be rather cautious not to confide all the adventures of one's life to an unknown man?"

"*That was always my practice.*"

"Can I not, by doing good, dispense with making a pilgrimage to St. James of Compostella?"

"*I have never been in that country.*"

"Is it necessary for me to imprison myself in a retreat with fools?"

"*As for me, I always made little journeys from town to town.*"

"Is it necessary for me to take sides either for the Greek Church or the Latin?"

"*When I was in the world I never made any difference between the Jew and the Samaritan.*"

"Well, if that is so, I take you for my only master." Then he made me a sign with his head which filled me with consolation. The vision disappeared, and a clear conscience stayed with me.

THE RIGHT TO LIFE (THE CASES AGAINST TORTURE AND CAPITAL PUNISHMENT)

Entrusting individuals with the capacity to reason also invigorated efforts to end the human carnage caused by waves of religious fanaticism during the Thirty Years' War (1618–1648). Because conflicting interpretations of revelation could not ensure respect for human life, British political philosopher Thomas Hobbes (1588–1679) sought to establish a system of peace by showing that individuals, once they entered a social covenant, should be guaranteed a right to life — i.e., a right to security. In Hobbes's *Leviathan* (1652) that need was seen to be so essential that individuals would choose to grant absolute power to a sovereign authority in exchange for effective protection. Yet, Hobbes maintained, if the sovereign failed to undertake this mission, or itself threatened the lives of its citizens, then the contract would be void. Despite Hobbes's minimal standard of what constitutes basic rights, his views were revolutionary for his time. By basing sovereignty on natural rights, Hobbes opened the door to three hundred years of debate over what would become the liberal basis of human rights (see Section 5.7).

In *Treatise on Crimes and Punishment* (1766), Italian criminologist and economist Cesare Beccaria (1738–1794) offered further reflection on the protection of individual life, arguing against torture and the death penalty. Indebted to Montesquieu, Beccaria's work was the first succinct treatise on rights governing criminal justice. Punishment, he claimed, should be related to the severity of the offense, imposed only when a defendant's guilt was proven, and only insofar as it promoted security and order. Any penalty exceeding these purposes, he maintained, was tyrannical. Torture was therefore an unacceptable method to seek truth and justice. Well in advance of his time, Becarria was also the first modern writer to argue for the abolition of capital punishment. "The death penalty," he wrote, "is not a matter of right." It is an act of war of society against the citizen that becomes necessary under extreme circumstances, "when the national stands to gain or lose its freedom, or in periods of anarchy" (see Section 5.8).

5.5 UNITED NATIONS UNIVERSAL DECLARATION OF HUMAN RIGHTS (1948): ARTICLES 3 AND 5–12

Article 3

Everyone has the right to life, liberty and the security of person.

Article 5

No one shall be subjected to torture or to cruel, inhuman or degrading treatment or punishment.

Article 6

Everyone has the right to recognition everywhere as a person before the law.

Article 7

All are equal before the law and are entitled without any discrimination to equal protection of the law. All are entitled to equal protection against any discrimination in violation of this Declaration and against any incitement to such discrimination.

Article 8

Everyone has the right to an effective remedy by the competent national tribunals for acts violating the fundamental rights granted him by the constitution or by law.

Article 9

No one shall be subjected to arbitrary arrest, detention or exile.

Article 10

Everyone is entitled to full equality to a fair and public hearing by an independent and impartial tribunal, in the determination of his rights and obligations and of any criminal charge against him.

Article 11

1. Everyone charged with a penal offense has the right to be presumed innocent until proved guilty according to law in a public trial at which he has had all the guarantees necessary for his defense.

2. No one shall be held guilty of any penal offense on account of any act or omission which did not constitute a penal offense, under national or international law, at the time when it was committed. Nor shall a heavier penalty be imposed than the one that was applicable at the time the penal offense was committed.

Article 12

No one shall be subjected to arbitrary interference with his privacy, family, home or correspondence, nor to attacks upon his honor and reputation. Everyone has the right to the protection of the law against such interference or attacks.

5.6 UNITED NATIONS INTERNATIONAL COVENANT ON CIVIL AND POLITICAL RIGHTS (1966): PART III

Article 6

1. Every human being has the inherent right to life. This right shall be protected by law. No one shall be arbitrarily deprived of his life.

2. In countries which have not abolished the death penalty, sentence of death may be imposed only for the most serious crimes in accordance with law in force at the time of the commission of the crime and not contrary to the provisions of the present Covenant and to the Convention on the Prevention and Punishment of the Crime of Genocide. This penalty can only be carried out pursuant to a final judgment rendered by a competent court.

3. When deprivation of life constitutes the crime of genocide, it is understood that nothing in this article shall authorize any State Party to the present Covenant to derogate in any way from any obligation assumed under the provisions of the Convention on the Prevention and Punishment of the Crime of Genocide.

4. Anyone sentenced to death shall have the right to seek pardon or commutation of the sentence. Amnesty, pardon or commutation of the sentence of death may be granted in all cases.

5. Sentence of death shall not be imposed for crimes committed by persons below eighteen years of age and shall not be carried out on pregnant women.

6. Nothing in this article shall be invoked to delay or to prevent the abolition of capital punishment by any State Party to the present Covenant.

5.7 THOMAS HOBBES: ON THE INALIENABLE RIGHT TO LIFE (*THE LEVIATHAN*, 1652)

Chapter XIV: Of the First and Second Natural Laws, and of Contracts

Right nature of what.

The RIGHT OF NATURE, which writers commonly call *jus naturale*, is the liberty each man has to use his own power, as he will himself, for the preservation of his own nature — that is to say, of his own life — and consequently of doing anything which, in his own judgment and reason, he shall conceive to be the aptest means thereunto.

Liberty what.

By LIBERTY is understood, according to the proper signification of the word, the absence of external impediments; which impediments may oft take away part of a man's power to do what he would, but cannot hinder him from using the power left him according as his judgment and reason shall dictate to him.

A law of nature what.

Difference of right and law.

A LAW OF NATURE, *lex naturalis*, is a precept or general rule, found out by reason, by which a man is forbidden to do that which is destructive of his life or takes away the means of preserving the same and to omit that by which he thinks it may be best preserved. For though they that speak of this subject use to confound *jus* and *lex*, *right* and *law*, yet they ought to be distinguished; because RIGHT consists in liberty to do or to forbear, whereas LAW determines and binds to one of them; so that law and right differ as much as obligation and liberty, which in one and the same matter are inconsistent.

Naturally every man has right to every thing.

The fundamental law of nature.

And because the condition of man is a condition of war of every one against every one — in which case everyone is governed by his own reason and there is nothing he can make use of that may not be a help unto him in preserving his life against his enemies — it follows that in such a condition every man has a right to everything, even to one another's body. And therefore, as long as this natural right of every man to everything endures, there can be no security to any man, how strong or wise soever he be, of living out the time which nature ordinarily allows men to live. And consequently it is a precept or general rule of reason *that every man ought to endeavor peace, as far as he has hope of obtaining it; and when he cannot obtain it, that he may seek and use all helps and advantages of war.* The first branch of which rule contains the first and fundamental law of nature, which is to *seek peace and follow it.* The second, the sum of the right of nature, which is, *by all means we can to defend ourselves.*

The second law of nature.

From this fundamental law of nature, by which men are commanded to endeavor peace, is derived this second law: *that a man be willing, when others are so too, as far forth as for peace and defense of himself he shall think it necessary, to lay down this right to all things, and be contented with so much liberty against other men as he would allow other men against himself.* For as long as every man holds this right of doing anything he likes, so long are all men in the condition of war. But if other men will not lay down their right as well as he, then there is no reason for anyone to divest himself of his, for that were to expose himself to prey, which no man is bound to, rather than to dispose himself to peace. This is that law of the gospel: *whatsoever you require that others should do to you, that do ye to them.* And that law of all men, *quod tibi fieri non vis, alteri ne feceris.*[1]

What it is to lay down a right.

Renouncing a right, what it is.

Transferring right what.

Obligation.

Duty.

Injustice.

To *lay down* a man's *right* to anything is to *divest* himself of the *liberty* of hindering another of the benefit of his own right to the same. For he that renounces or passes away his right gives not to any other man a right which he had not before — because there is nothing to which every man had not right by nature — but only stands out of his way, that he may enjoy his own original right without hindrance from him, not without hindrance from another. So that the effect which redounds to one man by another man's defect of right is but so much diminution of impediments to the use of his own right original. Right is laid aside either by *simply* renouncing it or by transferring it to another. By simply RENOUNCING, when he cares not to whom the benefit thereof redounds. By TRANSFERRING, when he intends the benefit thereof to some certain person or persons. And when a man has in either manner abandoned or granted away his right, then he is said to be OBLIGED or BOUND not to hinder those to whom such right is granted or abandoned from the benefit of it; and that he *ought*, and it is his DUTY, not to make void that voluntary act of his own; and that such hindrance is INJUSTICE and INJURY as being *sine jure*,[2] the right being before renounced or transferred. So that *injury* or *injustice* in the controversies of the world is somewhat like to that which in the disputations of scholars is called *absurdity*. For as it is there called an absurdity to contradict what one maintained in the beginning, so in the world it is called injustice and injury voluntarily to undo that which from the beginning he had voluntarily done. The way by which a man either simply renounces or transfers his right is a declaration or signification by some voluntary and sufficient sign or signs that he does so renounce or transfer, or has so renounced or transferred, the same to him that accepts it. And these signs are either words only or actions only; or as it happens most often, both words and actions. And the same are the BONDS by which men are bound and obliged — bonds that have their strength, not from their own nature, for nothing is more easily broken than a man's word, but from fear of some evil consequence upon the rupture.

Not all rights are alienable.

Whensoever a man transfers his right or renounces it, it is either in consideration of some right reciprocally transferred to himself or for some other good he hopes for thereby. For it is a voluntary act; and of the voluntary acts of every man, the object is some *good to himself.* And therefore there be some rights which no man can be understood by any words or other signs to have abandoned or transferred. As, first, a man cannot lay down the right of resisting them that assault him by force to take away his life, because he cannot be understood to aim thereby at any good to himself. The same may be said of wounds and chains and imprisonment, both because there is no benefit consequent to such patience as there is to the patience of suffering another to be wounded or imprisoned, as also because a man cannot tell, when he sees men proceed against him by violence, whether they intend his death or not. And, lastly, the motive and end for which this renouncing and transferring of right is introduced is nothing else but the security of a man's person in his life and in the means of so preserving life as not to be weary of it. And therefore if a man by words or other signs seems to despoil himself of the end for which those signs were intended, he is not to be understood as if he meant it or that it was his will, but that he was ignorant of how such words and actions were to be interpreted.

Contract what.

The mutual transferring of right is that which men call CONTRACT.

There is difference between transferring of right to the thing and transferring, or tradition — that is, delivery — of the thing itself. For the thing may be delivered together with the translation of the right, as in buying and selling with ready money or exchange of goods or lands, and it may be delivered some time after.

Covenant what.

Again, one of the contractors may deliver the thing contracted for on his part and leave the other to perform his part at some determinate time after and in the meantime be trusted, and then the contract on his part is called PACT or COVENANT; or both parts may contract now to perform hereafter, in which case he that is to perform in time to come, being trusted, his performance is called *keeping of promise* or faith, and the fading of performance, if it be voluntary, *violation of faith....*

Signs of contract are words both of the past, present, and future.

In contracts, the right passes riot only where the words are of the time present or past but also where they are of the future, because all contract is mutual translation or change of right, and therefore he that promises only because he has already received the benefit for which he promises is to be understood as if he intended the right should pass; for unless he had been content to have his words so understood, the other would not have performed his part first. And for that cause, in buying and selling and other acts of con-

tract a promise is equivalent to a covenant and therefore obligatory....

Covenants how made void.

Men are freed of their covenants two ways: by performing or by being forgiven. For performance is the natural end of obligation, and forgiveness the restitution of liberty, as being a retransferring of that right in which the obligation consisted.

Covenants extorted by fear are valid.

The former covenant to one makes void the later to another.

Covenants entered into by fear, in the condition of mere nature, are obligatory. For example, if I covenant to pay a ransom or service for my life to an enemy, I am bound by it; for it is a contract, wherein one receives the benefit of life, the other is to receive money or service for it; and consequently, where no other law, as in the condition of mere nature, forbids the performance, the covenant is valid. Therefore prisoners of war, if trusted with the payment of their ransom, are obliged to pay it; and if a weaker prince makes a disadvantageous peace with a stronger, for fear, he is bound to keep it; unless, as has been said before, there arises some new and just cause of fear to renew the war. And even in commonwealths, if I be forced to redeem myself from a thief by promising him money, I am bound to pay it till the civil law discharge me. For whatsoever I may lawfully do without obligation, the same I may lawfully covenant to do through fear; and what I lawfully covenant, I cannot lawfully break. A former covenant makes void a later. For a man that has passed away his right to one man today has it not to pass tomorrow to another; and therefore the later promise passes no right, but is null.

A man's covenant not to defend himself is void.

A covenant not to defend myself from force by force is always void. For, as I have showed before, no man can transfer or lay down his right to save himself from death, wounds, and imprisonment, the avoiding whereof is the only end of laying down any right; and therefore the promise of not resisting force in no covenant transfers any right, nor is obliging. For though a man may covenant thus: *unless I do so or so, kill me,* he cannot covenant thus: *unless I do so or so, I will not resist you when you come to kill me.* For man by nature chooses the lesser evil, which is danger of death in resisting, rather than the greater, which is certain and present death in not resisting. And this is granted to be true by all men, in that they lead criminals to execution and prison with armed men, notwithstanding that such criminals have consented to the law by which they are condemned.

No man obliged to accuse himself.

A covenant to accuse oneself, without assurance of pardon, is likewise invalid. For in the condition of nature, where every man is judge, there is no place for accusation; and in the civil state, the accusation is followed with punishment, which, being force, a man is not obliged not to resist. The same is also true of the accusation of those by whose condemnation a man falls into misery, as of a father, wife, or benefactor. For the testimony of such an accuser, if it be not willingly given, is presumed to be corrupted by nature, and therefore not to be received; and where a man's testimony is not to be credited, he is not bound to give it. Also accusations upon torture are not to be reputed as testimonies. For torture is to be used but as means of conjecture and light in the further examination and search of truth; and what is in that case confessed tends to the ease of him that is tortured, not to the informing of the torturers, and therefore ought not to have the credit of a sufficient testimony; for whether he deliver himself by true or false accusation, he does it by the right of preserving his own life....

---

[1] Matt. 7:12; Luke 6:31. The Latin expresses the same rule negatively: 'what you would not have done to you, do not do to others.
[2] Without legal basis.

5.8 CESARE BECCARIA: ON TORTURE AND THE DEATH PENALTY (*TREATISE ON CRIMES AND PUNISHMENTS*, 1766)

Chapter 2: The Right to Punish

Every punishment which is not derived from absolute necessity is tyrannous, says the great Montesquieu, a proposition which may be generalized as follows: every act of authority between one man and another which is not derived from absolute necessity is tyrannous. Here, then, is the foundation of the sovereign's right to punish crimes: the necessity of defending the repository of the public well-being from the usurpations of individuals. The juster the punishments, the more sacred and inviolable is the security and the greater the freedom which the sovereign preserves for his subjects. If we consult the human heart, we find in it the fundamental principles of the sovereign's true right to punish crimes, for it is vain to hope that any lasting advantage will accrue from public morality if it be not founded on ineradicable human sentiments. Any law which differs from them will always meet with a resistance that will overcome it in the end, in the same way that a force, however small, applied continuously, will always overcome a sudden shock applied to a body.

No man has made a gift of part of his freedom with the common good in mind; that kind of fantasy exists only in novels. If it were possible, each one of us would wish that the contracts which bind others did not bind us. Every man makes himself the center of all the world's affairs.

(The multiplication of the human race, however gradual, greatly exceeded the means that a sterile and untended nature provides for the satisfaction of man's ever-evolving needs, and brought primitive men together. The first unions inescapably gave rise to others to resist them, and so the state of war was translated from individuals to nations.)

Thus it was necessity which compelled men to give up a part of their freedom; and it is therefore certain that none wished to surrender to the public repository more than the smallest possible portion consistent with persuading others to defend him. The sum of these smallest possible portions constitutes the right to punish; everything more than that is no longer justice, but an abuse; it is a matter of fact not of right. Note that the word "right" is not opposed to the word "power," but the former is rather a modification of the latter, that is to say, the species which is of the greatest utility to the greatest number. And by "justice" I mean nothing other than the restraint necessary to hold particular interests together, without which they would collapse into the old state of unsociability. Any punishment that goes beyond the need to preserve this bond is unjust by its very nature. We must be careful not to attach any notion of something real to this word "justice," such as a physical force or an actual entity. It is simply a way whereby humans conceive of things, a way which influences beyond measure the happiness of all. Nor do I speak here of that justice which flows from God and whose direct bearing is on the punishments and rewards of the after-life.

Chapter 16: Of Torture

The torture of a criminal while his trial is being put together is a cruelty accepted by most nations, whether to compel him to confess a crime, to exploit the contradictions he runs into, to uncover his accomplices, to carry out some mysterious and incomprehensible metaphysical purging of his infamy, (or, lastly, to expose other crimes of which he is guilty but with which he has not been charged).

No man may be called guilty before the judge has reached his verdict; nor may society withdraw its protection from him until it has been determined that he has broken the terms of the compact by which that protection was extended to him. By what right, then, except that of force, does the judge have the authority to inflict punishment on a citizen while there is doubt about whether he is guilty or innocent? This dilemma is not a novelty: either the crime is certain or it is not; if it is certain, then no other punishment is called for than what is established by law and other torments are superfluous

because the criminal's confession is superfluous; if it is not certain, then an innocent man should not be made to suffer, because in law, such a man's crimes have not been proven. Furthermore, I believe it is a willful confusion of the proper procedure to require a man to be at once accuser and accused, in such a way that physical suffering comes to be the crucible in which truth is assayed, as if such a test could be carried out in the sufferer's muscles and sinews. This is a sure route for the acquittal of robust ruffians and the conviction of weak innocents. Such are the evil consequences of adopting this spurious test of truth, but a test worthy of a cannibal, that the ancient Romans, for all their barbarity on many other counts, reserved only for their slaves, the victims of a fierce and overrated virtue....

Another absurd ground for torture is the purging of infamy, that is, when a man who has been attainted by the law has to confirm his own testimony by the dislocation of his bones. This abuse should not be tolerated in the eighteenth century. It presupposes that pain, which is a sensation, can purge infamy, which is a mere moral relation. Is torture perhaps a crucible and the infamy some impurity? It is not hard to reach back in time to the source of this absurd law, because even the illogicalities which a whole nation adopts always have some connection with its other respected commonplaces. It seems that this practice derives from religious and spiritual ideas, which have had so much influence on the ideas of men in all nations and at all times. An infallible dogma tells us that the stains springing from human weakness, but which have not earned the eternal anger of the great Being, have to be purged by an incomprehensible fire. Now, infamy is a civil stain and, since pain and fire cleanse spiritual and incorporeal stains, why should the spasms of torture not cleanse the civil stain of infamy? I believe that the confession of guilt, which in some courts is a prerequisite for conviction, has a similar origin, for, before the mysterious court of penitence, the confession of sin is an essential part of the sacrament. It is thus that men abuse the clearest illuminations of revealed truth; and, since these are the only enlightenment to be found in times of ignorance, it is to them that credulous mankind will always turn and of them that it will make the most absurd and far-fetched use. But infamy is a sentiment which is subject neither to the law nor to reason, but to common opinion. Torture itself causes real infamy to its victims. Therefore, by this means, infamy is purged by the infliction of infamy.

The third ground for torture concerns that inflicted on suspected criminals who fall into inconsistency while being investigated, as if both the innocent man who goes in fear and the criminal who wishes to cover himself would not be made to fall into contradiction by fear of punishment, the uncertainty of the verdict, the apparel and magnificence of the judge, and by their own ignorance, which is the common lot both of most knaves and of the innocent; as if the inconsistencies into which men normally fall even when they are calm would not burgeon in the agitation of a mind wholly concentrated on saving itself from a pressing danger.

This shameful crucible of the truth is a standing monument to the law of ancient and savage times, when ordeal by fire, by boiling water and the lottery of armed combat were called the *judgments* of God, as if the links in the eternal chain which originates from the breast of the First Mover could be continually disrupted and uncoupled at the behest of frivolous human institutions. The only difference which there might seem to be between torture and ordeal by fire or boiling water is that the result of the former seems to depend on the will of the criminal, and that of the latter on purely physical and external factors; but this difference is only apparent and not real. Telling the truth in the midst of spasms and beatings is as little subject to our will as is preventing without fraud the effects of fire and boiling water. Every act of our will is always proportional to the force of the sensory impression which gives rise to it; and the sensibility of every man is limited. Therefore, the impression made by pain may grow to such an extent that, having filled the whole of the sensory field, it leaves the torture victim no freedom to do anything but choose the quickest route to relieving himself of the immediate pain. Thus the criminal's replies are as necessitated as are the effects of fire and boiling water. And thus the sensitive but guiltless man will admit guilt if he believes that, in that way, he can make the pain stop. All distinctions between the guilty and the innocent disappear as a consequence of the use of the very means which was meant to discover them.

(It would be redundant to make this point twice as clear by citing the numerous cases of innocent men who have confessed their guilt as a result of the convulsions of torture. There is no nation nor age which cannot cite its own cases, but men do not change nor do they think out the consequences of their practices. No man who has pushed his ideas beyond what is necessary for life, has not sometimes headed towards nature, obeying her hidden and indistinct calls; but custom, that tyrant of the mind, repulses and frightens him.)...

A strange consequence which necessarily follows from the use of torture is that the innocent are put in a worse position than the guilty. For, if both are tortured, the former has everything against him. Either he confesses to the crime and is convicted, or he is acquitted and has suffered an unwarranted punishment. The criminal, in contrast, finds himself in a favorable position, because if he staunchly withstands the torture he must be acquitted and so has commuted a heavier sentence into a lighter one. Therefore, the innocent man cannot but lose and the guilty man may gain.

The law which calls for torture is a law which says: *Men, withstand pain, and if nature has placed in you an inextinguishable self-love, if she has given you an inalienable right to self-defense, I create in you an entirely opposite propensity, which is a heroic self-hatred, and I order you to denounce yourselves, telling the truth even when your muscles are being torn and your bones dislocated.*

(Torture is given to discover if a guilty man has also committed other crimes to those with which he is charged. The underlying reasoning here is as follows: *You are guilty of one crime, therefore you may be of a hundred others; this doubt weighs on me and I want to decide the matter with my test of the truth; the laws torture you because you are guilty, because you may be guilty, or because I want you to be guilty.)*

Finally, torture is applied to a suspect in order to discover his accomplices in crime. But if it has been proven that torture is not a fit means of discovering the truth, how can it be of any use in unmasking the accomplices, which is one of the truths to be discovered? As if a man who accuses himself would not more readily accuse others. And can it be right to torture a man for the crimes of others? Will the accomplices not be discovered by the examination of witnesses, the interrogation of the criminal, the evidence and the *corpus delicti*, in short, by the very means which ought to be used to establish the suspect's guilt? Generally, the accomplices flee as soon as their partner is captured; the uncertainty of their fate condemns them to exile and frees the nation of the danger of further offenses, while the punishment of the criminal in custody serves its sole purpose, which is that of discouraging with fear other men from perpetrating a similar crime.

Chapter 28: The Death Penalty

I am prompted by this futile excess of punishments, which have never made men better, to inquire whether the death penalty is really useful and just in a well-organized state. By what right can men presume to slaughter their fellows? Certainly not that right which is the foundation of sovereignty and the laws. For these are nothing but the sum of the smallest portions of each man's own freedom; they represent the general will which is the aggregate of the individual wills. Who has ever willingly given up to others the authority to kill him? How on earth can the minimum sacrifice of each individual's freedom involve handing over the greatest of all goods, life itself? And even if that were so, how can it be reconciled with the other principle which denies that a man is free to commit suicide, which he must be, if he is able to transfer that right to others or to society as a whole?

Thus, the death penalty is not a matter of *right*, as I have just shown, but is an act of war on the part of society against the citizen that comes about when it is deemed necessary or useful to destroy his existence. But if I can go on to prove that such a death is neither necessary nor useful, I shall have won the cause of humanity.

There are only two grounds on which the death of a citizen might be held to be necessary. First, when it is evident that even if deprived of his freedom, he retains such connections and such power as to endanger the security of the nation, when, that is, his existence may threaten a dangerous revolution in the established form of government. The death of a citizen becomes necessary, therefore, when the nation stands to gain or lose its freedom, or in periods of anarchy, when disorder replaces the laws. But when the rule of law calmly prevails, under a form of government behind which the people are united, which is secured from without and from within, both by its strength and, perhaps more efficacious than force itself, by public opinion, in which the control of power is in the hands of the true sovereign, in which wealth buys pleasures and not influence, then I do not see any need to destroy a citizen, unless his death is the true and only brake to prevent others from committing crimes, which is the second ground for thinking the death penalty just and necessary.

Although men, who always suspect the voice of reason and respect that of authority, have not been persuaded by the experience of centuries, during which the ultimate penalty has never dissuaded men from offending against society, nor by the example of the citizens of Rome, nor by the twenty years of the reign of the Empress Elizabeth of Muscovy, in which she set the leaders of all peoples an outstanding precedent, worth at least as much as many victories bought with the blood of her motherland's sons, it will suffice to consult human nature to be convinced of the truth of my claim.

It is not the intensity, but the extent of a punishment which makes the greatest impression on the human soul. For our sensibility is more easily and lastingly moved by minute but repeated impressions than by a sharp but fleeting shock. Habit has universal power over every sentient creature. Just as a man speaks and walks and goes about his business with its help, so moral ideas are only impressed on his mind by lasting and repeated blows. It is not the terrible but fleeting sight of a felon's death which is the most powerful brake on crime, but the long-drawn-out example of a man deprived of freedom, who having become a beast of burden, repays the society which he has offended with his labor. Much more potent than the idea of death, which men always regard as vague and distant, is the efficacious because often repeated reflection that *I too shall be reduced to so dreary and so pitiable a state if I commit similar crimes.*

For all its vividness, the impression made by the death penalty cannot compensate for the forgetfulness of men, even in the most important matters, which is natural and speeded by the passions. As a general rule, violent passions take hold of men but not for long; thus they are suited to producing those revolutions which make normal men into Persians or Spartans; whereas the impressions made in a free and peaceful state should be frequent rather than strong.

For most people, the death penalty becomes a spectacle and for the few an object of compassion mixed with scorn. Both these feelings occupy the minds of the spectators more than the salutary fear which the law claims to inspire. But with moderate and continuous punishments it is this last which is the dominant feeling, because it is the only one. The limit which the lawgiver should set to the harshness of punishments seems to depend on when the feeling of compassion at a punishment, meant more for the spectators than for the convict, begins to dominate every other in their souls.

(If a punishment is to be just, it must be pitched at just that level of intensity which suffices to deter men from crime. Now there is no-one who, after considering the matter, could choose the total and permanent loss of his own freedom, however profitable the crime might be. Therefore, permanent penal servitude in place of the death penalty would be enough to deter even the most resolute soul: indeed, I would say that it is more likely to. Very many people look on death with a calm and steadfast gaze, some from fanaticism, some from vanity, a senti-

ment that almost always accompanies a man to the grave and beyond, and some from a last desperate effort either to live no more or to escape from poverty. However, neither fanaticism nor vanity survives in manacles and chains, under the rod and the yoke or in an iron cage; and the ills of the desperate man are not over, but are just beginning. Our spirit withstands violence and extreme but fleeting pains better than time and endless fatigue. For it can, so to speak, condense itself to repel the former, but its tenacious elasticity is insufficient to resist the latter.

With the death penalty, every lesson which is given to the nation requires a new crime; with permanent penal servitude, a single crime gives very many lasting lessons. And, if it is important that men often see the power of the law, executions ought not to be too infrequent; they therefore require there to be frequent crimes; so that, if this punishment is to be effective, it is necessary that it not make the impression that it should make. That is, it must be both useful and useless at the same time. If it be said that permanent penal servitude is as grievous as death, and therefore as cruel, I reply that, if we add up all the unhappy moments of slavery, perhaps it is even more so, but the latter are spread out over an entire life, whereas the former exerts its force only at single moment. And this is an advantage of penal servitude, because it frightens those who see it more than those who undergo it. For the former thinks about the sum of unhappy moments, whereas the latter is distracted from present unhappiness by the prospect of future pain. All harms are magnified in the imagination, and the sufferer finds resources and consolations unknown and unsuspected by the spectators, who put their own sensibility in the place of the hardened soul of the wretch.)

A thief or murderer who has nothing to weigh against breaking the law except the gallows or the wheel reasons pretty much along the following lines. (I know that self-analysis is a skill which we acquire with education; but just because a thief would not express his principles well, it does not mean that he lacks them.) *What are these laws which I have to obey, which have such a gulf between me and the rich man: He denies me the penny I beg of him, brushing me off with the demand that I should work, something he knows nothing about. Who made these laws? Rich and powerful men, who have never condescended to visit the filthy hovels of the poor, who have never broken moldy bread among the innocent cries of starving children and a wife's tears. Let us break these ties, which are pernicious to most people and only useful to a few and idle tyrants; let us attack injustice at its source. I shall return to my natural state of independence; for a while I shall live free and happy on the fruits of my courage and industry; perhaps the day for suffering and repentance will come, but it will be brief, and I shall have one day of pain for many years of freedom and pleasure. King of a small band of men, I shall put to rights the iniquities of fortune, and I shall see these tyrants blanch and cower at one whom they considered, with insulting ostentation, lower than their horses and dogs.* Then, religion comes into the mind of the ruffian, who makes ill-use of everything, and, offering an easy repentance and near-certainty of eternal bliss, considerably diminishes for him the horror of the last tragedy.

But a man who sees ahead of him many years, or even the remainder of his life, passed in slavery and suffering before the eyes of his fellow citizens, with whom he currently lives freely; and sociably, the slave of those laws by which he was protected, will make a salutary calculation, balancing all of that against the uncertainty of the outcome of his crimes, and the shortness of the time in which he could enjoy their fruit. The continued example of those whom he now sees as the victims of their own lack of foresight will make a stronger impression on him than would a spectacle which hardens more than it reforms him.

The death penalty is not useful because of the example of savagery it gives to men. If our passions or the necessity of war have taught us how to spill human blood, laws, which exercise a moderating influence on human conduct, ought not to add to that cruel example, which is all the more grievous the more a legal killing is carried out with care and pomp. It seems absurd to me that the laws, which are the expression of the public will, and which hate and pun-

ish murder, should themselves commit one, and that, to deter citizens from murder, they should decree a public murder. What are the true and most useful laws? Those contracts and terms that everyone would want to obey and to propose so long as the voice of private interest, which is always listened to, is silent or in agreement with the public interest. What are everyone's feelings about the death penalty? We can read them in the indignation and contempt everyone feels for the hangman, who is after all the innocent executor of the public will, a good citizen who contributes to the public good, as necessary an instrument of public security within the state as the valiant soldier is without. What, then, is the root of this conflict? And why is this feeling ineradicable in men, in spite of reason? It is because, deep within their souls, that part which still retains elements of their primitive nature, men have always believed that no-one and nothing should hold the power of life and death over them but necessity, which rules the universe with its iron rod.

What are men to think when they see the wise magistrates and the solemn ministers of justice order a convict to be dragged to his death with slow ceremony, or when a judge, with cold equanimity and even with a secret complacency in his own authority, can pass by a wretch convulsed in his last agonies, awaiting the *coup de grâce*, to savor the comforts and pleasures of life? *Ah!*, they will say, *these laws are nothing but pretexts for power and for the calculated and cruel; formalities of justice; they are nothing but a conventional language for killing us all the more surely, like the pre-selected victims of a sacrifice to the insatiable god of despotism. Murder, which we have preached to us as a terrible crime, we see instituted without disgust and without anger. Let us profit from this example. From the descriptions we have been given of it, violent death seemed to be a terrible thing, but we see it to be the work of a minute. How much the less it will be for him who, unaware of its coming, is spared almost everything about it which is most painful!* This is the horrific casuistry which, if not clearly, at least confusedly, leads men — in whom, as we have seen, the abuse of religion can be more powerful than religion itself — to commit crimes.

If it is objected that almost all times and almost all places have used the death penalty for some crimes, I reply that the objection collapses before the truth, against which there is no appeal, that the history of mankind gives the impression of a vast sea of errors, among which a few confused truths float at great distances from each other. Human sacrifices were common to almost all nations; but who would dare to justify them? That only a few societies have given up inflicting the death penalty, and only for a brief time, is actually favorable to my argument, because it is what one would expect to be the career of the great truths, which last but a flash compared with the long and dark night which engulfs mankind. The happy time has not yet begun in which the truth, like error hitherto, is the property of the many. Up until now, the only truths which have been excepted from this universal rule have been those which the infinite Wisdom wished to distinguish from the others by revealing them. The voice of a philosopher is too weak against the uproar and the shouting of those who are guided by blind habit. But what I say will find an echo in the hearts of the few wise men who are scattered across the face of the earth. And if truth, in the face of the thousand obstacles which, against his wishes, keep it far from the monarch, should arrive at his throne, let him know that it arrives with the secret support of all men, and let him know that its glory will silence the blood-stained reputation of conquerors and that the justice of future ages will award him peaceful trophies above those of the Titusts, the Antonines and the Trajans....

THE RIGHT TO PROPERTY

The English, American, and French revolutions were fought to overturn feudal or monarchical monopolies and to advance individuals' rights to life, civil liberties, and property. While political thinkers and revolutionary leaders would generally perceive the right to property as inviolable, many would debate the extent to which it should be limited. As early as the English Revolution (1640–1648), Gerard Winstanley (1609–1676), a leader of the English Diggers, warned against abuses of the right to property. In his famous political tract entitled "A Declaration from the Poor Oppressed of England" (1649), he pointed out that the right to property, so adamantly defended by John Lillburn, the leader of the Levellers, would end up subjugating one group of individuals to another. He therefore called upon England to become "a common Treasury of livelihood to all, without respect of persons."

John Locke (1632–1704) reclaimed Lillburn's position during the conservative settlement of the Glorious Revolution (1688), arguing in his *Second Treatise* (1690) that every man has a property in his person and that the labor of his body is ultimately his own. He shared, however, the concerns of the Diggers when he warned against the excessive and wasteful accumulation of property. He hence urged the more fortunate to always leave enough for everyone's subsistence (see Selection 5.11).

To avoid the widening of social and economic gaps, French philosopher Jean-Jacques Rousseau (1712–1768) considered in his *Geneva Manuscript* (c. 1756) the necessary circumstances under which the state could legitimately claim private property on behalf of the common good (see Section 5.12). In the footsteps of Rousseau, the French revolutionary Maximilien de Robespierre (1758–1794) warned Jacobin compatriots in his April 24, 1793, speech, "On Property Rights," to revise the *French Declaration of the Rights of Man and Citizen* (1789) by adding a clause limiting the free accumulation of property. Though he regarded the right to property as inviolable, such a right, he claimed, "carries moral responsibilities." He proposed work or relief for the needy, a progressive tax on incomes, and universal education, all to be secured by the state. In short, "property rights, should not be exercised as to prejudice the security, or the liberty, or the existence or the property of our fellowmen."

5.9   UNITED NATIONS UNIVERSAL DECLARATION OF HUMAN RIGHTS (1948): ARTICLE 17

Article 17

1. Everyone has the right to own property alone as well as in association with others.
2. No one shall be arbitrarily deprived of his property.

5.10   GERARD WINSTANLEY "A DECLARATION FROM THE POOR OPPRESSED OF ENGLAND" (1649)

WE whose names are subscribed, do in the name of all the poor oppressed people in *England*, declare unto you, that call your selves Lords of Manors, and Lords of the Land, That in regard the King of Righteousness, our Maker, hath inlightened our hearts so far, as to see, That the earth was not made purposely for you, to be Lords of it, and we to be your Slaves, Servants, and Beggers; but it was made to be a common Livelihood to all, without respect of persons: And that your buying and selling of Land, and the Fruits of it, one to another, is *the cursed thing*, and was brought in by War; which hath, and still does establish murder, and theft, in the hands of some branches of Mankind over others, which is the greatest outward burden, and unrighteous power, that the Creation groans under: For the power of enclosing Land, and owning Propriety, was brought into the Creation by your Ancestors by the Sword; which first did murder their fellow Creatures, Men, and after plunder or steal away their Land, and left this Land successively to you, their Children. And therefore, though you did not kill or thieve, yet you hold that cursed thing in your hand, by the power of the Sword; and so you justify the wicked deeds of your Fathers; and that sin of your Fathers, shall be visited upon the Head of you, and your Children, to the third and fourth Generation, and longer too, tell your bloody and thieving power be rooted out of the Land.

And further, in regard the King of Righteousness hath made us sensible of our burdens, and the cries and groanings of our hearts are come before him: We take it as a testimony of love from him, that our hearts begin to be freed from slavish fear of men, such as you are; and that we find Resolutions in us, grounded upon the inward law of Love, one towards another, To Dig and Plough up the Commons, and waste Lands through England; and that our conversation shall be so unblameable, That your Laws shall not reach to oppress us any longer, unless you by your Laws will shed the innocent blood that runs in our veins.

For though you and your Ancestors got your Propriety by murder and theft, and you keep it by the same power from us, that have an equal right to the Land with you, by the righteous Law of Creation, yet we shall have no occasion of quarreling (as you do) about that disturbing devil, called Particular Propriety: For the Earth, with all her Fruits of Corn, Cattle, and such like, was made to be a common Storehouse of Livelihood to all Mankind, friend and foe, without exception.

And to prevent all your scrupulous Objections, know this, That we must neither buy nor sell; Money must not any longer (after our work of the Earths community is advanced) be the great god, that hedges in some, and hedges out others; for Money is but part of the Earth: And surely, the Righteous Creator, who is King, did never ordain, That unless some of Mankind, do bring that Mineral (Silver and Gold) in their hands, to others of their own kind, that they should neither be fed, nor be clothed; no surely, For this was the project of Tyrantflesh (which Land-lords are branches of) to set his Image upon Money. And they make this unrighteous Law, That none should buy or sell, eat, or be clothed, or have any comfortable Livelihood among men, unless they did bring his Image stamped upon Gold or Silver in their hands....

For after our work of the Earthly community is advanced, we must make use of Gold and Silver, as we do of other metals, but not to buy and sell withal; for buying and selling is the great cheat, that robs and steals the Earth one from another: It is that which makes some Lords, others Beggers, some Rulers, others to be ruled; and makes great Murderers and Thieves to be imprisoners, and hangers of little ones, or of sincere-hearted men.

And while we are made to labor the Earth together, with one consent and willing mind; and while we are made free, that every one, friend and foe, shall enjoy the benefit of their Creation, that is, To have food and payment from the Earth, their Mother; and every one subject to give account of this thoughts, words and actions to none, but to the one only righteous Judge, and Prince of Peace, the Spirit of Righteousness that dwells, and that is now rising up to rule in every Creature, and in the whole Globe. We say, while we are made to hinder no man of his Privileges given him in his Creation, equal to one, as to another; what Law then can you make, to take hold upon us, but Laws of Oppression and Tyranny, that shall enslave or spill the blood of the Innocent? And so your Selves, your Judges, Lawyers, and Justices, shall be found to be the greatest Transgressors, in and over Mankind.

But to draw nearer to declare our meaning, what we would have, and what we shall endeavor to the uttermost to obtain, as moderate and righteous Reason directs us; seeing we are made to see our Privileges, given us in our Creation, which have hitherto been denied to us, and our Fathers, since the power of the Sword began to rule, And the secrets of the Creation have been locked up under the traditional, Parrat-like speaking, from the Universities, and Colleges for Scholars, And since the power of the murdering, and thieving Sword, formerly, as well as now of late years, hath set up a Government, and maintains that Government; for what are prisons, and putting others to death, but the power of the Sword; to enforce people to that Government which was got by Conquest and Sword, and cannot stand of it self, but by the same murdering power? That Government that is got over people by the Sword, and kept by the Sword, is not set up by the King of Righteousness to be his Law, but by Covetousness, the great god of the world; who hath been permitted to reign for a time, times, and dividing of time, and his government draws to the period of the

last term of his allotted time; and then the Nations shall see the glory of that Government that shall rule in Righteousness, without either Sword or Spear,

And seeing further, the power of Righteousness in our hearts, seeking the Livelihood of others, as well as our selves, hath drawn forth our bodies to begin to dig, and plough, in the Commons and waste Land, for the Reasons already declared,

And seeing and finding our selves poor, wanting Food to feed upon, while we labor the Earth, to cast in Seed, and to wait till the first Crop comes up; and wanting Ploughs, Carts, Corn, and such materials to plant the Commons withal, we are willing to declare our condition to you, and to all, that have the Treasury of the Earth, locked up in your Bags, Chests, and Barns, and will offer up nothing to this public Treasury; but will rather see your fellow-Creatures starve for want of Bread, that have an equal right to it with your selves, by the Law of Creation: But this by the way we only declare to you, and to all that follow the subtle art of buying and selling the Earth, with her Fruits, merely to get the Treasury thereof into their hands, to lock it up from them, to whom it belongs; that so, such coveteous, proud, unrighteous, selfish flesh, may be left without excuse in the day of Judgment.

And therefore, the main thing we aim at, and for which we declare our Resolutions to go forth, and act, is this, To lay hold upon, and as we stand in need, to cut and fell, and make the best advantage we can of the Woods and Trees, that grow upon the Commons, To be a stock for our selves, and our poor Brethren, through the Land of England, to plant the Commons withal; and to provide us bread to eat, till the Fruit of our labors in the Earth bring forth increase; and we shall meddle with none of your Proprieties (but what is called Commonage) till the Spirit in you, make you cast up your Lands and Goods, which were got, and still is kept in your hands by murder, and theft; and then we shall take it from the Spirit, that hath conquered you, and not from our Swords, which is an abominable, and unrighteous power, and a destroyer of the Creation: But the Son of man comes not to destroy, but to save.

And we are moved to send forth this Declaration abroad, to give notice to every one, whom it concerns, in regard we hear and see, that some or you, that have been Lords of Manors, do cause the Trees and Woods that grow upon the Commons, which you pretend a Royalty unto, to be cut down and sold; for your own private use, whereby the Common Land, which your own mouths do say belongs to the poor, is impoverished, and the poor oppressed people robbed of their Rights, while you give them cheating words, by telling some of our poor oppressed Brethren, That those of us that have begun to Dig and Plough up the Commons, will hinder the poor; and so blind their eyes, that they see not their Privilege, while you, and the rich Free-holders, make the most profit of the Commons, by your overstocking of them with Sheep and Cattle; and the poor that have the name to own the Commons have the least share therein; nay, they are checked by you, if they cut Wood, Heath, Turf, or Furseys, in places about the Common, where you disallow.

Therefore we are resolved to be cheated no longer, nor be held under the slavish fear of you no longer, seeing the Earth was made for us, as well as for you: And if the Common Land belongs to us who are the poor oppressed, surely the woods that grow upon the Commons belong to us likewise: therefore we are resolved to try the uttermost in the light of reason, to know whether we shall be free men, or slaves. If we lie still, and let you steal away our birthrights, we perish; and if we Petition we perish also, though we have paid taxes, given free quarter, and ventured our lives to preserve the Nation's freedom as much as you, and therefore by the law of contract with you, freedom in the land is our portion as well as yours, equal with you: And if we strive for freedom, and your murdering, governing Laws destroy us, we can but perish.

Therefore we require, and we resolve to take both Common Land, and Common woods to be a livelihood for us, and look upon you as equal with us, not above us, knowing very well, that England, the land of our Nativity, is to be a common Treasury of livelihood to all, without respect of persons....

Signed for and in the behalf of all the poor oppressed people of England, and the whole world.

5.11   JOHN LOCKE: ON PROPERTY (*THE SECOND TREATISE*, 1690)

Chapter II

4. To understand political power right and derive it from its original, we must consider what state all men are naturally in, and that is a state of perfect freedom to order their actions and dispose of their possessions and persons as they think fit, within the bounds of the law (of nature), without asking leave or depending upon the will of any other man. A state also of equality, wherein all the power and jurisdiction is reciprocal, no one having more than another; there being nothing more evident than that creatures of the same species and rank, promiscuously born to all the same advantages of nature and the use of the same faculties, should also be equal one amongst another without subordination or subjection; unless the lord and master of them all should, by any manifest declaration of his will, set one above another, and confer on him by an evident and dear appointment an undoubted right to dominion and sovereignty....

6. But though this be a state of liberty, yet it is not a state of license; though man in that state have an uncontrollable liberty to dispose of his person or possessions, yet he has not liberty to destroy himself, or so much as any creature in his possession, but where some nobler use than its bare preservation calls for it. The state of nature has a law of nature to govern it, which obliges every one; and reason, which is that law, teaches all mankind who will but consult it that, being all equal and independent,

no one ought to harm another in his life, health, liberty, or possessions....

Chapter V

26. God, who has given the world to men in common, has also given them reason to make use of it to the best advantage of life and convenience. The earth and all that is therein is given to men for the support and comfort of their being. And though all the fruits it naturally produces and beasts it feeds belong to mankind in common, as they are produced by the spontaneous hand of nature; and nobody has originally a private dominion exclusive of the rest of mankind in any of them, as they are thus in their natural state; yet, being given for the use of men, there must of necessity be a means to appropriate them some way or other before they can be of any use or at all beneficial to any particular man. The fruit or venison which nourishes the wild Indian, who knows no enclosure and is still a tenant in common, must be his, and so his, i.e., a part of him, that another can no longer have any right to it before it can do him any good for the support of his life.

27. Though the earth and all inferior creatures be common to all men, yet every man has a property in his own person; this nobody has any right to but himself. The labor of his body and the work of his hands, we may say, are properly his. Whatsoever then he removes out of the state that nature has provided and left it in, he has mixed his labor with, and joined to it something that is his own, and thereby makes it his property. It being by him removed from the common state nature has placed it in, it has by this labor something annexed to it that excludes the common right of other men. For this labor being the unquestionable property of the laborer, no man but he can have a right to what that is once joined to, at least where there is enough and as good left in common for others.

28. He that is nourished by the acorns he picked up under an oak, or the apples he gathered from the trees in the wood, has certainly appropriated them to himself. Nobody can deny but the nourishment is his. I ask, then, When did they begin to be his? When he digested or when he ate or when he boiled or when he brought them home? Or when he picked them up? And it is plain, if the first gathering made them not his, nothing else could. That labor put a distinction between them and common; that added something to them more than nature, the common mother of all, had done; and so they became his private right. And will anyone say he had no right to those acorns or apples he thus appropriated because he had not the consent of all mankind to make them his? Was it a robbery thus to assume to him-self what belonged to all in common? If such a consent as that was necessary, man had starved, notwithstanding the plenty God had given him. We see in commons, which remain so by compact, that it is the taking any part of what is common and removing it out of the state nature leaves it in which begins the property, without which the common is of no use. And the taking of this or that part does not depend on the express consent of all the commoners. Thus the grass my horse has bit, the turfs my servant has cut, and the ore I have I digged in any place where I have a right to them in common with others, become my property without the assignation or consent of anybody. The labor that was mine, removing them out of that common state they were in, has fixed my property in them.

29. By making an explicit consent of every commoner necessary to any one's appropriating to himself any part of what is given in common, children or servants could not cut the meat which their father or master had provided for them in common without assigning to every one his peculiar part. Though the water running in the fountain be every one's, yet who can doubt but that

in the pitcher is his only who drew it out? His labor has taken it out of the hands of nature where it was common and belonged equally to all her children, and has thereby appropriated it to himself.

30. Thus this law of reason makes the deer that Indian's who has killed it; it is allowed to be his goods who has bestowed his labor upon it, though before it was the common right of every one. And amongst those who are counted the civilized part of mankind, who have made and multiplied positive laws to determine property, this original law of nature, for the beginning of property in what was before common, still takes place; and by virtue thereof what fish any one catches in the ocean, that great and still remaining common of mankind, or what ambergris any one takes up here, is, by the labor that removes it out of that common state nature left it in, made his property who takes that pains about it. And even amongst us, the hare that anyone is hunting is thought his who pursues her during the chase; for, being a beast that is still looked upon as common and no man's private possession, whoever has employed so much labor about any of that kind as to find and pursue her has thereby removed her from the state of nature wherein she was common, and has begun a property.

31. It will perhaps be objected to this that "if gathering the acorns, or other fruits of the earth, etc., makes a right to them, then any one may engross as much as he will." To which I answer: not so. The same law of nature that does by this means give us property does also bound that property, too. "God has given us all things richly" (I Tim. vi. 17), is the voice of reason confirmed by inspiration. But how far has he given it us? To enjoy. As much as any one can make use of to any advantage of life before it spoils, so much he may by his labor fix a property in; whatever is beyond this is more than his share and belongs to others. Nothing was made by God for man to spoil

or destroy. And thus considering the plenty of natural provisions there was a long time in the world, and the few spenders, and to how small a part of that provision the industry of one man could extend itself and engross it to the prejudice of others, especially keeping within the bounds set by reason of what might serve for his use, there could be then little room for quarrels or contentions about property so established.

32. But the chief matter of property being now not the fruits of the earth and the beasts that subsist on it, but the earth itself, as that which takes in and carries with it all the rest, I think it is plain that property in that, too, is acquired as the former. As much land as a man tills, plants, improves, cultivates, and can use the product of, so much is his property. He by his labor does, as it were, enclose it from the common. Nor will it invalidate his right to say everybody else has an equal title to it, and therefore he cannot appropriate, he cannot enclose, without the consent of all his fellow commoners — all mankind. God, when he gave the world in common to all mankind, commanded man also to labor, and the penury of his condition required it of him. God and his reason commanded him to subdue the earth, i.e., improve it for the benefit of life, and therein lay out something upon it that was his own, his labor. He that in obedience to this command of God subdued, tilled, and sowed any part of it, thereby annexed to it something that was his property, which another had no title to, nor could without injury take from him....

34. God gave the world to men in common, but since he gave it them for their benefit and the greatest conveniences of life they were capable to draw from it, it cannot be supposed he meant it should always remain common and uncultivated. He gave it to the use of the industrious and rational — and labor was to be his title to it — not to the fancy or covetousness of the quarrelsome and contentious. He that had

as good left for his improvement as was already taken up needed not complain, ought not to meddle with what was already improved by another's labor; if he did, it is plain he desired the benefit of another's pains which he had no right to, and not the ground which God had given him in common with others to labor on, and whereof there was as good left as that already possessed, and more than he knew what to do with, or his industry could reach to.

35. It is true, in land that is common in England or any other country where there are plenty of people under government who have money and commerce, no one can enclose or appropriate any part without the consent of all his fellow commoners; because this is left common by compact, i.e., by the law of the land, which is not to be violated. And though it be common in respect of some men, it is not so to all mankind, but is the joint property of this country or this parish. Besides, the remainder after such enclosure would not be as good to the rest of the commoners as the whole was when they could all make use of the whole; whereas in the beginning and first peopling of the great common of the world it was quite otherwise. The law man was under was rather for appropriating. God commanded, and his wants forced, him to labor. That was his property which could not be taken from him wherever he had fixed it. And hence subduing or cultivating the earth and having dominion, we see, are joined together. The one gave title to the other. So that God, by commanding to subdue, gave authority so far to appropriate; and the condition of human life which requires labor and material to work on necessarily introduces private possessions.

36. The measure of property nature has well set by the extent of men's labor and the conveniences of life. No man's labor could subdue or appropriate all, nor could his enjoyment consume more than a small part, so that it was impossible for any man, this way, to entrench upon the right of another, or acquire to himself a property to the prejudice of his neighbor, who would still have room for as good and as large a possession — after the other had taken out his — as before it was appropriated. This measure did confine every man's possession to a very moderate proportion, and such as he might appropriate to himself without injury to anybody, in the first ages of the world, when men were more in danger to be lost by wandering from their company in the then vast wilderness of the earth than to be straitened for want of room to plant in. And the same measure may be allowed still without prejudice to anybody, as full as the world seems; for supposing a man or family in the state they were at first peopling of the world by the children of Adam or Noah, let him plant in some inland, vacant places of America; we shall find that the possessions he could make himself, upon the measures we have given, would not be very large, nor, even to this day, prejudice the rest of mankind, or give them reason to complain or think themselves injured by this man's encroachment, though the race of men have now spread themselves to all the corners of the world and do infinitely exceed the small number which was at the beginning. Nay, the extent of ground is of so little value without labor that I have heard it affirmed that in Spain itself a man may be permitted to plough, sow, and reap, without being disturbed, upon land he has no other title to but only his making use of it. But, on the contrary, the inhabitants think themselves beholden to him who by his industry on neglected and consequently waste land has increased the stock of corn which they wanted. But be this as it will, which I lay no stress on, this I dare boldly affirm — that the same rule of property, viz., that every man should have as much as he could make use of, would hold still in the world without straitening anybody, since there is land enough in the world to suffice double the inhabitants, had not the invention of money and the

tacit agreement of men to put a value on it introduced — by consent — larger possessions and a right to them; which how it has done, I shall by-and-by show more at large.

37. This is certain, that in the beginning, before the desire of having more than man needed had altered the intrinsic value of things which depends only on their usefulness to the life of man, or had agreed that a little piece of yellow metal which would keep without wasting or decay should be worth a great piece of flesh or a whole heap of corn, though men had a right to appropriate, by their labor, each one to himself as much of the things of nature as he could use, yet this could not be much, nor to the prejudiced of others, where the same plenty was still left to those who would use the same industry. To which let me add that he who appropriates land to himself by his labor does not lessen but increase the common stock of mankind; for the provisions serving to the support of human life produced by one acre of enclosed and cultivated land are — to speak much, within compass — ten times more than those which are yielded by an acre of land of an equal richness lying waste in common. And therefore he that encloses land, and has a greater plenty of the conveniences of life from ten acres than he could have from a hundred left to nature, may truly be said to give ninety acres to mankind; for his labor now supplies him with provisions out of ten acres which were by the product of a hundred lying in common. I have here rated the improved land very low in making its product but as ten to one, when it is much nearer a hundred to one; for I ask whether in the wild woods and uncultivated waste of America, left to nature, without any improvement, tillage, or husbandry, a thousand acres yield the needy and wretched inhabitants as many conveniences of life as ten acres equally fertile land do in Devonshire, where they are well cultivated.

Before the appropriation of land, he who gathered as much of the wild fruit, killed, caught, or tamed as many of the beasts as he could; he that so employed his pains about any of the spontaneous products of nature as any way to alter them from the state which nature put them in, by placing any of his labor on them, did thereby acquire a propriety in them; but, if they perished in his possession without their due use, if the fruits rotted or the venison putrified before he could spend it, he offended against the common law of nature and was liable to be punished; he invaded his neighbor's share, for he had no right further than his use called for any of them and they might serve to afford him conveniences of life.

5.12 JEAN-JACQUES ROUSSEAU: ON THE LIMITS OF PROPERTY (*THE GENEVA MANUSCRIPT* OR THE FIRST DRAFT OF THE SOCIAL CONTRACT, 1756)

Book I: Preliminary Concepts of the Social Body

This passage from the state of nature to the social state produces a remarkable change in man, by substituting justice for instinct in his behavior and giving his actions moral relationships which they did not have before. Only then, [when the voice of duty replaces physical impulse, and right replaces appetite,] does man, who until that time only considered himself find, that he is forced to act upon other principles and to consult his reason before heeding his inclinations. But although in this state he deprives himself of several advantages given him by nature, he gains such great ones, his faculties are exercised and developed, his ideas broadened, his feelings ennobled, and his whole soul elevated to such a point that if the abuses of this new condition did not often degrade him even beneath the condition he left, he ought ceaselessly to bless the happy moment that tore him away from it forever, and that changed him from a stupid, limited animal into an intelligent being and a man.

Let us reduce the pros and cons to easily compared terms. What man loses by the social contract is his natural freedom and an unlimited right to everything he needs; what he gains is civil freedom and the proprietorship of everything he possesses. In order not to be mistaken in these estimates, one must distinguish carefully between natural freedom, which is limited only by the force of the individual, and civil freedom, which is limited by the general will; and between possession, which is only the effect of force or the right of the first occupant, and property, which can only be based on a legal title.

On Real Estate

Each member of the community gives himself to it at the moment of its formation, just as he currently is — both himself and all his force, which includes the goods he holds. It is not that by this act possession, in changing hands, changes its nature and becomes property in the hands of the sovereign. But as the force of the State is incomparably greater than that of each private individual, public possession is by that very fact stronger and more irrevocable, without being more legitimate, at least in relation to Foreigners. For in relation to its members, the State is master of all their goods through a solemn convention, the most sacred right known to man. But with regard to other States, it is so only through the right of the first occupant, which it derives from the private individuals, a right less absurd, less odious than that of conquest and yet which, when well examined, proves scarcely more legitimate.

So it is that the combined and contiguous lands of private individuals become public territory, and the right of sovereignty, extending from the subjects to the ground they occupy, comes to include both property and persons, which places those who possess land in a greater dependency and turns even their force into security for their loyalty. This advantage does not appear to be well-known to Ancient monarchs, who seem to have considered themselves leaders of men rather than masters of the country.

Thus they only called themselves Kings of the Persians, the Scythians, the Macedonians, whereas ours more cleverly call themselves Kings of France, Spain, England. By thus holding the land, they are quite sure to hold its inhabitants.

What is admirable in this alienation is that far from plundering private individuals of their goods, by accepting them the community thereby only assures them of legitimate disposition, changes usurpation into a true right, and use into property. Then, with their title respected by all the members of the State and maintained with all its force against Foreigners, through a transfer that is advantageous to the community and even more so to themselves, they have, so to speak, acquired all they have given — an enigma easily explained by the distinction between the rights of the sovereign and of the proprietor to the same resource.

It can also happen that men start to unite before possessing anything, and that subsequently taking over a piece of land sufficient for all, they use it in common or else divide it among themselves either equally or according to certain proportions established by the sovereign. But however the acquisition is made, the right of each private individual to his own goods is always subordinate to the community's right to all, without which there would be neither solidity in the social bond nor real force in the exercise of sovereignty.

I shall end this chapter with a comment that should serve as the basis of the whole social system. It is that rather than destroying natural equality, the fundamental compact on the contrary substitutes a moral and legitimate equality for whatever physical inequality nature may have placed between men, and that although they may be naturally unequal in force or in genius, they all become equal through convention and by right.

5.13 MAXIMILIEN DE ROBESPIERRE: "ON PROPERTY RIGHTS" (1793)[1]

First, I shall propose to you a few articles that are necessary to complete your theory on property; and do not let this word "property" alarm anyone. Mean spirits, you whose only measure of value is gold, I have no desire to touch your treasures, however impure may have been the source of them. You must know that the agrarian law, of which there has been so much talk, is only a bogey created by rogues to frighten fools. I can hardly believe that it took a revolution to teach the world that extreme disparities in wealth lie at the root of many ills and crimes, but we are not the less convinced that the realization of an equality of fortunes is a visionary's dream. For myself, I think it to be less necessary to private happiness than to the public welfare. It is far more a question of lending dignity to poverty than of making war on wealth. Fabricius' cottage has no need to envy the palace of Crassus. I would as gladly be one of the sons of Aristides, reared in the Prytaneum at the cost of the Republic, than to be the heir presumptive of Xerxes, born in the filth of courts and destined to occupy a throne draped in the degradation of the peoples and dazzling against the public misery.

Let us then in good faith pose the principles that govern the rights of property; it is all the more necessary to do so because there are none that human prejudice and vice have so consistently sought to shroud in mystery.

Ask that merchant in human flesh what property is. He will tell you, pointing to the long bier that he calls a ship and in which he has herded and shackled men who still appear to be alive: "Those are my property; I bought them at so much a head." Question that nobleman, who has lands and ships or who thinks that the world has been turned upside down since he has had none, and he will give you a similar view of property.

Question the august members of the Capetian dynasty.[2] They will tell you that the most sacred of all property rights is without doubt the hereditary right that they have enjoyed since ancient times to oppress, to degrade, and to attach to their person legally and royally the 25 million people who lived, at their good pleasure, on the territory of France.

But to none of these people has it ever occurred that property carries moral responsibilities. Why should our Declaration of Rights appear to contain the same error in its definition of liberty, "the most valued property of man, the most sacred of the rights that he holds from nature"? We have justly said that this right was limited by the rights of others. Why have we not applied the same principle to property, which is a social institution, as if the eternal laws of nature were less inviolable than the conventions evolved by man? You have drafted numerous articles in order to ensure the greatest freedom for the exercise of property, but you have not said a single word to define its nature and its legitimacy, so that your declaration appears to have been made not for ordinary men, but for capitalists, profiteers, speculators and tyrants. I propose to you to rectify these errors by solemnly recording the following truths:

1. Property is the right of each and every citizen to enjoy and to dispose of the portion of goods that is guaranteed to him by law.
2. The right of property is limited, as are all other rights, by the obligation to respect the property of others.
3. It may not be so exercised as to prejudice the security, or the liberty, or the existence, or the property of our fellow men.
4. All moldings in property and all commercial dealings which violate this principle are unlawful and immoral.

You also speak of taxes in such a way as to establish the irrefutable principle that they can only be the expression of the will of the people or of its representatives. But you omit an article that is indispensable to the general interest: you neglect to establish the principle of a progressive tax. Now, in matters of public finance, is there a principle more solidly grounded in the nature of things and in eternal justice than that which imposes on citizens the obligations to contribute progressively to state expenditure according to their incomes — that is, according to the material advantages that they draw from the social system?

I propose that you should record this principle in an article conceived as follows: "Citizens whose incomes do not exceed what is required for their subsistence are exempted from contributing to state expenditure; all others must support it progressively according to their wealth."

The Committee[3] has also completely neglected to record the obligations of brotherhood that bind together the men of all nations, and their right to mutual assistance. It appears to have been unaware of the roots of the perpetual alliance that unite the peoples against tyranny. It would seem that your declaration has been drafted for a human herd planted in an isolated corner of the globe and not for the vast family of nations to which nature has given the earth for its use and habitation.

I propose that you fill this great gap by adding the following articles. They cannot fail to win the regard of all peoples, though they may, is true, have the disadvantage of estranging you irrevocably from kings. I confess that this disadvantage does not frighten me, nor will it frighten all others who have no desire to be reconciled to them. Here are four articles:

1. The men of all countries are brothers, and the different people must help one another according to their ability, as though they were citizens of a single state.
2. Whoever oppresses a single nation declares himself the enemy of all.
3. Whoever makes war on a people to arrest the progress of liberty and to destroy the rights of man must be prosecuted by all, not as ordinary enemies, but as rebels, brigands and assassins.
4. Kings, aristocrats and tyrants, whoever they be, are slaves in rebellion against the sovereign of the earth, which is the human race, and against the legislator of the universe, which is nature....

[1] April 24, 1793.
[2] The French royal family.
[3] The Constitutional Committee of the National Convention.

CHAPTER 6

How to Promote a Liberal Conception of Human Rights

JUST WAR, FREE TRADE, AND REPUBLICAN STATES

If life, liberty, and property were the principal revolutionary pursuits of the Enlightenment, considerations on how to protect or maintain these achievements, within and beyond national borders, would
also preoccupy the greatest minds of that era. What should be the criteria for a just war? And how
should a just war be waged? Could free trade and republican states, based on the separation of
powers, prevent wars and perpetuate peace? These were questions that thinkers from Hugo Grotius
to Immanuel Kant debated, offering insights that continue to shape today's discussions over war
and peace.

Dutch jurist and political thinker Hugo Grotius (1583–1645) was an early contributor to these discussions. His lasting fame rests on his *Law of War and Peace* (1625). Anxious to put an end to the
religious wars of the Reformation, Grotius, inspired by the Greek and Roman natural law theorists
and by medieval scholars like Aquinas, developed a just war theory. He began by distinguishing the
laws of nations from laws within the state. The laws of nations defined moral human conduct not
only within individual states, but also within the larger society of humankind, of which states were
only part. Yet unlike municipal laws, these laws of nations were advisory rather than compulsory.
They informed nations of their range of permissible actions, as well as the mutual advantage of
abiding by the rule of nature and reason. He went on to stipulate criteria for distinguishing justifiable from unjustifiable wars and called upon heads of state to temper their conduct during wartime.
Grotius's contribution to international law and human rights transcended his time to exert a contemporary influence.

While drafting new laws of nations was a commendable endeavor, the constitutions of states also
needed to be reframed to prevent tyranny and the occurrence of war. In light of the abusive character of the king's authority before the Glorious Revolution, John Locke's *Second Treatise* (1690)
argued that individual rights would be reliably protected only in a government in which the three
basic powers — legislative, executive, and federative — were separated. The separation of powers
could not only avert the rightful rebellion of oppressed and unrepresented peoples against a tyrant,
but also restrain whimsical wars waged by an unrestrained executive (see Section 6.3).

Drawing from the lessons of the Seven Years' War (1756–1763), Rousseau believed that a state
should be seen as more than the aggregation of atomistic individuals, as Locke had envisioned.
Instead, a representative and peaceful state should reflect the general will, a will based on organic
and mutual cooperation of the people (*The Geneva Manuscript*, c. 1756). Further, to avert animosity between states generated by rivalries over trade, Rousseau's *Consideration on Government of
Poland* (1772) called, against the new commercial spirit of his time, for economic self-sufficiency
and independence, as a better way to advance humanity's natural predisposition toward peace (*The
State of War*, c. 1753–1755) (see Sections 6.4 to 6.6).

Adam Smith's (1723–1790) *The Wealth of the Nations* (1776), however, would ultimately prevail
as the most influential theory on capitalism and free trade. Central to his thesis was the idea that

capital is best employed for the production and distribution of wealth under conditions of noninterference by governments (i.e., laissez-faire). Concerned that state monopolies or any other monopolies would generate economic inefficiency and injustice, Smith defended the long-term benefits of economic competition. Contrary to Rousseau, Smith encouraged individuals to pursue their commercial self-interest under the supervision of an "invisible hand" (*The Theory of Moral Sentiments*, 1759). The resulting economic competition, he believed, would ultimately lead to the greatest possible economic efficiency and societal wealth (see Sections 6.7 and 6.8 on free trade and mutual advantage).

The influence of John Locke and Adam Smith can be found in the writings of the famous English and American political thinker Thomas Paine (1737–1809), also known for his internationalist activism during the American and French revolutions. His *Rights of Man* (1792), a classic in the literature of human rights, not only supported basic universal rights — life, liberty, and property — but also argued that republican governance, the separation of powers, and the proliferation of commerce were the best means to achieve peace. The spreading spirit of republicanism and markets, he suggested, "may prompt a confederation for nations to abolish [war]" (see Section 6.9).

Revolutionary warfare was, however, an essential means to that end, argued Maximilien de Robespierre (1758–1794) in his speech to the national convention (December 4, 1793). Anticipating modern debates about emergency laws, Robespierre argued that certain liberties may be provisionally suspended during wartime. Those who attack the nature of revolutionary laws, Robespierre explained, are "foolish or perverse sophists; their only object is to resurrect tyranny and to destroy the fatherland. When they invoke the literal application of constitutional principles, it is only to violate them with impunity" (see Section 6.10).

German political philosopher Immanuel Kant (1724–1804), who had welcomed the aspirations of the French revolutionaries, later became a critic of the French revolutionary government. Since the preservation of the life of an individual was always an end in itself, life could not be sacrificed for a higher cause. Hence, rights within and between nations could only be achieved by peaceful means. Like Paine before him, Kant considered in *Perpetual Peace* (1795) why republican states, with their separation of powers, offered the only political structure in which individuals could preserve their basic rights and prevent leaders from waging arbitrary wars. To secure a just peace among nations, Kant imagined in *The Metaphysics of Morals* (1797) the formation of a confederation of republican states that would prevent aggression, encourage the expansion of commerce, and promote republican governance, a combination that would ultimately lead to perpetual peace (see Sections 6.11 and 6.12).

6.1 UNITED NATIONS UNIVERSAL DECLARATION OF HUMAN RIGHTS (1948): PREAMBLE

Whereas recognition of the inherent dignity and of the equal and inalienable rights of all members of the human family is the foundation of freedom, justice and peace in the world,

Whereas disregard and contempt for human rights have resulted in barbarous acts which have outraged the conscience of mankind, and the advent of a world in which human beings shall enjoy freedom of speech and belief and freedom from fear and want has been proclaimed as the highest aspiration of the common people,

Whereas it is essential, if man is not to be compelled to have recourse, as a last resort; to rebellion against tyranny and oppression, that human rights should be protected by the rule of law,

Whereas it is essential to promote the development of friendly relations between nations,

Whereas the peoples of the United Nations have in the Charter reaffirmed their faith in fundamental human rights, in the dignity and worth of the human person and in the equal rights of men and women and have determined to promote social progress and better standards of life in larger freedom...

6.2   HUGO GROTIUS (*THE LAW OF WAR AND PEACE*, 1625)

Prolegomena

1. THE municipal law of Rome and of other states has been treated by many, who have undertaken to elucidate it by means of commentaries or to reduce it to a convenient digest. That body of law, however, which is concerned with the mutual relations among States or rulers of states, whether derived from nature, or established by divine ordinances, or having its origin in custom and tacit agreement, few have touched upon. Up to the present time no one has treated it in a comprehensive and systematic manner; yet the welfare of mankind demands that this task be accomplished....

15. Since it is a rule of law of nature to abide by pacts (for it was necessary that among men there be some method of obligating themselves one to another, and no other natural method can be imagined), out of this source the bodies of municipal law have arisen. For those who had associated themselves with some group or had subjected themselves to a man or to men, had, either expressly promised, or from the nature of the transaction must be understood impliedly to have promised, that they would conform to that which should have been determined, in the one case by the majority, in the other by those upon whom authority had been conferred.

16. What is said, therefore, in accordance with the view not only of Carneades but also of others, that

     Expediency is, as it were, the mother
     Of what is just and fair,[1]

     Is not true, if we wish to speak accurately. For the very nature of man, which even if we had no lack of anything would lead us into the mutual relations of society, is the mother of the law of nature. But the mother of municipal law is that obligation which arises from mutual consent; and since this obligation derives its force from the law of nature, nature may be considered, so to say, the great-grandmother of municipal law.

     The law of nature nevertheless has the reinforcement of expediency; for the Author of nature willed that as individuals we should be weak, and should lack many things needed in order to live properly, to the end that we might be the more constrained to cultivate the social life. But expediency afforded an opportunity also for municipal law, since that kind of association of which we have spoken, and subjection, to authority, have their roots in expediency. From this it follows that those who prescribe laws for others in so doing are accustomed to have, or ought to have, some advantage in view.

17. But just as the laws of each state have in view the advantage of that state, so by mutual consent it has become possible that certain laws should originate as between all states, or a great many States; and it is apparent that the laws thus originating had in view the advantage, not of particular states, but of the great society of states. And this is what is called the law of nations, whenever we distinguish that term from the law of nature.

     This division of law Carneades passed over altogether. For he divided all law into the law of nature and the law of particular countries. Nevertheless if undertaking to treat of the body of law which is maintained between states — for he added a statement in regard to war and things acquired by means of war — he would surely have been obliged to make mention of this law.

18. Wrongly, moreover, does Carneades ridicule justice as folly. For since, by his own admission, the national who in his own country obeys its laws is not foolish, even though, out of regard for that law, he may be obliged to forgo certain things advantageous for himself, so that nation is not foolish which does not press its own advantage to the

point of disregarding the laws common to nations. The reason in either case is the same. For just as the national, who violates the law of his country in order to obtain an immediate advantage, breaks down that by which the advantages of himself and his posterity are for all future time assured, so the state which transgresses the laws of nature and of nations cuts away also the bulwarks which safeguard its own future peace. Even if no advantage were to be contemplated from the keeping of the law, it would be a mark of wisdom, not of folly, to allow ourselves to be drawn towards that to which we feel that our nature leads....

25. Least of all should that be admitted which some people imagine, that in war all laws are in abeyance. On the contrary war ought not to be undertaken except for the enforcement of rights; when once undertaken, it should be carried on only within the bounds of law and good faith.... But in order that wars may be justified, they must be carried on with not less scrupulousness than judicial processes are wont to be.

26. Let the laws be silent, then, in the midst of arms, but only the laws of the State, those that the courts are concerned with, that are adapted only to a state of peace; not those other laws, which are of perpetual validity and suited to all times. It was exceedingly well said by Dio of Prusa, that between enemies written laws, that is laws of particular states, are not in force, but that unwritten laws are in force, that is, those which nature prescribes, or the agreement of nations as established....

28. Fully convinced, by the considerations which I have advanced, that there is a common law among nations, which is valid alike for war and in war, I have had many and weighty reasons for undertaking to write upon this subject. Throughout the Christian world I observed a lack of restraint in relation to war, such as even barbarous races should be ashamed of; I observed that men rush to arms for slight causes, or no

cause at all, and that when arms have, once been taken up there is no longer any respect for law, divine or human; it is as if, in accordance with a general decree, frenzy had openly been let loose for the committing of all crimes....

Book II—Chapter I: The Causes of War: Defense of Self and Property

II. — *Justifiable causes include defense, the obtaining of that which belongs to us or is our due, and the inflicting of punishment*

2. Authorities generally assign to wars three justifiable causes, defense, recovery of property, and punishment. All three you may find in Camillus's declaration with reference to the Gauls: "All things which it is right to defend, to recover, and to avenge." In this enumeration the obtaining of what is owed to us was omitted, unless the word "recover" is used rather freely....

III. — *War for the defense of life is permissible*

We said above that if an attack by violence is made on one's person, endangering life, and no other way of escape is open, under such circumstances war is permissible, even though it involve the slaying of the assailant. As a consequence of the general acceptance of this principle we showed that in some cases a private war may be lawful.

This right of self-defense, it should be observed, has its origin directly, and chiefly, in the fact that nature commits to each his own protection, not in the injustice or crime of the aggressor. Wherefore, even if the assailant be blameless, as for instance a soldier acting in good faith, or one who mistakes me for some one else, or one who is rendered irresponsible by madness or by sleeplessness — this, we read, has actually happened to some — the right of self-defense is not thereby taken away; it is enough that I am not under obligation to suffer what such an assailant attempts, any more than

I should be if attacked by an animal belonging to another.

IV. — *War in defense of life is permissible only against an actual assailant*

1. It is a disputed question whether innocent persons can be cut down or trampled upon when by getting in the way they hinder the defense or flight by which alone death can be averted. That this is permissible, is maintained even by some theologians. And certainly, if we look to nature alone, in nature there is much less regard for society than concern for the preservation of the individual....

V. — *War in defense of life is permissible only when the danger is immediate and certain, not when it is merely assumed*

1. The danger, again, must be immediate and imminent in point of time. I admit, to be sure, that if the assailant seizes weapons in such a way that his intent to kill is manifest the crime can be forestalled; for in morals as in material things a point is not to be found which does not have a certain breadth. But those who accept fear of any sort as justifying anticipatory slaying are themselves greatly deceived, and deceive others....

VIII. — *Not to take advantage of the right of defense is permissible*

We said above, that while it is permissible to kill him who is making ready to kill, yet the man is more worthy of praise who prefers to be killed rather than to kill.

This principle, however, is by some conceded in such a way that an exception is made in the case of a person whose life is useful to many. But I should deem it unsafe to extend this rule, which is inconsistent with long suffering, so as to include all those whose lives are necessary for others. And so I should think that the exception ought to be restricted to those whose duty it is to ward off violence from others, such as members of an escort on a journey, who were hired with that purpose in view, and public rulers, to whom the verses of Lucan may be applied [translation by Ridley]:

When on thy breath so many nations hang
For life and safety, and so great a world
Calls thee its master, to have courted death
Proves want of heart.[2]

XI. — *By the law of nature it is permissible to kill in defense of property*

We may now come to injuries that are attempted upon property.

If we have in view expletive justice only, I shall not deny that in order to preserve property a robber can even be killed, in case of necessity. For the disparity between property and life is offset by the favorable position of the innocent party and the odious role of the robber, as we have said above. From this it follows, that if we have in view this right only, a thief fleeing with stolen property can be felled with a missile, if the property cannot otherwise be recovered. In his speech against Aristocrates, Demosthenes exclaims: "In the name of the gods is not this a hard and unjust thing, contrary not only to written laws but also to the law common to all men, that I am not permitted to use force against the man who, in the manner of an enemy, seizes and carries off my property?"

If, furthermore, we leave divine and human law out of account, regard for others, viewed as a principle of conduct, interposes no hindrance to such action, unless the stolen property is of extremely slight value and consequently worthy of no consideration. This exception is by some rightly added.

Chapter XXII: On Unjust Causes [of Wars]

I. — *The distinction between justifiable and persuasive causes is explained*

1. We said above, when we set out to treat the causes of wars, that some were justifiable, others persuasive. Polybius, who was the first to observe this distinction, calls the former "pretexts," because they are wont to be openly

alleged (Livy sometimes employs the term "claim"), and the latter by the name of the class, "causes."

2. Thus in the war of Alexander against Darius the "pretext" was the avenging of the injuries which the Persians had inflicted upon the Greeks, while the "cause" was the desire for renown, empire, and riches, to which was added a great expectation of an easy victory arising from the expeditions of Xenophon and Agesilaus. The "pretext" of the Second Punic War was the dispute over Saguntum, but the cause was the anger of the Carthaginians at the agreements which the Romans had extorted from them in times of adversity, and the encouragement which they derived from their successes in Spain, as was observed by Polybius....

II. — *Wars which lack causes of either sort are wars of savages*

There are some who rush into war without a cause of either sort, led, as Tacitus says, by the desire of incurring danger for its own sake. But the offense of these men is more than human; Aristotle calls it "the savagery of wild beasts." Concerning such persons Seneca wrote: "I can say that this is not cruelty, but ferocity which delights in savagery. We can call it madness; for there are various sorts of madness, and none is more unmistakable than that which turns to the slaughter and butchery of men."

Altogether similar to this expression of opinion is that of Aristotle, in the last book of the *Nicomachean Ethics*: "For anyone would seem to be absolutely murderous if he should make enemies of his friends in order that there might be fighting and bloodshed." Said Dio of Prusa: "To wage war and to fight without a pretext, what else is this than utter madness and a craving for evils arising therefrom?" ...

III. — *Wars which have persuasive but not justifying causes are wars of robbers*

1. In most cases those who go to war have persuasive causes, either with or without justifiable causes. There are some indeed who clearly ignore justifiable causes. To these we may apply the dictum uttered by the Roman jurists, that the man is a robber who, when asked the origin of his possession, adduces none other than the fact of possession.

With regard to those who advocate war Aristotle says: "Do they often times give no thought to the injustice of enslaving neighbors and those who have done no wrong?" ...

XII. — *An unjust cause of war also is the desire to rule others against their will on the pretext that it is for their good*

Not less iniquitous is it to desire by arms to subdue other men, as if they deserved to be enslaved, and were such as the philosophers at times call slaves by nature. For even if something is advantageous for any one, the right is not forthwith conferred upon me to impose this upon him by force. For those who have the use of their reason ought to have the free choice of what is advantageous or not advantageous, unless another has acquired a certain right over them.

With infants the case is clearly different; for since they do not have the right of exercising "independence of action" and of directing their own movements, nature confers the control over them upon persons who undertake it and are fitted therefore.

XIII. — *An unjust cause of war is the title to universal empire which some give to the Emperor, and which is shown to be inapplicable*

1. I should hardly trouble to add that the title which certain persons give to the Roman Emperor is absurd, as if he had the right of ruling over even the most distant and hitherto unknown peoples, were it not that Bartolus, long considered first among jurists, had dared to pronounce him a heretic who denies to the Emperor this title. His ground, forsooth, is that the Emperor at times calls himself lord of the world and that in the sacred writings that empire,

which later writers call Romania, is designated as "the inhabited world." Of like character is this expression:

Now the whole earth the victorious Roman held, as are many similar expressions used in a broad sense, or in hyperbole, or in high prais'e; as when, in the same Holy Writ, Judaea alone often appears under the designation of "the inhabited world." ...

Book III—Chapter IV

XIX.— *Whether rape is contrary to the law of nations*

1. You may read in many places that the raping of women in time of war is permissible, and in many others that it is not permissible. Those who sanction rape have taken into account only the injury done to the person of another, and have judged that it is not inconsistent with the law of war that everything which belongs to the enemy should be at the disposition of the victor. A better conclusion has been reached by others, who have taken into consideration not only the injury but the unrestrained lust of the act; also, the fact that such acts do not contribute to safety or to punishment, and should consequently not go unpunished in war any more than in peace.

The latter view is the law not of all nations, but of the better ones. Thus Marcellus, before capturing Syracuse, is said to have taken pains for the protection, of chastity, even in the case of the enemy....

Chapter XI: Moderation with Respect to the Right of Killing in a Lawful War

I. — *In a lawful war certain acts are devoid of moral justice; a condition which is explained*

1. Not even in a lawful war ought we to admit that which is said in the line,

He, who refuses what is just, yields all.

Cicero's point of view is better: "There are certain duties which must be performed even toward those from whom you have received an injury. There is in fact a limit to vengeance and to punishment." The same writer praises the ancient days of Rome, when the issues of wars were either mild or in accordance with necessity.

Seneca calls those persons cruel who "have a reason for punishing, but observe no limit." Aristides, in his second speech *On Leuctra*, says: "Men may, men may indeed be unjust in avenging themselves, if they carry vengeance beyond measure. He, who in punishing goes so far as to do what is unjust, becomes a second wrongdoer." ...

IV. — *In this matter it is an obligation of humaneness not to make the fullest use of one's right*

1. But we must keep in mind that which, we have recalled elsewhere also, that the rules of love are broader than the rules of law. He who is rich will be guilty of heartlessness if, in order that he himself may exact the last penny, he deprives a needy debtor of all his small possessions; and even much more guilty if the debtor has incurred the debt by his goodness — for instance, if he has gone surety for a friend — and has used none of the money for his own advantage, "for," as Quintilian the Father says, "the peril of a bondsman is worthy of commiseration." Nevertheless so hard a creditor does nothing contrary to his right according to a strict interpretation.

2. Therefore humanity requires that we leave to them that do not share in the guilt of the war, and that have incurred no obligation in any other way than as sureties, those things which we can dispense with more easily than they, particularly if it is quite clear that they will not recover from their own state what they have lost in this way....

Chapter XIV: Moderation in Regard to Prisoners of War

I. — *To what extent, in accordance with moral justice, it is permissible to take men captive*

1. In those places where custom sanctions the captivity and slavery of men, this ought to be limited primarily, if we have regard to moral justice, in the same way as in the case of property; with the result that, in fact, such acquisition may be permitted so far as the amount of either an original or derivative debt allows, unless perhaps on the part of the men themselves there is some special crime which equity would suffer to be punished with loss of liberty. To this degree, then, and no further, he who wages a lawful war has a right over the captured subjects of the enemy, and this right he may legitimately transfer to others.

2. Furthermore in this case also it will be the task of equity and goodness to employ those distinctions which were noted above, when we discussed the question of killing enemies. Demosthenes, in his letter "For the Children of Lycurgus," praises Philip of Macedon for not having enslaved all who were among his enemies. "For," said Demosthenes, "he did not consider the same punishment for all either fair or right, but, examining the case in the light of what each had deserved, he acted in such matters as a judge."

---

[1] In regard to this passage, Acron, or some other ancient interpreter of Horace (*Sat*. I, iii. 98): "The poet is writing in opposition to the teachings of the Stoics. He wishes to show that justice does not have its origin in nature but is born of expediency." For the opposite view, see Augustine's argument, *On Christian Doctrine*, Book III, chap. xiv.

[2] Curtius, Book X (IX, vi. 8): "But while you so eagerly expose your life to manifest dangers forgetting that you are dragging down into ruin the lives of so many citizens."

6.3 JOHN LOCKE: ON THE SEPARATION OF POWERS AND REBELLION (*THE SECOND TREATISE*, 1690)

Chapter II

7. And that all men may be restrained from invading others rights and from doing hurt to one another, and the law of nature be observed, which wills the peace and preservation of all mankind, the execution of the law of nature is, in that state, put into every man's hands, whereby everyone has a right to punish the transgressors of that law to such a degree as may hinder its violation; for the law of nature would, as all other laws that concern men in this world, be in vain if there were nobody that in that state of nature had a power to execute that law and thereby preserve the innocent and restrain offenders. And if anyone in the state of nature may punish another for any evil he has done, everyone may do so; for in that state of perfect equality, where naturally there is no superiority or jurisdiction of one over another, what any may do in prosecution of that law, everyone must needs have a right to do.

8. And thus in the state of nature one man comes by a power over another; but yet no absolute or arbitrary power to use a criminal, when he has got him in his hands, according to the passionate heats or boundless extravagance of his own will; but only to reattribute to him, so far as calm reason and conscience dictate, what is proportionate to his transgression, which is so much as may serve for reparation and restraint; for these two are the only reasons why one man may lawfully do harm to another, which is that we call punishment. In transgressing the law of nature, the offender declares himself to live by another rule than that of reason and common equity, which is that measure God has set to the actions of men for their mutual security; and so he becomes dangerous to mankind, the tie

which is to secure them from injury and violence being slighted and broken by him. Which being a trespass against the whole species and the peace and safety of it provided for by the law of nature, every man upon this score, by the right he has to preserve mankind in general, may restrain, or, where it is necessary, destroy things noxious to them, and so may bring such evil on any one who has transgressed that law, as may make him repent the doing of it and thereby deter him, and by his example others, from doing the like mischief. And in this case, and upon this ground, *every man has a right to punish the offender and be executioner of the law of nature....*

Chapter X: Of the Forms of a Commonwealth

132. The majority, having, as has been shown, upon men's first uniting into society, the whole power of the community naturally in them, may employ all that power in making laws for the community from time to time, and executing those laws by officers of their own appointing: and then the form of the government is a perfect democracy; or else may put the power of making laws into the hands of a few select men, and their heirs or successors: and then it is an oligarchy; or else into the hands of one man: and then it is a monarchy; if to him and his heirs: it is an hereditary monarchy; if to him only for life, but upon his death the power only of nominating a successor to return to them: an elective monarchy. And so accordingly of these the community may make compounded and mixed forms of government, as they think good. And if the legislative power be at first given by the majority to one or more persons only for their lives, or any limited time, and then the supreme power to revert to them again — when it is so reverted, the community may dispose of it again anew into what hands they please and so constitute a new form of government. For the form of govern-

ment depending upon the placing of the supreme power, which is the legislative — it being impossible to conceive that an inferior power should prescribe to a superior, or any but the supreme make laws — according as the power of making laws is placed, such is the form of the commonwealth.

133. By commonwealth, I must be understood all along to mean, not a democracy or any form of government, but any independent community which the Latins signified by the word *civitas*, to which the word which best answers in our language is "commonwealth," and most properly expresses such a society of men, which "community" or "city" in English does not, for there may be subordinate communities in government; and city amongst us has quite a different notion from commonwealth; and, therefore, to avoid ambiguity, I crave leave to use the word commonwealth in that sense in which I find it used by King James the First; and I take it to be its genuine signification, which if anybody dislike, I consent with him to change it for a better.

Chapter XII: Of the Legislative, Executive, and Federative Power of the Commonwealth

143. The legislative power is that which has a right to direct how the force of the commonwealth shall be employed for preserving the community and the members of it. But because those laws which are constantly to be executed, and whose force is always to continue, may be made in a little time, therefore there is no need that the legislative should be always in being, not having always business to do. And because it may be too great a temptation to human frailty, apt to grasp at power, for the same persons who have the power of making laws to have also in their hands the power to execute them, whereby they may exempt themselves from obedience to the laws they make, and suit the law, both in its making and execu-

tion, to their own private advantage, and thereby come, to have a distinct interest from the rest of the community contrary to the end of society and government; therefore, in well ordered commonwealths, where the good of the whole is so considered as it ought, the legislative power is put into the hands of diverse persons who, duly assembled, have by themselves, or jointly with others, a power to make laws; which when they have done, being separated again, they are themselves subject to the laws they have made, which is a new and near tie upon them to take care that they make them for the public good.

144. But because the laws that are at once and in a short time made have a constant and lasting force and need a perpetual execution or an attendance thereunto; therefore, it is necessary there should be a power always in being which should see to the execution of the laws that are made and remain in force. And thus the legislative and executive power come often to be separated.

145. There is another power in every commonwealth which one may call natural, because it is that which answers to the power every man naturally had before he entered into society for though in a commonwealth the members of it are distinct persons still in reference to one another, and as such are governed by the laws of the society, yet, in reference to the rest of mankind, they make one body which is as every member of it before was, still in the state of nature with the rest of mankind. Hence it is that the controversies that happen between any man of the society with those that are out of it are managed by the public, and an injury done to a member of their body engages the whole in the reparation of it. So that, under this consideration, the whole community is one body in the state of nature in respect of all other states or persons out of its community.

146. This, therefore, contains the power of war and peace, leagues and alliances, and all the transactions with all persons and communities without the commonwealth, and may be called "federative," if anyone pleases. So the thing be understood, I am indifferent as to the name.

147. These two powers, executive and federative, though they be really distinct in themselves, yet one comprehending the execution of the municipal laws of the society within itself upon all that are parts of it, the other the management of the security and interest of the public without, with all those that it may receive benefit or damage from, yet they are almost united. And though this federative power in the well or ill management of it be of great moment to the commonwealth, yet it is much less capable to be directed by antecedent, standing, positive laws than the executive, and so must necessarily be left to the prudence and wisdom of those whose hands it is in to be managed for the public good; for the laws that concern subjects one amongst another, being to direct their actions, may well enough precede them. But what is to be done in reference to foreigners, depending much upon their actions and the variation of designs and interests, must be left in great part to the prudence of those who have this power committed to them, to be managed by the best of their skill for the advantage of the commonwealth.

148. Though, as I said, the executive and federative power of every community be really distinct in themselves, yet they are hardly to be separated and placed at the same time in the hands of distinct persons; for both of them requiring the force of the society for their exercise, it is almost impracticable to place the force of the commonwealth in distinct and not subordinate hands, or that the executive and federative power should be placed in persons that might act separately, whereby the force of the public would be under different commands, which would be apt some time or other to cause disorder and ruin.

Chapter XIX

211. He that will with any clearness speak of the dissolution of government ought in the first place to distinguish between the dissolution of the society and the dissolution of the government. That which makes the community and brings men out of the loose state of nature into one politic society is the agreement which everybody has with the rest to incorporate and act as one body, and so be one distinct commonwealth. The usual and almost only way whereby this union is dissolved is the inroad of foreign force making a conquest upon them; for in that case, not being able to maintain and support themselves as one entire and independent body, the union belonging to that body which consisted therein must necessarily cease, and so every one return to the state he was in before, with a liberty to shift for himself and provide for his own safety, as he thinks fit, in some other society. Whenever the society is dissolved, it is certain the government of that society cannot remain. Thus conquerors' swords often cut up governments by the roots and mangle societies to pieces, separating the subdued or scattered multitude from the protection of and dependence on that society which ought to have preserved them from violence. The world is too well instructed in, and too forward to allow of, this way of dissolving of governments to need any more to be said of it; and there wants not much argument to prove that where the society is dissolved, the government cannot remain — that being as impossible as for the frame of a house to subsist when the materials of it are scattered and dissipated by a whirlwind, or jumbled into a confused heap by an earthquake.

212. Besides this overturning from without, governments are dissolved from within....

222. The reason why men enter into society is the preservation of their property; and the end why they choose and authorize a legislative is that there may be laws made and rules set as guards and fences to the properties of all the members of the society to limit the power and moderate the dominion of every part and member of the society; for since it can never be supposed to be the will of the society that the legislative should have a power to destroy that which every one designs to secure by entering into society, and for which the people submitted themselves to legislators of their own making. Whenever the legislators endeavor to take away and destroy the property of the people, or to reduce them to slavery under arbitrary power, they put themselves into a state of war with the people who are thereupon absolved from any further obedience, and are left to the common refuge which God has provided for all men against force and violence. Whensoever therefore, the legislative shall transgress this fundamental rule of society, and either by ambition, fear, folly, or corruption, endeavor to grasp themselves, or put into the hands of any other, an absolute power over the lives, liberties, and estates of the people, by this breach of trust they forfeit the power the people had put into their hands for quite contrary ends, and it devolves to the people, who have a right to resume their original liberty and, by the establishment of a new legislative, such as they shall think fit, provide for their own safety and security, which is the end for which they are in society. What I have said here concerning the legislative in general holds true also concerning the supreme executor, who having a double trust put in him — both to have a part in the legislative and the supreme execution of the law — acts against both when he goes about to set up his own arbitrary will as the law of the society. He acts also contrary to his trust when he either employs the force, treasure, and offices of the society to corrupt the representatives and gain them to his purposes, or openly pre-engages the electors and prescribes to their choice such whom he has by solicitations,

threats, promises, or otherwise won to his designs, and employs them to bring in such who have promised beforehand what to vote and what to enact. Thus to regulate candidates and electors, and new-model the ways of election, what is it but to cut up the government by the roots, and poison the very fountain of public security? For the people, having reserved to themselves the choice of their representatives, as the fence to their properties could do it for no other end but that they might always be freely chosen, and, so chosen, freely act and advise as the necessity of the commonwealth and the public good should upon examination and mature debate be judged to require. This those who give their votes before they hear the debate and have weighed the reasons on all sides are not capable of doing. To prepare such an assembly as this, and endeavor to set up the declared abettors of his own will for the true representatives of the people and the lawmakers of the society, is certainly as great a breach of trust and as perfect a declaration of a design to subvert the government as is possible to be met with. To which if one shall add rewards and punishments visibly employed to the same end, and all the arts of perverted law made use of to take off and destroy all that stand in the way of such a design, and will not comply and consent to betray the liberties of their country, it will be past doubt what is doing. What power they ought to have in the society who thus employ it contrary to the trust that went along with it in its first institution is easy to determine; and one cannot but see that he who has once attempted any such thing as this cannot any longer be trusted.

223. To this perhaps it will be said that, the people being ignorant and always discontented, to lay the foundation of government in the unsteady opinion and uncertain humor of the people is to expose it to certain ruin; and no government will be able long to subsist if the people may set up a new legislative whenever they take offense at the old one. To this I answer: Quite the contrary. People are not so easily got out of their old forms as some are apt to suggest. They are hardly to be prevailed with to amend the acknowledged faults in the frame they have been accustomed to. And if there be any original defects, or adventitious ones introduced by time or corruption, it is not an easy thing to get them changed, even, when all the world sees there is an opportunity for it. This slowness and aversion in the people to quit their old constitutions has in the many revolutions which have been seen in this kingdom, in this and former ages, still kept us to, or after some interval of fruitless attempts still brought us back again to, our old legislative of king, lords, and commons; and whatever provocations have made the crown be taken from some of our princes' heads, they never carried the people so far as to place it in another line.

224. But it will be said this hypothesis lays a ferment for frequent rebellion. To which answer: First, no more than any other hypothesis; for when the people are made miserable, and find themselves exposed to the ill-usage of arbitrary power, cry up their governors as much as you will for sons of Jupiter, let them be sacred or divine, descended or authorized from heaven, give them out from whom or what you please, the same will happen. The people generally ill-treated, and contrary to right, will be ready upon any occasion to ease themselves of a burden that sits heavy upon them. They will wish and seek for the opportunity, which in the change, weakness, and accidents of human affairs seldom delays long to offer itself. He must have lived but a little while in the world who has not seen examples of this in his time, and he must have read very little who cannot produce examples of it in all sorts of governments in the world.

225. Secondly, I answer, such revolutions happen not upon every little misman-

agement in public affairs. Great mistakes in the ruling part, many wrong and inconvenient laws, and all the slips of human frailty will be born by the people without mutiny or murmur. But if a long train of abuses, prevarications, and artifices, all tending the same way, make the design visible to the people, and they cannot but feel what they lie under and see whither they are going, it is not to be wondered that they should then rouse themselves and endeavor to put the rule into such hands which may secure to them the ends for which government was at first erected, and without which ancient names and specious forms are so far from being better that they are much worse than the state of nature or pure anarchy — the inconveniences being all as great and as near, but the remedy farther off and more difficult.

226. Thirdly, I answer that this doctrine of a power in the people of providing for their safety anew by a new legislative, when their legislators have acted contrary to their trust by invading their property, is the best fence against rebellion, and the probablest means to hinder it; for rebellion being an opposition, not to persons, but authority which is founded only in the constitutions and laws of the government, those, whoever they be, who by force break through, and by force justify their violation of them, are truly and properly rebels; for when men, by entering into society and civil government, have excluded force and introduced laws for the preservation of property, peace, and unity amongst themselves, those who set up force again in opposition to the laws do rebel are — that is, bring back again the state of war — and are properly rebels; which they who are in power, by the pretense they have to authority, the temptation of force they have in their hands, and the flattery of those about them, being likeliest to do, the properest way to prevent the evil is to show them the danger and injustice of it who are under the greatest temptation to run into it.

227. In both the forementioned cases, when either the legislative is changed or the legislators act contrary to the end for which they were constituted, those who are guilty are guilty of rebellion; for if any one by force takes away the established legislative of any society, and the laws of them made pursuant to their trust, he thereby takes away the umpirage which every one had consented to for a peaceable decision of all their controversies, and a bar to the state of war amongst them. They who remove or change the legislative take away this decisive power which nobody can have but by the appointment and consent of the people, and so destroying the authority which the people did, and nobody else can set up, and introducing a power which the people has not authorized, they actually introduce a state of war which is that of force without authority; and thus by removing the legislative established by the society — in whose decisions the people acquiesced and united as to that of their own will — they unite the knot and expose the people anew to the state of war. And if those who by force take away the legislative are rebels, the legislators themselves, as has been shown, can be no less esteemed so, when they who were set up for the protection and preservation of the people, their liberties and properties, shall by force invade and endeavor to take them away; and so they putting themselves into a state of war with those who made them the protectors and guardians of their peace, are properly, and with the greatest aggravation, *rebellantes*, rebels.

228. But if they who say "it lays a foundation for rebellion" mean that it may occasion civil wars or intestine broils, to tell the people they are absolved from obedience when illegal attempts are made upon their liberties or properties, and may oppose the unlawful violence of those who were their magistrates when they invade their properties contrary to the trust put in them, and that therefore this doctrine is not

to be allowed, being so destructive to the peace of the world; they may as well say, upon the same ground, that honest men may not oppose robbers or pirates because this may occasion disorder or bloodshed. If any mischiefs come in such cases, it is not to be charged upon him who defends his own right, but on him that invades his neighbor's. If the innocent honest man must quietly quit all he has, for peace's sake, to him who will lay violent hands upon it, I desire it may be considered what a kind of peace there will be in the world, which consists only in violence and rapine, and which is to be maintained only for the benefit of robbers and oppressors. Who would not think it an admirable peace betwixt the mighty and the mean when the lamb without resistance yielded his throat to be torn by the imperious wolf. Polyphemus' den gives us a perfect pattern of such a peace and such a government, wherein Ulysses and his companions had nothing to do but quietly to suffer themselves to be devoured. And no doubt Ulysses, who was a prudent man, preached up passive obedience, and exhorted them to a quiet submission by representing to them of what concernment peace was to mankind, and by showing the inconveniences which might happen if they should offer to resist Polyphemus, who had now the power over them.

229. The end of government is the good of mankind. And which is best for mankind? That the people should be always exposed to the boundless will of tyranny, or that the rulers should be sometimes liable to be opposed when they grow exorbitant in the use of their power and employ it for the destruction and not the preservation of the properties of their people? ...

240. Here, it is like, the common question will be made: Who shall be judge whether the prince or legislative act contrary to their trust? This, perhaps, ill-affected and factious men may spread amongst the people, when the prince only makes use of his due prerogative. To this I reply: The people shall be judge; for who shall be judge whether his trustee or deputy acts well and according to the trust reposed in him but he who deputes him and must, by having deputed him, have still a power to discard him when he fails in his trust? If this be reasonable in particular cases of private men, why should it be otherwise in that of the greatest moment where the welfare of millions is concerned, and also where the evil, if not prevented, is greater and the redress very difficult, dear, and dangerous?

241. But further, this question, Who shall be judge? cannot mean that there is no judge at all; for where there is no judicature on earth to decide controversies amongst men, God in heaven is Judge. He alone, it is true, is Judge of the right. But every man is judge for himself, as in all other cases, so in this, whether another has put himself into a state of war with him, and whether he should appeal to the Supreme Judge, as Jephthah did.

242. If a controversy arise betwixt a prince and some of the people in a matter where the law is silent or doubtful, and the thing be of great consequence, I should think the proper umpire in such a case should be the body of the people; for in cases where the prince has a trust reposed in him and is dispensed from the common ordinary rules of the law, there if any men find themselves aggrieved and think the prince acts contrary to or beyond that trust, who so proper to judge as the body of the people (who, at first, lodged that trust in him) how far they meant it should extend? But if the prince, or whoever they be in the administration, decline that way of determination, the appeal then lies nowhere but to heaven; force between either persons who have no known superior on earth, or which permits no appeal to a judge on earth, being properly a state of war wherein the appeal lies only to heaven; and in that state the injured party must judge for himself when he will think fit to

make use of that appeal and put himself upon it.

243. To conclude, the power that every individual gave the society when he entered into it can never revert to the individuals again as long as the society lasts, but will always remain in the community, because without this there can be no community, no commonwealth, which is contrary to the original agreement; so also when the society has placed the legislative in any assembly of men, to continue in them and their successors with direction and authority for providing such successors, the legislative can never revert to the people while that government lasts, because having provided a legislative with power to continue for ever, they have given up their political power to the legislative and cannot resume it. But if they have set limits to the duration of their legislative and made this supreme power in any person or assembly only temporary, or else when by the miscarriages of those in authority it is forfeited, upon the forfeiture, or at the determination of the time set, it reverts to the society, and the people have a right to act as supreme and continue the legislative in themselves, or erect a new form, or under the old form place it in new hands, as they think good.

6.4   JEAN-JACQUES ROUSSEAU: ON THE GENERAL WILL AND COMMERCIAL INEQUITY (*THE GENEVA MANUSCRIPT*, 1756)

Chapter III: On the Fundamental Compact

Man is born free, but everywhere is in chains. One who believes himself the master of others is nonetheless a greater slave than they. How did this change occur? No one knows. What can make it legitimate? It is not impossible to say. If I were to consider only force, as others do, I would say that as long as the people is constrained to obey and does so; it does well. As soon as it can shake off the yoke and does so, it does

even better. For in recovering its freedom by means of the same right used to steal it, either the people is well justified in taking it back, or those who took it away were not justified in doing so. But the social order is a sacred right that serves as a basis for all the others. However, this right does not have its source in nature; it is therefore based on a convention. The problem is to know what this convention is and how it could have been formed.

As soon as man's needs exceed his faculties and the objects of his desire expand and multiply, he must either remain eternally unhappy or seek a new form of being from which he can draw the resources he no longer finds in himself. As soon as obstacles to our self-preservation prevail, by their resistance, over the force each individual can use to conquer them, the primitive state can no longer subsist and the human race would perish if art did not come to nature's rescue. Since man cannot engender new forces but merely unite and direct existing ones, he has no other means of self-preservation except to form, by aggregation, a sum of forces that can prevail over the resistance; set them to work by a single motivation; make them act conjointly; and direct them toward a single object. This is the fundamental problem which is solved by the institution of the State.

If, then, these conditions are combined and everything that is not of the essence of the social Compact is set aside, one will find that it can be reduced to the following terms: "Each of us puts his will, his goods, his force, and his person in common, under the direction of the general will, and in a body we all receive each member as an inalienable part of the whole." Instantly, in place of the private person of each contracting party, this act of association produces a moral and collective body, composed of as many members as there are voices in the assembly, and to which the common self gives formal unity, life, and will. This public person, formed thus by the union of all the others, generally assumes the name body politic which its members call *State* when it is passive, *Sovereign* when active, *Power* when comparing it to similar bodies. As for the members themselves, they take the name *People* collectively, and individually are called *Citizens* as members of the *City* or participants in the sovereign authority, and *Subjects* as subject to the Laws of the State. But these terms, rarely used with complete precision, are often mistaken for one another, and it is enough to know how to distinguish them when the meaning of discourse so requires.

This formula shows that the primitive act of confederation includes a reciprocal engagement between the public and private individuals, and that each individual, contracting with himself so to speak, finds that he is doubly engaged, namely toward private individuals as a member of the sovereign and toward the sovereign as a member of the State. But it must be noted that the maxim of Civil Right that no one can be held responsible for engagements toward himself cannot be applied here, because there is a great difference between being obligated to oneself, or to a whole of which one is a part. It must further be noted that the public deliberation that can obligate all of the subjects to the sovereign — due to the two different relationships in which each of them is considered — cannot for the opposite reason obligate the sovereign toward itself, and that consequently it is contrary to the nature of the body politic for the sovereign to impose on itself a law that it cannot break. Since the sovereign can only be considered in a single relationship, it is then in the situation of a private individual contracting with himself. It is apparent from this that there is not, nor can there be, any kind of fundamental Law that is obligatory for the body of People. This does not mean that this body cannot perfectly well enter an engagement toward another, at least insofar as this is not contrary to its nature, because with reference to the foreigner, it becomes a simple Being or individual.

As soon as this multitude is thus united in a body, one could not harm any of its members without attacking the body in some part of its existence, and it is even less possible to harm the body without the members feeling the effects. For in addition to the common life in question, all risk also that part of themselves which is not currently at the disposition of the sovereign and which they enjoy in safety only under public protection. Thus duty and interest equally obligate the two contracting parties to be of mutual assistance, and the same persons should seek to combine in this double relationship all the advantages that are dependent on it. But there are some distinctions to be made insofar as the sovereign, formed solely by the private individuals composing it, never has any interest contrary to theirs, and as a consequence the sovereign power could never need a guarantee toward the private individuals, because it is impossible for the body ever to want to harm its members. The same is not true of the private individuals with reference to the sovereign, for despite the common interest, nothing would answer for their engagements to the sovereign if it did not find ways to be assured of their fidelity. Indeed, each individual can, as a man, have a private will contrary to or differing from the general will he has as a Citizen. His absolute and independent existence can bring him to view what he owes the common cause as a free contribution, the loss of which will harm others less than its payment burdens him; and considering the moral person which constitutes the state as a Being produced by reason because it is not a man, he might wish to enjoy the rights of the Citizen without wanting to fulfill the duties of a subject, an injustice whose spread would soon cause the ruin of the body politic.

In order for the social contract not to be an ineffectual formula, therefore, the sovereign must have some guarantees, independently of the consent of the private individuals, of their engagements toward the common cause. The oath is ordinarily the first of such guarantees, but since it comes from a totally different order of things and since each man, according to his inner maxims, modifies to his liking the obligation it imposes on him, it is rarely relied on in political institutions; and it is with reason that more real assurances, derived from the thing itself, are preferred. So the fundamental compact tacitly includes this engagement, which alone can give force to all the others: that whoever refuses to obey the general will shall be constrained to do so by the entire body. But it is important here to remember carefully that the particular, distinctive character of this compact is that the people contracts only with itself; that is, the people in a body, as sovereign, with the private individuals composing it, as subjects — a condition that creates all the ingenuity and functioning of the political machine, and alone renders legitimate, reasonable, and without danger engagements that without it would be absurd, tyrannical, and subject to the most enormous abuse....

6.5   JEAN-JACQUES ROUSSEAU: ON THE GENERAL WILL AND COMMERCIAL INEQUITY (*THE STATE OF WAR*, C. 1753–1755)

Man is naturally peaceful and timid; at the least danger, his first reaction is to flee; he only fights through the force of habit and experience. Honor, interest, prejudices, vengeance, all those passions which make him brave danger and death, are remote from him in the state of nature. It is only when he has entered into society with other men that he decides to attack another, and he only becomes a soldier after he has become a citizen. There are no strong natural dispositions to make war on all one's fellow men. But I am lingering too long over a system both revolting and absurd, which has already been refuted a hundred times.

There is then no general war between men; and the human species has not been created solely in order to engage in mutual destruction. It remains to consider war of an accidental and exceptional nature which can arise between two or more individuals....

I can conceive that, in the unarbitrated quarrels which can arise in the state of nature, a man whose anger has been roused can sometimes kill another, either by open force or by surprise. But if a real war were to take place, imagine the strange position which this same man would have to be in if he could only preserve his life at the expense of that of another....

Everything inclines natural man to peace; the sole needs he knows are eating and sleeping, and only hunger drags him from idleness. He is made into a savage continually

ready to torment his fellow men because of passions of which he knows nothing. On the contrary, these passions, aroused in the bosom of society by everything that can inflame them, are considered not to exist there at all. A thousand writers have dared to say that the body politic is passionless, and that there is no other *raison d'etat* than reason itself. As if no one saw that, on the contrary, the essence of society consists in the activity of its members, and that a state without movement would be nothing but a corpse. As if all the world's histories do not show us that the best-constituted societies are also the most active and that the continual action and reaction of all their members, whether within or without, bear witness to the vigor of the whole body.

6.6   JEAN-JACQUES ROUSSEAU: ON THE GENERAL WILL AND COMMERCIAL INEQUITY (*CONSIDERATION ON GOVERNMENT OF POLAND*, 1772)

Chapter XI: The Economic System

... But if perchance you wish to be a free nation, a peaceful nation, a wise nation, a nation that fears nobody and needs nobody, a nation that is sufficient unto itself and happy, then you must use another method altogether, namely this: keep alive — or bring back to life — simple customs, wholesome tastes, and a spirit that is martial but not ambitious. Instill courage and unselfishness into the hearts of your people. Employ the masses of your population in agriculture and the arts necessary for life. Cause money to become an object of contempt and, if possible, useless besides; and make it your business, with an eye to the great things you are to accomplish, to discover some more powerful and dependable incentive. As you travel this path, to be sure, the reports of your celebrations, your negotiations, and your exploits will fill no newspapers. No philosophers will fawn upon you. No poets will write songs about you. You will seldom be the talk of Europe, which may even profess to view you with disdain. You will live, however, in an atmosphere of true abundance, of justice, and of freedom. No one will pick quarrels with you. People will, rather, fear you, while pretending not to....

Rich peoples, in point of fact, have always been beaten and taken over by poor peoples. Is it certain that money is what keeps things going in a good government? Systems of finance are a modern invention; they have produced nothing, so far as I can see, that is good or great either. The governments of ancient times were ignorant of the very word "finance," and yet they accomplished things with men that are wonderful to contemplate. Money, at best, merely supplements men; and that which supplements is never so valuable as that which is supplemented. Poles do this for me: let the others have all the money in the world, or at least content yourselves with such of it as the others — since they need your wheat more than you need their gold — will find it necessary to give you. Believe me: to live abundantly is better than to live opulently. Be better off than mere wealth will ever make you, by providing yourselves with plenty. Tend your fields, and do not bother your heads about other things. You will harvest your gold soon enough, and in larger amounts than you need for the oil and wine you want. For, with those exceptions, Poland has in quantity — or is in position to produce — pretty much everything it requires.

Heads and hearts and hands are what you need to keep yourselves happy and free; they are the makings of a strong state and a prosperous people. Systems of finance produce venal hearts; for once a man makes up his mind that he is interested only in gain, he profits more by playing the knave than by being an honest man. Where money is used, it is easily diverted and concealed; what is intended for one purpose is utilized for another; those who handle money soon learn how to divert it — and what are all the officials assigned to keep watch on them, except so many more rascals whom one sends along to go shares with them? If all riches were public and obvious, if gold, in moving from place to place, left behind it visible traces that were impossible to conceal, money would be the most convenient instrument there could be for purchasing services, courage, fidelity, virtues....

6.7 ADAM SMITH: ON FREE TRADE AND MUTUAL ADVANTAGE (*THE WEALTH OF NATIONS*, 1776)

Book I

Chapter II: The Principle Which Occasions the Division of Labor

This division of labor, from which so many advantages are derived, is not originally the effect of any human wisdom, which foresees and intends that general opulence to which it gives occasion. It is the necessary, though very slow and gradual, consequence of a certain propensity in human nature which has in view, no such extensive utility; the propensity to truck, barter, and exchange one thing for another....

When an animal wants to obtain something either of a man or of another animal, it has no other means of persuasion but to gain the favor of those whose service it requires. A puppy fawns upon its dam, and a spaniel endeavors by a thousand attractions to engage the attention of its master who is at dinner, when it wants to be fed by him. Man sometimes uses the same arts with his brethren, and when he has no other means of engaging them to act according to his inclinations, endeavors by every servile and fawning attention to obtain their good will. He has not time, however, to do this upon every occasion. In civilized society, he stands at all times in need of the co-operation and assistance of great multitudes, while his whole life is scarce sufficient to gain the friendship of a few persons. In almost every other race of animals each individual, when it is grown up to maturity, is entirely independent, and in its natural state has occasion for the assistance of no other living creature. But man has almost constant occasion for the help of his brethren, and it is in vain for him to expect it from their benevolence only. He will be more likely to prevail if he can interest their self-love in his favor, and show them that it is for their own advantage to do for him what he requires of them. Whoever offers to another a bargain of any kind, proposes to do this. Give me that which I want, and you shall have this which you want, is the meaning of every such offer; and it is in this manner that we obtain from one another the far greater part of those good offices which we stand in need of. It is not from the benevolence of the butcher, the brewer, or the baker, that we expect our dinner, but from their regard to their own interest. We address ourselves, not to their humanity, but to their self-love and never talk to them of our own necessities, but of their advantages. Nobody but a beggar chooses to depend chiefly upon the benevolence of his fellow-citizens. Even a beggar does not depend upon it entirely. The charity of well-disposed people, indeed, supplies him with the whole fund of his subsistence. But if though this principle ultimately provides him with all the necessaries of life which he has occasion for, it neither does nor can provide him with them as he has occasion for them. The greater part of his occasional wants are supplied in the same manner as those of other people, by treaty, by barter, and by purchase. With the money which one man gives him he purchases food. The old clothes which another bestows upon him he exchanges for other old clothes which suit him better, or for lodging, or for food, or for money, with which he can buy either food, clothes, or lodging, as he has occasion.

As it is by treaty, by barter, and by purchase, that we obtain from one another the greater part of those mutual good offices which we stand in need of, so it is this same trucking disposition which originally gives occasion to the division of labor.

Chapter III: Division of Labor Limited by Extent of the Market

Capitals are increased by parsimony, and diminished by prodigality and misconduct. Whatever a person saves from his revenue he adds to his capital, and either employs it himself in maintaining an additional number of productive hands, or enables some other person to do so by lending it to him for an interest, that is, for a share of the profits. As the capital of an individual can be increased only by what he saves from his annual revenue or his annual gains, so the capital of a society, which is the same with that of all the individuals who compose it, can be increased only in the same manner.

Parsimony, and not industry, is the immediate cause of the increase of capital. Industry, indeed, provides the subject which parsimony accumulates. But whatever industry might acquire, if parsimony did not save and store up, the capital would never be the greater. Parsimony, by increasing the fund which is destined for the maintenance of productive hands, tends to increase the number of those hands whose labor adds to the value of the subject upon which it is bestowed. It tends therefore to increase the exchangeable value of the annual produce of the land and labor of the country. It puts into motion an additional quantity of industry, which gives an additional value to the annual produce....

Great nations are never impoverished by private, though they sometimes are by public prodigality and misconduct. The whole, or almost the whole public revenue, is in most countries employed in maintaining unproductive hands. Such are the people who compose a numerous and splendid court, a great ecclesiastical establishment, great fleets and armies, who in time of peace produce nothing, and in time of war acquire nothing which can compensate the expense of maintaining them, even while the war lasts. Such people, as they themselves produce nothing, are all maintained by the produce of other men's labor. When multiplied to an unnecessary number, they may in a particular year consume so great a share of this produce as not to leave a sufficiency for maintaining the productive laborers, who should reproduce it next year. The next year's produce will be less than that of the foregoing, and if the same disorder should continue, that of the third year will be still less than that of the second. Those unproductive hands who should be maintained by a part only of the spare revenue of the people, may consume so great a share of their whole revenue, and thereby oblige so great a number to encroach upon their capitals, the funds destined for the maintenance of productive labor, that all the frugality and good conduct of individuals may not be able to compensate the waste and degradation of produce occasioned by this violent and forced encroachment....

Book IV

Chapter II: Of Restraints upon the Importation from Foreign Countries of Such Goods as Can Be Produced at Home

... Every individual is continually exerting himself to find out the most advantageous employment for whatever capital he can command. It is his own advantage, indeed, and not that of the society, which he has in view. But the study of his own advantage, naturally, or rather necessarily, leads him to prefer that employment which is most advantageous to the society.

I. Every individual endeavors to employ his capital as near home as he can, and consequently as much as he can in the support of domestic industry, provided always that he can thereby obtain the ordinary, or not a great deal less than the ordinary profits of stock.

Thus, upon equal or nearly equal profits, every wholesale merchant naturally prefers the home trade to the foreign trade of consumption, and the foreign trade of consumption to the carrying trade. In the home trade his capital is never so long out of his sight as it frequently is in the foreign trade of consumption. He can know better the character and situation of the person whom he trusts, and if he should happen to be deceived, he knows better the laws of the country from which he must seek redress. In the carrying trade, the capital of the merchant is, as it were, divided between two foreign countries, and no part of it is ever necessarily brought home, or placed under his own immediate view and command. The capital which an Amsterdam merchant employs in carrying corn from Konnigsberg to Lisbon, and fruit and wine from Lisbon to Konnigsberg, must generally be the one half of it at Konnigsberg and the other half at Lisbon. No part of it need ever come to Amsterdam. The natural residence of such a merchant should either be at Konnigsberg or Lisbon, and it can only be some very particular circumstances

which can make him prefer the residence of Amsterdam. The uneasiness, however, which he feels at being separated so far from his capital, generally determines him to bring part both of the Konnigsberg goods which he destines for the market of Lisbon, and the Lisbon goods which he destines for that of Konnigsberg, to Amsterdam, and though this necessarily subjects him to a double charge of loading and unloading, as well as to the payment of some duties and customs, yet for the sake of having some part of his capital always under his own view and command, he willingly submits to this extraordinary charge; and it is in this manner that every country which has any considerable share of the carrying trade, becomes always the emporium, or general market, for the goods of all the different countries whose trade it carries on. The merchant, in order to save a second loading and unloading, endeavors always to sell in the home market as much of the goods of all those different countries as he can, and thus, so far as he can, to convert his carrying trade into a foreign trade of consumption. A merchant, in the same manner, who is engaged in the foreign trade of consumption, when he collects goods for foreign markets, will always be glad, upon equal or nearly equal profits, to sell as great a part of them at home as he can. He saves himself the risk and trouble of exportation, when, so far as he can, he thus converts his foreign trade of consumption into a home trade. Home is in this manner the center, if I may say so, round which the capitals of the inhabitants of every country are continually circulating, and towards which they are always tending, though by particular causes they may sometimes be driven off and repelled from it toward more distant employments. But a capital employed in the home trade, it has already been shown, necessarily puts into motion a greater quantity of domestic industry, and gives revenue and employment to a greater number of the inhabitants of the country, than an equal capital employed in the foreign trade of consumption: and one employed in the foreign trade of consumption has the same advantage over an equal capital employed in the carrying trade. Upon equal or only nearly equal profits, therefore, every individual naturally inclines to employ his capital in the manner in which it is likely to afford the greatest support to domestic industry, and to give revenue and employment to the greatest number of people of his own country.

II. Every individual who employs his capital in the support of domestic industry, necessarily endeavors so to direct that industry, that its produce may be of the greatest possible value.

The produce of industry is what it adds to the subject or materials upon which it is employed. In proportion as the value of this produce is great or small, so will likewise be the profits of the employer. But it is only for the sake of profit that any man employs a capital in the support of industry, and he will always, therefore, endeavor to employ it in the support of that industry of which the produce is likely to be of the greatest value, or to exchange for the greatest quantity either of money or of other goods.

But the annual revenue of every society is always precisely equal to the exchangeable value of the whole annual produce of its industry, or rather is precisely the same thing with that exchangeable value. As every individual, therefore, endeavors as much as he can both to employ his capital in the support of domestic industry, and so to direct that industry that its produce may be of the greatest value, every individual necessarily labors to render the annual revenue of the society as great as he can. He generally, indeed, neither intends to promote the public interest, nor knows how much he is promoting it. By preferring the support of domestic to that of foreign industry, he intends only his own security and by directing that industry in such a manner as its produce may be of the greatest value, he intends only his own gain, and he is in this, as in many other cases, led by an invisible hand to promote an end which was no part of his intention. Nor is it always the worse for the society that it was no part of it. By pursuing his own interest he frequently promotes that of the society more effectually than when he really intends to promote it. I have never known much good done by those who affected to trade for the public good. It is an affectation, indeed, not

very common among merchants, and very few words need be employed in dissuading them from it.

What is the species of domestic industry which his capital can employ, and of which the produce is likely to be of the greatest value, every individual, it is evident, can, in this local situation, judge much better than any statesman or lawgiver can do for him. The statesman, who should attempt to direct private people in what manner they ought to employ their capitals, would not only load himself with a most unnecessary attention, but assume an authority which could safely be trusted to no single person, to no council or senate whatever, and would nowhere be so dangerous as in the hands of a man who had folly and presumption enough to fancy himself fit to exercise it....

Were all nations to follow the liberal system of free exportation and free importation, the different states into which a great continent was divided would so far resemble the different provinces of a great empire. As among the different provinces of a great empire the freedom of the inland trade appears, both from reason and experience; not only the best palliative of a dearth, but the most effectual preventative of a famine; so would the freedom of the exportation and importation trade be among the different states into which a great continent was divided. The larger the continent, the easier the communication through all the different parts of it, both by land and by water, the less would any one particular part of it ever be exposed to either of these calamities: the scarcity of any one country being more likely to be relieved by the plenty of some other. But very few countries have entirely adopted this liberal system. The freedom of the corn trade is almost everywhere more or less restrained, and, in many countries, is confined by such absurd regulations, as frequently aggravate the unavoidable misfortune of a dearth into the dreadful calamity of a famine. The demand of such countries for corn may frequently become so great and so urgent, that a small state in their neighborhood, which happened at the same time to be laboring under some degree of dearth, could not venture to supply them without exposing itself to the like dreadful calamity. The very bad policy of one country may thus render it in some measure dangerous and imprudent to establish what would otherwise be the best policy in another. The unlimited freedom of exportation would be much less dangerous in great states, in which, the growth being much greater, the supply could seldom be much affected by any quantity of corn that was likely to be exported. In a Swiss canton, or in some of the little states of Italy, it may, perhaps, sometimes be necessary to restrain the exportation of corn. In such great countries as France or England it scarce ever can. To hinder, besides, the farmer from sending his goods at all times to the best market, is evidently to sacrifice the ordinary laws of justice to an idea of public utility, to a sort of reasons of state; an act of legislative authority which ought to be exercised only, which can be pardoned only, in cases of the most urgent necessity. The price at which the exportation of corn is prohibited, if it is ever to be prohibited, ought always to be a very high price.

The laws concerning corn may everywhere be compared to the laws concerning religion. The people feel themselves so much interested in what relates either to their subsistence in this life, or to their happiness in a life to come, that government must yield to their prejudices, and, in order to preserve the public tranquility, establish that system which they approve of. It is upon this account, perhaps, that we so seldom find a reasonable system established with regard to either of those two capital objects....

The improvement and prosperity of Great Britain, which has been so often ascribed to those laws, may very easily be accounted for by other causes. That security which the laws in Great Britain give to every man, that he shall enjoy the fruits of his own labor, is alone sufficient to make any country flourish, notwithstanding these and twenty other absurd regulations of commerce; and this security was perfected by the revolution, much about the same time that the bounty was established. The natural effort of every individual to better his own condition, when suffered to exert itself with freedom and security, is so powerful a principle, that it is

alone, and without any assistance, not only capable of carrying on the society to wealth and prosperity, but of surmounting a hundred impertinent obstructions with which the folly of human laws too often encumbers its operations; though the effect of these obstructions is always more or less either to encroach upon its freedom, or to diminish its security. In Great Britain industry is perfectly secure; and though far from being perfectly free, it is as free or freer than in any other part of Europe....

It is thus that the private interests and passions of individuals naturally dispose them to turn their stock towards the employments which in ordinary cases are most advantageous to the society. But, if from this natural preference, they should turn too much of it towards those employments, the fall of profit in them and the rise of it in all others, immediately dispose them to alter this faulty distribution. Without any intervention of law, the private interests and passions of men naturally lead them to divide and distribute the stock of every society, among all the different employments carried on in it, as nearly as possible in the proportion which is most agreeable to the interest of the whole society.

All the different regulations of the mercantile system necessarily derange more or less this natural and most advantageous distribution of stock. But those which concern the trade to America and the East Indies derange it, perhaps, more than any other; because the trade to those two great continents absorbs a greater quantity of stock than any other two branches of trade. The regulations, however, by which this derangement is effected in those two different branches of trade are not altogether the same. Monopoly is the great engine of both: but it is a different sort of monopoly. Monopoly of one kind or another seems to be the sole engine of the mercantile system.

In the trade to America every nation endeavors to engross as much as possible the whole market of its own colonies, by fairly excluding all other nations from any direct trade to them. During the greater part of the sixteenth century, the Portuguese endeavored to manage the trade of the East Indies in the same manner, by claiming the sole right of sailing in the Indian seas, on account of the merit of having first found out the road to them. The Dutch still continue to exclude all other European nations from any direct trade to their spice islands. Monopolies of this kind are evidently established against all other European nations, who are thereby not only excluded from a trade to which it might be convenient for them to turn some part of their stock, but are obliged to buy the goods which that trade deals in somewhat dearer than if they could import them themselves directly from the countries which produce them....

But since the fall of the power of Portugal, no European nation has claimed the exclusive right of sailing in the Indian seas, of which the principal ports are now open to the ships of all European nations. Except in Portugal, however, and within these few years, in France, the trade to the East Indies has in every European country been subjected to an exclusive company. Monopolies of this kind are properly established against the very nation which erects them. The greater part of that nation are thereby not only excluded from a trade to which it might be convenient for them to turn some part of their stock, but are obliged to buy the goods which that trade deals in somewhat dearer than if it was open and free to all their countrymen. Since the establishment of the English East Indian Company, for example, the other inhabitants of England, over and above being excluded from the trade, must have paid in the price of the East India goods which they have consumed, not only for all the extraordinary profits which the company may have made upon those goods in consequence of their monopoly, but for all the extraordinary waste which the fraud and abuse, inseparable from the management of the affairs of so great a company, must necessarily have occasioned. The absurdity of this second kind of monopoly, therefore, is much more manifest than that of the first. [East India Company dissolved.]

Both these kinds of monopolies derange more or less the natural distribution of the stock of the society; but they do not always derange it in the same way.

Monopolies of the first kind always attract to the particular trade in which they are established, a greater proportion of the stock, of the society than what would go to that trade of its own accord.

Monopolies of the second kind may sometimes attract stock towards the particular trade in which they are established, and sometimes repel it from that trade according to different circumstances. In poor countries they naturally attract towards that trade more stock than would otherwise go to it. In rich countries they naturally repel from it a good deal of stock which would otherwise go to it....

All systems either of preference or of restraint, being thus completely taken away, the obvious and simple system of natural liberty establishes itself of its own accord. Every man, as long as he does not violate the laws of justice, is left perfectly free to pursue his own interest his own way, and to bring both his industry and capital into competition with those of any other man, or order of men. The sovereign is completely discharged from a duty, in the attempting to perform which, he must always be deposed to innumerable delusions, and for the proper performance of which no human wisdom or knowledge could ever be sufficient: the duty of superintending the industry of private people, and of directing it towards the employments most suitable to the interest of the society. According to the system of natural liberty, the sovereign has only three duties to attend to; three duties of great importance, indeed, but plain and intelligible to common understandings: I. the duty of protecting the society from the violence and invasion of other independent societies; II. the duty of protecting, as far as possible, every member of the society from the injustice or oppression of every other member of it, or the duty of establishing an exact administration of justice; and III. the duty of erecting and maintaining certain public works and certain public institutions, which it can never be for the interest of any individual, or small number of individuals, to erect and maintain, because the profit could never repay the expense to any individual or small number of individuals, though it may frequently do much more than repay it to a great society....

6.8 ADAM SMITH: ON FREE TRADE AND MUTUAL ADVANTAGE (*THE THEORY OF MORAL SENTIMENTS*, 1759)

Part IV

Chapter 1

... The earth, by these labors of mankind, has been obliged to redouble her natural fertility, and to maintain a greater multitude of inhabitants. It is to no purpose that the proud and unfeeling landlord views his extensive fields, and without a thought for the wants of his brethren, in imagination consumes himself the whole harvest that grows upon them. The homely and vulgar proverb, that the eye is larger than the belly, never was more fully verified than with regard to him. The capacity of his stomach bears no proportion to the immensity of his desires, and will receive no more than that of the meanest peasant. The rest he is obliged to distribute among those who prepare, in the nicest manner, that little which he himself makes use of, among those who fit up the palace in which this little is to be consumed, among those who provide and keep in order all the different baubles and trinkets which are employed in the economy of greatness; all of whom thus derive from his luxury and caprice that share of the necessaries of life which they would in vain have expected from his humanity or his justice. The produce of the soil maintains at all times nearly that number of inhabitants which it is capable of maintaining. The rich only select from the heap what is most precious and agreeable. They consume little more than the poor; and in spite of their natural selfishness and rapacity, though they mean only their own conveniency, though the sole end which they propose from the labors of all the thousands whom they employ be the gratification of their own vain and insatiable desires, they divide with the poor the produce of all their improvements. They are led by an invisible hand to make nearly the same distribution of the necessaries of life which would have been made had the earth been divided into equal portions among all its inhabitants; and thus, without intending it, without knowing it, advance the interest of the society, and afford means to the multiplication of the species. When providence divided the earth among a few lordly masters, it neither forgot nor abandoned those who seemed to have been left out in the partition. These last, too, enjoy their share of all that it produces. In what constitutes the real happiness of human life, they are in no respect inferior to those who would seem so much above them. In ease of body and peace of mind, all the different ranks of life are nearly upon a level, and the beggar, who suns himself by the side of the highway, possesses that security which kings are fighting for....

6.9 THOMAS PAINE: ON JUST REVOLUTIONARY WARS, COMMERCE AND REPUBLICANISM (*THE RIGHTS OF MAN*, 1792)

... If any generation of men ever possessed the right of dictating the mode by which the world should be governed for ever, it was the first generation that existed; and if that generation did it not, no succeeding generation can show any authority for doing it, nor can set any up. The illuminating and divine principle of the equal rights of man (for it has its origin from the Maker of man) relates, not only to the living individuals, but to generations of men succeeding each other. Every generation is equal in rights to generations which preceded it, by the same rule that every individual is born equal in rights with his contemporary....

Man did not enter into society to become worst than he was before, nor to have fewer rights than he had before, but to have those rights better secured. His natural rights are the foundation of all his civil rights. But in order to pursue this distinction with more precision, it will be necessary to mark the different qualities of natural and civil rights.

A few words will explain this. Natural rights are those which appertain to man in right of his existence. Of this kind are all the intellectual rights, or rights of the mind, and also all those rights of acting as an individual for his own comfort and happiness, which are not injurious to the natural rights of others. Civil rights are those which appertain to man in right of his being a member of society. Every civil right has for its foundation some natural right pre-existing in the individual, but to the enjoyment of which his individual power is not, in all cases, sufficiently competent. Of this kind are all those which relate to security and protection.

From this short review it will be easy to distinguish between that class of natural rights which man retains after entering into society and those which he throws into the common stock as a member of society.

The natural rights which he retains are all those in which the *power* to execute is as perfect in the individual as the right itself. Among this class, as is before mentioned, are all the intellectual rights, or rights of the mind; consequently religion is one of those rights. The natural rights which are not retained, are all those in which, though the right is perfect in the individual, the power to execute them is defective. They answer not his purpose. A man, by natural right, has a right to judge in his own cause; and so far as the right of the mind is concerned, he never surrenders it. But what availeth it him to judge, if he has not power to redress? He therefore deposits this right in the common stock of society, and takes the arm of society, of which he is a part, in preference and in addition to his own. Society *grants* him nothing. Every man is a proprietor in society, and draws on the capital as a matter of right.

From these premises two or three certain conclusions will follow:

First, That every civil right grows out of a natural right; or, in other words, is a natural right exchanged.

Secondly, That civil power properly considered as such is made up of the aggregate of that class of the natural rights of man, which becomes defective in the individual in point of power, and answers not his purpose, but when collected to a focus becomes competent to the purpose of every one.

Thirdly, That the power produced from the aggregate of natural rights, imperfect in power in the individual, cannot be applied to invade the natural rights which are retained in the individual, and in which the power to execute is as perfect as the right itself.

We have now, in a few words, traced man from a natural individual to a member of society, and shown, or endeavored to show, the quality of the natural rights retained, and of those which are exchanged for civil rights. Let us now apply these principles to governments....

From the Revolutions of America and France, and the symptoms that have appeared in other countries, it is evident that the opinion of the world is changing with respect to systems of Government, and that revolutions are not within the compass of political calculations. The progress of time and circumstances, which men assign to the accomplishment of great changes, is too mechanical to measure the force of the mind, and the rapidity of reflection, by which revolutions are generated: All the old governments have received a shock from those that already appear, and which were once more improbable, and are a greater subject of wonder, than a general revolution in Europe would be now.

When we survey the wretched condition of man, under the monarchical and hereditary systems of Government, dragged from his home by one power, or driven by another, and impoverished by taxes more than by enemies, it becomes evident that those systems are bad, and that a general revolution in the principle and construction of Governments is necessary.

What is government more than the management of the affairs of a Nation? It is not, and from its nature cannot be, the property of any particular man or family, but of the whole community, at whose expense it is supported; and though by force and contrivance it has been usurped into an inheritance, the usurpation cannot alter the right of things. Sovereignty, as a matter of right, appertains to the Nation only, and not to any individual; and a Nation has at all times an inherent indefensible right to abolish any form of Government it finds inconvenient, and to establish such as accords with its interest, disposition and happiness. The romantic and barbarous distinction of men into Kings and subjects, though it may suit the condition of courtiers, cannot that of citizens; and is exploded by the principle upon which Governments are now founded. Every citizen is a member of the Sovereignty, and, as such, can acknowledge no personal subjection; and his obedience can be only to the laws.

When men think of what Government is, they must necessarily suppose it to possess a knowledge of all the objects and matters upon which its authority is to be exercised. In this view of Government, the republican system, as established by America and France, operates to embrace the whole of a Nation; and the knowledge necessary to the interest of all the parts is to be found in the center, which the parts by representation form: But the old Governments are on a construction that excludes knowledge as well as happiness; Government by Monks, who knew nothing of the world beyond the walls of a Convent, is as consistent as government by Kings.

What were formerly called Revolutions were little more than a change of persons, or an alteration of local circumstances. They rose and fell like things of course, and had nothing in their existence or their fate that could influence beyond the spot that produced them. But what we now see in the world, from the Revolutions of America and France, are a renovation of the natural order of things, a system of principles as universal as truth and the existence of man, and combining moral with political happiness and national prosperity.

"I. *Men are born, and always continue, free and equal in respect of their rights. Civil distinctions, therefore, can be founded only on public utility.*

"II. *The end of all political associations is the preservation of the natural and imprescriptible rights of man; and these rights are liberty, property, security, and resistance of oppression.*

"III. *The nation is essentially the source of all sovereignty; nor can any* INDIVIDUAL, *or* ANY BODY OF MEN, *be entitled to any authority which is not expressly derived from it.*"

In these principles, there is nothing to throw a Nation into confusion by inflaming ambition. They are calculated to call forth wisdom and abilities, and to exercise them for the public good, and not for the emolument or aggrandisement of particular descriptions of men or families. Monarchical sovereignty, the enemy of mankind, and the source of misery, is abolished; and the sovereignty itself is restored to its natural and original place, the Nation. Were this the case throughout Europe, the cause of wars would be taken away.

It is attributed to Henry the Fourth of France, a man of enlarged and benevolent heart, that he proposed, about the year 1610, a plan for abolishing war in Europe. The plan consisted in constituting an European Congress, or as the French authors style it, a Pacific Republic; by appointing delegates from the several Nations who were to act as a Court of arbitration in any disputes that might arise between nation and nation.

Had such a plan been adopted at the time it was proposed, the taxes of England and France, as two of the parties, would have been at least ten millions sterling annually to each Nation less than they were at the commencement of the French Revolution.

To conceive a cause why such a plan has not been adopted (and that instead of a Congress for the purpose of *preventing* war, it has been called only to *terminate* a war, after a fruitless expense of several years) it will be necessary to consider the interest of Governments as a distinct interest to that of Nations.

Whatever is the cause of taxes to a Nation, becomes also the means of revenue to Government. Every war terminates with an addition of taxes, and consequently with an addition of revenue; and in any event of war, in the manner they are now commenced and concluded, the power and interest of Governments are increased. War, therefore, from its productiveness, as it easily furnishes the pretense of necessity for taxes and appointments to places and offices, becomes a principal part of the system of old Governments; and to establish any mode to abolish war, however advantageous it might be to Nations, would be to take from such Government the most lucrative of its branches. The frivolous matters upon which war is made, show the disposition and avidity of Governments to uphold the system of war, and betray the motives upon which they act.

Why are not Republics plunged into war, but because the nature of their Government does not admit of an interest distinct from that of the Nation? Even Holland, though an ill-constructed Republic, and with a commerce extending over the world, existed nearly a century without war: and the instant the form of Government was changed in France, the republican principles of peace and domestic prosperity and economy arose with the new Government; and the same consequences would follow the cause in other Nations.

As war is the system of Government on the old construction, the animosity which Nations reciprocally entertain, is nothing more than what the policy of their Governments excites to keep up the spirit of the system. Each Government accuses the other of perfidy, intrigue, and ambition, as a means of heating the imagination of their respective Nations, and incensing them to hostilities. Man is not the enemy of man, but through the medium of a false system of Government. Instead, therefore, of exclaiming against the ambition of Kings, the exclamation should be directed against the principle of such Governments; and instead of seeking to reform the individual, the wisdom of a Nation should apply itself to reform the system.

Whether the forms and maxims of Governments which are still in practice, were adapted to the condition of the world at the period they were established, is not in this case the question. The older they are, the less correspondence can they have with the present state of things. Time, and change of circumstances and opinions, have the same progressive effect in rendering modes of Government obsolete as they have upon customs and manners. Agriculture, commerce, manufactures, and the tranquil arts, by which the prosperity of Nations is best promoted, require a different system of Government, and a different species of knowledge to direct its operations, than what might have been required in the former condition of the world.

As it is not difficult to perceive, from the enlightened state of mankind, that hereditary Governments are verging to their decline, and that Revolutions on the broad basis of national sovereignty and Government by representation, are making their way in Europe, it would be an act of wisdom to anticipate their approach, and produce Revolutions by reason and accommodation, rather than commit them to the issue of convulsions.

From what we now see, nothing of reform in the political world ought to be held improbable. It is an age of Revolutions, in which everything may be looked for. The intrigue of Courts, by which the system of war is kept up, may provoke a confederation of Nations to abolish it and an European Congress to patronize the progress of free Government, and promote the civilization of Nations with each other, is an event nearer in probability, than once were the revolutions and alliance of France and America.

6.10 MAXIMILIEN DE ROBESPIERRE "ON REVOLUTIONARY GOVERNMENT" (1793)[1]

Citizen Representatives of the People,

… We shall first outline the principles and the needs underlying the creation of a revolutionary government; next we shall expound the cause that threatens to throttle it at birth.

The theory of revolutionary government is as new as the Revolution that created it. It is as pointless to seek its origins in the books of the political theorists, who failed to foresee this revolution, as in the laws of the tyrants, who are happy enough to abuse their exercise of authority without seeking out its legal justification. And so this phrase is for the aristocracy a mere subject of terror or a term of slander, for tyrants an outrage and for many an enigma. It behooves us to explain it to all in order that we may rally good citizens, at least, in support of the principles governing the public interest.

It is the function of government to guide the moral and physical energies of the nation toward the purposes for which it was established. The object of constitutional government is to preserve the Republic; the object of revolutionary government is to establish it.

Revolution is the war waged by liberty against its enemies; a constitution is that which crowns the edifice of freedom once victory has been won and the nation is at peace.

The revolutionary government has to summon extraordinary activity to its aid precisely because it is at war. It is subjected to less binding and less uniform regulations, because the circumstances in which it finds itself are tempestuous and shifting, above all because it is compelled to deploy, swiftly and incessantly, new resources to meet new and pressing dangers.

The principal concern of constitutional government is civil liberty; that of revolutionary government, public liberty. Under a constitutional government little more is required than to protect the individual against abuses by the state, whereas revolutionary government is obliged to defend the state itself against the factions that assail it from every quarter.

To good citizens revolutionary government owes the full protection of the state; to the enemies of the people it owes only death.

These ideas are in themselves sufficient to explain the origin and the nature of the laws that we term revolutionary. Those who call them arbitrary or tyrannical are foolish or perverse sophists who seek to reconcile white with black and black with white: they prescribe the same system for peace and war, for health and sickness; or rather their only object is to resurrect tyranny and to destroy the fatherland. When they invoke the literal application of constitutional principles, it is only to violate them with impunity. They are cowardly assassins who, in order to strangle the Republic in its infancy without danger to themselves, try to throttle it with vague maxims which they have no intention of observing....

The task of firmly establishing the French Republic is not a child's game. It cannot be the work of indifference or idle fancy, nor can it be the chance outcome of the impact of all the rival claims of individuals or of all the revolutionary interests and groups. It took wisdom as well as power to create the universe. By handing over to men drawn from your own ranks the formidable task of continuously watching over the destinies of France, you have assumed the obligation of lending them the full support of your confidence and strength. If the revolutionary government is not sustained by the energy, intelligence, patriotism and good will of all the people's representatives, how will it summon up the strength to meet and defeat that arrayed against it by Europe's invading armies and by all the enemies of liberty who are pressing in on every side?

Woe unto us if we open our minds to the treacherous insinuations of our enemies, whose only hope of victory lies in our division. Woe unto us if we break the bond of union instead of knitting it more closely and if we allow private interest or injured vanity to guide us rather than fatherland and truth.

Thanks to five years of treason and tyranny, thanks to our credulity and lack of foresight and to the pusillanimity that followed too brief an exercise of vigor, Austria and England, Russia, Prussia and Italy have had time to set up in our country a secret government to challenge the authority of our own. They have also their committees, their treasury and their undercover agents. This government assumes whatever strength we deny to ours; it has the unity which ours has lacked, the policies that we have been too often willing to forego, the sense of continuity and concert whose need we have too often failed to appreciate....

With these aims in view, we propose the following decree:[2]

The National Convention decrees: ...

Article II.   The Committee of Public Safety shall, without delay, present its report on the means proposed to improve the organization of the Revolutionary Tribunal.

Article III.   The benefits and rewards granted by earlier decrees to the defenders of the country wounded in its defense, or to their widows or children, are increased by one third.

Article IV.   There shall be established a commission with the task of assuring to them the enjoyment of the rights provided by the law....

[1] December 4, 1793

[2] The proposed decree has been adopted by the National Convention.

6.11   IMMANUAL KANT: ON REPUBLICAN PEACE AND INTERNATIONAL LAW (*PERPETUAL PEACE*, 1795)

First Definitive Article of a Perpetual Peace:

The Civil Constitution of Every State Shall Be Republican.

A *republican constitution* is founded upon three principles: firstly, the principle of *freedom* for all members of a society (as men); secondly, the principle of the *dependence* of everyone upon a single common legislation (as subjects); and thirdly, the principle of legal *equality* for everyone (as citizens). It is the only constitution which can be derived from the idea of an original contract, upon which all rightful legislation of a people must be founded. Thus as far as right is concerned, republicanism is in itself the original basis of every kind of civil constitution, and it only remains to ask whether it is the only constitution which can lead to a perpetual peace.

The republican constitution is not only pure in its origin (since it springs from the pure concept of right); it also offers a prospect of attaining the desired result, i.e. a perpetual peace, and the reason for this is as follows—If, as is inevitably the case under this constitution, the consent of the citizens is required to decide whether or not war is to be declared, it is very natural that they will have great hesitation in embarking on so dangerous an enterprise. For this would mean calling down on themselves all the miseries of war, such as doing the fighting themselves, supplying the costs of the war from their own resources, painfully making good the ensuing devastation, and, as the crowning evil, having to take upon themselves a burden of debt which will embitter peace itself and which can never be paid off on account of the constant threat of new wars. But under a constitution where the subject is not a citizen, and which is therefore not republican, it is the simplest thing in the world to go to war. For the head of state is not a fellow citizen, but the owner of the state, and a war will not force him to make the slightest sacrifice so far as his banquets, hunts, pleasure palaces and court festivals are concerned. He can thus decide on war, without any significant reason, as a kind of amusement, and unconcernedly leave it to the diplomatic corps (who are always ready for such purposes) to justify the war for the sake of propriety....

6.12   IMMANUAL KANT: ON REPUBLICAN PEACE AND INTERNATIONAL LAW (*THE METAPHYSICS OF MORALS*, 1797)

Section I. The Right of a State

§46

The legislative power can belong only to the united will of the people. For since all right is supposed to emanate from this power, the laws it gives must be absolutely incapable of doing anyone an injustice. Now if someone makes dispositions for another person, it is always possible that he may thereby do him an injustice, although this is never possible in the case of decisions he makes for himself (for *volenti non fit iniuria*). Thus only the unanimous and combined will of everyone whereby each decides the same for all and all decide the same for each — in other words, the general united will of the people — can legislate.

The members of such a society (*societas civilis*) or state who unite for the purpose of legislating are known as *citizens* (*cives*), and the three rightful attributes which are inseparable from the nature of a citizen as such are as follows: firstly, lawful *freedom* to obey no law other than that to which he has given his consent; secondly, civil *equality* in recognizing no-one among the people as superior to himself, unless it be someone whom he is just as morally entitled to bind by law as the other is to bind him; and thirdly, the attribute of civil *independence* which allows him to owe his existence and sustenance not to the arbitrary will of anyone else among the people, but purely to his own rights and powers as a member of the commonwealth (so that he may not, as a civil personality, be represented by anyone else in matters of right).

Fitness to vote is the necessary qualification which every citizen must possess. To be fit to vote, a person must have an independent position among the people. He must therefore be not just a part of the commonwealth, but a member of it; i.e. he must by his own free will actively participate in a community of other people. But this latter quality makes it necessary to distinguish between the *active* and the *passive* citizen, although the latter concept seems to contradict the definition of the concept of a citizen altogether. The following examples may serve to overcome this difficulty. Apprentices to merchants or tradesmen, servants who are not employed by the state, minors (*naturaliter vel civiliter*), women in general and all those who are obliged to depend for their living (i.e. for food and protection) on the offices of others (excluding the state) — all of these people have no civil personality, and their existence is, to speak, purely inherent. The woodcutter whom I employ on my premises; the blacksmith in India who goes from house to house with his hammer, anvil and bellows to do work with iron, as opposed to the European carpenter or smith who can put the products of his work up for public sale; the domestic tutor as opposed to the academic, the tithe-holder as opposed to the farmer; and so on — they are all mere auxiliaries to the commonwealth, for they have to receive orders or protection from other individuals, so that they do not possess civil independence.

This dependence upon the will of others and consequent inequality does not, however, in any way conflict with the freedom and equality of all men as *human beings* who together constitute a people. On the contrary, it is only by accepting these conditions that such a people can become a state and enter into a civil constitution. But all are not equally qualified within this constitution to possess the right to vote, i.e. to be citizens and not just subjects among other subjects. For from the fact that as passive members of the state, they can demand to be treated by all others in accordance with laws of natural freedom and equality, it does not follow that they also have a right to influence or organize the state itself as active members, or to co-operate in introducing particular laws. Instead, it only means that the positive laws to which the voters agree, of whatever sort they may be, must not be at variance with the natural laws of freedom and with the corresponding equality of all members of the people whereby they are allowed to work their way up from their passive condition to an active one....

§ 47
B

Can the sovereign be regarded as the supreme proprietor of the land, or must he be regarded only as one who exercises supreme command over the people by means of laws? Since the land is the ultimate condition under which it is alone possible to possess external objects as one's own, while the possession and use of such objects in turn constitutes the primary hereditary right, all such rights must be derived from the sovereign as *lord of the land*, or rather as the supreme proprietor (*dominus territorii*). The people, as a mass of subjects, also belong to him (i.e. they are his people), although they do not belong to him as an owner by the right of property, but as a supreme commander by the right of persons.

But this supreme ownership is only an idea of the civil union, designed to represent through concepts of right the need to unite the private property of all members of the people under a universal public owner; for this makes it possible to define particular ownership by means of the necessary formal principle of *distribution* (division of the land), rather than by principles of *aggregation* (which proceeds empirically from the parts to the whole). The principles of right require that the supreme proprietor should not possess any land as private property (otherwise he would become a private person), for all land belongs exclusively to the people (not collectively, but distributively). Nomadic peoples, however, would be an exception to this rule, for they do not have any private property in the shape of land. Thus the supreme commander cannot own any *domains*, i.e. land reserved for his private use or for the maintenance of his court. For since the extent of his lands would then depend on his own discretion, the state would run the risk of finding all landed property in the hands of the government, and all the subjects would be treated as serfs bound to the soil (*glebae adscripti*) or holders of what always remained the property of someone else; they would consequently appear devoid of all freedom (*servi*). One can thus say of a lord of the land that he *possesses nothing* of his own (except his own person). For if he owned something on equal terms with anyone else in the state, he could conceivably come into conflict with this other person without there being any judge to settle it. But it can also be said that he *possesses everything*, because he has the right to exercise command over the people, to whom all external objects (*divisim*) belong, and to give each person whatever is his due.

It follows from this that there can be no corporation, class or order within the state which may as an owner hand down land indefinitely, by appropriate statues, for the exclusive use of subsequent generations. The state can at all times repeal such statutes, with the one condition that it must compensate those still alive. The *order of knights* (either as a corporation or simply as a class of eminently distinguished individual persons) and the *order of the clergy* (i.e., the church) can never acquire ownership of land to pass on their successors by virtue of the privileges with which they have been favored; they may acquire only the temporary use of it....

C

Indirectly, i.e. in so far as he takes the duty of the people upon himself, the supreme commander has the right to impose taxes upon the people for their own preservation, e.g. for the *care of the poor*, for *foundling hospitals* and *church activities*, or for what are otherwise known as charitable or pious institutions.

For the general will of the people has united to form a society which must constantly maintain itself, and to this end, it has subjected itself to the internal power of the state so as to preserve those members of the society who cannot do so themselves. The nature of the state thus justifies the government in compelling prosperous citizens to provide the means of preserving those who are unable to provide themselves with even the most rudimentary necessities of nature. For since their existence itself is an act of submission to the protection of the commonwealth and to the care it must give them to enable them to live, they have committed themselves in such a way that the state has a right to make them contribute their share to maintaining their fellow citizens. This may be done by taxing the citizens' property or their commercial transactions, or by instituting funds and using the interest from them — not for the needs of the state (for it is rich), but for the needs of the people. The contributions should not be *purely* voluntary (for we are here concerned only with the *rights* of the state as against subjects), they must in fact be compulsory political impositions. Some voluntary contributions such as lotteries, which are made from profit-seeking motives, should not be permitted, since they create greater than usual numbers of poor who become a danger to public property.

It might at this point be asked whether the poor ought to be provided for by *current contributions* so that each generation would support its own members, or by gradually accumulated *capital funds* and *pious foundations* at large (such as widows' homes, hospitals, etc.). Funds must certainly not be raised by begging, which has close affinities with robbery, but by lawful taxation. The first arrangement (that of current contributions) must be considered the only one appropriate to the rights of the state, for no-one who wishes to be sure of his livelihood can be exempt from it. These contributions increase with the numbers of poor, and they do not make poverty a means of support for the indolent (as is to be feared in the case of pious foundations), so that the government need not impose an *unjust* burden on the people.

As for the support of the children abandoned through need or through shame (and who may even be murdered for such reasons), the state has a right to make it a duty for the people not to let them perish knowingly, even although they are an unwelcome increase to the state's population. But whether this can justly be done by taxing bachelors of both sexes (i.e. single person of *means*) as a class which is partly responsible for the situation, using the proceeds to set up foundling hospitals, or whether any other method is preferable (although it is scarcely likely that any means of preventing the evil can be found) — this is a problem which has not yet been successfully solved without prejudice to right or to morality....

Section II: International Right

§53

The human beings who make up a nation can, as natives of the country, be represented as analogous to descendants from a common ancestry (*congeniti*) even if this is not in fact the case. But in an intellectual sense or for the purposes of right, they can be thought of as the offspring of a common mother (the republic), constituting, as it were, a single family (*gens, natio*) whose members (the citizens) are all equal by birth. These citizens will not intermix with any neighboring people who live in a state of nature, but will consider them ignoble, even though such savages for their own part may regard themselves as superior on account of the lawless freedom they have chosen. The latter likewise constitute national groups, but they do not constitute states.

What we are now about to consider under the name of international right or the right of nations is the right of *states* in relation to another (although it is not strictly correct to speak, as we usually do, of the *right of nations*; it should rather be called the *right of states — ius publicum civitatum*). The situation in question is that in which one state, as a moral person, is considered as existing in a state of nature in relation to another state, hence in a condition of constant war. International right is thus concerned partly with the right to make war, partly with the right of war itself, and partly with questions of right after a war, i.e. with the right of states to compel each other to abandon their warlike condition and to create a constitution which will establish an enduring peace. A state of nature among individuals or families (in their relations with one another) is different from a state of nature among entire nations, because international right involves not only the relationship between one state and another within a larger whole, but also the relation-ship between individual persons in one state and individuals in the other or between such individuals and the other state as a whole. But this difference between international right and the right of individuals in a mere state of nature is easily deducible from the latter concept without need of any further definitions.

§ 54

The elements of international right are as follows. Firstly, in their external relationships with one another, states, like lawless savages, exist in a condition devoid of right. Secondly, this *condition* is one of war (the right of the stronger), even if there is no actual war or continuous active fighting (i.e. hostilities). But even although neither of two states is done any injustice by the other in this condition, it is nevertheless in the highest degree unjust in itself, for it implies that neither wishes to experience anything better. Adjacent states are thus bound to abandon such a condition. Thirdly, it is necessary to establish a federation of peoples in accordance with the idea of an original social contract, so that states will protect one another against external aggression while refraining from interference in one-another internal disagreements. And fourthly, this association must not embody a sovereign power as in a civil constitution, but only a partnership or *confederation*. It must therefore be an alliance which can be terminated at any time, so that it has to be renewed periodically. This right is derived *in subsidium* from another original right, that of preventing oneself from lapsing into a state of actual war with one's partners in the confederation (*foedus Amphictyonum*).

§ 55

If we consider the original right of free states in the state of nature to make war upon one another (for example, in order to bring about a condition closer to that governed by right), we must first ask what right the state has *as against its own subjects* to employ them in a war on other states, and to expend or hazard their possessions or even their lives in the process. Does it not then depend upon their own judgment whether they wish to go to war or not? May they simply be sent thither at the sovereign's supreme-command?

This right might seem an obvious consequence of the right to do what one wishes with one's own property. Whatever someone has himself substantially *made* is his own undisputed property. These are the premises from which a mere jurist would deduce the right in question.

A country may yield various *natural products*, some of which, because of their very *abundance*, must also be regarded as *artifacts* of the state. For the country would not yield them in such quantities if there were no state or proper government in control and if the inhabitants still lived in a state of nature. For example, domestic poultry (the most useful kind of fowl), sheep, pigs, cattle, etc. would be completely unknown in the country I live in (or would only rarely be encountered) if there were no government to guarantee the inhabitants their acquisitions and possessions. The same applies to the number of human beings, for there can only be few of them in a state of nature, as in the wilds of America, even if we credit them with great industry (which they do not have). The inhabitants would be very sparsely scattered, for no-one could spread very far a field with his household in a land constantly threatened with devastation by other human beings, wild animals, or beasts of prey. There would thus be no adequate support for so large a population as now inhabits a country.

Now one can say that vegetables (e.g. potatoes) and domestic animals, in quantity at least, are *made* by human beings, and that they may therefore be used, expended or consumed (i.e. killed) at will. One might therefore appear justified in saying that the supreme power in the state, the sovereign, has the right to lead his subjects to war as if on a hunt, or into battle as if on an excursion, simply because they are for the most part produced by the sovereign himself.

But while this legal argument (of which monarchs are no doubt dimly aware) is certainly valid in the case of animals, which can be the *property* of human beings, it is absolutely impermissible to apply it to human beings themselves, particularly in their capacity as citizens. For a citizen must always be regarded as a co-legislative member of the state (i.e. not just as a means, but also as an end in himself), and he must therefore give his free consent through his representatives not only to the waging of war in general, but also to every particular declaration of war. Only under this limiting condition may the state put him to service in dangerous enterprises.

We shall therefore have to derive the right under discussion from the *duty* of the sovereign towards the people, not vice versa. The people must be seen to have given their consent to military action, and although they remain passive in this capacity (for they allow themselves to be directed) they are still acting spontaneously and they represent the sovereign himself.

§ 56

In the state of nature, the *right to make war* (i.e. to enter into hostilities) is the permitted means by which one state prosecutes its rights against another. Thus if a state believes that it has been injured by another state, it is entitled to resort to violence, for it cannot in the state of nature gain satisfaction through *legal proceedings*, the only means of settling disputes in a state governed by right. Apart from an actively inflicted injury (the first aggression, as distinct from the first hostilities), a state may be subjected to *threats*. Such threats may arise if another state is the first to make *military preparations*, on which the right of *anticipatory attack* (*ius praeventionis*) is based, or simply if there is an alarming increase of power (*potentia tremenda*) in another state which has acquired new territories. This is an injury to the less powerful state by the mere fact that the other state, even without offering any active offense, is *more powerful*; and any attack upon it is legitimate in the state of nature. On this is based the right to maintain a balance of power among all states which have active contact with one another.

Those *active injuries* which give a state the *right to make war* on another state include any unilateral attempt to gain satisfaction for an affront which the people of one state have offered to the people of the other. Such an act of *retribution* (*retorsio*) without any attempt to obtain compensation from the other state by peaceful means is similar in form to starting war without prior declaration. For if one wishes to find any rights in wartime, one must assume the existence of something analogous to a contract; in other words, one must assume that the other party has *accepted* the declaration of war and that both parties therefore wish to prosecute their rights in this manner.

§ 57

The most problematic task in international right is that of determining rights in wartime. For it is very difficult to form any conception at all of such rights and to imagine any law whatsoever in this lawless state without involving oneself in contradictions (*inter arma silent leges*). The only possible solution would be to conduct the war in accordance with principles which would still leave the states with the possibility of abandoning the state of nature in their external relations and of entering a state of right.

No war between independent states can be a *punitive* one (*bellum punitivum*). For a punishment can only occur in a relationship between a superior (*imperantis*) and a subject (*subditum*), and this is not the relationship which exists between states. Nor can there be a *war of extermination* (*bellum internecium*) or a *war of subjugation* (*bellum subiugatorium*); for these would involve the moral annihilation of a state, and its people would either merge with those of the victorious state or be reduced to bondage. Not that this expedient, which a state might resort in order to obtain peace, would in itself contradict the rights of a state. But the fact remains that the only concept of antagonism which the idea of international right includes is that of an antagonism regulated by principles of external freedom. This requires that violence be used only to preserve one's existing property, but not as a method of further acquisition; for the latter procedure would create a threat to one state by augmenting the power of another.

The attacked state is allowed to use any means of defense except those whose use would render its subjects unfit to be citizens. For if it did not observe this condition, it would render itself unfit in the eyes of international right to function as a person in relation to other states and to share equal rights with them. It must accordingly be prohibited for a state to use its own subjects as spies, and to use them, or indeed foreigners, as poisoners or assassins (to which class the so-called sharpshooters who wait in ambush on individual victims also belong), or even just to spread false reports. In short, a state must not use such treacherous methods as would destroy that confidence which is required for the future establishment of a lasting peace.

It is permissible in war to impose levies and contributions on the conquered enemy, but not to plunder the people, i.e. to force individual persons to part with their belongings (for this would be robbery, since it was not the conquered people who waged the war, but the state of which they were subjects which waged it *through them*). Bills of receipt should be issued for any contributions that are exacted, so that the burden imposed on the country or province can be distributed proportionately when peace is concluded.

§ 58

The right which applies *after* a war, i.e. with regard to the peace treaty at the time of its conclusion and also to its later consequences, consists of the following elements. The victor sets out the conditions, and these are drawn up in a *treaty* on which agreement is reached with the defeated party in order that peace may be concluded. A treaty of this kind is not determined by any pretended right which the victors possesses over his opponent because of an alleged injury the latter has done him; the victor should not concern himself with such questions, but should rely only on his own power for support. Thus he cannot claim compensation for the costs of war, for he would then have to pronounce his opponent unjust in waging it. And even if this argument should occur to him, he could not make use of it, or else he would have to maintain that the war was a punitive one, which would in turn mean that he had committed an offense in waging it himself. A peace treaty should also provide for the exchange of prisoners without ransom, whether the numbers on both sides are equal or not.

The vanquished state and its subjects cannot forfeit their civil freedom through the conquest of the country. Consequently, the former cannot be degraded to the rank of a colony or the latter to the rank of bondsmen. Otherwise, the war would have been a punitive one, which is self-contradictory.

A *colony* or province is a nation which has its own constitution, legislation and territory, and all members of any other state are no more than foreigners on its soil, even if the state to which they belong has supreme *executive* power over the colonial nation. The state with executive power is called the *mother state*. The daughter state is *ruled* by it, although it *governs* itself through its own parliament, which in turn functions under the presidency of a viceroy (*civitas hybrida*). The relationship of Athens to various islands was of this kind, as is that of Great Britain towards Ireland at the present moment.

It is even less possible to infer the rightful existence of *slavery* from the military conquest of a people, for one would then have to assume that the war had been a punitive one. Least of all would this justify hereditary slavery, which is completely absurd, for the guilt of a person's crime cannot be inherited.

It is implicit in the very concept of a peace treaty that it includes an *amnesty*.

§ 59

The *rights of peace* are as follows: firstly, the right to remain at peace when nearby states are at war (i.e. the right of *neutrality*); secondly, the right to secure the continued maintenance of peace once it has been concluded (i.e. the right of *guarantee*); and thirdly, the right to form *alliances* or confederate leagues of several states for the purpose of communal defense against any possible attacks from internal or external sources — although these must never become leagues for promoting aggression and internal expansion.

§ 60

The rights of a state against an *unjust enemy* are unlimited in quantity or degree, although they do have limits in relation to quality. In other words, while the threatened state may not employ *every* means to assert its own rights, it may employ an intrinsically permissible means to whatever degree its own strength allows. But what can the expression of "an unjust enemy" mean in relation to the concepts of international right, which requires that every state should act as judge of its own cause just as it would do in a state of nature? It must mean someone whose publicly expressed will, whether expressed in word or in deed, displays a maxim which would make peace among nations impossible and would lead to a perpetual state of nature if it were made into a general rule. Under this heading would come violations of public contracts, which can be assumed to affect the interests of all nations. For they are a threat to their freedom, and a challenge to them to unite

against such misconduct and to deprive the culprit of the power to act in a similar way again. But this does *not* entitle them to *divide up the offending state among themselves* and to make it disappear, as it were, from the face of the earth. For this would be an injustice against the people, who cannot lose their original right to unite into a commonwealth. They can only be made to accept a new constitution of nature that is unlikely to encourage their warlike inclinations.

Besides, the expression "an unjust enemy" is a *pleonasm* if applied to any situation in a state of nature, for this state is itself one of injustice. A just enemy would be one whom I could not resist without injustice. But if this were so, he would not be my enemy in any case.

§ 61

Since the state of nature among nations (as among individual human beings) is a state which one ought to abandon in order to enter a state governed by law, all international rights, as well as all the external property of states such as can be acquired or preserved by war, are purely *provisional* until the state of nature has been abandoned. Only within a universal *union of states* (analogous to the union through which a nation becomes a state) can such rights and property acquire *peremptory* validity and a true *state of peace* be attained. But if an international state of this kind extends over too wide an area of land, it will eventually become impossible to govern it and thence to protect each of its members, and the multitude of corporations this would require must again lead to a state of war. It naturally follows that *perpetual peace*, the ultimate end of all international alliances designed to *approach* the idea itself by a continual process, are not impracticable. For this is a project based upon duty, hence also upon the rights of man and of states, and it can indeed be put into execution.

Such a *union of several states* designed to preserve peace may be called a *permanent congress of states*, and all neighboring states are free to join it. A congress of this very kind (at least as far as the formalities of international right in relation to the preservation of peace are concerned) found expression in the assembly of the States General at The Hague in the first half of this century. To this assembly, the ministers of most European courts and even of the smallest republics brought their complaints about any aggression suffered by one of their number at the hands of another. They thus thought of all Europe as a single federated state, which they accepted as an arbiter in all their public disputes. Since then, however, international right has disappeared from cabinets, surviving only in books, or it has been consigned to the obscurity of the archives as a form of empty deduction after violent measures have already been employed.

In the present context, however, a *congress* merely signifies a voluntary gathering of various states which can be *dissolved* at any time, not an association which, like that of the American states, is based on a political constitution and is therefore indissoluble. For this is the only means of realizing the idea of public international right as it ought to be instituted, thereby enabling the nations to settle their disputes in a civilized manner by legal proceedings, not in a barbaric manner (like that of the savages) by acts of war.

Section III: Cosmopolitan Right

§ 62

The rational idea, as discussed above, of a *peaceful* (if not exactly amicable) international community of all those of the earth's peoples who can enter into active relations with one another, is not a philanthropic principle of ethics, but a principle of *right*. Through the spherical shape of the planet they inhabit (*globus terraqueus*), nature has confided them all within an area of definite limits. Accordingly, the only conceivable way in which anyone can possess habitable land on earth is by possessing a part within a determinate whole in which everyone has an original right to share. Thus all nations are *originally* members of a community of the land. But this is not a *legal community* of possession (*communio*) and utilization of the land, nor a community of ownership. It is a community of reciprocal action (*commercium*) which is physically possible, and each member of it accordingly has constant relations with all the others. Each may offer to have commerce with the rest, and they all have a right to make such overtures without being treated by foreigners as enemies. This right, in so far as it affords the prospect that all nations may unite for the purpose of creating certain universal laws to regulate the intercourse they may have with one another, may be termed *cosmopolitan* (*ius cosmopoliticum*).

The oceans may appear to cut nations off from the community of their fellows. But with the art of navigation, they constitute the greatest natural incentive to international commerce, and the greater the number of neighboring coastlines there are (as in the Mediterranean), the livelier this commerce will be. Yet these visits to foreign shores, and even more so, attempts to settle on them with a view to linking them with the motherland, can also occasion evil and violence in one part of the globe with ensuing repercussions which are felt everywhere else. But although such abuses are possible, they do not deprive the world's citizens of the right to *attempt* to enter into a community with everyone else and to visit all regions of the earth with this intention. This does not, however, amount to a right to settle on another nation's territory (*ius incolatus*), for the latter would require a special contract.

But one might ask whether a nation may establish a *settlement alongside another nation* (*accolatus*) in newly discovered regions, or whether it may take possession of land in the vicinity of a nation which has already settled in the same area, even without the latter's consent. The answer is that the right to do so is incontestable, so long as such settlements are established sufficiently far away from the territory of the original nation for neither party to interfere with the other in their use of the land. But if the nations involved are pastoral or hunting peoples (like the Hottentots, the Tunguses, and most native American nations) who rely upon large tracts of wasteland for their sustenance, settlements should not be established by violence, but only by treaty; and even then, there must be no attempt to exploit the ignorance of the natives in persuading them to give up their territories. Nevertheless, there are plausible enough arguments for the use of violence on the grounds that it is in the best interests of the world as a whole. For on the one hand, it may bring culture to uncivilized peoples (this is the excuse with which even Busching tries to extenuate the bloodshed which accompanied the introduction of Christianity into Germany); and on the other, it may help us to purge our country of depraved characters, at the same time affording the hope that they or their offspring will become reformed in another continent (as in New Holland). But all these supposedly good intentions cannot wash away the stain of injustice from the means which are used to implement them. Yet one might object that the whole world would perhaps still be in a lawless condition if men had had any such compunction about using violence when they first created a law-governed state. But this can as little annul the above condition of right as can the plea of political revolutionaries that the people are entitled to reform constitutions by force if they have become corrupt, and to act completely unjustly for once and for all, in order to put justice on a more secure basis and ensure that it flourishes in the future.

Conclusion

If a person cannot prove that a thing exists, he may attempt to prove that it does not exist. If neither approach succeeds (as often happens), he may still ask whether it is in *his interest to assume* one or other possibility as a hypothesis, either from theoretical or from practical considerations. In other words, he may wish on the one hand simply to explain a certain phenomenon (as the astronomer, for example, may wish to explain the sporadic movements of the planets), or on the other, to achieve a certain end which may itself be either *pragmatic* (purely technical) or *moral* (i.e., an end which it is our duty to take as a maxim). It is, of course, self-evident that no-one is duty-bound to make an *assumption* (*supposition*) that the end in question can be realized, since this would involve a purely theoretical and indeed problematic judgment; for no-one can be obliged to accept a given belief. But we can have a duty to act in accordance with the idea of such an end, even if there is not the slightest theoretical probability of its realization, provided that there is no means of demonstrating that it cannot be realized either.

Now, moral-practical reason within us pronounces the following irresistible veto: *There shall be no war*, either between individual human beings in the state of nature, or between separate states, which, although internally law-governed, still live in a lawless condition in their external relationships with one another. For war is not the way in which anyone should pursue his rights. Thus it is

no longer a question of whether perpetual peace is really possible or not, or whether we are not perhaps mistaken in our theoretical judgment if we assume that it is. On the contrary, we must simply act as if it could really come about which is perhaps impossible, and turn our efforts towards realizing it and towards establishing that constitution which seems most suitable for this purpose (perhaps that of republicanism in all states, individually and collectively). By working towards this end, we may hope to terminate the disastrous practices of war, which up till now has been the main object to which all states, without exception, have accommodated their internal institutions. And even if the fulfillment of this pacific intention were forever to remain a pious hope, we should still not be deceiving ourselves if we made it our maxim to work unceasingly towards it, for it is our duty to do so. To assume, on the other hand, that the moral law within us might be misleading, would give rise to the execrable wish to dispense with all reason and to regard ourselves, along with our principles, as subject to the same mechanism of nature as the other animal species.

It can indeed be said that this task of establishing a universal and lasting peace is not just a part of the theory of right within limits of pure reason, but its entire ultimate purpose. For the condition of peace is the only state in which the property of a large number of people living together as neighbors under a single constitution can be guaranteed by laws. The rule on which this constitution is based must not simply be derived from the experience of those who have hitherto fared best under it, and then set up as a norm for others. On the contrary, it should be derived *a priori* by reason from the absolute ideal of a rightful association of men under public laws. For all particular examples are deceptive (an example can only illustrate a point, but does not prove anything), so that one must have recourse to metaphysics. And even those who scorn metaphysics admit its necessity involuntarily when they say, for example (as they often do): "The best constitution is that in which the power rests with laws instead of with men." For what can be more metaphysically sublime than this idea, although by admission of those who express it, it also has a well-authenticated objective reality which can easily be demonstrated from particular instances as they arise. But no attempt should be made to put it into practice overnight by revolution, i.e., by forcibly overthrowing a defective constitution which has existed in the past; for there would then be an interval of time during which the condition of right would be nullified. If we try instead to give it reality by means of gradual reforms carried out in accordance with definite principles, we shall see that it is the only means of continually approaching the supreme political good — perpetual peace.

CHAPTER 7

Human Rights for Whom?

Those who were marginalized from the political and economic process would eventually challenge their exclusion from prevailing conceptions of universal human rights. Despite Kant's effort to defend universal collective responsibility to protect the needy from economic hardship, he entrusted, in the revolutionary spirit of his time, only "active citizens" — i.e., property-holding males — with the right to vote, as opposed to "passive citizens" — i.e., all females and men without property. The question of who constitutes an active citizen was the subject of great debates and social upheavals throughout the Enlightenment and beyond. The indigenous populations of the European colonies, African slaves, the propertyless, women, Jews (among other religious minorities), and their defenders would demand their full-fledged rights under the transforming rainbow of universalism.

The fate of Native Americans had already alarmed a Spanish Dominican missionary in the Americas, Bartolomé de Las Casas (1474–1566), the first European to expose the oppression of the Indians by the Europeans, as he called for the abolition of Indian slavery. In his *Defense of the Indians* (c. 1548), addressed to Charles V, the emperor of Spain, Las Casas argued against theologian and royal historian Ginés de Sepúlveda's defense of the enslavement of American Indians. Challenging Sepúlveda's belief that Indians were wicked, he pointed out that "if such a huge part of mankind is barbaric, it would follow that God's design has for the most part been ineffective." Following Aristotelian thought and Evangelical faith, he asserted the ability of all of God's creatures to reason and to be brought gently to Christianity. Las Casas advanced a view of Christianity that supports human emancipation.

The same sentiments prevailed in Hugo Grotius's *The Law of War and Peace* (1625). There, he affirmed the rights of strangers and refugees — rights that would later be embodied in the Universal Declaration of Human Rights and other international legal documents. "It ought to be permissible, for those who pass through a country, by water or by land," wrote Grotius, "to sojourn for a time, for the sake of health, or for any other good reasons." Moreover, "those who have been driven from their homes" have the right to acquire a permanent residence in another country, in submission to the government there (see Section 7.3).

Strangers and refugees, and particularly former slaves, were hardly welcome even in countries like England, known for its relatively liberal laws. Olaudah Equiano, a.k.a. Gustavus Vassa (1745–1797), wrote in *Interesting Narrative* (1789) about his continuing ill treatment both as a former slave and as a stranger on English soil. His ability to convey with eloquence the horrendous condition of slaves on slave ships and plantations, deeply moved a section of English society and helped galvanize the antislavery cause (see Section 7.4).

The case against slavery was also strengthened by the purely economic argument offered by Adam Smith in his *Wealth of Nations* (1776). For Smith, emancipating both slaves and serfs and allowing them to acquire property would increase their productivity. "A slave...who can acquire nothing but his maintenance," explained Smith, "consults his own ease by making the land produce as little as possible over and above that maintenance." With a similar logic, he argued against the tithe (the landlords' tax imposed on serfs to cultivate their lands) as nothing more than a "great hindrance" to productivity (see Section 7.5).

Despite the progress of the French Revolution in this regard, new taxes or property requirements were imposed on male citizens (the only sex eligible to be considered active citizens) as a prerequisite for visiting or holding public office. Maximilien de Robespierre was one of the first during the

Enlightenment to defend universal male suffrage without such a sine qua non. In a speech to the National Convention in September 1791, Robespierre argued that the rights attached to citizens "do not depend on the fortune each man possesses, nor on the amount of tax for which he is assessed, because it is not taxes that make citizens: citizenship merely obliges a man to contribute to public expenditure in proportion to his means" (see Section 7.6).

Robespierre's plea for universal male suffrage was rejected, a fate that also greeted the French playwright and pamphleteer Olympe de Gouge's (1748–1793) earlier quest for women's rights. Gouge had fought for women's rights during the French Revolution, criticizing the French Declaration of the Rights of Man and the Citizen for its exclusion of women's rights and concerns. In her 1790 "Declaration of the Rights of Women," addressed to Queen Marie-Antoinette, whom she had hoped to convert to the women's cause, Gouge asserted women's natural rights as equal to the rights of male citizens enjoyed in the 1789 declaration. At a time in which women were still viewed as passive citizens, dependent socially and economically on men, she added special provisos to protect women (e.g., the requirement that fathers recognize their children, and various other protections to be secured by the state for unmarried women). Opposed to the execution of Louis XVI, she herself was guillotined in 1793.

The English writer Mary Wollstonecraft (1759–1797) brought Gouge's fight to Great Britain. Wollstonecraft's essays in *A Vindication of the Rights of Woman* (1792) were passionate and insightful pleas for educational, social, and political equality for women. Focusing on the limited opportunities afforded middle class women, she deplored their dependence upon their husbands, their acquisition of manners rather than morals, and the requirements that they remain innocent and blindly submit to authority. It was essential for women, explained Wollstonecraft, to strengthen their minds and moral sense of responsibility through public co-education. Like men, they should be exposed to more challenging intellectual and professional activities (including political ones). In short, she concludes: "Make women rational creatures and free citizens, and they will become good wives and mothers; that is, if men do not neglect the duties of husbands and fathers."

The Jews (or at least male Jews) would fare better than women in the law. Amidst heated opposition to the emancipation of Jews, Adrien Duport made a speech to the National Assembly in 1791 to persuade his colleagues that the Jewish question should not be a special issue, particularly after "having declared ... how all peoples of the earth could become French citizens and how all French citizens could become active citizens." Duport's motion to allow Jews to become active citizens was passed on September 27, 1791, making France the first country to emancipate its Jewish population (see Section 7.9).

7.1 UNITED NATIONS UNIVERSAL DECLARATION OF HUMAN RIGHTS (1948): ARTICLES 2 AND 4

Article 2

Everyone is entitled to all the rights and freedoms set forth in this Declaration, without distinction of any kind, such as race, color, sex, language, religion, political or other opinion, national or social origin, property, birth or other status.

Furthermore, no distinction shall be made on the basis of political, jurisdictional or international status of the country or territory to which a person belongs, whether it be independent, non-self-governing or under any other limitation of sovereignty.

Article 4

No one shall be held in slavery or servitude; slavery and the slave trade shall be prohibited in all their forms.

7.2 BARTOLOMÉ DE LAS CASAS
(*IN DEFENSE OF THE INDIANS*, C. 1548)

Illustrious Prince:

... I have thought advisable to bring to the attention of Your Highness that there has come into my hands a certain brief synopsis in Spanish of a work that Ginés de Sepúlveda is reported to have written in Latin. In it he gives four reasons, each of which, in his opinion, proves beyond refutation that war against the Indians is justified, provided that it be waged properly and the laws of war be observed, just as, up to the present, the kings of Spain have commanded that it be waged and carried out....

If Sepúlveda's opinion (that campaigns against the Indians are lawful) is approved, the most holy faith of Christ, to the reproach of the name Christian, will be hateful and detestable to all the peoples of that world to whom the word will come of the inhuman crimes that the Spaniards inflict on that unhappy race, so that neither in our lifetime nor in the future will they want to accept our faith under any condition, for they see that its first heralds are not pastors but plunderers, not fathers but tyrants, and that those who profess it are ungodly, cruel, and without pity in their merciless savagery....

For now, as a sort of assault on the first argument for Sepúlveda's position, we should recognize that there are four kinds of barbarians, according to the Philosopher in Books 1 and 3 of the *Politics* and in Book 7 of the *Ethics*, and according to Saint Thomas and other doctors in various places.

First, barbarian in the loose and broad sense of the word means any cruel, inhuman, wild, and merciless man acting against human reason out of anger or native disposition, so that, putting aside decency, meekness, and humane moderation, he becomes hard, severe, quarrelsome, unbearable, cruel, and plunges blindly into crimes that only the wildest beasts of the forest would commit. Speaking of this kind of barbarian, the Philosopher says in the *Politics* that just as the man who obeys right reason and excellent laws is superior to all the animals, so too, if he leaves the path of right reason and law, he is the wickedest, worst, and most inhuman of all animals.[1]...

Indeed, our Spaniards are not unacquainted with a number of these practices. On the contrary, in the absolutely inhuman things they have done to those nations they have surpassed all other barbarians....

The second kind of barbarian includes those who do not have a written language that corresponds to the spoken one, as the Latin language does with ours, and therefore they do not know how to express in it what they mean. For this reason they are considered to be uncultured and ignorant of letters and learning....

The third kind of barbarian, in the proper and strict meaning of the word, are those who, either because of their evil and wicked character or the barrenness of the region in which they live, are cruel, savage, sottish, stupid, and strangers to reason. They are not governed by law or right, do not cultivate friendships, and have no state or politically organized community. Rather, they are without ruler, laws, and institutions....

Barbarians of this kind (or better, wild men) are rarely found in any part of the world and are few in number when compared with the rest of mankind, as Aristotle notes at the beginning of the seventh book of the *Ethics*. This kind of barbarian is savage, imperfect, and the worst of men, and they are mistakes of nature or freaks in a rational nature....

And since a rational nature is provided for and guided by divine providence for its own sake in a way superior to that of other creatures, not only in what concerns the species but also each individual, it evidently follows that it would be impossible to find in a rational nature such a freak or mistake of nature, that is, one that does not fit the common notion of man, except very rarely and in far fewer instances than in other creatures. For the good and all-powerful God, in his love for mankind, has created all things for man's use and protects him whom he has endowed with so many qualities by a singular affection and care (as we have said), and guides his actions and enlightens each one's mind and disposes him for virtue in accordance with the ability given to him....

Again, if we believe that such a huge part of mankind is barbaric, it would follow that God's design has for the most part been ineffective, with so many thousands of men deprived of the natural light that is common to all peoples. And so there would be a great reduction in the perfection of the entire universe — something that is unacceptable and unthinkable for any Christian....

We find that for the most part men are intelligent, far sighted, diligent, and talented, so that it is impossible for a whole region or country to be slow witted and stupid, moronic, or suffering from similar natural defects or abnormalities....

The Philosopher [Aristotle] adds that it is lawful to catch or hunt barbarians of this type like wild beasts so that they might be led to the right way of life. Two points must be noted here. First, to force barbarians to live in a civilized and human way is not lawful for anyone and everyone, but only for monarchs and the rulers of states. Second, it must be borne in mind that barbarians must not be compelled harshly in the manner described by the Philosopher, but are to be gently persuaded and lovingly drawn to accept the best way of life. For we are commanded by divine law to love our neighbor as ourselves, and since we want our own vices to be corrected and uprooted gently, we should do the same to our brothers, even if they are barbarians....

From Christ, the eternal truth, we have the command "You must love your neighbor as yourself."[2] And again Paul says "Love is not selfish,"[3] but seeks the things of Jesus Christ. Christ seeks souls, not property. He who alone is the immortal king of kings thirsts not for riches, not for ease and pleasures, but for the salvation of mankind, for which, fastened to the wood of the cross, he offered his life. He who wants a large part of mankind to be such that, following Aristotle's teachings, he may act like a ferocious executioner toward them, press them into slavery, and through them grow rich, is a despotic master, not a Christian; a son of Satan, not of God; a plunderer, not a shepherd; a person who is led by the spirit of the devil, not heaven. If you seek Indians so that gently, mildly, quietly, humanely, and in a Christian manner you may instruct them in the word of God and by your labor bring them to Christ's flock, imprinting the gentle Christ on their minds, you perform the work of an apos-

tle and will receive an imperishable crown of glory from our sacrificed lamb. But if it be in order that by sword, fire, massacre, trickery, violence, tyranny, cruelty, and an inhumanity that is worse than barbaric you may destroy and plunder utterly harmless peoples who are ready to renounce evil and receive the word of God, you are children of the devil and the most horrible plunderers of all. "My yoke," says Christ, "is easy and my burden light."[4] You impose intolerable burdens and destroy the creatures of God, you who ought to be life to the blind and light to the ignorant. Listen to Dionysius: "One should teach the ignorant, not torture them, just as we do not crucify the blind but lead them by the hand"; and a little later: "It is extremely shocking, therefore, that the one whom Christ, the highest goodness, seeks when lost in the mountains, calls back when he strays, and, no sooner found, carries back on his sacred shoulders, is tormented, rejected, and cast aside by you."[5]

This is the way the Apostles spread the gospel and brought the whole world to the feet of Christ, as is clear from the Acts of the Apostles....

Now if we shall have shown that among our Indians of the western and southern shores (granting that we call them barbarians and that they are barbarians) there are important kingdoms, large numbers of people who live settled lives in a society, great cities, kings, judges and laws, persons who engage in commerce, buying, selling, lending, and the other contracts of the law of nations, will it not stand proved that the Reverend Doctor Sepulveda has spoken wrongly and viciously against peoples like these, either out of malice or ignorance of Aristotle's teaching, and, therefore, has falsely and perhaps irreparably slandered them before the entire world? From the fact that the Indians are barbarians it does not necessarily follow that they are incapable of government and have to be ruled by others, except to be taught about the Catholic faith and to be admitted to the holy sacraments. They are not ignorant, inhuman, or bestial. Rather, long before they had heard the word Spaniard they had properly organized states, wisely ordered by excellent laws, religion, and custom. They cultivated friendship and, bound together in common fellowship, lived in populous cities in which they wisely administered the affairs of both peace and war justly and equitably, truly governed by laws that at very many points surpass ours....

[T]hey are so skilled in every mechanical art that with every right they should be set ahead of all the nations of the known world on this score, so very beautiful in their skill and artistry are the things this people produces in the grace of its architecture, its painting, and its needlework....

In the liberal arts that they have been taught up to now, such as grammar and logic, they are remarkably adept. With every kind of music they charm the ears of their audience with wonderful sweetness. They write skillfully and quite elegantly, so that most often we are at a loss to know whether the characters are handwritten or printed....

Since every nation by the eternal law has a ruler or prince, it is wrong for one nation to attack another under pretext of being superior in wisdom or to overthrow other kingdoms. For it acts contrary to the eternal law, as we read in Proverbs: "Do not displace the ancient landmark, set up by your ancestors."[6] This is not an act of wisdom, but of great injustice and a lying excuse for plundering others. Hence every nation, no matter how barbaric, has the right to defend itself against a more civilized one that wants to conquer it and take away its freedom. And, moreover, it can lawfully punish with death the more civilized as a savage and cruel aggressor against the law of nature. And this war is certainly more just than the one that, under pretext of wisdom, is waged against them....

Sepulveda's final argument that everyone can be compelled, even when unwilling, to do those things that are beneficial to him, if taken without qualification, is false in the extreme....

The Christian faith brings the grace of the Holy Spirit, which wipes away all wickedness, filth, and foolishness from human hearts. This is clear in the case of the Roman people, who sought to enact laws for all other nations in order to dominate them and who were, at one time, highly praised for their reputation for political skill and wisdom. Now this people itself was ruled by heinous vices and detestable practices, especially in its shameful games and hateful sacrifices, as in the games and plays held in the circus and in the

obscene sacrifices to Priapus and Bacchus. In these everything was so disgraceful, ugly, and repugnant to sound reason that they far outdistanced all other nations in insensitivity of mind and barbarism. This is explained clearly and at length by Saint Augustine and by Lactantius when he speaks about the religion of the Romans and Greeks, who wanted to be considered wiser than all the other nations of the world. He [Lactantius] writes that they habitually worshiped and offered homage to their gods by prostituting their children in the *gymnasia* so that anyone could abuse them at his pleasure. And he adds: "Is there anything astonishing in the fact that all disgraceful practices have come down from this people for whom these vices were religious acts, things which not only were not avoided but were even encouraged?"[7]...

When, therefore, those who are devoid of Christian truth have sunk into vices and crimes and have strayed from reason in many ways, no matter how well versed they may be in the skills of government, and certainly all those who do not worship Christ, either because they have not heard his words even by hearsay or because, once they have heard them, reject them, all these are true barbarians....

In keeping with this Paul says: "All government comes from God."[8] However, as long as unbelievers do not accept the Christian faith or are not cleansed by the waters of baptism, and especially those who have never heard anything about the Church or the Catholic people, they are in no way disposed or proportionate recipients for the exercise of the Pope's power or his contentious jurisdiction. For it is wanting in that case. And even if it is not, what can it accomplish, since it is the power that Christ granted his Vicar for building up the Church? There is also the absence of the "how" and the "when," which are necessary circumstances for the exercise of apostolic power, since the unbelievers are not yet subjects capable of duly and correctly receiving jurisdictional acts.

Consequently, the other circumstances needed for the proper and correct exercise of the above-mentioned acts are lacking, that is, a subject people and the matter over which [these acts] may be exercised. This is habitual possession of jurisdiction, with respect that is, to some persons who are not yet subjects but who, becoming such, are a fit subject and matter upon whom the acts of jurisdiction must be duly exercised. For example, if a teacher is the rector of a college that has not yet been founded, he has habitual jurisdiction. But after the college has been established and completed, he can actually exercise this jurisdiction. This is the teaching of those who are skilled in the law when they speak about jurisdiction as possessed, as it were, habitually and actually. This is also the case of the pastor of a church that has no parishioners. He is habitually a pastor and rector, but when his parish has parishioners he can actually use and exercise his jurisdiction, because then there is a matter, a subject, a people suited to the exercise of this jurisdiction, and from this potency or habit he can actualize his jurisdiction.

The Pope, then, does not have this subject-material (that is, a people or parishioners) among unbelievers who are completely outside the competence of the Church, because he has nothing to do with judging those outside.[9] Therefore he has no actual jurisdiction over these persons. However, as soon as they enter Christ's sheepfold they belong to the jurisdiction of the Christian Church, they are a part and members of the Christian people, as is evident from what has been said. And then the Pope can judge them by his power and, in the contained in law, compel them by his jurisdiction.[10]

Thus unbelievers who are completely outside the Church are not subject to the Church, nor do they belong to its territory or competence....

[O]ur main conclusion is proved principally by the fact that it is not the business of the Church to punish worshipers of idols [Indians] because of their idolatry whenever it is not its business to punish unbelief, because the unbelief of Jews and Saracens is much more serious and damnable than the unbelief of idolaters [Indians]. In the former, the definition of unbelief and the gravity of the sin are truly verified, whereas in the latter there is the obstacle of ignorance and deprivation in reference to hearing the word of God (as has already been explained). The Jews and the Saracens have heard the words of Christ, and the preaching of apostolic men and the words of gospel truth have daily beat against their hard hearts. But since they do not embrace the teaching of the gospel because of the previously mentioned pertinacity and insolence of

their minds, they are guilty of a wicked malice. However, the worshipers of idols, at least in the case of the Indians, about whom this disputation has been undertaken, have never heard the teaching of Christian truth even through hearsay; so they sin less than the Jews or Saracens, for ignorance excuses to some small extent....

Therefore since the Church does not punish the unbelief of the Jews even if they live within the territories of the Christian religion, much less will it punish idolaters who inhabit an immense portion of the earth, which was unheard of in previous centuries, who have never been subjects of either the Church or her members, and who have not even known what the Church is. For an argument that what is true of the greater [is therefore true of the lesser] is valid, as is evident in the Philosopher and among the doctors....

1 Aristotle, Book I, chap. 2.
2 Matthew 22:39.
3 Corinthians 13:5.
4 Matthew 11:30.
5 *Epistola ad demophilum monacbum.*
6 Hebrew Bible, Proverbs 22:28.
7 *Divinarum Institutionum*, Book I, chap. 20.
8 Romans 13:1.
9 1 Corinthians 5:12, a text that will be discussed later at greater length.
10 Decretals, 2, I, 13.

7.3 HUGO GROTIUS: ON THE RIGHT OF THE STRANGER AND THE REFUGEE (*THE LAW OF WAR AND PEACE*, 1625)

Book II, Chapter II

XV. — The right of temporary sojourn

1. To those who pass through a country, by water or by land, it ought to be permissible to sojourn for a time, for the sake of health, or for any other good reason; for this also finds place among the advantages which involve no detriment. So in Virgil, when the Trojans were forbidden to sojourn in Africa, Illoneus dared to appeal to the gods as judges. The Greeks viewed as well founded the complaint of the people of Megara against the Athenians, who

forbade the Megarians to enter their harbors, "contrary to common right," as Plutarch says. To the Lacedaemonians no cause for war seemed more just.

2. A natural consequence of this is that it is permissible to build a temporary hut, for example on the seashore, even if we admit that possession of the coast has been taken by a people. For when Pomponius said that an order of the praetor must be obtained before one would be allowed to erect any building on a public shore or in the sea reference was made to permanent structures. To such the lines of the poet refer:
The fish are conscious that a narrower bound
Is drawn the seas around by masses huge hurled down into the deep.

XVI. *Those who have been driven from their homes have the right to acquire a permanent residence, in another country, in submission to the government there in authority.*

Furthermore a permanent residence ought not to be denied to foreigners who, expelled from their homes, are seeking a refuge, provided that they submit themselves to the established government and observe any regulations which are necessary in order to avoid strafes. This fair distinction the divine poet observes when he represents Aeneas as offering the following terms:

Latinus, as my sire, his arms shall keep, and as my sire his sovereign sway shall hold
Inviolate.

In the work of the Halicarnassian, Latinus himself says that the cause of Aeneas is just, if Aeneas had been forced to come to his country by the lack of an abiding-place.

"It is characteristic of barbarians to drive away strangers," says Strabo, following Eratosthenes; and in this respect the Spartans failed to gain approval. In the opinion of Ambrose, also, those who keep foreigners out of their city are by no means worthy of approval....

7.4 OLAUDAH EQUIANO: ON THE MEMOIRS OF AN AFRICAN SLAVE (*THE INTERESTING NARRATIVE*, 1789)

The first object which saluted my eyes when I arrived on the coast was the sea, and a slave-ship, which was then riding at anchor, and waiting for its cargo. These filled me with astonishment, which was soon converted into terror, which I am yet at a loss to describe, nor the then feelings of my mind. When I was carried on board I was immediately handled, and tossed up, to see if I were sound, by some of the crew; and I was now persuaded that I had gotten into a world of bad spirits, and that they were going to kill me. Their complexions too differing so much from ours, their long hair, and the language they spoke, which was very different from any I had ever heard, united to confirm me in this belief. Indeed, such were the horrors of my views and fears at the moment, that, if ten thousand worlds had been my own, I would have freely parted with them all to have exchanged my condition with that of the meanest slave in my own country. When I looked round the ship too, and saw a large furnace of copper boiling, and a multitude of black people of every description chained together, every one of their countenances expressing dejection and sorrow, I no longer doubted of my fate, and, quite overpowered with horror and anguish, I fell motionless on the deck and fainted. When I recovered a little, I found some black people about me, who I believed were some of those who brought me on board, and had been receiving their pay; they talked to me in order to cheer me, but all in vain. I asked them if we were not to be eaten by those white men with horrible looks, red faces, and long hair? They told me I was not....

Soon after this, the blacks who brought me on board went off, and left me abandoned to despair. I now saw myself deprived of all chance of returning to my native country, or even the least glimpse of hope of gaining the shore, which I now considered as friendly: and I even wished for my former slavery in preference to my present situation, which was filled with horrors of every kind, still heightened by my ignorance of what I was to undergo. I was not long suffered to indulge my grief; I was soon put down under the decks, and there I received such a salutation in my nostrils as I had never experienced in my life; so that with the loathsomeness of the stench, and crying together, I became so sick and low that I was not able to eat, nor had I the least desire to taste any thing. I now wished for the last friend, Death, to relieve me; but soon, to my grief, two of the white men offered me eatables; and, on my refusing to eat, one of them held me fast by the hands, and laid me across, I think, the windlass, and tied my feet, while the other flogged me severely. I had never experienced any thing of this kind before; and although, not being used to the water, I naturally feared that element the first time I saw it; yet, nevertheless, could I have got over the nettings would have jumped over the side, but I could not; and, besides, the crew used to watch us very closely who were not chained down to the decks, lest we should leap into the water; and I have seen some of these poor African prisoners most severely cut for attempting to do so, and hourly whipped for not eating. This indeed was often the case with myself. In a little time after, amongst the poor chained men, I found some of my own nation, which in a small degree gave ease to my mind. I inquired of these what was to be done with us? They gave me to understand we were to be carried to these white people's country to work for them. I then was a little revived, and thought, if it were no worse than working, my situation was not so desperate: but still I feared I should be put to death, the white people looked and acted, as I thought, in so savage a manner; for I had never seen among any people such instances of brutal cruelty; and this not only shown towards us blacks, but also to some of the whites themselves. One white man in particular I saw, when we were permitted to be on deck, flogged so unmercifully with a large rope near the foremast, that he died in consequence of it; and they tossed him over the side as they would have done a brute. This made me fear these people the more; and expected nothing less than to be treated in the same manner....

Every circumstance I met with served only to render my state more painful, and heighten my apprehensions, and my opinion of the cruelty of the whites. One day they had taken a number of fishes; and when they had killed and satisfied themselves with as many as they thought fit, to our astonishment who were on the deck, rather than give any of them to us to eat, as we expected, they tossed the remaining fish into the sea again, although we begged and prayed for some as well as we could, but in vain; and some of my countrymen, being pressed by hunger, took an opportunity, when they thought no one saw them, of trying to get a little privately; but they were discovered, and the attempt procured them some very severe floggings.

One day, when we had a smooth sea, and moderate wind, two of my wearied countrymen, who were chained together (I was near them at the time), preferring death to such a life of misery, somehow made through the nettings, and jumped into the sea: immediately another quite dejected fellow, who, on account of his illness, was suffered to be out of irons, also followed their example; and I believe many more would very soon have done the same, if they had not been prevented by the ship's crew, who were instantly alarmed. Those of us that were the most active were, in a moment, put down under the deck; and there was such a noise and confusion amongst the people of the ship as I never heard before, to stop her, and get the boat out to go after the slaves. However, two of the wretches were drowned, but they got the other, and afterwards flogged him unmercifully, for thus attempting to prefer death to slavery. In this manner we continued to undergo more hardships than I can now relate; hardships which are inseparable from this accursed trade. — Many a time we were near suffocation, from the want of fresh air, which we were often without for whole days together. This and the stench of the necessary tubs, carried off many....

Many merchants and planters now came on board, though it was in the evening. They put us in separate parcels, and examined us attentively. They also made us jump, and pointed to the land, signifying we were to go there....

The buyers rush at once into the yard where the slaves are confined, and make choice of that parcel they like best. The noise and clamor with which this is attended, and the eagerness visible in the countenances of the buyers, serve not a little to increase the apprehensions of the terrified Africans, who may well be supposed to consider them as the ministers of that destruction to which they think themselves devoted. In this manner, without scruple, are relations and friends separated, most of them never to see each other again. I remember in the vessel in which I was brought over, in the men's apartment, there were several brothers, who, in the sale, were sold in different lots; and it was very moving on this occasion to see and hear their cries at parting. O, ye nominal Christians! might not an African ask you, learned you this from your God? who says unto you, Do unto all men as you would men should do unto you? Is it not enough that we are torn from our country and friends to toil for your luxury and lust of gain? Must every tender feeling be likewise sacrificed to your avarice? Are the dearest friends and relations, now rendered more dear by their separation from their kindred, still to be parted from each other, and thus prevented from cheering the gloom of slavery with the small comfort of being together and mingling their sufferings and sorrows? Why are parents to lose their children, brothers their sisters, or husbands their wives? Surely this is a new refinement in cruelty, which, while it has no advantage to atone for it, thus aggravates distress, and adds fresh horrors even to the wretchedness of slavery.

7.5   ADAM SMITH: ON SLAVERY AND SERFDOM (*THE WEALTH OF NATIONS*, 1776)

Book III, Chapter 2

... The pride of man makes him love to domineer, and nothing mortifies him so much as to be obliged to condescend to persuade his inferiors. Wherever the law allows it, and the nature of the work can afford it, therefore, he will generally prefer the service of slaves to that of freemen. The planting of sugar and tobacco can afford the expense of slave-cultivation. The raising of corn, it seems, in the present times, cannot. In the English colonies, of which the principal produce is corn, the far greater part of the work is done by freemen. The late resolution of the Quakers in Pennsylvania to set at liberty all their negro slaves may satisfy us that their number cannot be very great. Had they made any considerable part of their property, such a resolution could never have been agreed to. In our sugar colonies, on the contrary, the whole work is done by slaves, and in our tobacco colonies a very great part of it. The profits of a sugar-plantation in any of our West Indian colonies are generally much greater than those of any other cultivation that is known either in Europe or America; and the profits of a tobacco plantation, though inferior to those of sugar, are superior to those of corn, as has already been observed. Both can afford the expense of slave-cultivation, but sugar can afford it still better than tobacco. The number of negroes accordingly is much greater, in proportion to that of whites, in our sugar than in our tobacco colonies.

To the slave cultivators of ancient times gradually succeeded a species of farmers known at present in France by the name of Metayers. They are called in Latin, Coloni Partiarii. They have been so long in disuse in England that at present I know no English name for them. The proprietor furnished them with the seed, cattle, and instruments of husbandry, the whole stock, in short, necessary for cultivating the farm. The produce was divided equally between the proprietor and the farmer, after setting aside what was judged necessary for keeping up the stock, which was restored to the proprietor when the farmer either quitted, or was turned out of the farm.

Land occupied by such tenants is properly cultivated at the expense of the proprietor as much as that occupied by slaves. There is, however, one very essential difference between them. Such tenants, being freemen, are capable of acquiring property, and having a certain proportion of the produce of the land, they have a plain interest that the whole produce should be as great as possible, in order that their own proportion may be so. A slave, on the contrary, who can acquire nothing but his maintenance, consults his own ease by making the land produce as little as possible over and above that maintenance. It is probable that it was partly upon account of this advantage, and partly upon account of the encroachments which the sovereign, always jealous of the great lords, gradually encouraged their villains to make upon their authority, and which seem at last to have been such rendered this species of servitude altogether inconvenient, that tenure in villanage gradually wore out through the greater part of Europe. The time and manner, however, in which so important a revolution was brought about, is one of the most obscure points in modern history. The church of Rome claims great merit in it; and it is certain that so early as the twelfth century, Alexander III published a bull for the general emancipation of slaves. It seems, however, to have been rather a pious exhortation than a law to which exact obedience was required from the faithful. Slavery continued to take place almost universally for several centuries afterwards, till it was gradually abolished by the joint operation of the two interests above mentioned, that of the proprietor on the one hand, and that of the sovereign on the other. A villain enfranchised, and at the same time allowed to continue in possession of the land, having no stock of his own, could cultivate it only by means of what the landlord advanced to him, and must, therefore, have been what the French call a metayer.

It could never, however, be the interest even of this last species of cultivators to lay out, in the further improvement of the land, any part of the little stock which they might save from their own share of the produce, because the lord, who laid out nothing, was to get one-half of whatever it produced. The tithe, which is but a tenth of the produce, is found to be a very great hindrance to improvement. A tax, therefore, which amounted to one-half must have been an effectual bar to it. It might be the interest of a metayer to make the land produce as much as could be brought out of it by means of the stock furnished by the proprietor; but it could never be his interest to mix any part of his own with it. In France, where five parts out of six of the whole kingdom are said to be still occupied by this species of cultivators, the proprietors complain that their metayers take every opportunity of employing the master's cattle rather in carriage than in cultivation; because in the one case they get the whole profits to themselves, in the other they share them with their landlord. This species of tenants still subsist in some parts of Scotland. They are called steel-bow tenants. Those ancient English tenants, who are said by Chief Baron Gilbert and Doctor Blackstone who have been rather bailiffs of the landlord than farmers properly so called, were probably of the same kind.

To this species of tenancy succeeded, though by very slow degrees, farmers properly so called, who cultivated the land with their own stock, paying a rent certain to the landlord. When such farmers have a lease for a term of years, they may sometimes find it for their interest to lay out part of their capital in the further improvement of the farm; because they may sometimes expect to recover it, with a large profit, before the expiration of the lease The possession even of such farmers, however, was long extremely precarious, and still is so in many parts of Europe. They could before the expiration of their term be legally outed of their lease by a new purchaser; in England even by the fictitious action of a common recovery. If they were turned out illegally by the violence of their master, the action by which they obtained redress was extremely imperfect. It did not always reinstate them in the possession of the land but gave them damages which never amounted to the real loss. Even in England, the country perhaps of Europe where the yeomanry has always been most respected; it was not till about the 14th of Henry VII that the action of adjustment was invented, by which the tenant recovers, not damages only but possession, and in which his claim is not necessarily concluded by the uncertain decision of a single assize. This action has been found so effectual a remedy that, in the modern practice, when the landlord has occasion to sue for the possession of the land, he seldom makes use of the actions which properly belong to him as landlord, the writ of right or the writ of entry, but sues in the name of his tenant by the writ of adjustment. In England, therefore, the security of the tenant is equal to that of the proprietor. In England, besides, a lease for life of forty shillings a year value is a freehold, and entitles the lessee to vote for a member of parliament; and as a great part of the yeomanry have freeholds of this kind, the whole order becomes respectable to their landlords on account of the political consideration which this gives them. There is, I believe, nowhere in Europe, except in England, any instance of the tenant building upon the land of which he had no lease, and trusting that the honor of his landlord would take no advantage of so important an improvement. Those laws and customs so favorable to the yeomanry have perhaps contributed more to the present grandeur of England than all their boasted regulations of commerce taken together....

7.6 MAXIMILIEN DE ROBESPIERRE: ON THE PROPERTYLESS AND MALE SUFFRAGE (1791)

Why are we gathered in this legislative assembly? Doubtless to restore to the French nation the exercise of imprescriptible rights that belongs to every citizen. This is the main purpose of every political constitution. If it fulfills this obligation, it is just and free; if it fails to do so, it is nothing but a conspiracy against mankind.

You recognized this truth yourselves, and in a striking manner, when you decided, before beginning your great work, that a solemn declaration must be made of the sacred rights that serve as the immutable foundations on which it rests.

All men are born and remain free, and are equal at law.

Sovereignty derives from the nation as a whole.

The law is the expression of the general will. All citizens have the right to contribute to its making, either directly by themselves or through their freely elected representatives.

All citizens are admissible to every public office, and no distinction is made between them except in respect of their virtues and talents.

These are the principles that you have enshrined. It will now be readily seen which are the measures that I wish to combat; it is enough to test them against these immutable laws of human society.

1. Can the law be termed an expression of the general will when the greater number of those for whom it is made can have no hand in its making? No. And yet to forbid such men as do not pay a tax equal to three days' wages the right even to choose the electors whose task it is to appoint the members of the legislative assembly — what is this but to deprive a majority of Frenchmen of the right to frame the laws? This provision is therefore essentially unconstitutional and antisocial.

2. Can men be said to enjoy equal rights when some are endowed with the exclusive right to be elected members of the legislative body or of other public institutions, others merely with that of electing them, while the rest are deprived of all these rights at once? No. Yet such are the monstrous distinctions drawn between them by the decrees that make man active or passive, or half active and half passive, according to the varying degrees of fortune that permit him to pay three days' wages in taxes, ten days, or a silver mark. All these provisions are, then, essentially unconstitutional and antisocial.

3. Are men admissible to all public posts, and is no distinction made except such as derive from their virtues and talents, when an inability to pay the required tax excludes them from every public office regardless of the virtues and talents that they may possess? No. All these provisions are therefore essentially unconstitutional and antisocial.

4. And again, is the nation sovereign when the greater part of the persons composing it is deprived of the political rights from which sovereignty derives its essence? No. And yet you have just seen that these same decrees deny them to the majority of Frenchmen. What would remain of your Declaration of Rights if these decrees were allowed to continue? It would become an empty formula. What would the nation become? A slave; for it is freedom to obey laws of which one is oneself the maker, but it is slavery to be compelled to submit to the will of another. What would your constitution become? One fit for an aristocracy. For aristocracy is that state in which one part of the citizens is sovereign and the rest is subject. And what kind of an aristocracy? The most intolerable of all: an aristocracy of the Rich.

All men *born* and *domiciled* in France are members of the body politic termed the French nation; that is to say, they are French citizens. They are so by the nature of things and by the first principle of the law of nations. The rights attaching to this title do not depend on the fortune that each man possesses, or on the amount of tax for which he is assessed, because it is not taxes that make us citizens: citizenship merely obliges a man to contribute to public expenditure in proportion to his means. You may give the citizens new laws, but you may not deprive them of their citizenship.

The upholders of the system that I am denouncing have themselves realized this truth; for, not daring to challenge the title of citizen in those whom they condemn to political disinheritance, they have confined themselves to destroying the principle of equality inherent in that title by drawing a distinction between active and passive citizens. Trusting in the ease with which men may be governed by words, they have sought to lead us off the scent by using this new expression as a cover for the most flagrant violation of the rights of man.

But who can be so stupid as not to perceive that such a phrase can neither invalidate the principle nor solve the problem? For, in the idiom of these subtle politicians, it is exactly the same thing to declare that certain citizens shall not be active as to say that they shall no longer exercise the rights attaching to the title of citizen. Well, I shall ask them once more by what right they may thus strike their fellow citizens and constituents with paralysis and reduce them to inactivity; and I shall not cease protesting against this barbaric and insidious phrase which, if we do not hasten to efface it, will disgrace our language and our code of laws, so that the word "liberty" itself may not become meaningless and laughable.

What need I add to such self-evident truths? Nothing in regard to the representatives of a nation whose wishes and opinions have already anticipated my demand; but I still must reply to the contemptible sophisms by means of which the prejudices and ambitions of a certain class of men seek to buttress the disastrous doctrine that I here denounce. It is to them only that I now wish to speak.

The people, men of no property...the dangers of corruption...the example of England and of other nations reputed free: these are the arguments that are being used to confound justice and to combat reason.

One single sentence should be an adequate reply: the people, that great multitude whose cause I plead, have rights whose origin is the same as yours. Who has given you power to take them away?...

Nay, more. From the very efforts made by the enemies of the Revolution to degrade the people in your esteem and to degrade yours in the people's, by suggesting to you measures intended to stifle its voice or to weaken its energy, or to lead its patriotism astray, by hiding your decrees from it in order to prolong its ignorance of its rights; from the unwavering patience with which it has borne all its misfortunes in the expectation of a happier state of things; from this we learn that the people is the sole support of liberty. Who, then, could tolerate the idea of seeing it despoiled of its rights by the very revolution that is due to its courage and to the tender and generous devotion with which it defended its representatives! Is it to the rich and to the great that you owe this glorious insurrection that saved France and yourselves? Were not the soldiers who rallied to the service of the nation at arms men of the people? And to what class did their leaders belong, those who would have led them against you? ... Did the people then take up arms to help you to defend its rights and its dignity, or was it to give you power to encompass its destruction? Did it aid you to break the yoke of feudal aristocracy in order to fall back under the yoke of an aristocracy of wealth?

Up to now, I have adopted the language of those who seem to mean by the word "people" a class of men set aside from their fellows and to whom they attach a certain label of contempt or inferiority. It is now time that I express myself more precisely, in recalling that the system we condemn disfranchises nine-tenths of the nation and that it even excludes from the lists of those it terms active citizens vast numbers of men who, even in the bad old days of pride and prejudice, were honored and distinguished for their education, their industry, even for their fortunes.

Such is, in fact, the nature of this institution that it provides for the most ridiculous anomalies; for, while taking wealth as the measure of the rights of citizenship, it departs from this very rule by attaching them to what are called direct taxes, although it is evident that a man who pays substantial indirect taxes may enjoy a larger fortune than one who is subjected to a moderate direct tax. But who would have thought it possible that the sacred rights of man should be made to depend on the changing nature of financial systems, on the variations and diversities that our system presents in the different parts of the same State? What sort of system is it where a man who is a citizen in one part of France ceases to be one either in part or in whole if he moves to another and where a man who is one today will no longer be one tomorrow if he should suffer an adverse turn of fortune!

What sort of system is it in which an honest man, despoiled by an unjust oppressor, sinks into the class of the *helots* while his despoiler is raised by this very crime into the ranks of the citizens; in which a father, as the number of his children increases, sees with a growing certainty that he will not be able to leave them this title owing to the constant diminution of his divided inheritance; in which every father's son throughout half our land recovers his fatherland only at the point where he loses his father!...In short, what is the worth of my much vaunted right to belong to the sovereign body if the assessor of taxes has the power to deprive me of it by reducing my contribution by a cent and if it is subject at once to the caprice of man and the inconsistency of fortune?...

7.7   OLYMPE DE GOUGES ("THE DECLARATION OF THE RIGHTS OF WOMAN," 1790)

To the Queen: Madame,

Little suited to the language one holds to with kings, I will not use the adulation of courtiers to pay you homage with this singular production. My purpose, Madame, is to speak frankly to you; I have not awaited the epoch of liberty to thus explain myself; I bestirred myself as energetically in a time when the blindness of despots punished such noble audacity. When the whole empire accused you and held you responsible for its calamities, I alone in a time of trouble and storm, I alone had the strength to take up your defense. I could never convince myself that a princess, raised in the midst of grandeur, had all the vices of baseness. Yes, Madame, when I saw the sword raised against you, I threw my observations between that sword and you, but today when I see who is observed near the crowd of useless hirelings, and [when I see] that she is restrained by fear of the laws, I will tell you, Madame, what I did not say then.

If the foreigner bears arms into France, you are no longer in my eyes this falsely accused Queen, this attractive Queen, but an implacable enemy of the French. Oh, Madame, bear in mind that you are mother and wife; employ all your credit for the return of the Princes. This credit, if wisely applied, strengthens the father's crown, saves it for the son, and reconciles you to the love of the French. This worthy negotiation is the true duty of a queen. Intrigue, cabals, bloody projects will precipitate your fall, if it is possible to suspect that you are capable of such plots.

Madame, may a nobler function characterize you, excite your ambition, and fix your attentions. Only one whom chance has elevated to an eminent position can assume the task of lending weight to the progress of the Rights of Woman and of hastening its success. If you were less well informed, Madame, I might fear that your individual interests would outweigh those of your sex. You love glory; think, Madame, the greatest crimes immortalize one as much as the greatest virtues, but what a different fame in the annals of history. The one is ceaselessly taken as an example, and the other is eternally the execration of the human race.

It will never be a crime for you to work for the restoration of customs, to give your sex all the firmness of which it is capable. This is not the work of one day, unfortunately for the new regime. This revolution will happen only when all women are aware of their deplorable fate, and of the rights they have lost in society. Madame, support such a beautiful cause; defend this unfortunate sex, and soon you will have half the realm on your side, and at least one-third of the other half.

Those, Madame, are the feats by which you should show and use your credit. Believe me, Madame, our life is a pretty small thing, especially for a Queen, when it is not embellished by people's affection and by the eternal delights of good deeds.

If it is true that the French arm all the powers against their own Fatherland, why? For frivolous prerogatives, for chimeras. Believe, Madame, if I judge by what I feel — the monarchical party will be destroyed by itself, it will abandon all tyrants, and all hearts will rally around the fatherland to defend it.

There are my principles, Madame. In speaking to you of my fatherland, I lose sight of the purpose of this dedication. Thus, any good citizen sacrifices his glory and his interests when he has none other than those of his country.

I am with the most profound respect, Madame,

Your most humble and most obedient servant,

de Gouges

THE RIGHTS OF WOMAN

Man, are you capable of being just? It is a woman who poses the Declaration of the Rights...below question; you will not deprive her of that right at least. Tell me, who gives you sovereign empire to oppress my sex? Your strength? Your talents? Observe the Creator in his wisdom; survey in all her grandeur that nature with whom you seem to want to be in harmony, and give me, if you dare, an example of this tyrannical empire. Go back to the animals, consult the elements, study plants, finally glance at all the modifications of organic matter, and surrender to the evidence when offer you the means; search, probe, and distinguish, if you can, the sex in the administration of nature. Everywhere you will find them mingled, everywhere they cooperate in harmonious togetherness in this immortal masterpiece.

Man alone has raised his exceptional circumstances to a principle. Bizarre, blind, bloated with science and degenerated — in a century of enlightenment and wisdom — into the crassest ignorance, he wants to command as a despot a sex which is in full possession of its intellectual faculties; he pretends to enjoy the Revolution and to claim his rights to equality in order to say nothing more about it.

Declaration of the Rights of Woman and the Female Citizen

For the National Assembly to decree in its last sessions, or in those of the next legislature:

Preamble

Mothers, daughters, sisters [and] representatives of the nation demand to be constituted into a national assembly. Believing that ignorance, omission, or scorn for the rights of woman are the only cause of public misfortunes and of the corruption of governments, [the women] have resolved to set forth in a solemn declaration the natural inalienable, and sacred rights of woman in order that this declaration constantly exposed before all the members of the society, will ceaselessly remind them of their rights and duties; in order that the authoritative acts of women and the authoritative acts of men may be at any moment compared with and respectful of the purpose of all political institutions and in order that citizens' demands, henceforth based on simple and incontestable principles, will always support the constitution, good morals, and the happiness of all.

Consequently, the sex that is as superior in beauty as it is in courage during the sufferings of maternity recognizes and declares in the presence and under the auspices of the Supreme Being, the following Rights of Woman and of Female Citizens.

Article I
Woman is born free and lives equal to man in her rights. Social distinctions can be based only on the common utility.

Article II
The purpose of any political association is the conservation of the natural and imprescriptible rights of woman and man; these rights are liberty, property, security, and especially resistance to oppression.

Article III
The principle of all sovereignty rests essentially with the nation, which is nothing but the union of woman and man; no body and no individual can exercise any authority which does not come expressly from it [the nation].

Article IV
Liberty and justice consist of restoring all that belongs to others; thus, the only limits on the exercise of the natural rights of woman are perpetual male tyranny; these limits are to be reformed by the laws of nature and reason.

Article V
Laws of nature and reason proscribe all acts harmful to society; everything which is not prohibited by these wise and divine laws cannot be prevented, and no one can be constrained to do what they do not command.

Article VI
The law must be the expression of the general will; all female and male citizens must contribute either personally or through their representatives to its formation; it must be the same for all: male and female citizens, being equal in the eyes of the law, must be equally admitted to all honors, positions, and public employment according to their capacity and without other distinctions besides those of their virtues and talents.

Article VII
No woman is an exception; she is accused, arrested, and detained in cases determined by law. Women, like men, obey this rigorous law.

Article VIII
The law must establish only those penalties that are strictly and obviously necessary, and no one can be punished except by virtue of a law established and promulgated prior to the crime and legally applicable to women.

Article IX
Once any woman is declared guilty, complete rigor is [to be] exercised by the law.

Article X
No one is to be disquieted for his very basic opinions; woman has the right to mount the scaffold; she must equally have the right to mount the rostrum, provided that her demonstrations do not disturb the legally established public order.

Article XI
The free communication of thoughts and opinions is one of the most precious rights of woman, since that liberty assures the recognition of children by their fathers. Any female citizen thus may say freely, I am the mother of a child which belongs to you, without being forced by a barbarous prejudice to hide the truth; [an exception may be made] to respond to the abuse of this liberty in cases determined by the law.

Article XII
The guarantee of the rights of woman and the female citizen implies a major benefit; this guarantee must be instituted for the advan-

tage of all, and not for the particular benefit of those to whom it is entrusted.

Article XIII

For the support of the public force and the expenses of administration, the contributions of woman and man are equal; she shares all the duties [corvées] and all the painful tasks; therefore, she must have the same share in the distribution of positions, employment, offices, honors, and jobs [industrie].

Article XIV

Female and male citizens have the right to verify, either by themselves or through their representatives, the necessity of the public contribution. This can only apply to women if they are granted an equal share, not only of wealth, but also of public administration, and in the termination of the proportion, the base, the collection, and the duration of the tax.

Article XV

The collectivity of women, joined for tax purposes to the aggregate of men, has the right to demand an accounting of his administration from any public agent.

Article XVI

No society has a constitution without the guarantee of rights and the separation of powers; the constitution is null if the majority of individuals comprising the nation have not cooperated in drafting it.

Article XVII

Property belongs to both sexes whether united or separate; for each it is an inviolable and sacred right; no one can be deprived of it, since it is the true patrimony of nature, unless the legally determined public need obviously dictates it, and then only with a just and prior indemnity.

Postscript

Woman, wake up; the tocsin of reason is being heard throughout the whole universe; discover your rights. The powerful empire of nature is no longer surrounded by prejudice, fanaticism, superstition, and lies. The flame of truth has dispersed all the clouds of folly and usurpation. Enslaved man has multiplied his strength and needs recourse to yours to break his chains. Having become free, he has become unjust to his companion. Oh, women, women! When will you cease to be blind? What advantage have you received from the Revolution? A more pronounced scorn, a more marked disdain. In the centuries of corruption you ruled only over the weakness of men. The reclamation of your patrimony, based on the wise decrees of nature — what have you to dread from such a fine undertaking? The bon mot of the legislator of the marriage of Cana? Do you fear that our French legislators, correctors of that morality, long ensnared by political practices now out of date, will only say again to you: women, what is there in common between you and us? Everything, you will have to answer. If they persist in their weakness in putting this non sequitur in contradiction to their principles, courageously oppose the force of reason to the empty pretentions of superiority; unite yourselves beneath the standards of philosophy; deploy all the energy of your character, and you will soon see these haughty men, not groveling at your feet as servile adorers, but proud to share with you the treasures of the Supreme Being. Regardless of what barriers confront you, it is in your power to free yourselves; you have only to want to. Let us pass now to the shocking tableau of what you have been in society; and since national education is in question at this moment, let us see whether our wise legislators will think judiciously about the education of women.

Women have done more harm than good. Constraint and dissimulation have been their lot. What force had robbed them of, ruse returned to them; they had recourse to all the resources of their charms, and the most irreproachable person did not resist them. Poison and the sword were both subject to them; they commanded in crime as in fortune. The French government, especially, depended throughout the centuries on the nocturnal administration of women; the cabinet kept no secret from their indiscretion; ambassadorial post, command, ministry, presidency, pontificate, college of cardinals; finally, anything which characterizes the folly of men, profane and sacred, all have been subject to the cupidity and ambition of this sex, formerly contemptible and respected, and since the revolution, respectable and scorned. In this sort of contradictory situation, what remarks could I not make! I have but a moment to make them, but this moment will fix the attention of the remotest posterity. Under the Old Regime, all was vicious, all was guilty; but could not the amelioration of conditions be perceived even in the substance of vices? A woman only had to be beautiful or amiable; when she possessed these two advantages, she saw a hundred fortunes at her feet. If she did not profit from them, she had a bizarre character or a rare philosophy which made her scorn wealth; then she was deemed to be like a crazy woman; the most indecent made herself respected with gold; commerce in women was a kind of industry in the first class [of society], which, henceforth, will have no more credit. If it still had it, the revolution would be lost, and under the new relationships we would always be corrupted; however, reason can always be deceived [into believing] that any other road to fortune is closed to the woman whom a man buys, like the slave on the African coasts. The difference is great; that is known. The slave is commanded by the master; but if the master gives her liberty without recompense, and at an age when the slave has lost all her charms, what will become of this unfortunate woman? The victim of scorn, even the doors of charity are closed to her; she is poor and old, they say; why did she not know how to make her fortune? Reason finds other examples that are even more touching. A young, inexperienced woman, seduced by a man whom she loves, will abandon her parents to follow him; the ingrate will leave her after a few years, and the older she has become with him, the more human is his inconstancy; if she has children, he will likewise abandon them. If he is rich, he will consider himself excused from sharing his fortune with his noble victims. If some involvement binds him to his duties, he will deny them, trusting that the laws will support him. If he is married, any other obligation loses its rights. Then what laws remain to extirpate vice all the way to its root? The law of dividing wealth and public administration between men and women. It can easily be seen that one who is born into a rich family gains very much from such equal sharing. But the one born into a poor family with merit and virtue — what is her lot? Poverty and opprobrium. If she does not precisely excel in music or painting, she cannot be admitted to any public function when she has all the capacity for it. I do not want to give only a sketch of things; I will go more deeply into this in the new edition of all my political writings, with notes, which I propose to give to the public in a few days.

I take up my text again on the subject of morals. Marriage is the tomb of trust and love. The married woman can with impurity give bastards to her husband, and also give them the wealth which does not belong to them. The woman who is unmarried has only one feeble right; ancient and inhuman laws refuse to her for her children the right to the name and the wealth of their father; no new laws have been made in this matter. If it is considered a paradox and an impossibility on my part to try to give my sex an honorable and just consistency, I leave it to men to attain glory for dealing with this matter; but while we wait, the way can be prepared through national education, the restoration of morals, and conjugal conventions.

Form for a Social Contract between Man and Woman

We, ___ and ___, moved by our own will, unite ourselves for the duration of our lives, and for the duration of our mutual inclinations, under the following conditions: We intend and wish to make our wealth communal, meanwhile reserving to ourselves the right to divide it in favor of our children and of those toward whom we might have a particular inclination, mutually recognizing that our property belongs directly to our children, from whatever bed they come, and that all of them without distinction have the right to bear the name of the fathers and mothers who have acknowledged them, and we are charged to subscribe to the law which punishes the renunciation of one's own blood. We likewise obligate ourselves, in case of separation, to divide our wealth and to set aside in advance the portion the law indicates for our children, and in the event of a perfect union, the one who dies will divest himself of half his property in his children's favor, and if one dies childless, the survivor will inherit by right, unless the dying person has disposed of half the common property in favor of one whom he judged deserving.

That is approximately the formula for the marriage act I propose for execution. Upon reading this strange document, I see rising up against me the hypocrites, the prudes, the clergy, and the whole infernal sequence. But how it [my proposal] offers to the wise the moral means of achieving the perfection of a happy government! I am going to give in a few words the physical proof of it. The rich, childless Epicurean finds it very good to go to his poor neighbor to augment his family. When there is a law authorizing a poor man's wife to have a rich one adopt their children, the bonds of society will be strengthened and morals will be purer. This law will perhaps save the community's wealth and hold back the disorder which drives so many victims to the almshouses of shame, to a low station, and into degenerate human principles where nature has groaned for so long. May the detractors of wise philosophy then cease to cry out against primitive morals, or may they lose their point in the source of their citations.

Moreover, I would like a law which would assist widows and young girls deceived by the false promises of a man to whom they were attached; I would like, I say, this law to force an inconstant man to hold to his obligations or at least [to pay] an indemnity equal to his wealth. Again, I would like this law to be rigorous against women, at least those who have the effrontery to have recourse to a law which they themselves had violated by their misconduct, if proof of that were given. At the same time, as I showed in *Le Bonheur primitif de l'homme*, in 1788, that prostitutes should be placed in designated quarters. It is not prostitutes who contribute the most to the depravity of morals, it is the women of society. In regenerating the latter, the former are changed. This link of fraternal union will first bring disorder, but in consequence it will produce at the end a perfect harmony.

I offer a foolproof way to elevate the soul of women; it is to join them to all the activities of man; if man persists in finding this way impractical, let him share his fortune with woman, not at his caprice, but by the wisdom of laws. Prejudice falls, morals are purified, and nature regains all her rights. Add to this the marriage of priests and the strengthening of the king on his throne, and the French government cannot fail.

It would be very necessary to say a few words on the troubles which are said to be caused by the decree in favor of colored men in our islands. There is where nature shudders with horror; there is where reason and humanity have still not touched callous souls; there, especially, is where division and discord stir up their inhabitants. It is not difficult to divine the instigators of these incendiary fermentations; they are even in the midst of the National Assembly; they ignite the fire in Europe which must inflame America. Colonists make a claim to reign as despots over the men whose fathers and brothers they are; and, disowning the rights of nature, they trace the source of [their rule] to the scantiest tint of their blood. These inhuman colonists say: our blood flows in their veins, but we will shed it all if necessary to glut our greed or our blind ambition. It is in these places nearest to nature where the father scorns the son; deaf to the cries of blood, they stifle all its attraction; what can be hoped from the resistance opposed to them? To constrain [blood] violently is to render it terrible; to leave [blood] still enchained is to direct all calamities towards America. A divine hand seems to spread liberty abroad throughout the realms of man; only the law has the right to curb this liberty if it degenerates into license, but it must be equal for all; liberty must hold the National Assembly to its decree dictated by prudence and justice. May it act the same way for the state of France and render her as attentive to new abuses as she was to the ancient ones which each day become more dreadful. My opinion would be to reconcile the executive and legislative power, for it seems to me that the one is everything and the other is nothing — whence comes, unfortunately perhaps, the loss of the French Empire. I think that these two powers, like man and woman, should be united but equal in force and virtue to make a good household....

7.8 MARY WOLLSTONECRAFT (*A VINDICATION OF THE RIGHTS OF WOMEN*, 1792)

Introduction

I have turned over various books written on the subject of education, and patiently observed the conduct of parents and the management of schools; but what has been the result? — a profound conviction that the neglected education of my fellow-creatures is the grand source of the misery I deplore, and that women, in particular, are rendered weak and wretched by a variety of concurring causes, originating from one hasty conclusion. The conduct and manners of women, in fact, evidently prove that their minds are not in a healthy state; for, like the flowers which are planted in too rich a soil, strength and usefulness are sacrificed to beauty; and the flaunting leaves, after having pleased a fastidious eye, fade, disregarded on the stalk, long before the season when they ought to have arrived at maturity. One cause of this barren blooming I attribute to a false system of education, gathered from the books written on this subject by men who, considering females rather as women than human creatures, have been more anxious to make them alluring mistresses than affectionate wives and rational mothers; and the understanding of the sex has been so bubbled by this specious homage, that the civilized women of the present century, with a few exceptions, are only anxious to inspire love, when they ought to cherish a nobler ambition, and by their abilities and virtues exact respect.

In a treatise, therefore, on female rights and manners, the works which have been particularly written for their improvement must not be overlooked, especially when it is asserted, in direct terms, that the minds of women are enfeebled by false refinement; that the books of instruction, written by men of genius, have had the same tendency as more frivolous productions; and that, in the true style of Mahometanism, they are treated as a kind of subordinate beings, and not as a part of the human species, when improvable reason is allowed to be the dignified distinction which raises men above the brute creation, and puts a natural scepter in a feeble hand.

Yet, because I am a woman, I would not lead my readers to suppose that I mean violently to agitate the contested question respecting the quality or inferiority of the sex; but as the subject lies in my way, and I cannot pass it over without subjecting the main tendency of my reasoning to misconstruction, I shall stop a moment to deliver, in a few words, my opinion. In the government of the physical world it is observable that the female in point of strength is, in general, inferior to the male. This is the law of Nature; and it does not appear to be suspended or abrogated in favor of woman. A degree of physical superiority cannot, therefore, be denied, and it is a noble prerogative! But not content with this natural pre-eminence, men endeavor to sink us still lower, merely to render us alluring objects for a moment; and women, intoxicated by the adoration which men, under the influence of their senses, pay them, do not seek to obtain a durable interest in their hearts, or to become the friends of the fellow-creatures who find amusement in their society....

The most perfect education, in my opinion, is such an exercise of the understanding as is best calculated to strengthen the body and form the heart. Or, in other words, to enable the individual to attain such habits of virtue as will render it independent. In fact, it is a farce to call any being virtuous whose virtues do not result from the exercise of its own reason. This was Rousseau's opinion respecting men; I extend it to women, and confidently assert that they have been drawn out of their sphere by false refinement, and not by an endeavor to acquire masculine qualities....

But in the education of women, the cultivation of the understanding is always subordinate to the acquirement of some corporeal accomplishment. Even when enervated by confinement and false notions of modesty, the body is prevented from attaining that grace and beauty which relaxed half-formed limbs never exhibit. Besides, in youth their faculties are not brought forward by emulation; and having no serious scientific study, if they have natural sagacity, it is turned too soon on life and manners. They dwell on effects and modifications, without tracing them back to causes; and complicated rules to adjust behavior are a weak substitute for simple principles.

As a proof that education gives this appearance of weakness to females, we may instance the example of military men, who are, like them, sent into the world before their minds have been stored with knowledge, or fortified by principles. The consequences are similar; soldiers acquire a little superficial knowledge, snatched from the muddy current of conversation, and from continually mixing with society, they gain what is termed a knowledge of the world; and this acquaintance with manners and customs has frequently been confounded with a knowledge of the human heart. But can the crude fruit of casual observation, never brought to the test of judgment, formed by comparing speculation and experience, deserve such a distinction? Soldiers, as well as women, practice the minor virtues with punctilious politeness. Where is then the sexual difference, when the education has been the same? All the difference that I can discern arises from the superior advantage of liberty which enables the former to see more of life....

The great misfortune is this, that they both acquire manners before morals, and a knowledge of life before they have from reflection any acquaintance with the grand ideal outline of human nature. The consequence is natural. Satisfied with common nature, they become a prey to prejudices, and taking all their opinions on credit, they blindly submit to authority. So that if they have any sense, it is a kind of instinctive glance that catches proportions, and decides with respect to manners, but fails when arguments are to be pursued below the surface, or opinions analyzed....

Strengthen the female mind by enlarging it, and there will be an end to blind obedience; but as blind obedience is ever sought for by power, tyrants and sensualists are in the right when they endeavor to keep woman in the dark, because the former only want slaves, and the latter a plaything. The sensualist, indeed, has been the most dangerous of tyrants, and women have been duped by their lovers, as princes by their ministers, whilst dreaming that they reigned over them....

Women are therefore to be considered either as moral beings, or so weak that they must be entirely subjected to the superior faculties of men....

It appears to me necessary to dwell on these obvious truths, because females have been insulated, as it were; and while they have been stripped of the virtues that should clothe humanity, they have been decked with artificial graces that enable them to exercise a short-lived tyranny. Love, in their bosoms, taking place of every nobler passion, their sole ambition is to be fair, to raise emotion instead of inspiring respect; and this ignoble desire, like the servility in absolute monarchies, destroys all strength of character. Liberty is the mother of virtue, and if women be, by their very constitution, slaves, and not allowed to breathe the sharp invigorating air of freedom, they must ever languish like exotics, and be reckoned beautiful flaws in nature....

I, therefore, will venture to assert that till women are more rationally educated, the progress of human virtue and improvement in knowledge must receive continual checks. And if it be granted that woman was not created merely to gratify the appetite of man, or to be the upper servant, who provides his meals and takes care of his linen, it must follow that the first care of those mothers or fathers who really attend to the education of females should be, if not to strengthen the body, at least not to destroy the constitution by mistaken notions of beauty and female excellence; nor should girls ever be allowed to imbibe the pernicious notion that a defect can, by any chemical process of reasoning, become an excellence....

But should it be proved that woman is naturally weaker than man, whence does it follow that it is natural for her to labor to become still weaker than nature intended her to be? Arguments of this cast are an insult to common sense, and savor of passion. The *divine right* of husbands, like the divine right of kings, may, it is to be hoped, in this enlightened age, be contested without danger; and though conviction may not silence many boisterous disputants, yet, when any prevailing prejudice is attacked, the wise will consider, and leave the narrow-minded to rail with thoughtless vehemence at innovation....

In order to preserve [women's] innocence, as ignorance is courteously termed, truth is hidden from them, and they are made to assume an artificial character before their faculties have acquired any strength. Taught from their infancy that beauty is woman's scepter, the mind shapes itself to the body, and roaming round its gilt cage, only seeks to adore its prison. Men have various employments and pursuits which engage their attention, and give a character to the opening mind; but women, confined to one, and having their thoughts constantly directed to the most insignificant part of themselves, seldom extend their views beyond the triumph of the hour. But were their understanding once emancipated from the slavery to which the pride and sensuality of man and their short-sighted desire, like that of dominion in tyrants, of present sway, has subjected them, we should probably read of their weaknesses with surprise....

Let not men then in the pride of power, use the same arguments that tyrannic kings and venal ministers have used, and fallaciously assert that woman ought to be subjected because she has always been so. But, when man, governed by reasonable laws, enjoys his natural freedom, let him despise woman, if she do not share it with him; and, till that glorious period arrives, in descanting on the folly of the sex, let him not overlook his own.

Women, it is true, obtaining power by unjust means, by practicing or fostering *vice*, evidently lose the rank which reason would assign them, and they become either abject slaves or capricious tyrants. They lose all simplicity, all dignity of mind, in acquiring power, and act as men are observed to act when they have been exalted by the same means.

It is time to effect a revolution in female manners — time to restore to them their lost dignity — and make them, as a part of the human species, labor by reforming themselves to reform the world. It is time

to separate unchangeable morals from local manners. If men be demi-gods, why let us serve them! And if the dignity of the female soul be as disputable as that of animals — if their reason does not afford sufficient light to direct their conduct whilst unerring instinct is denied — they are surely of all creatures the most miserable! and, bent beneath the iron hand of destiny, must submit to be a *fair defect* in creation. But to justify the ways of Providence respecting them, by pointing out some irrefragable reason for thus making such a large portion of mankind accountable and not accountable, would puzzle the subtilest casuist....

Supposing a woman, trained up to obedience, be married to a sensible man, who directs her judgment without making her feel the servility of her subjection, to act with as much propriety by this reflected light as can be expected when reason is taken at secondhand, yet she cannot ensure the life of her protector; he may die and leave her with a large family. A double duty devolves on her; to educate them in the character of both father and mother; to form their principles and secure their property. But, alas! she has never thought, much less acted for herself. She has only learned to please men, to depend gracefully on them; yet, encumbered with children, how is she to obtain another protector — a husband to supply the place of reason. A rational man, for we are not treading on romantic ground, though he may think her a pleasing docile creature, will not choose to marry *a family* for love, when the world contains many more pretty creatures. What is then to become of her? She either falls an easy prey to some mean fortune-hunter, who defrauds her children of their paternal inheritance, and renders her miserable; or becomes the victim of discontent and blind indulgence. Unable to educate her sons, or impress them with respect; for it is not a play on words to assert, that people are never respected, though filling an important station, who are not respectable; she pines under the anguish of unavailing impotent regret. The serpent's tooth enters into her very soul, and the vices of licentious youth bring her with sorrow, if not with poverty also, to the grave.

This is not an overcharged picture; on the contrary, it is a very possible case, and something similar must have fallen under every attentive eye.

I have, however, taken it for granted, that she was well disposed, though experience shows, that the blind may as easily be led into a ditch as along the beaten road. But supposing, no very improbable conjecture, that a being only taught to please must still find her happiness in pleasing; what an example of folly, not to say vice, will she be to her innocent daughters! The mother will be lost in the coquette, and, instead of making friends of her daughters, view them with eyes askance, for they are rivals — rivals more cruel than any other, because they invite a comparison, and drive her from the throne of beauty, who has never thought of a seat on the bench of reason.

It does not require a lively pencil, or the discriminating outline of a caricature, to sketch the domestic miseries and petty vices which such a mistress of a family diffuses. Still she only acts as a woman ought to act, brought up according to Rousseau's system. She can never be reproached for being masculine, or turning out of her sphere; nay, she may observe another of his grand rules, and, cautiously preserving her reputation free from spot, be reckoned a good kind of woman. Yet in what respect can she be termed good? She abstains, it is true, without any great struggle, from committing gross crimes; but how does she fulfill her duties? Duties! In truth she has enough to think of to adorn her body and nurse a weak constitution.

With respect to religion, she never presumed to judge for herself; but conformed, as a dependent creature should, to the ceremonies of the Church which she was brought up in, piously believing that wiser heads than her own have settled that business; and not to doubt is her point of perfection. She therefore pays her tithe of mint and cumin — and thanks her God that she is not as other women are. These are the blessed effects of a good education! These the virtues of man's helpmate!

I must relieve myself by drawing a different picture.

Let fancy now present a woman with a tolerable understanding, for I do not wish to leave the line of mediocrity, whose constitution, strengthened by exercise, has allowed her body to acquire its full vigor; her mind, at the same time, gradually expanding itself to comprehend the moral duties of life, and in what human virtue and dignity consist.

Formed thus by the discharge of the relative duties of her station, she marries from affection, without losing sight of prudence, and looking beyond matrimonial felicity, she secures her husband's respect before it is necessary to exert mean arts to please him and feed a dying flame, which nature doomed to expire when the object became familiar, when friendship and forbearance take place of a more ardent affection. This is the natural death of love, and domestic peace is not destroyed by struggles to prevent its extinction. I also suppose the husband to be virtuous; or she is still more in want of independent principles.

Fate, however, breaks this tie. She is left a widow, perhaps, without a sufficient provision; but she is not desolate! The pang of nature is felt; but after time has softened sorrow into melancholy resignation, her heart turns to her children with redoubled fondness, and anxious to provide for them, affection gives a sacred heroic cast to her maternal duties. She thinks that not only the eye sees her virtuous efforts from whom all her comfort now must flow, and whose approbation is life; but her imagination, a little abstracted and exalted by grief, dwells on the fond hope that the eyes which her trembling hand closed, may still see how she subdues every wayward passion to fulfill the double duty of being the father as well as the mother of her children. Raised to heroism by misfortunes, she represses the first faint dawning of a natural inclination, before it ripens into love, and in the bloom of life forgets her sex — forgets the pleasure of an awakening passion, which might again have been inspired and returned. She no longer thinks of pleasing, and conscious dignity prevents her from priding herself on account of the praise which her conduct demands. Her children have her love, and her brightest hopes are beyond the grave, where her imagination often strays.

I think I see her surrounded by her children, reaping the reward of her care. The intelligent eye meets hers, whilst health and innocence smile on their chubby cheeks, and as they grow up the cares of life are lessened by their grateful attention. She lives to see the virtues which she endeavored to plant on principles, fixed into habits, to see her children attain a strength of character sufficient to enable them to endure adversity without forgetting their mother's example.

The task of life thus fulfilled, she calmly waits for the sleep of death, and rising from the grave, may say — "Behold, thou gavest me a talent, and here are five talents."

I wish to sum up what I have said in a few words, for I here throw down my gauntlet, and deny the existence of sexual virtues, not excepting modesty. For man and woman, truth, if I understand the meaning of the word, must be the same; yet the fanciful female character, so prettily drawn by poets and novelists, demanding the sacrifice of truth and sincerity, virtue becomes a relative idea, having no other foundation than utility, and of that utility men pretend arbitrarily to judge, shaping it to their own convenience.

Women, I allow, may have different duties to fulfill; but they are human duties, and the principles that should regulate the discharge of them, I sturdily maintain, must be the same.

To become respectable, the exercise of their understanding is necessary, there is no other foundation for independence of character; I mean explicitly to say that they must only bow to the authority of reason, instead of being the modest slaves of opinion.

In the superior ranks of life how seldom do we meet with a man of superior abilities, or even common acquirements? The reason appears to me clear, the state they are born in was an unnatural one. The human character has ever been formed by the employments the individual, or class, pursues; and if the faculties are not sharpened by necessity, they must remain obtuse. The argument may fairly be extended to women; for, seldom occupied by serious business, the pursuit of pleasure gives that insignificancy to their character which renders the society of the great so insipid. The same want of firmness, produced by a similar cause, forces them both to fly from themselves to noisy pleasures, and artificial passions, till vanity takes place of every social affection, and the characteristics of humanity can scarcely be discerned. Such are the blessings of civil governments, as they are at present organized, that wealth and female softness equally tend to debase mankind, and are produced by the same cause; but allowing women to be rational creatures, they should be incited to acquire virtues which they may call their own, for how can a rational being be ennobled by anything that is not obtained by its own exertions?...

Though I consider that women in the common walks of life are called to fulfill the duties of wives and mothers, by religion and reason, I cannot help lamenting that women of a superior cast have not a road open by which they can pursue more extensive plans of usefulness and independence. I may excite laughter, by dropping an hint, which I mean to pursue, some future time, for I really think that women ought to have representatives, instead of being arbitrarily governed without having any direct share allowed them in the deliberations of government....

But, as the whole system of representation is now, in this country, only a convenient handle for despotism, they need not complain, for they are as well represented as a numerous class of hard-working mechanics, who pay for the support of royalty when they can scarcely stop their children's mouths with bread. How are they represented whose very sweat supports the splendid stud of an heir-apparent, or varnishes the chariot of some female favorite who looks down on shame? Taxes on the very necessaries of life, enable an endless tribe of idle princes and princesses to pass with stupid pomp before a gaping crowd, who almost worship the very parade which costs them so dear....

But what have women to do in society? I may be asked, but to loiter with easy grace; surely you would not condemn them all to suckle fools and chronicle small beer! No. Women might certainly study the art of healing, and be physicians as well as nurses. And midwifery, decency seems to allot to them, though I am afraid, the word midwife, in our dictionaries, will soon give place to *accoucheur*, and one proof of the former delicacy of the sex be effaced from the language.

They might also study politics, and settle their benevolence on the broadest basis; for the reading of history will scarcely be more useful than the perusal of romances, if read as mere biography; if the character of the times, the political improvements, arts, etc., be not observed. In short, if it be not considered as the history of man; and not of particular men, who filled a niche in the temple of fame, and dropped into the black rolling stream of time, that silently sweeps all before it into the shapeless void called — eternity. — For shape, can it be called, "that shape hath none"?

Business of various kinds, they might likewise pursue, if they were educated in a more orderly manner, which might save many from common and legal prostitution. Women would not then marry for a support, as men accept of places under Government, and neglect the implied duties; nor would an attempt to earn their own subsistence, a most laudable one! sink them almost to the level of those poor abandoned creatures who live by prostitution. For are not milliners and mantua-makers reckoned the next class? The few employments open to women, so far, from being liberal, are menial; and when a superior education enables them to take charge of the education of children as governesses, they are not treated like the tutors of sons, though even clerical tutors are not always treated in a manner calculated to render them respectable in the eyes of their pupils, to say nothing of the private comfort of the individual. But as women educated like gentlewomen, are never designed for the humiliating situation which necessity sometimes forces them to fill; these situations are considered in the light of a degradation; and they know little of the human heart, who need to be told, that nothing so painfully sharpens sensibility as such a fall in life....

Parental Affection

Woman, however, a slave in every situation to prejudice, seldom exerts enlightened maternal affection; for she either neglects her children, or spoils them by improper indulgence. The affection of some women for their children is, as I have before termed it, frequently very brutish: for it eradicates every spark of humanity. Justice, truth, everything is sacrificed by these Rebekahs, and for the sake of their own children they violate the most sacred duties, forgetting the common relationship that binds the whole family on earth together. Yet, reason seems to say, that they who suffer one duty, or affection, to swallow up the rest, have not sufficient heart or mind to fulfill that one conscientiously. It then loses the venerable aspect of a duty, and assumes the fantastic form of a whim....

[U]nless the understanding of woman be enlarged, and her character rendered more firm, by being allowed to govern her own conduct, she will have sufficient sense or command of temper to manage her children properly....

On National Education

The good effects resulting from attention to private education will ever be very confined, and the parent who really puts his own hand to the plough, will always, in some degree, be disappointed, till education becomes a grand national concern. A man cannot retire into a desert with his child, and if he did he could not bring himself back to childhood, and become the proper friend and playfellow of an infant or youth. And when children are confined to the society of men and women, they very soon acquire that kind of premature man-hood which stops the growth of every vigorous power of mind or body. In order to open their faculties they should be excited to think for themselves; and this can only be done by mixing a number of children together, and making them jointly pursue the same objects....

This train of reasoning brings me back to a subject, on which I mean to dwell, the necessity of establishing proper day-schools.

But, these should be national establishments, for whilst schoolmasters are dependent on the caprice of parents, little exertion can be expected from them, more than is necessary to please ignorant people. Indeed, the necessity of a master's giving the parents some sample of the boy's abilities, which during the vacation is shown to every visitor, is productive of more mischief than would at first be supposed. For it is seldom done entirely, to speak with moderation, by the child itself; thus the master countenances falsehood, or winds the poor machine up to some extraordinary exertion, that injures the wheels, and stops the progress of gradual improvement. The memory is loaded with unintelligible words, to make a show of, without the understanding's acquiring any distinct ideas: but only that education deserves emphatically to be termed cultivation of mind, which teaches young people how to begin to think. The imagination should not be allowed to debauch the understanding before it gained strength, or vanity will become the forerunner of vice: for every way of exhibiting the acquirements of a child is injurious to its moral character....

When...I call women slaves, I mean in a political and civil sense: for indirectly they obtain too much power, and are debased by their exertions to obtain illicit sway.

Let an enlightened nation then try what effect reason would have to bring them back to nature, and their duty; and allowing them to share the advantages of education and government with man, see whether they will become better, as they grow wiser and become free. They cannot be injured by the experiment, for it is not the power of man to render them more insignificant than they are at present....

To render this practicable, day-schools for particular ages should be established by Government, in which boys and girls might be educated together. The school for the younger children, from five to nine years of age, ought to be absolutely free and open to all classes....

To prevent any of the distinctions of vanity, they should be dressed alike, and all obliged to submit to the same discipline, or leave the school. The schoolroom ought to be surrounded by a large piece of ground, in which the children might be usefully exercised, for at this age they should not be confined to any sedentary employment for more than an hour at a time. But these relaxations might all be rendered a part of elementary education, for many things improve and amuse the senses, when introduced as a kind of show, to the principles of which, dryly laid down, children would turn a deaf ear. For instance, botany, mechanics, and astronomy; reading, writing, arithmetic, natural history, and some simple experiments in natural philosophy, might fill up the day; but these pursuits should never encroach on gymnastic plays in the open air. The elements of religion, history, the history of man, and politics, might also be taught by conversations in the Socratic form....

These would be schools of morality — and the happiness of man, allowed to flow from the pure springs of duty and affection, what advances might not the human mind make? Society can only be happy and free in proportion as it is virtuous; but the present distinctions, established in society, corrode all private, and blast all public virtue.

I have already inveighed against the custom of confining girls to their needle, and shutting them out from all political and civil employments; for by thus narrowing their minds they are rendered unfit to fulfill the peculiar duties which Nature has assigned them....

I speak of the improvement and emancipation of the whole sex, for I know that the behavior of a few women, who, by accident, or following a strong bent of nature, have acquired a portion of knowledge superior to that of the rest of their sex, has often been overbearing; but there have been instances of women who, attaining knowledge, have not discarded modesty, nor have they always pedantically appeared to despise the ignorance which they labored to disperse in their own minds. The exclamations then which any advice respecting female learning commonly produces, especially from pretty women, often arise from envy. When they chance to see that even the luster of their eyes, and the flippant sportiveness of refined coquetry, will not always secure them attention during a whole evening, should a woman of a more cultivated understanding endeavor to give a rational turn to the conversation, the common source of consolation is that such women seldom get husbands. What arts have I not seen silly women use to interrupt by *flirtation* — a very significant word to describe such a maneuver — a rational conversation, which made the men forget that they were pretty women.

But, allowing what is very natural to man, that the possession of rare abilities is really calculated to excite over-weening pride, disgusting in both men and women, in what a state of inferiority must the female faculties have rusted when such a small portion of knowledge as those women attained, who have sneeringly been termed learned women, could be singular? — sufficiently so to puff up the possessor, and excite envy in her contemporaries, and some of the other sex....

The conclusion which I wish to draw is obvious. Make women rational creatures and free citizens, and they will quickly become good wives and mothers — that is, if men do not neglect the duties of husbands and fathers.

Discussing the advantages which a public and private education combined, as I have sketched, might rationally be expected to produce, I have dwelt most on such as are particularly relative to the female world, because I think the female world oppressed; yet the gangrene, which the vices engendered by oppression have produced, is not confined to the morbid part, but pervades society at large; so that when I wish to see my sex become more like moral agents, my heart bounds with the anticipation of the general diffusion of that sublime contentment which only morality can diffuse.

7.9 "ADMISSION OF JEWS TO RIGHTS OF CITIZENSHIP" (1791)

Duport: I have one very short observation to make to the Assembly, which appears to be of the highest importance and which demands all its attention. You have regulated by the Constitution, Sirs, the quali-

ties deemed necessary to become a French citizen, and an active citizen: that sufficed, I believe, to regulate all the incidental questions that could have been raised in the Assembly relative to certain professions, to certain persons. But there is a decree of adjournment that seems to strike a blow at these general rights: I speak of the Jews. To decide the question that concerns them, it suffices to lift the decree of adjournment that you have rendered and which seems to suspend the question in their regard. Thus, if you had not rendered a decree of adjournment on the question of the Jews, it would not have been necessary to do anything; for, having declared by your Constitution how all peoples of the earth could become French citizens and how all French citizens could become active citizens, there would have been no difficulty on this subject.

I ask therefore that the decree of adjournment be revoked and that it be declared relative to the Jews that they will be able to become active citizens, like all the peoples of the world, by fulfilling the conditions prescribed by the Constitution. I believe that freedom of worship no longer permits any distinction to be made between the political rights of citizens on the basis of their beliefs and I believe equally that the Jews cannot be the only exceptions to the enjoyment of these rights, when pagans, Turks, Muslims, Chinese even, men of all the sects, in short, are admitted to these rights.

Decree of the National Assembly, 27 September 1791

The National Assembly, considering that the conditions necessary to be a French citizen and to become an active citizen are fixed by the Constitution, and that every man meeting the said conditions, who swears the civic oath, and engages himself to fulfill all the duties that the Constitution imposes, has the right to all of the advantages that the Constitution assures;

Revokes all adjournments, reservations, and exceptions inserted into the preceding decrees relative to Jewish individuals who will swear the civic oath which will be regarded as a renunciation of all the privileges and exceptions introduced previously in their favor.

PART III

The Socialist Contribution and the Industrial Age

INTRODUCTION

With the British sociologist T. H. Marshall (1893–1981), Part III introduces readers to an analysis of human rights based on social and economic changes. In his *Citizenship and Social Classes* (1950), Marshall provides an invaluable introduction to the development of citizenship, institutions, and rights in relationship to the changing nature of capitalism. He divides the notion of citizenship into three components: civil, political, and social rights. The first part is rooted in the Enlightenment, stretching backward to include the Habeas Corpus, the Toleration Act, and the abolition of censorship of the press. The second component is associated with the institution of voting rights, which emerged with the First British Reform Act of 1832. The development of the third component began with the demand for free public education, which, along other social rights, gained wider currency during the nineteenth century. But it was only during the twentieth century, Marshall argued, that social rights achieved equal partnership with the civil and political elements of citizenship — as reflected in the institution of the welfare state in the United States and Europe and the promulgation of Articles 20 to 26 of the 1948 United Nations Declaration of Human Rights.

The call for broadening human rights during the nineteenth century coincided with the deplorable conditions experienced by the growing working class converging around new industrial sites. Placing the concept of civil and economic rights inherited from the Enlightenment in its historical and socioeconomic context, socialist radicals and reformers fought to extend universal suffrage and social rights to the dispossessed. While oscillating between calls for political reform and class war, they established, under Karl Marx's leadership, a new socialist international organization (the International) to orchestrate worldwide working class action. One goal was to oppose the drift toward wars driven by geopolitical and imperialist interests. Under the organic principle of human emancipation, the new international organization was also devoted to ending slavery and to advancing the rights of children, women, and marginalized minorities.

III.1   T. H. MARSHALL: ON CIVIL, POLITICAL, AND SOCIAL RIGHTS
(*CITIZENSHIP AND SOCIAL CLASSES*, 1950)

The Development of Citizenship to the End of the Nineteenth Century

I shall be running true to type as a sociologist if I begin by saying that I propose to divide citizenship into three parts. But the analysis is, in this case, dictated by history even more clearly than by logic. I shall call these three parts, or elements, civil, political and social. The civil element is composed of the rights necessary for individual freedom — liberty of the person, freedom of speech, thought and faith, the right to own property and to conclude valid contracts, and the right to justice. The last is of a different order from the others, because it is the right to defend and assert all one's rights on terms of equality with others and by due process of law. This shows us that the institutions most directly associated with civil rights are the courts of justice. By the political element I mean the right to participate in the exercise of political power, as a member of a body invested with political authority or as an elector of the members of such a body. The corresponding institutions are parliament and councils of local government. By the social element I mean the whole range from the right to a modicum of economic welfare and security to the right to share to the full in the social heritage and to live the life of a civilized being according to the standards prevailing in the society. The institutions most closely connected with it are the educational system and the social services.[1]

In early times these three strands were wound into a single thread. The rights were blended because the institutions were amalgamated. As Maitland said: "The further back we trace our history the more impossible it is for us to draw strict lines, of demarcation between the various functions of the State: the same institution is a legislative assembly, a governmental council and a court of law ... Everywhere, as we pass from the ancient to the modern, we see what the fashionable philosophy calls differentiation."[2]...

When the three elements of citizenship parted company they were soon barely on speaking terms. So complete was the divorce between them that it is possible, without doing too much violence to historical accuracy, to assign the formative period in the life of each to a different century — civil rights to the eighteenth, political to the nineteenth and social to the twentieth. These periods must, of course, be treated with reasonable elasticity, and there is some evident overlap, especially between the last two.

To make the eighteenth century cover the formative period of civil rights it must be stretched backwards to include Habeas Corpus, the Toleration Act, and the abolition of the censorship of the press; and it must be extended forwards to include Catholic Emancipation, the repeal of the Combination Acts, and the successful end of the battle for the freedom of the press associated with the names of Cobbett and Richard Carlile. It could then be more accurately, but less briefly, described as the period between the Revolution and the first Reform Act. By the end of that period, when political rights made their first infantile attempt to walk in 1832, civil rights had come to man's estate and bore, in most essentials, the appearance that they have today.[3]...

By the beginning of the nineteenth century this principle of individual economic freedom was accepted as axiomatic. You are probably familiar with the passage quoted by the Webbs from the report of the Select Committee of 1811, which states that:

No interference of the legislature with the freedom of trade, or with the perfect liberty of every individual to dispose of his time and of his labor in the way and on the terms which he may judge most conducive to his own interest, can take place without violating general principles of the first importance to the prosperity and happiness of the community.[4]

The repeal of the Elizabethan statutes followed quickly, as the belated recognition of a revolution which had already taken place.

The story of civil rights in their formative period is one of the gradual addition of new rights to a status that already existed and was held to appertain to all adult members of the community — or perhaps one should say to all male members, since the status of women, or at least of married women, was in some important respects peculiar. This democratic, or universal, character of the status arose naturally from the fact that it was essentially the status of freedom, and in seventeenth-century England all men were free. Servile status, or villeinage by blood, had lingered on as a patent anachronism in the days of Elizabeth, but vanished soon afterwards. This change from servile to free labor has been described by Professor Tawney as "a high landmark in the development both of economic and political society," and as "the final triumph of the common law" in regions from which it had been excluded for four centuries. Henceforth the English peasant "is a member of a society in which there is, nominally at least, one law for all men."[5] The liberty which his predecessors had won by fleeing into the free towns had become his by right. In the towns the terms "freedom" and "citizenship" were interchangeable. When freedom became universal, citizenship grew from a local into a national institution.

The story of political rights is different both in time and in character. The formative period began, as I have said, in the early nineteenth century, when the civil rights attached to the status of freedom had already acquired sufficient substance to justify us in speaking of a general status of citizenship. And, when it began, it consisted, not in the creation of new rights to enrich a status already enjoyed by all, but in the granting of old rights to new sections of the population. In the eighteenth century political rights were defective, not in content, but in distribution — defective, that is to say, by the standards of democratic citizenship. The Act of 1832 did little, in a purely quantitative sense, to remedy that defect. After it was passed the voters still amounted to less than one-fifth of the adult male population. The franchise was still a group monopoly, but it had taken the first step towards becoming a

monopoly of a kind acceptable to the ideas of nineteenth-century capitalism — a monopoly which could, with some degree of plausibility, be described as open and not closed. A closed group monopoly is one into which no man can force his way by his own efforts; admission is at the pleasure of the existing members of the group. The description fits a considerable part of the borough franchise before 1832; and it is not too wide of the mark when applied to the franchise based on freehold ownership of land. Freeholds are not always to be had for the asking, even if one has the money to buy them, especially in an age in which families look on their lands as the social, as well as the economic, foundation of their existence. Therefore the Act of 1832, by abolishing rotten boroughs and by extending the franchise to leaseholders and occupying tenants of sufficient economic substance, opened the monopoly by recognizing the political claims of those who could produce the normal evidence of success in the economic struggle.

It is clear that, if we maintain that in the nineteenth century citizenship in the form of civil rights was universal, the political franchise was not one of the rights of citizenship. It was the privilege of a limited economic class, whose limits were extended by each successive Reform Law. It can nevertheless be argued that citizenship in this period was not politically meaningless. It did not confer a right, but it recognized a capacity. No sane and law-abiding citizen was debarred by personal status from acquiring and recording a vote. He was free to earn, to save, to buy property or to rent a house) and to enjoy whatever political rights were attached to these economic achievements. His civil rights entitled him, and electoral reform increasingly enabled him, to do this.

It was, as we shall see, appropriate that nineteenth-century capitalist society should treat political rights as a secondary product of civil rights. It was equally appropriate that the twentieth century should abandon this position and attach political rights directly and independently to citizenship as such. This vital change of principle was put into effect when the Act of 1918, by adopting manhood suffrage, shifted the basis of political rights from economic substance to personal status. I say "manhood" deliberately in order to emphasize the great significance of this reform quite apart from the second, and no less important, reform introduced at the same time — namely the enfranchisement of women. But the Act of 1918 did not fully establish the political equality of all in terms of the rights of citizenship. Remnants of an inequality based on differences of economic substance lingered on until, only last year, plural voting (which had already been reduced to dual voting) was finally abolished.

When I assigned the formative periods of the three elements of citizenship each to a separate century — civil rights to the eighteenth, political to the nineteenth and social to the twentieth — I said that there was a considerable overlap between the last two. I propose to confine what I have to say now about social rights to this overlap, in order that I may complete my historical survey to the end of the nineteenth century, and draw my conclusions from it, before turning my attention to the second half of my subject, a study of our present experiences and their immediate antecedents. In this second act of the drama social rights will occupy the center of the stage.

The original source of social rights was membership of local communities and functional associations. This source was supplemented and progressively replaced by a Poor Law and a system of wage regulation which were nationally conceived and locally administered. The latter — the system of wage regulation — was rapidly decaying in the eighteenth century, not only because industrial change made it administratively impossible, but also because it was incompatible with the new conception of civil rights in the economic sphere, with its emphasis on the right to work where and at what you pleased under a contract of your own making. Wage regulation infringed this individualist principle of the free contract of employment.

The Poor Law was in a somewhat ambiguous position. Elizabethan legislation had made of it something more than a means for relieving destitution and suppressing vagrancy, and its constructive aims suggested an interpretation of social welfare reminiscent of the more primitive, but more genuine, social rights which it had largely superseded. The Elizabethan Poor Law was, after all, one item in a broad program of economic planning whose general object was, not to create a new social order, but to preserve the existing one with the minimum of essential change. As the pattern of the old order dissolved under the blows of a competitive economy, and the plan disintegrated, the Poor Law was left high and dry as an isolated survival from which the idea of social rights was gradually drained away. But at the very end of the eighteenth century there occurred a final struggle between the old and the new, between the planned (or patterned) society and the competitive economy. And in this battle citizenship was divided against itself; social rights sided with the old and civil with the new.

In his book *Origins of Our Time*, Karl Polanyi attributes to the Speenhamland system of poor relief an importance which some readers may find surprising. To him it seems to mark and symbolize the end of an epoch. Through it the old order rallied its retreating forces and delivered a spirited attack into the enemy's country. That, at least, is how I should describe its significance in the history of citizenship. The Speenhamland system offered, in effect, a guaranteed minimum wage and family allowances, combined with the right to work or maintenance. That, even by modern standards, is a substantial body of social rights, going far beyond what one might regard as the proper province of the Poor Law. And it was fully realized by the originators of the scheme that the Poor Law was being invoked to do what wage regulation was no longer able to accomplish. For the Poor Law was the last remains of a system which tried to adjust real income to the social needs and status of the citizen and not solely to the market value of his labor. But this attempt to inject an element of social security into the very structure of the wage system through the instrumentality of the Poor Law was doomed to failure, not only because of its disastrous practical consequences, but also because it was utterly obnoxious to the prevailing spirit of the times.

In this brief episode of our history we see the Poor Law as the aggressive champion of the social rights of citizenship. In the succeeding phase we find the attacker driven back far behind his original position. By the Act of 1834 the Poor Law renounced all claim to trespass on the territory of the wages system, or to interfere with the forces of the free market. It offered relief only to those who, through age or sickness, were incapable of continuing the battle, and to those other weaklings who gave up the struggle, admitted defeat, and cried for mercy. The tentative move towards the concept of social security was reversed. But more than that, the minimal social rights that remained were detached from the status of citizenship. The Poor Law treated the claims of the poor, not as an integral part of the rights of the citizen, but as an alternative to them — as claims which could be met only if the claimants ceased to be citizens in any true sense of the word. For paupers forfeited in practice the civil right of personal liberty, by internment in the workhouse, and they forfeited by law any political rights they might possess. This disability of defranchisement remained in being until 1918, and the significance of its final removal has, perhaps, not been fully appreciated. The stigma which clung to poor relief expressed the deep feelings of a people who understood that those who accepted relief must cross the road that separated the community of citizens from the outcast company of the destitute.

The Poor Law is not an isolated example of this divorce of social rights from the status of citizenship. The early Factory Acts show the same tendency. Although in fact they led to an improvement of working conditions and a reduction of working hours to the benefit of all employed in the industries to which they applied, they meticulously refrained from giving this protection directly to the adult male — the citizen *par excellence*. And they did so out of respect for his status as a citizen, on the grounds that enforced protective measures curtailed the civil right to conclude a free contract of employment. Protection was confined to women and chil-

dren, and champions of women's rights were quick to detect the implied insult. Women were protected because they were not citizens. If they wished to enjoy full and responsible citizenship, they must forgo protection. By the end of the nineteenth century such arguments had become obsolete, and the factory code had become one of the pillars in the edifice of social rights.

The history of education shows superficial resemblances to that of factory legislation. In both cases the nineteenth century was, for the most part, a period in which the foundations of social rights were laid, but the principle of social rights as an integral part of the status of citizenship was either expressly denied or not definitely admitted. But there are significant differences. ...

The education of children has a direct bearing on citizenship, and, when the State guarantees that all children shall be educated, it has the requirements and the nature of citizenship definitely in mind. It is trying to stimulate the growth of citizens in the making. The right to education is a genuine social right of citizenship, because the aim of education during childhood is to shape the future adult. Fundamentally it should be regarded, not as the right of the child to go to school, but as the right of the adult citizen to have been educated. And it follows that the growth of public elementary education during the nineteenth century was the first decisive step on the road to the re-establishment of the social rights of citizenship in the twentieth....

The Early Impact of Citizenship on Social Class

So far my aim has been to trace in outline the development of citizenship in England to the end of the nineteenth century. For this purpose I have divided citizenship into three elements, civil, political and social. I have tried to show that civil rights came first, and were established in something like their modern form before the first Reform Act was passed in 1832. Political rights came next, and their extension was one of the main features of the nineteenth century, although the principle of universal political citizenship was not recognized until 1918. Social rights, on the other hand, sank to a vanishing point in the eighteenth and early nineteenth centuries. Their revival began with the development of public elementary education, but it was not until the twentieth century that they attained to equal partnership with the other two elements in citizenship. ...

[1] By this terminology, what economists sometimes call "income from civil rights" would be called "income from social rights." Cf. H. Dalton, *Some Aspects of the Inequality of Incomes in Modern Communities*, Part 3, Chapters 3 and 4.

[2] F. Maitland, *Constitutional History of England*, p. 105.

[3] The most important exception is the right to strike, but the conditions which made this right vital for the workman and acceptable to political opinion had not yet fully come into being.

[4] Sidney and Beatrice Webb, *History of Trade Unionism*.

[5] R. H. Tawney, *Agrarian Problem in the Sixteenth Century*, 1916, pp. 43–44.

III.2 UNITED NATIONS UNIVERSAL DECLARATION OF HUMAN RIGHTS (1948): ARTICLES 20–26

Article 20

1.   Everyone has the right to freedom of peaceful assembly and association.

2.   No one may be compelled to belong to an association.

Article 21

1.   Everyone has the right to take part in the Government of his country, directly or through freely chosen representatives.

2.   Everyone has the right of equal access to public service in his country.

3.   The will of the people shall be the basis of the authority of government; this will shall be expressed in periodic and genuine elections which shall be by universal and equal suffrage and shall be held by secret vote or by equivalent free voting procedures.

Article 22

Everyone, as a member of society, has the right to social security and is entitled to realization, through national effort and international cooperation and in accordance with the organization and resources of each State, of the economic, social and cultural rights indispensable for his dignity and the free development of his personality.

Article 23

1.   Everyone has the right to work, to free choice of employment, to just and favorable conditions of work and to protection against unemployment.

2.   Everyone, without any discrimination, has the right to equal pay for equal work.

3.   Everyone who works has the right to just and favorable remuneration insuring for himself and his family an existence worthy of human dignity, and supplemented, if necessary, by other means of social protection.

4.   Everyone has the right to form and to join trade unions for the protection of his interests.

Article 24

Everyone has the right to rest and leisure, including reasonable limitation of working hours and periodic holidays with pay.

Article 25

1.   Everyone has the right to a standard of living adequate for the health and well-being of himself and of his family, including food, clothing, housing and medical care and necessary social services, and the right to security in the event of unemployment, sickness, disability, widowhood, old age or other lack of livelihood in circumstances beyond, his control.

2.   Motherhood and childhood are entitled to special care and assistance. All children, whether born in or out of wedlock, shall enjoy the same social protection.

Article 26

1.   Everyone has the right to education. Education shall be free, at least in the elementary and fundamental stages. Elementary education shall be compulsory. Technical and professional education shall be made generally available and higher education shall be equally accessible to all on the basis of merit.

2.   Education shall be directed to the full development of the human personality and to the strengthening of respect for human rights and fundamental freedoms. It shall promote understanding, tolerance and friendship among all nations, racial or religious groups, and shall further the activities of the United Nations for the maintenance of peace.

3.   Parents have a prior right to choose the kind of education that shall be given to their children.

CHAPTER 8

Challenging the Liberal Vision of Rights

Following the Enlightenment's revolutionary heritage, this second generation of rights activists proceeded by articulating how the morality, law, and economic interests of the bourgeoisie had been so far intertwined. In that spirit, the German socialist Friederich Engels (1820–1895), Karl Marx's lifelong intellectual and political companion, opposed the liberal and ahistorical character of human rights defended by German philosophers such as Eugen Dühring. "The concept of truth," Engels asserted in *The Anti-Dühring* (1878), "had varied so much from nation to nation and from age to age, that they have often been in direct contradiction of each other." He further maintained that moral theories of rights are the product of the dominant class at any given stage of economic development. A real human morality, he wrote, is possible only when class antagonisms are transcended in both ideological and material terms. Thus, the notions of free will and freedom are empty if they are not discussed in terms of historical necessity or of material contingencies and possibilities.

Working class conditions and legal rights, socialists argued, were greatly restricted by the new contingencies of capitalism. The unlimited pursuit of property rights, they maintained, mainly benefited those who were initially advantaged and precluded achievement of the universal political equality advocated by liberalism. Thus, efforts to address inequities in voting rights went hand in hand with hopes to redress economic and social disparities. Unsurprisingly, the political rights demands of the Chartist movement, a working class movement that gained its name from the People's Charter of 1838, rallied many radical associations to its cause. The charter demanded political rights, including manhood suffrage, voting by secret ballot, and an end to the need for a property qualification for parliament. From the Chartist movement to the Paris Commune to the establishment of labor parties throughout Europe and the United States, these demands would meet enormous opposition (see Section 8.2).

The June 1848 revolution that led to the restriction of manhood suffrage in France was one of these instances. The German socialist philosopher and activist Karl Marx (1818–1833) supported the Chartist movement in England and wrote in *The New York Daily Tribune* (1850) that the "carrying of universal suffrage in England would be a far more socialistic measure than anything which has been honored with that name on the Continent." Many labor activists echoed his views. In Germany, for instance, prominent socialist writer and political leader Ferdinand Lassalle (1825–1864) advocated popular suffrage in his "Working Class Program," a program originally described in a speech in Berlin in 1862 that was then illegally published as a pamphlet. Lassalle, rejecting Marx's great skepticism regarding the ability of the German state to reform, believed that the working class could free itself through increased political participation (see Section 8.4).

Among the various struggles for universal suffrage, the Paris Commune represents an important episode. The Commune of 1871 was the result of a civil uprising involving all the various revolutionary movements within Paris, accompanying the defeat of the French in the Franco-Prussian War. In the face of growing food shortages and incessant Prussian bombardment, the Parisian working class opted to elect a self-governing commune. They presented the "Manifesto of the Paris Commune" (1871), calling for universal manhood suffrage and a fairer, if not necessarily socialist, management of the economy. After two months of resistance, the government crushed the Paris Commune, leaving 30,000 dead and exiling 7,000 prisoners to the French colony of New Caledonia.

The bloodshed in Paris further galvanized the growing European labor movement, which regarded the right to vote as a political means to improve the social and economic conditions of the working class. For some on the left of the political spectrum, however, attainment of full political equality would require the repudiation of another right that had been central to the earlier Enlightenment tradition: the right to property. Thus, French socialist anarchist Pierre-Joseph Proudhon (1809–1865) went so far as to declare that property was theft. In *What Is Property? or, An Inquiry into Principle of Right and of Government* (1840), he favored the basic rights celebrated by the French Declaration of the Rights of Man and Citizen (1789), namely, the rights to liberty, equality, and security. Yet, "the rich man's right to property," he insisted, is irrationally favored over the "poor man's desire for property. What a contradiction!" While Proudhon emphasized mutual cooperation between social associations, he did not in fact condemn all types of property. He maintained that the rights of farmers to possess the land they work and of craftspeople to own their tools and workshops were essential for the preservation of liberty, as long as their possessions did not lead to the exploitation of the labor of others.

In the same spirit as Proudhon's efforts to improve the fate of the dispossessed, the French socialist politician and historian Louis Blanc (1811–1882) published *The Organization of Labor* (1840), a study that advocated a system of worker-owned workshops, to be started with state subsidies. When Blanc helped create such workshops, and as Parisian workers rallied in defense of workers' rights, the French provisional government violently crushed the 1848 uprising in a bloodbath on what became known as June Day. In exile, Blanc wrote his introduction to the 1848 edition of *The Organization of Labor*, insisting forcefully that unless rooted in material well-being, civil and political rights were devoid of substance (see Section 8.7).

In that same tradition, Karl Marx encapsulated in his various speeches and writings many demands for social and economic rights that were not then secured by capitalism, including the right to the limitation of the working day (1866), the right to freedom of association (1866), universal health care and national public education for both sexes (1866–1869), the prohibition of child labor, the establishment of factory health and safety measures, the regulation of prison labor, and the establishment of effective liability law (1891). It is worth noting that these political, social, and economic demands would later be embodied in key international human rights documents: the 1948 U.N. Universal Declaration of Human Rights, the 1966 U.N. Covenant for Civil and Political Rights, and the 1966 Covenant for Economic, Social, and Cultural Rights.

A HISTORICAL MATERIALIST APPROACH

8.1 FRIEDRICH ENGELS (*THE ANTI-DÜHRING*, 1878)

IX. Morality and Law — Eternal Truths

... If we have not made much progress with truth and error, we can make even less with good and bad. This antithesis belongs exclusively to the domain of morals, that is, a domain belonging to the history of mankind, and it is precisely in this field that final and ultimate truths are most sparsely sown. The conceptions of good and bad have varied so much from nation to nation and from age to age that they have often been in direct contradiction to each other. But all the same, someone may object, good is not bad and bad is not good; if good is confused with bad there is an end to all morality, and everyone can do and leave undone whatever he cares. This is also, stripped of all oracular phrases, Herr Dühring's opinion. But the matter cannot be so simply disposed of. If it was such an easy business there would certainly be no dispute at all over good and bad; everyone would know what was good and what was bad. But how do things stand today? What morality is preached to us today? There is first Christian-feudal morality, inherited from past periods of faith; and this again has two main subdivisions, Catholic and Protestant moralities, each of which in turn has no lack of further subdivisions from the Jesuit-Catholic and Orthodox-Protestant to loose "advanced" moralities. Alongside of these we find the modern bourgeois morality and with it too the proletarian morality of the future, so that in the most advanced European countries alone the past, present and future provide three great groups of moral theories which are in force simultaneously and alongside of one another. Which is then the true one? Not one of them, in the sense of having absolute validity; but certainly that morality which contains the maximum of durable elements is the one which, in the present, represents the overthrow of the present, represents the future: that is, the proletarian.

But when we see that the three classes of modern society, the feudal aristocracy, the bourgeoisie and the proletariat, each have their special morality, we can only draw the conclusion that men, consciously or unconsciously, derive their moral ideas in the last resort from the practical relations on which their class position is based — from the economic relations in which they carry on production and exchange.

But nevertheless there is much that is common to the three moral theories mentioned above — is this not at least a portion of a morality which is externally fixed? These moral theories represent three different stages of the same historical development, and have therefore a common historical background, and for that reason alone they necessarily have much in common. Even more. In similar or approximately similar stages of economic development moral theories must of necessity be more or less in agreement. From the moment when private property in movable objects developed, in all societies in which this private property existed there must be this moral law in common: Thou shall not steal. Does this law thereby become an eternal moral law? By no means. In a society in which the motive for stealing has been done away with, in which therefore at the very most only lunatics would ever steal, how the teacher of morals would be laughed at who tried solemnly to proclaim the eternal truth: Thou shall not steal!

We therefore reject every attempt to impose on us any moral dogma whatsoever as an eternal, ultimate and forever immutable moral law on the pretext that the moral world too has its permanent principles which transcend history and the differences between nations. We maintain on the contrary that all former moral theories are the product, in the last analysis, of the economic stage which society had reached at that particular epoch. And as society has hitherto moved in class antagonisms, morality was always a class morality; it has either justified the domination and the interests of the ruling class, or, as soon as the oppressed class has become powerful enough, it has represented the revolt against this domination and the future interests of the oppressed. That in this process there has on the whole been progress in morality, as in all other branches of human knowledge, cannot be doubted. But we have not yet passed beyond class morality. A really human morality which transcends class antagonisms and their legacies in thought becomes possible only at a stage of society which has not only overcome class contradictions but has even forgotten them in practical life. And now it is possible to appreciate the presumption shown by Herr Dühring in advancing his claim, from the midst of the old class society and on the eve of a social revolution, to impose on the future classless society an eternal morality which is independent of time and changes in reality. Even assuming — what we do not know up to now — that he understands the structure of the society of the future at least in its main outlines.

Finally, one more revelation, which is 'absolutely original' but for that reason no less "going to, the roots of things." With regard to the origin of evil, we have "the fact that the *type of the cat* with the guile associated with it is found in animal form, and the similar fact that a similar type of character is found also in human beings.... There is therefore nothing mysterious about evil, unless someone wants to scent out something mysterious in the existence of that *cat* or of any animal of prey." Evil is — the cat. The devil therefore has no horns or cloven hoof, but claws and green eyes. And Goethe committed an unpardonable error in presenting Mephistopheles as a black dog instead of the said cat. Evil is the cat! That is morality, not only for all worlds, but also — of no use to anyone!

X.   Morality and Law — Equality

… The idea that all men, as men, have something in common, and that they are therefore equal so far as these common characteristics go, is of course primeval. But the modern demand for equality is something entirely different from that; this consists rather in deducing from those common characteristics of humanity, from that equality of men as men, a claim to equal political or social status for all human beings, or at least for all citizens of a state or all members of a society. Before the original conception of relative equality could lead to the conclusion that men should have equal rights in the state and in society, before this conclusion could appear to be something even natural and self-evident, however, thousands of years had to pass and did pass. In the oldest primitive communities equality of rights existed at most for members of the community; women, slaves and strangers were excluded from this equality as a matter of course. Among the Greeks and Romans the inequalities of men were of greater importance than any form of equality. It would necessarily have seemed idiotic to the ancients that Greeks and barbarians, freemen and slaves, citizens and dependents, Roman citizens and Roman subjects (to use a comprehensive term) should have a claim to equal political status. Under the Roman Empire all these distinctions gradually disappeared, except the distinction between freemen and slaves, and in this way there arose, for the freemen at least, that equality as between private individuals on the basis of which Roman law developed — the complete elaboration of law based on private property which we know. But so long as the distinction between freemen and slaves existed, there could be no talk of drawing legal conclusions from the fact of general equality *as men*; and we saw this again quite recently, in the slave-owning states of the North American Union.

Christianity knew only *one* point in which all men were equal: that all were equally born in original sin — which corresponded perfectly with its character as the religion of the slaves and the oppressed. Apart from this is recognized, at most, the equality of the elect, which however was only stressed at the very beginning. The traces of common ownership which are also found in the early stages of the new religion can be ascribed to the solidarity of a prescribed sect rather than to real equalitarian ideas. Within a very short time the establishment of the distinction between priests and laymen put an end even to this tendency to Christian equality. The overrunning of Western Europe by the Germans abolished for centuries ideas of equality, through the gradual building up of a complicated social and political hierarchy such as had never before existed. But at the same time the invasion drew Western and Central Europe into the course of historical development, created for the first time a compact cultural area, and within this area also for the first time a system of predominant national states exerting mutual influence on each other and mutually holding each other in check. Thereby it prepared the ground on which alone the question of the equal status of men, of the rights of man, could at a later period be raised.

The feudal middle ages also developed in its womb the class which was destined in the future course of its evolution to be the standard-bearer of the modern demand for equality: the bourgeoisie. Itself in its origin one of the "estates" of the feudal order, the bourgeoisie developed to predominantly handicraft industry and the exchange of products within feudal society to a relatively high level, when at the end of the fifteenth century the great maritime discoveries opened to it a new and more comprehensive career. Trade beyond the confines of Europe, which had previous been carried on only between Italy and the Levant, was now extended to America and India, and soon surpassed in importance both the mutual exchange between the various European countries and the internal trade within each separate country. American gold and silver flooded Europe and forced its way like a disintegrating element into every fissure, hole and pore of feudal society. Handicraft industry could no longer satisfy the rising demand; in the leading industries of the most advanced countries it was replaced by manufacture.

But this mighty revolution in the economic conditions of life in society was not followed immediately by any corresponding change in its political structure. The state order remained feudal, while society became more and more bourgeois. Trade on a large scale, that is to say, international and, even more, world trade, requires free owners of commodities who are unrestricted in their movements and have equal rights as traders exchange their commodities on the basis of laws that are equal for them all, at least in each separate place. The transition from handicraft to manufacture presupposes the existence of a number of free workers — free on the one hand from the fetters of the guild and on the other from the means whereby they could themselves utilize their labor power: workers who can contract with their employers for the hire of their labor power, and as parties to the contract have rights equal with his. And finally the equality and equal status of a human labor, because and in so far as it is *human* labor, found its unconscious but clearest expression in the law of value of modern bourgeois economics, according to which the value of a commodity is measured by the socially necessary labor embodied in it.[1] But where economic relations required freedom and equality of rights, the political system opposed them at every step with guild restrictions and special privileges. Local privileges, differential duties, exceptional laws of all kinds affected in trading not only foreigners or people living in the colonies, but often enough also whole categories of the nationals of each country; the privileges of the guilds everywhere and ever anew formed barriers to the path of development of manufacture. Nowhere was the path open and the chances equal for the bourgeois competitors — and yet this was the first and ever more pressing need.

The demand for liberation from feudal fetters and the establishment of equality of rights by the abolition of feudal inequalities was bound soon to assume wider dimensions from the moment when the economic advance of society first placed it on the order of the day. If it was raised in the interests of industry and trade, it was also necessary to demand the same equality of rights for the great mass of the peasantry who, in every degree of bondage from total serfdom upwards, were compelled to give the greater part of their labor time to their feudal lord without payment and in addition to render innumerable other dues to him and to the state. On the other hand, it was impossible to avoid the demand for the abolition also of feudal privileges, the freedom from taxation of the nobility, the political privileges of the various feudal estates. And as people were no longer living in a world empire such as the Roman Empire had been, but in a system of independent states dealing with each other on an equal footing and at approximately the same degree of bourgeois development, it was a matter of course that the demand for equality should assume a general character reaching out beyond the individual state, that freedom and equality should be proclaimed as *human rights*. And it is significant of the specifically bourgeois character of these human rights that the American Constitution, the first to recognize the rights of man, in the same breath confirmed the slavery of the colored races in America: class privileges were proscribed, race privileges sanctified.

As is well known, however, from the moment when, like a butterfly from the chrysalis, the bourgeoisie arose out of the burghers of the feudal period, when this "estate" of the Middle Ages developed into a class of modern society, it was always and inevitably accompanied by its shadow, the proletariat. And in the same way the bourgeois demand for equality was accompanied by the proletarian demand for equality. From the moment when the bourgeois demand for the abolition of class *privileges* was put forward, alongside of it appeared the proletarian demand for the abolition of the *classes themselves* — at first in religious form, basing itself on primitive Christianity, and later drawing support from the bourgeois equalitarian theories themselves. The proletarians took the bourgeoisie at their word: equality must not be merely apparent, must not apply merely to the sphere of the state, but must also be real, must be extended to the social and economic sphere. And especially since the time when the French bourgeoisie, from the Great Revolution on, brought bourgeois equality to the forefront, the French proletariat has answered it blow for blow with the demand for social and economic equality, and equality has become the battle-cry particularly of the French proletariat.

The demand for equality in the mouth of the proletariat has therefore a double meaning. It is either — as was especially the case at the very start, for example in the peasants war — the spontaneous reaction against the crying social inequalities, against the contrast of rich and poor, the feudal lords and their serfs, surfeit and starvation; as such it is this simple expression of the revolutionary instinct, and finds its justification in that, and indeed only in that. Or, on the other hand, the proletarian demand for equality has arisen as the reaction against the bourgeois demand for equality, drawing more or less correct and more far-reaching demands from this bourgeois demand, and serving as an agitation means in order to rouse the workers against the capitalists on the basis of the capitalists' own assertions; and in this case it stands and falls with bourgeois equality itself. In both cases the real content of the proletarian demand for equality is the demand for the *abolition of classes*. Any demand for equality which goes beyond that, of necessity passes into absurdity. We have given examples of this, and shall find enough additional ones later when we come to Herr Dühring's fantasies of the future.

The idea of equality, therefore, both in its bourgeois and in its proletarian form, is itself a historical product, the creation of which required definite historical conditions; which in turn themselves presuppose a long previous historical development. It is therefore anything but an eternal truth. And if today it is taken for granted by the general public — in one sense or another — if, as Marx says, it "already possesses the fixity of a popular prejudice," this is not the consequence of its axiomatic truth, but the result of the general diffusion and the continued appropriateness of the ideas of the eighteenth century. If therefore Herr Dühring is

able without more ado to make his famous two men conduct their economic relations on the basis of equality, this is because it seems quite natural to popular prejudice. And in fact Herr Dühring calls his philosophy *natural* because it is derived from things which seem to him quite natural. But why they seem to him quite natural is a question which he does not ask.

XI.   Morality and Law — Freedom and Necessity

... It is difficult to deal with morality and law without coming up against the question of so-called free will, of human responsibility, of the relation between freedom and necessity. And the philosophy of reality also has not only one but even two solutions of this problem.

"All false theories of freedom must be replaced by what we know from experience is the nature of the relation between rational judgment on the one hand and instinctive impulse on the other, a relation which *so to speak* unites them into a single mean force. The fundamental facts of this form of dynamics must be drawn from observation, and for the calculation in advance of events which have not yet occurred must also be estimated *as closely as possible*, in general both as to their nature and magnitude. In this way the foolish delusions of inner freedom, which have been a source of worry and anxiety for thousands of years, are not only thoroughly cleared away, but are also replaced by something positive, which can be made use of for the practical regulation of life."— On this basis freedom consists in rational judgment pulling a man to the right while irrational impulses pull him to the left, and in this parallelogram of forces the actual movement follows the direction of the diagonal. Freedom is therefore the mean between judgment and impulse, reason and unreason, and its degree in each individual case can be determined on the basis of experience by a "personal equation," to use an astronomical expression. But a few pages later on we find: "We base moral responsibility on freedom, which however in our view means nothing more than susceptibility to conscious motives in accordance with our natural and acquired intelligence. All such motives operate with the inevitable force of natural law, not withstanding our awareness of the possible contradiction in the actions; but it is precisely on this inevitable compulsion that we rely when we bring in the moral lever."

This second definition of freedom, which quite unceremoniously gives a knock-out blow to the other, is again nothing but an extremely superficial rendering of the Hegelian conception of the matter. Hegel was the first to state correctly the relation between freedom and necessity. To him, freedom is the appreciation of necessity. "Necessity is *blind* only *in so far as it is not understood.*" Freedom does not consist in the dream of independence of natural laws, but in the knowledge of these laws, and in the possibility this gives of systematically making them work towards definite ends. This holds good in relation both to the laws of external nature and to those which govern the bodily and mental existence of men themselves — two classes of laws which we can separate from each other at most only in thought but not in reality. Freedom of the will therefore means nothing but the capacity to make decisions with real knowledge of the subject. Therefore the *freer* a man's judgment is in relation to a definite question, with so much the greater *necessity* is the content of this judgment determined; while the uncertainty, rounded on ignorance, which seems to make an arbitrary choice among many different and conflicting possible decisions, shows by this precisely that it is not free, that it is controlled by the very object it should itself control. Freedom therefore consists in the control over ourselves and over external nature which is found on knowledge of natural necessity; it is therefore necessarily a product of historical development. The first men who separated themselves from the animal kingdom were in all essentials as unfree

as the animals themselves, but each step forward in civilization was a step towards freedom. On the threshold of human history stands the discovery that mechanical motion can be transformed into heat the production of fire by friction; at the close of the development so far gone through stands the discovery that heat can be transformed into mechanical motion: the steam-engine. And, in spite of the gigantic and liberating revolution in the social world which the steam engine is carrying through — and which is not yet half completed — it is beyond question that the generation of fire by friction was of even greater effectiveness for the liberation of mankind. For the generation of fire by friction gave man for the first time control over one of the forces of Nature, and thereby separated him for ever from the animal kingdom. The steam engine will never bring about such a mighty leap forward in human development, however important it may seem in our eyes as representing all those powerful productive forces dependent on it — forces which alone make possible a state of society in which there are no longer class distinctions or anxiety over the means of subsistence for the individual, and in which for the first time there can be talk of real human freedom and of an existence in harmony with the established laws of Nature. But how young the whole of human history still is, and how ridiculous it would be to attempt to ascribe any absolute validity to our present views, is evident from the simple fact that all past history can be characterized as the history of the epoch from the practical discovery of the transformation of mechanical motion into heat up to that of the transformation of heat into mechanical motion....

[1] This tracing of the origin of the modern ideas of equality to the economic condition of bourgeois society was first developed by Marx in *Capital* [note by F. Engels].

THE STRUGGLE FOR VOTING RIGHTS

8.2 CHARTISM: ON THE PETITION FOR VOTING RIGHTS (1838)[1]

To the Honorable the Commons of Great Britian and Ireland. The Petition of the undersigned Members of the Working Men's Association and others sheweth —

That the only *rational use* of the institutions and laws of society is justly to protect, encourage, and support all that can be made to contribute to *the happiness of all the people.*

That, as the object to be obtained is mutual benefit, so ought the enactment of laws to be by mutual consent.

That obedience to laws can only be *justly enforced* on the certainty that those who are called on to obey them have had, either personally or by their representatives, the power to enact, amend, or repeal them.

That all those who are excluded from this share of political power are not justly included within the operation of the laws; to them the laws are only despotic enactments, and the legislative assembly from whom they emanate can only be considered parties to an unholy compact, devising plans and schemes for taxing and subjecting the many.

That the universal political right of every human being is superior and stands apart from all customs, forms, or ancient usage; a fundamental right not in the power of man to confer, or justly to deprive him of.

That to take away this sacred right from the *person* and to vest it in *property*, is a willful perversion of justice and common sense, as the creation and security of property *are the consequences of society* — the great object of which is human happiness.

That any constitution or code of laws, formed in violation of men's political and social rights, are not rendered sacred by time nor sanctified by custom.

That the ignorance which originated, or permits their operation, forms no excuse for perpetuating the injustice; nor can aught but force or fraud sustain them, when any considerable number of the people perceive and feel their degradation.

That the intent and object of your petitioners are to present such facts before your Honorable house as will serve to convince you and the country at large that you do not represent the people of these realms; and to appeal to your sense of right and justice as well as to every principle of honor, for directly making such legislative enactments as shall cause the mass of the people to be represented; with the view of securing *the greatest amount of happiness to all classes of society....*

Your petitioners therefore respectfully submit to your Honorable House that these facts afford abundant proofs that you do not represent the numbers or the interests of the millions; but that the persons composing it have interests for the most part foreign or directly opposed to the true interests of the great body of the people.

That perceiving the tremendous power you possess over the lives, liberty and labor of the unrepresented millions — perceiving the *military* and *civil forces* at your command — *the revenue* at your disposal — the *relief of the poor in* your hands — the *public press* in your power, by enactments expressly excluding the working classes alone — moreover, the power of delegating to others the whole control of the *monetary arrangements* of the Kingdom, by which the laboring classes may be silently plundered or suddenly suspended from employment — seeing all these elements of power wielded by your Honorable House as at present constituted, and fearing the consequences that may result if a thorough reform is not speedily had recourse to, your petitioners earnestly pray your Honorable House *to enact the following as the law of these realms,* with such other essential details as your Honorable House shall deem necessary.

[1] Petition adopted at the Crown and Anchor Meeting.

A Law for Equally Representing the People of Great Britain and Ireland

Equal Representation

That the United Kingdom be divided into 200 electoral districts; dividing, as nearly as possible, an equal number of inhabitants; and that each district do send a representative to Parliament.

Universal Suffrage

That every person producing proof of his being 21 years of age, to the clerk of the parish in which he has resided six months, shall be entitled to have his name registered as a voter. That the time for registering in each year be from the 1st of January to the 1st of March.

Annual Parliaments

That a general election do take place on the 24th of June in each year, and that each vacancy be filled up a fortnight after it occurs. That the hours for voting be from six o'clock in the morning till six o'clock in the evening.

No Property Qualifications

That there shall be no property qualification for members; but on requisition, signed by 200 voters, in favor of any candidate being presented to the clerk of the parish in which they reside, such candidate shall be put in nomination. And the list of all the candidates nominated throughout the district shall be stuck on the church door in every parish, to enable voters to judge of their qualification.

Vote by Ballot

That each voter must vote in the parish in which he resides. That each parish provide as many balloting boxes as there are candidates proposed in the district; and that a temporary place be fitted up in each parish church for the purpose of secret voting. And, on the day of election, as each voter passes orderly on to the ballot, he shall have given to him, by the officer in attendance, a balloting ball, which he shall drop into the box of his favorite candidate. At the close of the day the votes shall be counted, by the proper officers, and the numbers stuck on the church doors. The following day the clerk of the district and two examiners shall collect the votes of all the parishes throughout the district, and cause the name of the successful candidate to be posted in every parish of the district.

Sittings and Payments to Members

That the members do take their seats in Parliament on the first Monday in October next after the election, and continue their sittings every day (Sundays excepted) till the business of the sitting is terminated, but not later than the 1st of September. They shall meet every day (during the Session) for business at 10 o'clock in the morning, and adjourn at 4. And every member shall be paid quarterly out of the public treasury £400 a year. That all electoral officers shall be elected by universal suffrage. By passing the foregoing as the law of the land, you will confer a great blessing on the people of England; and your petitioners, as is duty bound, will ever pray.

8.3   KARL MARX: ON UNIVERSAL SUFFRAGE (1852)

... We now come to the Chartists, the politically active portion of the British working class. The six points of the Charter which they contend for contain nothing but the demand of universal suffrage, and of the conditions without which universal suffrage would be illusory for the working class, such as the ballot, payment of members, annual general elections. But universal suffrage is the equivalent for political power for the working class of England, where the proletariat forms the large majority of the population, where, in a long, though underground, civil war, it has gained a clear consciousness of its position as a class, and where even the rural districts know no longer any peasants, but only landlords, industrial capitalists (farmers), and hired laborers. The carrying of universal suffrage in England would, therefore, be a far more socialistic measure than anything which has been honored with that name on the Continent.

Its inevitable result, here, is the political supremacy of the working class....

8.4 FERDINAND LASSALLE: ON UNIVERSAL AND DIRECT SUFFRAGE (*THE WORKING CLASS PROGRAM*, 1862)

...We will now consider the principle of the working class as the ruling principle of the community only in three of its relations: —

(1) In relation to the formal means of its realization.
(2) In relation to its moral significance.
(3) In relation to the political conception of the object of the State, which is inherent in that principle.

We cannot on this occasion enter upon its other aspects, and even those to which we have referred can be only very cursorily examined in the short time that remains to us.

The formal means of carrying out this principle is the universal and direct suffrage which we have already discussed. I say universal and *direct* suffrage, gentlemen, not that mere universal suffrage which we had in the year 1848. The introduction of two degrees in the electoral act, namely, original electors and electors simply, is nothing but an ingenious method purposely introduced with the object of falsifying as far as possible the will of the people by means of the electoral act.

It is true that even universal and direct suffrage is no magic wand, gentlemen, which is able to protect you from temporary mistakes.

We have seen in France two bad elections following one another, in 1848 and 1849. But universal and direct suffrage is the *only* means which in the long run of itself corrects the mistakes to which its momentary wrong use may lead. It is that spear which heals the wounds it itself has made. It is impossible in the long run with universal and direct suffrage that the elected body should be any other than the exact and true likeness of the people which has elected it.

The people must therefore at all times regard universal and direct suffrage as its indispensable political weapon, as the most fundamental and important of its demands.

I will now glance at the *moral* significance of the principle of society which we are considering.

It is possible that the idea of converting the principle of the *lower classes* of society into the ruling principle of the State and the community may appear to be extremely dangerous and immoral, and to threaten the destruction of morality and education by a "modern barbarism."

And it is no wonder that this idea should be so regarded at the present day since even public opinion, gentlemen — I have already indicated by what means, namely, the newspapers — receives its impressions from the mint of *capital*, and from the hands of the privileged wealthy Bourgeoisie.

Nevertheless this fear is only a prejudice, and it can be proved on the contrary, that the idea would exhibit the greatest advance and triumph of morality that the history of the world has ever recorded.

That view is a prejudice I repeat, and it is simply the prejudice of the *present time* which is dominated by privilege.

At another time, namely, that of the first French Republic of the year 1793 (of which I have already told you that I cannot enter into further particulars on this occasion, but that it was destined to perish by its own want of definite aims) the *opposite* prejudice prevailed. It was then a current dogma that all the upper classes were immoral and corrupt, and that only the lower classes were good and moral. In the new declaration of the rights of man issued by the French convention, that powerful constituent assembly of France, this was actually laid down by a special article, namely, article nineteen, which runs as follows, "Toute institution qui ne suppose le peuple bon, et le magistrat corruptible, est vicieuse." ["Every institution which does not assume that the people are good and the magistracy contemptible is vicious."] You see that this is exactly the opposite to the happy faith now required, according to which there is no greater sin than to doubt of the goodwill and the virtue of the Government, while it is taken for granted that the *people* are a sort of tiger and a sink of corruption.

At the time of which we are speaking the opposite dogma had advanced so far, that almost every one who had a whole coat on his back was thought to be a bad man, or at least an object of suspicion; and virtue, purity, and patriotic morality were thought to be possessed only by those who had no decent clothes. It was the period of sansculottism.[1]

This view, gentlemen, is in fact founded on *a truth*, but it presents itself in an *untrue* and *perverted* form. Now there is nothing more dangerous than a truth which presents itself in an untrue perverted form. For in whatever way we deal with it, we are certain to go wrong. If we adopt such a truth in its untrue perverted form, it will lead at certain times to most pernicious destruction, as was the case with sansculottism. But if we regard the whole statement as untrue on account of its untrue perverted form, then we are much worse. For we have rejected a *truth*, and, in the case before us, a truth without the recognition of which not a single sound step in our political life can be taken.

The only course that remains open to us, therefore, is to set aside the untrue and perverted form of the statement, and to bring its true essence into distinct relief....

History, gentlemen, is a struggle with nature; with the misery, the ignorance, the poverty, the weakness, and consequent slavery in which we were involved when the human race came upon the scene in the beginning of history. The progressive *victory* over this weakness — this is the development of freedom which history displays to us.

In this struggle we should never have made one step forward, nor shall we ever advance one step more by acting the principle of *each one for himself, each one alone*.

It is *the State* whose function it is to carry on *this development of freedom*, this development of the human race until its freedom is attained.

The State is this unity of individuals into a moral whole, a unity which increases a million-fold the strength of *all* the individuals who are comprehended in it, and multiplies a million times the power which would be at the disposal of them *all* as individuals.

The object of the State, therefore, is not only to *protect* the personal freedom and property of the individual with which he is supposed according to the idea of the Bourgeoisie to have entered the State. On the contrary, the object of the State is precisely this, to place the individuals *through this* union in a position to attain to *such objects*, and reach such a *stage of existence* as they *never* could have reached as individuals; to make them capable of acquiring an amount of *education, power*, and *freedom* which would have been wholly unattainable by them as individuals.

Accordingly the object of the State is to bring man to positive expansion, and progressive development, in other words, to bring the destiny of man — that is the culture of which the human race is *capable* — into *actual existence*; it is the *training and development* of the human race to freedom.

[1] Editor: Popular class during the French revolution.

8.5 MANIFESTO OF THE PARIS COMMUNE (1871)

To the French people:

In the painful and terrible conflict that again threatens Paris with the horrors of a siege and bombardment; that causes French blood to flow, sparing neither our brothers, our wives nor our children; crushed beneath cannonballs and rifle shot, it is necessary that public opinion not be divided, that the national conscience be troubled....

The Commune has the obligation to affirm and determine the aspirations and wishes of the populace of Paris, to define the character of the movement of March 18, misunderstood, unknown and slandered by the politicians seated at Versailles....

What does it ask for?

The recognition and consolidation of the Republic, the only form of government compatible with the rights of the people and the normal and free development of society.

The absolute autonomy of the Commune extended to all localities in France and assuring to each one its full rights, and to every Frenchman the full exercise of his faculties and abilities as man, citizen and producer.

The only limit to the autonomy of the Commune should be the equal right to autonomy for all communes adhering to the contract, whose association shall insure French unity.

The inherent rights of the Commune are:

The vote on communal budgets, receipts and expenses; the fixing and distribution of taxes; the direction of public services; the organization of its magistracy, internal police and education; the administration of goods belonging to the Commune.

The choice by election or competition of magistrates and communal functionaries of all orders, as well as the permanent right of control and revocation.

The absolute guarantee of individual freedom and freedom of conscience.

The permanent intervention of citizens in communal affairs by the free manifestation of their ideas, the free defense of their interests, with guarantees given for these manifestations by the Commune, which alone is charged with overseeing and assuring the free and fair exercise of the right to gather and publicize.

The organization of urban defense and the National Guard, which elects its chiefs and alone watches over the maintenance of order in the city.

Paris wants nothing else as a local guarantee, on condition, of course, of finding in the great central administration — the delegation of federated Communes — the realization and the practice of the same principles.

But as an element of its autonomy, and profiting by its freedom of action, within its borders it reserves to itself the right to operate the administrative and economic reforms called for by the populace as it wills; to create the institutions needed to develop and spread instruction, production, exchange and credit; to universalize power and property in keeping with the needs of the moment, the wishes of those concerned and the facts furnished by experience.

Our enemies are fooling themselves or are fooling the country when they accuse Paris of wanting to impose its will or its supremacy over the rest of the nation and to pretend to a dictatorship, which would be a veritable attack on the independence and sovereignty of other communes....

THE STRUGGLE FOR ECONOMIC AND SOCIAL RIGHTS

8.6 PIERRE-JOSEPH PROUDHON (*WHAT IS PROPERTY? OR, AN INQUIRY INTO THE PRINCIPLE OF RIGHT AND OF GOVERNMENT*, 1840)

Chapter I: Method Pursued in This Work — The Idea of a Revolution

If I were asked to answer the following question: *What is slavery?* and I should answer in one word, *It is murder*, my meaning would be understood at once. No extended argument would be required to show that the power to take from a man his thought, his will, his personality, is a power of life and death; and that to enslave a man is to kill him. Why, then, to this other question: *What is property?* may I not likewise answer, *It is robbery*, without the certainty of being misunderstood; the second proposition being no other than a transformation of the first?

I undertake to discuss the vital principle of our government and our institutions, property: I am in my right. I may be mistaken in the conclusion which shall result from my investigations: I am in my right. I think best to place the last thought of my book first: still am I in my right.

Such an author teaches that property is a civil right, born of occupation and sanctioned by law; another maintains that it is a natural right, originating in labor, — and both of these doctrines, totally opposed as they may seem, are encouraged and applauded. I contend that neither labor, nor occupation, nor law, can create property; that it is an effect without a cause: am I censurable? ...

Nevertheless, I build no system. I ask an end to privilege, the abolition of slavery, equality of rights, and the reign of law. Justice, nothing else; that is the alpha and omega of my argument: to others I leave the business of governing the world....

Chapter II: Property Considered as a Natural Right — Occupation and Civil Law as Efficient

Bases of Property
Definitions

The Roman law defined property as the right to use and abuse one's own within the limits of the law — *jus utendi et abutendi re suâ, quatcnus juris ratio patitur.* A justification of the word *abuse* has been attempted, on the ground that it signifies, not senseless and immoral abuse, but only absolute domain. Vain distinction! invented as an excuse for property, and powerless against the frenzy of possession, which it neither prevents nor represses. The proprietor may, if he chooses, allow his crops to rot under foot; sow his field with salt; milk his cows on the sand; change his vineyard into a desert, and use his vegetable-garden as a park: do these things constitute abuse, or not? In the matter of property, use and abuse are necessarily indistinguishable.

According to the Declaration of Rights, published as a preface to the Constitution of '93, property is "the right to enjoy and dispose at will of one's goods, one's income, and the fruit of one's labor and industry."

Code Napoleon, article 544: "Property is the right to enjoy and dispose of things in the most absolute manner, provided we do not overstep the limits prescribed by the laws and regulations."

These two definitions do not differ from that of the Roman law: all give the proprietor an absolute right over a thing; and as for the restriction imposed by the code, — *provided we do not overstep the limits prescribed by the laws and regulations,* — its object is not to limit property, but to prevent the domain of one proprietor from interfering with that of another. That is a confirmation of the principle, not a limitation of it.

There are different kinds of property: 1. Property pure and simple, the dominant and seigniorial power over a thing; or, as they term it, *naked property.* 2. *Possession.* "Possession," says Duranton, "is a matter of fact, not of right." Toullier: "Property is a right, a legal power; possession is a fact." The tenant, the farmer, the commandite the usufructuary, are possessors; the owner who lets and lends for use, the heir who is to come into possession on the death of a usufructuary, are proprietors. If I may venture the comparison: a lover is a possessor, a husband is a proprietor.

This double definition of property — domain and possession — is of the highest importance; and it must be clearly understood, in order to comprehend what is to follow.

From the distinction between possession and property arise two sorts of rights: the *jus in re,* the right *in* a thing, the right by which I may reclaim the property which I have acquired, in whatever hands I find it; and the *jus ad rem,* right *to* a thing, which gives me a claim to become a proprietor. Thus the right of the partners to a marriage over each other's person is the *jus in re*; that of two who are betrothed is only the *jus ad rem.* In the first, possession and property are united; the second includes only naked property. With me who, as a laborer, have a right to the possession of the products of Nature and my own industry — and who, as a proletaire, enjoy none of them — it is by virtue of the *jus ad rem* that I demand admittance to the *jus in re.*

This distinction between the *jus in re* and the *jus ad rem* is the basis of the famous distinction between *possessoire* and *petitoire,*

— actual categories of jurisprudence, the whole of which is included within their vast boundaries. *Petitoire* refers to every thing relating to property; *possessoire* to that relating to possession. In writing this memoir against property, I bring against universal society an *action petitoire*: I prove that those who do not possess today are proprietors by the same title as those who do possess; but, instead of inferring there from that property should be shared by all, I demand, in the name of general security, its entire abolition. If I fail to win my case, there is nothing left for us (the proletarian class and myself) but to cut our throats: we can ask nothing more from the justice of nations; for, as the code of procedure (art. 26) tells us in its energetic style, *the plaintiff who has been non-suited in an action petitoire, is debarred thereby from bringing an action possessoire*. If, on the contrary, I gain the case, we must then commence an *action possessoire*, that we may be reinstated in the enjoyment of the wealth of which we are deprived by property. I hope that we shall not be forced to that extremity; but these two actions cannot be prosecuted at once, such a course being prohibited by the same code of procedure.

Before going to the heart of the question, it will not be useless to offer a few preliminary remarks.

§ 1. — Property as a Natural Right.

The Declaration of Rights has placed property in its list of the natural and inalienable rights of man, four in all: *liberty, equality, property, security*. What rule did the legislators of '93 follow in compiling this list? None. They laid down principles, just as they discussed sovereignty and the laws; from a general point of view, and according to their own opinion. They did every thing in their own blind way.

If we can believe Toullier: "The absolute rights can be reduced to three: *security, liberty, property*." Equality is eliminated by the Rennes professor; why? Is it because *liberty* implies it, or because property prohibits it? On this point the author of "Droit Civil Explique" is silent: it has not even occurred to him that the matter is under discussion.

Nevertheless, if we compare these three or four rights with each other, we find that property bears no resemblance whatever to the others; that for the majority of citizens it exists only potentially, and as a dormant faculty without exercise; that for the others, who do enjoy it, it is susceptible of certain transactions and modifications which do not harmonize with the idea of a natural right; that, in practice, governments, tribunals, and laws do not respect it; and finally that everybody, spontaneously and with one voice, regards it as chimerical.

Liberty is inviolable. I can neither sell nor alienate my liberty; every contract, every condition of a contract, which has in view the alienation or suspension of liberty, is null: the slave, when he plants his foot upon the soil of liberty, at that moment becomes a free man. When society seizes a malefactor and deprives him of his liberty, it is a case of legitimate defense: whoever violates the social compact by the commission of a crime declares himself a public enemy; in attacking the liberty of others, he compels them to take away his own. Liberty is the original condition of man; to renounce liberty is to renounce the nature of man: after that, how could we perform the acts of man?

Likewise, equality before the law suffers neither restriction nor exception. All Frenchmen are equally eligible to office: consequently, in the presence of this equality, condition and family have, in many cases, no influence upon choice. The poorest citizen can obtain judgment in the courts against one occupying the most exalted station. Let the millionaire, Ahab, build a chateau upon the vineyard of Naboth: the court will have the power, according to the circumstances, to order the destruction of the chateau, though it has cost millions; and to force the trespasser to restore the vineyard to its original state, and pay the damages. The law wishes all property, that has been legitimately acquired, to be kept inviolate without regard to value, and without respect for persons.

The charter demands, it is true, for the exercise of certain political rights, certain conditions of fortune and capacity; but all publicists know that the legislator's intention was not to establish a privilege, but to take security. Provided the conditions fixed by law are complied with, every citizen may be an elector, and every elector eligible. The right, once acquired, is the same for all; the law compares neither persons nor votes. I do not ask now whether this system is the best; it is enough that, in the opinion of the charter and in the eyes of every one, equality before the law is absolute, and, like liberty, admits of no compromise.

It is the same with the right of security. Society promises its members no half-way protection, no sham defense; it binds itself to them as they bind themselves to it. It does not say to them, "I will shield you, provided it costs me nothing; I will protect you, if I run no risks thereby." It says, "I will defend you against everybody; I will save and avenge you, or perish myself." The whole strength of the State is at the service of each citizen; the obligation which binds them together is absolute.

How different with property! Worshipped by all, it is acknowledged by none: laws, morals, customs, public and private conscience, all plot its death and ruin.

To meet the expenses of government, which has armies to support, tasks to perform, and officers to pay, taxes are needed. Let all contribute to these expenses: nothing more just. But why should the rich pay more than the poor? That is just, they say, because they possess more. I confess that such justice is beyond my comprehension.

Why are taxes paid? To protect all in the exercise of their natural rights — liberty, equality, security, and property; to maintain order in the State; to furnish the public with useful and pleasant conveniences.

Now, does it cost more to defend the rich man's life and liberty than the poor man's? Who, in time of invasion, famine, or plague, causes more trouble, — the large proprietor who escapes the evil without the assistance of the State, or the laborer who sits in his cottage unprotected from danger?

Is public order endangered more by the worthy citizen, or by the artisan and journeyman? Why, the police have more to fear from a few hundred laborers, out of work, than from two hundred thousand electors!...

But they say, the courts and the police force are established to restrain this mob; government is a company, not exactly for insurance, for it does not insure, but for vengeance and repression. The premium which this company exacts, the tax, is divided in proportion to property; that is, in proportion to the trouble which each piece of property occasions the avengers and repressers paid by the government.

This is any thing but the absolute and inalienable right of property. Under this system the poor and the rich distrust, and make war upon, each other. But what is the object of the war? Property. So that property is necessarily accompanied by war upon property. The liberty and security of the rich do not suffer from the liberty and security of the poor; far from that, they mutually strengthen and sustain each other. The rich man's right of property, on the contrary, has to be continually defended against the poor man's desire for property. What a contradiction!...

To sum up: liberty is an absolute right, because it is to man what impenetrability is; to matter, — a *sine qua non* of existence; equality is an absolute right, because without equality there is no society; security is an absolute right, because in the eyes of every man his own liberty and life are as precious as another's. These three rights are absolute; that is, susceptible of neither increase nor diminution; because in society each associate receives as much as he gives, — liberty for liberty, equality for equality, security for security, body for body, soul for soul, in life and in death.

But property, in its derivative sense, and by the definitions of law, is a right outside of society; for it is clear that, if the wealth of each was social wealth, the conditions would be equal for all, and it would be a contradiction to say: *Property is a man's right to dispose at will of social property.* Then if we are associated for the sake of liberty, equality, and security, we are not associated for the sake of property; then if property is a *natural* right, this natural right is not *social*, but *anti-social*. Property and society are utterly irreconcilable institutions. It is as impossible to associate two proprietors as to join two magnets by their opposite poles. Either society must perish, or it must destroy property....

Certain classes do not relish investigation into the pretended titles to property, and its fabulous and perhaps scandalous history. They wish to hold to this proposition: that property is a fact; that it always has been, and always will be. With that proposition the *savant* Proudhon[1] commenced his "Treatise on the Right of Usufruct," regarding the origin of property as a useless question. Perhaps I would subscribe to this doctrine, believing it inspired by a commendable love of peace, were all my fellow-citizens in comfortable circumstances; but, no! I will not subscribe to it....

§ 8. — That, from the Stand-point of Justice, Labor destroys Property.

... The isolated man can supply but a very small portion of his wants; all his power lies in association, and in the intelligent combination of universal effort. The division and co-operation of labor multiply the quantity and the variety of products; the individuality of functions improves their quality.

There is not a man, then, but lives upon the products of several thousand different industries; not a laborer but receives from society at large the things which he consumes, and, with these, the power to reproduce. Who, indeed, would venture the assertion, "I produce, by my own effort, all that I consume; I need the aid of no one else"? The farmer, whom the early *economists* regarded as the only real producer — the farmer, housed, furnished, clothed, fed, and assisted by the mason, the carpenter, the tailor, the miller, the baker, the butcher, the grocer, the blacksmith, etc. — the farmer, I say, can he boast that he produces by his own unaided effort?

The various articles of consumption are given to each by all; consequently, the production of each involves the production of all. One product cannot exist without another; an isolated industry is an impossible thing. What would be the harvest of the farmer, if others did not manufacture for him barns, wagons, ploughs, clothes, etc.? Where would be the *savant* without the publisher; the printer without the type-caster and the machinist; and these, in their turn, without a multitude of other industries? ... Let us not prolong this catalogue — so easy to extend — lest we be accused of uttering commonplaces. All industries are united by mutual relations in a single group; all productions do reciprocal service as means and end; all varieties of talent are but a series of changes from the inferior to the superior.

Now, this undisputed and indisputable fact of the general participation in every species of product makes all individual productions common; so that every product, coming from the hands of the producer, is mortgaged in advance by society. The producer himself is entitled to only that portion of his product, which is expressed by a fraction whose denominator is equal to the number of individuals of which society is composed. It is true that in return this same producer has a share in all the products of others, so that he has a claim upon all, just as all have a claim upon him; but is it not clear that this reciprocity of mortgages, far from authorizing property, destroys even possession? The laborer is not even possessor of his product; scarcely has he finished it, when society claims it.

"But," it will be answered, "even if that is so — even if the product does not belong to the producer — still society gives each laborer an equivalent for his product; and this equivalent, this salary, this reward, this allowance, becomes his property. Do you deny that this property is legitimate? And if the laborer, instead of consuming his entire wages, chooses to economize, — who dare question his right to do so?"

The laborer is not even proprietor of the price of his labor, and cannot absolutely control its disposition. Let us not be blinded by a spurious justice. That which is given the laborer in exchange for his product is not given him as a reward for past labor, but to provide for and secure future labor. We consume before we produce. The laborer may say at the end of the day, "I have paid yesterday's expenses; to-morrow I shall pay those of today." At every moment of his life, the member of society is in debt; he dies with the debt unpaid: — how is it possible for him to accumulate? ...

On Government

§ 3. —Determination of the Third Form of Society. Conclusion.

Then, no government, no public economy, no administration, is possible, which is based upon property.

Communism seeks *equality* and *law*. Property, born of the sovereignty of the reason, and the sense of personal merit, wishes above all things *independence* and *proportionality*.

But communism, mistaking uniformity for law, and levelism for equality, becomes tyrannical and unjust. Property, by its despotism and encroachments, soon proves itself oppressive and anti-social.

The objects of communism and property are good — their results are bad. And why? Because both are exclusive, and each disregards two elements of society. Communism rejects independence and proportionality; property does not satisfy equality and law.

Now, if we imagine a society based upon these four principles, — equality, law, independence, and proportionality, — we find:

1. That *equality*, consisting only in *equality of conditions*, that is, of *means*, and not in *equality of comfort*, — which it is the business of the laborers to achieve for themselves, when provided with equal means, — in no way violates justice and *équité*.
2. That *law*, resulting from the knowledge of facts, and consequently based upon necessity itself, never clashes with independence.
3. That individual *independence*, or the autonomy of the private reason, originating in the difference in talents and capacities, can exist without danger within the limits of the law.
4. That *proportionality*, being admitted only in the sphere of intelligence and sentiment, and not as regards material objects, may be observed without violating justice or social equality.

This third form of society, the synthesis of communism and property, we will call *liberty*.[2] In determining the nature of liberty, we do not unite communism and property indiscriminately; such a process would be absurd eclecticism. We search by analysis for those elements in each which are true, and in harmony with the laws of Nature and society, disregarding the rest altogether; and the result gives us an adequate expression of the natural form of human society, — in one word, liberty.

Liberty is equality, because liberty exists only in society; and in the absence of equality there is no society.

Liberty is anarchy, because it does not admit the government of the will, but only the authority of the law; that is, of necessity.

Liberty is infinite variety, because it respects all wills within the limits of the law. Liberty is proportionality, because it allows the utmost latitude to the ambition for merit, and the emulation of glory....

Liberty is not opposed to the rights of succession and bequest. It contents itself with preventing violations of equality. "Choose," it tells us, "between two legacies, but do not take them both." All our legislation concerning transmissions, entailments, adoptions, and, if I may venture to use such a word, *coadjutoreries*, requires remodeling.

Liberty favors emulation, instead of destroying it. In social equality, emulation consists in accomplishing under like conditions; it is its own reward. No one suffers by the victory.

Liberty applauds self-sacrifice, and honors it with its votes, but it can dispense with it. Justice alone suffices to maintain the social equilibrium. Self-sacrifice is an act of supererogation. Happy, however, the man who can say, "I sacrifice myself."[3]

Liberty is essentially an organizing force. To insure equality between men and peace among nations, agriculture and industry, and the centers of education, business, and storage, must be distributed according to the climate and the geographical position of the country, the nature of the products, the character and natural talents of the inhabitants, in proportions so just, so wise, so harmonious, that in no place shall there ever be either an excess or a lack of population, consumption, and products. There commences the science of public and private right, the true political economy....

I have accomplished my task; property is conquered, never again to arise. Wherever this work is read and discussed, there will be deposited the germ of death to property; there, sooner or later, privilege and servitude will disappear, and the despotism of will give place to the reign of reason. What sophisms, indeed, what prejudices (however obstinate) can stand before the simplicity of the following propositions: —

I. Individual *possession*[4] is condition of social life; five thousand years of property demonstrate it. *Property* is the suicide of society. Possession is a right; property is against right. Suppress property while maintaining possession, and, by this simple modification of the principle, you will revolutionize law, government, economy, and institutions; you will drive evil from the face of the earth.

II. All having an equal right of occupancy, possession varies with the number of possessors; property cannot establish itself.

III. The effect of labor being the same for all, property is lost in the common prosperity.

IV. All human labor being the result of collective force, all property becomes, in consequence, collective and unitary. To speak more exactly, labor destroys property.

V. Every capacity for labor being, like every instrument of labor, an accumulated capital, and a collective property, inequality of wages and fortunes (on the ground of inequality of capacities) is, therefore, injustice and robbery.

VI. The necessary conditions of commerce are the liberty of the contracting parties and the equivalence of the products exchanged. Now, value being expressed by the amount of time and outlay which each product costs, and liberty being inviolable, the wages of laborers (like their rights and duties) should be equal.

VII. Products are bought only by products. Now, the condition of all exchange being equivalence of products, profit is impossible and unjust. Observe this elementary principle of economy, and

pauperism, luxury, oppression, vice, crime, and hunger will disappear from our midst.

VIII. Men are associated by the physical and mathematical law of production, before they are voluntarily associated by choice. Therefore, equality of conditions is demanded by justice; that is, by strict social law: esteem, friendship, gratitude, admiration, all fall within the domain of *equitable* or *proportional* law only.

IX. Free association, liberty — whose sole function is to maintain equality in the means of production and equivalence in exchanges — is the only possible, the only just, the only true form of society.

X. Politics is the science of liberty. The government of man by man (under whatever name it be disguised) is oppression. Society finds its highest perfection in the union of order with anarchy....

[1] Translator: The Proudhon here referred to is J. B.V. Proudhon, a distinguished French jurist and distant relative of the author.

[2] *Libertas, liberare, libratio, libra* — liberty, to liberate, libration, balance (pound) — words which have a common derivation. Liberty is the balance of rights and duties. To make a man free is to balance him with others, that is, to put him on their level.

[3] In a monthly publication, the first number of which has just appeared under the name of "L'Egalitaire," self-sacrifice is laid down as a principle of equality. This is a confusion of ideas. Self-sacrifice, taken alone, is the last degree of inequality. To seek equality in self-sacrifice is to confess that equality is against nature. Equality must be based upon justice, upon strict right, upon the principles invoked by the proprietor himself; otherwise it will never exist. Self-sacrifice is superior to justice; but it cannot be imposed as law, because it is of such a nature as to admit of no reward. It is, indeed, desirable that everybody shall recognize the necessity of self-sacrifice, and the idea of "L'Egalitaire" is an excellent example. Unfortunately, it can have no effect. What would you reply, indeed, to a man who should say to you, "I do not want to sacrifice myself"? Is he to be compelled to do so? When self-sacrifice is forced, it becomes oppression, slavery, the exploitation of man by man. Thus have the proletaires sacrificed themselves to property.

[4] Individual possession is no obstacle to extensive cultivation and unity of exploitation. If I have not spoken of the drawbacks arising from small estates, it is because I thought it useless to repeat what so many others have said, and what by this time all the world must know. But I am surprised that the economists, who have so clearly shown the disadvantages of spade-husbandry, have failed to see that it is caused entirely by property; above all, that they have not perceived that their plan for mobilizing the soil is a first step towards the abolition of property.

8.7 LOUIS BLANC: ON THE MATERIAL BASIS FOR RIGHTS (*ORGANIZATION OF LABOR*, 1848 EDITION)

... But if it is necessary to become engaged in a program of social reform, it is no less necessary to pursue one of political reform. For if the first is the *end*, the second is the *means*. It is not enough to discover scientific processes appropriate for inaugurating the principle of association and for organizing labor in accordance with the rules of reason, justice and humanity. One must also find a way to realize the principle that has been adopted, and to enable the processes that have been discovered through study to bear fruit. Now, power is organized force. Power depends upon chambers, tribunals, soldiers — in other words, upon the triple force of laws, judgments and bayonets. Not to use it as an instrument is to encounter it as an obstacle.

Besides, the emancipation of the proletarians is a most complicated task; it is involved with too many questions, it upsets too many habits, it is contrary, not in reality but in appearance, to too many interests, for anyone to believe seriously that it could be brought about by a series of partial efforts and isolated attempts. All the force of the State must be applied in this task. The proletarians lack the instruments of labor, which they need in order to emancipate themselves: the function of the government is to provide them with these. If we had to define the State as we see it, we would say that the State is the banker for the poor.

Now, is it true, as M. de Lamartine[1] was not afraid to point out in a recent manifesto, that this conception "consists in seizing, in the name of the State, property and sovereignty over industries and labor, in suppressing all free will on the part of citizens who own property, who sell, buy, or consume; in arbitrarily creating or distributing products, in establishing maximum prices, in regulating wages, in completely substituting a dispossessed citizenry for an industrial and proprietary State"?

As God is our witness, we have never proposed anything of the sort! And if it is we that M. de Lamartine was pretending to refute, then he probably has not done us the honor of reading our work. What we ask, as will be seen further on, is that the State — once it has been democratically constituted — create social workshops, destined to replace the individual workshops gradually and without any sudden upheavals; we ask that the social workshops be governed by statutes incorporating the principle of association and having the form and power of law. But once it is founded and set in motion, the social workshop will be sufficient unto itself and will no longer have recourse to anything but its own organizing principle. After the first year, the associated laborers would freely choose administrators and leaders from among themselves; they would work out the division of the receipts among themselves; they would be occupied in discovering ways to expand the enterprise. How can anyone say that such a system opens the way to arbitrariness and tyranny? The State would found the social workshop, provide it with laws, and watch over the execution of those laws, to see that they are carried out for the good of everyone; but that would be the limit of its role. Is such a role, can such a role be tyrannical? Today, when the government arrests a thief who has been discovered in somebody's house, does anyone accuse the government of tyranny? Does anyone reproach it for having entered the domain of individual life, for having penetrated into the private affairs of families? Well, in our system, the State would be, with respect to the social workshops, only what it is today with respect to society as a whole. It would watch over the inviolability of the pertinent statutes, just as today it watches over the inviolability of the laws. It would be the supreme protector of the principle of association, without at the same time being allowed or enabled to absorb into itself the action of the associated laborers, just as today it is the supreme protector of the property principle, though it does not absorb into itself the action of the property-owners.

But are we for having the State intervene, at least from the standpoint of initiative, in the economic reformation of society? Have we avowed that our goal is to undermine competition, to withdraw industry from the regime of *laissez-faire, laissez-passer*? Most certainly, and far from denying it, we proclaim it aloud. Why? Because we want freedom.

Yes, freedom! That is what must be won; but real freedom, freedom for all, the freedom that is sought in vain wherever those immortal sisters, equality and fraternity, are absent.

If we were to ask why the freedom of the state of nature was judged false and destroyed, the first child who came along would be able to give us the right answer. The freedom of the state of nature was, *in fact*, only an abominable oppression, because it allied itself with inequality of strength, because it made the weak man the victim of the vigorous, the impotent man the prey of the agile. Now, in the present social regime, instead of the inequality of physical strength, we have inequality of the means of development; instead of the battle of body against body, we have that of capital against capital; instead of the abuse of physical superiority, we have the abuse of a superiority created by social conventions. In place of the weak we have the ignorant; in place of the impotent, the poor. Where, then, is freedom?

It most certainly exists for those who have the means of enjoying it and making it bear fruit, for those who own the soil, who have money, credit, and the thousand resources that culture and intelligence provide; these people have so much that they can even abuse it. But is it the same for that interesting and numerous class that has neither land, nor capital, nor credit, nor instruction — that has, in other words, nothing that would enable the individual to manage for himself and develop his faculties? And when society is thus divided, with immense strength on one side and immense weakness on the other, then competition is unleashed in its midst, competition that pits the rich against the poor, the wily speculator against the naive laborer, the client of some slick banker against the usurer's serf, the thoroughly accoutered athlete against the unarmed combatant, the nimble man against the paralytic! And this disorderly and permanent shock of power against impotence, this anarchy in the midst of oppression, this invisible tyranny unsurpassed in harshness by tyrannies that can be seen by the human eye — this is what they call freedom!

In other words, the son of a poor man, pulled by hunger off the road that takes him to school, forced to sell short his body and soul at the nearby spinning-mill in order to add a few pennies to the family earnings — this boy is free to develop his intelligence, if he wants to.

In other words, the worker, who will die if the debate goes on for too long, is free to discuss conditions with his employer! ...

These days, it is said, nothing succeeds like success. This is true, and to say that the social order is characterized by such an aphorism is enough to condemn it. For all notions of justice and humanity are turned upside down when the more ways of getting rich a person has the less he needs to use them, while the fewer ways of escaping misery he possesses the more miserable he is. Has the accident of birth thrown you among us in a completely deprived condition? Toil, suffer, die: no one allows credit to a poor man, and the doctrine of *laissez-faire* guarantees that he will be abandoned. Were you born in the midst of opulence? Have a good time, enjoy yourself, sleep: your money is making money for you. Nothing succeeds like success!

But the poor man, you say, has the *right* to better his position? So! and what difference does it make, if he has not the *power* to do so? What does the *right* to be cured matter to a sick man whom no one is curing?

Right, considered abstractly, is the mirage that has kept the people in an abused condition since 1789. Right is the dead metaphysical protection that replaced, for the people, the living protection that was owed them. Right, sterilely and pompously proclaimed in the charters, has only served to mask whatever was unjust about the inauguration of a regime of individualism, and whatever was barbarous about the abandonment of the poor man. It is because freedom was defined by the word "right" that people came to designate men who were slaves of hunger, cold, ignorance, chance, as "free" men. Let us say it then for once and for all: freedom consists, not only in the RIGHTS that have been accorded, but also in the POWER given men to develop and exercise their faculties, under the reign of justice and the safeguard of law.

And let it be noted that this is not a vain distinction; its meaning is profound, its consequences are immense. For, once it is admitted that a man must have the *power* to develop and exercise his faculties in order to be really free, the upshot is that society owes every one of its members both instruction, without which the human mind *cannot* grow, and the instruments of labor, without which human activity *cannot* achieve its fullest development. Now, how will society be made to give suitable instruction and the necessary instruments of labor to every one of its members, if not by the intervention of the State? It is therefore in the name of freedom that we are asking for the rehabilitation of the principle of authority. We want a strong government because, in the regime of inequality within which we are still vegetating, there are weak persons who need a social force to protect them. We want a government that will intervene in industry, because in an area where people make loans only to the rich, a social banker is needed who will lend to the poor. In a word, we are invoking the idea of power because the freedom of the future must be a reality.

For the rest, do not be deceived; this necessity for the intervention of governments is relative; it derives solely from this state of weakness, misery and ignorance into which earlier tyrannies have plunged the people.

If the dearest hope of our hearts is not deceived, a day will come when a strong and active government will no longer be needed, because there will no longer be inferior and subordinate classes in society. Until then, the establishment of a tutelary authority is indispensable. The seed-bed of socialism can be fertilized only by the wind of politics.

O, rich men, you are deceived when you become aroused against those who dedicate their waking hours to the calm and peaceful solution of social problems. Yes, the sacred cause of the poor man is your cause too. A solidarity of heavenly origin binds you to their misery through fear and links you by your own interest to their future deliverance. Only their emancipation is capable of opening up to you the real treasure, that of tranquil joy, which you have not known as yet; the virtue of the principle of fraternity is precisely that, as it lessens the sorrows of the poor, it adds to your joys. "Watch out," you have been told, "watch out for the war of the have-nots against those who have." Ah! if this unholy war were really a possibility, what then would one be forced to think, good God! of the social order that had given rise to it? Miserable sophists! They do not perceive that this regime whose defense they discuss in whispers would be condemned beyond repeal if its danger really merited the stigma of their alarm! What, then! there would be such an excess of suffering among *those who have not*, such hatred in their souls, and such an impetuous desire to revolt in the depths of society, that to pronounce the word "fraternity," Christ's word, would be a terrible imprudence, and would serve as a signal for some new *Jacquerie*! No, rest assured, violence is to be feared only where discussion is not permitted. Order has no better protection than study. Thank heaven, people today understand that, if anger sometimes chastises evil, it is nevertheless incapable of bringing about good, that a blind and ferocious impatience would only pile up ruins under which the seeds of the ideas of justice and love would smother to death. It is not a question of taking wealth away; it is a question of fertilizing it so that it becomes universal. It is a question of raising the level of humanity for the good of all, without exception.

[1] Editor: M. de Lamartine (1790–1869), a romantic poet and a member of the provisional government in France.

8.8   KARL MARX: ON LIMITATION OF THE WORKING DAY (1866)[1]

A preliminary condition, without which all further attempts at improvement and emancipation must prove abortive, is the *limitation of the working day*.

It is needed to restore the health and physical energies of the working class, that is, the great body of every nation, as well as to secure them the possibility of intellectual development, sociable intercourse, social and political action.

We propose *8 hours work* as the *legal limit* of the working day. This limitation being generally claimed by the workmen of the United States of America, the vote of the Congress will raise it to the common platform of the working classes all over the world.

For the information of continental members, whose experience of factory law is comparatively short-dated, we add that all legal restrictions will fail and be broken through by Capital if the *period of the day* during which the 8 working hours must be taken, be not fixed. The length of that period ought to be determined by the 8 working hours and the additional pauses for meals. For instance, if the different interruptions for meals amount to *one hour*, the legal period of the day ought to embrace 9 hours, say from 7 a.m. to 4 p.m., or from 8 a.m. to 5 p.m., etc. Nightwork to be but exceptionally permitted, in trades or branches of trades specified by law. The tendency must be to suppress all nightwork.

This paragraph refers only to adult persons, male or female, the latter, however, to be rigorously excluded from all *nightwork whatever*, and all sort of work hurtful to the delicacy of the sex, or exposing their bodies to poisonous and otherwise deleterious agencies. By adult persons we understand all persons having reached or passed the age of 18 years.

[1] Instructions for the Delegates to the Geneva Congress (1866).

8.9   KARL MARX: ON FREEDOM OF ASSOCIATION AND TRADE UNIONS (1866)[1]

(a)   Their past.

Capital is concentrated social force, while the workman has only to dispose of his working force. The *contract* between capital and labor can therefore never be struck on equitable terms, equitable even in the sense of a society which places the ownership of the material means of life and labor on one side and the vital productive energies on the opposite side. The only social power of the workmen is their number. The force of numbers, however, is broken by disunion. The disunion of the workmen is created and perpetuated by their *unavoidable competition among themselves*.

Trades' Unions originally sprang up from the *spontaneous* attempts of workmen at removing or at least checking that competition, in order to conquer such terms of contract as might raise them at least above the condition of mere slaves. The immediate object of Trades' Unions was therefore confined to everyday necessities to expediences for the obstruction of the incessant encroachments of capital, in one word, to questions of wages and time of labor. This activity of the Trades' Unions is not only legitimate, it is necessary. It cannot be dispensed with so long as the present system of production lasts. On the contrary, it must be generalized by the formation and the combination of Trades' Unions throughout all countries. On the other hand, unconsciously to themselves, the Trades' Unions were forming *centers of organization* of the working class, as the medieval municipalities and communes did for the middle class. If the Trades' Unions are required for the guerilla fights between capital and labor, they are still more important as *organized agencies for superseding the very system of wages labor and capital rule.*

(b) Their present.

Too exclusively bent upon the local and immediate struggles with capital, the Trades' Unions have not yet fully understood their power of acting against the system of wages slavery itself. They therefore kept too much aloof from general social and political movements. Of late, however, they seem to awaken to some sense of their great historical mission, as appears, for instance, from their participation, in England, in the recent political movement from the enlarged views taken of their function in the United States, and from the following resolution passed at the recent great conference of Trades' delegates at Sheffield:

That this Conference, fully appreciating the efforts made by the International Association to unite in one common bond of brotherhood the working men of all countries, most earnestly recommend to the various societies here represented, the advisability of becoming affiliated to that body, believing that it is essential to the progress and prosperity of the entire working community.

(c) Their future.

Apart from their original purposes, they must now learn to act deliberately as organizing centers of the working class in the broad interest of its *complete emancipation.* They must aid every social and political movement tending in that direction. Considering themselves and acting as the champions and representatives of the whole working class, they cannot fail to enlist the non-society men into their ranks. They must look carefully after the interests of the worst paid trades, such as the agricultural laborers, rendered powerless by exceptional circumstances.

They must convince the world at large that their efforts, far from being narrow and selfish, aim at the emancipation of the downtrodden millions.

[1] Instructions for the Delegates to the Geneva Congress (1866).

8.10   KARL MARX: ON EDUCATION FOR BOTH SEXES (1866)[1]

We consider the tendency of modern industry to make children and juvenile persons of both sexes co-operate in the great work of social production, as a progressive, sound and legitimate tendency, although under capital it was distorted into an abomination. In a rational state of society every *child whatever,* from the age of 9 years, ought to become a productive laborer in the same way that no able-bodied adult person ought to be exempted from the general law of nature, viz.: to work in order to be able to eat, and work not only with the brain but with the hands too.

However, for the present, we have only to deal with the children and young persons of both sexes divided into *three classes*, to be treated differently;[2] the first class to range from 9 to 12; the second, from 13 to 15 years; and the third, to comprise the ages of 16 and 17 years. We propose that the employment of the first class in any workshop or housework be legally restricted to *two*; that of the second, to *four*; and that of the third, to *six* hours. For the third class, there must be a break of at least one hour for meals or relaxation.

It may be desirable to begin elementary school instruction before the age of 9 years; but we deal here only with the most indispensable antidotes against the tendencies of a social system which degrades the working man into a mere instrument for the accumulation of capital, and transforms parents by their necessities into slave-holders, sellers of their own children. The *right* of children and juvenile persons must be vindicated. They are unable to act for themselves. It is, therefore, the duty of society to act on their behalf.

If the middle and higher classes neglect their duties toward their offspring, it is their own fault. Sharing the privileges of these classes, the child is condemned to suffer from their prejudices.

The case of the working class stands quite different. The working man is no free agent. In too many cases, he is even too ignorant to understand the true interest of his child, or the normal conditions of human development. However, the more enlightened part of the working class fully understands that the future of its class, and, therefore, of mankind, altogether depends upon the formation of the rising working generation. They know that, before everything else, the children and juvenile workers must be saved from the crushing effects of the present system. This can only be effected by converting *social reason* into *social force*, and, under given circumstances, there exists no other method of doing so, than through *general laws*, enforced by the power of the state. In enforcing such laws, the working class do not fortify governmental power. On the contrary, they transform that power, *now* used against them, into their own agency. They effect by a general act what they would vainly attempt by a multitude of isolated individual efforts.

Proceeding from this standpoint, we say that no parent and no employer ought to be allowed to use juvenile labor, except when combined with education.

By education we understand three things.

Firstly: *Mental education.*

Secondly: *Bodily education,* such as is given in schools of gymnastics, and by military exercise.

Thirdly: *Technological[3] training,* which imparts the general principles of all processes of production, and simultaneously, initiates the child and young person in the practical use and handling of the elementary instruments of all trades.

A gradual and progressive course of mental, gymnastic, and technological training ought to correspond to the classification of the juvenile laborers. The costs of the tech-nological schools ought to be partly met by the sale of their products.

The combination of paid productive labor, mental education, bodily exercise and poly-technic training, will raise the working class far above the level of the higher and middle classes.

It is self-understood that the employment of all persons from 9 to 17 years (inclusively) in nightwork and all health-injuring trades must be strictly prohibited by law.

[1] Instructions for the Delegates to the Geneva Congress (1866).

[2] Editor: Instead of this sentence the French and German texts have two sentences ending the preceding paragraph and beginning a new one: "However, for the present, we have only to deal with the children and young persons belonging to the working class.

"We deem it necessary, basing on physiology, to divide children and young persons of both sexes." The rest proceeds as in the English text.

[3] Editor: The German text has *polytechnical.*

8.11   KARL MARX: ON NATIONAL EDUCATION (1869)[1]

[I]

Cit. Marx said there was a peculiar difficulty connected with this question. On the one hand a change of social circumstances was required to establish a proper system of education, on the other hand a proper system of education was required to bring about a change of social circumstances; we must therefore commence where we were.

The question treated at the congresses was whether education was to be national or private. National education had been looked upon as governmental, but that was not necessarily the case. In Massachusetts every township was bound to provide schools for primary education for all the children. In towns of more than 5,000 inhabitants higher schools for technical education had to be provided, in larger towns still higher. The state contributed something but not much. In Massachusetts one-eighth of the local taxes went for education, in New York one-fifth. The school committees who administered the schools were local, they appointed the schoolmasters and selected the books. The fault of the American system was that it was too much localized, the education given depended upon the state of culture prevailing in each district. There was a cry for a central supervision. The taxation for schools was compulsory, but the attendance of children was not. Property had to pay the taxes and the people who paid the taxes wanted that the money was usefully applied. Education might be national without being governmental. Government might appoint inspectors whose duty it was to see that the laws were obeyed, just as the factory inspectors looked after the observance of the factory acts, without any power of interfering with the course of education itself.

The Congress might without hesitation adopt that education was to be compulsory. As to children being prevented from working, one thing was certain: it would not reduce wages and people would get used to it.

The Proudhonists maintained that gratuitous education was nonsense, because the state had to pay for it; of course somebody had to pay, but not those who could least afford it. Was not in favor of gratuitous college education.

As Prussian education had been talked so much of he would conclude by observing that the Prussian system was only calculated to make good soldiers.

[II]

Cit. Marx said: upon certain points we were unanimous.

The discussion had started with the proposition to reaffirm the Geneva resolution which demanded that mental education should be combined with bodily labor, with gymnastics and technological training; nothing had been said against that.

The technological training advocated by proletarian writers was meant to compensate for the deficiencies occasioned by the division [of] labor which prevented apprentices from acquiring a thorough knowledge of their business. This had been taken hold of and misconstrued into what the middle class understood by technical education.

As to Mrs. Law's Church budget[2] it would be good policy for the Congress to declare against the Church.

Cit. Milner's proposition[3] was not suitable to be introduced in connection with the schools; it was a kind of education that the young must get from the adults in the everyday struggle of life. He could not accept Warren as a bible, it was a question upon which few could agree. We might add that such education cannot be given at school, but must be given by adults.

Nothing could be introduced either in primary or higher schools that admitted of party and class interpretation. Only subjects such as the physical sciences, grammar, etc., were fit matter for schools. The rules of grammar, for instance, could not differ, whether explained by a religious Tory or a free thinker. Subjects that admitted of different conclusions must be excluded and left for the adults to such teachers as Mrs. Law, who gave instruction in religion.[4]

[1] Minutes of the General Council Meetings of August 10 and 17, 1869, International.

[2] Harriet Law's proposition moved at the General Council meeting of August 17, 1869, meant the transfer of the Church's property and income to schools.

[3] George Milner proposed at the Council meetings of August 10 and 17, 1869, that the children should be taught bourgeois political economy, which was unacceptable from the proletarian viewpoint and in practice would only increase the ideological influence of the ruling bourgeoisie on the rising generation. Milner particularly stressed the need to give the pupils an idea of the "value of labor" and distribution. He referred, in particular, to the American Utopian Socialist Warren, who preached the theory of "just exchange."

[4] Editor: In the report of the General Council meeting of August 17, 1869, published in *The Bee-Hive*, No. 410, August 21, 1869, this part of Marx's speech is given as follows: "As to political economy, religion and other questions, they could not be admitted into the primary, nor even the higher schools; that was a kind of education which must rest with the adult, and must be left to the lecture room, to such schoolmasters as Mrs. Law."

8.12 KARL MARX: ON SOCIAL AND ECONOMIC RIGHTS (*CRITIQUE OF THE GOTHA PROGRAM*, 1891)

... B. "The German Workers' Party demands as the intellectual and moral basis of the state:

1. Universal and *equal elementary education* through the state. Universal compulsory school attendance. Free instruction."

    Equal elementary education? What idea lies behind these words? Is it believed that in present-day society (and it is only with this one has to deal) education can be *equal* for all classes? Or is it demanded that the upper classes also shall be compulsorily reduced to the modicum of education — the elementary school — that alone is compatible with the economic conditions not only of the wage workers but of the peasants as well.

    "Universal compulsory school attendance. Free instruction." The former exists even in Germany, the second in Switzerland and in the United States in the case of elementary schools. If in some states of the latter country the higher educational institutions are also "free," that only means in fact defraying the cost of the education of the upper classes from the general tax receipts....

2. The paragraph on the schools should at least have demanded technical schools (theoretical and practical) in combination with the elementary school.

    "*Elementary education through the state*" is altogether objectionable. Defining by a general law the financial means of the elementary schools, the qualifications of the teachers, the branches of instruction, etc., and, as happens in the United States, supervising the fulfillment of these legal prescriptions by means of state inspectors, is a very different thing from appointing the state as the educator of the people! Government and church should rather be equally excluded from any influence on the school....

    "*Normal working day*" In no other country has the Workers' Party restricted itself to such an indefinite demand, but has always fixed the length of the working day that it considers normal under the given circumstances.

3. "*Restriction of women's labor and prohibition of child labor*"

    The standardization of the working day must already include the restriction of women's labor, in so far as it relates to the duration, intervals, etc., of the working day; otherwise it could only mean the exclusion of women's labor from branches of industry that are specifically unhealthy for the female body or are objectionable morally for the female sex. If that is what was meant, then it ought to have been stated.

    "*Prohibition of child labor*"! Here it was absolutely essential to state the age limits.

    A *general prohibition* of child labor is incompatible with the existence of large-scale industry and hence an empty, pious aspiration.

    Its realization — if it were possible — would be reactionary, since, with a strict regulation of the working time according to the different age groups and other safety measures for the protection of children, an early combination of productive labor with education is one of the most potent means for the transformation of present-day society.

4. "*State supervision of factory, workshop and domestic industry*"

    In regard to the Prusso-German state it should definitely have been demanded that the inspectors are only to be removable by a court of law; that any worker can denounce them to the courts for neglect of duty; that they must belong to the medical profession.

5. "*Regulation of prison labor*"

    A petty demand in a general workers' program. In any case, it should have been clearly stated that there is no intention from fear of competition to allow ordinary criminals to be treated like beasts, and especially that there is no desire to deprive them of their sole means of betterment, productive labor. This was surely the least one might have expected from socialists.

6. *"An effective liability law"*

It should have been stated what is understood by an "effective" liability law.

Incidentally, in connection with the normal working day, the part of factory legislation that deals with health regulations and safety measures has been overlooked. The liability law only comes into operation when these regulations are infringed....

CHAPTER 9

How to Promote a Socialist Perspective of Human Rights

Free Trade, Just War, and International Organizations

ON FREE TRADE'S VIRTUES AND INJUSTICES

The prevailing Enlightenment idea that republican institutions and commerce based on free trade would be sufficient to promote human rights domestically and globally, and would also extirpate war, was severely challenged during the industrial revolution. The expansion of capitalism, coinciding with the political and economic exclusion of disenfranchised masses and colonial wars, showed the insufficiency of the Enlightenment vision. In the face of miserable living conditions for ordinary workers in the industrializing world, and widespread suffering in the colonies of the capitalist powers, socialists debated whether workers' rights could be achieved through political reform or only by violent revolution.

With respect to free trade, Karl Marx (1818–1883) characterized that central underpinning of the liberal worldview as both progressive and pernicious. In the *Communist Manifesto* (1848), he and Engels welcomed the revolutionary virtues of the bourgeoisie in promoting the "cosmopolitan character of production and consumption in every country" and credited the bourgeoisie for its progressive ability to eradicate parochial and feudal social structures. Marx's speech "On the Question of Free Trade" (1848), arguing for the repeal of the protectionist Corn Laws in Britain, proclaimed that in a revolutionary sense alone: "I am in favor of Free Trade." His reason was that free trade would provide new political space for working class solidarity across borders. That support was offered despite his belief that initially "the Freedom of Capital" meant the freedom to crush workers' rights and wage wars to conquer new markets. In the long run, however, "the weapons with which the bourgeoisie felled feudalism to the ground are now turned against the bourgeoisie itself." (See Section 9.1).

9.1   KARL MARX (*THE COMMUNIST MANIFESTO*, 1848)

... Each step in the development of the bourgeoisie was accompanied by a corresponding political advance of that class. An oppressed class under the sway of the feudal nobility, an armed and self-governing association in the medieval commune;[1] here independent urban republic (as in Italy and Germany), there taxable "third estate" of the monarchy (as in France), afterward, in the period of manufacture proper, serving either the semi-feudal or the absolute monarchy as a counterpoise against the nobility, and, in fact, cornerstone of the great monarchies in general, the bourgeoisie has at last, since the establishment of Modern Industry and of the world market, conquered for itself, in the modern representative State, exclusive political sway. The executive of the modern State is but a committee for managing the common affairs of the whole bourgeoisie.

nexus - connection or series of connections linking two or more things

ossify - turn into bone or bony tissue : become stagnant or rigid

The bourgeoisie, historically, has played a most revolutionary part.

The bourgeoisie, wherever it has got the upper hand, has put an end to all feudal, patriarchal, idyllic relations. It has pitilessly torn asunder the motley feudal ties that bound man to his "natural superiors," and has left remaining no other nexus between man and man than naked self-interest, than callous "cash payment." It has drowned the most heavenly ecstasies of religious fervor, of chivalrous enthusiasm, of philistine sentimentalism, in the icy water of egotistical calculation. It has resolved personal worth into exchange value, and in place of the numberless indefeasible chartered freedoms has set up that single, unconscionable freedom — Free Trade. In one word, for exploitation, veiled by religious and political illusions, it has substituted naked, shameless, direct, brutal exploitation.

The bourgeoisie has stripped of its halo every occupation hitherto honored and looked up to with reverent awe. It has converted the physician, the lawyer, the priest, the poet, the man of science, into its paid wage-laborers.

The bourgeoisie has torn away from the family its sentimental veil, and has reduced the family relation to a mere money relation.

The bourgeoisie has disclosed how it came to pass that the brutal display of vigor in the Middle Ages, which Reactionists so much admire, found its fitting complement in the most slothful indolence. It has been the first to show what man's activity can bring about. It has accomplished wonders far surpassing Egyptian pyramids, Roman aqueducts and Gothic cathedrals; it has conducted expeditions that put in the shade all former Exoduses of nations and crusades.

The bourgeoisie cannot exist without constantly revolutionizing the instruments of production, and thereby the relations of production and with them the whole relations of society. Conservation of the old modes of production in unaltered form was, on the contrary, the first condition of existence for all earlier industrial classes. Constant revolutionizing of production, uninterrupted disturbance of all social conditions, everlast-

Rousseau

ing uncertainty and agitation distinguish the bourgeois epoch from all earlier ones. All fixed, fast-frozen relations, with their train of ancient and venerable prejudices and opinions, are swept away, all new-formed ones become antiquated before they can ossify. All that is solid melts into air, all that is holy is profaned, and man is at last compelled to face with sober senses his real conditions of life and his relations with his kind.

The need of a constantly expanding market for its products chases the bourgeoisie over the whole surface of the globe. It must nestle everywhere, settle everywhere, establish connections everywhere.

The bourgeoisie has through its exploitation of the world market given a cosmopolitan character to production and consumption in every country. To the great chagrin of Reactionists, it has drawn from under the feet of industry the national ground on which it stood. All old-established national industries have been destroyed or are daily being destroyed. They are dislodged by new industries, whose introduction becomes a life and death question for all civilized nations, by industries that no longer work up indigenous raw material but raw material drawn from the remotest zones; industries whose products are consumed, not only at home, but in every quarter of the globe. In place of the old wants, satisfied by the production of the country, we find new wants, requiring for their satisfaction the products of distant lands and climes. In place of the old local and national seclusion and self-sufficiency, we have intercourse in every direction, universal interdependence of nations. And as in material, so also in intellectual production. The intellectual creations of individual nations become common property. National one-sidedness and narrow-mindedness become more and more impossible, and from the numerous national and local literatures there arises a world literature.

The bourgeoisie, by the rapid improvement of all instruments of production, by the immensely facilitated means of communication, draws all, even the most barbarian, nations into civilization. The cheap prices of its commodities are the heavy artillery with which it batters down all Chinese walls,

Is Marx against world literature? He sees value in nationalism?

Or do his readers value nationalism

with which it forces the barbarians' intensely obstinate hatred of foreigners to capitulate. It compels all nations, on pain of extinction, to adopt the bourgeois mode of production; it compels them to introduce what it calls civilization into their midst, i.e., to become bourgeois themselves. In a word, it creates a world after its own image.

The bourgeoisie has subjected the country to the rule of the towns. It has created enormous cities, has greatly increased the urban population as compared with the rural, and has thus rescued a considerable part of the population from the idiocy of rural life. Just as it has made the country dependent on the towns, so it has made barbarian and semi-barbarian countries dependent on the civilized ones, nations of peasants on nations of bourgeois, the East on the West.

The bourgeoisie keeps doing away more and more with the scattered state of the population, of the means of production, and of property. It has agglomerated population, centralized means of production, and has concentrated property in a few hands. The necessary consequence of this was political centralization. Independent or but loosely connected provinces with separate interests, laws, governments, and systems of taxation became lumped together into one nation, with one government, one code of laws, one national class interest, one frontier and one customs tariff.

The bourgeoisie during its rule of scarce one hundred years has created more massive and more colossal productive forces than have all preceding generations together. Subjection of nature's forces to man, machinery, application of chemistry to industry and agriculture, steam navigation, railways, electric telegraphs, clearing of whole continents for cultivation, canalization of rivers, whole populations conjured out of the ground — what earlier century had even a presentiment that such productive forces slumbered in the lap of social labor?

We see then: the means of production and of exchange, of the foundation of which the bourgeoisie built itself up, were generated in feudal society. At a certain stage in the development of these means of production and of exchange, the conditions under which feudal society produced and exchanged, the feudal organization of agriculture and manufacturing industry, in a word, the feudal relations of property became no longer compatible with the already developed productive forces; they became so many fetters. They had to be burst asunder; they were burst asunder.

Into their place stepped free competition, accompanied by a social and political constitution adapted to it and by the economic and political sway of the bourgeois class.

A similar movement is going on before our own eyes. Modern bourgeois society with its relations of production, of exchange and of property, a society that has conjured up such gigantic means of production and of exchange, is like the sorcerer who is no longer able to control the powers of the nether world whom he has called up by his spells. For many a decade past the history of industry and commerce is but the history of the revolt of modern productive forces against modern conditions of production, against the property relations that are the conditions for the existence of the bourgeoisie and of its rule. It is enough to mention the commercial crises that by their periodical return put on trial, each time more threateningly, the existence of the entire bourgeois society. In these crises a great part not only of the existing products, but also of the previously created productive forces, are periodically destroyed. In these crises there breaks out an epidemic that in all earlier epochs would have seemed an absurdity — the epidemic of over-production. Society suddenly finds itself put back into a state of momentary barbarism; it appears as if a famine, a universal war of devastation had cut off the supply of every means of subsistence; industry and commerce seem to be destroyed; and why? Because there is too much civilization, too much means of subsistence, too much industry, too much commerce. The productive forces at the disposal of society no longer tend to further the development of the conditions of bourgeois property; on the contrary, they have become too powerful for these conditions, by which they are fettered, and as soon as they overcome these fetters, they bring disorder into the whole of bourgeois society, endanger the existence of bourgeois property. The conditions of bourgeois society are too narrow to comprise the wealth created by them. And how does the bourgeoisie get over these crises? On the one hand by enforced destruction of a mass of productive forces; on the other, by the conquest of new market and by the more thorough exploitation of the old ones. That is to say, by paving the way for more extensive and more destructive crises and by diminishing the means whereby crises are prevented.

The weapons with which the bourgeoisie felled feudalism to the ground are now turned against the bourgeoisie itself....

[1] "Commune" was the name taken in France by the nascent towns even before they had conquered from their feudal lords and masters local self-government and political rights as the "Third Estate." Generally speaking, for the economic development of the bourgeoisie, England is here taken as the typical country; for its political development, France [1888]. This was the name given their urban communities by the townsmen of Italy and France, after they had purchased or wrested their initial rights of self-government from their feudal lords.[1890].

9.2 KARL MARX ("SPEECH ON THE QUESTION OF FREE TRADE," 1848)[1]

... To sum up what is Free Trade under the present conditions of society? Freedom of Capital. When you have torn down the few national barriers which still restrict the free development of capital, you will merely have given it complete freedom of action. So long as you let the relation of wages-labor to capital exist, no matter how favorable the conditions under which you accomplish the exchange of commodities, there will always be a class which exploits and a class which is exploited. It is really difficult to understand the presumption of the Free Traders who imagine that the more advantageous application of capital will abolish the antagonism between industrial capitalists and wage-workers. On the contrary. The only result will be that the antagonism of these two classes will stand out more clearly.

Let us assume for a moment that there are no more Corn Laws or national and munici-

pal import duties; that in a word all the accidental circumstances which to-day the workingman may look upon as a cause of his miserable condition have vanished, and we shall have removed so many curtains that hide from his eyes his true enemy.

He will see that capital released from all trammels will make him no less a slave than capital trammeled by import duties.

Gentlemen! Do not be deluded by the abstract word Freedom! Whose freedom? Not the freedom of one individual in relation to another, but freedom of Capital to crush the worker.

Why should you desire farther to sanction unlimited competition with this idea of freedom, when the idea of freedom itself is only the product of a social condition based upon Free Competition?

We have shown what sort of fraternity Free Trade begets between the different classes of one and the same nation. The fraternity which Free Trade would establish between the nations of the earth would not be more real, to call cosmopolitan exploitation universal brotherhood is an idea that could only be engendered in the brain of the bourgeoisie. Every one of the destructive phenomena to which unlimited competition gives rise within any one nation is reproduced in more gigantic proportions in the market of the world. We need not pause any longer upon Free Trade sophisms on this subject, which are worth just as much as the arguments of our prize essayists Messrs. Hope, Morse, and Greg.

For instance, we are told that Free Trade would create an international division of labor, and thereby give to each country those branches of production most in harmony with its natural advantages.

You believe perhaps, gentlemen, that the production of coffee and sugar is the natural destiny of the West Indies.

Two centuries ago, nature, which does not trouble itself about commerce, had planted neither sugar-cane nor coffee trees there. And it may be that in less than half a century you will find there neither coffee nor sugar, for the East Indies, by means of cheaper production, have already successfully broken down this so-called natural destiny of the West Indies.

And the West Indies, with their natural wealth, are as heavy a burden for England as the weavers of Dacca, who also were destined from the beginning of time to weave by hand.

One other circumstance must not be forgotten, namely that, just as everything has become a monopoly, there are also nowadays some branches of industry which prevail over all others, and secure to the nations which especially foster them the command of the market of the world. Thus in the commerce of the world cotton alone has much greater commercial importance than all the other raw materials used in the manufacture of clothing. It is truly ridiculous for the Free Traders to refer to the few specialties in each branch of industry, throwing them into the balance against the product used in everyday consumption, and produced most cheaply in those countries in which manufacture is most highly developed.

If the Free Traders cannot understand how one nation can grow rich at the expense of another, we need not wonder, since these same gentlemen also refuse to understand how in the same country one class can enrich itself at the expense of another.

Do not imagine, gentlemen, that in criticizing freedom of commerce we have the least intention of defending Protection.

One may be opposed to constitutionalism without being in favor of absolutism.

Moreover, the Protective system is nothing but a means of establishing manufacture upon a large scale in any given country, that is to say, of making it dependent upon the market of the world; and from the moment that dependence upon the market of the world is established, there is more or less dependence upon Free Trade too. Besides this, the Protective system helps to develop free competition within a nation. Hence we see that in countries where the bourgeoisie is beginning to make itself felt as a class, in Germany for example, it makes great efforts to obtain Protective duties. They serve the bourgeoisie as weapons against feudalism and absolute monarchy, as a means for the concentration of its own powers for the realization of Free Trade within the country.

But, generally speaking, the Protective system in these days is conservative, while the Free Trade system works destructively. It breaks up old nationalities and carries antagonism of proletariat and bourgeoisie to the uttermost point. In a word, the Free Trade system hastens the Social Revolution. In this revolutionary sense alone, gentlemen, I am in favor of Free Trade.

[1] Delivered to the Democratic Association of Brussels at its public meeting of January 9, 1848. First published in French as a pamphlet in the beginning of February 1848 in Brussels. Printed according to the American edition of 1889 and checked with the 1848 French edition.

JUST WAR: (CLASS) WAR OR POLITICAL REFORM?

Like Locke before him, Karl Marx (1848) depicted revolutions as an inevitable means to redress oppression. "The history of all existing hitherto society," he developed, "is the history of class struggles ... between oppressor and oppressed" (see Section 9.3). In *The Class Struggle in France* (1850), he explained his belief that a dictatorship of the proletariat would be "the necessary transit point to the abolition of class distinctions generally." Yet Karl Marx was not completely averse to the idea of reform. In his speech "The Possibility of a Nonviolent Revolution," delivered in Amsterdam (1872), his call for revolutionary means included caveats, namely, that in some countries, such as America, England, and Holland, workers might attain their objectives peacefully. That question of reform versus revolution would be echoed in fierce arguments that divided the political Left.

The exiled Polish socialist leader in Germany, Rosa Luxemburg (1870–1924), captured the revolutionary trend of that debate, advocating desertion by troops ordered to battle in World War I and the revolutionary overthrow of the capitalist regimes responsible for the war. In her *Junius Pamphlet*, published in 1916, she condemned World War I as imperialist, revealing the horrific results of capitalist colonial rivalries for the lives of the working class. She further denounced the collaboration of European social democratic parties, which had abandoned their longstanding pledges to oppose the impending war among the leading capitalist states and had instead rushed to proclaim loyalty to their countries when the fighting began in August 1914. Luxemburg's pamphlet was written in 1915 and smuggled out of prison, where she had been sentenced for several years for giving an antiwar speech. Once out of prison, she led the Spartacus League (1914–1918) in grassroots demonstrations against the war. Though she warned against a premature effort to take over Berlin in 1919, she joined the uprising when it occurred. Soon after the German government crushed the rebellion, she was murdered by right-wing soldiers in 1919 (see Section 9.6).

In the same period, a crucial episode in the ongoing debate on what means were acceptable for achievement of socialist human rights ends was the Russian Revolution of February 1917. Though the influential German Social-Democratic leader Karl Kautsky (1854–1938) regarded himself as a follower of Marx, he distinguished himself from other Marxists by condemning, in *The Dictatorship of the Proletariat* (1918), the dictatorial outcome of the Bolshevik Revolution as an unacceptable means to attain power and establish socialist rights. Building on Kantian ethics, he argued that democracy and socialism, or political reform, should be perceived as "means toward the same ends." A nondemocratic organization of social labor, he insisted, is conducive to dictatorial power and the gradual decline of popular support. He thus argued that the political will and maturity of the working class — which depend upon the level of industrialization and parliamentary democracy — are essential prerequisites for achieving socialist rights (see Section 9.7).

Leon Trotsky (1879–1939), the principal organizer of the Red Army during the Russian civil war (1918–1921), attacked Kautsky's view of moral standards as inapplicable during the revolutionary process. In *Their Morals and Ours* (1938), he explained how violence had to be understood in terms of its objective, rather than as an isolated means. There is a difference, he maintained, "between a slaveholder who through cunning and violence shackles a slave in chains, and a slave who through cunning and violence breaks the chains." "Does this imply that all means are permissible?" he asked. "That is permissible," he answered, "which really leads to the liberation of humanity." "A means," he continued, "can only be justified by its ends," which include the power of humanity over nature and the abolition of the exploitation of one person by another. In this respect, Trotsky intended to set himself apart from Stalin's oppressive regime. Yet at the same time, Trotsky denounced the "moral absolutism" and "hypocrisy" of liberals and social democrats regarding the conduct of the Bolsheviks, at a time when their revolution was endangered by a civil war waged on a five-thousand-mile front. Trotsky's contribution to the successful defense of that revolution went unrewarded, however, as Joseph Stalin (1879–1953) consolidated his rule, purging and murdering his rivals, including Trotsky. The Bolshevik dream of international socialist rights had yielded to a repressive bureaucratic state.

9.3   KARL MARX (*THE COMMUNIST MANIFESTO*, 1848)

Bourgeois and Proletarians

The history of all hitherto existing society is the history of class struggles. Freeman and slave, patrician and plebeian, lord and serf, guild-master and journeyman, in a word, oppressor and oppressed, stood in constant opposition to one another, carried on an uninterrupted, now hidden, now open fight, a fight that each time ended, either in a revolutionary reconstitution of society at large, or in the common ruin of the contending classes.

In the earlier epochs of history, we find almost everywhere a complicated arrangement of society into various orders, a manifold gradation of social rank. In ancient Rome we have patricians, knights, plebeians, slaves, in the Middle Ages, feudal lords, vassals, guild-masters, journeymen, apprentices, serfs; in almost all of these classes, again, subordinate gradations.

The modern bourgeois society that has sprouted from the ruins of feudal society has not done away with class antagonisms. It has but established new classes, new conditions of oppression, new forms of struggle in place of the old ones.

Our epoch, the epoch of the bourgeoisie, possesses, however, this distinctive feature: It has simplified the class antagonisms. Society as a whole is more and more splitting up into two great hostile camps, into two great classes directly facing each other — bourgeoisie and proletariat.

From the serfs of the Middle Ages sprang the chartered burghers of the earliest towns. From these burgesses the first elements of the bourgeoisie were developed.

The discovery of America, the rounding of the Cape, opened up fresh ground for the rising bourgeoisie. The East Indian and Chinese markets, the colonization of America, trade with the colonies, the increase in the means of exchange and in commodities generally, gave to commerce, to navigation, to industry, an impulse never before known, and thereby, to the revolutionary element in the tottering feudal society, a rapid development....

We see, therefore, how the modern bourgeoisie is itself the product of a long course of development, of a series of revolutions in the modes of production and of exchange....

Altogether, collisions between the classes of the old society further the course of development of the proletariat in many ways. The bourgeoisie finds itself involved in a constant battle. At first with the aristocracy; later on, with those portions of the bourgeoisie itself whose interests have become antagonistic to the progress of industry; at all times with the bourgeoisie of foreign countries. In all these battles it sees itself compelled to appeal to the proletariat, to ask for its help, and thus, to drag it into the political arena. The bourgeoisie itself, therefore, supplies the proletariat with its own elements of political and general education, in other words, it furnishes the proletariat with weapons for fighting the bourgeoisie....

9.4   KARL MARX (*THE CLASS STRUGGLES IN FRANCE*, 1850)

... So swiftly had the march of the revolution ripened conditions that the friends of reform of all shades, the most moderate claims of the middle classes, were compelled to group themselves round the banner of the most extreme party of revolution, round the *red flag*....

Since it dreams of the peaceful achievement of its Socialism — allowing, perhaps, for a second February Revolution lasting a brief day or so — the coming historical process naturally appears to it as an *application of systems*, which the thinkers of society, whether in companies or as individual inventors, devise or have devised. Thus they become the eclectics or adepts of the existing socialist *systems*, of *doctrinaire Socialism*, which was the theoretical expression of the proletariat only as long as it had not yet developed further into a free historical movement of its own.

Thus, while *utopia, doctrinaire Socialism*, which subordinates the whole movement to one of its elements, which puts the cerebrations of the individual pedant in place of common, social production and, above all, wishes away the necessities of the revolutionary class struggles by petty tricks or great sentimental rhetoric — while this doctrinaire Socialism, which basically only idealizes present-day society, makes a shadowless picture of it and seeks to oppose its ideal to its reality, while this Socialism is ceded by the proletariat to the petty bourgeoisie, while the internal struggle between the different socialist leaders reveals each so-called system to be the pretentious adherence to one transitional position on the path, to social upheaval as opposed to another — the *proletariat* increasingly organizes itself around *revolutionary Socialism,* around *Communism,* for which the bourgeoisie itself has invented the name of *Blanqui.* This Socialism is the *declaration of the permanence of the revolution,* the *class dictatorship* of the proletariat as the necessary transit point to the *abolition of class distinctions generally,* to the abolition of all the relations of production on which they rest, to the abolition of all the social relations that correspond to these relations of production, to the revolutionizing of all the ideas that result from these social relations....

9.5   KARL MARX: ("ON THE POSSIBILITY OF A NON-VIOLENT REVOLUTION," 1872)[1]

In the 18th century the kings and potentates were in the habit of assembling at The Hague to discuss the interests of their dynasties.

It is there that we decided to hold our workers' congress despite the attempts to intimidate us. In the midst of the most reactionary population we wanted to affirm the existence, the spreading and hope for the future of our great Association.

When our decision became known, there was talk of emissaries we had sent to prepare the ground. Yes, we have emissaries everywhere, we do not deny it, but the majority of them are unknown to us. Our emissaries in The Hague were the workers, whose labor is so exhausting, just as in Amsterdam they

are workers too, workers who toil for sixteen hours a day. Those are our emissaries, we have no others; and in all the countries in which we make an appearance we find them ready to welcome us, for they understand very quickly that the aim we pursue is the improvement of their lot.

The Hague Congress has achieved three main things:

It has proclaimed the necessity for the working classes to fight the old disintegrating society in the political as well as the social field; and we see with satisfaction that henceforth this resolution of the London Conference will be included in our Rules.

A group has been formed in our midst which advocates that the workers should abstain from political activity.

We regard it as our duty to stress how dangerous and fatal we considered those principles to be for our cause.

One day the worker will have to seize political supremacy to establish the new organization of labor; he will have to overthrow the old policy which supports the old institutions if he wants to escape the fate of the early Christians who, neglecting and despising politics, never saw their kingdom on earth.

But we by no means claimed that the means for achieving this goal were identical everywhere. We know that the institutions, customs and traditions in the different countries must be taken into account; and we do not deny the existence of countries like America, England, and if I knew your institutions better I might add Holland, where the workers may achieve their aims by peaceful means. That being true we must also admit that in most countries on the Continent it is force which must be the lever of our revolution; it is force which will have to be resorted to for a time in order to establish the rule of the workers.

The Hague Congress has endowed the General Council with new and greater powers. Indeed, at a time when the kings are assembling in Berlin and when from this meeting of powerful representatives of feudalism and the past there must result new and more severe measures of repression against us; at a time when persecution is being organized, the Hague Congress rightly believed that it was wise and necessary to increase the powers of its General Council and to centralize, in view of the impending struggle, activity which isolation would render impotent. And, by the way, who but our enemies could take alarm at the authority of the General Council? Has it a bureaucracy and an armed police to ensure that it is obeyed? Is not its authority solely moral, and does it not submit its decisions to the Federations which have to carry them out? In these conditions, kings, with no army, no police, no magistracy, and reduced to having to maintain their power by moral influence and authority, would be feeble obstacles to the progress of the revolution.

Finally, the Hague Congress transferred the seat of the General Council to New York. Many, even of our friends, seemed to be surprised at such a decision. Are they then forgetting that America is becoming the world of workers *par excellence*; that every year half a million men, workers, emigrate to that other continent, and that the International must vigorously take root in that soil where the worker predominates? Moreover, the decision taken by the Congress gives the General Council the right to co-opt those members whom it judges necessary and useful for the good of the common cause. Let us rely on its wisdom to choose men equal to the task and able to carry with a steady hand the banner of our Association in Europe.

Citizens, let us bear in mind this fundamental principle of the International: solidarity! It is by establishing this life-giving principle on a reliable base among all the workers in all countries that we shall achieve the great aim which we pursue. The revolution must display solidarity, and we find a great example of this in the Paris Commune, which fell because there did not appear in all the centers, in Berlin, Madrid, etc., a great revolutionary movement corresponding to this supreme uprising of the Paris proletariat.

For my part I will persist in my task and will constantly work to establish among the workers this solidarity which will bear fruit for the future. No, I am not withdrawing from the International, and the rest of my life will be devoted, like my efforts in the past, to the triumph of the social ideas which one day, be sure of it, will bring about the universal rule of the proletariat.

[1] On the Hague Congress [a correspondent's report of a speech given at a meeting in Amsterdam on September 8, 1872].

9.6 ROSA LUXEMBURG: ON WORLD WAR I AND IMPERIALISM (*THE JUNIUS PAMPHLET*, 1916)

Have we ever had a different conception of the role to be played by the working class in the great world war? Have we forgotten how we were wont to describe the coming event, only a few short years ago? "Then will come the catastrophe. All Europe will be called to arms, and sixteen to eighteen million men, the flower of the nations, armed with the best instruments of murder will make war upon each other. But I believe that behind this march there looms the final crash. Not we, but they themselves will bring it. They are driving things to the extreme, they are leading us straight into a catastrophe. They will harvest what they have sown. The *Goetterdaemmerung* of the bourgeois world is at hand. Be sure of that. It is coming." Thus spoke Bebel, the speaker of our group in the Reichstag in the Morocco debate.

An official leaflet published by the party, *Imperialism and Socialism*, that was distributed in hundreds of thousands of copies only a few years ago, closes with the words: "Thus the struggle against militarism daily becomes more and more clearly a decisive struggle between capital and labor. War, high prices and capitalism — peace, happiness for all, socialism! Yours is the choice. History is hastening onward toward a decision. The proletariat must work unceasingly at its world mission, must strengthen the power of its organization and the clearness of its understanding. Then, come what will, whether it will succeed, by its power, in saving humanity from the horrible cruelties of the world war, or whether capitalism shall sink back into history, as it was born, in blood and violence, the historic moment will find the working class prepared, and preparedness is everything."

The official handbook for socialist voters, in 1911, the date of the last Reichstag elections, contains, on page 42, the following comments on the expected world war: "Do our rulers and our ruling classes dare to demand this awful thing of the people? Will not a cry of horror, of fury and of indignation fill the country and lead the people to put an end to this murder? Will they not ask: 'For whom and for what? Are we insane that we should be treated thus or should tolerate such treatment?' He who dispassionately considers the possibility of a great European world war can come to no other conclusion.

"The next European war will be a game of *va banque*, whose equal the world has never seen before. It will be, in all probability, the last war."

With such words the Reichstag representatives won their 110 seats in the Reichstag.

When in the summer of 1911, the *Panther* made its spring to Agadir, and the noisy clamor of German imperialists brought Europe to the precipice of war, an international meeting in London, on the fourth of August, adopted the following resolution: "The German, Spanish, English, Dutch and French delegates of labor organizations hereby declare their readiness to oppose every declaration of war with every means in their power. Every nationality here represented pledges itself, in accordance with the decisions of its national and international congresses to oppose all criminal machinations on the part of the ruling classes."

But when in November 1912, the International Peace Congress met at Basel, when the long train of labor representatives entered the Minster, a presentiment of the coming hour of fate made them shudder and the heroic resolve took shape in every breast.

The cool, skeptical Victor Adler cried out: "Comrades, it is most important that we here, at the common source of our strength, that we, each and every one of us, take from hence the strength to do in his country what he can, through the forms and means that are at his disposal, to oppose this crime of war, and if it should be accomplished, if we should really be able to prevent war, let this be the cornerstone of our coming victory. That is the spirit that animates the whole International." ...

[But] on the thirtieth of July 1914 the central organ of the German social democracy cried out: "The socialist proletariat rejects all responsibility for the events that are being precipitated by a ruling class that is blinded, and on the verge of madness. We know that for us new life will spring from the ruins. But the responsibility falls upon the rulers of today.

"For them it is a question of existence!

World history is the last judgment!"

And then came the awful, the incredible fourth of August, 1914.

Did it *have* to come? An event of such importance cannot be a mere accident. It must have its deep, significant, objective causes. But perhaps these causes may be found in the errors of the leader of the proletariat, the social democracy itself, in the fact that our readiness to fight has flagged, convictions have forsaken us....

Friedrich Engels once said: "Capitalist society faces a dilemma, either an advance to socialism or a reversion to barbarism." What does a "reversion to barbarism" mean at the present stage of European civilization? We have read and repeated these words thoughtlessly without a conception of their terrible import. At this moment one glance about us will show us what a reversion to barbarism in capitalist society means. *This world war* means a reversion to barbarism. The triumph of imperialism leads to the destruction of culture, sporadically during a modern war, and forever, if the period of world wars that has just begun is allowed to take its damnable course to the last ultimate consequence. Thus we stand today, as Friedrich Engels prophesied more than a generation ago, before the awful proposition: either the triumph of imperialism and the destruction of all culture, and, as in ancient Rome, depopulation, desolation, degeneration, a vast cemetery; or, the victory of socialism, that is, the conscious struggle of the international proletariat against imperialism, against its methods, against war. This is the dilemma of world history, its inevitable choice, whose scales are trembling in the balance awaiting the decision of the prole-tariat. Upon it depends the future of culture and humanity. In this war imperialism has been victorious. Its brutal sword of mur-der has dashed the scales, with overbearing brutality, down into the abyss of shame and misery. If the proletariat learns *from* this war and in this war to exert itself, to cast off its serfdom to the ruling classes, to become the lord of its own destiny, the shame and misery will not have been in vain.

The modern working class must pay dearly for each realization of its historic mis-sion. The road to the Golgotha of its class liberation is strewn with awful sacrifices. The June combatants, the victims of the Commune, the martyrs of the Russian Rev-olution — an endless line of bloody shad-ows. They have fallen on the field of honor, as Marx wrote of the heroes of the Com-mune, to be enshrined forever in the great heart of the working class. Now millions of proletarians are falling on the field of dis-honor, of fratricide, of self-destruction, the slave-song on their lips. And that too has not been spared us. We are like the Jews whom Moses led through the desert. But we are not lost, and we will be victorious if we have not forgotten how to learn. And if the modern leaders of the proletariat do not know how to learn, they will go down "to make room for those who will be more able to cope with the problems of a new world." ...

In refuting the existence of the class strug-gle, the social democracy has denied the very basis of its own existence. What is the very breath of its body, if not the class struggle? What role could it expect to play in the war, once having sacrificed the class struggle, the fundamental principle of its existence? The social democracy has destroyed its mission, for the period of the war, as an active politi-cal party, as a representative of working-class politics. It has thrown aside the most important weapon it possessed, the power of criticism of the war from the peculiar point of view of the working class. Its only mission now is to play the role of the gendarme over the working class under a state of military rule.

German freedom, that same German free-dom for which, according to the declaration of the Reichstag group, Krupp cannons are now fighting, has been endangered by this attitude of the social democracy far beyond the period of the present war. The leaders of the social democracy are convinced that democratic liberties for the working class will come as a reward for its allegiance to the fatherland. But never in the history of the world has an oppressed class received politi-cal rights as a reward for service rendered to the ruling classes. History is full of examples of shameful deceit on the part of the ruling classes, even when solemn promises were made before the war broke out. The social democracy has not assured the extension of liberty in Germany. It has sacrificed those liberties that the working class possessed before the war broke out....

The events that bore the present war did not begin in July 1914 but reach back for decades. Thread by thread they have been woven together on the loom of an inexo-rable natural development until the firm net of imperialist world politics has encir-cled five continents. It is a huge historical complex of events, whose roots reach deep down into the Plutonic deeps of economic creation, whose outermost branches spread out and point away into a dimly dawning new world, events before whose all-embrac-ing immensity, the conception of guilt and retribution, of defense and offense, sink into pale nothingness.

Imperialism is not the creation of any one or of any group of states. It is the product of a particular stage of ripeness in the world development of capital, an innately inter-national condition, an indivisible whole, that is recognizable only in all its relations, and from which no nation can hold aloof at will. From this point of view only is it pos-sible to understand correctly the question of "national defense" in the present war.

The national state, national unity and independence were the ideological shield under which the capitalist nations of central Europe constituted themselves in the past century. Capitalism is incompatible with economic and political divisions, with the accompanying splitting up into small states. It needs for its development large, united ter-ritories, and a state of mental and intellectual development in the nation that will lift the demands and needs of society to a plane corresponding to the prevailing stage of capitalist production, and to the mechanism of modern capitalist class rule. Before capitalism could develop, it sought to create for itself a territory sharply defined by national limitations. This program was carried out only in France at the time of the great revolution, for in the national and political heritage left to Europe by the feudal middle ages, this could be accomplished only by revolutionary measures. In the rest of Europe this nationalization, like the revolutionary movement as a whole, remained the patchwork of half-kept promises. The German Empire, modern Italy, Austria-Hungary, and Turkey, the Russian Empire and the British world empire are all living proofs of this fact. The national program could play a historic role only so long as it represented the ideological expression of a growing bourgeoisie, lusting for power, until it had fastened its class rule, in some way or other, upon the great nations of central Europe and had created within them the necessary tools and conditions of its growth. Since then, imperialism has buried the old bourgeois democratic program completely by substituting expansionist activity irrespective of national relationships for the original program of the bourgeoisie in all nations. The national phase, to be sure, has been preserved, but its real content, its function, has been perverted into its very opposite. Today the nation is but a cloak that covers imperialistic desires, a battle cry for imperialistic rivalries, the last ideological measure with which the masses can be persuaded to play the role of cannon fodder in imperialistic wars.

This general tendency of present-day capitalist policies determines the policies of the individual states as their supreme blindly operating law, just as the laws of economic competition determine the conditions under which the individual manufacturer shall produce.

Let us assume for a moment, for the sake of argument, for the purpose of investigating this phantom of "national wars" that controls social democratic politics at the present time, that in one of the belligerent states, the war at its outbreak was purely one of national defense. Military success would immediately demand the occupation of foreign territory. But the existence of influential capitalist groups interested in imperialistic annexations will awaken expansionist appetites as the war goes on. The imperialistic tendency that, at the beginning of hostilities, may have been existent only in embryo, will shoot up and expand in the hothouse atmosphere of war until they will in a short time determine its character, its aims and its results.

Furthermore, the system of alliance between military states that has ruled the political relations of these nations for decades in the past makes it inevitable that each of the belligerent parties, in the course of war, should try to bring its allies to its assistance, again purely from motives of self-defense. Thus one country after another is drawn into the war, inevitably new imperialistic circles are touched and others are created. Thus England drew in Japan, and, spreading the war into Asia, has brought China into the circle of political problems and has influenced the existing rivalry between Japan and the United States, between England and Japan, thus heaping up new material for future conflicts. Thus Germany has dragged Turkey into the war, bringing the question of Constantinople, of the Balkans and of Western Asia directly into the foreground of affairs.

Even he who did not realize at the outset that the world war, in its causes, was purely imperialistic, cannot fail to see after a dispassionate view of its effects that war, under the present conditions, automatically and inevitably develops into a process of world division. This was apparent from the very first. The wavering balance of power between the two belligerent parties forces each, if only for military reasons, in order to strengthen its own position, or in order to frustrate possible attacks, to hold the neutral nations in check by intensive deals in peoples and nations, such as the German-Austrian offers to Italy, Rumania, Bulgaria and Greece on the one hand, and the English-Russian bids on the other. The "national war of defense" has the surprising effect of creating, even in the neutral nations, a general transformation, of ownership and relative power, always in direct line with expansionist tendencies. Finally the fact that all modern capitalist states have colonial possessions that will, even though the war may have begun as a war of national defense, be drawn into the conflict from purely military considerations, the fact that each country will strive to occupy the colonial possessions of its opponent, or at least to create disturbances therein, automatically turns every war into an imperialistic world conflagration.

Thus the conception of even that modest, devout fatherland-loving war of defense that has become the ideal of our parliamentarians and editors is pure fiction, and shows, on their part, a complete lack of understanding of the whole war and its world relations...

Thus the serious dilemma between the national interests and international solidarity of the proletariat, the tragic conflict that made our parliamentarians fall "with heavy heart" to the side of imperialistic warfare, was a mere figment of the imagination, a bourgeois nationalist fiction. Between the national interests and the class interests of the proletariat, in war and in peace, there is actually complete harmony. Both demand the most energetic prosecution of the class struggle, and the most determined insistence on the social, democratic program.

But what action should the party have taken to give to our opposition to the war and to our war demands weight and emphasis? Should it have proclaimed a general strike? Should it have called upon the soldiers to refuse military service? Thus the question is generally asked. To answer with a simple yes or no were just as ridiculous as to decide: "When war breaks out we will start a revolution." Revolutions are not "made" and great movements of the people are not produced according to technical recipes that repose in the pockets of the party leaders. Small circles of conspirators may organize a riot for a certain day and a certain hour, can give their small group of supporters the signal to begin. Mass movements in great historical crises cannot be initiated by such primitive measures.

The best prepared mass strike may break down miserably at the very moment when the party leaders give the signal, may collapse completely before the first attack. The success of the great popular movements depends, aye, the very time and circumstance of their inception is decided, by a number of economic, political and psychological factors. The existing degree of tension between the classes, the degree of intelligence of the masses and the degree or ripeness of their spirit of resistance — all these factors, which are incalculable, are premises that cannot be artificially created by any party. That is the difference between the great historical upheavals, and the small show-demonstrations that a well-disciplined party can carry out in times of peace, orderly, well-trained performances, responding obediently to the baton in the hands of the party leaders. The great historical hour itself creates the forms that will carry the revolutionary movements to a successful outcome, creates and improvises new weapons, enriches the arsenal of the people with weapons unknown and unheard of by the parties and their leaders....

The high stage of world industrial development in capitalist production finds expression in the extraordinary technical development and destructiveness of the instruments of war, as in their practically uniform degree of perfection in all belligerent countries. The international organization of war industries is reflected in the military instability that persistently brings back the scales, through all partial decisions and variations, to their true balance, and pushes a general decision further and further into the future. The indecision of military results, moreover, has the effect that a constant stream of new reserves, from the belligerent nations as well as from nations hitherto neutral, are sent to the front. Everywhere war finds material enough for imperialist desires and conflicts, itself creates new material to feed the conflagration that spreads out like a prairie fire. But the greater the masses, and the greater the number of nations that are dragged into this world war, the longer will it rage.

All of these things together prove, even before any military decision of victory or defeat can be established, that the result of the war will be: the economic ruin of all participating nations, and, in a steadily growing measure, of the formally neutral nations, a phenomenon entirely distinct from the earlier wars of modern times. Every month of war affirms and augments this effect, and thus takes away, in advance, the expected fruits of military victory for a decade to come. This, in the last analysis, neither victory nor defeat can alter; on the contrary, it makes a purely military decision altogether doubtful, and increases the likelihood that the war will finally end through a general and extreme exhaustion. But even a victorious Germany, under such circumstances, even if its imperialist war agitators should succeed in carrying on the mass murder to the absolute destruction of their opponents, even if their most daring dreams should be fulfilled — would win but a Pyrrhic victory. A number of annexed territories, impoverished and depopulated, and a grinning ruin under its own roof, would be its trophies. Nothing can hide this, once the painted stage properties of financial war bond transactions, and the Potemkin villages of an "unalterable prosperity" kept up by war orders, are pushed aside.

The most superficial observer cannot but see that even the most victorious nation cannot count on war indemnities that will stand in any relation to the wounds that the war has inflicted. Perhaps they may see in the still greater economic ruin of the defeated opponents, England and France, the very countries with which Germany was most closely united by industrial relations, upon whose recuperation its own prosperity so much depends, a substitute and an augmentation for their victory. Such are the circumstances under which the German people, even after a victorious war, would be required to pay, in cold cash, the war bonds that were "voted" on credit by the patriotic parliament; i.e., to take upon their shoulders an immeasurable burden of taxation, and a strengthened military dictatorship as the only permanent tangible fruit of victory....

Capitalist desire for imperialist expansion, as the expression of its highest maturity in the last period of its life, has the economic tendency to change the whole world into capitalistically producing nations, to sweep away all superannuated, precapitalistic methods of production and society, to subjugate all the riches of the earth and all means of production to capital, to turn the laboring masses of the peoples of all zones into wage slaves. In Africa and in Asia, from the most northern regions to the southernmost point of South America and in the South Seas, the remnants of old communistic social groups, of feudal society, of patriarchal systems, and of ancient handicraft production are destroyed and stamped out by capitalism. Whole peoples are destroyed, ancient civilizations are leveled to the ground, and in their place profiteering in its most modern forms is being established.

This brutal triumphant procession of capitalism through the world, accompanied by all the means of force, of robbery, and of infamy, has one bright phase: it has created the premises for its own final overthrow, it has established the capitalist world rule upon which, alone, the socialist world revolution can follow. This is the only cultural and progressive aspect of the great so-called works of culture that were brought to the primitive countries. To capitalist economists and politicians, railroads, matches, sewerage systems and warehouses are progress and culture. Of themselves such works, grafted upon primitive conditions, are neither culture nor progress, for they are too dearly paid for with the sudden economic and cultural ruin of the peoples who must drink down the bitter cup of misery and horror of two social orders, of traditional agricultural landlordism, of supermodern, superrefined capitalist exploitation, at one and the same time. Only as the material conditions for the destruction of capitalism and the abolition of class society can the effects of the capitalist triumphal march through the world bear the stamp of progress in a historical sense. In this sense imperialism, too, is working in our interest.

The present world war is a turning point in the course of imperialism. For the first time the destructive beasts that have been loosed by capitalist Europe over all other parts of the world have sprung with one awful leap, into the midst of the European nations. A cry of horror went up through the world when Belgium, that priceless little jewel of European culture, when the venerable monuments of art in northern France, fell into fragments before the onslaughts of a blind and destructive force. The "civilized world" that has stood calmly by when this same imperialism doomed tens of thousands of heroes to destruction, when the desert of Kalahari shuddered with the insane cry of the thirsty and the rattling breath of the dying, when in Putumayo, within ten years, forty thousand human beings were tortured to death by a band of European industrial robber barons, and the remnants of a whole people were beaten into cripples, when in China an ancient civilization was delivered into the hands of destruction and anarchy, with fire and slaughter, by the European soldiery, when Persia gasped in the noose of the foreign rule of force that closed inexorably about her throat, when in Tripoli the Arabs were mowed down, with fire and swords, under the yoke of capital while their homes were razed to the ground — this civilized world has just begun to know that the fangs of the imperialist beast are deadly, that its breath is frightfulness, that its tearing claws have sunk deeper into the breasts of its own mother, European culture. And this belated recognition is coming into the world of Europe in the distorted form, of bourgeois hypocrisy, that leads each nation to recognize infamy only when it appears in the uniform of the other. They speak of German barbarism, as if every people that goes out for organized murder did not change into a horde of barbarians! They speak of Cossack horrors, as if war itself were not the greatest of all horrors, as if the praise of human slaughter in a socialist periodical were not mental Cossackdom in its very essence.

But the horrors of imperialist bestiality in Europe have had another effect, that has brought to the "civilized world" no horror-stricken eyes, no agonized heart. It is the mass destruction of the European proletariat. Never has a war killed off whole nations; never, within the past century, has it swept over all of the great and established lands of civilized Europe. Millions of human lives were destroyed in the Vosges, in the Ardennes, in Belgium, in Poland, in the Carpathians and on the Save; millions have been hopelessly crippled. But nine-tenths of these millions come from the ranks of the working class of the cities and the farms. It is our strength, our hope that was mowed down there, day after day, before the scythe of death. They were the best, the most intelligent, the most thoroughly schooled forces of international socialism, the bearers of the holiest traditions, of the highest heroism, the modern labor movement, the vanguard of the whole world proletariat, the workers of England, France, Belgium, Germany and Russia who are being gagged and butchered in masses....

9.7   KARL KAUTSKY: ON POLITICAL REFORM AND SOCIALISM (*THE DICTATORSHIP OF THE PROLETARIAT*, 1918)

The Problem

For the first time in world history, the present Russian Revolution has made a socialist party the ruler of a great country. This is a far mightier event than the proletariat seizure of power over Paris in March 1871. But the Paris Commune surpasses the Soviet Republic in one important respect — it was the work of the whole proletariat. All socialist tendencies took part in it, none excluded itself or was excluded.

By contrast, the socialist party now ruling Russia today came to power in a struggle against other socialist parties. It exercises its power while excluding other socialist parties from its ruling bodies.

The antagonism between the two socialist tendencies does not rest on petty personal jealousies — it is the antagonism between two fundamentally different methods: the democratic and the dictatorial. Both tendencies have the same goal: to liberate the proletariat and therefore mankind by means of socialism. But the path followed by one is considered by the other to be a wrong path, which leads to ruin.

It is impossible to confront such a gigantic event as the proletarian struggle in Russia without taking part. Every one of us feels the necessity of taking sides, of being passionately committed. This is particularly necessary given that the problems occupying our Russian comrades today will be of practical significance for Western Europe tomorrow — in fact they already have a decisive influence on our propaganda and tactics.

We shall therefore examine what is the significance of democracy for the proletariat; what is meant by the dictatorship of the proletariat; and what conditions the dictatorship as a form of government creates for the proletariat's struggle for liberation.

Democracy and the Conquest of Political Power

In order to distinguish between democracy and socialism — by which is meant the socialization of the means of production and of production — it is sometimes argued that it is the latter which is the final goal and aim of our movement, while democracy is only a means towards this end and one which may, in certain cases, serve no purpose and even prove a hindrance.

However, a closer analysis reveals that it is not socialism as such which is our goal, but rather the abolition of "every form of exploitation and oppression, whether it be that of a class, a party, a sex or a race" (Erfurt Program).

We seek to achieve this goal by supporting the proletarian class struggle because as the lowest class, the proletariat cannot free itself without removing all the causes of exploitation and oppression, and because, of all exploited and oppressed classes, it is the industrial proletariat which is increasingly gathering the strength, the force and the urge to struggle, and whose victory is inevitable. This is why today every genuine opponent of exploitation and oppression, whatever his class of origin, must join the proletarian class struggle.

If in this struggle, we set ourselves the aim of the socialist mode of production, it is because under the present technical and economic conditions, this appears to be the only means of achieving our goal. If it were to be shown that we are mistaken in this matter and that the liberation of the proletariat and of humanity could be achieved solely or most appropriately on the basis of private property in the means of production, as Proudhon still believed, then we should be obliged to abandon socialism. This would not involve giving up our final goal at all: indeed the very interests of this goal would dictate that we abandon socialism.

Democracy and socialism cannot therefore be distinguished on the basis that one is a means and the other an end. Both are means towards the same end.

This distinction between them lies elsewhere. Without democracy, socialism as a means towards the liberation of the proletariat is inconceivable. Yet it is possible to have socialized production without democracy. Under primitive conditions it was possible for a communist economy to form a direct basis for despotism, as Engels pointed out in 1875 in connection with the village communism which has continued to exist in Russia and India down to our own day.

Under the so-called 'culture' system Dutch colonial policy in Java for a time based the organization of the agricultural production for the government which exploited the people, on a form of land communism.

The most striking example of a non-democratic organization of social labor is provided, however, by the Jesuit state of Paraguay in the eighteenth century. The Jesuits, as the ruling class, organized the labor of the native Indian population in a truly remarkable manner, using dictatorial powers, but without using force, for they had succeeded in gaining the support of their subjects.

Bur for modern man a patriarchal system of this kind would be intolerable. Such a system is only possible under conditions where the ruler far surpassed the ruled in terms of knowledge and where the latter are absolutely unable to raise themselves to the same level. A class or stratum which is waging a struggle for freedom cannot regard such a system of tutelage as its goal but most decisively reject it.

And so, for us, socialism without democracy is out of the question. When we speak of modern socialism we mean not only the social organization of production but also the democratic organization of society. Accordingly, for us, socialism is inseparably linked with democracy. There can be no socialism without democracy.

And yet this proposition cannot simply be reversed. Democracy is quite possible without socialism. Even pure democracy is conceivable without socialism — for example, in small peasant communities, where there is complete equality of economic conditions for everyone, on the basis of private property in the means of production.

Why should democracy be an inappropriate means for achieving socialism?

It is a question of the conquest of political power. It is argued that if, in a democratic state previously ruled by the bourgeoisie, there is a possibility of the social democrats gaining a majority in parliamentary elections, the ruling classes will employ all means of force at their disposal to impede the rule of democracy. For this reason it is claimed that the proletariat cannot gain political power by means of democracy but only by means of revolution.

There is no doubt that, whenever the proletariat in a democratic state is gaining in strength, it is to be expected that the ruling classes will attempt to frustrate, by the use of force, the utilization of democracy by the rising class. But this does not prove the uselessness of democracy for the proletariat. If, under the above-mentioned conditions, the ruling classes have recourse to force, they do so precisely because they fear the consequences of democracy. Their acts of violence would in fact subvert democracy.

So the fact that we expect the ruling classes to attempt to destroy democracy does not represent grounds for asserting the worthlessness of democracy for the proletariat. Instead it points to the necessity for the proletariat to defend democracy tooth and nail. Of course, if the proletariat is told that democracy is basically a useless ornament, then it will not make the effort necessary to defend it. However, the majority of the proletariat is far too attached to its democratic rights to stand idly by while they are taken away. On the contrary, it is much more likely that they will defend their rights with such vigor that, if their opponents seek to abolish the rights of the people by acts of violence, their resolute defense will lead to a political overthrow. The more the proletariat cherishes democracy, the more passionately it adheres to it, the more likely is this to come about.

On the other hand, it must not be thought that the course of events here described is inevitable in all cases. We need not be so faint-hearted. The more democratic the state is, the greater is the extent to which the instruments for exercising state power — including the military — are dependent upon the will of the people (the militia). Even in a democracy these instruments of power may be used to repress proletarian movements by force, in cases where the proletariat is still numerically weak — for example in an agrarian state, or where it is politically weak through lack of organization or consciousness. But if the proletariat in a democratic state reaches the stage where it becomes able in terms of strength and numbers to conquer political power through the use of existing liberties, then the 'capitalist dictatorship' will find itself hard-pressed to summon the resources necessary to abolish democracy by force.

Marx, in fact, considered it possible, and indeed probable, that in England, as in America, the proletariat would achieve political power by peaceful means. After the 1872 Hague congress of the International, he spoke at a public meeting in Amsterdam and said, among other things:

The worker will one day have to be in possession of political power in order to found the new organization of labor. He has to subvert the old political forms which maintain the institutions in force, if he does not wish to be like the Christians of old who neglected and despised such things, and to renounce the "kingdom of this world."

However, we have never claimed that the ways of achieving this goal must be everywhere the same.

We know that the account must be taken of the institutions, the manners and the traditions of the various countries and we do not deny that there are countries such as America, England and perhaps, if I were better acquainted with your system, I might add Holland to the list, where the workers may be able to achieve their ends by peaceful means. But this is not true of all countries.

Whether or not Marx's expectation will be fulfilled remains to be seen.

Undoubtedly, in the states referred to above, there do exist sections of the propertied classes which have a growing inclination to use force against the proletariat. But there are also other growing sections which respect the increasing power of the proletariat and desire to control its mood by means of concessions. Even though, for its duration, the War everywhere represented a constraint upon the political freedom of the popular masses, it nevertheless enabled the English proletariat to gain a considerable extension of voting rights. There is still no way of predicting today how democracy in the various states will influence the way in which the proletariat conquers power and to what extent it will mean that violent methods can be avoided by both sides in favor of peaceful ones. But there is no question of democracy losing its importance in the process. The forms of transition will certainly be very different in, on the one hand, a democratic republic where the people's rights have been firmly established for decades, if not for centuries, where these rights were conquered and retained or advanced by revolution and where, as a result, the ruling classes have learned to respect them, and, on the other hand, a community where a military despotism has hitherto enjoyed unrestrained control over the people through the use of the most powerful instruments and is thus accustomed to holding them in check.

But this influence of democracy on the mode of transition to a proletarian regime does not exhaust its importance for us in the pre-socialist period. Its most important function for us in this period is its indulgence on the maturing of the proletariat.

Democracy and the Maturity of the Proletariat

Socialism requires specific historical conditions which make it possible and necessary. This is no doubt generally recognized. Yet there is certainly no unanimity among us concerning the question of what the conditions are which must be fulfilled in order for a modern form of socialism to take shape in a country which is ripe for socialism. This lack of unity of such an important question is not a calamity — indeed it is a matter for rejoicing that we now have to occupy ourselves with the problem. For this requirement stems from the fact that for most of us socialism is now no longer something which we expect to happen in a few centuries, as so many recent converts were assuring us at the beginning of the War. Socialism has now taken its place as a practical question on today's agenda.

And so what are the prerequisites for the transition to socialism?

Every conscious human action presupposes a will. The will to socialism is the first condition for bringing it about. This will is brought into being by the existence of large-scale industry. Where small industry predominates in society, the majority of the population consists of its owners. The number of those who own nothing is small and the aspirations of the man without property is to own a small enterprise. Under certain circumstances this aspiration can take on a revolutionary form but in such cases the revolution will not be a socialist one for it will simply set out to redistribute the existing wealth in a manner which ensures that everyone becomes an individual owner. Small industry always produces the desire to retain or gain private ownership of the means of production on the part of individual workers and not the will for collective ownership, i.e. socialism.

This will is first implanted in the masses when large-scale industry is already highly developed and its predominance over small industry unquestionable; when the dissolution of large-scale industry would be a retrograde, indeed an impossible, step; when the workers in the large-scale industry can aspire to ownership of the means of production only in collective forms; and when the small industries which exist are deteriorating so fast that their owners can no longer drive a good living from them. Under these conditions the will to socialism begins to grow.

But at the same time it is also large-scale industry which provides the material possibility for the establishment of socialism. The greater the number of separate enterprises in the country and the greater the extent to which they are independent of each other, the more difficult it is to organize them collectively. This difficulty diminishes as the number of businesses falls and as relations between them become closer and more unified. Finally, in addition to the will and the material conditions which may be said to represent the raw materials of socialism, something else is required: the strength which actually brings it into being. Those who want socialism must become strong — stronger than those who do not want it.

This factor, too, is produced by the development of large-scale industry. It means an increase in the number of proletarians, who have an interest in socialism and a reduction in the number of capitalists, that is, a reduction relative to the number of proletarians. In relation to the non-proletarian intermediate strata — small farmers and petty bourgeoisie — the number of capitalists may for a time increase. But the fastest growing class in the state is the proletariat.

All these factors arise directly from economic development. They do not arise of themselves without human co-operation, but they do arise without the intervention of the proletariat, solely through the activities of the capitalists who have an interest in the growth of their large scale industries.

To begin with, this development is industrial and confined to the towns. There is only distant echo 0f it in agriculture. It is not from agriculture but from industry and the towns that socialism will gain its impetus. But in order for it to come about a fourth factor — in addition to the three already mentioned — is required: not only must the proletariat have an interest in socialism, not only must it have to hand the required material conditions and possess the strength necessary to bring socialism into being, but it must also have the capacity to maintain it in existence and to develop it along the appropriate lines. Only then can socialism be realized as a permanent mode of production.

If socialism is to be a possibility, then the maturity of the proletariat must be found together with the maturity of the material conditions provided by the appropriate stage of industrial development. The factor will not, however, be produced automatically by industrial development and the workings of the capitalist urge for profit without any intervention on the part of the proletariat. It must be obtained actively by means of opposition to capital.

As long as small industry predominates, there are two categories of propertyless persons. For the first category, consisting of apprentices and the sons of peasants, their lack of property condition is only a temporary condition. They expect to own property one day and so private ownership is in their interest. For the rest, the propertyless are made up of the lumpenproletariat, a class of parasites superfluous to — and indeed a burden upon — society, for they lack education, consciousness and cohesion. They are doubtless prepared to expropriate the owners where they can but they have neither the will nor the ability to set up a new type of economy.

The capitalist mode of production makes use of these propertyless hordes whose numbers increase dramatically in the early stages of capitalism. From useless, and indeed dangerous parasites, capitalism transforms them into the indispensable economic foundation of production and thereby of society. In this process both their numbers and their strength increase but they nevertheless remain ignorant, coarse and lacking in ability. Capitalism even attempts to force the whole working class down to this level. Overwork, the monotonous and soul-destroying character of work, female and child labor — by these means capitalism often succeeds in reducing the working classes below the level of the former lumpenproletariat. The pauperization of the proletariat is then accelerated to an alarming degree.

This pauperization gave rise to the first impulse towards socialism as an attempt to put an end to the increasing misery of the masses. However, it also seemed that this misery would render the proletariat forever incapable of emancipating itself. Bourgeois pity was to bring about its salvation by means of socialism.

It rapidly became apparent that nothing was to be expected from this pity. Only those who had an interest in socialism, namely the proletarians, could be expected to have sufficient strength to put socialism into practice. But had they not been reduced to despair? No, not all of them. There were still some strata which had retained the strength and courage necessary for the battle against misery. This small band was to succeed where the Utopians had failed and was to conquer state power and bring socialism to the proletariat by means of a coup. This was the conceptions of Blanqui and Weitling. The proletarians, too ignorant and depraved to organize and rule themselves, were to be organized and ruled from above by a government composed of their elite, in somewhat the same manner as the Jesuits in Paraguay had organized and ruled the Indians ...

The proletarian class struggle as a mass struggle presupposes democracy. If not necessary "unconditional" and "pure democracy," at least that degree of democracy which is required to organize the masses and keep them regularly informed. This can never be done adequately by secret methods. Individual tracts are not a substitute for a thriving daily press. Masses cannot be organized clandestinely and, above all, a secret organization cannot be a democratic one. Such an organization invariably leads to the dictatorship of one individual or of a group of leaders. The common members are reduced to the function of executive instruments. Such a situation of this kind might become necessary for the oppressed strata if there was a complete lack of democracy but it would not further self-government of the masses but instead the Messiah-complexes of the leaders and their dictatorial habits....

In his letter of May 1875 criticizing the Gotha party program Marx writes:

Between capitalist and communist society lies the period of the revolutionary transformation of the one into the other. This period is also one of political transition in which the state can be nothing but the *revolutionary dictatorship of the proletariat*.

Unfortunately Marx failed to state precisely how he envisaged this dictatorship. Taken literally the word signifies the abolition (*Aufhebung*) of democracy. It can also be taken literally to mean the sovereign rule of a single person unfettered by any sort of law. A rule which should be distinguished from despotism by being regarded as a temporary emergency measure and not as a permanent institution of the state.

The use by Marx of the expression "dictatorship of the proletariat," that is the dictatorship of a class and not of a single person, makes it clear that he did not mean a dictatorship in the literal sense.

In the passage quoted above Marx was not talking about a *form of government* but of a *state of affairs* which most necessarily arise wherever the proletariat achieves political power. The fact that he did not have a form of government in mind is attested to, surely, by his opinion that in England and America the transition could occur peacefully and democratically.

Of course democracy does not as yet guarantee a peaceful transition but the latter is certainly not possible without democracy.

It is however quite unnecessary to resort to guesswork to discover Marx's views on the dictatorship of the proletariat. If he did not explain more fully what he understood by the expression in 1875 it might well have been because he had already done so some years earlier in 1871 in his pamphlet *On the Civil War in France* where he wrote:

The Commune was essentially a working-class government, the result of the struggle between the producing class against the appropriating class; at last the political form under which to work out the economic emancipation of labor had emerged.

Thus the Paris Commune was "the dictatorship of the proletariat" as Engels explicitly stated in his introduction to the third edition of Marx's pamphlet.

The commune was not so much the abolition of democracy as the widest application of democracy on the basis of universal suffrage. Government power was to be subject to universal suffrage.

> The Commune was composed of town councilors elected from the various wards of Paris by *universal suffrage* ... *Universal suffrage* was to serve the people constituted in communes just as individual suffrage serves every other employer in his choice of workmen etc.

Time and again in this pamphlet Marx talks about universal suffrage of all the people rather than of the franchise of a specially privileged class. For him the dictatorship of the proletariat was a state of affairs which necessarily arose in a real democracy because of the overwhelming numbers of the proletariat.

Marx must not therefore be quoted by those who support dictatorship in opposition to democracy. Of course having said that it has still not been shown that they are wrong. They must however look for other arguments in support of their case.

In examining this question one must be careful not to confuse dictatorship as a *state of affairs* with dictatorship as a *form of government*. It is only the question of dictatorship as a form of government which is a subject of dispute in our ranks. Dictatorship as a form of government means depriving the opposition of their rights by abolishing their franchise, the freedom of the press and freedom of association. The question is whether the victorious proletariat needs to employ these measures and whether they will merely facilitate or are in fact indispensable to the building of socialism.

In the first instance it must be noted that when we speak of dictatorship as a form of government this cannot include the dictatorship of a class, for, as we have already seen, a class can only rule not govern. If one wishes to signify by dictatorship not merely a condition of rule but a specific form of government then one must either talk of the dictatorship of a single person or an organi-

zation or of a proletarian party — but not of the proletariat. The problem immediately becomes complicated when the proletariat splits into different parties. Then the dictatorship of one of these parties is in no way the dictatorship of the proletariat any longer but a dictatorship of one part of the proletariat over another. The situation becomes still more complex if the socialist parties are split over their relations vis-à-vis non-proletarian strata, if for instance one party was to come to power by means of an alliance between city proletarians and peasants. In this instance the dictatorship of the proletariat assumes very strange forms.

What are the reasons for thinking that the rule of the proletariat should and must of necessity take a form which is incompatible with democracy? Anyone who quotes Marx on the dictatorship of the proletariat must not forget that Marx is not dealing with a state of affairs that can only arise in special circumstances but with one that must occur in any event.

Now it may be assumed that as a rule the proletariat will only come to power when it represents the majority of the population or at least has its support. Next to its economic indispensability the proletariat's weapon in its political struggles consists in the huge mass of its numbers. It can only expect to carry the day against the resources of the ruling classes where it has the masses, that is the majority of the population, behind it. Marx and Engels were both of this opinion and that is why they declared in the *The Communist Manifesto*:

> All previous movements were movements of minorities or in the interests of minorities. The proletarian movement is the independent movement of the immense majority in the interests of the immense majority.

This was also true of the Paris Commune. The first act of the new revolutionary regime was an appeal to the electorate. The poll was held in conditions of the greatest freedom and gave large majorities for the Commune in nearly all the districts of Paris. Sixty-five revolutionaries were elected as against twenty-one candidates from the opposition;

of the latter fifteen were clearly reactionaries and six were Radical Republicans of the Gambetta faction. The sixty-five revolutionaries represented all the existing tendencies of French socialism. No matter how much they fought against each other no one group exercised a dictatorship over the others.

A government so strongly rooted in the masses has not the slightest reason to encroach upon democratic rights. It will not always be able to dispense with the use of force in instances where force is being used to crush democracy. Force can only be met with force.

However a government which knows that the masses are behind it will only use force to protect democracy and not to suppress it. It would be quite suicidal to dispense with universal suffrage, which is a government's surest foundation and a powerful source of tremendous moral authority.

Thus the suspension (*Aufhebung*) of democracy by dictatorship can only be a matter for consideration in exceptional circumstances, such as when an unusual combination of favorable circumstances enables a proletarian party to seize power even though the majority of the population does not support it or is in fact positively against it.

Such a chance victory is hardly possible where the people have been schooled in politics for decades and where the idea of political parties is well established. Surely such a state of affairs is merely indicative of very backward conditions. What if after a seizure of power the electorate votes against the socialist government? Should the latter do what has up until now been demanded of each and every government, that is bow to the will of the people and to resume its struggle for power on a democratic basis with resolute determination; or ought it to suppress democracy so as to stay in power?...

9.8   LEON TROTSKY (*THEIR MORALS AND OURS*, 1938)

Moral Precepts Obligatory upon All

Whoever does not care to return to Moses, Christ, or Mohammed; whoever is not satisfied with eclectic *hodge-podges* must acknowledge that morality is a product of social development; that there is nothing immutable about it; that it serves social interests; that these interests are contradictory; that morality more than any other form of ideology has a class character.

But do not elementary moral precepts exist, worked out in the development of humanity as a whole and indispensable for the existence of every collective body? Undoubtedly such precepts exist but the extent of their action is extremely limited and unstable. Norms "obligatory upon all" become the less forceful the sharper the character assumed by the class struggle. The highest form of the class struggle is civil war, which explodes into midair all moral ties between the hostile classes.

Under "normal" conditions a "normal" person observes the commandment: "Thou shalt not kill!" But if one kills under exceptional conditions for self-defense, the jury acquits that person. If one falls victim to a murderer, the court will kill the murderer. The necessity of courts, as well as that of self-defense, flows from antagonistic interests. In so far as the state is concerned, in peaceful times it limits itself to *legalized* killings of individuals so that in time of war it may transform the "obligatory" commandment, "Thou shalt not kill!" into its opposite. The most "humane" governments, which in peaceful times "detest" war, proclaim during war that the highest duty of their armies is the extermination of the greatest possible number of people.

The so-called "generally recognized" moral precepts in essence preserve an algebraic, that is, an indeterminate character. They merely express the fact that people in their individual conduct are bound by certain common norms that flow from their being members of society. (The highest generalization of these norms is the "categorical imperative" of Kant. But in spite of the fact that it occupies a high position in the philosophic Olympus this imperative does not embody anything categoric because it embodies nothing concrete. It is a shell without content.)

This vacuity in the norms obligatory upon all arises from the fact that in all decisive questions people feel their class membership considerably more profoundly and more directly than their membership in "society." The norms of "obligatory" morality are in reality filled with class, that is, antagonistic content. The moral norm becomes the more categoric the less it is "obligatory upon all." The solidarity of workers, especially of strikers or barricade fighters, is incomparably more "categoric" than human solidarity in general.

The bourgeoisie, which far surpasses the proletariat in the completeness and irreconcilability of its class consciousness, is vitally interested in imposing its moral philosophy upon the exploited masses. It is exactly for this purpose that the concrete norms of the bourgeois catechism are concealed under moral abstractions patronized by religion, philosophy, or by that hybrid which is called "common sense." The appeal to abstract norms is not a disinterested philosophical mistake but a necessary element in the mechanics of class deception. The exposure of this deceit which retains the tradition of thousands of years is the first duty of a proletarian revolutionist....

Morality and Revolution

Among the liberals and radicals there are not a few individuals who have assimilated the methods of the materialist interpretation of events and who consider themselves Maoists. This does not hinder them, however, from remaining bourgeois journalists, professors, or politicians. A Bolshevik is inconceivable, of course, without the materialist method, in the sphere of morality as well. But this method serves him not solely for the interpretation of events but rather for the creation of a revolutionary party of the proletariat. It is impossible to accomplish this task without complete independence from the bourgeoisie and their morality. Yet bourgeois public opinion now actually reigns in full sway over the official workers' movement from William Green in the United States, Leon Blum and Maurice Thorez in France, to Garcia Oliver in Spain. In this fact the reactionary character of the present period reaches its sharpest expression.

A revolutionary Marxist cannot begin to approach his historical mission without having broken morally from bourgeois public opinion and its agencies in the proletariat. For this, moral courage of a different caliber is required from that of opening wide one's mouth at meetings and yelling, "Down with Hitler!" "Down with Franco!" It is precisely this resolute, completely thought-out, inflexible rupture of the Bolsheviks from conservative moral philosophy not only of the big but of the petty bourgeoisie that mortally terrorizes democratic phrasemongers, drawing-room prophets, and lobbying heroes. From this derive their complaints about the "amoralism" of the Bolsheviks.

Their identification of bourgeois morals with morals "in general" can best of all, perhaps, be verified at the extreme left wing of the petty bourgeoisie, precisely in the centrist parties of the so-called London Bureau. Since this organization "recognizes" the program of proletarian revolution, our disagreements with it seem, at first glance, secondary. Actually their "recognition" is valueless because it does not bind them to anything. They "recognize" the proletarian revolution as the Kantians recognized the categorical imperative, that is, as a holy principle but not applicable to daily life. In the sphere of practical politics they unite with the worst enemies of the revolution (reformists and Stalinists) for the struggle against us. All their thinking is permeated with duplicity and falsehood. If the centrists, according to a general rule, do not raise themselves to imposing crimes it is only because they forever remain in the byways of politics: they are, so to speak, petty pickpockets of history. For this reason they consider themselves called upon to regenerate the workers' movement with a new morality.

At the extreme left wing of this "left" fraternity stands a small and politically completely insignificant grouping of German emigres who publish the paper *Neuer Weg* (The New Road). Let us bend down lower and listen to these "revolutionary" indicters of Bolshevik amoralism. In a tone of ambiguous pseudopraise the *Neuer Weg* proclaims that the Bolsheviks are distinguished advantageously from other parties by their absence of hypocrisy — they openly declare what others quietly apply in fact, that is, the principle "the end justifies the means." But according to the convictions of *Neuer Weg* such a "bourgeois" precept is incompatible with a "healthy socialist movement." "Lying and worse are not permissible means of struggle, as Lenin still considered them." The word "still" evidently signifies that Lenin did not succeed in overcoming his delusions only because he failed to live until the discovery of The New Road.

In the formula, "lying and worse," "worse" evidently signifies violence, murder, and so on, since under equal conditions violence is worse than lying, and murder — the most extreme form of violence. We thus come to the conclusion that lying, violence, murder, are incompatible with a "healthy socialist movement." What, however, is our relation to revolution? Civil war is the most severe of all forms of war. It is unthinkable not only without violence against tertiary figures but, under contemporary technique, without killing old men, old women, and children. Must one be reminded of Spain? The only possible answer of the "friends" of Republican Spain sounds like this: Civil war is better than fascist slavery. But this completely correct answer merely signifies that the *end* (democracy or socialism) justifies, under certain conditions, such *means* as violence and murder. Not to speak about lies! Without lies war would be as unimaginable as a machine without oil. In order to safeguard even the session of the Cortes (February 1, 1938) from fascist bombs, the Barcelona government several times deliberately deceived journalists and their own population. Could it have acted in any other way? Whoever accepts the end: victory over Franco, must accept the means: civil war with its wake of horrors and crimes.

Nevertheless, lying and violence "in themselves" warrant condemnation? Of course, even as does the class society which generates them. A society without social contradictions will naturally be a society without lies and violence. However there is no way of building a bridge to that society save by revolutionary, that is, violent means. The revolution itself is a product of class society and of necessity bears its traits. From the point of view of "eternal truths" revolution is of course "antimoral." But this merely means that idealist morality is counterrevolutionary, that is, in the service of the exploiters.

"Civil war," the philosopher caught unawares will perhaps respond, "is however a sad exception. But in peaceful times a healthy socialist movement should manage without violence and lying." Such an answer however represents nothing less than a pathetic evasion. There is no impervious demarcation between "peaceful" class struggle and revolution. Every strike embodies in an unexpanded form all the elements of civil war. Each side strives to impress the opponent with an exaggerated picture of its resoluteness to struggle and its material resources. Through their press, agents, and spies the capitalists labor to frighten and demoralize the strikers. From their side, the workers' pickets, where persuasion does not avail, are compelled to resort to force. Thus "lying and worse" are an inseparable part of the class struggle even in its most elementary form. It remains to be added that the very conception of *truth* and *lie* was born of social contradictions....

Revolution and the Institution of Hostages

Lincoln's significance lies in his not hesitating before the most severe means, once they were found to be necessary, in achieving a great historic aim posed by the development of a young nation. The question lies not even in which of the warring camps caused or itself suffered the greatest number of victims. History has different yardsticks for the cruelty of the Northerners and the cruelty of the Southerners in the Civil War. (A slaveholder who through cunning and violence shackles a slave in chains, and a slave who through cunning and violence breaks the chains — let not the contemptible eunuchs tell us that they are equals before a court of morality!)

After the Paris Commune had been drowned in blood and the reactionary knaves of the whole world dragged its banner in the filth of vilification and slander, there were not a few democratic Philistines who, adapting themselves to reaction, slandered the Communards for shooting sixty-four hostages headed by the Paris archbishop. Marx did not hesitate a moment in defending this bloody act of the Commune. In a circular issued by the General Council of the First International, which seethes with the fiery eruption of lava, Marx first reminds us of the bourgeoisie adopting the institution of hostages in the struggle against both colonial peoples and their own toiling masses and afterward refers to the systematic execution of the Commune captives by the frenzied reactionaries, continuing: "... the Commune, to protect their [the captives'] lives, was obliged to resort to the Prussian practice of securing hostages."...

When the October Revolution was defending itself against the united forces of imperialism on a 5,000-mile front, the workers of the whole world followed the course of the struggle with such ardent sympathy that in their forums it was extremely risky to indict the "disgusting barbarism" of the institution of hostages. Complete degeneration of the Soviet state and the triumph of reaction in a number of countries was necessary before the moralists crawled out of their crevices ... to aid Stalin. If it is true that the repressions safeguarding the privileges of the new aristocracy have the same moral value as the revolutionary measures of the liberating struggle, then Stalin is completely justified, if ... if the proletarian revolution is not completely condemned.

Seeking examples of immorality in the events of the Russian civil war, Messrs. Moralists find themselves at the same time constrained to close their eyes to the fact that the Spanish revolution also produced an institution of hostages, at least during that period when it was a genuine revolution of the masses. If the indicters dare not attack the Spanish workers for their "disgusting barbarism," it is only because the ground of the Pyrennean peninsula is still too hot for them, it is considerably more convenient to

return to 1919. This is already history, the old men have forgotten and the young ones have not yet learned. For the same reason pharisees of various hues return to Kronstadt and Makhkno with such obstinancy — here exists a free outlet for moral effluvia!

Dialectical Interdependence of End and Means

A means can be justified only by its end. But the end in its turn needs to be justified. From the Marxist point of view, which expresses the historical interests of the proletariat, the end is justified if it leads to increasing the power of humanity over nature and to the abolition of the power of one person over another.

"We are to understand then that in achieving this end anything is permissible?" demands the philistine sarcastically, demonstrating that he understood nothing. That is permissible, we answer, which *really* leads to the liberation of humanity. Since this end can be achieved only through revolution, the liberating morality of the proletariat of necessity is endowed with a revolutionary character. It irreconcilably counteracts not only religious dogma but all kinds of idealistic fetishes, these philosophic gendarmes of the ruling class. It deduces a rule for conduct from the laws of the development of society, thus primarily from the class struggle, this law of all laws.

"Just the same," the moralist continues to insist, "does it mean that in the class struggle against capitalists all means are permissible: lying, frame-up, betrayal, murder, and so on?" Permissible and obligatory are those and only those means, we answer, which unite the revolutionary proletariat, fill their hearts with irreconcilable hostility to oppression, teach them contempt for official morality and its democratic echoers, imbue them with consciousness of their own historic mission, raise their courage and spirit of self-sacrifice in the struggle. Precisely from this it flows that not all means are permissible. When we say that the end justifies the means, then for us the conclusion follows that the great revolutionary end spurns those base means and ways which set one part of the working class against other parts, or attempt to make the masses happy without their participation; or lower the faith of the masses in themselves and their organization, replacing it by worship for the "leaders." Primarily and irreconcilably, revolutionary morality rejects servility in relation to the bourgeoisie and haughtiness in relation to the toilers, that is, those characteristics in which petty-bourgeois pedants and moralists are thoroughly steeped.

These criteria do not, of course, give a ready answer to the question as to what is permissible and what is not permissible in each separate case. There can be no such automatic answers. Problems of revolutionary morality are fused with the problems of revolutionary strategy and tactics. The living experience of the movement under the clarification of theory provides the correct answer to these problems.

Dialectical materialism does not know dualism between means and end. The end flows naturally from the historical movement. Organically the means are subordinated to the end. The immediate end becomes the means for a further end. In his play *Franz von Sickingen*, Ferdinand Lassalle puts the following words into the mouth of one of the heroes:

Do not only show the goal, show the path as well.

For so closely interwoven with one another are path and goal

That a change in one means a change in the other,

And a different path gives rise to a different goal.

Lassalle's lines are not at all perfect. Still worse is the fact that in practical politics Lassalle himself diverged from the above expressed precept — it is sufficient to recall that he went as far as secret agreements with Bismarck! But the dialectical interdependence between means and end is expressed entirely correctly in the above-quoted sentences. Seeds of wheat must be sown in order to yield an ear of wheat.

Is individual terror, for example, permissible or impermissible from the point of view of "pure morals"? In this abstract form the question does not exist at all for us. Conservative Swiss bourgeois even now render official praise to the terrorist William Tell. Our sympathies are fully on the side of Irish, Russian, Polish, or Hindu terrorists in their struggle against national and political oppression. The assassinated Kirov, a rude satrap, does not call forth any sympathy. Our relation to the assassin remains neutral only because we know not what motives guided him. If it became known that Nikolaev acted as a conscious avenger for workers' rights trampled upon by Kirov, our sympathies would be fully on the side of the assassin. However, not the question of subjective motives but that of objective efficacy has for us the decisive significance. Are the given means really capable of leading to the goal? In relation to individual terror, both theory and experience bear witness that such is not the case. To the terrorist we say: It is impossible to replace the masses; only in the mass movement can you find effective expression for your heroism. However, under conditions of civil war, the assassination of individual oppressors ceases to be an act of individual terror. If, we shall say, a revolutionist bombed General Franco and his staff into the air, it would hardly evoke moral indignation even from the democratic eunuchs. Under the conditions of civil war a similar act would be politically completely effective. Thus, even in the sharpest question — murder of man by man — moral absolutes prove futile. Moral evaluations, along with political ones, flow from the inner needs of struggle.

The liberation of the workers can come only through the workers themselves. There is, therefore, no greater crime than deceiving the masses, palming off defeats as victories, friends as enemies, bribing workers' leaders, fabricating legends, staging false trials, in a word, doing what the Stalinists do. These means can serve only one end: lengthening the domination of a clique already condemned by history. But they cannot serve to liberate the masses. That is why the Fourth International wages a life and death struggle against Stalinism.

The masses, of course, are not at all impeccable. Idealization of the masses is foreign to us. We have seen them under different conditions, at different stages and in addition in the biggest political shocks. We have observed their strong and weak sides. Their strong side — resoluteness, self-sacrifice, heroism — has always found its clearest expression in times of revolutionary upsurge. During this period the Bolsheviks headed the masses. Afterward a different historical chapter loomed when the weak side of the oppressed came to the forefront: heterogeneity, insufficiency of culture, narrowness of world outlook. The masses tired of the tension, became disillusioned, lost faith in themselves — and cleared the road for the new aristocracy. In this epoch the Bolsheviks ("Trotskyists") found themselves isolated from the masses. Practically speaking, we went through two such big historic cycles: 1897–1905, years of flood tide; 1907–1913, years of the ebb; 1917–1923, a period of upsurge unprecedented in history; finally, a new period of reaction, which has not ended even today. In these immense events the "Trotskyists" learned the rhythm of history, that is, the dialectics of the class struggle. They also learned, it seems, and to a certain degree successfully, how to subordinate their subjective plans and programs to this objective rhythm. They learned not to fall into despair over the fact that the laws of history do not depend upon their individual tastes and are not subordinated to their own moral criteria. They learned to subordinate their individual tastes to the laws of history. They learned not to become frightened by the most powerful enemies if their power is in contradiction to the needs of historical development. They know how to swim against the stream in the deep conviction that the new historic flood will carry them to the other shore. Not all will reach that shore, many will drown. But to participate in this movement with open eyes and with an intense will — only this can give the highest moral satisfaction to a thinking being!

INTERNATIONAL ORGANIZATIONS

The question of whether the state (even a socialist one) could secure rights in a capitalist-dominated world had already been the subject of prolonged debates in nineteenth-century labor circles. Whereas anarchists rejected the state as a vehicle for human rights, socialists were split between proponents of the revolutionary overthrow of the capitalist state and advocates of reform. Despite differences over tactics, most ultimately endorsed the development of an internationalist socialist organization able to synchronize global activism in support of workers' rights.

A year before the establishment of the First International (1864), Pierre-Joseph Proudhon, reflecting the anarchist trend, proposed in *The Principle of Federalism* (1863) establishing a federation as a way to balance two opposites: liberty and authority. Federation, he claimed, should guarantee the states their sovereignty, liberty, territory, security, and mutual prosperity. Yet the federal power should never exceed that of local or provincial authorities. He predicted that federal systems that guarantee political rights while excluding economic and labor protections would serve mainly to increase the power of private capital and commerce. To avoid financial exploitation under the umbrella of federalism, he proposed an agroindustrial system that, by means of social cooperatives (mutualism) and credit unions, would secure "the right to work and to education, and an organization of work which would allow each laborer to become a skilled worker and an artisan, and each wage earner to become his own master."

To achieve this ideal would require nothing less than the solidarity of the working class across national boundaries. "Workers of the world, unite!" Karl Marx wrote in *The Communist Manifesto* (1848) and in his 1864 "Inaugural Address of the Working Men's International Association" (or the First International). The numerous setbacks experienced by impoverished workers between 1848 and 1864, Marx explained, required an institution that would foster international solidarity and organized class action around political and welfare rights.

That vision of internationalism was taken to a new level when British Fabian socialist Leonard Woolf (1880–1969) proposed, in *International Government* (1916), building on the tradition of Hugo Grotius, Immanuel Kant, and Karl Marx, an international institution to enforce world peace. Writing soon before Woodrow Wilson's (1856–1924) proposal for a League of Nations, he argued that the only alternative to war was the development of an international organization, one that would involve a degree of submission by each nation "to the expressed will of other nations." Furthermore, he also warned against "dosing international society with law in treaties unless you have a judge handy to decide the legal disputes." He thus suggested for the first time the establishment of an international high court, to which the nations would agree to submit, not all their possible differences and disputes, but only such as were, by their very nature, legal or justiciable (see Section 9.11).

9.9 PIERRE-JOSEPH PROUDHON (*THE PRINCIPLE OF FEDERALISM*, 1863)

Isolation of the Idea of Federation

Since in theory and in history authority and liberty succeed one another in a polar movement; since the former declines imperceptibly and withdraws, while the latter expands and becomes prominent; since this dual movement leads to a subordination such that authority becomes progressively the instrument of liberty; since, in other words, the liberal or contractual system gains the upper hand day by day over the authoritarian system, it is the idea of contract that we must take to be the principal idea in politics....

The political contract does not attain its full dignity and morality except where (1) it is *synallagmatic* and *commutative*, (2) it is confined, in its object, within definite limits — two conditions which are held to exist in the democratic system, but which, even there, are generally only a fiction. Can one say that in a representative and centralized democracy, or in a constitutional monarchy with restricted franchise, or even more in a communist republic such as Plato's the political contract binding the citizen to the state can be equal and reciprocal? Can one say that these contracts, which remove from the citizens a half or two-thirds of their sovereignty and a quarter of their product, are confined within just limits? It would be closer to the truth to say that, as experience shows only too often, contracts in such systems are excessive, *onerous*, for they provide no compensation for a good many of those who are parties to them;

and *aleatory*, for the promised advantage, inadequate as it is, is not even guaranteed.

In order for the political contract to become synallagmatic and commutative as the idea of democracy requires, in order for it to remain within reasonable limits and to become profitable and convenient for all, the citizen who enters the association must (1) have as much to gain from the state as he sacrifices to it, (2) retain all his liberty, sovereignty, and initiative, except that which he must abandon in order to attain that special object for which the contract is made, and which the state must guarantee. So confined and understood, the political contract is what I shall call a federation.

Federation, from the Latin *foedus*, genitive *foederis*, which means pact, contract, treaty, agreement, alliance, and so on, is an agreement by which one or more heads of family, one or more towns, one or more groups of towns or states, assume reciprocal and equal commitments to perform one or more specific tasks, the responsibility for which rests exclusively with the officers of the federation....

The contract of federation has the purpose, in general terms, of guaranteeing to the federated states their sovereignty, their territory, the liberty of their subjects; of settling their disputes; of providing by common means for all matters of security and mutual prosperity; thus, despite the scale of the interests involved, it is essentially limited. The authority responsible for its execution can never overwhelm the constituent members; that is, the federal powers can never exceed in number and significance those of local or provincial authorities, just as the latter can never outweigh the rights and prerogatives of man and citizen. If it were otherwise, the community would become communistic; the federation would revert to centralized monarchy; the federal authority, instead of being a mere delegate and subordinate function as it should be, will be seen as dominant; instead of being confined to a specific task, it will tend to absorb all activity and all initiative; the confederated states will be reduced to administrative districts, branches, or local offices. Thus transformed, the body politic may be termed republican, democratic, or what you will; it will no longer be a state constituted by a plenitude of autonomies, it will no longer be a confederation. The same will hold, with even greater force, if for reasons of false economy as a result of deference, or for any other reason the federated towns, cantons or states charge one among their number with the administration and government of the rest. The republic will become unitary, not federal, and will be on the road to despotism.[1]...

The whole science of constitutions is here. I shall summarize it in three propositions.

1. Form groups of a modest size, individually sovereign, and unite them by a federal pact.
2. Within each federated state organize government on the principle of organic separation; that is, separate all powers that can be separated, define everything that can be defined, distribute what has been separated and defined among distinct organs and functionaries; leave nothing undivided; subject public administration to all the constraints of publicity and control.
3. Instead of absorbing the federated states and provincial and municipal authorities within a central authority, reduce the role of the center to that of general initiation, of providing guarantees and supervising, and make the execution of its orders subject to the approval of the federated governments and their responsible agents — just as, in a constitutional monarchy, every order by the king must be countersigned by a minister in order to become effective....

The federal system is applicable to all nations and all ages, for humanity is progressive in each of its generations and peoples; the policy of federation, essentially the policy of progress, consists in ruling every people, at any given moment, by decreasing the sway of authority and central power to the point permitted by the level of consciousness and morality....

Economic Sanctions: The Agro-Industrial Federation

But there is more to be said. However impeccable in its logic the federal constitution may be, and whatever practical guarantees it may supply, it will not survive if economic factors tend persistently to dissolve it. In other words, political right requires to be buttressed by economic right. If the production and distribution of wealth are given over to chance; if the federal order serves merely to preserve the anarchy of capital and commerce; if, as a result of this misguided anarchy, society comes to be divided into two classes — one of landlords, capitalists, and entrepreneurs, the other of wage-earning proletarians, one rich, the other poor — then the political order will still be unstable. The working class, the most numerous and poorest of the classes, will eventually regard it as nothing but a trick; the workers will unite against the bourgeois, who in turn will unite against the workers; and federation will degenerate into unitary democracy, if the people are stronger, or, if the bourgeoisie is victorious, into a constitutional monarchy.

The anticipation of such a social war had led to the establishment of strong governments, so admired by theorists, who have seen confederations as frail things incapable of defending power from mass aggression, that is, of preserving government policy in defiance of the rights of the nation....

The twentieth century will open the age of federations, or else humanity will undergo another purgatory of a thousand years. The real problem to be resolved is not political but economic....

The reader may expect me to present a scheme of economic science as applied to federations, and to show in detail all that has to be done from this perspective. I shall simply say that after reforming the political order the federal government must necessarily proceed to a series of reforms in the economic realm. Here, in a few words, is what these reforms must be.

Just as, in a political context, two or more independent states may federate in order to guarantee mutually their territorial integrity or to protect their liberty, so too, in an economic context, confederation may be intended to provide reciprocal security in commerce and industry, or a *customs union*; or the object may be to construct and maintain means of transportation, such as roads, canals, and railways, or to organize credit, insurance, and so on. The purpose of such specific federal arrangements is to protect the citizens of the federated states from capitalist and financial exploitation, both within them and from the outside; in their aggregate they form, as opposed to the financial feudalism in the ascendant today, what I will call *an agro-industrial federation*.

I shall not go into this topic in any depth. Those of my readers who have followed my work to any extent for the last fifteen years will understand well enough what I mean. The purpose of industrial and financial feudalism is to confirm, by means of the monopoly of public services, educational privilege, the division of labor, interest on capital, inequitable taxation, and so on, the political neutralization of the masses, wage-labor or economic servitude, in short inequality of condition and wealth. The agro-industrial federation, on the other hand, will tend to foster increasing equality, by organizing all public services in an economical fashion and in hands other than the state's, through mutualism in credit and insurance, the equalization of the tax burden, guaranteeing the right to work and to education, and an organization of work which allows each laborer to become a skilled worker and an artist, each wage-earner to become his own master.

Such a revolution, it is clear, cannot be the work of a bourgeois monarchy or a unitary democracy; it will be accomplished by federation. It does not spring from the *unilateral* contract or the contract of *goodwill*, nor from the institutions of *charity*, but from bilateral and commutative contract.

Considered in itself, the idea of an industrial federation which serves to complement and support political federation is most strikingly justified by the principles of economics. It is the application on the largest possible scale of the principles of mutualism, division of labor, and economic solidarity, principles which the will of the people will have transformed into positive laws....

1. The Helvetian Confederation consists of twenty-five sovereign states (nineteen cantons, six half-cantons), containing a population of two million, four hundred thousand inhabitants. It is therefore governed by twenty-five constitutions, comparable to our charters or constitutions of 1791, 1793, 1795, 1799, 1814, 1830, 1848, 1852, together with a federal constitution to which of course there is no parallel in France. The spirit of this constitution, which conforms to the principles outlined above, is contained in the following articles:

"Article 2. The purpose of confederation is to secure the independence of the nation against foreign powers, to maintain internal peace and order, to protect the rights and liberties of its members, and to increase their common prosperity."

"Article 3. The cantons are sovereign within the limits of federal sovereignty, and as such they exercise all rights which have not been delegated to the federal power."

"Article 5. The confederation guarantees to the cantons their territory, their sovereignty within the limits established by Article 3, their constitutions, the liberty and rights of their inhabitants, the constitutional rights of their citizens, as well as the rights and powers which the people have conferred."

Thus a confederation is not exactly a state; it is a group of sovereign and independent states, associated by a pact of mutual guarantees. Nor is a federal constitution the same as what is understood in France by a charter or constitution, an abridged statement of public law; the pact contains the conditions of association, that is, the rights and reciprocal obligations of the states. What is called federal authority, finally, is no longer a government; it is an agency created by the states for the joint execution of certain functions which the states abandon, and which thus become federal powers.

In Switzerland the federal authority resides in a deliberative assembly elected by the citizens of the twenty-five cantons, and an executive council composed of seven members appointed by the assembly. The members of the assembly and the federal council are elected for three-year terms; since the federal constitution can be revised at any time, the powers of office, no less than its occupants, may be altered. Thus the federal power is in the full sense of the word an agent, under the strict control of his principals, whose power varies at their pleasure.

9.10   KARL MARX ("INAUGURAL ADDRESS OF THE WORKING MEN'S INTERNATIONAL ASSOCIATION," 1864)

Working Men,

It is a great fact that the misery of the working masses has not diminished from 1848 to 1864, and yet this period is unrivaled for the development of its industry and the growth of its commerce....

In all countries of Europe it has now become a truth demonstrable to every unprejudiced mind, and only decried by those whose interest it is to hedge other people in a fool's paradise, that no improvement of machinery, no appliance of science to production, no contrivances of communication, no new colonies, no emigration, no opening of markets, no free trade, nor all these things put together, will do away with the miseries of the industrious masses; but that, on the present false base, every fresh development of the productive powers of labor must tend to deepen social contrasts and point social antagonisms. Death of starvation rose almost to the rank of an institution, during this "intoxicating" epoch of economical progress, in the metropolis of the British Empire. That epoch is marked in the annals of the world by the quickened return, the widening compass, and the deadlier effects of the social pest called a commercial and industrial crisis.

After the failure of the revolutions of 1848, all party organizations and party journals of the working classes were, on the Continent, crushed by the iron hand of force, the most advanced sons of labor fled in despair to the Transatlantic Republic, and the short-lived dreams of emancipation vanished before an epoch of industrial fever, moral marasm, and political reaction. The defeat of the continental working classes, partly owed to the diplomacy of the English Government, acting then as now in fraternal solidarity with the Cabinet of St. Petersburg, soon spread its contagious effects on this side of the Channel. While the rout of their continental brethren unmanned the English working classes, and broke their faith in their own cause, it restored to the landlord and the money-lord their somewhat shaken confidence. They insolently withdrew concessions already advertised. The discoveries of new goldlands led to an immense exodus, leaving an irreparable void in the ranks of the British proletariat. Others of its formerly active members were caught by the temporary bribe of greater work and wages, and turned into "political blacks." All the efforts made at keeping up, or remodeling, the Chartist Movement, failed signally; the press organs of the working class died one by one of the apathy of the masses, and, in point of fact, never before seemed the English working class so thoroughly reconciled to a state of political nullity. If, then, there had been no solidarity of action between the British and the continental working classes, there was, at all events, a solidarity of defeat.

And yet the period passed since the revolutions of 1848 has not been without its compensating features. We shall here only point to two great facts.

After a thirty years' struggle, fought with most admirable perseverance, the English working classes, improving a momentous split between the landlords and money-lords, succeeded in carrying the Ten Hours' Bill. The immense physical, moral, and intellectual benefits hence accruing to the factory operatives, half-yearly chronicled in the reports of the inspectors of factories, are now acknowledged on all sides. Most of the continental governments had to accept the English Factory Act in more or less modified forms, and the English Parliament itself is every year compelled to enlarge its sphere of action. But besides its practical import, there was something else to exalt the marvelous success of this working men's measure. Through their most notorious organs of science, such as Dr. Ure, Professor Senior, and other sages of that stamp, the middle class had predicted, and to their hearts content proved, that any legal restriction of the hours of labor must sound the death knell of British industry, which, vampire like, could but live by sucking blood, and children's blood, too. In olden times, child murder was a mysterious rite of the religion of Moloch, but it was practiced on some very solemn occasions only, once a year perhaps, and then Moloch had no exclusive bias for the children of the poor. This struggle about the legal restriction of the hours of labor raged the more fiercely since, apart from frightened avarice, it told indeed upon the great contest between the blind rule of the supply and demand laws which form the political economy of the middle class, and social production controlled by social foresight, which forms the political economy of the working class. Hence the Ten Hours' Bill was not only a great practical success; it was the victory of a principle; it was the first time that in broad daylight the political economy of the middle class succumbed to the political economy of the working class.

But there was in store a still greater victory of the political economy of labor over the political economy of property. We speak of the co-operative movement, especially the co-operative factories raised by the unassisted efforts of a few bold "hands." The value of these great social experiments cannot be over-rated. By deed, instead of by argument, they have shown that production on a large scale, and in accord with the behests of modern science, may be carried on without the existence of a class of masters employing a class of hands; that to bear fruit, the means of labor need not be monopolized as a means of dominion over, and of extortion against, the laboring man himself; and that, like slave labor, like serf labor, hired labor is but a transitory and inferior form, destined to disappear before associated labor plying its toil with a willing hand, a ready mind, and a joyous heart. In England, the seeds of the co-opera-

tive system were sown by Robert Owen; the working men's experiments, tried on the Continent, were, in fact, the practical upshot of the theories, not invented, but loudly proclaimed, in 1848.

At the same time, the experience of the period from 1848 to 1864 has proved beyond doubt that, however excellent in principle, and however useful in practice, co-operative labor, if kept within the narrow circle of the casual efforts of private workmen, will never be able to arrest the growth in geometrical progression of monopoly, to free the masses, nor even to perceptibly lighten the burden of their miseries. It is perhaps for this very reason that plausible noblemen, philanthropic middle-class spouters, and even keen political economists, have all at once turned nauseously complimentary to the very co-operative labor system they had vainly tried to nip in the bud by deriding it as the Utopia of the dreamer, or stigmatizing it as the sacrilege of the Socialist. To save the industrious masses, co-operative labor ought to be developed to national dimensions, and, consequently, to be fostered by national means. Yet, the lords of land and the lords of capital will always use their political privileges for the defense and perpetuation of their economical monopolies. So far from promoting, they will continue to lay every possible impediment in the way of the emancipation of labor. Remember the sneer with which, last session, Lord Palmerston put down the advocates of the Irish Tenants' Right Bill. The House of Commons, cried he, is a house of landed proprietors.

To conquer political power has therefore become the great duty of the working classes. They seem to have comprehended this, for in England, Germany, Italy, and France there have taken place simultaneous revivals, and simultaneous efforts are being made at the political reorganization of the working men's party.

One element of success they possess — numbers; but numbers weigh only in the balance, if united by combination and led by knowledge. Past experience has shown how disregard of that bond of brotherhood which ought to exist between the workmen of different countries, and incite them to stand firmly by each other in all their struggles for emancipation, will be chastised by the common discomfiture of their incoherent efforts. This thought prompted the working men of different countries assembled on September 28, 1864, in public meeting at St. Martin's Hall, to found the International Association.

Another conviction swayed that meeting.

If the emancipation of the working classes requires their fraternal concurrence of different nations, how are they to fulfill that great mission with a foreign policy in pursuit of criminal designs, playing upon national prejudices, and squandering in piratical wars the people's blood and treasure? It was not the wisdom of the ruling classes, but the heroic resistance to their criminal folly by the working classes of England that saved the West of Europe from plunging headlong into an infamous crusade for the perpetuation and propagation of slavery on the other side of the Atlantic. The shameless approval, mock sympathy, or idiotic indifference, with which the upper classes of Europe have witnessed the mountain fortress of the Caucasus falling a prey to, and heroic Poland being assassinated by, Russia; the immense and unresisted encroachments of that barbarous power, whose head is at St. Petersburg, and whose hands are in every Cabinet of Europe, have taught the working classes the duty to master themselves the mysteries of international politics; to watch the diplomatic acts of their respective Governments; to counteract them, if necessary, by all means in their power; when unable to prevent, to combine in simultaneous denunciations, and to vindicate the simple laws of morals and justice, which ought to govern the relations of private individuals, as the rules paramount of the intercourse of nations.

The fight for such a foreign policy forms part of the general struggle for the emancipation of the working classes.

Proletarians of all countries, Unite!

9.11   LEONARD S. WOOLF: ON INTERNATIONAL GOVERNMENT AND INTERNATIONAL COURT (*INTERNATIONAL GOVERNMENT,* 1916)

Chapter III: International Law

... Ever since the time of Grotius there have been many customs and rules in the society of nations observed and admitted, by the nations, but at the beginning of the nineteenth century there were not even rudimentary organs, legislative or judicial, which could lay these rules down as law. In the nineteenth century there has been a rapid development in two directions.

In the first place, nations have attempted to substitute agreements or treaties for general rules. Treaties clearly do not, as a rule, *make* International Law; they are like contracts or agreements between individuals. Owing to the want of any law-making organ, nations have tried to regulate their relations to one another by an enormous number of such separate agreements. The efficacy of this system will be discussed when I deal with treaties. In the second place, for the first time in history, during the nineteenth century attempts were made on a considerable scale to make International Law in conferences and congresses. The success of these attempts will be considered when I come to deal with conferences and congresses; here it is sufficient to note that these nineteenth-century assemblies are undoubtedly the first signs of the growth of an International Legislative organ.

It is unnecessary for our immediate purpose to examine more closely into International Law, but it is advisable to state shortly a few facts about it which really require no detailed proof, but have great bearing upon our inquiry. A large number of its rules are quite definitely admitted, are acted upon every day, and really do help to regulate pacifically international society. On the other hand, much of it is vague and uncertain. This is due largely to two facts: there is no recognized international organ for making International Law, and no judicial organ for interpreting it. The consequences are two: whenever new circumstances arise which require a new rule of conduct for nations, the nations concerned have to set about making the new rule by bargaining and negotiation. If they cannot agree, either it remains uncertain what the law is, or the question has to be settled by war. Secondly, when there is already a rule, but nations disagree as to its interpretation, they again have to attempt by bargaining and negotiation to come to some agreement as to how it shall be interpreted. And, again, if they cannot agree, the only method left is to cut the knot by war.

Chapter IV: Treaties

Treaties perform in international society the part of anaesthetics in surgery; they get the patient into a condition which makes it possible to operate; but, unfortunately, up to the present, the means and instruments for operating have been wanting. It is no good giving gas to a man with toothache unless you have a dentist with his nippers on the premises; and it is no good dosing international society with law in treaties unless you have a judge handy to decide the legal disputes.

Chapter V: Conferences, Congresses, and the Concert of Europe

...Any form of international organization in which conferences or any other kind of deliberative and legislative organ are to decide on questions which at present are very likely to lead to war is useless, unless there is agreement as to what questions are to be so decided and machinery for submitting them automatically for decision. To say that such an organ is only to deal with international questions is to shirk the difficulty. Owing to our existing conception of "States," "nations," and "nationality," there will always be a wide divergence of opinion whether a question involving nationality is, or when it becomes, international....

The simplest way out of the difficulty is, of course, to say that the position of nationalities within States is always a right subject for international legislation....

[Y]et practically everyone, from Foreign Secretaries to public-house politicians, is obsessed by the mysterious sovereignty of sovereign Powers. The ordinary view is that the action of a nation is to be determined solely by its own ideals and desires. In a sense, therefore, any international question is not international, but domestic, and a sovereign Power always has to consider only two things — what it desires and whether it is strong enough to enforce its desire. But the whole of an international organization and authority implies an agreement that each nation is willing that its action will be, in part, determined by what other nations desire. Any kind of conference which is to *decide* things involves the submission of one nation to the expressed will of other nations. Perhaps the main thing is that we should see that we do not cease to be a nation, or, at any rate, a nation with "national honor," because we make that submission.

Part III: Articles Suggested for Adoption by an International Conference at the Termination of the Present War

... The new world that we have to face at the conclusion of the war will, perforce, start from the ruins of the old. All that will be immediately practicable can be presented as only a more systematic development of the rapidly multiplying Arbitration Treaties of the present century, and the conclusions of the two Conventions at The Hague. Only on some such lines, it is suggested, can we reasonably hope, at this juncture, to get the Governments of the world to come into the proposed agreement.

The alternative to war is law. What we have to do is to find some way of deciding differences between States, and of securing the same acquiescence in the decision as is now shown by individual citizens in a legal judgment. This involves the establishment of a Supernational Authority, which is the essence of our proposals.

What is suggested is, first, the establishment of an International High Court, to which the nations shall agree to submit, not all their possible differences and disputes, but only such as are, by their very nature, "legal" or "justiciable." Experience warrants the belief that the decisions of such a judicial tribunal, *confined to the issues which the litigant States had submitted to it*, would normally be accepted by them. Provision is made, however, for a series of "sanctions other than war," principally economic and social in character, by which all the constituent States could bring pressure to bear on any State not obeying a decision of the Court.

Alongside the International High Court, but without authority over it, there should be an International Council, composed of representatives of such of the forty or fifty independent sovereign States of the world as may choose voluntarily to take part. It is proposed that this International Council should be differently regulated and organized according (1) as it acts as a World Legislature for codifying and amending international law, and for dealing with questions interesting only America or Europe respectively; or (2) is invoked by any constituent State, to mediate in any dispute not of a nature to be submitted to the International High Court. It is not suggested that the enactments or the decisions of the International Council should, except to a very limited extent, be binding on States unwilling to ratify or acquiesce in them. Subject to the provisions made to prevent the proceedings being brought to naught by a tiny and unimportant minority, on matters of secondary importance, it is suggested that the International Council must content itself, at any rate at the outset, with that "greatest common measure" which commands general assent.

Provision is made for an International Secretariat and an International Official Gazette, in which all treaties or agreements will be immediately published, no others being recognized or regarded as enforceable.

In view of the fact that no fewer than twenty-one out of the forty to fifty independent sovereign States of the world are in America, the suggestion is made that there should be separate Councils for Europe and America respectively, with suitable provision in each case for the safeguarding of the interests of other States. Moreover, as the position of the eight Great Powers (Austria-Hungary, the British Empire, France, Germany, Italy, Japan, Russia, and the United States), which govern among them three-fourths of all the population of the world and control nine-tenths of its armaments, differs so greatly from that of the other two-score States, provision is made both for their meeting in separate Councils and for ratification of all proceedings by the Council of the Great Powers. It is nowhere suggested that any one of the eight Great Powers can — except by its own express ratification — be made subject to any enactment or decision of the International Council that it may deem to impair its independence or its territorial integrity, or to require any alteration of its internal laws.

It follows, accordingly, that each State retains the right to go to war if, after due delay, it chooses to do so.

What the several States are asked to bind themselves to are (a) to submit all disputes of the "legal" or "justiciable" kind (but no others) to the decision of the International High Court, unless some special tribunal is preferred and agreed to; (b) to lay before the International Council for inquiry, mediation, and eventual report, all disputes not "justiciable" by the International High Court or other tribunal; (c) in no case to proceed to any warlike operation, or commit any act of aggression, until twelve months after the dispute had been submitted to one or the other body; (d) to put in operation, if and when required, the sanctions (other than war) decreed by the International High Court; and, possibly the most essential of all these proposals, (e) *to make common cause, even to the extent of war, against any constituent State which violates this fundamental agreement.*

It remains to be said only that the adoption of this plan of preventing war — the establishment of the proposed Supernational Authority — is not dependent on, and need not wait for, the adhesion of all the independent sovereign States of the world.

CHAPTER 10

Human Rights for Whom?

Despite many revolutionary setbacks, the nineteenth century raised the political consciousness of marginalized individuals and their champions, who had been eclipsed by the march of capitalism and authoritarian governments. Difficult industrial working conditions included the harsh treatment of children in the workplace, stirring support for laws limiting the working day of children and for providing public education. At the same time, the fight to broaden manhood suffrage intensified the political demands of the suffragette movement. As nation-states were consolidated, oppressed national minorities, including the Jews, demanded civil and political rights. As wars continued to ravage Europe, champions of human rights also began to clamor for the rights of wounded soldiers and prisoners of war.

British socialist Robert Owen (1771–1858), who had become manager and part owner of the largest mills of Scotland, the New Lanark, sought ways to pragmatically implement his social vision. In his "Address to the Inhabitants of Lanark" (1816), Owen promised to improve the living conditions of his workers and their children. He placed great importance upon the education of the young and the improvement of their health and spirit — an attitude that was shared by many labor advocates, who realized with Owen that an uneducated working class would never be able to improve its political and economic situation (see Section 10.1).

Improving the political condition of minorities like the Jews also became a focus of attention in socialist circles. In *On the Jewish Question* (1843), Karl Marx rejected the idea that groups have intrinsic rights — religious or cultural — in isolation from the overall society. Opposing the liberal premises of the French Declaration of the Rights of Man and Citizen (1789), he asserted that the eighteen-century claim for human emancipation required a division between man as an egoistic being in civil society and man as an abstract citizen in the state. Jews, or any other group, he believed, could not claim individual emancipation while the rest of society suffered from exploitation. In this spirit, Marx congratulated the American President for ending slavery, thereby creating the social and political space needed for class solidarity between workers and emancipated slaves (see Section 10.3).

German socialist and co-founder of the German Social Democratic Party, August Bebel (1840–1913), pursued Marx's and Engel's position regarding the rights of another group: women. In *Women and Socialism* (1883) Bebel warned the women's suffrage movement of his time that their frustrations would not end once they reached their political objectives, and that voting rights for women and equal career opportunities were essential but not sufficient for women's civil emancipation. Only a minority of middle class women, he maintained, would be able to pursue higher education or civil service, leaving millions of women in misery. Women, he argued, cannot achieve real equality under capitalism, as long as women work for free in the household and gain low wages in the workplace. He thus encouraged all proletarian women to reach greater emancipation by joining their male worker's struggle for a socialist transformation of society. Only such efforts would ensure full rights for women, including economic and intellectual independence and socialized childcare. In a socialist society, he wrote, "nurses, teachers, women friends, the rising female generation, all these will stand by her when she is in need of assistance."

Clara Zetkin (1857–1933), a prominent figure in the German and international workers' movement, offered a valuable analysis of women's right demands as shaped by their social classes. "There is a women question," she stated, "for women of the proletariat, of the bourgeoisie and the intelligentsia, and of the Upper Thousands; it takes various forms depending upon the class situation of these strata." Yet like Bebel, she believed that the struggle of middle class suffragettes would be incomplete if women did not earn their economic independence vis-à-vis their husbands (see Section 10.5).

The socialization of childcare was one such prerequisite for economic independence, argued Bolshevik leader Lenin (1878–1924). Echoing Bebel and Zetkin, Lenin proposed in 1919 ways to achieve the emancipation of women, including freeing them from domestic housework. "Public dining rooms, *crèches*, kindergartens," he wrote, "are examples of ... the simple everyday means, which assume nothing pompous, grandiloquent or solemn, but which in fact can emancipate women, which can in fact lessen and abolish their inferiority to their role in social production and in social life" (see Section 10.6).

While not a socialist, Swiss businessman and social activist Henry Dunant (1828–1919) left a lasting humanitarian legacy that also broadened the scope of human rights. A witness to the suffering of unclaimed wounded and dying soldiers in the aftermath of the Battle of Solferino (1859), he called for the creation of the International Committee of the Red Cross (ICRC), an international medical agency established to help the wounded regardless of their side in a conflict. The 1864 Geneva Convention resulted in large measure from Dunant's *Memory of Solferino* (1862) and his humanitarian proposals for the treatment of prisoners in wartime. (See the selection on the rights of wounded soldiers in Section 10.7 and the selection from the Geneva Convention in Sections 15.9 and 15.10.)

10.1 ROBERT OWEN: ON CHILDREN ("ADDRESS TO THE INHABITANTS OF LANARK," 1816)

... This Institution,[1] when all its parts shall be completed, is intended to produce permanently beneficial effects; and, instead of longer applying temporary expedients for correcting some of your most prominent external habits, to effect a complete and thorough improvement in the internal as well as external character of the whole village. For this purpose the Institution has been devised to afford the means of receiving your children at an early age, as soon almost as they can walk. By this means many of you, mothers of families, will be enabled to earn a better maintenance or support for your children; you will have less care and anxiety about them; while the children will be prevented from acquiring any bad habits, and gradually prepared to learn the best.

The middle room of the story below will be appropriated to their accommodation; and in this their chief occupation will be to play and amuse themselves in severe weather: at other times they will be permitted to occupy the enclosed area before the building; for, to give children a vigorous constitution, they ought to be kept as much as possible in the open air. As they advance in years, they will

be taken into the rooms on the right and left, where they will be regularly instructed in the rudiments of common learning; which, before they shall be six years old, they may be taught in a superior manner.

These stages may be called the first and second preparatory schools: and when your children shall have passed through them, they will be admitted into this place (intended also to be used as a chapel), which, with the adjoining apartment, is to be the general schoolroom for reading, writing, arithmetic, sewing, and knitting; all which, on the plan to be pursued, will be accomplished to a considerable extent by the time the children are ten years old; before which age, none of them will be permitted to enter the works.

For the benefit of the health and spirits of the children both boys and girls will be taught to dance, and the boys will be instructed in military exercises; those of each sex who may have good voices will be taught to sing, and those among the boys who have a taste for music will be taught to play upon some instrument; for it is intended to give them as much diversified innocent amusement as the local circumstances of the establishment will admit.

The rooms to the east and west on the story below will also be appropriated in bad weather for relaxation and exercise during some part of the day, to the children who, in the regular hours of teaching, are to be instructed in these apartments.

In this manner is the Institution to be occupied during the day in winter. In summer, it is intended that they shall derive knowledge from a personal examination of the works of nature and of art, by going out frequently with some of their masters into the neighborhood and country around.

After the instruction of the children who are too young to attend the works shall have been finished for the day, the apartments shall be cleaned, ventilated, and in winter lighted and heated, and in all respects made comfortable, for the reception of other classes of the population. The apartments on this floor are then to be appropriated for the use of the children and youth of both sexes who have been employed at work during the day, and who may wish still further to improve themselves in reading, writing, arithmetic, sewing, or knitting; or to learn any of the useful arts: to instruct them in which, proper masters and mistresses, who are appointed, will attend for two hours every evening.

The three lower rooms, which in winter will also be well lighted and properly heated, will be thrown open for the use of the adult part of the population, who are to be provided with every accommodation requisite to enable them to read, write, account, sew, or play, converse, or walk about. But strict order and attention to the happiness of every one of the party will be enforced, until such habits shall be acquired as will render any formal restriction unnecessary; and the measures thus adopted will soon remove such necessity....

When you and your children shall be in the full possession of all that I am preparing for you, you will acquire superior habits; your minds will gradually expand; you will be enabled to judge accurately of the cause and consequences of my proceedings, and to estimate them at their value. You will then become desirous of living in a more perfect state of society, — a society which will possess within itself the certain means of preventing the existence of any injurious passions, poverty, crime, or misery; in which

every individual shall be instructed, and his powers of body and mind directed, by the wisdom derived from the best previous experience, so that neither bad habits nor erroneous sentiments shall be known; — in which age shall receive attention and respect, and in which every injurious distinction shall be avoided, — even variety of opinions shall not create disorder or any unpleasant feeling; — a society in which individuals shall acquire increased health, strength, and intelligence, — in which their labor shall be always advantageously directed, — and in which they will possess every rational enjoyment.

In due time communities shall be formed possessing such characters, and be thrown open to those among you, and to individuals of every class and denomination, whose wretched habits and whose sentiments of folly have not been too deeply impressed to be obliterated or removed, and whose minds can be sufficiently relieved from the pernicious effects of the old system, to permit them to partake of the happiness of the new....

[1] Editor: Owen refers here to the new restructured community of Lanark.

10.2   KARL MARX (ON THE JEWISH QUESTION, 1843)

Bruno Bauer, *Die Judenfrage*, Braunschweig, 1843

The German Jews desire emancipation. What kind of emancipation do they desire? Civic, political emancipation.

Bruno Bauer replies to them: No one in Germany is politically emancipated. We ourselves are not free. How are we to free you? You Jews are *egoists* if you demand a special emancipation for yourselves as Jews. As Germans, you ought to work for the political emancipation of Germany, and as human beings, for the emancipation of mankind, and you should feel the particular kind of your oppression and your shame not as an exception to the rule, but on the contrary as a confirmation of the rule.

Or do the Jews demand the same status as *Christian subjects of the state*? In that case they recognize that the *Christian state* is justified and they recognize too the regime of general oppression. Why should they disapprove of their special yoke if they approve of the general yoke? Why should the German be interested in the liberation of the Jew, if the Jew is not interested in the liberation of the German?

The *Christian* state knows only *privileges*. In this state the Jew has the privilege of being a Jew. As a Jew, he has rights which the Christians do not have. Why should he want rights which he does not have, but which the Christians enjoy?

In wanting to be emancipated from the Christian state, the Jew is demanding that the Christian state should give up its *religious* prejudice. Does he, the Jew, give up *his* religious prejudice? Has he then the right to demand that someone else should renounce his religion?

By its very nature, the Christian state is incapable of emancipating the Jew; but, adds Bauer, by his very nature the Jew cannot be emancipated. So long as the state is Christian and the Jew is Jewish, the one is as incapable of granting emancipation as the other is of receiving it.

The Christian state can behave towards the Jew only in the way characteristic of the Christian state, that is, by granting privileges, by permitting the separation of the Jew from the other subjects, but making him feel the pressure of all the other separate spheres of society, and feel it all the more intensely because he is in *religious* opposition to the dominant religion. But the Jew, too, can behave towards the state only in a Jewish way, that is, by treating it as something alien to him, by counterposing his imaginary nationality to the real nationality, by counterposing his illusory law to the real law, by deeming himself justified in separating himself from mankind, by abstaining on principle from taking part in the historical movement, by putting his trust in a future which has nothing in common with the future of mankind in general, and by seeing himself as a member of the Jewish people, and the Jewish people as the chosen people.

On what grounds then do you Jews want emancipation? On account of your religion? It is the mortal enemy of the state religion. As citizens? In Germany there are no citizens. As human beings? But you are no more human beings than those to whom you appeal.

Bauer has posed the question of Jewish emancipation in a new form, after giving a critical analysis of the previous formulations and solutions of the question. What, he asks, is the *nature* of the Jew who is to be emancipated and of the Christian state that is to emancipate him? He replies by a critique of the Jewish religion, he analyzes the *religious* opposition between Judaism and Christianity, he elucidates the essence of the Christian state — and he does all this audaciously, trenchantly, wittily, and with profundity, in a style of writing that is as precise as it is pithy and vigorous.

How then does Bauer solve the Jewish question? What is the result? The formulation of a question is its solution. The critique of the Jewish question is the answer to the Jewish question. The summary, therefore, is as follows:

We must emancipate ourselves before we can emancipate others.

The most rigid form of the opposition between the Jew and the Christian is the *religious* opposition. How is an opposition resolved? By making it impossible. How is *religious* opposition made impossible? By *abolishing religion*. As soon as Jew and Christian recognize that their respective religions are no more than *different stages in the development of the human mind*, different snake skins cast off by *history*, and that *man* is the snake who sloughed them, the relation of Jew and Christian is no longer religious but is only a critical, *scientific* and human relation. *Science* then constitutes their unity. But contradictions in science are resolved by science itself.

The *German* Jew in particular is confronted by the general absence of political emancipation and the strongly marked Christian character of the state. In Bauer's conception, however, the Jewish question has a universal significance, independent of specifically German conditions. It is the question of the relation of religion to the state, of the *contradiction between religious constraint and political emancipation.* Emancipation from religion is laid down as a condition, both to the Jew who wants to be emancipated politically, and to the state which is to effect emancipation and is itself to be emancipated....

If Bauer asks the Jews: Have you from your standpoint the right to want *political emancipation?* we ask the converse question: Does the standpoint of political emancipation give the right to demand from the Jew the abolition of Judaism and from man the abolition of religion? ...

We do not turn secular questions into theological questions. We turn theological questions into secular ones. History has long enough been merged in superstition, we now merge superstition in history. The question of the *relation of political emancipation to religion* becomes for us the question of the *relation of political emancipation to human emancipation.* We criticize the religious weakness of the political state by criticizing the political state in its *secular* form, *apart* from its weaknesses as regards religion. The contradiction between the state and a *particular religion*, for instance *Judaism*, is given by us a human form as the contradiction between the state and *particular secular* elements; the contradiction between the state and *religion in general* as the contradiction between the state and its *presuppositions* in general.

The *political* emancipation of the Jew, the Christian, and in general of *religious* man is the *emancipation of the state* from Judaism, from Christianity, from *religion* in general. In its own form, in the manner characteristic of its nature, the state as a *state* emancipates itself from religion by emancipating itself from the *state religion*, that is to say, by the state as a state not professing any religion, but, on the contrary, asserting itself as state. The *political* emancipation from religion is not a religious emancipation that has been carried through to completion and is free from contradiction, because political emancipation is not a form of *human* emancipation which has been carried through to completion and is free from contradiction.

The limits of political emancipation are evident at once from the fact that the *state* can free itself from a restriction without man being *really* free from this restriction, that the state can be a *free state*[1] without man being a *free man....*

The *political* elevation of man above religion shares all the defects and all the advantages of political elevation in general....

The state allows private property, education, occupation, to *act* in their *way*, i.e., as private property, as education, as occupation, and to exert the influence of their special nature. Far from abolishing these *real* distinctions, the state only exists on the presupposition of their existence; it feels itself to be a *political state* and asserts its *universality* only in opposition to these elements of its being....

The perfect political state is, by its nature, man's *species-life*, as *opposed* to his material life. All the preconditions of this egoistic life continue to exist in *civil society outside* the sphere of the state, but as qualities of civil society. Where the political state has attained its true development, man — not only in thought, in consciousness, but in *reality*, in *life* — leads a twofold life, a heavenly and an earthly life: life in the *political community*, in which he considers himself a *communal being*, and life in *civil society*, in which he acts as a *private individual*, regards other men as a means, degrades himself into a means, and becomes the plaything of alien powers. The relation of the political state to civil society is just as spiritual as the relation of heaven to earth. The political state stands in the same opposition to civil society, and it prevails over the latter in the same way as religion prevails over the narrowness of the secular world, i.e., by likewise having always to acknowledge it, to restore it, and allow itself to be dominated by it. In his *most immediate* reality, in civil society, man is a secular being. Here, where he regards himself as a real individual, and is so regarded by others, he is a *fictitious* phenomenon. In the state, on the other hand, where man is regarded as a species-being, he is the imaginary member of an illusory sovereignty, is deprived of his real individual life and endowed with an unreal universality.

Man, as the adherent of a *particular* religion, finds himself in conflict with his citizenship and with other men as members of the community. This conflict reduces itself to the *secular* division between the *political* state and *civil society*....

Political emancipation is, of course, a big step forward. True, it is not the final form of human emancipation in general, but it is the final form of human emancipation *within* the hitherto existing world order. It goes without saying that we are speaking here of real, practical emancipation.

Man emancipates himself *politically* from religion by banishing it from the sphere of public law to that of private law. Religion is no longer the spirit of the *state*, in which man behaves — although in a limited way, in a particular form, and in a particular sphere — as a species-being, in community with other men. Religion has become the spirit of *civil society*, of the sphere of egoism, of *helium omnium contra omnes*. It is no longer the essence of *community*, but the essence of *difference*. It has become the expression of man's *separation* from his *community*, from himself and from other men — as it was *originally*. It is only the abstract avowal of specific perversity, *private whimsy*, and arbitrariness. The endless fragmentation of religion in North America, for example, gives it even *externally* the form of a purely individual affair. It has been thrust among the multitude of private interests and ejected from the community as such. But one should be under no illusion about the limits of political emancipation. The division of the human being into a *public man* and a *private man*, the *displacement* of religion from the state into civil society, this is not a stage of political emancipation but its *completion*; this emancipation therefore neither abolishes the *real* religiousness of man, nor strives to do so.

The *decomposition* of man into Jew and citizen, Protestant and citizen, religious man and citizen, is neither a deception directed *against* citizenhood, nor is it a circumvention of political emancipation, it is *political emancipation* itself, the *political* method of emancipating oneself from religion. Of course, in periods when the political state as such is born violently out of civil society, when political liberation is the form in which men strive to achieve their liberation, the state can and must go as far as the *abolition of religion*, the *destruction* of religion. But it can do so only in the same way that it proceeds to the abolition of private property, to the maximum, to confiscation, to progressive taxation, just as it goes as far as the abolition of life, the *guillotine*. At times of special self-confidence, political life seeks to suppress its prerequisite, civil society and the elements composing this society, and to constitute itself as the real species-life of man devoid of contradictions. But it can achieve this only by coming into *violent* contradiction with its own conditions of life, only by declaring the revolution to be *permanent*, and therefore the political drama necessarily ends with the re-establishment of religion, private property, and all elements of civil society, just as war ends with peace.

Indeed, the perfect Christian state is not the so-called *Christian* state, which acknowledges Christianity as its basis, as the state religion, and therefore adopts an exclusive attitude towards other religions. On the contrary, the perfect Christian state is the *atheistic* state, the *democratic* state, the state which relegates religion to a place among the other elements of civil society. The state which is still theological, which still officially professes Christianity as its creed, which still does not dare to proclaim itself *as a state*, has, in its *reality* as a state, not yet succeeded in expressing the *human* basis — of which Christianity is the high-flown expression — in a *secular, human* form. The so-called Christian state is simply nothing more than a *non-state*, since it is not Christianity as a religion, but only the *human background* of the Christian religion, which can find its expression in actual human creations....

Therefore we do not say to the Jews as Bauer does: You cannot be emancipated politically without emancipating yourselves radically from Judaism. On the contrary, we tell them: Because you can be emancipated politically without renouncing Judaism completely and incontrovertibly, *political emancipation* itself is not *human* emancipation. If you Jews want to be emancipated politically without emancipating yourselves humanly, the half-hearted approach and contradiction is not in you alone, it is inherent in the *nature* and *category* of political emancipation. If you find yourself within the confines of this category, you share in a general confinement. Just as the state *evangelizes* when, although it is a state, it adopts a Christian attitude towards the Jews, so the Jew *acts politically* when, although a Jew, he demands civic rights.

But if a man, although a Jew, can be emancipated politically and receive civic rights, can he lay claim to the so-called *rights of man* and receive them? Bauer *denies* it....

According to Bauer, man has to sacrifice the *"privilege of faith"* to be able to receive the universal rights of man. Let us examine for a moment the so-called rights of man, to be precise, the rights of man in their authentic form, in the form which they have among those who *discovered* them, the North Americans and the French. These rights of man are in part *political* rights, rights which can only be exercised in a community with others. Their content is *participation* in the *community*, and specifically in the *political* community, in the *life of the state*. They come within the category of *political freedom*, the category of *civic rights*, which, as we have seen, in no way presuppose the incontrovertible and positive abolition of religion, nor therefore of Judaism. There remains to be examined the other part of the rights of man, the Rights of Man insofar as these differ from the Rights of the Citizen.

Included among them is freedom of conscience, the right to practice any religion one chooses. *The privilege of faith* is expressly recognized either as a right of man or as the consequence of a right of man, that of liberty.

Declaration of the Rights of Man and of the Citizen, 1791, Article 10: "No one is to be subjected to annoyance because of his opinions, even religious opinions." "The freedom of every man to practice the *religion* of which he is an adherent" is guaranteed as a right of man in Section I of the Constitution of 1791.

Declaration of the Rights of Man, etc., 1793, includes among the rights of man, Article 7: "The free exercise of religion." Indeed, in regard to man's right to express his thoughts and opinions, to hold meetings, and to exercise his religion, it is even stated: "The necessity of proclaiming these *rights* presupposes either the existence or the recent memory of despotism." Compare the Constitution of 1795, Section XIV, Article 354.

Constitution of Pennsylvania, Article 9, § 3: "All men have received from nature the imprescriptible *right* to worship the Almighty according to the dictates of their conscience, and no one can be legally compelled to follow, establish or support against his will any religion or religious ministry. No human authority can, in any circumstances, intervene in a matter of conscience or control the forces of the soul."

Constitution of New Hampshire, Articles 5 and 6: "Among these natural rights some are by nature inalienable since nothing can replace them. The rights of conscience are among them."

Incompatibility between religion and the rights of man is to such a degree absent from the concept of the *rights* of man that, on the contrary, a man's *right to be religious* in any way he chooses, to practice his own particular religion, is expressly included among the rights of man. The *privilege of faith* is a *universal right of man*.

The *droits de l'homme*, the rights of man, are as *such* distinct from the *droits du citoyen*, the rights of the citizen. Who is *homme* as distinct from *citoyen*? None other than the *member of civil society*. Why is the *member of civil society* called "man," simply man; why are his rights called the *rights of man*? How is this fact to be explained? From the relationship between the political state and civil society, from the nature of political emancipation.

Above all, we note the fact that the so-called *rights of man*, the *droits de l'homme* as distinct from the *droits du citoyen*, are nothing but the rights of a *member of civil society*, i.e., the rights of egoistic man, of man separated from other men and from the community. Let us hear what the most radical Constitution, the Constitution of 1793, has to say:

Declaration of the Rights of Man and of the Citizen, Article 2. "These rights, etc., (the natural and imprescriptible rights) are: *equality, liberty, security, property*."

What constitutes *liberty*?

Article 6. "Liberty is the power which man has to do everything that does not harm the rights of others," or ... "Liberty consists in being able to do everything which does not harm others."

Liberty, therefore, is the right to do everything that harms no one else. The limits within which anyone can act *without harming* someone else are defined by law, just as the boundary between two fields is determined by a boundary post. It is a question of the liberty of man as an isolated monad, withdrawn into himself. Why is the Jew, according to Bauer, incapable of acquiring the rights of man?

"As long as he is a Jew, the restricted nature which makes him a Jew is bound to triumph over the human nature which should link him as a man with other men, and will separate him from non-Jews."

But the right of man to liberty is based not on the association of man with man, but on the separation of man from man. It is the right of this separation, the *right* of the *restricted* individual, withdrawn into himself.

The practical application of man's right to liberty is man's right to *private property*.

What constitutes man's right to private property?

Article 16 (Constitution of 1793): "The right of *property* is that which every citizen has of enjoying and of disposing *at his discretion* of his goods and income, of the fruits of his labor and industry."

The right of man to private property is, therefore, the right to enjoy one's property and to dispose of it at one's discretion (*à son gré*), without regard to other men, independently of society, the right of self-interest. This individual liberty and its application form the basis of civil society. It makes every man see in other men not the *realization* of his own freedom, but the *barrier* to it. But, above all, it proclaims the right of man

"of enjoying and of disposing *at his discretion* of his goods and income, of the fruits of his labor and industry."

There remain the other rights of man: *égalité* and *sûreté*.[2]

Égalité, used here in its non-political sense, is nothing but the equality of the *liberté* described above, namely: each man is to the same extent regarded as such a self-sufficient monad. The Constitution of 1795 defines the concept of this equality, in accordance with its significance, as follows:

Article 3 (Constitution of 1795): "Equality consists in the law being the same for all, whether it protects or punishes."

And *sûreté*?

Article 8 (Constitution of 1793): "Security consists in the protection afforded by society to each of its members for the preservation of his person, his rights, and his property."

Security is the highest social concept of civil society, the concept of *police*, expressing the fact that the whole of society exists only in order to guarantee to each of its members the preservation of his person, his rights, and his property. It is in this sense that Hegel calls civil society "the state of need and reason."[3]

The concept of security does not raise civil society above its egoism. On the contrary, security is the *insurance* of its egoism.

None of the so-called rights of man, therefore, go beyond egoistic man, beyond man as a member of civil society, that is, an individual withdrawn into himself, into the confines of his private interests and private caprice, and separated from the community. In the rights of man, he is far from being conceived as a species-being; on the contrary, species-life itself, society, appears as a framework external to the individuals, as a restriction of their original independence. The sole bond holding them together is natural necessity, need and private interest, the preservation of their property and their egoistic selves.

It is puzzling enough that a people which is just beginning to liberate itself, to tear down all the barriers between its various sections, and to establish a political community, that such a people solemnly proclaims (Declaration of 1791) the rights of egoistic man separated from his fellow men and from the community, and that indeed it repeats this proclamation at a moment when only the most heroic devotion can save the nation, and is therefore imperatively called for, at a moment when the sacrifice of all the interests of civil society must be the order of the day, and egoism must be punished as a crime. (*Declaration of the Rights of Man*, etc., of 1793.) This fact becomes still more puzzling when we see that the political emancipators go so far as to reduce citizenship, and the *political community*, to a mere *means* for maintaining these so-called rights of man, that therefore the *citoyen* is declared to be the servant of egoistic *homme*, that the sphere in which man acts as a communal being is degraded to a level below the sphere in which he acts as a partial being, and that, finally, it is not man as *citoyen*, but man as bourgeois who is considered to be the *essential* and *true* man.

"The *aim* of all *political association* is the *preservation* of the natural and imprescriptible rights of man." (*Declaration of the Rights*, etc., of 1791, Article 2.) "*Government* is instituted in order to guarantee man the enjoyment of his natural and imprescriptible rights." (*Declaration*, etc., of 1793, Article 1.)

Hence even in moments when its enthusiasm still has the freshness of youth and is intensified to an extreme degree by the force of circumstances, political life declares itself to be a mere *means*, whose purpose is the life of civil society. It is true that its revolutionary practice is in flagrant contradiction with its theory. Whereas, for example, security is declared one of the rights of man, violation of the privacy of correspondence is openly declared to be the order of the day. Whereas the "*unlimited* freedom of the press" (Constitution of 1793, Article 122) is guaranteed as a consequence of the right of man to individual liberty, freedom of the press is totally destroyed, because "freedom of the press should not be permitted when it endangers public liberty." (Robespierre jeune, *Histoire parlementaire de la Révolution français* by Buchez and Roux, vol. 28, p. 159.) That is to say, therefore: The right of man to liberty ceases to be a right as soon as it comes into conflict with political life, whereas in theory *political* life is only the guarantee of human rights, the rights of the individual, and therefore must be abandoned as soon as it comes into contradiction with its aim, with these rights of man. But practice is merely the exception, theory is the rule. But even if one were to regard revolutionary practice as the correct presentation of the relationship, there would still remain the puzzle of why the relationship is turned upside-down in the minds of the political emancipators and the *aim* appears as the means, while the means appears as the aim. This optical illusion of their consciousness would still remain a puzzle, although now a psychological, a theoretical puzzle.

The puzzle is easily solved.

Political emancipation is at the same time the *dissolution* of the old society on which the state alienated from the people, the sovereign power, is based. Political revolution is a revolution of civil society. What was the character of the old society? It can be described in one word — feudalism. The character of the old civil society was *directly political*, that is to say, the elements of civil life, for example, property, or the family, or the mode of labor, were raised to the level of elements of political life in the form of seigniory, estates, and corporations. In this form they determined the relation of the individual to the *state as a whole*, i.e., his *political* relation, that is, his relation of separation and exclusion from the other components of society. For that organization of national life did not raise property or labor to the level of social elements; on the contrary, it completed their *separation* from the state as a whole and constituted them as *discrete* societies within society. Thus, the vital functions and conditions of life of civil society remained nevertheless political, although political in the feudal sense, that is to say, they secluded the individual from the state as a whole and they converted the *particular* relation of his corporation to the state as a whole into his general relation to the life of the nation, just as they converted his particular civil activity and situation into his general activity and situation. As a result of this organization, the unity of the state, and also the consciousness, will and activity of this unity, the general power of the state, are likewise bound to appear as the *particular* affair of a ruler isolated from the people, and of his servants.

The political revolution which overthrew this sovereign power and raised state affairs to become affairs of the people, which constituted the political state as a matter of *general* concern, that is, as a real state, necessarily smashed all estates, corporations, guilds, and privileges, since they were all manifestations of the separation of the people from the community. The political revolution thereby *abolished* the *political character of civil society*. It broke up civil society into its simple component parts; on the one hand, the *individuals*; on the other hand, the *material* and *spiritual elements* constituting the content of the life and social position of these individuals. It set free the political spirit, which had been, as it were, split up, partitioned and dispersed in the various blind alleys of feudal society. It gathered the dispersed parts of the political spirit, freed it from its intermixture with civil life, and established it as the sphere of the community, the *general* concern of the nation, ideally independent of those *particular* elements of civil life. A person's *distinct* activity and distinct situation in life were reduced to a merely individual significance. They no longer constituted the general relation of the individual to the state as a whole. Public affairs as such, on the other hand, became

the general affair of each individual, and the political function became the individual's general function.

But the completion of the idealism of the state was at the same time the completion of the materialism of civil society. Throwing off the political yoke meant at the same time throwing off the bonds which restrained the egoistic spirit of civil society. Political emancipation was at the same time the emancipation of civil society from politics, from having even the *semblance* of a universal content.

Feudal society was resolved into its basic element — man, but man as he really formed its basis — *egoistic* man.

This *man*, the member of civil society, is thus the basis, the precondition, of the political state. He is recognized as such by this state in the rights of man.

The liberty of egoistic man and the recognition of this liberty, however, is rather the recognition of the *unrestrained* movement of the spiritual and material elements which form the content of his life.

Hence man was not freed from religion, he received religious freedom. He was not freed from property, he received freedom to own property. He was not freed from the egoism of business, he received freedom to engage in business.

The *establishment of the political state* and the dissolution of civil society into independent *individuals* — whose relations with one another depend on *law*, just as the relations of men in the system of estates and guilds depended on *privilege* — is accomplished by *one and the same act*. Man as a member of civil society, *unpolitical* man, inevitably appears, however, as the *natural* man. The *droits de l'homme* appear as *droits naturels*, because *conscious activity* is concentrated on the *political act*. Egoistic man is the *passive* result of the dissolved society, a result that is simply *found in existence*, an object of *immediate certainty*, therefore a natural object. The political revolution resolves civil life into its component parts, without *revolutionizing* these components themselves or subjecting them to criticism. It regards civil society, the world of needs, labor, private interests, civil law, as the basis *of its existence*, as a *precondition* not requiring further substantiation and therefore as its *natural basis*. Finally, man as a member of civil society is held to be man *in the proper sense*, *homme* as distinct from the *citoyen*, because he is man in his sensuous, individual, *immediate* existence, whereas political man is only abstract, artificial man, man as an *allegorical, juridical* person. The real man is recognized only in the shape of the *egoistic* individual, the *true* man is recognized only in the shape of the *abstract citoyen*.

Therefore Rousseau correctly describes the abstract idea of political man as follows: "Whoever dares undertake to establish a people's institutions must feel himself capable of *changing*, as it were, *human nature*, of *transforming* each individual, who by himself is a complete and solitary whole, into a *part* of a larger whole, from which, in a sense, the individual receives his life and his being, of substituting a *limited* and *mental existence* for the physical and independent existence. He has to take from *men his own powers*, and give him in exchange alien powers which he cannot employ without the help of the other men." [Editor: *Control Social*, Book II, London, 1782, p. 67.)

All emancipation is a *reduction* of the human world and relationships to *man himself*.

Political emancipation is the reduction of man, on the one hand, to a member of civil society, to an egoistic, *independent* individual, and, on the other hand, to a *citizen*, a juridical person.

Only when the real, individual man reabsorbs in himself the abstract citizen, and as an individual human being has become a *species-being* in his everyday life, in his particular work, and in his particular situation, only when man has recognized and organized his *"forces pro-pres"* as *social* forces, and consequently no longer separates social power from himself in the shape of *political* power, only then will human emancipation have been accomplished....

---

[1] A pun on the word *Freistaat*, i.e., republic, for if it is taken literally, it means "free state."

[2] Editor: Equality and security.

[3] Editor: Hegel, *Grundlinien der Philosophie des Rechts, Werke*, Bd. VIII, S. 242.

10.3 KARL MARX: LETTER TO PRESIDENT ABRAHAM LINCOLN ON THE ABOLITION OF SLAVERY (1865)[1]

Sir: — We congratulate the American people upon your reelection by a large majority. If resistance to the Slave Power was the reserved watchword of your first election, the triumphant war cry of your reelection is, Death to Slavery.

From the commencement of the titanic American strife the workingmen of Europe felt instinctively that the star-spangled banner carried the destiny of their class. The contest for the territories which opened the dire epopee, was it not to decide whether the virgin soil of immense tracts should be wedded to the labor of the immigrant or prostituted by the tramp of the slave driver?

When an oligarchy of 300,000 slaveholders dared to inscribe, for the first time in the annals of the world, "slavery" on the banner of armed revolt; when on the very spots where hardly a century ago the idea of one great democratic republic had first sprung up, whence the first declaration of the Rights of Man issued, and the first impulse given to the European revolution of the 18th century; when on those very spots counterrevolution, with systematic thoroughness, gloried in rescinding "the ideas entertained at the time of the formation of the old Constitution," and maintained "slavery to be a beneficent institution, indeed the only solution of the great problem of the relation of labor to capital," and cynically proclaimed property in man "the cornerstone of the new edifice"; then the working classes of Europe understood at once, even before the fanatic partisanship of the upper classes for the Confederate gentry had given its dismal warning, that the slaveholders' rebellion was to sound the tocsin for a general holy crusade of property against labor, and that for the men of labor, with their hopes for the future, even their past conquests were at stake in that tremendous conflict on the other side of the Atlantic. Everywhere they bore therefore patiently the hardships imposed upon them by the cotton crisis, opposed enthusiastically the proslavery intervention, importunities of their "betters," and from most parts of Europe contributed their quota of blood to the good cause.

While the workingmen, the true political power of the North, allowed slavery to defile their own republic; while before the Negro, mastered and sold without his concurrence, they boasted it the highest prerogative of the white-skinned laborer to sell himself and choose his own master; they were unable to attain the true freedom of labor or to support their European brethren in their struggle for emancipation, but this barrier to progress has been swept off by the red sea of civil war.

The workingmen of Europe feel sure that as the American War of Independence initiated a new era of ascendancy for the middle class, so the American antislavery War will do for the working classes. They consider it an earnest of the epoch to come, that it fell to the lot of Abraham Lincoln, the single-minded son of the working class, to lead his country through the matchless struggle for the rescue of an enchained race and the reconstruction of a social world.

[1]This address was signed by all the members of the General Council of the International Workingmen's Association (the First International) and was forwarded to President Lincoln through Charles Francis Adams, the minister of the United States in London. It was published in the *Bee-Hive*, London, January 7, 1865.

10.4 AUGUST BEBEL (*WOMAN AND SOCIALISM*, 1883)

Introduction

We are living in an age of great social transformations that are steadily progressing. In all strata of society we perceive an unsettled state of mind and an increasing restlessness, denoting a marked tendency toward profound and radical changes. Many questions have arisen and are being discussed with growing interest in ever widening circles. One of the most important of these questions and one that is constantly coming into greater prominence, is the woman question.

The woman question deals with the position that woman should hold in our social organism, and seeks to determine how she can best develop her powers and her abilities, in order to become a useful member of human society, endowed with equal rights and serving society according to her best capacity. From our point of view this question coincides with that other question: In what manner should society be organized to abolish oppression, exploitation, misery and need, and to bring about the physical and mental welfare of individuals and of society as a whole? To us then, the woman question is only one phase of the general social question that at present occupies all intelligent minds; its final solution can only be attained by removing social extremes and the evils which are a result of such extremes.

Nevertheless, the woman question demands our special consideration. What the position of woman has been in ancient society, what her position is to-day and what it will be in the coming social order, are questions that deeply concern at least one half of humanity. Indeed, in Europe they concern a majority of organized society, because women constitute a majority of the population. Moreover, the prevailing conceptions concerning the development of woman's social position during successive stages of history are so faulty, that enlightenment on this subject has become a necessity. Ignorance concerning the position of woman, chiefly accounts for the prejudice that the woman's movement has to contend with among all classes of people, by no means least among the women themselves. Many even venture to assert that there is no woman question at all, since woman's position has always been the same and will remain the same in the future, because nature has destined her to be a wife and a mother and to confine her activities to the home. Everything that is beyond the four narrow walls of her home and is not closely connected with her domestic duties, is not supposed to concern her.

In the woman question then we find two contending parties, just as in the labor question, which relates to the position of the workingman in human society. Those who wish to maintain everything as it is, are quick to relegate woman to her so-called "natural profession," believing that they have thereby settled the whole matter. They do not recognize that millions of women are not placed in a position enabling them to fulfill their natural function of wifehood and motherhood.... They furthermore do not recognize that to millions of other women their "natural profession" is a failure, because to them marriage has become a yoke and a condition of slavery, and they are obliged to drag on their lives in misery and despair. But these wiseacres are no more concerned by these facts than by the fact that in various trades and professions millions of women are exploited far beyond their strength, and must slave away their lives for a meager subsistence. They remain deaf and blind to these disagreeable truths, as they remain deaf and blind to the misery of the proletariat, consoling themselves and others by the false assertion that it has always been thus and will always continue to be so. That woman is entitled, as well as man, to enjoy all the achievements of civilization, to lighten her burdens, to improve her condition, and to develop all her physical and mental qualities, they refuse to admit. When, furthermore, told that woman — to enjoy full physical and mental freedom — should also be economically independent, should no longer depend for subsistence upon the good will and favor of the other sex, the limit of their patience will be reached. Indignantly they will pour forth a bitter endictment of the "madness of the age" and its "crazy attempts at emancipation." These are the old ladies of both sexes who cannot overcome the narrow circle of their prejudices. They are the human owls that dwell wherever darkness prevails, and cry out in terror whenever a ray of light is cast into their agreeable gloom.

Others do not remain quite as blind to the eloquent facts. They confess that at no time woman's position has been so unsatisfactory in comparison to general social progress, as it is at present. They recognize that it is necessary to investigate how the condition of the self-supporting woman can be improved; but in the case of married women they believe the social problem to be solved. They favor the admission of unmarried women only into a limited number of trades and professions. Others again are more advanced and insist that competition between the sexes should not be limited to the inferior trades and professions, but should be extended to all higher branches of learning and the arts and sciences as well. They demand equal educational opportunities and that women should be admitted to all institutions of learning, including the universities. They also favor the appointment of women to government positions, pointing out the results already achieved by women in such positions, especially in the United States. A few are even coming forward to demand equal political rights for women. Woman, they argue, is a human being and a member of organized society as well as man, and the very fact that men have until now framed and administered the laws to suit their own purposes and to hold woman in subjugation, proves the necessity of woman's participation in public affairs.

It is noteworthy that all these various endeavors do not go beyond the scope of the present social order. The question is not propounded whether any of these proposed reforms will accomplish a decisive and essential improvement in the condition of women. According to the conceptions of bourgeois, or capitalistic society, the civic equality of men and women is deemed an ultimate solution of the woman question. People are either unconscious of the fact, or deceive themselves in regard to it, that the admission of women to trades and industries is already practically accomplished and is being strongly favored by the ruling classes in their own interest. But under prevailing conditions woman's invasion of industry has the detrimental effect of increasing competition on the labor market, and the result is a reduction in wages for both male and female workers. It is clear then, that this cannot be a satisfactory solution.

Men who favor these endeavors of women within the scope of present society, as well as the bourgeois women who are active in the movement, consider complete civic equality of women the ultimate goal. These men and women then differ radically from those who, in their narrow-mindedness, oppose the movement. They differ radically from those men who are actuated by petty motives of selfishness and fear of competition, and therefore try to prevent women from obtaining higher education and from gaining admission to the better paid professions. But there is no difference of class between them, such as exists between the worker and the capitalist.

If the bourgeois suffragists would achieve their aim and would bring about equal rights for men and women, they would still fail to abolish that sex slavery which marriage, in its present form, is to countless numbers of women; they would fail to abolish prostitution; they would fail to abolish the economic dependence of wives. To the great majority of women it also remains a matter of indifference whether a few thousand members of their sex, belonging to the more favored classes of society, obtain higher learning and enter some learned profession, or hold a public office. The general condition of the sex as a whole is not altered thereby.

The female sex as such has a double yoke to bear. Firstly, women suffer as a result of their social dependence upon men, and the inferior position allotted to them in society; formal equality before the law alleviates this condition, but does not remedy it. Secondly, women suffer as a result of their economic dependence, which is the lot of women in general, and especially of the proletarian woman as it is of the proletarian men.

We see, then, that all women, regardless of their social position, represent that sex which during the evolution of society has been oppressed and wronged by the other sex, and therefore it is to the common interest of all women to remove their disabilities by changing the laws and institutions of the present state and social order. But a great majority of women is furthermore deeply and personally concerned in a complete reorganization of the present state and social order which has for its purpose the abolition of wage-slavery, which at present weighs most heavily upon the women of the proletariat, as also the abolition of sex-slavery, which is closely connected with our industrial conditions and our system of private ownership.

The women who are active in the bourgeois suffrage movement, do not recognize the necessity of so complete a transformation. Influenced by their privileged social position, they consider the more radical aims of the proletarian woman's movement dangerous doctrines that must be opposed. The class antagonism that exists between the capitalist and working class and that is increasing with the growth of industrial problems, also clearly manifests itself then within the women's movement. Still these sister-women, though antagonistic to each other on class lines, have a great many more points in common than the men engaged in the class struggle, and though they march in separate armies they may strike a united blow. This is true in regard to all endeavors pertaining to all equal rights of woman under the present social order; that is, her right to enter any trade or profession adapted to her strength and ability, and her right to civic and political equality. These are, as we shall see, very important and very far-reaching aims. Besides striving for these aims, it is in the particular interest of proletarian women to work hand in hand with proletarian men for such measures and institutions that tend to protect the working woman from physical and mental degeneration, and to preserve her health and strength for a normal fulfillment of her maternal function. Furthermore, it is the duty of the proletarian woman to join the men of her class in the struggle for a thorough-going transformation of society, to bring about an order that by its social institutions will enable both sexes to enjoy complete economic and intellectual independence.

Our goal then is, not only to achieve equality of men and women under the present social order, which constitutes the sole aim of the bourgeois woman's movement, but to go far beyond this, and to remove all barriers that make one human being dependent upon another, which includes the dependence of one sex upon the other. *This* solution of the woman question is identical with the solution of the social question. They who seek a complete solution of the woman question must, therefore, join hands with those who have inscribed upon their banner the solution of the social question in the interest of all mankind — the Socialists.

The Socialist Party is the only one that has made the full equality of women, their liberation from every form of dependence and oppression, an integral part of its program; not for reasons of propaganda, but from necessity. *For there can be no liberation of mankind without social independence and equality of the sexes....*

Woman in the Future

In the new society woman will be entirely independent, both socially and economically. She will not be subjected to even a trace of domination and exploitation, but will be free and man's equal, and mistress of her own lot. Her education will be the same as man's, with the exception of those deviations that are necessitated by the differences of sex and sexual functions. Living under normal conditions of life, she may fully develop and employ her physical and mental faculties. She chooses an occupation suited to her wishes, inclinations and abilities, and works under the same conditions as man. Engaged as a practical working woman in some field of industrial activity, she may, during a second part of the day, be educator, teacher or nurse, during a third she may practice a science or an art, and during a fourth she may perform some administrative function. She studies, works, enjoys pleasures and recreation with other women or with men, as she may choose or as occasions may present themselves.

In the choice of love she is as free and unhampered as man. She woos or is wooed, and enters into a union prompted by no other considerations but her own feelings. This union is a private agreement, without the interference of a functionary, just as marriage has been a private agreement until far into the middle ages. Here Socialism will create nothing new, it will merely reinstate, on a higher level of civilization and under a different social form, what generally prevailed before private property dominated society.

Man shall dispose of his own person, provided that the gratification of his impulses is not harmful or detrimental to others. The satisfaction of the sexual impulse is as much the private concern of each individual, as the satisfaction of any other natural impulse. No one is accountable to any one else, and no third person has a right to interfere. What I eat and drink, how I sleep and dress is my private affair, and my private affair also is my intercourse with a person of the opposite sex. Intelligence and culture, personal independence, — qualities that will become natural, owing to the education and conditions prevailing in the new society, — will prevent persons from committing actions that will prove detrimental to themselves. Men and women of future society will possess far more self-control and a better knowledge of their own natures, than men and women of to-day. The one fact alone, that the foolish prudery and secrecy connected with sexual matters will disappear, will make the relation of the sexes a far more natural and healthful one. If between a man and woman who have entered into a union, incompatibility, disappointment or revulsion should appear, morality commands a dissolution of the union which has become unnatural, and therefore immoral. As all those circumstances will have vanished that have so compelled a great many women either to choose celibacy or prostitution, men can no longer dominate over women. On the other hand, the completely changed social conditions will have removed the many hindrances and harmful influences that affect married life to-day and frequently prevent its full development or make it quite impossible.

The impediments, contradictions and unnatural features in the present position of woman are being recognized by ever wider circles, and find expression in our modern literature on social questions, as well as in modern fiction; only the form in which it is expressed sometimes fails to answer the purpose. That present day marriage is not suited to its purpose, is no longer denied by any thinking person. So it is not surprising that even such persons favor a free choice of love and a free dissolution of the marriage relation, who are not inclined to draw the resulting conclusions that point to a change of the entire social system. They believe that freedom in sexual intercourse is justifiable among members of the privileged classes only....

Compulsory marriage is the normal marriage to bourgeois society. It is the only "moral" union of the sexes; any other sexual union is "immoral." Bourgeois marriage is, — this we have irrefutably proved, — the result of bourgeois relations. Closely connected with private property and the right of inheritance, it is contracted to obtain "legitimate" children. Under the pressure of social conditions it is forced also upon those who have nothing to bequeath. It becomes a social law, the violation of which is punished by the state, by imprisonment of the men or women who have committed adultery and have become divorced.

But in Socialistic society there will be nothing to bequeath, unless house furnishings and personal belongings should be regarded as hereditary portions; so the modern form of marriage becomes untenable from this point of view also. This also settles the question of inheritance, which Socialism will not need to abolish. Where there is no private property, there can be no right of inheritance. So woman will *be free*, and the children she may have will not impair her freedom, they will only increase her pleasure in life. Nurses, teachers, women friends, the rising female generation, all these will stand by her when she is in need of assistance....

For thousands of years human society has passed through all phases of development, only to return to its starting point: communistic property and complete liberty and fraternity: but no longer only for the members of the gens, but for all human beings. That is what the great progress consists of. What bourgeois society has striven for in vain, in what it failed and was bound to fail, — to establish liberty, equality and fraternity for all, — will be realized by Socialism. Bourgeois society could merely advance the theory, but here, as in many other things, practice was contrary to the theories. Socialism will unite theory and practice.

But as mankind returns to the starting point of its development, it will do so on an infinitely higher level of civilization. If primitive society had common ownership in the gens and the clan, it was but in a coarse form and an undeveloped stage. The course of development that man has since undergone, has reduced common property to small and insignificant remnants, has shattered the gens and has finally atomized society; but in its various phases it has also greatly heightened the productive forces of society and the extensiveness of its demands; it has transformed the gentes and the tribes into nations, and has thereby again created a condition that is in glaring contradiction to the requirements of society. It is the task of the future to remove this contradiction by re-establishing the common ownership of property and the means of production on the broadest basis.

Society takes back what it has at one time possessed and has itself created, but it enables all to live in accordance with the newly created conditions of life on the highest level of civilization. In other words, it grants to all what under more primitive conditions has been the privilege of single individuals or classes. Now woman, too, is restored to the active position maintained by her in primitive society; only she no longer is mistress, but man's equal.

"The end of the development of the state resembles the beginnings of human existence. Primitive equality is reinstated. The maternal material existence opens and closes the cycle of human affairs." Thus Backofen says in his book on the Matriarchate....

So men, proceeding from the most varied standpoints, arrive at the same conclusions, as a result of their scientific investigations. The complete emancipation of woman, and her establishment of equal rights with man is one of the aims of our cultured development, whose realization no power on earth can prevent. But it can be accomplished only by means of a transformation that will abolish the rule of man over man, including the rule of the capitalist over the laborer. Then only can humanity attain its fullest development. The "golden age" of which men have been dreaming, and for which they have been yearning for thousands of years, will come at last. Class rule will forever be at an end and with it the rule of man over woman.

10.5   CLARA ZETKIN: ON WOMEN'S RIGHTS AND SOCIAL CLASSES (1896)[1]

Through the researches by Bachofen, Morgan and others, it seems established that the social subjection of women coincided with the rise of private property. The antagonism inside the family between the man as owner and the woman as non-owner was the foundation for the economic dependence of the female sex and its lack of social rights.

In the family, he is the bourgeois; the wife represents the proletariat.[2] Nevertheless there could be no talk of a women's question in the modern sense of the term. It was the capitalist mode of production that first brought about the social transformation which raised the modern women's question; it smashed to smithereens the old family economy that in pre-capitalist times had provided the great mass of women with the sustenance and meaningful content of life. Indeed, we must not apply to the old-time household work of women the conception that is linked with women's work in our own day, viz. the conception that it is something petty and of no account. As long as the old-time family still existed, within its framework women found a meaningful content of life in productive work, and hence their lack of social rights did not impinge on their consciousness, even though the development of their individualities was narrowly limited....

There is a women's question for the women of the proletariat, of the middle bourgeoisie, of the intelligentsia, and of the Upper Ten Thousand; it takes various forms depending on the class situation of these strata.

What form is taken by the women's question among the women of the Upper Ten Thousand? A woman of this social stratum, by virtue of her possession of property, can freely develop her individuality; she can live in accordance with her inclinations. As a wife, however, she is still always dependent on the man. The sexual tutelage of a former age has survived, as a leftover, in family law, where the tenet *"And he shall be thy lord"* is still valid.

And how is the family of the Upper Ten Thousand constituted so that the woman is legally subjected to the man? This family lacks moral premises in its very foundation. Not the individuality but money is decisive in its doings. Its law reads: What capital brings together, let no sentimental morality put asunder. (*"Bravo!"*) Thus, in the morality of marriage, two prostitutions count as one virtue. This is matched also by the style of family life. Where the wife is no longer forced to perform duties, she shunts her duties as spouse, mother and housekeeper onto paid servants. When the women of these circles entertain a desire to give their lives serious content, they must first raise the demand for free and independent control over their property. This demand therefore is in the center of the demands raised by the women's movement of the Upper Ten Thousand. These women fight for the achievement of this demand against the men of their own class — exactly the same demand that the bourgeoisie fought for against all privileged classes: a struggle for the elimination of all social distinctions based on the possession of wealth....

And how does the women's question manifest itself in the ranks of the small and middle bourgeoisie, and in the bourgeois intelligentsia? Here it is not a matter of property dissolving the family, but mainly the phenomena accompanying capitalist production. As the latter completes its triumphal progress, in the mass the middle and small bourgeoisie are more and more driven to ruin. In the bourgeois intelligentsia there is a further circumstance that makes for the worsening of the conditions of life: Capital needs an intelligent and scientifically trained labor force; it therefore favored over-production in proletarian brain-workers, and contributed to the fact that the previously respectable and remunerative social position of members of the liberal professions is increasingly disappearing. To the same degree, however, the number of marriages is continually decreasing; for while the material bases are worsening on the one hand, on the other the individual's demands on life are increasing, and therefore the men of these circles naturally think twice and thrice before they decide to marry. The age limits for starting one's own family are getting jacked up higher and higher, and men are pushed into marriage to a lesser degree as social arrangements make a comfortable bachelor existence possible even without a legal wife. Capitalist exploitation of proletarian labor power ensures, through starvation wages, that a large supply of prostitutes answers the demand from this same aspect of the male population. Thus the number of unmarried women in middle-class circles is continually increasing. The women and daughters of these circles are thrust out into society to establish a life for themselves, not only one that provides bread but also one that can satisfy the spirit.

In these circles the woman does not enjoy equality with the man as owner of private property, as obtains in the higher circles. Nor does she enjoy equality as a workingwoman, as obtains in proletarian circles. The women of these circles must, rather, first fight for their economic equality with the men, and they can do this only through two demands; through the demand for equality in occupational education and through the demand for sex equality in carrying on an occupation. Economically speaking, this means nothing else than the realization of free trade and free competition between men and women. The realization of this demand awakens a conflict of interest between the women and men of the middle class and the intelligentsia. The competition of women in the liberal professions is the driving force behind the resistance of the men against the demands of the bourgeois women's-rightsers. It is pure fear of competition; all other grounds adduced against intellectual labor by women are mere pretexts — women's smaller brain, or their alleged natural vocation as mothers. This competitive battle pushes the women of these strata to demand political rights, so as to destroy all limitations still militating against their economic activity, through political struggle.

In all this I have indicated only the original, purely economic aspect. We would do the bourgeois women's movement an injustice if we ascribed it only to purely economic motives. No, it also has a very much deeper intellectual and moral side. The bourgeois woman not only demands to earn her own bread, but she also wants to live a full life

intellectually and develop her own individuality. It is precisely in these strata that we meet those tragic and psychologically interesting "Neva" figures, where the wife is tired of living like a doll in a doll house, where she wants to take part in the broader development of modern culture; and on both the economic and intellectual-moral sides the strivings of the bourgeois women's-righters are entirely justified.

For the proletarian woman, it is capital's need for exploitation, its un-ceasing search for the cheapest labor power, that has created the women's question.[3] ...This is also how the woman of the proletariat is drawn into the machinery of contemporary economic life, this is how she is driven into the workshop and to the machine. She entered economic life in order to give the husband some help in earning a living — and the capitalist mode of production transforms her into an undercutting competitor; she wanted to secure a better life for her family — and in consequence brought greater misery to the proletarian family; the proletarian woman became an independent wage-earner because she wanted to give her children a sunnier and happier life — and she was in large part torn away from her children. She became completely equal to the man as labor-power: the machine makes muscular strength unnecessary, and everywhere women's labor could operate with the same results for production as man's labor. And since she was a cheap labor force and above all a willing labor force that only in the rarest cases dared to kick against the pricks of capitalist exploitation, the capitalists multiplied the opportunities to utilize women's labor in industry to the highest degree.

The wife of the proletarian, in consequence, achieved her economic independence. But, in all conscience, she paid for it dearly, and thereby gained nothing at the same time, practically speaking. If in the era of the family the man had the right — think back to the law in the Electorate of Bavaria — to give the wife a bit of a lashing now and then, capitalism now lashes her with scorpions. In those days the dominion of the man over the woman was mitigated by personal relationships, but between worker and employer there is only a commodity relationship. The woman of the proletariat has achieved her economic independence, but neither as a person nor as a woman or wife does she have the possibility of living a full life as an individual. For her work as wife and mother she gets only the crumbs that are dropped from the table by capitalist production.

Consequently, the liberation struggle of the proletarian woman cannot be — as it is for the bourgeois woman — a struggle against the men of her own class. She does not need to struggle, as against the men of her own class, to tear down the barriers erected to limit her free competition. Capital's need for exploitation and the development of the modern mode of production have wholly relieved her of this struggle. On the contrary; it is a question of erecting new barriers against the exploitation of the proletarian woman; it is a question of restoring and ensuring her rights as wife and mother. The end-goal of her struggle is not free competition with men but bringing about the political rule of the proletariat. Hand in hand with the men of her own class, the proletarian woman fights against capitalist society. To be sure, she also concurs with the demands of the bourgeois women's movement. But she regards the realization of these demands only as a means to an end, so that she can get into the battle along with the workingmen and equally armed.

Bourgeois society does not take a stance of basic opposition to the demands of the bourgeois women's movement: this is shown by the reforms in favor of women already introduced in various states both in private and public law. If the progress of these reforms is especially slow in Germany, the cause lies, for one thing, in the competitive economic struggle in the liberal professions which the men fear, and, secondly, in the very slow and weak development of bourgeois democracy in Germany, which has not measured up to its historical tasks because it is spellbound by its class fear of the proletariat. It fears that the accomplishment of such reforms will advantage only the Social-Democracy. The less a bourgeois democracy lets itself be hypnotized by this fear, the readier it is for

reform. We see this in England. England is the sole country that still possesses a really vigorous bourgeoisie, whereas the German bourgeoisie, trembling with fear of the proletariat, renounces reforms in the political and social fields. Moreover, Germany is still blanketed by a widespread petty-bourgeois outlook; the philistine pigtail of prejudice hangs close on the neck of the German bourgeoisie....

[1] Originally titled "Only with Proletarian Women will Socialism be Victorious."
[2] Engels, *Origin of the Family*, near end of Chapter 2.
[3] Editor: These suspension points are in the text.

10.6 VLADIMIR I. LENIN: ON THE EMANCIPATION OF WOMEN (1919)[1]

... Take position of women. Not a single democratic party in the world, not even in any of the most advanced bourgeois republics, has done in this sphere in tens of years a hundredth part of what we did in the very first year we were in power. In the literal sense, we did not leave a single brick standing of the despicable laws which placed women in a state of inferiority compared with men, of the laws restricting divorce, of the disgusting formalities attending divorce proceedings, of the laws on illegitimate children and on searching for their fathers, etc. To the shame of the bourgeoisie and of capitalism, be it said numerous survivals of these laws, exist in all civilized countries. We have the right a thousand times to be proud of what we have done in this sphere. But the more thoroughly we have cleared the ground of the lumber of the old, bourgeois, laws and institutions, the more apparent has it become to us that we have only cleared the ground for the structure; the structure itself has not been built as yet.

Notwithstanding all the liberating laws that have been passed, woman continues to be a *domestic slave*, because *petty housework* crushes, strangles, stultifies and degrades her, chains her to the kitchen and to the nursery, and wastes her labor on barbarously unproductive, petty, nerve-racking, stultifying and crushing drudgery. The real *emancipation of women*, real Communism, will begin only when a mass struggle (led by the proletariat which is in power) is started against this petty domestic economy, or rather when it is *transformed on a mass scale* into large-scale socialist economy.

Do we in practice devote sufficient attention to this question, which, theoretically, is indisputable for every Communist? Of course not. Do we devote sufficient care to the *young shoots* of Communism which have already sprung up in this sphere? Again we must say emphatically, No! Public dining rooms, *crèches*, kindergartens — these are examples of the shoots, the simple everyday means, which assume nothing pompous, grandiloquent or solemn, but which can *in fact emancipate women*, which can in fact lessen and abolish their inferiority to men in regard to their role in social production and in social life. These means are not new, they (like all the material prerequisites for socialism) were created by large-scale capitalism; but under capitalism they remained, first, a rarity, and second, and what is particularly important, either *profit-making* enterprises, with all the worst features of speculation, profiteering, cheating and fraud, or the "acrobatics of bourgeois philanthropy," which the best workers quite rightly hated and despised.

There is no doubt that the number of these institutions in our country has greatly increased and that they are *beginning* to change in character. There is no doubt that there is far more *organizing talent* among the working women and peasant women than we are aware of, people who are able to organize in a practical way and enlist large numbers of workers, and a still larger number of consumers, for this purpose without the abundance of phrases, fuss, squabbling and chatter about plans, systems, etc., which our swelled-headed "intelligentsia" or half-baked "Communists" always suffer from. But we do not *nurse* these new shoots with sufficient care.

Look at the bourgeoisie! How well it is able to advertise what it requires! See how what the capitalists regard as "model" enterprises are praised in millions of copies of *their* newspapers; see how "model" bourgeois enterprises are transformed into objects of national pride! Our press does not take the trouble, or hardly takes the trouble, to describe the best dining rooms or *crèches*, to secure by daily exhortation the transformation of some of them into models. It does not give them enough publicity, does not describe in detail what saving in human labor, what conveniences for, the consumer, what a saving in products, what emancipation of women from domestic slavery and what an improvement in sanitary conditions can be achieved with *exemplary Communist labor* for the whole of society, for all the toilers.

[1] June 28, 1919.

10.7 J. HENRY DUNANT: ON THE RIGHTS OF WOUNDED SOLDIERS (*A MEMORY OF SOLFERINO*, 1876)

… At the entrance to the church was a Hungarian who never ceased to call out, begging for a doctor in heartbreaking Italian. A burst of grapeshot had ploughed into his back which looked as if it had been furrowed with steel claws, laying bare a great area of red quivering flesh. The rest of his swollen body was all black and green, and he could find no comfortable position to sit or lie in. I moistened great masses of lint in cold water and tried to place this under him, but it was not long before gangrene carried him off.…

The feeling one has of one's own utter inadequacy in such extraordinary and solemn circumstances is unspeakable. It is, indeed, excessively distressing to realize that you can never do more than help those who are just before you — that you must keep waiting men who are calling out and begging you to come. When you start to go somewhere, it is hours before you get there, for you are stopped by one begging for help, then by another, held up at every step by the crowd of poor wretches who press before and about you. Then you find yourself asking: "Why go to the right, when there are all these men on the left who will die without a word of kindness or comfort, without so much as a glass of water to quench their burning thirst?"

The moral sense of the importance of human life; the humane desire to lighten a little the torments of all these poor wretches, or restore their shattered courage; the furious and relentless activity which a man summons up at such moments: all these combine to create a kind of energy which gives one a positive craving to relieve as many as one can....

If an international relief society had existed at the time the [Battle of] Solferino, what endless good they could have done!...

There is need, therefore, for voluntary orderlies and volunteer nurses, zealous, trained and experienced, whose position would be recognized by the commanders or armies in the field, and their mission facilitated and supported. The personnel of military field hospitals is always inadequate, and would still be inadequate if the number of aids were two or three times as many, and this will always be the case. The only possible way is to turn to the public. It is inevitable, it will always be inevitable, for it is through the cooperation of the public that we can expect to attain the desired goal. The imploring appeal must therefore be made to men of all countries and of all classes, to the mighty ones of this world, and to the poorest workman: for all can, in one way or another, each in his own sphere and within his own limitations, do something to help the good work forward. Such an appeal is made to ladies as well as to men — to the mighty princess seated on the steps of the throne — to the poor devoted orphan serving maid — to the poor widow alone in the world and anxious to devote her last strength to the welfare of her neighbor. It is an appeal which is addressed equally to General and Corporal: to the philanthropist and to the writer who, in the quiet of his study, can give his talent to publications relating to a question which concerns all the human race and in a more particular sense, concerns every nation, every district, and every family, since no man can say with certainty that he is forever safe from the possibility of war....It is the more important to reach an agreement and concert measures in advance, because

when hostilities once begin, the belligerents are already ill-disposed to each other, and thenceforth regard all questions from the one limited standpoint of their own subjects.

Humanity and civilization call imperiously for such an organization as is here suggested. It seems as if the matter is one of actual duty, and that in carrying it out the cooperation of every man of influence, and the good wishes at least of every decent person, can be relied upon with assurance. Is there in the world a prince or a monarch who would decline to support the proposed societies, happy to be able to give full assurance to his soldiers that they will be at once properly cared for if they should be wounded? Is there any Government that would hesitate to give its patronage to a group endeavoring in this manner to preserve the lives of useful citizens, for assuredly the soldier who receives a bullet in the defense of his country deserves all that country's solicitude? Is there a single officer, a single general, considering his troops as "his boys," who would not be anxious to facilitate the work of volunteer helpers? Is there a military commissary, or a military doctor, who would not be grateful for the assistance of a detachment of intelligent people, wisely and properly commanded and tactful in their work?

Last of all — in an age when we hear so much of progress and civilization, is it not a matter of urgency, since unhappily we cannot always avoid wars, to press forward in a human and truly civilized spirit the attempt to prevent, or at least to alleviate, the horrors of war?

The practical execution of this proposal, on a large scale, would certainly call for somewhat considerable funds, but there would never be difficulty about the necessary money. In wartime, all and sundry would hasten to give their contributions or bring their mite in response to the committee's appeals. There is no coldness or indifference among the public when the country's sons are fighting. After all, the blood that is being spilled in battle is the same that runs in the veins of the whole nation. It must not be thought, therefore, that there is any danger of the enterprise being checked by obstacles of this kind. It is not there that the difficulty lies. The whole problem lies in serious preparation for work of this kind, and in the actual formation of the proposed societies.

If the new and frightful weapons of destruction which are now at the disposal of the nations, seem destined to abridge the duration of future wars, it appears likely, on the other hand, that future battles will only become more and more murderous. Moreover, in this age when surprise plays so important a part, is it not possible that wars may arise, from one quarter or another, in the most sudden and unexpected fashion? And do not these considerations alone constitute more than adequate reason for taking precautions against surprise?

PART IV

The Right to Self-Determination and the Imperial Age

INTRODUCTION

While the struggle for self-determination became a central feature of world politics during the twentieth century, it was hardly a new concept. The great human rights activist, stateswoman, and diplomat Eleanor Roosevelt (1884–1962) understood that well, offering in her "Universal Validity of Man's Right to Self-Determination" (1952) an insightful historical introduction to that subject — an introduction that will inform the selections of Part IV. While self-determination was invoked in the nineteenth-century writings of German and other European nationalists, and redefined later by European socialists, Roosevelt explained, it was its promotion by U.S. President Woodrow Wilson that made it a principle of international diplomacy. Yet Wilson's support for self-determination did not extend to those living under colonial rule, and demands for the right to self-determination in the colonized world were put on the backburner at the Treaty of Versailles (1919).

The tragic events of World War II, however, greatly weakened the imperial powers of Europe, leaving them unable to resist the intensifying claims to self-determination that had arisen in Asia, Africa, and the Americas. If self-determination must now be recognized as an inalienable right, Roosevelt maintained, it needed to be considered in relation to its impact on other nationalities, to ensure its consistency with the framework of universality and responsibility. In this context, Roosevelt asked questions similar to those posed earlier by Rosa Luxemburg and Lenin:

> Does self-determination mean the right of secession? Does self-determination constitute a right of fragmentation or a justification for the fragmentation of nations? Does self-determination mean the right of people to sever association with another power regardless of the economic effect upon both parties, regardless of the effect upon their internal stability and their external security, regardless of the effect upon their neighbors or the international community? Obviously not.

Her questions illuminate the often overlooked problems associated with the codification of the right to self-determination in Article 1 of both the U.N. Covenant of Civil and Political Rights (1966) and the U.N. Covenant of Economic, Social, and Cultural Rights (1966).

Anticipating the difficulties of nation building, Luxembourg noted that self-determination is more than the right of a people to compose their own laws, but also "the process by which people agree to finance their own affairs, spread their burden among themselves, and see that individual contributions to the common good are made." A visionary, she warned that self-determination should be regarded as a process in which self-governance is only gradually attained, and that by "mistaking the form [of governance] for the substance, we might in fact jeopardize the very rights we seek to promote."

Drawing on Eleanor Roosevelt's historical milestones in the emergence of a right to self-determination, selections are included from John Stuart Mill to convey the nineteenth-century liberal understanding of self-determination; Rosa Luxemburg and Vladimir Lenin for their still pertinent socialist perspectives on human rights; Woodrow Wilson, the League of Nations, and the Polish Minority Treaty, as relevant illustrations of the interwar consensus among the major powers on the right to self-determination; and, finally, Mahatma Gandhi, Sati' al-Husri, Kawme Nkrumah, and Frantz Fanon for their respective Asian, Arab, and African anticolonial contributions on the right to a homeland.

IV.1   ELEANOR ROOSEVELT ("THE UNIVERSAL VALIDITY OF MAN'S RIGHT TO SELF-DETERMINATION," 1952)[1]

... The desire of every people to determine its own destiny, free from dictation or control by others, is one of the most deep-seated of all human feelings. Throughout history groups of individuals having common bonds of language, religion, and culture have developed a sense of solidarity as a people and have tended to resent any effort of the outsider, the foreigner, to interfere with them. So strong is this feeling that men of many peoples have at various times been willing to lay down their lives to be free from domination by others.

The fact that wars have sometimes resulted from the failure of one people to respect the wishes of another led us all as members of the United Nations to agree that one of our major purposes is "to develop friendly relations among nations based on respect for the principle of equal rights and self-determination of peoples." In our present discussion we find ourselves faced with the problem not only of giving greater moral weight to this principle but at the same time giving it clearer definition so that it may have universal validity in the complex world of today.

While the underlying concept of self-determination is, I suppose, as old as human society, the term "self-determination" is relatively new. It appears to have been used first with regard to the nineteenth-century struggle of certain European peoples for a separate national existence. It occurs in the writings of the radical German philosophers of 1848 as *Selbstbestimmungsrecht*, which was translated into English as "the right of self-determination of nations" in a resolution adopted by a Conference of European Socialists in 1915. As a number of speakers, including the representatives of Egypt and the United Kingdom have pointed out, this phrase was given wide currency as a principle of international diplomacy by an American President, Woodrow Wilson. However, as several speakers have also reminded us, Woodrow Wilson from the beginning recognized that the principle of self-determination has its limitations. Because I think it important that we keep President Wilson's thought in this matter clearly in mind, I should like to quote again the statement he made in setting forth his four principles before the U.S. Congress on February 11, 1918. He asserted that all well defined national aspirations shall be accorded the utmost satisfaction that can be afforded them without introducing new, or perpetuating old, elements of discord and antagonism that would be likely in time to break the peace of Europe and consequently the world.

Today we discuss the question of self-determination in quite a different and much more complex setting. The stage is no longer Europe alone; it is worldwide. In a single resolution of a few paragraphs, we are setting forth certain guidelines for the respect of a principle, not only in Europe but in Asia, Africa, and the Americas as well. Consider for a moment the wide variety of cultures of the peoples with whose self-determination we are concerned — the culture of the spear and the earthen hut, the culture of vast rural peasantries, the complex culture of industrial cities, and confused combinations of culture. The complexity would seem to me enough to make us cautious lest we be too precise, narrow, or rigid in drawing up rules for promoting respect for the principle of self-determination.

In this debate, as with any resolution we adopt, we are molding for generations to come a principle of international conduct. If self-determination is a right which belongs to all people, it is inappropriate for us to express ourselves here in a general resolution with respect only to certain people. Our words and phrases must be made to apply as much to those who once exercised the right and had it snatched from them as to those who have never possessed it.

We, like others before us, would ask ourselves therefore, what may constitute a "people" to whom the principle of self-determination shall be applied. What are their characteristics? What are their cultural or political or geographical boundaries?

In our search for an answer we find the very concept of a "people" undergoing rapid evolution. Possibly the very first group of human beings seeking to maintain itself as an entity free from the control of others was the family or kinship group. The trend of history, in varying degrees and with numerous setbacks, seems to have been that larger and larger groups of once separate peoples have been formed and have come to think of themselves as a single people. Almost every nation represented at this table is composed of disparate elements of population that have been combined in one way or another into a unified or federated political system.

Here differences among formerly separate peoples either have been or are being submerged and new and larger peoples are emerging. This process of evolution and merger is still going on. It is a trend which diminishes the possibilities of conflict. Must we not exercise the greatest care lest anything we do here tend to freeze the pattern of peoples along present lines and thus instead of promoting the unity of mankind, emphasize certain obstacles to such unity?

We in the United States have gained the conviction from our own experience that the combination of peoples is a process of enrichment. Right here in New York City the number of persons of Irish descent total nearly 550,000, more than in the city of Dublin; the Italian population, similarly defined, is well over 1,000,000 and exceeds the population of Naples. New York has more people of Jewish origin than all Israel. Our 12,000 Arabic-speaking people are the equivalent of a small Middle Eastern city. Yet, as I am sure you have seen demonstrated many times, their children are not Irishmen, Italians, Jews or Arabs. They are Americans.

We do not claim for one moment that the process of creating a new people is easy or that we have fully succeeded in doing so for all elements of the population, but we know it can be done and we are convinced that this process is to be preferred to clinging over-zealously to the separateness of peoples.

At the same time we believe it is possible and desirable to retain a good deal of diversity within large political entities. Through our federated system of government, each state and each community preserves for its people the maximum voice in their own affairs. Louisiana has continued its legal system adopted from France, passed on from the earnest settlers of the region. Arizona and New Mexico have Spanish as one of the official languages of their legislatures. Throughout the country, people worship in Norwegian and Russian, publish newspapers in German and Greek, broadcast over the radio in a variety of tongues. In every state, county, and town the people decide for themselves who shall teach in their schools and what shall be taught. Their policemen come from their own communities and are subject to their control.

This is self-determination exercised to a high degree, yet without sacrificing cooperation in the larger fields of common interest. Each element of the national community contributes to the national government, takes part in it, and helps to shape the decisions which lead to a national destiny. Yet it must be equally clear that to grant the automatic exercise of the absolute right of political self-determination to every distinct section of our population would be detrimental to the interests of the population as a whole. And such considerations would apply to the territories whose future rises or falls with ours.

In this context we might ask ourselves: Does self-determination mean the right of secession? Does self-determination constitute a right of fragmentation or a justification for the fragmentation of nations? Does self-determination mean the right of people to sever association with another power regardless of the economic effect upon both parties, regardless of the effect upon their internal stability and their external security, regardless of the effect upon their neighbors or the international community? Obviously not.

As I have suggested, the concept of self-determination of peoples is a valid vital principle, but like most other principles it cannot be applied in absolute or rigid terms. Surely it is not consonant with realities to suggest that there are only two alternatives — independence or slavery. Just as the concept of individual human liberty carried to its logical extreme would mean anarchy, so the principle of self-determination of peoples given unrestricted application could result in chaos. Is either principle thereby invalidated? Certainly not! On the contrary, we feel sure that human freedoms can find their fullest expression only in the context of responsibility.

The resolution before us, in at least one other respect, raises the question of absolutes. It speaks of granting the right of self-determination, upon a "demand for self-government," by ascertaining the wishes of the people through a plebiscite.

We are compelled to ask, is this not an extremely limited concept of self-determination? Is the demand for self-government the only question on which the people should be consulted? Is the plebiscite the only method of consultation?

Were self-determination synonymous with self-government, we would find these questions easier to answer. But self-determination, as applied to non-self-governing territories, whose peoples have not had the opportunity to attain their full political growth, is a much more complicated matter. It has application at all stages along the road to self-government.

Self-determination is a process. It is in essence the process of democracy as contrasted with the process of dictation in any society developed or underdeveloped. It is, as has been said by other speakers, a process which involves responsibilities as well as rights. It is the process by which people develop their own laws and provide their own justice. This means not merely the right to compose a code of law, nor even the actual writing of a code; it also means general agreement to abide by the laws in the inter-

ests of society as a whole, even though one's individual or group freedoms are thereby limited. Self-determination is the process by which people agree to finance their own affairs, spread their burdens among themselves, and see that individual contributions to the common good are made. Self-determination is the building of roads and schools; not just deciding to build them, but finding the engineers, the money, the workmen, the teachers, and seeing the job through.

These matters are the essence of self-determination. If self-determination can be increasingly developed in all phases of the life of a people, their self-governing or independent institutions, when achieved, will be strong and lasting. If we conceive of self-determination as synonymous with self-government, we ignore the nature of the process by which true self-government is attained. Mistaking the form for the substance, we might in fact jeopardize the very rights we seek to promote.

There are not only many aspects of the life of any people to which the principle of self-determination can be applied; there are also many ways of learning the wishes of the people, and they must be appropriate to the question involved, as well as to the literacy and understanding of the citizens.

Furthermore, as I indicated a moment ago, it would be unfortunate if we limited our concept of self-determination to the non-self-governing world. We have seen in our own time flagrant examples of peoples and nations, vigorous and proud and independent, which have been overrun by a conqueror and subjected to his dictatorial control. These peoples and nations are entitled to the restoration of their independence.

At a time in history when the freedoms of so many individuals and peoples have been destroyed or are seriously threatened, it is, in the view of my delegation, important that the United Nations reaffirm the principle of self-determination and promote international respect for it. It is important that it do so for all peoples, and not solely for peoples in some form of colonial status. In considering the recommendations to this end drafted by the Commission on Human Rights, my delegation would strongly urge that we consider them within the framework of universality and of responsibility lest we frustrate the very purpose for which the principle of self-determination was set forth in the charter — that is, "to develop friendly relations among nations."

[1] Department of State Bulletin, December 8, 1952.

IV.2 UNITED NATIONS UNIVERSAL DECLARATION OF HUMAN RIGHTS (1948): PREAMBLE, ARTICLES 1–2, 15

Preamble

Whereas recognition of the inherent dignity and of the equal and inalienable rights of all members of the human family is the foundation of freedom, justice and peace in the world, ...

The General Assembly,

Proclaims this Universal Declaration of Human Rights as a common standard of achievement for all peoples and all nations, to the end that every individual and every organ of society, keeping this Declaration constantly in mind, shall strive by teaching and education to promote respect for these rights and freedoms and by progressive measures, national and international, to secure their universal and effective recognition and observance, both among the peoples of Member States themselves and among the peoples of territories under their jurisdiction.

Article 1

All human beings are born free and equal in dignity and rights. They are endowed with reason and conscience and should act towards one another in a spirit of brotherhood.

Article 2

Everyone is entitled to all the rights and freedoms set forth in this Declaration, without distinction of any kind, such as race, color, sex, language, religion, political or other opinion, national or social origin, property, birth or other status.

Furthermore, no distinction shall be made on the basis of the political, jurisdictional or international status of the country or territory to which a person belongs, whether it be independent, trust, non-self-governing or under any other limitation of sovereignty.

Article 15

1.   Everyone has the right to a nationality.

2.   No one shall be arbitrarily deprived of his nationality nor denied the right to change his nationality.

IV.3 UNITED NATIONS INTERNATIONAL COVENANT OF CIVIL AND POLITICAL RIGHTS AND THE INTERNATIONAL COVENANT ON ECONOMIC, SOCIAL, AND CULTURAL RIGHTS (1966)

Adopted by the General Assembly in 1966; entry into force, 1976.

Article 1

1.   All peoples have the right of self-determination. By virtue of that right they freely determine their political status and freely pursue their economic, social and cultural development.

2.   All peoples may, for their own ends, freely dispose of their natural wealth and resources without prejudice to any obligations arising out of international economic co-operation, based upon the principle of mutual benefit, and international law. In no case may a people be deprived of its own means of subsistence.

3.   The States Parties to the present Covenant, including those having responsibility for the administration of Non-Self-Governing and Trust Territories, shall promote the realization of the right of self-determination, and shall respect that right, in conformity with the provisions of the Charter of the United Nations.

CHAPTER 11

On the National Question

The British political theorist John Stuart Mill (1806–1873) called for the right to self-determination only in particular instances. In *Consideration on Representative Government* (1861), he argued that the homogeneity of national identity, of a "united public opinion," was necessary for the establishment of free political institutions. The unified nation, rather than the multinational state, constituted the fundamental political unity. Its existence was a necessary precondition for free government. The other prerequisites were economic and social development, and those nations that lagged behind, like India, were legitimate objects of an "enlightened" colonialism for which the British provided a model.

As early as 1909, Rosa Luxemburg, the exiled Polish socialist leader in Germany, provided a socialist view of the right to self-determination. In *The National Question and Autonomy* (1909), she maintained that socialist concessions to claims for national rights were usually pointless and counterproductive. Yet in opposition to future Soviet leader Joseph Stalin, she favored claims to self-determination by oppressed people only so long as their economies could survive independence. Attacking the Polish nationalists of her day, Luxemburg argued that secession from Russia would undermine the interests of the Polish proletariat. Such rights were utopian for industrially backward countries, like Poland and Czechoslovakia, whose economic development depended on the market of their mother country. Luxemburg also warned that any alliance of the working class with the nationalist bourgeoisie of oppressed countries would subvert the future establishment of democratic and socialist regimes.

In *The Right of Nations to Self-Determination* (1914), Lenin embraced some aspects of Luxemburg's views while diverging from others. With Luxemburg, he argued that nationalism from above was different than nationalism from below, distinguishing the oppressive nationalism of tsarist Russia from the justifiable nationalism of oppressed Poland. Yet unlike Luxemburg, he maintained that the right to national self-determination should not be determined by economic factors alone. Lenin further argued against Luxemburg that workers among the oppressed nationalities in the pursuit of secession should consider tactical alliances with elements of the bourgeoisie.

From a very different ideological perspective, President Woodrow Wilson (1856–1924) proclaimed, in his "Fourteen Points Address" to Congress (1918), the right of ethnic groups to national self-determination: "It is the principle of justice to all peoples and nationalities, and their right to live on equal terms of liberty and safety with another, whether they be strong or weak." These rights, he hoped, could be realized by a League of Nations, which would establish national borders around homogenous ethnic groups, thereby presumably removing a major cause of war.

Inspired by Wilson, the League of Nations was established after World War I in the hope that an international organization could preserve peace, provide security, and facilitate human cooperation worldwide. The Covenant of the League of Nations (1919) called for humane working conditions, the prohibition of traffic in women and children, the prevention and control of disease, and the just treatment of colonial peoples. The League of Nations placed the people of the colonies under a system of mandates administered by the victorious colonial powers, which agreed to bring the mandated territories toward self-government. The administering powers were responsible for ensuring racial and religious impartiality in the territories under their supervision. The right to immediate self-determination after World War I, however, was still limited to European nationalities.

The League of Nation's attempt to advance the Wilsonian vision of self-determination, based on the concept of national cohesion, led to the reestablishment of Poland and the carving out of independent states from the old Austro-Hungarian Empire. The Polish Minority Treaty (1919), ratified by the members of the league, endorsed Poland's right to self-determination and encouraged efforts to protect minorities. Article 7, for example, stipulated that all Polish nationalities should be equal before the law and enjoy the same civil and political rights without distinction as to race, language, or religion. Similarly, Articles 10 and 11 offered protection for the Jewish minority. In the end, however, the concept of a right to self-determination proved destructive of those who most needed protection in Europe. It helped rationalize, for example, Nazi Germany's absorption of Austria and then its occupation of Czechoslovakia's Sudetenland, in terms of the right to national unity of German peoples. Indeed, such interpretations raised the question of whether the right to self-determination would inevitably provide justifications for undermining a universal approach to advancing human rights.

As Europe was descending into a second World War, colonized people seized the opportunity to call for their right to a homeland. The preeminent Indian nationalist and pacifist leader Mahatma Gandhi (1869–1948) made his first strong bid for Indian self-determination before the end of World War II. Choosing a path that was unique for his time, he proposed that passive resistance is ... superior to the forces of weapons, for without drawing a drop of blood it produces far-reaching results; it is the reverse of resistance by arms" ("Passive Resistance," 1909). Passive resistance, Gandhi asserted in the same spirit as the ancient Greek Stoic Epictectus, required one's ability to stand up for one's principles by courageously facing death. India, he further argued in "Appeal to the Nation" (1924), should be ready to sacrifice itself for its independence, but only through nonviolent means. That was because, he maintained, there cannot be any separation between "Means and Ends" (1909–1947). One cannot expect to achieve independence against tyranny by using the same tools as one's oppressor. Although Gandhi called for the equal distribution of wealth, he believed, unlike many revolutionary socialists, that equality could be achieved by means of passive resistance (see Section 11.10). If socialism, he claimed, is an end "as pure as crystal," it requires "crystal-like" means to achieve it (*Harijan*, 1947).

The question of national independence and national unity was also an important concern in the colonized countries of the Middle East. In the early twentieth century, fragmented European spheres of domination gradually supplanted the Ottoman Empire's control over the Arab world. In "Muslim Unity and Arab Unity" (1944), Arab nationalist thinker Sati' al-Husri saw the unification of the Arab world as a necessary means of resisting foreign domination. Inspired by German Romantic thinkers, Sati' al-Husri approached the unity of the Arab world on a cultural and romantic plane. The whole Arab world, he hoped, would be combined into one nationally conscious and politically assertive community, united by a common geography, language, history, and tradition.

By that time, another notable independence movement was stirring in French Indochina. In 1919, at the Versailles Peace talks following World War I, Vietnamese nationalist Ho Chi Minh had appealed unsuccessfully for the independence of French Indochina. Following the Japanese occupation of Vietnam (an occupation in which Vichy France continued to administer the country), Ho retuned to Vietnam to lead the Viet Minh Independence movement. Following the defeat of Germany and Japan in 1945, and the French refusal to allow independence, Ho drew upon the most famous words of the U.S. Declaration of Independence, reminding the international community that "all men are created equal; they are endowed by their Creator with certain unalienable Rights; among these are Life, Liberty, and the pursuit of Happiness" (Declaration of Independence of the Democratic Republic of Vietnam, 1945). These inalienable rights, he maintained, must be extended to all peoples, including the Vietnamese.

The anticolonization struggle was also raging on the African continent. Kwame Nkrumah (1909–1972), the leader of the first black African country (Ghana) to shake off the chains of colonial rule, became an inspiring figure for oppressed Africans. Pushing for pan-African unity, he delivered a memorable speech on decolonization at the United Nations in 1960. Looking to the United Nations as the only organization that offered hope for the future of humankind, he asked the members of the General Assembly to cast their eyes across Africa: "The colonialists and imperialists are still there. In this twentieth century of enlightenment, some nations still extol the vain glories of colonialism and imperialism." It is the responsibility of the United Nations, he declared, to call upon all imperial powers to liberate their colonies (speech on decolonization and the United Nations, 1960).

The brutality of colonialism was vividly recounted by the West Indian psychoanalyst and social philosopher Frantz Fanon (1925–1961). The Algerian war of independence against France (1954–1962) had taught Fanon the importance of violent struggle as a means to empower colonized peoples. Violence, he argued in the *Wretched of the Earth* (1963), was a "cleansing force" that "frees the native from his inferiority complex and from his despair and inaction." Yet, as a result of internalizing the forces of colonial domination, the local elite tend to perpetuate — even after decolonization — the unequal social and economic structures they had inherited. Yet while acknowledging that independence would create new problems, Fanon maintained that the very process of fighting for nationhood could awaken political consciousness, forge an indigenous cultural identity, and ultimately make possible true independence based on equitable political and economic arrangements.

11.1   JOHN STUART MILL
(*CONSIDERATIONS ON REPRESENTATIVE GOVERNMENT*, 1861)

Chapter XVI: Of Nationality, as Connected with Representative Government

A portion of mankind may be said to constitute a Nationality, if they are united among themselves by common sympathetics, which do not exist between them and any others — which make them co-operate with each other more willingly than with other people, desire to be under the same government, and desire that it should be government by themselves or a portion of themselves, exclusively. This feeling of nationality may have been generated by various causes. Sometimes it is the effect of identity of race and descent. Community of language, and community of religion, greatly contribute to it. Geographical limits are one of its causes. But the strongest of all is identity of political antecedents; the possession of a national history, and consequent community of recollections; collective pride and humiliation, pleasure and regret, connected with the same incidents in the past. None of these circumstances however are either indispensable, or necessarily sufficient by themselves. Switzerland has a strong sentiment of nationality, though the cantons are of different races, different languages, and different religions. Sicily has, throughout history, felt itself quite distinct in nationality from Naples, notwithstanding identity of religion, almost identity of language, and

a considerable amount of common historical antecedents. The Flemish and the Walloon provinces of Belgium, notwithstanding diversity of race and language, have a much greater feeling of common nationality, than the former have with Holland, or the latter with France. Yet in general the national feeling is proportionally weakened by the failure of any of the causes which contribute to it. Identity of language, literature, and, to some extent, of race and recollections, have maintained the feeling of nationality in considerable strength among the different portions of the German name, though they have at no time been really united under the same government; but the feeling has never reached to making the separate States desire to get rid of their autonomy. Among Italians an identity far from complete, of language and literature, combined with a geographical position which separates them by a distinct line from other countries, and, perhaps more than everything else, the possession of a common name, which makes them all glory in the past achievements in arts, arms, politics, religious primacy, science, and literature, of any who share the same designation, give rise to an amount of national feeling in the population, which, though still imperfect, has been sufficient to produce the great events now passing before us, notwithstanding a great mixture of races, and although they have never, in either ancient or modern history, been under the same government, except while that government extended or was extending itself over the greater part of the known world.

Where the sentiment of nationality exists in any force, there is a prima facie case for uniting all the members of the nationality under the same government, and a government to themselves apart. This is merely saying that the question of government ought to be decided by the governed. One hardly knows what any division of the human race should be free to do, if not to determine, with which of the various collective bodies of human beings they choose to associate themselves. But, when a people are ripe for free institutions, there is a still more vital consideration. Free institutions are next to impossible in a country made up of different nationalities. Among a people without fellow-feeling, especially if they read and speak different languages, the united public opinion, necessary to the working of representative government, cannot exist. The influences which form opinions and decide political acts are different in the different sections of the country. An altogether different set of leaders have the confidence of one part of the country and of another. The same books, newspapers, pamphlets, speeches, do not reach them. One action does not know what opinions, or what instigations, are circulating in another. The same incidents, the same acts, the same system of government, affect them in different ways; and each fears more injury to itself from the other nationalities, than from the common arbiter, the State. Their mutual antipathies are generally much stronger than jealousy of the government. That any one of them feels aggrieved by the policy of the common ruler is sufficient to determine another to support that policy. Even if all are aggrieved, none feel that they can rely on the others for fidelity in a joint resistance; the strength of none is sufficient to resist alone, and each may reasonably think that it consults its own advantage most by bidding for the favor of the government against the rest. Above all, the grand and only effectual security in the last resort against the despotism of the government is in that case wanting: the sympathy of the army with the people. The military are the part of every community in whom, from the nature of the case, the distinction between their fellow countrymen and foreigners is the deepest and strongest. To the rest of the people, foreigners are merely strangers; to the soldier, they are men against whom he may be called, at a week's notice, to fight for life or death. The difference to him is that between friends and foes — we may almost say between fellow men and another kind of animals: for as respects the enemy, the only law is that of force, and the only mitigation, the same as in the case of other animals — that of simple humanity. Soldiers to whose feelings half or three-fourths of the subjects of the same government are foreigners, will have no more scruple in mowing them down, and no more desire to ask the reason why, than they would have in doing the same thing against declared enemies. An army composed of various nationalities has no other patriotism than devotion to the flag. Such armies have been the executioners of liberty through the whole duration of modern history. The sole bond which holds them together is their officers, and the government which they serve; and their only idea, if they have any, of public duty, is obedience to orders. A government thus supported, by keeping its Hungarian regiments in Italy and its Italian in Hungary, can long continue to rule in both places with the iron rod of foreign conquerors.

If it be said that so broadly marked a distinction between what is due to a fellow countryman and what is due merely to a human creature is more worthy of savages than of civilized beings, and ought, with the utmost energy, to be contended against, no one holds that opinion more strongly than myself. But this object, one of the worthiest to which human endeavor can be directed, can never, in the present state of civilization, be promoted by keeping different nationalities of anything like equivalent strength, under the same government. In a barbarous state of society, the case is sometimes different. The government may then be interested in softening the antipathies of the races, that peace may be preserved, and the country more easily governed. But when there are either free institutions, or a desire for them, in any of the peoples artificially tied together, the interest of the government lies in an exactly opposite direction. It is then interested in keeping up and unvenoming their antipathies; that they may be prevented from coalescing, and it may be enabled to use some of them as tools for the enslavement of others. The Austrian Court has now for a whole generation made these tactics its principal means of government; with what fatal success, at the time of the Vienna insurrection and the Hungarian contest, the world knows too well. Happily there are now signs that improvement is too far advanced to permit this policy to be any longer successful.

For the preceding reasons, it is in general a necessary condition of free institutions that the boundaries of governments should coincide in the main with those of nationalities. But several considerations are liable to conflict in practice with this general principle. In the first place, its application is often precluded by geographical hindrances. There are parts even of Europe, in which different nationalities are so locally intermingled, that it is not practible for them to be under separate governments. The population of Hungary is composed of Magyars, Slovacks, Croats, Serbs, Roumans, and in some districts, Germans, so mixed up as to be incapable of local separation; and there is no course open to them but to make a virtue of necessity, and reconcile themselves to living together under equal rights and laws. Their community of servitude, which dates only from the destruction of Hungarian independence in 1849, seems to be ripening and disposing them for such an equal union. The German colony of East Prussia is cut off from Germany by part of the ancient Poland, and being too weak to maintain separate independence, must, if geographical continuity is to be maintained, be either under a non-German government, or the intervening Polish territory must be under a German one. Another considerable region in which the dominant element of the population is German, the provinces of Courland, Esthonia, and Livonia, is condemned by its local situation to form part of a Slavonian state. In Eastern Germany itself there is a large Slavonic population: Bohemia is principally Slavonic, Silesia and other districts partially so. The most united country in Europe, France, is far from being homogeneous: indepen-

dently of the fragments of foreign nationalities at its remote extremities, it consists, as language and history prove, of two portions, one occupied almost exclusively by a Gallo-Roman population, while in the other the Frankish, Burgundian, and other Teutonic races form a considerable ingredient.

When proper allowance has been made for geographical exigencies, another more purely moral and social consideration offers itself. Experience proves that it is possible for one nationality to merge and be absorbed in another: and when it was originally an inferior and more backward portion of the human race, the absorption is greatly to its advantage. Nobody can suppose that it is not more beneficial to a Breton, or a Basque of French Navarre, to be brought into the current of the ideas and feelings of a highly civilized and cultivated people — to be a member of the French nationality, admitted on equal terms to all the privileges of French citizenship, sharing the advantages of French protection, and the dignity and prestige of French power — than to sulk on his own rocks, the half-savage relic of past times, revolving in his own little mental orbit, without participation or interest in the general movement of the world. The same remark applies to the Welshman or the Scottish Highlander, as members of the British nation.

Whatever really tends to the admixture of nationalities, and the blending of their attributes and peculiarities in a common union, is a benefit to the human race. Not by extinguishing types, of which, in these cases, sufficient examples are sure to remain, but by softening their extreme forms, and filling up the intervals between them. The united people, like a crossed breed of animals (but in a still greater degree, because the influences in operation are moral as well as physical), inherits the special aptitudes and excellences of all its progenitors, protected by the admixture from being exaggerated into the neighboring vices. But to render this admixture possible, there must be peculiar conditions. The combinations of circumstances which occur, and which affect the result, are various.

The nationalities brought together under the same government may be about equal in numbers and strength, or they may be very unequal. If unequal, the least numerous of the two may either be the superior in civilization, or the inferior. Supposing it to be superior, it may either, through that superiority, be able to acquire ascendancy over the other, or it may be overcome by brute strength and reduced to subjection. This last is a sheer mischief to the human race, and one which civilized humanity with one accord should rise in arms to prevent. The absorption of Greece by Macedonia was one of the greatest misfortunes which ever happened to the world: that of any of the principal countries of Europe by Russia would be a similar one.

If the smaller nationality, supposed to be the more advanced in improvement, is able to overcome the greater, as the Macedonians, reinforced by the Greeks, did Asia, and the English India, there is often a gain to civilization; but the conquerors and the conquered cannot in this case live together under the same free institutions. The absorption of the conquerors in the less advanced people would be an evil: these must be governed as subjects, and the state of things is either a benefit or a misfortune, according as the subjugated people have or have not reached the state in which it is an injury not to be under a free government, and according as the conquerors do or do not use their superiority in a manner calculated to fit the conquered for a higher stage of improvement. This topic will be particularly treated of in a subsequent chapter.

When the nationality which succeeds in overpowering the other is both the most numerous and the most improved; and especially if the subdued nationality is small, and has no hope of reasserting its independence; then, if it is governed with any tolerable justice, and if the members of the more powerful nationality are not made odious by being invested with exclusive privileges, the smaller nationality is gradually reconciled to its position, and becomes amalgamated with the larger. No Bas-Breton, nor even any Alsatian, has the smallest wish at the present day to be separated from France. If all Irish-

men have not yet arrived at the same disposition towards England, it is partly because they are sufficiently numerous to be capable of constituting a respectable nationality by themselves; but principally because, until of late years, they had been so atrociously governed, that all their best feelings combined with their bad ones in rousing bitter resentment against the Saxon rule. This disgrace to England, and calamity to the whole empire, has, it may be truly said, completely ceased for nearly a generation. No Irishman is now less free than an Anglo-Saxon, nor has a less share of every benefit either to his country or to his individual fortunes, than if he were sprung from any other portion of the British dominions. The only remaining real grievance of Ireland, that of the State Church, is one which half, or nearly half, the people of the larger island have in common with them. There is now next to nothing, except the memory of the past, and the difference in the predominant religion, to keep apart two races, perhaps the most fitted of any two in the world to be the completing counterpart of one another. The consciousness of being at last treated not only with equal justice but with equal consideration is making such rapid way in the Irish nation as to be wearing off all feelings that could make them insensible to the benefits which the less numerous and less wealthy people must necessarily derive from being fellow citizens instead of foreigners to those who are not only their nearest neighbors, but the wealthiest, and one of the freest, as well as most civilized and powerful, nations of the earth.

The cases in which the greatest practical obstacles exist to the blending of nationalities are when the nationalities which have been bound together are clearly equal in numbers and in the other elements of power. In such cases, each, confiding in its strength, and feeling itself capable of maintaining an equal struggle with any of the others, is unwilling to be merged in it: each cultivates with party obstinacy its distinctive peculiarities; obsolete customs, and even declining languages, are revived, to deepen the separation; each deems itself tyrannized over if any authority is exercised within itself by functionaries of a rival race; and whatever is given to one of the conflicting nationalities is considered to be taken from all the rest. When nations, thus divided, are under a despotic government which is a stranger to all of them, or which, though sprung from one, yet feeling greater interest in its own power than in any sympathies of nationality, assigns no privilege to either nation and chooses its instruments indifferently from all; in the course of a few generations, identity of situation often produces harmony of feeling, and the different races come to feel towards each other as fellow countrymen; particularly if they are dispersed over the same tract of country. But if the era of aspiration to free government arrives before this fusion has been effected, the opportunity has gone by for effecting it. From that time, if the unrecognized nationalities are geographically separate, and especially if their local position is such that there is no natural fitness or convenience in their being under the same government (as in the case of an Italian province under a French or German yoke), there is not only an obvious propriety, but, if either freedom or concord is cared for, a necessity, for breaking the connection altogether. There may be cases in which the provinces, after separation, might usefully remain united by a federal tie: but it generally happens that if they are willing to forge complete independence, and become members of a federation, each of them has other neighbors with whom it would prefer to connect itself, having more sympathies in common, if not also greater community of interest....

Chapter XVIII: Of the Government of Dependencies by a Free State

Free States, like all others, may possess dependencies, acquired either by conquest or by colonization; and our own is the greatest instance of the kind in modern history. It is a most important question, how such dependencies ought to be governed.

It is unnecessary to discuss the case of small posts, like Gibraltar, Aden, or Heligoland, which are held only as naval or military positions. The military or naval object is in this case paramount, and the inhabitants cannot, consistently with it, be admitted to the government of the place; though they ought to be allowed all liberties and privileges compatible with that restriction, including the free management of municipal affairs; and as a compensation for being locally sacrificed to the convenience of the governing State, should be admitted to equal rights with its native subjects in all other parts of the empire.

Outlying territories of some size and population, which are held as dependencies, that is, which are subject, more or less, to acts of sovereign power on the part of the paramount country, without being equally represented (if represented at all) in its legislature, may be divided into two classes. Some are composed of people of similar civilization to the ruling country; capable of, and ripe for, representative government: such as the British possessions in America and Australia. Others, like India, are still at a great distance from that state.

In the case of dependencies of the former class, this country has at length realized, in rare completeness, the true principle of government. England has always felt under a certain degree of obligation to bestow on such of her outlying populations as were of her own blood and language, and on some who were not, representative institutions formed in imitation of her own: but until the present generation, she has been on the same bad level with other countries as to the amount of self-government which she allowed them to exercise through the representative institutions that she conceded to them. She claimed to be the supreme arbiter even of their purely internal concerns, according to her own, not their, ideas of how those concerns could be best regulated. This practice was a natural corollary from the vicious theory of colonial policy — once common to all Europe, and not yet completely relinquished by any other people — which regarded colonies as valuable by affording markets for our commodities, that could be kept entirely to ourselves: a privilege we valued so highly, that we thought it worth purchasing by allowing to the colonies the same monopoly of our market for their own productions, which we claimed for our commodities in theirs.

This notable plan for enriching them and ourselves, by making each pay enormous sums to the other, dropping the greatest part by the way, has been for some time abandoned. But the bad habit of meddling in the internal government of the colonies did not at once terminate when we relinquished the idea of making any profit by it. We continued to torment them, not for any benefit to ourselves, but for that of a section or faction among the colonists: and this persistence in domineering cost us a Canadian rebellion, before we had the happy thought of giving it up. England was like an ill brought-up elder brother, who persists in tyrannizing over the younger ones from mere habit, till one of them, by a spirited resistance, though with unequal strength, gives him notice to desist. We were wise enough not to require a second warning. A new era in the colonial policy of nations began with Lord Durham's Report; the imperishable memorial of that nobleman's courage, patriotism, and enlightened liberality, and of the intellect and practical sagacity of its joint authors, Mr. Wakefield and the lamented Charles Buller.[1]

It is now a fixed principle of the policy of Great Britain, professed in theory and faithfully adhered to in practice, that her colonies of European race, equally with the parent country, possess the fullest measure of internal self-government. They have been allowed to make their own free representative constitutions, by altering in any manner they thought fit the already very popular constitutions which we had given them. Each is governed by its own legislature and executive, constituted on highly democratic principles. The veto of the Crown and of Parliament, though nominally reserved, is only exercised (and that very rarely) on questions which concern the empire, and not solely the particular colony. How liberal a construction has been given to the distinction between imperial and colonial questions is shown by the fact that the whole of the unappropriated lands in the regions behind our American and Australian colonies have been given up to the uncontrolled disposal of the colonial communities; though they might, without injustice, have been kept in the hands of the Imperial Government, to be administered

for the greatest advantage of future emigrants from all parts of the empire. Every colony has thus as full power over its own affairs as it could have if it were a member of even the loosest federation; and much fuller than would belong to it under the Constitution of the United States, being free even to tax at its pleasure the commodities imported from the mother country. Their union with Great Britain is the slightest kind of federal union; but not a strictly equal federation, the mother country retaining to itself the powers of a Federal Government, though reduced in practice to their very narrowest limits. This inequality is, of course, as far as it goes, a disadvantage to the dependencies, which have no voice in foreign policy, but are bound by the decisions of the superior country. They are compelled to join England in war, without being in any way consulted previous to engaging in it....

Thus far, of the dependencies whose population is in a sufficiently advanced state to be fitted for representative government. But there are others which have not attained that state, and which, if held at all, must be governed by the dominant country, or by persons delegated for that purpose by it. This mode of government is as legitimate as any other, if it is the one which in the existing state of civilization of the subject people, most facilitates their transition to a higher stage of improvement. There are, as we have already seen, conditions of society in which a vigorous despotism is in itself the best mode of government for training the people in what is specifically wanting to render them capable of a higher civilization. There are others, in which the mere fact of despotism has indeed no beneficial effect, the lessons which it teaches having already been only too completely learnt; but in which, there being no spring of spontaneous improvement in the people themselves, their almost only hope of making any steps in advance depends on the chances of a good despot. Under a native despotism, a good despot is a rare and transitory accident: but when the dominion they are under is that of a more civilized people, that people ought to be able to supply it constantly. The ruling country ought to be able to do for its subjects all that could be done by a succession of absolute monarchs, guaranteed by irresistible force against the precariousness of tenure attendant on barbarous despotisms, and qualified by their genius to anticipate all that experience has taught to the more advanced nation. Such is the ideal rule of a free people over a barbarous or semi-barbarous one. We need not expect to see that ideal realized; but unless some approach to it is, the rulers are guilty of a dereliction of the highest moral trust which can devolve upon a nation: and if they do not even aim at it, they are selfish usurpers, on a par in criminality with any of those whose ambition and rapacity have sported from age to age with the destiny of masses of mankind.

As it is already a common, and is rapidly tending to become the universal, condition of the more backward populations, to be either held in direct subjection by the more advanced, or to be under their complete political ascendancy; there are in this age of the world few more important problems than how to organize this rule, so as to make it a good instead of an evil to the subject people; providing them with the best attainable present government, and with the conditions most favorable to future permanent improvement. But the mode of fitting the government for this purpose is by no means so well understood as the conditions of good government in a people capable of governing themselves. We may even say that it is not understood at all....

It is always under great difficulties, and very imperfectly, that a country can be governed by foreigners; even when there is no extreme disparity, in habits and ideas, between the rulers and the ruled. Foreigners do not feel with the people. They cannot judge, by the light in which a thing appears to their own minds, or the manner in which it affects their feelings, how it will affect the feelings or appear to the minds of the subject population. What a native of the country, of average practical ability, knows as it were by instinct, they have to learn slowly, and after all imperfectly, by study and experience. The laws, the customs, the social relations, for which they have to legislate, instead of

being familiar to them from childhood, are all strange to them....

The utmost they can do is to give some of their best men a commission to look after it; to whom the opinion of their own country can neither be much of a guide in the performance of their duty, nor a competent judge of the mode in which it has been performed....

[1] I am speaking here of the *adoption* of this improved policy, not, of course, of its original suggestion. The honor of having been its earliest champion belongs unquestionably to Mr. Roebuck.

11.2 ROSA LUXEMBURG (*THE NATIONAL QUESTION AND AUTONOMY*, 1909)

I. The Right of Nations to Self-Determination

Among other problems, the 1905 revolution in Russia has brought into focus the nationality question. Until now, this problem has been urgent only in Austria-Hungary. At present, however, it has become crucial also in Russia, because the revolutionary development made all classes and all political parties acutely aware of the need to solve the nationality question as a matter of practical politics. All the newly formed or forming parties in Russia, be they radical, liberal, or reactionary, have been forced to include in their programs some sort of a position on the nationality question, which is closely connected with the entire complex of the state's internal and external policies. For a workers' party, nationality is a question both of program and of class organization. The position a workers' party assumes on the nationality question, as on every other question, must differ in method and basic approach from the positions of even the most radical bourgeois parties, and from the positions of the pseudo-socialistic, petit bourgeois parties. Social democracy, whose political program is based on the scientific method of historical materialism and the class struggle, cannot make an exception with respect to the nationality question. Moreover, it is only by approaching the problem from the standpoint of scientific socialism that the politics of social democracy will offer a solution which is essentially uniform, even though the program must take into account the wide variety of forms of the nationality question arising from the social, historical, and ethnic diversity of the Russian empire.

In the program of the Social Democratic Labor Party (RSDLP) of Russia, such a formula, containing a general solution of the nationality question in all its particular manifestations, is provided by the ninth point; this says that the party demands a democratic republic whose constitution would insure, among other things, *that all nationalities forming the state have the right to self-determination.*

This program includes two more extremely important propositions on the same matter. These are the seventh point, which demands the abolition of classes and the full legal equality of all citizens without distinction of *sex, religion, race,* or *nationality,* and the eighth point, which says that the several ethnic groups of the state should have the right to schools conducted in their respective national languages at state expense, and the right to use their languages at assemblies and on an equal level with the state language in all state and public functions. Closely connected to the nationality question is the third point of the program, which formulates the demand for wide self-government on the local and provincial level in areas which are characterized by special living conditions and by the special composition of their populations. Obviously, however, the authors of the program felt that the equality of all citizens before the law, linguistic rights, and local self-government were not enough to solve the nationality problem, since they found it necessary to add a special paragraph granting each nationality the "right to self-determination."

What is especially striking about this formula is the fact that it doesn't represent anything specifically connected with socialism nor with the politics of the working class. "The right of nations to self-determination" is at first glance a paraphrase of the old slogan of bourgeois nationalism put forth in all

countries at all times: "the right of nations to freedom and independence."...

II.

The general and cliché-like character of the ninth point in the program of the Social Democratic Labor Party of Russia shows that this way of solving the question is foreign to the position of Marxian socialism. A "right of nations" which is valid for all countries and all times is nothing more than a metaphysical cliché of the type of "rights of man" and "rights of the citizen." Dialectic materialism, which is the basis of scientific socialism, has broken once and for all with this type of "eternal" formula. For the historical dialectic has shown that there are no "eternal" truths and that there are no "rights." In the words of Engels, "What is good in the here and now, is an evil somewhere else, and vice versa" — or, what is right and reasonable under some circumstances becomes nonsense and absurdity under others. Historical materialism has taught us that the real content of these "eternal" truths, rights, and formulae is determined only by the *material* social conditions of the environment in a given historical epoch.

On this basis, scientific socialism has revised the entire store of democratic clichés and ideological metaphysics inherited from the bourgeoisie. Present-day social democracy long since stopped regarding such phrases as "democracy," "national freedom," "equality," and other such beautiful things as eternal truths and laws transcending particular nations and times. On the contrary, Marxism regards and treats them only as expressions of certain definite historical conditions, as categories which, in terms of their material content and therefore their political value, are subject to constant change, which is the *only* "eternal" truth.

When Napoleon or any other despot of his ilk uses a plebiscite, the extreme form of political democracy, for the goals of Caesarism, taking advantage of the political ignorance and economic subjection of the masses, we do not hesitate for a moment to come out wholeheartedly against that "democracy," and are not put off for a moment by the majesty or the omnipotence of the people, which, for the metaphysicians of bourgeois democracy, is something like a sacrosanct idol.

When a German like Tassendorf or a tsarist gendarme, or a "truly Polish" National Democrat defends the "personal freedom" of strikebreakers, protecting them against the moral and material pressure of organized labor, we don't hesitate a minute to support the latter, granting them the fullest moral and historical right to *force* the unenlightened rivals into solidarity, although from the point of view of formal liberalism, those "willing to work" have on their side the right of "a free individual" to do what reason, or unreason, tells them.

When, finally, liberals of the Manchester School demand that the wage worker be left completely to his fate in the struggle with capital in the name of "the equality of citizens" we unmask that metaphysical cliché which conceals the most glaring economic inequality, and we demand, point-blank, the legal protection of the class of wage workers, thereby clearly breaking with formal "equality before the law."

The nationality question cannot be an exception among all the political, social, and moral questions examined in this way by modern socialism. It cannot be settled by the use of some vague cliché, even such a fine-sounding formula as "the right of all nations to self-determination." For such a formula expresses either absolutely nothing, so that it is an empty, non-committal phrase, or else it expresses the unconditional duty of socialists to support all national aspirations, in which case it is simply false.

On the basis of the general assumptions of historical materialism, the position of socialists with respect to nationality problems depends primarily on the concrete circumstances of each case, which differ significantly among countries, and also change in the course of time in each country....

A glaring example of how the change of historical conditions influences the evaluation and the position of socialists with respect to the nationality question is the so-called Eastern question. During the Crimean War in 1855, the sympathies of all democratic and

socialist Europe were on the side of the Turks and against the South Slavs who were seeking their liberty. The "right" of all nations to freedom did not prevent Marx, Engels, and Liebknecht from speaking against the Balkan Slavs and from resolutely supporting the integrity of the Turks. For they judged the national movements of the Slavic peoples in the Turkish empire not from the standpoint of the "eternal" sentimental formulae of liberalism, but from the standpoint of the material conditions which determined the *content* of these national movements....

III.

What is more, in taking such a stand Marx and Engels were not at all indulging in party or class egoism, and were not sacrificing entire nations to the needs and perspectives of Western European democracy, as it might have appeared.

It is true that it sounds much more generous, and is more flattering to the overactive imagination of the young "intellectual," when the socialists announce a general and universal introduction of freedom for all existing suppressed nations. But the tendency to grant all peoples, countries, groups, and all human creatures the right to freedom, equality, and other such joys by one sweeping stroke of the pen, is characteristic only of the youthful period of the socialist movement, and most of all of the phraseological bravado of anarchism.

The socialism of the modern working class, that is, scientific socialism, takes no delight in the radical and wonderful-sounding solutions of social and national questions, but examines primarily the real issues involved in these problems....

Actually, even if as socialists we recognized the immediate right of all nations to independence, the fates of nations would not change an iota because of this. The "right" of a nation to freedom as well as the "right" of the worker to economic independence are, under existing social conditions, only worth as much as the "right" of each man to eat off gold plates, which, as Nicolaus Chernyshevski wrote, he would be ready to sell at any moment for a ruble. In the 1840s the "right to work" was a favorite postulate of the Utopian Socialists in France, and appeared as an immediate and radical way of solving the social question. However, in the Revolution of 1848 that "right" ended, after a very short attempt to put it into effect, in a terrible fiasco, which could not have been avoided even if the famous "national workshops" had been organized differently. An analysis of the real conditions of the contemporary economy, as given by Marx in his *Capital*, must lead to the conviction that even if present-day governments were forced to declare a universal "right to work," it would remain only a fine-sounding phrase, and not one member of the rank and file of the reserve army of labor waiting on the sidewalk would be able to make a bowl of soup for his hungry children from that right.

Today, social democracy understands that the "right to work" will stop being an empty sound only when the capitalist regime is abolished, for in that regime the chronic unemployment of a certain part of the industrial proletariat is a necessary condition of production. Thus, social democracy does not demand a declaration of that imaginary "right" on the basis of the existing system, but rather strives for the abolition of the system itself by the class struggle, regarding labor organizations, unemployment insurance, etc., only as temporary means of help.

In the same way, hopes of solving all nationality questions within the capitalist framework by insuring to all nations, races, and ethnic groups the possibility of "self-determination" is a complete utopia. And it is a utopia from the point of view that the objective system of political and class forces condemns many a demand in the political program of social democracy to be unfeasible in practice. For example, important voices in the ranks of the international workers' movement have expressed the conviction that a demand for the universal introduction of the eight-hour day by legal enactment has no chance of being realized in bourgeois society because of the growing social reaction of the ruling classes, the general stagnation of social reforms, the rise of powerful organizations of businessmen, etc. Nonetheless, no one would dare call the demand for

the eight-hour day a utopia, because it is in complete accordance with the progressive development of bourgeois society.

However, to resume: The actual possibility of "self-determination" for all ethnic groups or otherwise defined nationalities is a utopia precisely because of the trend of historical development of contemporary societies. Without examining those distant times at the dawn of history when the nationalities of modern states were constantly moving about geographically, when they were joining, merging, fragmenting, and trampling one another, the fact is that all the ancient states without exception are, as a result of that long history of political and ethnic upheavals, extremely mixed with respect to nationalities. Today, in each state, ethnic relics bear witness to the upheavals and intermixtures which characterized the march of historical development in the past....Historical development, especially the modern development of capitalism, does not tend to return to each nationality its independent existence, but moves rather in the opposite direction....

The development of *world powers*, a characteristic feature of our times growing in importance along with the progress of capitalism, from the very outset condemns all small nations to political impotence. Apart from a few of the most powerful nations, the leaders in capitalist development, which possess the spiritual and material resources necessary to maintain their political and economic independence, "self-determination," the independent existence of smaller and petty nations, is an illusion, and will become even more so. The return of all, or even the majority of the nations which are today oppressed, to independence would only be possible if the existence of small states in the era of capitalism had any chances or hopes for the future. Besides, the big-power economy and politics — a condition of survival for the capitalist states — turn the politically independent, formally equal, small European states into mutes on the European stage and more often into scapegoats. Can one speak with any seriousness of the "self-determination" of peoples which are formally independent, such as Montenegrins, Bulgarians,

Rumanians, the Serbs, the Greeks, and, as far as that goes, even the Swiss, whose very independence is the product of the political struggles and diplomatic game of the "Concert of Europe?" From this point of view, the idea of insuring all "nations" the possibility of self-determination is equivalent to reverting from Great-Capitalist development to the small medieval states, far earlier than the fifteenth and sixteenth centuries.

The other principal feature of modern development, which stamps such an idea as Utopian, is capitalist *imperialism*. The example of England and Holland indicates that under certain conditions a capitalist country can even completely skip the transition phase of "national state" and create at once, in its manufacturing phase, a colony-holding state. The example of England and Holland, which, at the beginning of the seventeenth century, had begun to acquire colonies, was followed in the eighteenth and nineteenth centuries by all the great capitalist states. The fruit of that trend is the continuous destruction of the independence of more and more new countries and peoples, of entire continents.

The very development of international trade in the capitalist period brings with it the inevitable, though at times slow ruin of all the more primitive societies, destroys their historically existing means of "self-determination," and makes them dependent on the crushing wheel of capitalist development and world politics....

A general attempt to divide all existing states into national units and to re-tailor them on the model of national states and statelets is a completely hopeless, and historically speaking, reactionary undertaking.

IV.

... In a class society, "the nation" as a homogeneous sociopolitical entity does not exist. Rather, there exist within each nation, classes with antagonistic interests and "rights." There literally is not one social area, from the coarsest material relationships to the most subtle moral ones, in which the possessing class and the class-conscious proletariat hold the same attitude,

and in which they appear as a consolidated "national" entity. In the sphere of economic relations, the bourgeois classes represent the interests of exploitation — the proletariat the interests of work. In the sphere of legal relations, the cornerstone of bourgeois society is private property, the interest of the proletariat demands the emancipation of the propertyless man from the domination of property. In the area of the judiciary, bourgeois society represents class "justice," the justice of the well-fed and the rulers; the proletariat defends the principle of taking into account social influences on the individual, of humaneness. In international relations, the bourgeoisie represents the politics of war and partition, and at the present stage, a system of trade war; the proletariat demands a politics of universal peace and free trade. In the sphere of the social sciences and philosophy, bourgeois schools of thought and the school representing the proletariat stand in diametric opposition to each other. The possessing classes have their worldview; it is represented by idealism, metaphysics, mysticism, eclecticism; the modern proletariat has its theory — dialectic materialism. Even in the sphere of so-called universal conditions — in ethics, views on art, on behavior — the interests, worldview, and ideals of the bourgeoisie and those of the enlightened proletariat represent two camps, separated from each other by an abyss. And whenever the formal strivings and the interests of the proletariat and those of the bourgeoisie (as a whole or in its most progressive part) seem identical — for example, in the field of democratic aspirations — there, under the identity of forms and slogans, is hidden the most complete divergence of contents and essential politics.

There can be no talk of a collective and uniform will, of the self-determination of the "nation" in a society formed in such a manner. If we find in the history of modern societies "national" movements, and struggles for "national interests," these are usually class movements of the ruling strata of the bourgeoisie, which can in any given case represent the interest of the other strata of the population only insofar as under the form of "national interests" it defends progressive forms of historical development, and insofar as the working class has not yet distinguished itself from the mass of the "nation" (led by the bourgeoisie) into an independent, enlightened political class....

For social democracy, the nationality question is, like all other social and political questions, primarily *a question of class interests*....

Society will win the ability to freely determine its national existence when it has the ability to determine its political being and the conditions of its creation. "Nations" will control their historical existence when human society controls its social processes.

Therefore, the analogy which is drawn by partisans of the "right of nations to self-determination" between that "right" and all democratic demands, like the right of free speech, free press, freedom of association and of assembly, is completely incongruous. These people point out that we support the freedom of association because we are the party of political freedom; but we still fight against hostile bourgeois parties. Similarly, they say, we have the democratic duty to support the self-determination of nations, but this fact does not commit us to support every individual tactic of those who fight for self-determination.

The above view completely overlooks the fact that these "rights," which have a certain superficial similarity, lie on completely different historical levels. The rights of association and assembly, free speech, the free press, etc., are the legal forms of existence of a mature bourgeois society. But "the right of nations to self-determination" is only a metaphysical formulation of an idea which in bourgeois society is completely nonexistent and can be realized only on the basis of a socialist regime....

V.

Let us take a concrete example in an attempt to apply the principle that the "nation" should "determine itself."

With respect to Poland at the present stage of the revolution, one of the Russian Social Democrats belonging to the editorial committee of the now defunct paper, *Iskra*, in 1906 explained the concept of the indispensable Warsaw constituent assembly in the following way:

If we start from the assumption that the political organization of Russia is the decisive factor determining the current oppression of the nationalities, then we must conclude that the proletariat of the oppressed nationalities and the annexed countries should be extremely active in the organization of an all-Russian constituent assembly.

This assembly could, if it wished, carry out its revolutionary mission, and break the fetters of force with which tsardom binds to itself the oppressed nationalities.

And there is no other satisfactory, that is, revolutionary way of solving that question than by implementing the rights of the nationalities to determine their own fate.[1] The task of a united proletarian party of all nationalities in the assembly will be to bring about such a solution of the nationality question, and this task can be realized by the Party only insofar as it is based on the movement of the masses, on the pressure they put on the constituent assembly....

The presentation by the proletariat of the demand for a constituent assembly for Poland should not be taken to mean that the Polish nation would be represented in the all-Russian assembly by any delegation of the Warsaw sejm.

I think that such representation in the all-Russian assembly would not correspond to the interests of revolutionary development. It would join the proletariat and bourgeois elements of the Polish sejm by bonds of mutual solidarity and responsibility, in contradiction to the real mutual relations of their interests.

In the all-Russian assembly, the proletariat and bourgeoisie of Poland should not be represented by one delegation. But this would occur even if a delegation were sent from the sejm to an assembly which included representatives of all the parties of the sejm proportionally to their numbers. In this case, the direct and independent representation of the Polish proletariat in the assembly would disappear, and the very creation of real political parties in Poland would be made difficult. Then the elections to the Polish sejm, whose main task is to define the political relations between Poland and Russia, would not show the political and social faces of the leading parties, as elections to an all-Russian assembly could do; for the latter type of elections would advance, besides the local, partial, historically temporary and specifically national questions, *the general questions of politics and socialism, which really divide contemporary societies.*[2]

The Russian Social Democratic Labor Party leaves the solution of the Polish question up to the Polish "nation." The Polish Socialists should not pick it up but try, as hard as they can, to solve this question according to the interests and will of the proletariat. However, the party of the Polish proletariat is organizationally tied to the all-state party, for instance, the Social Democracy of the Kingdom of Poland and Lithuania is a part of the Russian Social Democratic Labor Party....

Let us suppose for the sake of argument, that in the federal constituent assembly, two contradictory programs are put forth from Poland: the autonomous program of national democracy and the autonomous program of Polish social democracy, which are quite at odds with respect to internal tendency as well as to political formulation. What will the position of Russian social democracy be with regard to them? Which of the programs will it recognize as an expression of the will and "self-determination" of the Polish "nation?" Polish social democracy never had any pretensions to be speaking in the name of the "nation." National democracy comes forth as the expresser of the "national" will. Let us also assume for a moment that this party wins a majority at the elections to the constituent assembly by taking advantage of the ignorance of the petit bourgeois elements as well as certain sections of the proletariat. In this case, will the representatives of the all-Russian proletariat, complying with the requirements of the formula of their program, come out in favor of the proposals of national democracy and go against their own comrades from Poland? Or will they associate themselves with the program of the Polish proletariat, leaving the "right of nations" to one side as a phrase which binds them to nothing? Or will the Polish Social Democrats be forced, in order to reconcile these contradictions in their program, to come out in the Warsaw constituent assembly, as well as in their own agitation in Poland, in favor of their own autonomous program, but in the federal constituent assembly, as members well aware of the discipline of the Social Democratic Party of Russia, for the program of national democracy, that is, against their own program?

Let us take yet another example. Examining the question in a purely abstract form, since the author has put the problem on that basis, let us suppose, to illustrate the principle, that in the national assembly of the Jewish population of Russia — for why should the right to create separate constituent assemblies be limited to Poland, as the author wants? — the Zionist Party somehow wins a majority and demands that the all-Russian constituent assembly vote funds for the emigration of the entire Jewish community. On the other hand, the class representatives of the Jewish proletariat firmly resist the position of the Zionists as a harmful and reactionary utopia. What position will Russian social democracy take in this conflict?

It will have two choices. The "right of nations to self-determination" might be essentially identical with the determination of the national question by the proletariat in question — that is, with the nationality program of the concerned Social Democratic parties. In such a case, however, the formula of the "right of nations" in the program of the Russian party is only a mystifying paraphrase of the class position. Or, alternatively, the Russian proletariat as such could recognize and honor only the will of the national *majorities* of the nationalities under Russian subjugation, even though the proletariat of the respective "nations" should come out against this majority with their own class program. And in this case, it is a political dualism of a special type; it gives dramatic expression to the discord between the "national" and class positions; it points up the conflict between the position of the federal workers' party and that of the parties of the particular nationalities which make it up.

[1] Emphasis in the entire citation is Luxemburg's.

[2] Here as everywhere I speak of a definite manner of solving the nationality question for Poland, not touching those changes which may prove themselves indispensable while resolving this question for other nations. [*Note of the author of the cited article.*]

11.3   VLADIMIR I. LENIN (*THE RIGHT OF NATIONS TO SELF-DETERMINATION*, 1914)

What Is Self-Determination of Nations?

Naturally, this is the first question to arise when any attempt is made to consider what self-determination is, from a Marxist viewpoint. What is meant by that term? Should we seek for an answer in legal definitions deduced from all sorts of "general concepts" of law? Or should we seek an answer in the historical and economic study of the national movements? ...

Rosa Luxemburg, who declaims a great deal about the alleged abstract and metaphysical nature of the point in question ... succumb[s] to the sin of abstraction and metaphysics. It is Rosa Luxemburg herself who is continually straying into generalities about self-determination (including the very amusing speculation on the question of how the will of the nation is to be ascertained), without anywhere clearly and precisely asking herself whether the issue is determined by juridical definitions or by the experience of the national movements throughout the world.

A precise formulation of this question, which a Marxist cannot avoid, would at once have shaken nine-tenths of Rosa Luxemburg's arguments. This is not the first time national movements have arisen in Russia, nor are they peculiar to Russia alone. Throughout the world, the period of the final victory of capitalism over feudalism has been linked with national movements. The economic basis of those movements is the fact that in order to achieve complete victory for commodity production the bourgeoisie must capture the home market, must have politically united territories with a population speaking the same language, and all obstacles to the development of this language and to its consolidation in literature must be removed. Language is the most important means of human intercourse. Unity of language and its unimpeded development are most important conditions for genuinely free and extensive commercial intercourse on a scale commensurate with modern capitalism, for a free and broad grouping of the population in all its separate classes and lastly for the establishment of close connection between the market and each and every proprietor, big or little, seller and buyer.

Therefore, the tendency of every national movement is towards the formation of *national states*, under which these requirements of modern capitalism are best satisfied. The profoundest economic factors drive towards this goal, and therefore, for the whole of Western Europe, nay, for the entire civilized world, the *typical*, normal state for the capitalist period is the national state.

Consequently, if we want to learn the meaning of self-determination of nations, not by juggling with legal definitions, or "inventing" abstract definitions, but by examining the historical and economic conditions of the national movements, we shall inevitably reach the conclusion that self-determination of nations means the political separation of these nations from alien national bodies, the formation of an independent national state.

Later on we shall see still other reasons why it would be incorrect to understand the right to self-determination to mean anything but the right to separate state existence. At present, we must deal with Rosa Luxemburg's efforts to "dismiss" the unavoidable conclusion that the striving to form a national state rests on deep economic foundations....

For the question of the political self-determination of nations in bourgeois society, and of their independence as states, Rosa Luxemburg has substituted the question of their economic independence. This is as intelligent as if someone, in discussing the demand in the program for the supremacy of parliament, i.e., the assembly of people's representatives, in a bourgeois state, were to expound the perfectly correct conviction that big capital is supreme under any regime in a bourgeois country.

There is no doubt that the greater part of Asia, the most populous part of the world, consists either of colonies of the "Great Powers" or of states which are extremely dependent and oppressed as nations. But does this commonly known circumstance in any way shake the undoubted fact that in Asia itself the conditions for the most complete development of commodity production, for the freest, widest, and speediest growth of capitalism, have been created only in Japan, i.e., only in an independent national state? This state is a bourgeois state, therefore, it, itself, has begun to oppress other nations and to enslave colonies. We cannot say whether Asia will have time before the downfall of capitalism to become crystallized into a system of independent national states, like Europe; but it remains an undisputed fact that capitalism, having awakened Asia, has called forth national movements everywhere in that continent, too; that the tendency of these movements is towards the creation of national states there; that the best conditions for the development of capitalism are ensured precisely by such states. The example of Asia speaks *in favor* of Kautsky and *against* Rosa Luxemburg.

The example of the Balkan states also speaks against her, for everyone can see now that the best conditions for the development of capitalism in the Balkans are created precisely in proportion to the creation of independent national states in that peninsula.

Therefore, Rosa Luxemburg notwithstanding, the example of the whole of progressive, civilized mankind, the example of the Balkans, and the example of Asia prove that Kautsky's proposition is absolutely correct: The national state is the rule and the "norm" of capitalism; the heterogeneous nation state represents backwardness, or is an exception. From the standpoint of national relations, the best conditions for the development of capitalism are undoubtedly provided by the national state. This does not mean, of course, that such a state, based on bourgeois relations, could eliminate the exploitation and oppression of nations. It only means that Marxists cannot ignore the

powerful *economic* factors that give rise to the aspiration to create national states. It means that "self-determination of nations" in the program of the Marxists *cannot*, from a historical-economic point of view, have any other meaning than political self-determination, political independence, the formation of a national state....

While recognizing equality and an equal right to a national state, [the proletariat] attaches supreme value to the alliance of the proletarians of all nations, and evaluates every national demand, every national separation, *from the angle* of the class struggle of the workers. This call for practicalness is merely a call for the uncritical acceptance of bourgeois aspirations.

We are told: By supporting the right to secession you are supporting the bourgeois nationalism of the oppressed nations....

Our reply to this is: No, a "practical" solution of this question is important for the bourgeoisie. The important thing for the workers is to distinguish the *principles* of two trends. *If* the bourgeoisie of the oppressed nation fights against the oppressing one, we are always, in every case, and more resolutely than anyone else, *in favor*; for we are the staunchest and the most consistent enemies of oppression. But if the bourgeoisie of the oppressed nation stands for *its own* bourgeois nationalism we are opposed. We fight against the privileges and violence of the oppressing nation, but we do not condone the strivings for privileges on the part of the oppressed nation.

If we do not raise and advocate the slogan of the *right* to secession we shall play into the hands, not only of the bourgeoisie, but also of the feudal landlords and the despotism of the *oppressing* nation. Kautsky long ago advanced this argument against Rosa Luxemburg, and the argument is indisputable. When Rosa Luxemburg, in her anxiety not to "assist" the nationalistic bourgeoisie of Poland, rejects the *right* to secession in the program of the *Russian* Marxists, she is *in fact* assisting the Great-Russian Black-Hundreds. She is in fact assisting opportunist resignation to the privileges (and worse than privileges) of the Great Russians.

Carried away by the struggle against nationalism in Poland, Rosa Luxemburg has forgotten the nationalism of the Great Russians, although *this* nationalism is the most formidable at the present time, it is the nationalism that is less bourgeois and more feudal, and it is the principal obstacle to democracy and to the proletarian struggle. The bourgeois nationalism of *every* oppressed nation has a general democratic content which is directed *against* oppression, and it is this content that we support *unconditionally*, while strictly distinguishing it from the tendency towards national exceptionalism, while fighting against the tendency of the Polish bourgeoisie to oppress the Jews, etc., etc.

This is "impractical" from the standpoint of a bourgeois and a philistine; but it is the only policy in the national question that is practical, that is based on principles, and that really furthers democracy, liberty, and proletarian unity.

The recognition of the right to secession for all; the appraisal of each concrete question of secession from the point of view of removing all inequality, all privileges, all exceptionalism.

Let us examine the position of an oppressing nation. Can a nation be free if it oppresses other nations? It cannot. The interests of the freedom of the Great-Russian population demand a struggle against such oppression. The long, age-long history of the suppression of the movements of the oppressed nations, the systematic propaganda in favor of such suppression on the part of the "upper" classes, have created enormous obstacles to the cause of freedom of the Great-Russian people itself, in the form of prejudices, etc.

The Great-Russian Black-Hundreds deliberately foster and fan these prejudices. The Great-Russian bourgeoisie tolerates them or panders to them. The Great-Russian proletariat cannot achieve *its own* aims, cannot clear the road to freedom for itself unless it systematically combats these prejudices.

In Russia, the creation of an independent national state so far remains the privilege of one nation, the Great-Russian nation. We, the Great-Russian proletarians, defend no privileges, and we do not defend this privi-

lege. In our fight we take the given state as our basis; we unite the workers of all nations in the given state; we cannot vouch for any particular path of national development, we are marching to our class goal by *all* possible paths.

But we cannot advance to that goal unless we combat all nationalism, unless we fight for the equality of the workers of all nations. Whether the Ukraine, for example, is destined to form an independent state is a matter that will be determined by a thousand factors, which cannot be foreseen. Without attempting idle *"guesses,"* we firmly uphold what is beyond doubt: the right of the Ukraine to form such a state. We respect this right; we do not uphold the privileges of the Great Russians over the Ukrainians; we *teach* the masses to recognize that right, and to reject the *state* privileges of any nation.

In the leaps which all nations take in the period of bourgeois revolutions, clashes and struggle over the right to a national state are possible and probable. We proletarians declare in advance that we are *opposed* to Great-Russian privileges and this is what guides our entire propaganda and agitation.

In her quest for "practicalness" Rosa Luxemburg has overlooked the *principal* practical task both of the Great-Russian proletariat and of the proletariat of other nationalities: the task of daily agitation and propaganda against all state and national privileges and for the right, the equal right of all nations to their national state. This task is (at present) our principal task in the national question, for only in this way can we defend the interests of democracy and the alliance of all proletarians of all nations on an equal footing.

This propaganda may be "impractical" from the point of view of the Great-Russian oppressors as well as from the point of view of the bourgeoisie of the oppressed nations (both demand a *definite* "yes" or "no," and accuse the Social Democrats of being "vague"). In reality it is this propaganda, and only this propaganda, that ensures the really democratic, the really socialist education of the masses. Only such propaganda ensures the greatest chances of national peace in Russia, should she remain a heterogeneous national state, and the most peaceful (and for the proletarian class struggle, harmless) division into separate national states, should the question of such a division arise....

To accuse the supporters of freedom of self-determination, i.e., freedom to secede, of encouraging separatism, is as foolish and as hypocritical as accusing the advocates of freedom of divorce of wishing to destroy family ties. Just as in bourgeois society the defenders of privilege and corruption, on which bourgeois marriage rests, oppose freedom of divorce, so, in the capitalist state, repudiation of the right to self-determination, i.e., the right of nations to secede, is tantamount to defending the privileges of the dominating nation and police methods of administration as against democratic methods.

No doubt, the political corruption engendered by the relations prevailing in capitalist society sometimes leads members of parliament and journalists to indulge in frivolous and even in just nonsensical twaddle about a particular nation seceding. But only reactionaries can allow themselves to be frightened (or pretend to be frightened) by such twaddle. Those who stand by democratic principles, i.e., who insist that questions of state must be decided by the people, know very well that there is a very big difference between what the politicians prate about and what the people decide. The people know from daily experience the value of geographical and economic ties and the advantages of a big market and of a big state. They will, therefore, resort to secession only when national oppression and national friction make joint life absolutely intolerable and hinder all economic intercourse. In that case, the interests of capitalist development and of the freedom of the class struggle will be best served by secession....

The interests of the working class and of its struggle against capitalism demand complete solidarity and the closest unity of the workers of all nations; they demand strong opposition to the nationalistic policy of the bourgeoisie of every nationality. Hence, Social Democrats would be equally running counter to proletarian policy and subordinating the workers to the policy of the bour-

geoisie if they were to repudiate the right of nations to self-determination, i.e., the right of an oppressed nation to secede, or if they were to support all the national demands of the bourgeoisie of the oppressed nations. It makes no difference to the wage worker whether he is exploited chiefly by the Great-Russian bourgeoisie rather than by the non-Russian bourgeoisie, or by the Polish bourgeoisie rather than the Jewish bourgeoisie, etc. The wage worker who understands his class interests is equally indifferent to the state privileges of the Great-Russian capitalists and to the promises of the Polish or Ukrainian capitalists to set up an earthly paradise when they obtain state privileges. Capitalism is developing and will continue to develop, in one way or another, both in united heterogeneous states and in separate national states.

In any case the wage workers will be exploited. And in order to be able to fight successfully against exploitation, the proletariat must be free of nationalism, must be absolutely neutral, so to speak, in the struggle for supremacy that is going on among the bourgeoisie of the various nations. If the proletariat of any one nation gives the slightest support to the privileges of "its" national bourgeoisie, this will inevitably rouse distrust among the proletariat of the other nation; it will weaken the international class solidarity of the workers and divide them, to the delight of the bourgeoisie. And repudiation of the right to self-determination, or secession, inevitably means, in practice, supporting the privileges of the dominating nation....

To sum up: From the point of view of the theory of Marxism in general the question of the right of self-determination presents no difficulties. No one can seriously dispute the London resolution of 1896, or the fact that self-determination implies only the right to secession, or the fact that the formation of independent national states is the tendency of all bourgeois-democratic revolutions....

It is easy to understand that the recognition by the Marxists of the *whole of Russia*, and first and foremost by the Great Russians, of the *right* of nations to secede in no way precludes *agitation* against secession by

Marxists of a particular *oppressed* nation, just as the recognition of the right to divorce does not preclude agitation against divorce in a particular case....

Such a state of affairs sets the proletariat of Russia a twofold, or, rather, a two-sided task: first, to fight against all nationalism and, above all, against Great-Russian nationalism; to recognize not only complete equality of rights for all nations in general, but also equality of rights as regards forming an independent state, i.e., the right of nations to self-determination, to secession. And second, precisely in the interests of the successful struggle against the nationalism of all nations in *any* form, it sets the task of preserving the unity of the proletarian struggle and of the proletarian organizations, of amalgamating these organizations into an international association, in spite of the bourgeois strivings for national segregation.

Complete equality of rights for all nations: the right of nations to self-determination; the amalgamation of the workers of all nations — this is the national program that Marxism, the experience of the whole world, and the experience of Russia, teaches the workers.

11.4   WOODROW WILSON ("THE FOURTEEN POINTS ADDRESS," 1918)

An Address to a Joint Session of Congress

... It will be our wish and purpose that the processes of peace, when they are begun, shall be absolutely open and that they shall involve and permit henceforth no secret understandings of any kind. The day of conquest and aggrandizement is gone by; so is also the day of secret covenants entered into in the interest of particular governments and likely at some unlooked-for moment to upset the peace of the world. It is this happy fact, now clear to the view of every public man whose thoughts do not still linger in an age that is dead and gone, which makes it possible for every nation whose purposes are consistent with justice and the peace of the world to avow now or at any other time the objects it has in view.

We entered this war because violations of right had occurred which touched us to the quick and made the life of our own people impossible unless they were corrected and the world secured once for all against their recurrence. What we demand in this war, therefore, is nothing peculiar to ourselves. It is that the world be made fit and safe to live in; and particularly that it be made safe for every peace-loving nation which, like our own, wishes to live its own life, determine its own institutions, be assured of justice and fair dealing by the other peoples of the world as against force and selfish aggression. All the peoples of the world are in effect partners in this interest, and for our own part we see very clearly that unless justice be done to others it will not be done to us. The program of the world's peace, therefore, is our program; and that program, the only possible program, as we see it, is this:

I.   Open covenants of peace, openly arrived at, after which there shall be no private international understandings of any kind but diplomacy shall proceed always frankly and in the public view.

II. Absolute freedom of navigation upon the seas, outside territorial waters, alike in peace and in war, except as the seas may be closed in whole or in part by international action for the enforcement of international covenants.

III. The removal, so far as possible, of all economic barriers and the establishment of an equality of trade conditions among all the nations consenting to the peace and associating themselves for its maintenance.

IV. Adequate guarantees given and taken that national armaments will be reduced to the lowest point consistent with domestic safety.

V.   A free, open-minded, and absolutely impartial adjustment of all colonial claims, based upon a strict observance of the principle that in determining all such questions of sovereignty the interests of the populations concerned must have equal weight with the equitable claims of the government whose tide is to be determined.

VI. The evacuation of all Russian territory and such a settlement of all questions affecting Russia as will secure the best and freest cooperation of the other nations of the world in obtaining for her an unhampered and unembarrassed opportunity for the independent determination of her own political development and national policy and assure her of a sincere welcome into the society of free nations under institutions of her own choosing; and, more than a welcome, assistance also of every kind that she may need and may herself desire. The treatment accorded Russia by her sister nations in the months to come will be the acid test of their good will, of their comprehension of her needs as distinguished from their own interests, and of their intelligent and unselfish sympathy.

VII. Belgium, the whole world will agree, must be evacuated and restored, without any attempt to limit the sovereignty which she enjoys in common with all other free nations. No other single act will serve as this will serve to restore confidence among the nations in the laws which they have themselves set and determined for the government of their relations with one another. Without this healing act the whole structure and validity of international law is forever impaired.

VIII. All French territory should be freed and the invaded portions restored, and the wrong done to France by Prussia in 1871 in the matter of Alsace-Lorraine, which has unsettled the peace of the world for nearly fifty years, should be righted, in order that peace may once more be made secure in the interests of all.

IX. A readjustment of the frontiers of Italy should be effected along clearly recognizable lines of nationality.

X. The peoples of Austria-Hungary, whose place among the nations we wish to see safeguarded and assured, should be accorded the freest opportunity of autonomous development.

XI. Rumania, Serbia, and Montenegro should be evacuated; occupied territories restored; Serbia accorded free and secure access to the sea; and the relations of the several Balkan states to one another determined by friendly counsel along historically established lines of allegiance and nationality; and international guarantees of the political and economic independence and territorial integrity of the several Balkan states should be entered into.

XII. The Turkish portions of the present Ottoman Empire should be assured a secure sovereignty, but the other nationalities which are now under Turkish rule should be assured an undoubted security of life and an absolutely unmolested opportunity of autonomous development, and the Dardanelles should be permanently opened as a free passage to the ships and commerce of all nations under international guarantees.

XIII. An independent Polish state should be erected which should include the territories inhabited by indisputably Polish populations, which should be assured a free and secure access to the sea, and whose political and economic independence and territorial integrity should be guaranteed by international covenant.

XIV. A general association of nations must be formed under specific covenants for the purpose of affording mutual guarantees of political independence and territorial integrity to great and small states alike.

In regard to these essential rectifications of wrong and assertions of right we feel ourselves to be intimate partners of all the governments and peoples associated together against the Imperialists. We cannot be separated in interest or divided in purpose. We stand together until the end.

For such arrangements and covenants we are willing to fight and to continue to fight until they are achieved; but only because we wish the right to prevail and desire a just and stable peace such as can be secured only by removing the chief provocations to war, which this program does remove. We have no jealousy of German greatness, and there is nothing in this program that impairs it. We grudge her no achievement or distinction of learning or of pacific enterprise such as have made her record very bright and very enviable. We do not wish to injure her or to block in any way her legitimate influence or power. We do not wish to fight her either with arms or with hostile arrangements of trade if she is willing to associate herself with us and the other peace-loving nations of the world in covenants of justice and law and fair dealing. We wish her only to accept a place of equality among the peoples of the world, — the new world in which we now live, — instead of a place of mastery.

Neither do we presume to suggest to her any alteration or modification of her institutions. But it is necessary, we must frankly say, and necessary as a preliminary to any intelligent dealings with her on our part, that we should know whom her spokesmen speak for when they speak to us, whether for the Reichstag majority or for the military party and the men whose creed is imperial domination.

We have spoken now, surely, in terms too concrete to admit of any further doubt or question. *An evident principle runs through the whole program I have outlined. It is the principle of justice to all peoples and nationalities, and their right to live on equal terms of liberty and safety with one another, whether they be strong or weak. Unless this principle be made its foundation no part of the structure of international justice can stand.*[1] The people of the United States could act upon no other principle; and to the vindication of this principle they are ready to devote their lives, their honor, and everything that they possess. The moral climax of this the culminating and final war for human liberty has come, and they are ready to put their own strength, their own highest purpose, their own integrity and devotion to the test.

[1] Editor's emphasis.

11.5   THE COVENANT OF THE LEAGUE OF NATIONS (1919)

Preamble   The High Contracting Parties

Purposes   In order to promote international cooperation and to achieve international peace and
                        security by the acceptance of obligations not to resort to war, by the prescription of
methods   open, just and honorable relations between nations, by the firm establishment of the
enacting   understandings of international law as the actual rule of conduct among Governments,
clause   and by the maintenance of justice and a scrupulous respect for all treaty obligations in
                        the dealings of organized peoples with one another;

                        Agree to this Covenant of the League of Nations.

Article I

Membership   1. The original Members of the League shall be those of the Signatories which are
original   named in the Annex to this Covenant[1] and also such of those other States named in the
                        Annex as shall accede without reservation to this Covenant. Such accession shall be
                        effected by a Declaration deposited with the Secretariat within two months of the
                        coming into force of the Covenant. Notice thereof shall be sent to all other Members of
                        the League.
elections   2. Any fully self-governing State, Dominion or Colony not named in the Annex may
                        become a Member of the League if its admission is agreed to by two-thirds of the
                        Assembly, provided that it shall give effective guarantees of its sincere intention to
                        observe its international obligations and shall accept such regulations as may be
                        prescribed by the League in regard to its military, naval and air forces and armaments.[2]
withdrawals   3. Any Member of the League may, after two years' notice of its intention so to do,
                        withdraw from the League, provided that all its international obligations and all its
                        obligations under this Covenant shall have been fulfilled at the time of its withdrawal.[3]
                        ...

Article XXII

Mandates   1. To those colonies and territories which as a consequence of the late war have ceased
principle   to be under the sovereignty of the States which formerly governed them, and which are
                        inhabited by peoples not yet able to stand by themselves under the strenuous
                        conditions of the modern world, there should be applied the principle that the well-
                        being and development of such peoples form a sacred trust of civilization and that
                        securities for the performance of this trust should be embodied in this Covenant.
procedure   2. The best method of giving practical effect to this principle is that the tutelage of such
                        peoples should be entrusted to advanced nations which, by reason of their resources,
                        their experience or their geographical position, can best undertake this responsibility
                        and which are willing to accept it, and that this tutelage should be exercised by them
                        as Mandatories on behalf of the League.
types   3. The character of the mandate must differ according to the stage of the development
                        of the people, the geographical situation of the territory, its economic conditions and
                        other similar circumstances.
                        4. Certain communities formerly belonging to the Turkish Empire have reached a stage
                        of development where their existence as independent nations can be provisionally
                        recognized, subject to the rendering of administrative advice and assistance by a
                        Mandatory until such time as they are able to stand alone. The wishes of these
                        communities must be a principal consideration in the selection of the Mandatory.
Class B   5. Other peoples, especially those of Central Africa, are at such a stage that the
                        Mandatory must be responsible for the administration of the territory under conditions
                        which will guarantee freedom of conscience or religion, subject only to the
                        maintenance of public order and morals, the prohibition of abuses, such as the slave
                        trade, the arms traffic and the liquor traffic, and the prevention of the establishment of
                        fortifications or military and naval bases and of military training of the natives for other
                        than police purposes and the defense of territory, and will also secure equal
                        opportunities for the trade and commerce of other Members of the League.

Class C	6. There are territories, such as South-West Africa and certain of the South Pacific Islands, which, owing to the sparseness of their population, or their small size, or their remoteness from the centers of civilization, or their geographical contiguity to the territory of the Mandatory, or other circumstances, can be best administered under the laws of the Mandatory as integral portions of its territory, subject to the safeguards above mentioned in the interests of the indigenous population.
reports	7. In every case of mandate, the Mandatory shall render to the Council an annual report in reference to the territory committed to its charge.
Commission	8. The degree of authority, control or administration to be exercised by the Mandatory shall, if not previously agreed upon by the League, be explicitly defined in each case by the Council.

Article XXIII

Miscellaneous pledges	Subject to and in accordance with the provisions of international conventions existing or hereafter to be agreed upon, the Members of the League
Labor conditions	a) Will endeavor to secure and maintain fair and humane conditions of labor for men, women and children, both in their own countries and in all countries to which their commercial and industrial relations extend, and for that purpose will establish and maintain the necessary international organizations;
Treatment of natives	b) Undertake to secure just treatment of the native inhabitants of territories under their control;
Drug and vice traffic	c) Will entrust the League with the general supervision over the execution of agreements with regard to the traffic in women and children and the traffic in opium and other dangerous drugs;
Arms traffic	d) Will entrust the League with the general supervision of the trade in arms and ammunition with the countries in which the control of this traffic is necessary in the common interest;
Communications and transit	e) Will make provision to secure and maintain freedom of communications and of transit and equitable treatment for the commerce of all Members of the League. In this connection, the special necessities of the regions devastated during the war of 1914–1918 shall be borne in mind;
Health	f) Will endeavor to take steps in matters of international concern for the prevention and control of disease....

[1] The following states became members of the League under this clause:

Australia	India
Belgium	Italy
Bolivia	Japan
Brazil	Liberia
British Empire	New Zealand
Canada	Nicaragua
China	Panama
Cuba	Peru
Czechoslovakia	Poland
France	Portugal
Greece	Roumama
Guatemala	Kingdom of the Serbs, Croats, and Slovenes
Haiti	Siam
Honduras	South Africa
	Uruguay

[2] The following states became members of the League under this clause prior to January 1, 1927.

Abyssinia	Finland
Albania	Germany
Austria	Hungary
Bulgaria	Irish Free State
Costa Rica	Latvia
Dominican Republic	Lithuania
Estonia	

[3] In 1925 Costa Rica gave notice of withdrawal to take effect in 1927, and in 1926 Brazil and Spain gave notice of withdrawal to take effect in 1928.

11.6 POLISH MINORITY TREATY (1919)

Whereas, The Allied and Associated Powers have by the success of their arms restored to the Polish nation the independence of which it had been unjustly deprived; and

Whereas, By the proclamation of March 30, 1917, the Government of Russia assented to the re-establishment of an independent Polish State; and

Whereas, The polish State, which now, in fact, exercises sovereignty over those portions of the former Russian Empire which are inhabited by a majority of Poles, has already been recognized as a sovereign and independent State by the Principal Allied and Associated Powers; and

Whereas, Under the Treaty of Peace concluded with Germany by the Allied and Associated Powers, a Treaty of which Poland is a signatory, certain portions of the former German Empire will be incorporated in the territory of Poland; and

Whereas, Under the terms of the said Treaty of Peace, the boundaries of Poland not already laid down are to be subsequently determined by the Principal Allied and Associated Powers;

The United States of America, the British Empire, France, Italy and Japan, on the one hand, confirming their recognition of the Polish State, constituted within the said limits as a sovereign and independent member of the Family of Nations, and being anxious to ensure the execution of the provisions of Article 93 of the said Treaty of Peace with Germany;

Poland, on the other hand, desiring to conform her institutions to the principles of liberty and justice, and to give a sure guarantee to the inhabitants of the territory over which she has assumed sovereignty;

For this purpose the High Contracting Parties...have agreed as follows:

Chapter I

Article I

Poland undertakes that the stipulations contained in Articles 2 to 8 of this Chapter shall be recognized as fundamental laws, and that no law, regulation or official action shall conflict or interfere with these stipulations, nor shall any law, regulation or official action prevail over them.

Article 2

Poland undertakes to assure full and complete protection of life and liberty to all inhabitants of Poland without distinction of birth, nationality, language, race or religion.

All inhabitants of Poland shall be entitled to the free exercise, whether public or private, of any creed, religion or belief, whose practices are not inconsistent with public order or public morals.

Article 3

Poland admits and declares to be Polish nationals *ipso facto* and without the requirement of any formality, German, Austrian, Hungarian or Russian nationals habitually resident at the date of the coming into force of the present Treaty in territory which is or may be recognized as forming part of Poland, but subject to any provisions in the Treaties of Peace with Germany or Austria respectively relating to persons who became resident in such territory after a specified date.

Nevertheless, the persons referred to above who are over eighteen years of age will be entitled under the conditions contained in the said Treaties to opt for any other nationality which may be open to them. Option by a husband will cover his wife and option by parents will cover their children under eighteen years of age.

Persons who have exercised the above right to opt must, except where it is otherwise provided in the Treaty of Peace with Germany, transfer within the succeeding twelve months their place of residence to the State for which they have opted. They will be entitled to retain their immovable property in Polish territory. They may carry with them their movable property of every description. No export duties may be imposed upon them in connection with the removal of such property.

Article 4

Poland admits and declares to be Polish nationals *ipso facto* and without the requirement of any formality, persons of German, Austrian, Hungarian or Russian nationality who were born in the said territory of parents habitually resident there, even if at the date of the coming into force of the present Treaty they are not themselves habitually resident there.

Nevertheless, within two years after the coming into force of the present Treaty, these persons may make a declaration before the competent Polish authorities in the country in which they are resident, stating that they abandon Polish nationality, and they will then cease to be considered as Polish nationals. In this connection a declaration by a husband will cover his wife and a declaration by parents will cover their children under eighteen years of age.

Article 5

Poland undertakes to put no hindrance in the way of the exercise of the right which the persons concerned have, under the Treaties concluded or to be concluded by the Allied and Associated Powers with Germany, Austria, Hungary or Russia, to choose whether or not they will acquire Polish nationality.

Article 6

All persons born in Polish territory who are not born nationals of another State shall *ipso facto* become Polish nationals.

Article 7

All Polish nationals shall be equal before the law and shall enjoy the same civil and political rights without distinction as to race, language or religion.

Differences of religion, creed or confession shall not prejudice any Polish national in matters relating to the enjoyment of civil or political rights, as for instance admission to public employments, functions and honors, or the exercise of professions and industries.

No restriction shall be imposed on the free use by any Polish national of any language in private intercourse, in commerce, in religion, in the press or in publications of any kind, or at public meetings.

Notwithstanding any establishment by the Polish Government of an official language, adequate facilities shall be given to Polish nationals of non-Polish speech for the use of their language, either orally or in writing, before the courts.

Article 8

Polish nationals who belong to racial, religious or linguistic minorities shall enjoy the same treatment and security in law and in fact as the other Polish nationals. In particular they shall have an equal right to establish, manage and control at their own expense charitable, religious and social institutions, schools and other educational establishments, with the right to use their own language and to exercise their religion freely therein.

Article 9

Poland will provide in the public educational system in towns and districts in which a considerable proportion of Polish nationals of other than Polish speech are resident adequate facilities for ensuring that in the primary schools the instruction shall be given to the children of such Polish nationals through the medium of their own language. This provision shall not prevent the Polish Government from making the teaching of the Polish language obligatory in the said schools.

In towns and districts where there is a considerable proportion of Polish nationals belonging to racial, religious or linguistic minorities, these minorities shall be assured an equitable share in the enjoyment and application of the sums which may be provided out of public funds under the State, municipal or other budget, for educational, religious or charitable purposes.

The provisions of this Article shall apply to Polish citizens of German speech only in that part of Poland which was German territory on August 1st, 1914.

Article 10

Educational Committees appointed locally by the Jewish communities of Poland will, subject to the general control of the State, provide for the distribution of the proportional share of public funds allocated to Jewish schools in accordance with and for the organization and management of these schools.

The provisions of Article 9 concerning the use of languages in schools shall apply to these schools.

Article 11

Jews shall not be compelled to perform any act which constitutes a violation of their Sabbath, nor shall they be placed under any disability by reason of their refusal to attend courts of law or to perform any legal business on their Sabbath. This provision however shall not exempt Jews from such obligations as shall be imposed upon all other Polish citizens for the necessary purpose of military service, national defense, or the preservation of public order.

Poland declares her intention to refrain from ordering or permitting elections, whether general or local, to be held on a Saturday, nor will registration for electoral or other purposes be compelled to be performed on a Saturday.

Article 12

Poland agrees that the stipulations in the foregoing Articles, so far as they affect persons belonging to racial, religious or linguistic minorities, constitute obligations of international concern and shall be placed under the guarantee of the League of Nations. They shall not be modified without the assent of a majority of the Council of the League of Nations. The United States, the British Empire, France, Italy and Japan hereby agree not to withhold their assent from any modification in these Articles which is in due form assented to by a majority of the Council of the League of Nations....

11.7   MAHATMA GANDHI ("PASSIVE RESISTANCE," 1909)

... We simply want to find out what is right and to act accordingly. The real meaning of the statement that we are a law abiding nation is that we are passive resisters. When we do not like certain laws, we do not break the heads of law-givers but we suffer and do not submit to the laws. That we should obey laws whether good or bad is a newfangled notion. There was no such thing in former days. The people disregarded those laws they did not like and suffered the penalties for their breach. It is contrary to our manhood if we obey laws repugnant to our conscience. Such teaching is opposed to religion and means slavery. If the Government were to ask us to go about without any clothing, should we do so? If I were a passive resister, I would say to them that I would have nothing to do with their law. But we have so forgotten ourselves and become so compliant that we do not mind any degrading law.

A man who has realized his manhood, who fears only God, will fear no one else. Man-made laws are not necessarily binding on him. Even the Government does not expect any such thing from us. They do not say: "You must do such and such a thing," but they say: "If you do not do it, we will punish you." We are sunk so low that we fancy that it is our duty and our religion to do what the law lays down. If man will only realize that it is unmanly to obey laws that are unjust, no man's tyranny will enslave him. This is the key to self-rule or home-rule.

It is a superstition and ungodly thing to believe that an act of a majority binds a minority. Many examples can be given in which acts of majorities will be found to have been wrong and those of minorities to have been right. All reforms owe their origin to the initiation of minorities in opposition to majorities. If among a band of robbers a knowledge of robbing is obligatory, is a pious man to accept the obligation? So long as the superstition that men should obey unjust laws exists, so long will their slavery exist. And a passive resister alone can remove such a superstition.

To use brute force, to use gunpowder, is contrary to passive resistance, for it means that we want our opponent to do by force that which we desire but he does not. And if such a use of force is justifiable, surely he is entitled to do likewise by us. And so we should never come to an agreement. We may simply fancy, like the blind horse moving in a circle round a mill, that we are making progress. Those who believe that they are not bound to obey laws which are repugnant to their conscience have only the remedy of passive resistance open to them. Any other must lead to disaster.

READER: From what you say I deduce that passive resistance is a splendid weapon of the weak, but that when they are strong they may take up arms.

EDITOR: This is gross ignorance. Passive resistance, that is, soul-force, is matchless. It is superior to the force of arms. How, then, can it be considered only a weapon of the weak? Physical-force men are strangers to the courage that is requisite in a passive resister. Do you believe that a coward can ever disobey a law that he dislikes? Extremists are considered to be advocates of brute force. Why do they, then, talk about obeying laws? I do not blame them. They can say nothing else. When they succeed in driving out the English and they themselves become governors, they will want you and me to obey their laws. And that is a fitting thing for their constitution. But a passive resister will say he will not obey a law that is against his conscience, even though he may be blown to pieces at the mouth of a cannon.

What do you think? Wherein is courage required — in blowing others to pieces from behind a cannon, or with a smiling face to approach a cannon and be blown to pieces? Who is the true warrior — he who keeps death always as a bosom-friend, or he who controls the death of others? Believe me that a man devoid of courage and manhood can never be a passive resister.

This however, I will admit: that even a man weak in body is capable of offering this resistance. One man can offer it just as well as millions. Both men and women can indulge in it. It does not require the training of an army; it needs no jiu-jitsu. Control over the mind is alone necessary, and when that is attained, man is free like the king of the forest and his very glance withers the enemy.

Passive resistance is an all-sided sword, it can be used anyhow; it blesses him who uses it and him against whom it is used. Without drawing a drop of blood it produces far-reaching results. It never rusts and cannot be stolen. Competition between passive resisters does not exhaust. The sword of passive resistance does not require a scabbard. It is strange indeed that you should consider such a weapon to be a weapon merely of the weak.

READER: You have said that passive resistance is a specialty of India. Have cannons never been used in India?

EDITOR: Evidently, in your opinion, India means its few princes. To me it means its teeming millions on whom depends the existence of its princes and our own.

Kings will always use their kingly weapons. To use force is bred in them. They want to command, but those who have to obey commands do not want guns: and these are in a majority throughout the world. They have to learn either body-force or soul-force. Where they learn the former, both the rulers and the ruled become like so many madmen; but where they learn soul-force, the commands of the rulers do not go beyond the point of their swords, for true men disregard unjust commands. Peasants have never been subdued by the sword, and never will be. They do not know the use of the sword, and they are not frightened by the use of it by others. That nation is great which rests its head upon death as its pillow. Those who defy death are free from all fear. For those who are laboring under the delusive charms of brute-force, this picture is not overdrawn. The fact is that, in India, the nation at large has generally used passive resistance in all departments of life. We cease to cooperate with our rulers when they displease us. This is passive resistance....

READER: From what you say, then, it would appear that it is not a small thing to become a passive resister, and, if that is so, I should like you to explain how a man may become one.

EDITOR: To become a passive resister is easy enough but it is also equally difficult. I have known a lad of fourteen years become a passive resister; I have known also sick people do likewise; and I have also known physically strong and otherwise happy people unable to take up passive resistance. After a great deal of experience it seems to me that those who want to become passive resisters for the service of the country have to observe perfect chastity, adopt poverty, follow truth, and cultivate fearlessness.

Chastity is one of the greatest disciplines without which the mind cannot attain requisite firmness. A man who is unchaste loses stamina, becomes emasculated and cowardly. He whose mind is given over to animal passions is not capable of any great effort. This can be proved by innumerable instances. What, then, is a married person to do is the question that arises naturally; and yet it need not. When a husband and wife gratify the passions, it is no less an animal indulgence on that account. Such an indulgence, except for perpetuating the race, is strictly prohibited. But a passive resister has to avoid even that very limited indulgence because he can have no desire for progeny. A married man, therefore, can observe perfect chastity. This subject is not capable of being treated at greater length. Several questions arise: How is one to carry one's wife with one, what are her rights, and other similar questions. Yet those who wish to take part in a great work are bound to solve these puzzles.

Just as there is necessity for chastity, so is there for poverty. Pecuniary ambition and passive resistance cannot well go together. Those who have money are not expected to throw it away, but they *are* expected to be indifferent about it. They must be prepared to lose every penny rather than give up passive resistance....

11.8   MAHATHA GANDHI ("AN APPEAL TO THE NATION," 1924)[1]

Under the above heading Mr. Srish Chandra Chatterji and eighteen other signatories have issued a document which I copy below:

We are passing through a series of national crises the gravity of which can hardly be exaggerated. There are moments in the history of nations when a decisive move in the right direction often leads a nation to a triumphant goal and when that supreme moment is lost in vague imaginations or false and indecisive steps, it takes long centuries to retrieve the loss. India is passing through some such crisis and we are extremely fortunate that the crisis is not yet over. The whole world is shivering from the pains of Labor, the indications of a new life are manifest everywhere, and a regenerated India must find a place among the new-born nations of the world. This rejuvenated India cannot accept any over-lord, she must be a free and independent nation.

At a time when all the nations of the world are fighting for independence and liberty, at a time when our Indian heroes are championing the cause of India's independence abroad, it is simply ridiculous and shameful that we Indians should hesitate to accept independence as our only legitimate and logical goal; we therefore appeal to our nation to declare in the open Congress in unmistakable terms that independence and complete independence is our destined goal, let there be no ambiguous phrases to qualify it, let it be preached in all its nakedness. It is the moral force of this ideal that creates nations.

We must educate the country from this very moment in a way so that the people may realize the significance of a republic and a federation. We may postpone it for the future only at the risk of a great national calamity. We therefore appeal to the Congress delegates to define Swaraj as a Federated Republic of the United States of India.

We also appeal to the delegates of this Congress to delete the words "by peaceful and legitimate means" from the Congress creed, so that men holding every shade of opinion may have no difficulty in joining the only national organization in the country, though for the present it may be retained as a part of the actual program of Congress work. Our time is short and we cannot dilate upon this point at any length, but we only say that means are after all means and our object and means should not be confounded with each other.

We are further of opinion that mere changing of the creed and passing of resolutions would not bring us independence. We therefore request the representatives of our nation to engage the whole strength and the whole resources of the Congress in organizing a band for national workers who will devote all their time and all their energy in the service of their motherland and who must be ready to suffer and even be ready to sacrifice their lives for the national cause. When the Congress is backed by an organization of this kind then and then alone will the Congress have any strength and only then can we expect the voice of the Congress to be respected.

The other items in our program should be:

(1)   Boycott of British goods.

(2)   Establishment or helping in the establishment of factories and cottage industries on strictly co-operative basis.

(3)   Helping the laborers and peasants of our land in obtaining their grievances redressed and organizing them for their own economic good and moral prosperity.

(4)   And finally to organize a federation of all the Asiatic races in the immediate future.

I know that this "appeal to the nation" has been before the public for some time. It contains nothing new. Nevertheless, it represents the views not merely of the signatories but of a large number of educated Indians. It will not therefore be a waste of energy to examine the contents....

[1]July 17, 1924.

11.9   MAHATMA GANDHI ("MEANS AND ENDS," 1909–1947)

Your belief that there is no connection between the means and the end is a great mistake. Through that mistake even men who have been considered religious have committed grievous crimes. Your reasoning is the same as saying that we can get a rose through planting a noxious weed. If I want to cross the ocean, I can do so only by means of a vessel; if I were to use a cart for that purpose, both the cart and I would soon find the bottom. "As is the God, so is the votary" is a maxim worth considering. Its meaning has been distorted and men have gone astray. The means may be likened to a seed, the end to a tree; and there is just the same inviolable connection between the means and the end as there is between the seed and the tree. I am not likely to obtain the result flowing from the worship of God by laying myself prostrate before Satan. If, therefore, anyone were to say: "I want to worship God; it does not matter that I do so by means

of Satan," it would be set down as ignorant folly. We reap exactly as we sow.

Hind Swaraj, or *India Home Rule*, 1909

They say "means are after all means." I would say "means are after all everything." As the means so the end. There is no wall of separation between means and end. Indeed the Creator has given us control (and that too very limited) over means, none over the end. Realization of the goal is in exact proportion to that of the means. This is a proposition that admits of no exception.

Young India, July 17, 1924

I do not believe in short-violent-cuts to success.... However much I may sympathize with and admire worthy motives, I am an uncompromising opponent of violent methods even to serve the noblest of causes. There is, therefore, really no meeting-ground between the school of violence and myself. But my creed of nonviolence not only does not preclude me but compels me even to associate with anarchists and all those who believe in violence. But that association is always with the sole object of weaning them from what appears to me their error. For experience convinces me that permanent good can never be the outcome of untruth and violence. Even if my belief is a fond delusion, it will be admitted that it is a fascinating delusion.

Young India, December 11, 1924

Means and end are convertible terms in my philosophy of life.

Young India, December 26, 1924

... I do suggest that the doctrine [of nonviolence] holds good also as between States and States. I know that I am treading on delicate ground if I refer to the late war. But I fear I must in order to make the position clear. It was a war of aggrandizement, as I have understood, on either part. It was a war for dividing the spoils of the exploitation of weaker races — otherwise euphemistically called the world commerce.... It would be found that

before general disarmament in Europe commences, as it must some day, unless Europe
is to commit suicide, some nation will have
to dare to disarm herself and take large risks.
The level of nonviolence in that nation, if that
event happily comes to pass, will naturally
have risen so high as to command universal
respect. Her judgments will be unerring, her
decisions firm, her capacity for heroic self-sacrifice will be great, and she will want to live as
much for other nations as for herself.

Young India, October 8, 1925

Ahimsä and Truth are so intertwined that it
is practically impossible to disentangle and
separate them. They are like the two sides of
a coin or rather a smooth unstamped metal-
lic disc. Who can say, which is the obverse,
and which the reverse? Nevertheless, *ahimsä*
is the means; Truth is the end. Means to be
means must always be within our reach, and
so *ahimsä* is our supreme duty. If we take care
of the means, we are bound to reach the end
sooner or later. When once we have grasped
this point final victory is beyond question.
Whatever difficulties we encounter, whatever
apparent reverses we sustain, we may not give
up the quest for Truth which alone is being
God Himself.

Yeranda Mandir, 1935

Socialism is a beautiful word and, so far as
I am aware, in socialism all the members of
society are equal — none low, none high.
In the individual body, the head is not high
because it is the top of the body, nor are the
soles of the feet low because they touch the
earth. Even as members of the individual body
are equal, so are the members of society. This
is socialism.

In it the prince and the peasant, the wealthy
and the poor, the employer and the employee
are all on the same level. In terms of religion,
there is no duality in socialism. It is all unity.
Looking at society all the world over, there is
nothing but duality or plurality. Unity is con-
spicuous by its absence.... In the unity of my
conception there is perfect unity in the plurality of designs.

In order to reach this state, we may not look
on things philosophically and say that we
need not make a move until all are converted
to socialism. Without changing our life we
may go on giving addresses, forming parties
and hawk-like seize the game when it comes
our way. This is no socialism. The more we
treat it as game to be seized, the farther it
must recede from us.

Socialism begins with the first convert. If
there is one such you can add zeros to the
one and the first zero will account for ten and
every addition will account for ten times the
previous number. If, however, the beginner
is a zero, in other words, no one makes the
beginning, multiplicity of zeros will also produce zero value. Time and paper occupied in
writing zeros will be so much waste.

This socialism is as pure as crystal. It, therefore, requires crystal-like means to achieve it.
Impure means result in an impure end. Hence
the prince and the peasant will not be equaled
by cutting off the prince's head, nor can the
process of cutting off equalize the employer
and the employed. One cannot reach truth by
untruthfulness. Truthful conduct alone can
reach truth. Are not nonviolence and truth
twins? The answer is an emphatic "No." Non-
violence is embedded in truth and vice versa.
Hence has it been said that they are faces of
the same coin. Either is inseparable from the
other. Read the coin either way—the spelling of words will be different; the value is the
same. This blessed state is unattainable without perfect purity. Harbor impurity of mind
or body and you have untruth and violence
in you.

Therefore only truthful, nonviolent and pure-
hearted socialists will be able to establish a
socialistic society in India and the world.

Harijan, July 1947

11.10 MAHATMA GANDHI ("EQUAL DISTRIBUTION THROUGH NONVIOLENCE," 1940)

In last week's article on the Constructive Program I mentioned equal distribution of wealth
as one of the 13 items.

The real implication of equal distribution is that each man shall have the wherewithal to supply all his natural needs and no more. For example, if one man has a weak digestion and requires only a quarter of a pound of flour for his bread and another needs a pound, both should be in a position to satisfy their wants. To bring this ideal into being the entire social order has got to be reconstructed. A society based on non-violence cannot nurture any other ideal. We may not perhaps be able to realize the goal, but we must bear it in mind and work unceasingly to near it. To the same extent as we progress towards our goal we shall find contentment and happiness, and to that extent too shall we have contributed towards the bringing into being of a non-violent society.

It is perfectly possible for an individual to adopt this way of life without having to wait for others to do so. And if an individual can observe a certain rule of conduct, it follows that a group of individuals can do likewise. It is necessary for me to emphasize the fact that no one need wait for anyone else in order to adopt a right course. Men generally hesitate to make a beginning if they feel that the objective cannot be had in its entirety. Such an attitude of mind is in reality a bar to progress.

Now let us consider how equal distribution can be brought about through non-violence. The first step towards it is for him who has made this ideal part of his being to bring about the necessary changes in his personal life. He would reduce his wants to a minimum, bearing in mind the poverty of India. His earnings would be free of dishonesty. The desire for speculation would be renounced. His habitation would be in keeping with the new mode of life. There would be self-restraint exercised in every sphere of life. When he has done all that is possible in his own life, then only will he be in a position to preach this ideal among his associates and neighbors.

Indeed at the root of this doctrine of equal distribution must lie that of the trusteeship of the wealthy for the superfluous wealth possessed by them. For according to the doctrine they may not possess a rupee more than their neighbors. How is this to be brought about? Nonviolently? Or should the wealthy be dispossessed of their possessions? To do this we would naturally have to resort to violence. This violent action cannot benefit society.

Society will be the poorer, for it will lose the gifts of a man who knows how to accumulate wealth. Therefore the nonviolent way is evidently superior. The rich man will be left in possession of his wealth, of which he will use what he reasonably requires for his personal needs and will act as a trustee for the remainder to be used for the society. In this argument honesty on the part of the trustee is assumed.

As soon as a man looks upon himself as a servant of society, earns for its sake, spends for its benefit, then purity enters into his earnings and there is *ahimsa* in his venture. Moreover, if men's minds turn towards this way of life, there will come about a peaceful revolution in society, and that without any bitterness.

It may be asked whether history at any time records such a change in human nature. Such changes have certainly taken place in individuals. One may not perhaps be able to point to them in a whole society. But this only means that up till now there has never been an experiment on a large scale in nonviolence. Somehow or other the wrong belief has taken possession of us that *ahimsa* is pre-eminently a weapon for individuals and its use should therefore be limited to that sphere. In fact this is not the case. *Ahimsa* is definitely an attribute of society. To convince people of this truth is at once my effort and my experiment. In this age of wonders no one will say that a thing or idea is worthless because it is new. To say it is impossible because it is difficult is again not in consonance with the spirit of the age. Things undreamt of are daily being seen, the impossible is ever becoming possible. We are constantly being astonished these days at the amazing discoveries in the field of violence. But I maintain that far more undreamt of and seemingly impossible discoveries will be made in the field of nonviolence. The history of religion is full of such examples. To try to root out religion itself from society is a wild goose chase. And were such an attempt to succeed, it would mean the destruction of society. Superstition, evil customs and other imperfections creep in from age to age and mar religion for the time being. They come and go. But religion itself remains, because the existence of the world in a broad sense depends on religion. The ultimate definition of religion may be said to be obedience to the law of God. God and His law are synonymous terms. Therefore God signifies an unchanging and living law. No one has ever really found Him. But *avatars* and prophets have, by means of their *tapasya*, given to mankind a faint glimpse of the eternal Law.

If, however, in spite of the utmost effort, the rich do not become guardians of the poor in the sense of the term and the latter are more and more crushed and die of hunger, what is to be done? In trying to find the solution to this riddle I have lighted on nonviolent non-co-operation and civil disobedience as the right and infallible means. The rich cannot accumulate wealth without the co-operation of the poor in society. Man has been conversant with violence from the beginning, for he has inherited this strength from the animal in nature. It was only when he rose from the state of a quadruped (animal) to that of a biped (man) that the knowledge of the strength of *ahimsa* entered into his soul. This knowledge has grown within him slowly but surely. If this knowledge were to penetrate to and spread amongst the poor, they would become strong and would learn how to free themselves by means of nonviolence from the crushing inequalities which have brought them to the verge of starvation.

I scarcely need to write anything about non-co-operation and civil disobedience, for the readers of *Harijanbandhu* are familiar with these and their working.

Equal Distribution

Harijanbandhu, 24 Aug. 1940
Harijan, 25 Aug. 1940

11.11   SATI' AL-HUSRI ("MUSLIM UNITY AND ARAB UNITY," 1944)

I have read and heard many opinions and observations concerning Muslim unity and Arab unity, and which is to be preferred. I have been receiving for some time now various questions concerning this matter; Why, it is asked, are you interested in Arab unity, and why do you neglect Muslim unity? Do you not see that the goal of Muslim unity is higher than the goal of Arab unity, and that the power generated by Muslim union would be greater than that generated by Arab union? Do you not agree that religious

feeling in the East is much stronger than national feeling? Why, then, do you want us to neglect the exploitation of this powerful feeling and to spend our energies in order to strengthen a weak feeling? Do you believe that the variety of languages will prevent the union of the Muslims? Do you not notice that the principles of communism, socialism, Freemasonry, and other systems unite people, of different languages, races, countries, and climate; that none of these differences have prevented them from coming to understanding, from drawing nearer to one another, and from agreeing on one plan and one creed? Do you not know that every Muslim in Syria, Egypt, or Iraq believes that the Indian Muslim, the Japanese Muslim, or the European Muslim is as much his brother as the Muslim with whom he lives side by side? Whence, then, the impossibility of realizing Muslim union? Some say that Muslim unity is more powerful than any other and that its realization is easier than the realization of any other. What do you say to this? Some pretend, mistakenly, that the idea of Arab union is a plot the aim of which is to prevent the spread of the idea of Muslim union, in order to isolate some of the countries of the Muslim world and facilitate their continued subjugation. What is your opinion of this allegation?

I have heard and read, and I still hear and read, many similar questions which occur in conversations, in private letters, or in open letters. I have therefore thought to devote this essay to the full discussion of these problems and to the frank explanation of my view concerning them.

I think that the essential point which has to be studied and solved when deciding which to prefer, Muslim unity or Arab unity, may be summarized as follows: Is Muslim unity a reasonable hope capable of realization? Or is it a utopian dream incapable of realization? And assuming the first alternative, is its realization easier or more difficult than the realization of Arab unity? Does one of these two schemes exclude the other? And is there a way of realizing Muslim unity without realizing Arab unity? When we think about such questions and analyze them, we have, in the first place, to define clearly what we mean by Muslim unity and by Arab unity and to delimit without any ambiguity the use of the two expressions.

It goes without saying that Arab unity requires the creation of a political union of the different Arab countries, the inhabitants of which speak Arabic. As for Muslim unity, that naturally requires the creation of a political union of the different Muslim countries, the inhabitants of which profess the Muslim religion, regardless of the variety of their languages and races. It is also well known that the Muslim world includes the Arab countries, Turkey, Iran, Afghanistan, Turkestan, parts of India, the East Indies, the Caucasus, North Africa, as well as parts of central Africa, without considering a few scattered units in Europe and Asia, as in Albania, Yugoslavia, Poland, China, and Japan. Further, there is no need to show that the Arab countries occupy the central portion of this far-flung world.

Whoever will examine these evident facts and picture the map of the Muslim world, noticing the position of the Arab world within it, will have to concede that Arab unity is much easier to bring about than Muslim unity, and that this latter is not capable of realization, assuming that it can be realized, except through Arab unity. It is not possible for any sane person to imagine union among Cairo, Baghdad, Tehran, Kabul, Haiderabad, and Bukhara, or Kashgar, Persia, and Timbuctoo, without there being a union among Cairo, Baghdad, Damascus, Mecca, and Tunis. It is not possible for any sane person to conceive the possibility of union among Turks, Arabs, Persians, Malayans, and Negroes, while denying unity to the Arabs themselves. If, contrary to fact, the Arab world were more extensive and wider than the Muslim world, it would have been possible to imagine a Muslim union without Arab union, and it would have been permissible to say that Muslim union is easier to realize than Arab union. But as the position is the exact opposite, there is no logical scope whatever for such statements and speculations. We must not forget this truth when we think and speak concerning Muslim unity and Arab unity. The idea of Muslim unity is, it is true, wider and more inclusive than the concept of Arab unity, but it is not possible to advocate Muslim unity without advocating Arab unity. We have, therefore, the right to assert that whoever opposes Arab unity also opposes Muslim unity. As for him who opposes Arab unity, in the name of Muslim unity or for the sake of Muslim unity, he contradicts the simplest necessities of reason and logic.

Having established this truth, to disagree with which is not logically possible, we ought to notice another truth, which is no less important. We must not forget that the expression "unity," in this context, means political unity and we must constantly remember that the concept of Islamic unity greatly differs from that of Muslim brotherhood. Unity is one thing and affection another, political unity is one thing and agreement on a certain principle another. To advocate Muslim unity, therefore, is different from advocating the improvement of conditions in Islam and different also from advocating an increase in understanding, in affection, and in cooperation among Muslims. We can therefore say that he who talks about the principle of Muslim brotherhood, and discusses the benefits of understanding among the Muslims, does not prove that Muslim unity is possible. Contrariwise, he who denies the possibility of realizing Muslim unity does not deny the principle of Muslim brotherhood or oppose the efforts toward the awakening of the Muslims and understanding among them. What may be said concerning the ideal of brotherhood is not sufficient proof of the possibility of realizing Muslim unity. Further, it is not intelligent or logical to prove the possibility of realizing Muslim unity by quoting the example of Freemasonry or socialism or communism, because the Freemasons do not constitute a political unity and the socialist parties in the different European countries have not combined to form a new state. Even communism itself has not formed a new state, but has taken the place of the tsarist Russian state. We have, therefore, to distinguish quite clearly between the question of Muslim brotherhood and that of Muslim unity, and we must consider directly whether or not it is possible to realize Muslim unity in the political sense.

If we cast a general glance at history and review the influence of religions over the formation of political units, we find that the world religions have not been able to unify peoples speaking different languages, except in the Middle Ages, and that only in limited areas and for a short time. The political unity which the Christian church sought to bring about did not at any time merge the Orthodox world with the Catholic. Neither did the political unity which the papacy tried to bring about in the Catholic world last for any length of time. So it was also in the Muslim world; the political unity which existed at the beginning of its life was not able to withstand the changes of circumstance for any length of time. Even the Abbasid caliphate, at the height of its power and glory, could not unite all the Muslims under its political banner. Similarly, the lands ruled by this caliphate did not effectively preserve their political unity for very long. Nor was it long after the founding of the caliphate that its control over some of the provinces became symbolic rather than real; it could not prevent the secession of these provinces and their transformation into independent political units. It deserves to be mentioned in this connection that the spread of the Muslim religion in some areas took place after the Muslim caliphate lost effectively unity and real power, so much so that in some countries Islam spread in a manner independent of the political authority, at the hands of missionary tradesmen, holy men, and dervishes. In short, the Muslim world, within its present extensive limits, never at any time formed a political unity. If their political unity could not be realized in past centuries, when social life was simple and political relations were primitive, when religious customs controlled every aspect of behavior and thought, it will not be possible to realize it in this century, when social life has became complicated, political problems have become intractable, and science and technology have liberated themselves from the control of tradition and religious beliefs.

I know that what I have stated here will displease many doctors of Islam; I know that the indications of history which I have set out above will have no influence over the beliefs of a great many of the men of religion, because they have been accustomed to discuss these matters without paying heed to historical facts or to the geographical picture; nor are they used to distinguishing between the meaning of religious brotherhood and the meaning of political ties. They have been accustomed to confuse the principles of Islamic brotherhood, in its moral sense, and the idea of Islamic unity, in its political sense. I think it useless to try to persuade these people of the falsity of their beliefs, but I think it necessary to ask them to remember what reason and logic require in this respect. Let them maintain their belief in the possibility of realizing Islamic unity, but let them at the same time agree to the necessity of furthering Arab unity, at least as one stage toward the realization of the Islamic unity in which they believe. In any event, let them not oppose the efforts which are being made to bring about Arab unity, on the pretext of serving the Islamic unity which they desire. I repeat here what I have written above: Whoever opposes Arab unity, on the pretext of Muslim unity, contradicts the simplest requirements of reason and logic, and I unhesitatingly say that to contradict logic to this extent can be the result only of deceit or of deception. The deceit is that of some separatists who dislike the awakening of the Arab nation and try to arouse religious feeling against the idea of Arab unity, and the deception is that of the simple-minded, who incline to believe whatever is said to them in the name of religion, without realizing what hidden purposes might lurk behind the speeches. I therefore regard it as my duty to draw the attention of all the Muslim Arabs to this important matter and I ask them not to be deceived by the myths of the separatists on this chapter.

Perhaps the strangest and most misleading views that have been expressed regarding Arab unity and Islamic unity are the views of those who say that the idea of Arab unity was created to combat Islamic unity in order to isolate some Islamic countries, the better to exercise continuous power over them. I cannot imagine a view further removed from the realities of history and politics or more contradictory to the laws of reason and logic. The details I have mentioned above concerning the relation of Muslim unity to Arab unity are sufficient, basically, to refute such allegations. Yet I think it advisable to add to these details some observations for further proof and clarity. It cannot be denied that the British, more than any other state, have humored and indulged the Arab movement. This is only because they are more practiced in politics and quicker to understand the psychology of nations and the realities of social life. Before anybody else they realized the hidden powers lying in the Arab idea, and thought it wise, therefore, to humor it somewhat, instead of directly opposing it. This was in order to preserve themselves against the harm they might sustain through it and to make it more advantageous to their interests.

We must understand that British policy is a practical policy, changing with circumstances and always making use of opportunities. We must not forget that it was Great Britain who, many times, saved the Ottoman state, then the depository of the Islamic caliphate, from Russian domination. She it was who halted Egyptian armies in the heart of Anatolia to save the seat of the Muslim caliphate from these victorious troops, and she it was who opposed the union of Egypt with Syria at the time of Muhammad Ali. Whoever, then, charges that the idea of Arab unity is a foreign plot utters a greater falsehood than any that has ever been uttered, and he is the victim of the greatest of deceptions. We must know full well that the idea of Arab unity is a natural idea. It has not been artificially started. It is a natural consequence of the existence of the Arab nation itself. It is a social force drawing its vitality from the life of the Arabic language, from the history of the Arab nation, and from the connectedness of the Arab countries. No one can logically pretend that it is the British who created the idea of Arab unity, unless he can prove that it is the British who have created the Arabic language, originating the history of the Arab nation and putting together the geography of the Arab countries. The idea of Arab unity is a natural concept springing from the depths of social nature and not from the artificial views which can be invented by individuals or by states. It remained latent, like many natural and social forces, for many centuries, as a result of many historical factors which cannot be analyzed here. But everything indicates that this period is now at an end, that the movement has come into the open and will manifest itself with ever-increasing power. It will, without any doubt, spread all over the Arab countries, to whom it will bring back their ancient glory and primeval youth; it will indeed bring back what is most fertile, most powerful, and highest in these countries. This ought to be the faith of the enlightened among the speakers of the *dad*.

11.12 HO CHI MINH (DECLARATION OF INDEPENDENCE OF THE DEMOCRATIC REPUBLIC OF VIETNAM, 1945)[1]

All men are created equal; they are endowed by their Creator with certain unalienable Rights; among these are Life, Liberty, and the pursuit of Happiness.

This immortal statement was made in the Declaration of Independence of the United States of America in 1776. In a broader sense, this means: All the peoples on the earth are equal from birth, all the peoples have a right to live, to be happy and free.

The Declaration of the French Revolution made in 1791 on the Rights of Man and the Citizen also states: "All men are born free and with equal rights, and must always remain free and have equal rights."

Those are undeniable truths.

Nevertheless, for more than eighty years, the French imperialists, abusing the standard of Liberty, Equality, and Fraternity, have violated our Fatherland and oppressed our fellow citizens. They have acted contrary to the ideals of humanity and justice.

In the field of politics, they have deprived our people of every democratic liberty.

They have enforced inhuman laws; they have set up three distinct political regimes in the North, the Center, and the South of Viet-

Nam in order to wreck our national unity and prevent our people from being united.

They have built more prisons than schools. They have mercilessly slain our patriots; they have drowned our uprisings in rivers of blood.

They have fettered public opinion; they have practiced obscurantism against our people.

To weaken our race they have forced us to use opium and alcohol.

In the field of economics, they have fleeced us to the backbone, impoverished our people and devastated our land.

They have robbed us of our rice fields, our mines, our forests, and our raw materials. They have monopolized the issuing of bank notes and the export trade.

They have invented numerous unjustifiable taxes and reduced our people, especially our peasantry, to a state of extreme poverty.

They have hampered the prospering of our national bourgeoisie; they have mercilessly exploited our workers.

In the autumn of 1940, when the Japanese fascists violated Indochina's territory to establish new bases in their fight against the Allies, the French imperialists went down on their bended knees and handed over our country to them.

Thus, from that date, our people were subjected to the double yoke of the French and the Japanese. Their sufferings and miseries increased. The result was that, from the end of last year to the beginning of this year, from Quang Tri Province to the North of Viet-Nam, more than two million of our fellow citizens died from starvation. On March 9 [1945], the French troops were disarmed by the Japanese. The French colonialists either fled or surrendered, showing that not only were they incapable of "protecting" us, but that, in the span of five years, they had twice sold our country to the Japanese.

On several occasions before March 9, the Viet Minh League urged the French to ally themselves with it against the Japanese. Instead of agreeing to this proposal, the French colonialists so intensified their terrorist activities against the Viet Minh members that before fleeing they massacred a great number of our political prisoners detained at Yen Bay and Cao Bang.

Notwithstanding all this, our fellow citizens have always manifested toward the French a tolerant and humane attitude. Even after the Japanese *Putsch* of March, 1945, the Viet Minh League helped many Frenchmen to cross the frontier, rescued some of them from Japanese jails, and protected French lives and property.

From the autumn of 1940, our country had in fact ceased to be a French colony and had become a Japanese possession.

After the Japanese had surrendered to the Allies, our whole people rose to regain our national sovereignty and to found the Democratic Republic of Viet-Nam.

The truth is that we have wrested our independence from the Japanese and not from the French.

The French have fled, the Japanese have capitulated, Emperor Bao Dai has abdicated. Our people have broken the chains which for nearly a century have fettered them and have won independence for the Fatherland. Our people at the same time have overthrown the monarchic regime that has reigned supreme for dozens of centuries. In its place has been established the present Democratic Republic....

[1] September 2, 1945.

11.13 KWAME NKRUMAH (SPEECH ON DECOLONIZATION AT THE UNITED NATIONS, 1960)

Mr. President, Distinguished Delegates:

The great tide of history flows and as it flows it carries to the shores of reality the stubborn facts of life and man's relations, one with another. One cardinal fact of our time is the momentous impact of Africa's awakening upon the modern world. The flowing tide of African nationalism sweeps everything before it and constitutes a challenge to the colonial powers to make a just restitution for the years of injustice and crime committed against our continent.

But Africa does not seek vengeance. It is against her very nature to harbor malice. Over two hundred millions of our people cry out with one voice of tremendous power — and what do we say? We do not ask for death for our oppressors, we do not pronounce wishes of ill-fate for our slave-masters, we make an assertion of a just and positive demand. Our voice booms across the oceans and mountains, over the hills and valleys, in the desert places and through the vast expanse of mankind's habitation, and it calls out for the freedom of Africa. Africa wants her freedom, Africa must be free. It is a simple call, but it is also a signal lighting a red warning to those who would tend to ignore it.

For years and years Africa has been the footstool of colonialism and imperialism, exploitation and degradation. From the north to the south, from the east to the west, her sons languished in the chains of slavery and humiliation, and Africa's exploiters and self-appointed controllers of her destiny strode across our land with incredible inhumanity, without mercy, without shame, and without honor. Those days are gone and gone for ever, and now I, an African, stand before this august assembly of the United Nations and speak with a voice of peace and freedom, proclaiming to the world the dawn of a new era.

Mr. President, distinguished delegates, I wish to thank the General Assembly sincerely for this opportunity of addressing you. Let me say here and now that our tribulations and suffering harden and steel us, making us a bastion of indomitable courage, and fortifying our iron determination to smash our chains.

I look upon the United Nations as the only organization that holds out any hope for the future of mankind. Mr. President, distinguished delegates, cast your eyes across Africa's. The colonialists and imperialists are still there. In this twentieth century of enlightenment, some nations still extol the vain glories of colonialism and imperialism. As long as a single foot of African soil remains under foreign domination, the world shall know no peace. The United Nations must therefore face up to its responsibilities, and ask those who would bury their heads like the proverbial ostrich in their imperialist sands, to pull their heads out and look at the blazing African sun now traveling across the sky of Africa's redemption. The United Nations must call upon all nations that have colonies in Africa

to grant complete independence to the territories still under their control....

11.14 FRANTZ FANON (*THE WRETCHED OF THE EARTH*, 1963)

Concerning Violence

... Decolonization, which sets out to change the order of the world, is, obviously, a program of complete disorder. But it cannot come as a result of magical practices, or of a natural shock, or of a friendly understanding. Decolonization, as we know, is a historical process: that is to say that it cannot be understood, it cannot become intelligible nor clear to itself except in the exact measure that we can discern the movements which give it historical form and content. Decolonization is the meeting of two forces, opposed to each other by their very nature, which in fact owe their originality to that sort of sub-stantification which results from and is nourished by the situation in the colonies. Their first encounter was marked by violence and their existence together — that is to say the exploitation of the native by the settler — was carried on by dint of a great array of bayonets and cannons. The settler and the native are old acquaintances. In fact, the settler is right when he speaks of knowing "them" well. For it is the settler who has brought the native into existence and who perpetuates his existence. The settler owes the fact of his very existence, that is to say, his property, to the colonial system....

The naked truth of decolonization evokes for us the searing bullets and bloodstained knives which emanate from it. For if the last shall be first, this will only come to pass after a murderous and decisive struggle between the two protagonists. That affirmed intention to place the last at the head of things, and to make them climb at a pace (too quickly, some say) the well-known steps which characterize an organized society, can only triumph if we use all means to turn the scale, including, of course, that of violence.

You do not turn any society, however primitive it may be, upside down with such a program if you have not decided from the very beginning, that is to say from the actual formulation of that program, to overcome all the obstacles that you will come across in so doing. The native who decides to put the program into practice, and to become its moving force, is ready for violence at all times. From birth it is clear to him that this narrow world, strewn with prohibitions, can only be called in question by absolute violence.

The colonial world is a world divided into compartments. It is probably unnecessary to recall the existence of native quarters and European quarters, of schools for natives and schools for Europeans; in the same way we need not recall apartheid in South Africa. Yet, if we examine closely this system of compartments, we will at least be able to reveal the lines of force it implies. This approach to the colonial world, its ordering and its geographical layout will allow us to mark out the lines on which a decolonized society will be reorganized.

The colonial world is a world cut in two. The dividing line, the frontiers are shown by barracks and police stations. In the colonies it is the policeman and the soldier who are the official, instituted go-betweens, the spokesmen of the settler and his rule of oppression. In capitalist societies the educational system, whether lay or clerical, the structure of moral reflexes handed down from father to son, the exemplary honesty of workers who are given a medal after fifty years of good and loyal service, and the affection which springs from harmonious relations and good behavior — all these aesthetic expressions of respect for the established order serve to create around the exploited person an atmosphere of submission and of inhibition which lightens the task of policing considerably. In the capitalist countries a multitude of moral teachers, counselors and "bewilderers" separate the exploited from those in power. In the colonial countries, on the contrary, the policeman and the soldier, by their immediate presence and their frequent and direct action maintain contact with the native and advise him by means of rifle butts and napalm not to budge. It is obvious here that the agents of government speak the language of pure force. The intermediary does not lighten the oppression, nor seek to hide the domination; he shows them up and puts them into practice with the clear conscience of an upholder of the peace; yet he is the bringer of violence into the home and into the mind of the native.

The zone where the natives live is not complementary to the zone inhabited by the settlers. The two zones are opposed, but not in the service of a higher unity. Obedient to the rules of pure Aristotelian logic, they both follow the principle of reciprocal exclusivity. No conciliation is possible, for of the two terms, one is superfluous. The settlers' town is a strongly built town, all made of stone and steel. It is a brightly lit town; the streets are covered with asphalt, and the garbage cans swallow all the leavings, unseen, unknown and hardly thought about. The settler's feet are never visible, except perhaps in the sea; but there you're never close enough to see them. His feet are protected by strong shoes although the streets of his town are clean and even, with no holes or stones. The settler's town is a well-fed town, an easygoing town; its belly is always full of good things. The settlers' town is a town of white people, of foreigners.

The town belonging to the colonized people, or at least the native town, the Negro village, the medina, the reservation, is a place of ill fame, peopled by men of evil repute. They are born there, it matters little where or how; they die there, it matters not where, nor how. It is a world without spaciousness; men live there on top of each other, and their huts are built one on top of the other. The native town is a hungry town, starved of bread, of meat, of shoes, of coal, of light. The native town is a crouching village, a town on its knees, a town wallowing in the mire. It is a town of niggers and dirty Arabs. The look that the native turns on the settler's town is a look of lust, a look of envy; it expresses his dreams of possession — all manner of possession: to sit at the settler's table, to sleep in the settler's bed, with his wife if possible. The colonized man is an envious man. And this the settler knows very well; when their glances meet he ascertains bitterly, always on the defensive, "They want to take our place." It is true, for there is no native who does not dream at least once a day of setting himself up in the settler's place.

This world divided into compartments, this world cut in two is inhabited by two different species. The originality of the colonial context is that economic reality, inequality, and the immense difference of ways of life never come to mask the human realities. When you examine at close quarters the colonial context, it is evident that what parcels out the world is to begin with the fact of belonging to or not belonging to a given race, a given species. In the colonies the economic substructure is also a superstructure. The cause is the consequence; you are rich because you are white, you are white because you are rich....

The natives' challenge to the colonial world is not a rational confrontation of points of view. It is not a treatise on the universal, but the untidy affirmation of an original idea propounded as an absolute. The colonial world is a Manichean world. It is not enough for the settler to delimit physically, that is to say with the help of the army and the police force, the place of the native. As if to show the totalitarian character of colonial exploitation the settler paints the native as a sort of quintessence of evil. Native society is not simply described as a society lacking in values. It is not enough for the colonist to affirm that those values have disappeared from, or still better never existed in, the colonial world. The native is declared insensible to ethics; he represents not only the absence of values, but also the negation of values. He is, let us dare to admit, the enemy of values, and in this sense he is the absolute evil. He is the corrosive element, destroying all that comes near him; he is the deforming element, disfiguring all that has to do with beauty or morality; he is the depository of maleficent powers, the unconscious and irretrievable instrument of blind forces. Monsieur Meyer could thus state seriously in the French National Assembly that the Republic must not be prostituted by allowing the Algerian people to become part of it. All values, in fact, are irrevocably poisoned and diseased as soon as they are allowed in contact with the colonized race. The customs of the colonized people, their traditions, and their myths — above all, their myths — are the very sign of that poverty of spirit and of their constitutional depravity....

The violence with which the supremacy of white values is affirmed and the aggressiveness which has permeated the victory of these values over the ways of life and of thought of the native mean that, in revenge, the native laughs in mockery when Western values are mentioned in front of him. In the colonial context the settler only ends his work of breaking in the native when the latter admits loudly and intelligibly the supremacy of the white man's values. In the period of decolonization, the colonized masses mock at these very values, insult them, and vomit them up....

The native discovers that his life, his breath, his beating heart are the same as those of the settler. He finds out that the settler's skin is not of any more value than a native's skin; and it must be said that this discovery shakes the world in a very necessary manner. All the new, revolutionary assurance of the native stems from it. For if, in fact, my life is worth as much as the settler's, his glance no longer shrivels me up nor freezes me, and his voice no longer turns me into stone. I am no longer on tenterhooks in his presence; in fact, I don't give a damn for him. Not only does his presence no longer trouble me, but I am already preparing such efficient ambushes for him, that soon there will be no way out but that of flight.

We have said that the colonial context is characterized by the dichotomy which it imposes upon the whole people. Decolonization unifies that people by the radical decision to remove from it its heterogeneity, and by unifying it on a national, sometimes a racial, basis. We know the fierce words of the Senegalese patriots, referring to the maneuvers of their president, Senghor: "We have demanded that the higher posts should be given to Africans; and now Senghor is Africanizing the Europeans." That is to say that the native can see clearly and immediately if decolonization has come to pass or not, for his minimum demands are simply that the last shall be first....

Nowadays a theoretical problem of prime importance is being set, on the historical plane as well as on the level of political tactics, by the liberation of the colonies: when can one affirm that the situation is ripe for a movement of national liberation? In what form should it first be manifested? Because the various means whereby decolonization has been carried out have appeared in many different aspects, reason hesitates and refuses to say which is a true decolonization, and which a false. We shall see that for a man who is in the thick of the fight it is an urgent matter to decide on the means and the tactics to employ: that is to say, how to conduct and organize the movement. If this coherence is not present there is only a blind will toward freedom, with the terribly reactionary risks which it entails.

What are the forces which in the colonial period open up new outlets and engender new aims for the violence of colonized peoples? In the first place there are the political parties and the intellectual or commercial elites. Now, the characteristic feature of certain political structures is that they proclaim abstract principles but refrain from issuing definite commands. The entire action of these nationalist political parties during the colonial period is action of the electoral type: a string of philosophico-political dissertations on the themes of the rights of peoples to self-determination, the rights of man to freedom from hunger and human dignity, and the unceasing affirmation of the principle: "One man, one vote." The national political parties never lay stress upon the necessity of a trial of armed strength, for the good reason that their objective is not the radical overthrowing of the system. Pacifists and legalists, they are in fact partisans of order, the new order —but to the colonialist bourgeoisie they put bluntly enough the demand which to them is the main one: "Give us more power." On the specific question of violence, the elite are ambiguous. They are violent in their words and reformist in their attitudes. When the nationalist political leaders *say* something, they make quite clear that they do not really *think* it....

The peasantry is systematically disregarded for the most part by the propaganda put out by the nationalist parties. And it is clear that in the colonial countries the peasants alone are revolutionary, for they have nothing to lose and everything to gain. The starving peasant, outside the class system, is the first among the exploited to discover that only violence pays. For him there is no compromise, no possible coming to terms; colonization and decolonization are simply a question of relative strength. The exploited man sees that his liberation implies the use of all means, and that of force first and foremost.

At the decisive moment, the colonialist bourgeoisie, which up till then has remained inactive, comes into the field. It introduces that new idea which is in proper parlance a creation of the colonial situation: non-violence. In its simplest form this non-violence signifies to the intellectual and economic elite of the colonized country that the bourgeoisie has the same interests as they and that it is therefore urgent and indispensable to come to terms for the public good. Non-violence is an attempt to settle the colonial problem around a green baize table, before any regrettable act has been performed or irreparable gesture made, before any blood has been shed. But if the masses, without waiting for the chairs to be arranged around the baize table, listen to their own voice and begin committing outrages and setting fire to buildings, the elite and the nationalist bourgeois parties will be seen rushing to the colonialists to exclaim, "This is very serious! We do not know how it will end; we must find a solution — some sort of compromise."

This idea of compromise is very important in the phenomenon of decolonization, for it is very far from being a simple one. Compromise involves the colonial system and the young nationalist bourgeoisie at one and the same time. The partisans of the colonial system discover that the masses may destroy everything. Blown-up bridges, ravaged farms, repressions, and fighting harshly disrupt the economy. Compromise is equally attractive to the nationalist bourgeoisie, who since they are not clearly aware of the possible consequences of the rising storm, are genuinely afraid of being swept away by this huge hurricane and never stop saying to the settlers: ⌈We are still capable of stopping the slaughter; the masses still have confidence in us; act quickly if you do not want to put everything in jeopardy.⌉ One step more, and the leader of the nationalist party keeps his distance with regard to that violence. He loudly proclaims that he has nothing to do with these Mau-Mau, these terrorists, these throat-slitters. At best, he shuts himself off in a no man's land between the terrorists and the settlers and willingly offers his services as go-between; that is to say, that as the settlers cannot discuss terms with these Mau-Mau, he himself will be quite willing to begin negotiations. Thus it is that the rear guard of the national struggle, that very party of people who have never ceased to be on the other side in the fight, find themselves somersaulted into the vanguard of negotiations and compromise — precisely because that party has taken very good care never to break contact with colonialism....

But it so happens that for the colonized people this violence, because it constitutes their only work, invests their characters with positive and creative qualities. ⌈The practice of violence binds them together as a whole, since each individual forms a violent link in the great chain, a part of the great organism of violence which has surged upward in reaction to the settler's violence in the beginning.⌉ The groups recognize each other and the future nation is already indivisible. The armed struggle mobilizes the people; that is to say, it throws them in one way and in one direction.

The⌈ mobilization of the masses, when it arises out of the war of liberation, introduces into each man's consciousness the ideas of a common cause, of a national destiny, and of a collective history.⌉ In the same way the second phase, that of the building-up of the nation, is helped on by the existence of this cement which has been mixed with blood and anger. Thus we come to a fuller appreciation of the originality of the words used in these underdeveloped countries. During the colonial period the people are called upon to fight against oppression; after national liberation, they are called upon to fight against poverty, illiteracy, and underdevelopment.

The struggle, they say, goes on. The people realize that life is an unending contest....

The Pitfalls of National Consciousness

History teaches us clearly that the battle against colonialism does not run straight away along the lines of nationalism. For a very long time the native devotes his energies to ending certain definite abuses: forced labor, corporal punishment, inequality of salaries, limitation of political rights, etc. This right for democracy against the oppression of mankind will slowly leave the confusion of neo-liberal universalism to emerge, sometimes laboriously, as a claim to nationhood. It so happens that the unpreparedness of the educated classes, the lack of practical links between them and the mass of the people, their laziness, and, let it be said, their cowardice at the decisive moment of the struggle will give rise to tragic mishaps.

National consciousness, instead of being the all-embracing crystallization of the innermost hopes of the whole people, instead of being the immediate and most obvious result of the mobilization of the people, will be in any case only an empty shell, a crude and fragile travesty of what it might have been. The faults that we find in it are quite sufficient explanation of the facility with which, when dealing with young and independent nations, the nation is passed over for the race, and the tribe is preferred to the state. These are the cracks in the edifice which show the process of retrogression, that is so harmful and prejudicial to national effort and national unity. We shall see that such retrograde steps with all the weaknesses and serious dangers that they entail are the historical result of the incapacity of the national middle class to rationalize popular action, that is to say their incapacity to see into the reasons for that action....

The national economy of the period of independence is not set on a new footing. It is still concerned with the groundnut harvest, with the cocoa crop and the olive yield. In the same way there is no change in the marketing of basic products, and not a single industry is set up in the country. We go on sending out raw materials; we go on being Europe's small farmers, who specialize in unfinished products.

Yet the national middle class constantly demands the nationalization of the economy and of the trading sectors. This is because, from their point of view, nationalization does not mean placing the whole economy at the service of the nation and deciding to satisfy the needs of the nation. For them, nationalization does not mean governing the state with regard to the new social relations whose growth it has been decided to encourage. To them, nationalization quite simply means the transfer into native hands of those unfair advantages which are a legacy of the colonial period...

Seen through its eyes, its mission has nothing to do with transforming the nation; it consists, prosaically, of being the transmission line between the nation and a capitalism, rampant though camouflaged, which today puts on the mask of neo-colonialism. The national bourgeoisie will be quite content with the role of the Western bourgeoisie's business agent, and it will play its part without any complexes in a most dignified manner. But this same lucrative role, this cheap-Jack's function, this meanness of outlook and this absence of all ambition symbolize the incapability of the national middle class to fulfill its historic role of bourgeoisie. Here, the dynamic, pioneer aspect, the characteristics of the inventor and of the discoverer of new worlds which are found in all national bourgeoisies are lamentably absent....

The national bourgeoisie turns its back more and more on the interior and on the real facts of its undeveloped country, and tends to look toward the former mother country and the foreign capitalists who count on its obliging compliance. As it does not share its profits with the people, and in no way allows them to enjoy any of the dues that are paid to it by the big foreign companies, it will discover the need for a popular leader to whom will fall the dual role of stabilizing the regime and of perpetuating the domination of the bourgeoisie. The bourgeois dictatorship of underdeveloped countries draws its strength from the existence of a leader. We know that in the well-developed countries the bourgeois dictatorship is the result of the economic power of the bourgeoisie. In the underdeveloped countries on the contrary the leader stands for moral power, in whose shelter the thin and poverty-stricken bourgeoisie of the young nation decides to get rich.

The former colonial power increases its demands, accumulates concessions and guarantees and takes fewer and fewer pains to mask the hold it has over the national government. The people stagnate deplorably in unbearable poverty; slowly they awaken to the unutterable treason of their leaders. This awakening is all the more acute in that the bourgeoisie is incapable of learning its lesson. The distribution of wealth that it effects is not spread out between a great many sectors; it is not ranged among different levels, nor does it set up a hierarchy of half-tones....

There must be an economic program; there must also be a doctrine concerning the division of wealth and social relations. In fact, there must be an idea of man and of the future of humanity; that is to say that no demagogic formula and no collusion with the former occupying power can take the place of a program. The new peoples, unawakened at first but soon becoming more and more clear minded, will make strong demands for this program. The African people and indeed all underdeveloped peoples, contrary to common belief, very quickly build up a social and political consciousness. What can be dangerous is when they reach the stage of social consciousness before the stage of nationalism. If this happens, we find in underdeveloped countries fierce demands for social justice which paradoxically are allied with often primitive tribalism. The underdeveloped peoples behave like starving creatures; this means that the end is very near for those who are having a good time in Africa. Their government will not be able to prolong its own existence indefinitely. A bourgeoisie that provides nationalism alone as food for the masses fails in its mission and gets caught up in a whole series of mishaps. But if nationalism is not made explicit, if it is not enriched and deepened by a very rapid transformation into a consciousness of social and political needs, in other words into humanism, it leads up a blind alley. The bourgeois leaders of underdeveloped countries imprison national consciousness in sterile formalism. It is only when men and women are included on a vast scale in enlightened and fruitful work that form and body are given to that consciousness. Then the flag and the palace where sits the government cease to be the symbols of the nation. The nation deserts these brightly lit, empty shells and takes shelter in the country, where it is given life and dynamic power. The living expression of the nation is the moving consciousness of the whole of the people; it is the coherent enlightened action of men and women....

PART V

*H*uman Rights in the Era of Globalization

INTRODUCTION

The impact of globalization on human rights has provoked heated debates sifnce the end of the cold war, debates well illustrated by the lively exchange between *New York Times* journalist Thomas Friedman and the director of the French monthly periodical *Le Monde Diplomatique*, Ignacio Ramonet. Friedman maintains that poor countries will benefit from greater immersion in the global market, as growing trade reduces poverty, while fostering accountable and transparent institutions. Ramonet rejects Friedman's claim, arguing instead that globalization reflects the self-interest of the wealthiest states at the expense of the poor, leading to dangerous nationalist backlashes.

The debate between Friedman and Ramonet provides a useful introduction to the questions that globalization poses for human rights. Does economic globalization weaken or expand labor rights? Favor or hinder environmental rights? Bring peace or trigger war? Bridge or heighten cultural divisions? Is globalization compatible with security and human rights? The following provides a brief overview of the contending views on these questions, represented by the contribution to Part V.

V.1 THOMAS L. FRIEDMAN AND IGNACIO RAMONET ("DUELING GLOBALIZATIONS," 1999)

DOS CAPITAL

If there can be a statute of limitations on crimes, then surely there must be a statute of limitations on foreign-policy cliches. With that in mind, I hereby declare the "post-Cold War world" over....

Today's globalization system has some very different attributes, rules, incentives, and characteristics, but it is equally influential. The Cold War system was characterized by one overarching feature: division. The world was chopped up, and both threats and opportunities tended to grow out of whom you were divided from. Appropriately, that Cold War system was symbolized by a single image: the Wall. The globalization system also has one overarching characteristic: inte-

gration. Today, both the threats and opportunities facing a country increasingly grow from whom it is connected to. This system is also captured by a single symbol: the World Wide Web. So in the broadest sense, we have gone from a system built around walls to a system increasingly built around networks.

Once a country makes the leap into the system of globalization, its elite begin to internalize this perspective of integration and try to locate themselves within a global context. I was visiting Amman, Jordan, in the summer of 1998 when I met my friend, Rami Khouri, the country's leading political columnist, for coffee at the Hotel Inter-Continental. We sat down, and I asked him what was new. The first thing he said to me was "Jordan was just added to CNN's worldwide weather highlights." What Rami was saying was that it is important for Jordan to know that those institutions that think globally believe it is now worth knowing what the weather is like in Amman. It makes Jordanians feel more important and holds out the hope that they will profit by having more tourists or global investors visiting. The day after seeing Rami I happened to interview Jacob Frenkel, governor of the Bank of Israel and a University of Chicago-trained economist. He remarked to me: "Before, when we talked about macroeconomics, we started by looking at the local markets, local financial system, and the interrelationship between them, and then, as an afterthought, we looked at the international economy. There was a feeling that what we do is primarily our own business and then there are some outlets where we will sell abroad. Now, we reverse the perspective. Let's not ask what markets we should export to after having decided what to produce; rather, let's first study the global framework within which we operate and then decide what to produce. It changes your whole perspective."

Integration has been driven in large part by globalization's defining technologies: computerization, miniaturization, digitization, satellite communications, fiber optics, and the Internet. And that integration, in turn, has led to many other differences between the Cold War and globalization systems.

Unlike the Cold War system, globalization has its own dominant culture, which is why integration tends to be homogenizing. In previous eras, cultural homogenization happened on a regional scale—Romanization of Western Europe and the Mediterranean world, the Islamization of Central Asia, the Middle East, North Africa, and Spain by the Arabs, or the Russification of Eastern and Central Europe, and parts of Eurasia, under the Soviets. Culturally speaking, globalization is largely the spread (for better and for worse) of Americanization — from Big Macs and iMacs to Mickey Mouse....

Thomas L. Friedman

A New Totalitarianism

Friedman notes, and rightly so, that everything is now interdependent and that, at the same time, everything is in conflict. He also observes that globalization embodies (or infects) every trend and phenomenon at work in the world today — whether political, economic, social, cultural, or ecological. But he forgets to remark that there are groups from every nationality, religion, and ethnicity that vigorously oppose the idea of global unification and homogenization.

Furthermore, our author appears incapable of observing that globalization imposes the force of two powerful and contradictory dynamics on the world: fusion and fission. On the one hand, many states seek out alliances. They pursue fusion with others to build institutions, especially economic ones that provide strength — or safety — in numbers. Like the European Union, groups of countries in Asia, Eastern Europe, North Africa, North America, and South America are signing free-trade agreements and reducing tariff barriers to stimulate commerce, as well as reinforcing political and security alliances.

But set against the backdrop of this integration, several multinational communities are falling victim to fission, cracking or imploding into fragments before the astounded eyes of their neighbors. When the three federal states of the Eastern bloc — Czechoslovakia, the USSR, and Yugoslavia — broke apart, they gave birth to some 22 independent states! A veritable sixth continent!

The political consequences have been ghastly. Almost everywhere, the fractures provoked by globalization have reopened old wounds. Borders are increasingly contested, and pockets of minorities give rise to dreams of annexation, secession, and ethnic cleansing. In the Balkans and the Caucasus, these tensions unleashed wars (in Abkhazia, Bosnia, Croatia, Kosovo, Moldova, Nagorno-Karabakh, Slovenia, and South Ossetia)....

Magnates and Misfits

Globalization rests upon two pillars, or paradigms, which influence the way globalizers such as Friedman think. The first pillar is communication. It has tended to replace, little by little, a major driver of the last two centuries: progress. From schools to businesses, from families and law to government, there is now one command: Communicate.

The second pillar is the market. It replaces social cohesion, the idea that a democratic society must function like a clock. In a clock, no piece is unnecessary and all pieces are unified. From this eighteenth-century mechanical metaphor we can derive a modern economic and financial version. From now on, everything must operate according to the criteria of the "master market." Which of our new values are most fundamental? Windfall profits, efficiency, and competitiveness.

In this market-driven, interconnected world, only the strongest survive. Life is a fight, a jungle. Economic and social Darwinism, with its constant calls for competition, natural selection, and adaptation, forces itself on everyone and everything. In this new social order, individuals are divided into "solvent" or "nonsolvent" — i.e., apt to integrate into the market or not. The market offers protection to the solvents only. In this new order, where human solidarity is no longer an imperative, the rest are misfits and outcasts.

Thanks to globalization, only activities possessing four principal attributes thrive — those that are planetary, permanent, immediate, and immaterial in nature. These four characteristics recall the four principal attributes of God Himself. And in truth, globalization is set up to be a kind of modern divine critic, requiring submission, faith, worship, and new rites. The market dictates the Truth, the Beautiful, the Good, and the Just. The "laws" of the market have become a new stone tablet to revere.

Friedman warns us that straying from these laws will bring us to ruin and decay. Thus, like other propagandists of the New Faith, Friedman attempts to convince us that there is one way, and one way alone — the ultraliberal way — to manage economic affairs and, as a consequence, political affairs. For Friedman, the political is in effect the economic, the economic is finance,

and finances are markets. The Bolsheviks said, "All power to the Soviets!" Supporters of globalization, such as Friedman, demand, "All power to the market!" The assertion is so peremptory that globalization has become, with its dogma and high priests, a kind of new totalitarianism.

Ignacio Ramonet

DOS CAPITAL 2.0

Ignacio Ramonet makes several points in his provocative and impassioned anti-globalization screed. Let me try to respond to what I see as the main ones....

Frankly, I can and do make a much stronger case for the downsides of globalization than Ramonet does. I know that globalization is hardly all good, but unlike Ramonet, I am not utterly blind to the new opportunities it creates for people — and I am not just talking about the wealthy few. Ask the high-tech workers in Bangalore, India, or Taiwan, or the Bordeaux region of France, or Finland, or coastal China, or Idaho what they think of the opportunities created by globalization. They are huge beneficiaries of the very market forces that Ramonet decries. Don't they count? What about all the human rights and environmental nongovernmental organizations that have been empowered by the Internet and globalization? Don't they count? Or do only French truck drivers count?

Ramonet says I am "incapable of observing that globalization imposes the force of two powerful contradictory dynamics on the world: fusion and fission." Say what? Why does he think I called my book *The Lexus and the Olive Tree*? It is all about the interaction between what is old and inbred — the quest for community, nation, family, tribe, identity, and one's own olive tree — and the economic pressures of globalization that these aspirations must interact with today, represented by the Lexus. These age-old passions are bumping up against, being squashed by, ripping through, or simply learning to live in balance with globalization.

What Ramonet can accuse me of is a belief that for the moment, the globalization system has been dominating the olive-tree impulses in most places. Many critics have pointed out that my observation that no two countries have ever fought a war against each other while they both had a McDonald's was totally disproved by the war in Kosovo. This is utter nonsense. Kosovo was only a temporary exception that in the end proved my rule. Why did airpower work to bring the Balkan war to a close after only 78 days? Because NATO bombed the Serbian tanks and troops out of Kosovo? No way. Airpower alone worked because NATO bombed the electricity stations, water system, bridges, and economic infrastructure in Belgrade—a modern European city, a majority of whose citizens wanted to be integrated with Europe and the globalization system. The war was won on the power grids of Belgrade, not in the trenches of Kosovo. One of the first things to be reopened in Belgrade was the McDonald's. It turns out in the end the Serbs wanted to wait in line for burgers, not for Kosovo.

Ramonet falls into a trap that often ensnares French intellectuals, and others, who rail against globalization. They assume that the rest of the world hates it as much as they do, and so they are always surprised in the end when the so-called little people are ready to stick with it. My dear Mr. Ramonet, with all due respect to you and Franz Fanon, the fact is the wretched of the earth want to go to Disney World, not to the barricades. They want the Magic Kingdom, not Les Miserables. Just ask them.

Finally, Ramonet says that I believe all the problems of globalization will be solved by the "invisible hand of the market." I have no idea where these quotation marks came from, let alone the thought. It certainly is not from anything I have written. The whole last chapter of my book lays out in broad strokes what I believe governments — the American government in particular — must do to "democratize" globalization, both economically and politically. Do I believe that market forces and the Electronic Herd are very powerful today and can, at times, rival governments? Absolutely. But do I believe that market forces will solve everything? Absolutely not. Ramonet, who

clearly doesn't know a hedge fund from a hedge hog, demonizes markets to an absurd degree. He may think governments are powerless against such monsters, but I do not.

I appreciate the passion of Ramonet's argument, but he confuses my analysis for advocacy. My book is not a tract for or against globalization, and any careful reader will see that. It is a book of reporting about the world we now live in and the dominant international system that is shaping it — a system driven largely by forces of technology that I did not start and cannot stop. Ramonet treats globalization as a choice, and he implicitly wants us to choose something different. That is his politics. I view globalization as a reality, and I want us first to understand that reality and then, by understanding it, figure out how we can get the best out of it and cushion the worst. That is my politics....

Thomas L. Friedman

Let Them Eat Big Macs

It is truly touching when Thomas Friedman says, "The wretched of the earth want to go to Disney World, not to the barricades." Such a sentence deserves a place in posterity alongside Queen Marie-Antoinette's declaration in 1789, when she learned that the people of Paris were revolting and demanding bread: "Let them eat cake!"

My dear Mr. Friedman, do reread the 1999 Human Development Report from the United Nations Development Program. It confirms that 1.3 billion people (or one-quarter of humanity) live on less than one dollar a day. Going to Disney World would probably not displease them, but I suspect they would prefer, first off, to eat well, to have a decent home and decent clothes, to be better educated, and to have a job. To obtain these basic needs, millions of people around the world (their numbers grow more numerous each day) are without a doubt ready to erect barricades and resort to violence.

I deplore this kind of solution as much as Friedman does. But if we are wise, it should never come to that. Rather, why not allocate a miniscule part of the world's wealth to the "wretched of the earth"? If we assigned just 1 percent of this wealth for 20 years to the development of the most unhappy of our human brothers, extreme misery might disappear, and with it, risks of endemic violence.

But globalization is deaf and blind to such considerations — and Friedman knows it. On the contrary, it worsens differences and divides and polarizes societies. In 1960, before globalization, the most fortunate 20 percent of the planet's population were 30 times richer than the poorest 20 percent. In 1997, at the height of globalization, the most fortunate were 74 times richer than the world's poorest! And this gap grows each day. Today, if you add up the gross national products of all the world's underdeveloped countries (with their 600 million inhabitants) they still will not equal the total wealth of the three richest people in the world. I am sure, my dear Mr. Friedman, that those 600 million people have only one thing on their minds: Disney World!

It is true that there is more to globalization than just the downsides, but how can we overlook the fact that during the last 15 years of globalization, per capita income has decreased in more than 80 countries, or in almost half the states of the world? Or that since the fall of communism, when the West supposedly arranged an economic miracle cure for the former Soviet Union — more or less, as Friedman would put it, new McDonald's restaurants — more than 150 million ex-Soviets (out of a population of approximately 290 million) have fallen into poverty?

If you would agree to come down out of the clouds, my dear Mr. Friedman, you could perhaps understand that globaliza-

tion is a symptom of the end of a cycle. It is not only the end of the industrial era (with today's new technology), not only the end of the first capitalist revolution (with the financial revolution), but also the end of an intellectual cycle — the one driven by reason, as the philosophers of the eighteenth century defined it. Reason gave birth to modern politics and sparked the American and French Revolutions. But almost all that modern reason constructed — the state, society, industry, nationalism, socialism — has been profoundly changed. In terms of political philosophy, this transformation captures the enormous significance of globalization. Since ancient times, humanity has known two great organizing principles: the gods, and then reason. From here on out, the market succeeds them both.

Now the triumph of the market and the irresistible expansion of globalization cause me to fear an inevitable showdown between capitalism and democracy. Capitalism inexorably leads to the concentration of wealth and economic power in the hands of a small group. And this in turn leads to a fundamental question: How much redistribution will it take to make the domination of the rich minority acceptable to the majority of the world's population? The problem, my dear Mr. Friedman, is that the market is incapable of responding. All over the world, globalization is destroying the welfare state.

What can we do? How do we keep half of humanity from revolting and choosing violence? I know your response, dear Mr. Friedman: Give them all Big Macs and send them to Disney World!

Ignacio Ramonet

CHAPTER 12

Redefining Rights in the New Millennium

ON LABOR AND DEVELOPMENT RIGHTS

The American economist Milton Friedman, recipient of the Nobel Prize for Economics in 1976, epitomized the position that laissez-faire capitalism and globalization are crucial milestones for the spread of political freedom. In his 1991 address "Economic Freedom, Human Freedom, Political Freedom," he reiterated his view, advanced in *Capitalism and Freedom* (1962, 2002), that "history suggests only that capitalism is a necessary [if not sufficient] condition for political freedom." Reviewing developing economies, he warned that while economic freedom facilitates political freedom, once established, political freedom may succumb to collectivist pressure. In other words, political freedom has a tendency to destroy economic freedom.

From a different perspective on globalization, the American sociologist Charles Tilly argued in "Globalization Threatens Labor Rights" (1995) that because globalization has gradually undermined the capacity of states to monitor and control cross-border financial flows, states are losing the capacity to pursue effective social policies, including the enforcement of labor rights. The availability of low-wage foreign workers and the threat of capital flight have further intensified workers' insecurity, in effect pitting one labor rights community against another. Reaching a similar conclusion, Amnesty International observed in 1998 that "labor rights are human rights," as it sought to promote alliances between labor unions and human rights organizations, to carve a broader space for human rights solidarity against the pressures of competitive economic interests and the prevailing neoliberal economic trends associated with globalization (see Section 12.3).

The Indian economist and Nobel Prize recipient (1998) Amartya Kumar Sen has been a forceful voice against the neoliberal economic position on human and labor rights. Best known for his work on human development theory and welfare economics, he argued in his *Development as Freedom* (1999) that human rights (civil, political, and social rights) are inseparable elements of economic development. Sen offered a concept of human capability based on the premise, for example, that the right to vote is meaningless if the capability to vote (e.g., sufficient education, transportation to polls) does not exist. In other words, government and economic development policies should be evaluated in terms of the material and institutional capability available to citizens in their exercise of universal and indivisible.

12.1 MILTON FRIEDMAN ("ECONOMIC FREEDOM, HUMAN FREEDOM, POLITICAL FREEDOM," 1991)[1]

... In 1962, when ... *Capitalism and Freedom* was published, the general intellectual climate of opinion was very different than it has since become....

In the 1950s and 1960s, socialist thinking was dominant; those of us who rejected that view were regarded as fringe eccentrics. Since then, there has been a reaction against such socialist thinking and a recognition of the importance of private enterprise and of private property. Unfortunately, as I shall note later, the reaction has been more in the climate of opinion than in practice. Talk and rhetoric have been one thing; actual practice has been very different.

What I want to talk about ... is the relationship among economic freedom, human freedom, and political freedom. In *Capitalism and Freedom*, I wrote: "Historical evidence speaks with a single voice on the relation between political freedom and a free market. I know of no example in time or place of a society that has been marked by a large measure of political freedom that has not also used something comparable to a free market to organize the bulk of economic activity" (p. 9). I went on to point out that "history suggests only that capitalism is a necessary condition for political freedom. Clearly it is not a sufficient condition" (p. 10).

Both of those statements remain valid today, thirty years later. Over the centuries many non-free societies have relied on capitalism and yet have enjoyed neither human nor political freedom. Ancient Greece was fundamentally a capitalist society, but it had slaves. The U.S. South before the Civil War is another example of a society with slaves that relied predominantly on private property. Currently, South Africa has relied predominantly on private markets and private enterprise, yet it has not been a free society. Many Latin American countries are in the same position. They have been ruled by an oligarchy, and yet they have employed primarily private markets. So it is clear that capitalism is not a sufficient condition for human or political freedom, though it is a necessary condition.

While experience has not contradicted the statements I made, it has persuaded me that the dichotomy I stressed between economic freedom and political freedom is too simple. Even at this broad level, I am persuaded that it is important to consider a trichotomy: economic freedom, human freedom, and political freedom.

The example that persuaded me that the relationship was less simple than the one I had sketched in *Capitalism and Freedom* is Hong Kong as it developed in the 1950s and especially as it has developed in the period since *Capitalism and Freedom* was written. Hong Kong has been, though unfortunate, as the Mainland communist regime takes over, it will not remain, one of the freest, if not the freest, of countries in the world in every respect but one. Hong Kong has had an extraordinary degree of economic freedom: no tariffs and no import or export quotas, except as we in our wisdom have forced such quotas on Hong Kong in order to protect our industries from its efficiency. (It is truly absurd for the United States to force Hong Kong to limit the output of textiles so that our textile industry will not be bothered. That is no way for a great nation to behave.) Taxes have been very low, 10 to 12% of the national income. (In the United States today, government spending is 43% of the national income.) There are few regulations on business, no price controls, no wage controls.

Hong Kong's completely free economy has achieved marvels. Here is a place with no resources except a magnificent harbor, a small piece of land [with...] a population of 500,000 after World War II that has grown to a population close to six million over ten times as large and at the same time, the standard of life has multiplied more than fourfold. It has been one of the most rapidly growing countries in the world, a remarkable example of what free markets can do if left unrestricted. I may say that Hong Kong is not a place where most of us would want to live. It is not a place where most of the people there want to live. It is very crowded; it is a very small area. If other places would take them, the people would love to go. However, the remarkable thing is that under such adverse circumstances they have done so well.

In addition to economic freedom, Hong Kong has a great deal of human freedom. I have visited many times and I have never seen any evidence of suppression of freedom of speech, freedom of the press, or any other human freedom that we regard as important.

However, in one respect Hong Kong has no freedom whatsoever. It has no political freedom. The Chinese who fled to Hong Kong were not free people. They were refugees from the communist regime and they themselves had been citizens of a regime that was very far from a free society. They did not choose freedom; it was imposed on them. It was imposed on them by outside forces. Hong Kong was governed by officials of the British Colonial Office, not by self chosen representatives. In the past couple of years, in trying to persuade the world that Britain has not done a dastardly deed in turning Hong Kong over to the communists, the British administration has tried to institute a legislative council and to give some evidence of political representation. However, in general, over the whole of that period, there has been essentially no direct political representation.

That brings out an enormous paradox, the one that as I said caused me to rethink the relationship among different kinds of freedom. The British colonies that were given their political freedom after World War II have for the most part destroyed the other freedoms. Similarly, at the very time officials of the British Colonial Office were imposing economic freedom on Hong Kong, at home in Britain a socialist government was imposing socialism on Britain.... It shows how complex the relationship is between economic freedom and political freedom, and human freedom and political freedom. Indeed, it suggests that while economic freedom facilitates political freedom, political freedom, once established, has a tendency to destroy economic freedom.

Consider the example that I believe is most fascinating, India. It was given its political freedom by Britain over forty years ago. It has continued, with rare exceptions, to be a political democracy. It has continued to be a country where people are governed by representatives chosen at the ballot box, but it has had very little economic freedom and very limited human freedom. On the economic side, it has had extensive controls over exports and imports, over foreign exchange, over prices, over wages. There have been some reforms in the past year or so, but until recently you could not establish any kind of enterprise without getting a license from the government. The effect of such centralized control of the economy has been that the standard of life for the great bulk of the Indians is no higher today than it was forty years ago when India was given its political freedom.

The situation is even more extreme if you consider that Hong Kong, which I started with, got zero foreign aid during its growth. India has been a major recipient; it got some $55 billion of foreign aid over the past forty years. It is tempting to say that India failed to grow despite foreign aid. I believe that it was the other way: in part, India failed to grow because of foreign aid. Foreign aid provided the resources that enabled the government to impose the kind of economic policies it did.

What is true for India is true much more broadly. Foreign aid has done far more harm to the countries we have given it to than it has done good. Why? Because in every case, foreign aid has strengthened governments that were already too powerful. Mozambique, Tanzania, and many another African countries testify to the same effect as India.

To come back to Hong Kong, the only reason it did not get its political freedom is because the local people did not want political freedom. They knew very well that that meant the Chinese communists would take them over. In a curious way, the existence of the Chinese communist government was the major protection of the economic and human freedoms that Hong Kong enjoyed. Quite a paradoxical situation.

Hong Kong is by no means unique. Wherever the market plays a significant role, whether you have political freedom or not, human freedoms are more widespread and more extensive than where the market does not play any role. The totalitarian countries completely suppressed the market and also had the least human freedom.

Another fascinating example that brings out the complexity of the situation is Chile. Chile, as you know, was first taken over by Salvador Allende and a socialist group. Allende came into power as a result of an election in which no one of the three major parties was able to get a majority, and subsequent political maneuvering, along with his promise to abide by the constitution. No sooner in office, however, than he reneged on his promise and proceeded to try to convert Chile into a full fledged communist state. The important thing for my purpose is what happened after Allende's policies provoked the military to overthrow him and set up a military junta led by General Pinochet to run the country.

Almost all military juntas are adverse to economic freedom for obvious reasons. The military is organized from the top down: the general tells the colonel, the colonel tells the captain, the captain tells the lieutenant, and so on. A market economy is organized from the bottom up: the consumer tells the retailer, the retailer tells the wholesaler, the wholesaler tells the producer, and the producer delivers. The principles underlying a military organization are precisely the reverse of those underlying a market organization.

Pinochet and the military in Chile were led to adopt free market principles after they took over only because they did not have any other choice. They tried for a while to have military officers run the economy. However, inflation doubled in the first eight or nine months of their regime. When rates of inflation reached 700 to 1,000% they had to do something. By accident, the only group of economists in Chile who were not tainted by a connection with the Allende socialists were the so called Chicago boys. They were called Chicago boys because they consisted almost entirely of economists who had studied at the University of Chicago and had received their Ph.D. degrees at the University of Chicago. They were untainted because the University of Chicago was almost the only institution in the United States at the time in which the

economics department had a strong group of free market economists. So in desperation Pinochet turned to them.

I have nothing good to say about the political regime that Pinochet imposed. It was a terrible political regime. The real miracle of Chile is not how well it has done economically; the real miracle of Chile is that a military junta was willing to go against its principles and support a free market regime designed by principled believers in a free market. The results were spectacular. Inflation came down sharply. After a transitory period of recession and low output that is unavoidable in the course of reversing a strong inflation, output started to expand, and ever since, the Chilean economy has performed better than any other South American economy.

The economic development and the recovery produced by economic freedom in turn promoted the public's desire for a greater degree of political freedom is exactly what happened, if I may jump from one continent to another, in China after 1976 when the regime introduced a greater measure of economic freedom in one sector of the economy, agriculture, with great success. That, too, generated pressure for more political freedom and was one of the major factors underlying the dissatisfaction that led to Tiananmen Square.

In Chile, the drive for political freedom, that was generated by economic freedom and the resulting economic success, ultimately resulted in a referendum that introduced political democracy. Now, at long last, Chile has all three things: political freedom, human freedom and economic freedom. Chile will continue to be an interesting experiment to watch to see whether it can keep all three or whether, now that it has political freedom, that political freedom will tend to be used to destroy or reduce economic freedom.

In order to understand the paradox that economic freedom produces political freedom but political freedom may destroy economic freedom, it is important to recognize that free private markets have a far broader meaning than the usual restriction to narrowly economic transactions. Literally, a market is simply a place where people meet, where people get together to make deals with one another. Every country has a market. At its most extreme totalitarian stage Russia had a market. But there are different kinds of markets. A private market is one in which the people making deals are making them either on their own behalf or as agents for identifiable individuals rather than as agents of governments. In the Russian market, the market existed and deals were being made all over the lot, but people were dealing with one another not on their own behalf, not as representatives for other identifiable individuals, but supposedly as agents for the government, for the public at large. A private market is very different from a government market. In a strictly private market, all the deals are between individuals acting in their own interest or as agents for other identifiable individuals.

Finally, you can have a private market, but it may or may not be a free market The question is whether all the deals are strictly voluntary. In a free private market, all the deals are strictly voluntary. Many of the cases of private markets that I cited before were not cases of free private markets. You have a private market in many of the Latin American countries, but they are not free private markets. You have a private market in India, but it is not a free private market because many voluntary deals are not permitted. An individual can deal with another to exchange a good or service only if he has the permission of the government. I may say a completely free private market exists nowhere in the world. Hong Kong is perhaps the closest approximation to it. However, almost everywhere what you have, at best, is a partly free, largely hampered, private market.

A free private market is a mechanism for achieving voluntary cooperation among people. It applies to any human activity, not simply to economic transactions. We are speaking a language. Where did that language come from? Did some government entity construct the language and instruct people to use it? Was there some government commission that developed the rules of grammar? No, the language we speak developed through a free private market. People com-municated with one another, they wanted to talk with one another, the words they used gradually came to be one thing rather than another, and the grammar came to be one thing rather than another entirely as a result of free voluntary exchange.

Take another example, science. How did we develop the complicated structure of physics, economics, what will you? Again, it was developed and continues to develop as a result of a free private market in which scientists communicate with one another, exchange information with one another, because both parties to any exchange want to benefit.

A characteristic feature of a free private market is that all parties to a transaction believe that they are going to be better off by that transaction. It is not a zero sum game in which some can benefit only at the expense of others. It is a situation in which everybody thinks he is going to be better off.

A free private market is a mechanism for enabling a complex structure of cooperation to arise as an unintended consequence of Adam Smith's invisible hand, without any deliberate design. A free private market involves the absence of coercion. People deal with one another voluntarily, not because somebody tells them to or forces them to. It does not follow that the people who engage in these deals like one another, or know one another, or have any interest in one another. They may hate one another. Everyone of us, every day without recognizing it, engages in deals with people all over the world whom we do not know and who do not know us. No super planning agency is telling them to produce something for us. They may be of a different religion, a different color, a different race. The farmer who grows wheat is not interested in whether it is going to be bought by somebody who is black or white, somebody who is Catholic or Protestant; and the person who buys the wheat is not concerned about whether the person who grew it was white or black, Catholic or Protestant. So the essence of a free private market is that it is a situation in which everybody deals with one another because he or she believes he or she will be better off.

The essence of human freedom as of a free private market, is freedom of people to make their own decisions so long as they do not prevent anybody else from doing the same thing. That makes clear, I think, why free private markets are so closely related to human freedom. It is the only mechanism that permits a complex interrelated society to be organized from the bottom up rather than the top down. However, it also makes clear why free societies are so rare. Free societies restrain power. They make it very hard for bad people to do harm, but they also make it very hard for good people to do good. Implicitly or explicitly, most opponents of freedom believe that they know what is good for other people better than other people know for themselves, and they want the power to make people do what is really good for them.

The recent absolutely remarkable phenomenon of the collapse of communism in Eastern Europe raises in acute form the issues that we have been discussing. There is much talk in those countries about moving to a free market, but so far very limited success. In the past, free markets have developed in all sorts of ways out of feudalism, out of military juntas, out of autocracy and mostly they have developed by accident rather than by design. It was a pure accident that Hong Kong achieved a free market. Insofar as anyone designed it, it was the colonial officials who were sent there; but it was a pure accident that they were favorable to, or at least not hostile to, a free market. It was an accident that a free market developed in the United States, nothing natural about it. We might very well have gone down a very different road. We started to go down a very different road in the 1830s when there was widespread governmental activity in the building of canals, in the building of toll ways, and the taking over of banks; there were state banks in Ohio, Illinois, and so on. What happened is that in the Panic of 1837 they all went broke, and that destroyed people's belief that the way to run a country was by government. That had a great deal to do with the subsequent widespread belief that small government was the best government.

While free societies have developed by accident in many different ways, there is so far no example of a totalitarian country that has successfully converted to a free society. That is why what is going on in Eastern Europe is so exciting. We are witnessing something that we have not seen before. We know and they know what needs to be done. It is very simple. I tell the people in Eastern Europe when I see them that I can tell them what to do in three words: privatize, privatize, privatize. The problem is to have the political will to do so, and to do so promptly. It is going to be exciting to see whether they can do so.

However, the point that impresses me now and that I want to emphasize is that the problem is not only for them but for us. They have as much to teach us as we have to teach them. What was their problem under communism? Too big, too intrusive, too powerful a government. I ask you, what is our problem in the United States today? We have a relatively free system. This is a great country and has a great deal of freedom, but we are losing our freedom. We are living on our capital in considerable measure. This country was built up during 150 years and more in which government played a very small role. As late as 1929, total government spending in the United States never exceeded about 12% of the national income, about the same fraction as in Hong Kong in recent years. Federal government spending was about 3 to 4% of the national income except at the time of the Civil War and World War I. Half of that went for the military and half for everything else. State and local governments spent about twice as much. Again, local governments spent more than state governments. In the period between then and now, the situation has changed drastically. Total government spending, as I said, is 43% of national income, and two thirds of that is federal.

Moreover, in addition to what government spends directly, it exercises extensive control over the deals that people can make in the private market. It prevents you from buying sugar in the cheapest market; it forces you to pay twice the world price for sugar. It forces enterprises to meet all sorts of requirements about wages, hours, antipollution standards, and so on and on. Many of these may be good, but they are government dictation of how the resources shall be used. To put it in one word that should be familiar to us by now, it is socialist.

The United States today is more than 50% socialist in terms of the fraction of our resources that are controlled by the government. Fortunately, socialism is so inefficient that it does not control 50% of our lives. Fortunately, most of that is wasted. People worry about government waste; I don't. I just shudder at what would happen to freedom in this country if the government were efficient in spending our money. The really fascinating thing is that our private sector has been so effective, so efficient, that it has been able to produce a standard of life that is the envy of the rest of the world on the basis of less than half the resources available to all of us.

The major problems that face this country all derive from too much socialism. If you consider our educational system at the elementary and secondary level, government spending per pupil has more than tripled over the past thirty years in real terms after allowing for inflation, yet test scores keep declining, dropout rates are high, and functional illiteracy is widespread. Why should that be a surprise? Schooling at the elementary and secondary level is the largest socialist enterprise in the United States next to the military. Now why should we be better at socialism than the Russians? In fact, they ought to be better; they have had more practice at it. If you consider medical care, which is another major problem now, total spending on medical care has gone from 4% of the national income to 13%, and more than half of that increase has been in the form of government spending. Costs have multiplied and it is reasonably clear that output has not gone up in anything like the same ratio. Our automobile industry can produce all the cars anybody wants to drive and is prepared to pay for. They do not seem to have any difficulty, but our government cannot produce the roads for us to drive on. The aviation industry can produce the planes, the airlines can get the pilots, but the government somehow cannot provide the landing strips and the air traffic controllers. I challenge anybody to name a major problem in the United States that does not derive from excessive government.

Crime has been going up, our prisons are overcrowded; our inner cities are becoming unlivable all as a consequence of good intentions gone awry, the good intentions in this case being to prevent the misuse of drugs. The results: very little if any reduction in the use of drugs but a great many innocent victims. The harm which is being done by that program is far greater than any conceivable good. And the harm is not being done only at home. What business do we have destroying other countries such as Colombia because we cannot enforce our laws?

It is hard to be optimistic about how successful we can be in preserving our relatively free system. The collapse of the communist states in Eastern Europe was the occasion for a great deal of self-congratulation on our part. It introduced an element of complacency and smugness. We all said, "Oh my, how good we are! See, we must be doing everything right." But we did not learn the lesson that they had to teach us, and that lesson is that government has very real functions, but if it wanders beyond those functions and goes too far, it tends to destroy human and economic freedom.

I am nonetheless a long term optimist. I believe that the United States is a great country and that our problems do not arise from the people as such. They arise from the structure of our government. We are being misgoverned in all these areas but not because of bad motives or bad people. The people who run our government are the same kind of people as the people outside it. We mislead ourselves if we think we are going to correct the situation by electing the right people to government. We will elect the right people and when they get to Washington they will do the wrong things. You and I would; I am not saying that there is anything special about them.

The important point is that we in our private lives and they in their governmental lives are all moved by the same incentive: to promote our own self-interest. Armen Alchian once made a very important comment. He said, "You know, there is one thing you can trust everybody to do. You can trust everybody to put his interest above yours." That goes for those of us in the private sector; that goes for people in the government sector. The difference between the two is not in the people; it is not in the incentives. It is in what it is in the self-interest for different people to do. In the private economy, so long as we keep a free private market, one party to a deal can only benefit if the other party also benefits. There is no way in which you can satisfy your needs at the expense of somebody else. In the government market, there is another recourse. If you start a program that is a failure and you are in the private market, the only way you can keep it going is by digging into your own pocket. That is your bottom line. However, if you are in the government, you have another recourse. With perfectly good intentions and good will nobody likes to say: "I was wrong." You can say, "Oh, the only reason it is a failure is because we haven't done enough. The only reason the drug program is a failure is because we haven't spent enough money on it." And it does not have to be your own money. You have a very different bottom line. If you are persuasive enough, or if you have enough control over power, you can increase spending on your program at the expense of the taxpayer. That is why a private project that is a failure is closed down while a government project that is a failure is expanded.

The only way we are really going to change things is by changing the political structure. The most hopeful thing I see on that side is the great public pressure at the moment for term limits. That would be a truly fundamental change.

I want to close on a slightly optimistic note. About 200 years ago, an English newspaper wrote: "There are 775,300,000 people in the World. Of these, arbitrary governments command 741,800,000 and the free ones [comprise only] 33 1/2 million.... On the whole, slaves are three and twenty times more numerous than men enjoying, in any tolerable degree, the rights of human nature."[2] I know of no such precise estimate for the present, but I made a rough estimate

on the basis of the freedom surveys of Freedom House. I estimate that, while slaves still greatly outnumber free people, the ratio has fallen in the past two centuries from 23 to 1 to about 3 to 1. We are still very far from our goal of a completely free world, but, on the scale of historical time, that is amazing progress, more in the past two centuries than in the prior two millennia. Let's hope and work to make sure that that keeps up. Thank you.

[1] Address delivered on November 1, 1991.
[2] Cited in Forrest McDonald, *Novus Or do Seclorum* (Lawrence: University Press of Kansas, 1985), p.9.

12.2   CHARLES TILLY ("GLOBALIZATION THREATENS LABOR RIGHTS," 1995)

... I will argue that globalization threatens established rights of labor through its undermining of state capacity to guarantee those rights. In reasoning about the causal chains involved, I will draw heavily on inferences from Western European history, the history I know best. The paper takes a considerable excursion back into that history on the ground that here, as so often, historical perspective clarifies what is now happening to the world, and what might happen next. Based on a reading of European history, ideas informing this essay run as follows:...

2.   Although in Western countries some groups of workers enjoyed rights enforced by municipalities and other organizations prior to 1800, states were rarely parties to such contracts before the nineteenth century. Otherwise said, workers enjoyed few rights at a national scale.

In Europe before 1800, different groups of workers frequently exercised rights, thus defined, to monopolize the production and sale of some commodity within a stipulated set of markets, to regulate the entry of new producers and purveyors into their trades, to bargain collectively with local employers over conditions of production and remuneration, to gain preferential access to local food supplies in times of crisis, to glean, hunt, and/or *pasture* on common or deserted land, to pursue grievances through courts, to participate as groups in public festivities, to select members of cross trade councils, and to discipline renegade members of their own trades. In general workers did not enjoy shared worker-specific rights to organize trade unions, to strike against individual employers, to offer political candidates organized support, to address national political authorities directly, to bear arms, or to draw compensation for hardship from public funds. Although people exercised some individual rights as members of communities, churches, households, and other organizations, workers' rights generally took a categorical form, applying to individual workers only in so far as they qualified as bona fide members of local trades.

Before the nineteenth century, states rarely served as third parties to these rights. Instead, municipalities, parishes, local lords, sovereign courts, and similar smaller-scale authorities typically guaranteed the rights in question, arbitrated them, or served as their enforcers. In England, historians sometimes speak loosely as though the Statute of Laborers, Statute of Artificers, Poor Law, and Assize of Bread clearly established plebeian claims on the crown, but at most they justified appeals to those royally sanctioned autonomous intermediaries, county magistrates. Parliament did intervene in the food supply, for example, but almost exclusively by licensing or forbidding exports and authorizing commitment of food to troops; it left actual regulation of prices and supplies to local authorities. The crown, in its turn, intervened chiefly by sending armed forces to protect shipments or to break up crowds that were seizing grain. Eighteenth-century parliamentary legislation for Spitalfields weavers and merchant seamen stood out as exceptional, in no way giving other workers a warrant to call on the state for protection. Above all, workers' rights, where they existed, rested on the relations between particular groups of workers and municipalities, not national states.

3. Through intense struggles, incremental changes, and alterations in the organization of states, workers in capitalist countries acquired substantial collective rights after 1850 or so. Those rights expanded irregularly through World War II.

The situation changed profoundly during the nineteenth century. Especially as a consequence of greatly expanded war-making, states intervened much more directly in their populations' lives after 1750, thereby generating new resistance, struggle, bargaining, and settlements in the form of rights. Significantly expanded state capacity, furthermore, meant that the state became party to a much wider range of transactions than before and became more attractive as an object of new demands. States that could conscript, tax, and police could also regulate working conditions, organize schools, and build highways. At the same time, concentration and nationalization of capital gave workers connections and central objects of claims they had not previously known....

5. Those rights attached workers collectively to particular states, and therefore depended on the capacity of those states to enforce workers' claims on others, notably on capitalists.

The variant chronologies of workers' rights make my point: Rights to strike, to associate, to call down sanctions against poor working conditions, to seek legal enforcement of contracts, to collect unemployment benefits, to earn pensions all depended not on the general ethos of Europeans or Westerners but on some particular state's readiness to validate the rights in question. One proof lies in the capacity of states to suspend some or all of those rights in times of war or civil strife, as most European states did during World War I.[1] Another lies in the effective strategies for labor pursued by the leaders of different states, including Bismarck's simultaneous repression of trade-union organization and elaboration of insurance programs for sickness, accident, and old age. Similarly, workers' reliance on state power to exclude foreign labor and thus to reinforce domestic labor's right to work embedded a given country's workers in their own state's capacity to control its borders.

Of course, the degree of embeddedness in particular states varied from institution to institution and from state to state. Bo Rothstein points out, for example, that European workers' movements had a choice between two types of unemployment-insurance scheme: "(1) as a compulsory system administered by government agencies and (2) as a voluntary but publicly supported scheme administered by unions or union-dominated funds," the latter being called the Ghent system for its origins in that Belgian city's legal arrangement.[2] Sweden, Denmark, Finland, Iceland, and Belgium — in recent decades, the most highly unionized European countries — all adopted the Ghent system. In either system, the right to unemployment insurance depends ultimately on the state, much more so than in the nineteenth-century private accumulation of funds by unions and mutual-aid societies; in both systems workers surrender autonomy in favor of reliance on the state's greater financial capacity. However, the compulsory state system bypasses unions to establish direct connections between workers and state agencies, while the Ghent system establishes unions as privileged intermediaries.

Over the whole range of workers' rights — not only unemployment insurance but also health and welfare benefits, vocational training, occupational safety, minimum wages, unionization, and the right to strike — the actual exercise of rights depended heavily on the state's capacity and propensity to discipline capital. Much of labor politics in Western countries indeed pivots

precisely on demands that the state enforce such rights in the face of capitalist resistance. In return, states can count on commitment of workers to their international policies, as socialist internationalists learned with consternation on the eve of World War I: On the whole, workers abandoned pacifism and international solidarity in favor of support for their own countries' war efforts.

6. In general, the same states' capacity to pursue social policies, including the enforcement of workers' rights, also depended on the creation of substantial, effective controls over the stocks and flows of persons, diseases, other biota, pollutants, weapons, drugs, money, other capital, technology, information, commodities, political practices, and cultural forms within well-delimited territories.

In addition to state controls over capitalists, the concession of many rights to workers entailed greatly enlarged intervention of states in stocks and flows that had previously escaped any more than light, intermittent state influences. State-guaranteed vocational education depended on state regulation or creation of a wide variety of educational institutions, while unemployment compensation assumed both extensive monitoring of employment and accumulation of large financial reserves. These institutions in their turn implied state capacity to observe and control the accumulation, expenditure, and transfer of an enormous range of resources; otherwise the effects of government policies would become unpredictable and the ability of government to meet their commitments shaky at best. Michael Mann refers to this sort of capacity as "infrastructural power":

the institutional capacity of a central state, despotic or not, to penetrate its territories and logistically implement decisions. This is collective power, "power through" society, coordinating social life through state infrastructures. Weber implied this also increased their despotic power over society. But this is not necessarily so. Infrastructural power is a two-way street: It also enables civil society parties to control the state, as Marxists and pluralists emphasize. Increasing infrastructural power does not necessarily increase or reduce distributive, despotic power.[3]

Infrastructural power arises through delineation of state boundaries accompanied by monitoring and intervention in stocks and flows of a wide range of resources both within and across those boundaries.

7. After 1850 or so, capitalist states actually succeeded in imposing significant controls over most of these stocks and flows.

Mark me well: I am not arguing that the granting of rights to workers and to citizens in general caused the expansion of state power. I have in mind a rather different scenario. For millennia the rulers of most states acted chiefly to enhance their own war-making capacities, to maintain their own oligarchies in power, and to reinforce the perquisites of those oligarchies vis-à-vis the subject population; groups outside the ruling classes only gained autonomy or power when they served one of these activities, when they took advantage of contradictions among these activities (as when oligarchies became reluctant to wage war and crowns turned to merchants for loans) or when they were able to evade the state's reach.

After 1750 or so, however, a combination of (1) a great increase in the scale and cost of international war and (2) a strong turn toward recruitment of troops from among the country's own young men generated great expansions of state fiscal apparatus, consequent growth of state structures in general, widespread resistance, struggles between ordinary people and state officials over the means of war, and bargains establishing a modicum of citizens' rights. Expanded rights con-

fronted states whose extractive capacity had enormously increased, which meant that the self-interested work a well-organized group could do by means of state intervention likewise increased. The paradoxical result: intensified commitment to the state's survival coupled with intensified struggle to turn the state to group advantage.

This scenario played itself out in a thousand ways: in unprecedented state budgets, new bureaucracies, serious attempts to define and control borders, establishment of public educational systems, creation of censuses and central statistical offices, organization of national maps and cadasters, founding of museums, movement away from excise to direct taxes, formation of political parties, issuing of passports and visas, standardization of calendar and clock times, patenting of inventions, imposition of military conscription, uniformization of legal tenders, installation of labor inspectors, starting of public health services, surveys of poverty, and much more. In general, the efforts had two aspects: circumscription and central control.

"Circumscription" denotes an increase in a state's capacity to limit stocks and flows of resources within and across national frontiers; it rests, among other things, on delineation and surveillance of those frontiers. In the nineteenth century, European states acted much more vigorously to monitor and contain the accumulation, movement, and transfer of capital, goods, persons, ideas, and technologies; as a result, they acquired enhanced means of influencing technological innovation, employment, investment, and supplies of money. They started rationalizing their borders, requiring passports of people who crossed them, and controlling the passage of valuable resources as well.

"Central control" denotes a state's intervention in populations, organizations, and activities throughout its territory through surveillance, coordination, and command. During the nineteenth century European states elaborated extensive controls over communications systems, transportation, public health, urban form, schools, working conditions, welfare and a wide range of other social activities. Central control included the redefinition and standardization of culture, of shared understanding and their objectifications. From the nineteenth century onward, states promoted or undertook the organization of publications, ceremonies, museums, schools, and symbols favoring national identities, beliefs, histories, and languages; in the process, they came to define variant cultures as inferior, mistaken, and sometimes subversive. National narratives, furthermore, located the histories of particular states in the general history of Europe and of humanity.

8. As a result, citizens (including workers) demanded increasingly that states enact programs expanding and guaranteeing their rights, and thereby sanctioned even greater state control over such stocks and flows.

As this scenario implies, state budgets not only expanded, but shifted away from their previous enormous concentration on war and war-related debt service. They shifted toward collective goods such as highways, railroads, schools, and, eventually, welfare through a process of bargaining over disposition of expanded state capacity. After documenting the great expansion of fifteenth-century European states, Raymond Grew points out that in some respects rulers nevertheless withdrew from intervention: "A system of power based on law is endangered by laws it cannot enforce, and gradually, most nineteenth-century states abandoned efforts to control wages, consumption, prices, churches, strikes, labor organization, and the press."[4] What actually happened in these instances, however, was that states circumscribed without exerting much central control—set limits, but did not regulate much within those limits. In the case of strikes and labor organization, as we have seen, the very setting of limits constrained workers to abandon forms of organization and action they have previously employed. In fact, European states took similar circumscriptive approaches to wages, consumption, prices, churches, and the press.

9. Both the globalization of many economic activities and the creation of powerful supranational organizations are now undermining the capacity of states to monitor and control such stocks and flows — hence, undermining their capacity to pursue effective social policies, including the enforcement of workers' rights.

The news briefs with which this paper began indicate the swelling of a great flood, but they do not quite show how rising waters are affecting states' foundations. The effects are, I think, profound. With respect to labor migration, both the United States and the European Community have proved quite incapable of stemming the entry of illegal workers. With respect to capital, almost all states have proved vulnerable to threatened flights of investment and incompetent to monitor entries and exits of large amounts of money. With respect to illegal drugs, practically no country in the world has erected effective barriers to their movement, sale, or consumption. Weapons flow freely across state borders, as do diseases and pollutants. Television, radio, fax, and computer networks broadcast information, entertainment, and popular culture throughout the world despite efforts of many states to contain them. Astute pricing of interstate but intrafirm movements of goods allows multinational firms to evade taxation, while temporary employment, part-time employment, commission sales and subcontracting allow them to avoid statutory obligations to long-term employees. Multinational corporations, international banking syndicates, and large criminal organizations are engineering some of these changes, but so are multinational compacts such as the European Community.

A number of Western regimes, especially conservative regimes like those of Margaret Thatcher and Ronald Reagan, reacted to the decreasing effectiveness of state action by trying to shrink the state. As James Cronin remarks,

[W]hat is most distinctive historically about the Conservatives under Thatcher was their obsession with the state and with the institutional bases of power and policy. They displayed a particularly intense desire to limit the size and restructure the shape of the state itself, to reduce the extent to which government was held responsible for the economic and social welfare of its citizens, to diminish the capacity of the state to undertake or to avoid that responsibility and to eliminate those state institutions and policies that had provided support for Labor. In this they showed keen insight into recent politics and an intuitive understanding of the process by which the very structure of the state shapes politics: creating expectations and opportunities for placing demands upon government, opening or limiting the arena for political mobilization, offering or withdrawing the political recognition of interests that is so essential to their existence and successful mobilization.[5]

In other words, they responded to the state's overcommitment by denying commitments and destroying commitment-producing mechanisms.

Perhaps the most surprising effects of globalization on state activity, however, lie in the area of warfare. Given a Weberian conception of states as monopolists of violent means, one might have thought use of force the last place in which states would lose their grips. European states did, after all, accomplish an enormous disarming of their civilian populations between 1600 and 1900, while arming themselves so effectively that only defection of government troops made forceful seizures of power

possible. With the Gulf war, the United States bid to make itself arms purveyor to the world. Yet the very involvement of major states — the United States, Russia, China, the United Kingdom, and France represent about 80 percent of world trade in major conventional weapons[6] — promoted the acquisition of weapons by nonstate actors.

The process had two dimensions: the swelling of international weapons shipments and a shift toward forms of war, including civil war, involving other forces than disciplined national armies. Each dimension promoted the other. Even within Europe, the former zones of Yugoslavia and the Soviet Union have thrown up dozens of armed forces that do not belong to recognized states. In the rest of the world, irregular forces have become so prominent and powerful that guerrilla war has displaced the engagement of centrally disciplined government troops as the dominant form of warfare.[7] In Somalia, Liberia, Colombia, Mexico, Afghanistan, Sri Lanka, and many other places, so-called low-intensity conflict kills thousands of people every year.

States figure importantly in these conflicts not only as suppliers of arms, but also as supporters of intervention in the politics of other states, as inciters and objects of rebellion, as sponsors of death squads, as aspirations on the part of independence movements. Proliferation of genocide, politicide and expulsion of minorities as techniques of rule since 1945 bespeaks not disappearance but abuse of state power. Still, it is astonishing to what degree large-scale violence other than interstate war has increased since 1945, and to what extent states are losing their ability to contain that violence. The change testifies to weakened state capacity on a worldwide scale.

10. Current changes therefore threaten all rights embedded in slates, including workers' rights.

Jelle Visser and Bernhard Ebbinghaus point out that worker power and union densities have been falling since about 1980 in the capitalist world as a whole even including the historic social democracies. "From a weakened position at home," they add,

trade unions face the double challenge of Europe: the further political and economic integration of the 12 member states of the European Community, and the demand for aid, development and support from Central and Eastern European countries. With the advance of economic integration and a European monetary Union, national sovereignty in matters of economic and social policies risks being limited, and customary union avenues for protecting and enhancing employee welfare and security in the national agenda will become more and more restrained. The internationalization of organizations and markets has eroded, and will further reduce, the remaining zones of national autonomy in social and economic policy-making. Given the advance of multinational firms and within-firm centralization of decision-making on strategic issues, and the arrival of supranational decision-making in the European Community on the main economic and monetary issues, trade unions have no choice but to develop some transnational capacity for organization and action."[8]

But, they point out, the diversity of European union movements poses two serious obstacles to any such joint effort: First, the sheer difficulty of finding common formulas for such variously organized structures; second, the strategic division between relatively powerful labor movements (which have the capacity to act but much to lose by leveling) and relatively powerless ones (which are in no position to lead continental collective action). So far European workers have managed to create a European Trade Union Confederation with many members and few powers as well as a few multinational federations within such sectors as mining and metalworking. Still, their capacity for effec-

tive action at a European scale remains trivial.

The circumstances Visser and Ebbinghaus describe result precisely from the embedding of labor's rights in particular European states over the last 150 years. As the scale of economic action rises and the free flow of resources among European Community economics accelerates, the capacity of individual states to intervene on behalf of labor, the utility of any such intervention, and the power of organized labor relative to international capital all decline. Since rights depend on enforceability, all state-based rights decline. That emphatically includes the rights of workers....

15. If workers are to enjoy collective rights in the new world order, they will have to invent new strategies at the scale of international capital.

To the extent that (a) rights emerge from organized struggle and (b) the current struggle still pits labor against capital, only collective action at an international scale has much prospect of providing gains for labor, or even of stemming labor's losses. The governments involved as guarantors, furthermore, will have to be international agencies, compacts, or consortia of existing states. No individual state will have the power to enforce workers' rights in the fluid world that is emerging.

[1] Leopold Harimson and Giulio Sapelli, eds., *Strikes, Social Conflict and the First World War. An International Perspective* (Milan: Fondazione Giangiacomo Feltrinelli 1992).

[2] Bo Rothstein, "Labor-Market Institutions and Working-Class Strength," in *Structuring Politics. Historical Institutionalism in Comparative Analysis*, ed. Sven Steinmo, Kathleen Thelen, and Frank Longstreth (Cambridge: Cambridge University Press, 1992), 39–40.

[3] Michael Mann, *The Sources of Social Power II: The Rise of Classes and Nation-States, 1760–1914* (Cambridge: Cambridge University Press, 1993), 59.

[4] Raymond Grew, "The Nineteenth-Century European State," in *Statemaking and Social Movements. Essays in History and Theory*, ed. Charles Bright and Susan Harding (Ann Arbor, MI: University of Michigan, 1984), 101.

[5] James E. Cronin, *The Politics of State Expansion. War, State and Society in Twentieth-Century Britain* (London: Routledge 1991), 247.

[6] Ruth Leger Sivard, *World Military and Social Expenditures (New York: World Priorities, Inc. 1993)*, 19.

[7] Martin van Creveld, *The Transformation of War* (New York: Free Press, 1991).

[8] Jelle Visser and Bernhard Ebbinghaus, "Making the Most of Diversity? European Integration and Transnational Organization of Labor," in *Organized Interests and the European Community*, ed. Justin Greenwood, Jürgen R. Grote, and Karsten Ronit (London: Sage Publications, 1992), 206–207.publisher.

12.3   AMNESTY INTERNATIONAL ("AMNESTY INTERNATIONAL ON HUMAN RIGHTS AND LABOR RIGHTS," 1998)

Our rallying cry for May Day is "labor rights are human rights." This reminds us that people traditionally look to unions to protect their rights and the unions have the largest force of "human rights defenders" in the world. Human rights embrace the whole spectrum of standards that every person should expect as a minimum entitlement in any decent society, and they include rights in every realm of life, civil, political, social and cultural — from social security to health, from education to sexual orientation rights.

The broad human rights movement and the unions still have a lot to learn from each other and both could benefit from working more closely together. Organizing collectively into a union is one of the prime examples of action to prevent people's rights being violated and trade unions give us the models for mass action to respond to abuses of rights. Union solidarity action is a good illustration of organized activism by one branch of a movement to protect those at risk somewhere else. But apart from the campaigns of unions and rights organizations, what affects the state of labor rights and human rights are the same major social trends which are influencing every other aspect of life.

The theories of "neo-liberal economics" dominate current ideology and in reality, of the 100 largest economies in the world, 51 are now global corporations; only 49 are countries. The multi-nationals show the ever-increasing scope and power of globalization. They work on a super-national scale and organize their business like a world-wide game of Monopoly, moving their operations, plant, finance and workforce around like pieces on the map. They fragment production to suit their interests. They continue to gain more control over each process, more control over the workforce and more control over the market, merging, acquiring, and garnering more power. Mitsubishi is now larger than Indonesia, with the fourth largest population on earth. General Motors is bigger than Denmark, Toyota is bigger than Norway. Philip Morris is larger than New Zealand.

With the latest computer technologies they hold extensive data and monitor the behavior of millions of "citizen consumers"; with world-wide marketing and pin-sharp targeting, they manipulate and manage expectations, they penetrate our communities, our homes and our lives. They often push down wages and living standards, job-security and terms and conditions of employment.

Like super-powers, they have near-universal reach and supremacy and the rights of their staff, their suppliers, their customers and small businesses have all been subordinated to the rules of the new big game. Governments court these corporations and compete in offering them inducements. The human consequences of this new order are seen in the erosion of rights in the "maquiladoras" and sweatshops of Latin America, the factory/storage/living blocks of the export processing zones in the Far East. An alliance of women's organizations said: "While women who wear Nike shoes in the United States are encouraged to perform to their best, the Indonesian, Vietnamese and Chinese women making the shoes often suffer from inadequate wages, corporal punishment, forced overtime and/or sexual harassment." At the social and political level, the top 200 multi-national corporations have more economic power than the poorest four-fifths of humanity; the head of Microsoft has more money than twice the combined GDP of Uganda, Kenya and Tanzania. Through this sheer size, economic dominance and mobility, the multi-nationals can set the agenda for development, sway political decisions and have a major impact on the reality of human rights for very many people.

The global market means that governments have less control over economic matters. A lot of countries may look more social-democratic with the disappearance of many dictatorships, but the capacity and legitimacy of the state is in decline. At the same time traditional national governments are increasingly relinquishing power through privatizing public services, including parts of the military, security and police services as well as their utilities, major industries, etc. They have diminishing power to control mergers, take-overs and liquidations, may not know who plans to buy or sell a major industry or utility; a telephone, TV or water company may change ownership overnight.

"Peace-keeping" forces, prison detention and policing services are increasingly being privately run as corporations. Amnesty International and other NGOs have started developing techniques and learning from experience in exposing the involvement of corporations such as Shell, BP and Total in human rights violations in Nigeria, Colombia, Myanmar. This approach can effectively complement the efforts of unions and labor activists. Work on child labor exploitation, on apparel industries and sports goods have shown what is possible, although there is still much to be done to develop this area of work.

The sheer weight of national debt in many poor countries, alongside the power of IMF, large transnational corporations and overseas investors, leaves the governments with little power to make their own choices or control their nation's affairs. Rights and justice come very low on government priority lists compared to foreign debts. Human rights are undermined by extreme inequalities in power and wealth; injustice in access to food, fuel, shelter and the bare necessities of life go hand in hand with poverty and powerlessness leading to destitution, malnutrition, disease, illiteracy, unemployment.

The financial institutions like the IMF, the World Bank and the multi-national banks have a major impact on people's rights. More and more states have taken their loans and accepted the social policies they impose such as the infamous Structural Adjustment Programs, which include cuts in public expenditure, unemployment, lower wages, reductions in welfare and public services — health, education, social security, transport, etc.

International finance can move massive capital funds very quickly from one side of the world to the other, just to speculate, and people's rights suffer when the social fabric is torn apart by currency crises, national bank failure, government collapse. Let us hope that human rights will not be further eroded in the recently damaged "tiger economies" such as Indonesia and South Korea.

Thus overall, a new breed of world "super-bodies" seem to be emerging: the multi-national commercial corporations, the international banking and financial bodies and the regional inter-government economic organizations. These new super bodies normally share the same outlook, the same analysis and culture. Human rights and labor rights are not a priority on their agenda.

In some countries in recent years there have remained no effective social structures at all to protect rights of any sort, when the normal machinery of government collapsed altogether as a result of armed conflicts. Human rights suffer in these conditions, whether the reason is resistance to oppression, competition among regional powers or "warlordism." Witness the effects on all human rights in former Yugoslavia, Somalia, Rwanda, parts of the former Soviet Union, in Zaire, Sierra Leone or Liberia, East Timor. Amnesty International's "concerns" arise in the increasingly widespread "limited," "internal" or "low intensity" wars around the world.

Across the world, unprecedented numbers of people whose rights have been denied are on the move, migrant workers looking for a better life with basic rights and refugees fleeing violence or conditions of oppression. But their freedom of movement and their most basic rights are at risk as more and more barriers are erected to keep them out.

Human rights and labor rights are being affected by the amazing capacities and spread of computer and communications technologies, and by the applications of new science— genetic engineering, biotechnologies, wonder drugs, artificial intelligence. So many "great leaps forward," but as ever, the question will be for whose benefit are they developed and who will have access to them? Who do they liberate and whose rights do they threaten?

Changes and threats to the environment and to eco-systems have major implications for all our rights as humans. Rights at work are threatened by toxic chemicals, new materials and waste products, rights to health services are threatened by pollution of the atmosphere, the right to life, liberty and security are put in jeopardy by meltdowns like Chernobyl, the Ogoni's rights to own property and to freedom of movement are put at risk by soil contamination. And no one can avoid the effects of global warming. The actual effects of the economic system can make a mockery of its alleged rationality and rob us of our rights.

Amnesty International has a tradition of emphasizing the responsibilities of national governments, to "deliver" rights, to protect rights, to rectify violations. In the face of the decreasing functions and powers of governments, how should we respond, how can we globalize accountability?

Unions are familiar with the dilemma that the state is sometimes an ally, legislating or protecting norms, and sometimes the "enemy," sending police against demonstrations, demanding "registration" of unions, setting pay freezes, etc. The key issue is surely about accountability, the right to participate in government and the right to change it.

Labor rights and human rights organizations need to find ways of working which are effective with power structures that lie outside the familiar context of the company or the nation state. We have to influence decision-makers in distant multinational company HQs, in board-rooms of management accountancy firms and investment analysts. We have to influence the decisions of technical experts and diplomats in the World Trade Organization, the IMF, the World Bank and innumerable other remote, specialist agencies which are insulated from traditional democratic pressure. How should we adapt our campaigning to face this challenge?

With the intensive specialization of human rights into separate topics from health issues to social security, from education rights to nationality issues, this field of interest risks becoming very "professionalized." The whole base of activism on labor rights and human rights issues is at issue. In order to retain people acting unpaid, out of conviction, our movements need to learn how to enable members to take up the particular causes which they identify with, feel passionately about and want to pursue very specifically. We also need to hold on to traditional principles of solidarity for when mass support is needed. But trends in trade unions and in voluntary organizations are tending to reflect noticeable changes in active participation; smaller, more flexible, specialized self-organized groups are playing a much more activist role than the traditional cohorts of uniform monolithic branches. Another set of issues we must study and adapt to.

The last decade has seen a big increase in the number of non-governmental organizations working on labor rights, human rights, international affairs, single issues, on themes or for specific sectors, or particular campaigns, but nothing on a scale to match the changes we have to face. We need to learn to work much more closely with each other in the different branches of human rights, recognizing where we share, and where we differ over objectives, understanding differing specialist interests and strengths, differing structures and accountability.

As economic production, finance and control becomes more and more concentrated, it seems that when policies go wrong, they can lead to catastrophes on an ever increasing scale — massive economic crises, famines, environmental disasters, military conflicts, communal violence, mass killings and genocide erupt more suddenly and more disastrously than ever before. We need to adapt our movements to respond more quickly and more effectively to the massive scale of human rights violations and the sudden emergencies which arise today.

Historically there never was a period of halcyon days with equal rights in a society ruled by mutual respect: every age has been turbulent, beset with new risks and threats to people's rights. Those who care about rights face considerable challenges, we must adapt to reality or we'll be irrelevant.

12.4 AMARTYA SEN ("DEVELOPMENT AS FREEDOM," 1999)[1]

Let me start off with a distinction between two general attitudes to the process of development that can be found born in professional economic analysis and in public discussions and debates.[2] One view sees development as a "fierce" process, with much "blood, sweat and tears" — a world in which wisdom demands toughness. In particular, it demands calculated neglect of various concerns that are seen as "soft-headed" (even if the critics are often too polite to call them that). Depending on what the author's favorite poison is, the temptations to be *resisted* can include having social safety nets that protect the very poor, providing social services for the population at large, departing from rugged institutional guidelines in response to identified hardship, and favoring — "much too early" — political and civil rights and the "luxury" of democracy. These things, it is argued in this austere attitudinal mode, could be supported later on, when the development process has borne enough fruit: what is needed here and now is "toughness and discipline." The different theories that share this general outlook diverge from one another in pointing to distinct areas of softness that are particularly to be avoided, varying from financial softness to political relaxation, from plentiful social expenditures to complaisant poverty relief.

This hard-knocks attitude contrasts with an alternative outlook that sees development as essentially a "friendly" process. Depending on the particular version of this attitude, the congeniality of the process is seen as exemplified by such things as mutually beneficial exchanges (of which Adam Smith spoke eloquently), or by the working of social safety nets, or of political liberties, or of social development — or some combination or other of these supportive activities.

Constitutive and Instrumental Roles of Freedom

The approach of this book is much more compatible with the latter approach than with the former.[3] It is mainly an attempt to see development as a process of expanding the real freedoms that people enjoy. In this approach, expansion of freedom is viewed as both (1) the *primary end* and (2) the *principal means* of development. They can be called respectively the "constitutive role" and the "instrumental role" of freedom in development. The constitutive role of freedom relates to the importance of substantive freedom in enriching human life. The substantive freedoms include elementary capabilities like being able to avoid such deprivations as starvation, under-nourishment, escapable morbidity and premature mortality, as well as the freedoms that are associated with being literate and numerate, enjoying political participation and uncensored speech and so on. In this constitutive perspective, development involves expansion of these and other basic freedoms. Development, in this view, is the process of expanding human freedoms, and the assessment of development has to be informed by this consideration.

Let me refer here to an example that was briefly discussed in the introduction (and which involves an often raised question in the development literature) in order to illustrate how the recognition of the "constitutive" role of freedom can alter developmental analysis. Within the narrower views of development (in terms of, say, GNP growth or industrialization) it is often asked whether the freedom of political participation and dissent is or is not "conducive to development." In the light of the foundational view of development as freedom, this question would seem to be defectively formulated, since it misses the crucial understanding that political participation and dissent are *constitutive* parts of development itself. Even a very rich person, who is prevented from speaking freely, or from participating in public debates and decisions, is *deprived* of something that she has reason to value. The process of development, when judged by the enhancement of human freedom, has to include the removal of this person's deprivation. Even if she had no immediate interest in exercising the freedom to speak or to participate, it would still be a deprivation of her freedoms if she were to be left with no choice on these matters. Development seen as enhancement of freedom cannot but address such deprivations. The relevance of the deprivation of basic political freedoms or civil rights, for an adequate understanding of development, does not have to be established through their indirect contribution to *other* features of development (such as the growth of GNP or the promotion of industrialization). These freedoms are part and parcel of enriching the process of development.

This fundamental point is distinct from the "instrumental" argument that these freedoms and rights may *also* be very effective in contributing to economic progress. That instrumental connection is important as well ... but the significance of the instrumental role of political freedom as *means* to development does not in any way reduce the evaluative importance of freedom as an *end* of development.

The *intrinsic* importance of human freedom as the preeminent objective of development has to be distinguished from the *instrumental* effectiveness of freedom of different kinds to promote human freedom. Since the focus of the last chapter was mainly on the intrinsic importance of freedom, I shall now concentrate more on the effectiveness of freedom as *means* — not just as end. The instrumental role of freedom concerns the way different kinds of rights, opportunities, and entitlements contribute to the expansion of human freedom in general, and thus to promoting development. This relates not merely to the obvious connection

that expansion of freedom of each kind must contribute to development since development itself can be seen as a process of enlargement of human freedom in general. There is much more in the instrumental connection than this constitutive linkage. The effectiveness of freedom as an instrument lies in the fact that different kinds of freedom interrelate with one another, and freedom of one type may greatly help in advancing freedom of other types. The two roles are thus linked by empirical connections, relating freedom of one kind to freedom of other kinds.

Instrumental Freedoms

In presenting empirical studies in this work, I shall have the occasion to discuss a number of instrumental freedoms that contribute, directly or indirectly, to the overall freedom people have to live the way they would like to live. The diversities of the instruments involved are quite extensive. However, it may be convenient to identify five distinct types of freedom that may be particularly worth emphasizing in this instrumental perspective. This is by no means an exhaustive list, but it may help to focus on some particular policy issues that demand special attention at this time.

In particular, I shall consider the following types of instrumental freedoms: (1) *political freedoms*, (2) *economic facilities*, (3) *social opportunities*, (4) *transparency guarantees* and (5) *protective security*. These instrumental freedoms tend to contribute to the general capability of a person to live more freely, but they also serve to complement one another. While development analysis must, on the one hand, be concerned with the objectives and aims that make these instrumental freedoms consequentially important, it must also take note of the empirical linkages that tie the distinct types of freedom *together*, strengthening their joint importance. Indeed, these connections are central to a fuller understanding of the instrumental role of freedom. The claim that freedom is not only the primary object of development but also its principal means relates particularly to these linkages.

Let me comment a little on each of these instrumental freedoms. *Political freedoms*, broadly conceived (including what are called civil rights), refer to the opportunities that people have to determine who should govern and on what principles, and also include the possibility to scrutinize and criticize authorities, to have freedom of political expression and an uncensored press, to enjoy the freedom to choose between different political parties, and so on. They include the political entitlements associated with democracies in the broadest sense (encompassing opportunities of political dialogue, dissent and critique as well as voting rights and participatory selection of legislators and executives).

Economic facilities refer to the opportunities that individuals respectively enjoy to utilize economic resources for the purpose of consumption, or production, or exchange. The economic entitlements that a person has will depend on the resources owned or available for use as well as on conditions of exchange, such as relative prices and the working of the markets. Insofar as the process of economic development increases the income and wealth of a country, they are reflected in corresponding enhancement of economic entitlements of the population. It should be obvious that in the relation between national income and wealth, on the one hand, and the economic entitlements of individuals (or families), on the other, distributional considerations are important, in addition to aggregative ones. How the additional incomes generated are distributed will clearly make a difference.

The availability and access to finance can be a crucial influence on the economic entitlements that economic agents are practically able to secure. This applies all the way from large enterprises (in which hundreds of thousands of people may work) to tiny establishments that are run on micro credit. A credit crunch, for example, can severely affect the economic entitlements that rely on such credit.

Social opportunities refer to the arrangements that society makes for education, health care and so on, which influence the individual's substantive freedom to live better. These facilities are important not only for the conduct of private lives (such as living a healthy life and avoiding preventable morbidity and premature mortality), but also for more effective participation in economic and political activities. For example, illiteracy can be a major barrier to participation in economic activities that require production according to specification or demand strict quality control (as globalize trade increasingly does). Similarly, political participation may be hindered by the inability to read newspapers or to communicate in writing with others involved in political activities.

I turn now to the fourth category. In social interactions, individuals deal with one another on the basis of some presumption of what they are being offered and what they can expect to get. In this sense, the society operates on some basic presumption of trust. *Transparency guarantees* deal with the need for openness that people can expect: the freedom to deal with one another under guarantees of disclosure and lucidity. When that trust is seriously violated, the lives of many people — both direct parties and third parties — may be adversely affected by the lack of openness. Transparency guarantees (including the right to disclosure) can thus be an important category of instrumental freedom. These guarantees have a clear instrumental role in preventing corruption, financial irresponsibility and underhand dealings.

Finally, no matter how well an economic system operates, some people can be typically on the verge of vulnerability and can actually succumb to great deprivation as a result of material changes that adversely affect their lives. *Protective security* is needed to provide a social safety net for preventing the affected population from being reduced to abject misery, and in some cases even starvation and death. The domain of protective security includes *fixed* institutional arrangements such as unemployment benefits and statutory income supplements to the indigent as well as ad hoc arrangements such as famine relief or emergency public employment to generate income for destitutes.

Interconnections and Complementarity

These instrumental freedoms directly enhance the capabilities of people, but they also supplement one another, and can furthermore reinforce one another. These interlinkages are particularly important to seize in considering development policies.

The fact that the entitlement to economic transactions tends to be typically a great engine of economic growth has been widely accepted. But many other connections remain under-recognized, and they have to be seized more fully in policy analysis. Economic growth can help not only in raising private incomes but also in making it possible for the state to finance social insurance and active public intervention. Thus the contribution of economic growth has to be judged not merely by the increase in private incomes, but also by the expansion of social services (including, in many cases, social safety nets) that economic growth may make possible.[4]

Similarly, the creation of social opportunities, through such services as public education, health care, and the development of a free and energetic press, can contribute both to economic development and to significant reductions in mortality rates. Reduction of mortality rates, in turn, can help to reduce birth rates, reinforcing the influence of basic education — especially female literacy and schooling — on fertility behavior.

The pioneering example of enhancing economic growth through social opportunity, especially in basic education, is of course Japan. It is sometimes forgotten that Japan had a higher rate of literacy than Europe had even at the time of the Meiji restoration in the mid-nineteenth century, when industrialization had not yet occurred there but had gone on for many decades in Europe. Japan's economic development was clearly much helped by the human resource development related to the social opportunities that were generated. The so-called East Asian miracle involving other countries in East Asia was, to a great extent, based on similar causal connections.[5]

This approach goes against — and to a great extent undermines — the belief that has been so dominant in many policy circles that "human development" (as the process of expanding education, healthcare and other conditions of human life is often called) is really a kind of luxury that only richer countries can afford. Perhaps the most important impact of the type of success that the East Asian economies, beginning with Japan, have had is the total undermining of that implicit prejudice. These economies went comparatively early for massive expansion of education, and later also of health care, and this they did, in many cases, *before* they broke the restraints of general poverty. And they have reaped as they have sown. Indeed, as Hiromitsu Ishi has pointed out, the priority to human resource development applies particularly to the early history of Japanese economic development, beginning with the Meiji era (1868–1911), and that focus has not intensified with economic affluence as Japan has grown richer and much more opulent.[6] ...

[1] See Chapter 2

[2] I have discussed this contrast in an earlier paper, "Development Thinking at the Beginning of the 21st Century," in *Economic and Social Development into the XXI Century*, edited by Louis Emmerij (Washington, D.C.: Inter-American Development Bank, distributed by Johns Hopkins University Press, 1997). See also my "Economic Policy and Equity: An Overview," in *Economic Policy and Equity*, edited by Vito Tanzi, Ke-young Chu, and Sanjeev Gupta (Washington, D.C.: International Monetary Fund, 1999).

[3] This chapter served as the basis of a keynote address given at the World Bank Symposium on Global Finance and Development in Tokyo, March 1–2, 1999.

[4] On this see Jean Drèze and Amartya Sen, *Hunger and Public Action* (Oxford: Clarendon Press, 1989).

[5] On this see World Bank, *The East Asian Miracle: Economic Growth and Public Policy* (Oxford: Oxford University Press, 1993). See also Tanzi et al., *Economic Policy and Equity*.

[6] See Hiromitsu Ishi, "Trends in the Allocation of Public Expenditure in Light of Human Resource Development — Overview in Japan," mimeographed, Asian Development Bank, Manila, 1995. See also Carol Gluck, *Japan's Modern Myths: Ideology in the Late Meiji Period* (Princeton: Princeton University Press, 1985).

ON ENVIRONMENTAL RIGHTS

The inability of ordinary people in poor countries to control their environment and the use of their national resources is well exemplified by the dramatic events that led to the execution of Nigerian journalist and environmental activist Ken Saro-Wiwa (1941–1995). In 1990, Ken Saro-Wiwa founded the MOSOP, a movement to promote the rights of the Ogoni, demanding that they receive a share of the proceeds from the oil extracted from their lands by Shell, as well as compensation for environmental damage. After organizing a peaceful march of approximately 300,000 Ogoni, he was arrested and detained by the Nigerian government. Later accused of incitement to murder, Saro-Wiwa was imprisoned and sentenced in a specially convened trial that was widely criticized by human rights organizations. His eloquent trial speech, "On Environmental Rights of the Ogoni People of Nigeria" (1995), dramatized the struggle for economic development and environmental rights against the power of a global corporation to manipulate the policies of states.

In "Radicalism, Environmentalism and Wilderness Preservation: A Third World Critique" (1989–1999), Indian scholar Ramachandra Guha reveals the tensions within the ecological movement in the developing world. Guha argued that Third World development projects inspired by the deep ecological movement were antithetical to environmental positions associated with egalitarian justice. He illustrated his point by showing how a project called Tiger, a network of parks celebrated by the international conservation community, was considered a success by wilderness protection advocates. Yet the protection of tigers and other mammals, Guha explained, was only made possible thanks to the physical displacement of peasants and livestock. The resulting dislocation of peasants from their sources of livelihood, argued Guha, unveiled the distorting priorities of the global ecological movement. Guha's criticism found a voice in the Rio Declaration on Environment and Human Rights (1992) — a declaration that put "human beings at the centers of concerns for sustainable development" and affirms a human entitlement "to a healthy and productive life in harmony with nature."

12.5 KEN SARO-WIWA: ON ENVIRONMENTAL RIGHTS OF THE OGONI PEOPLE IN NIGERIA (1995)[1]

My name is Kenule Beeson Saro-Wiwa. I live at Simaseng place 9 Rumuibekwe road, port Harcourt. I am a writer, publisher, environmentalist and human rights activist.

I am the president of the Ethnic Minority Rights Organization of Africa (EMIROAF). I am also the current president of the Movement for the Survival of the Ogoni People (MOSOP) which was founded in 1990 to struggle non-violently for the political, economic and environmental rights of the Ogoni people. The motto of the movement is "Freedom, Peace and Justice." ...

The birthright of freedom and equality imprinted itself on my mind as I studied history in my first year at the University. Nigeria was a federation of ethnic groups. All ethnic groups are equal irrespective of size. I had followed, even as a schoolboy at Umuahia, the proceedings of the Willink Commission of Inquiry which investigated the fears of Nigeria's ethnic minorities and was expected to put forward proposals as to how to allay them as Nigeria marched to independence. I had noted the cries of the Ogoni people before the Commission. One of the men who spoke for the Ogoni before the commission, Kemte Giadom, has been before this Tribunal in a slightly diminished role. There was no doubt in the minds of the Ogoni leaders that the Ogoni required room, breathing space, in Nigeria and that their rights had to be specially protected. The colonial government was not very forthcoming and was probably less than honest. Oil had already been found in Ogoni and Olibiri at that time, yet the British used the fact of poverty to deny the ethnic groups in the Niger delta the right to self-determination which they keenly demanded and were entitled to. It was thought that this birthright would have to be secured after independence.

Now here we were, independent or said to be independent and the struggle for the national cake had become a living matter of life and death for the three major ethnic groups. But did they care who baked the cake? For the cake was a minority cake, baked in the belly of the Niger delta, in its plains and creeks where the heat from the ovens was roasting the inhabitants. Greed for the cake was to lead to internecine war, a war in which an estimated one million people died.

In that war which raged between July 1967 and January 1970, at least 30,000 Ogoni people or ten percent of the Ogoni population died. It was a very heavy price to pay for having oil on their land, for baking the cake for the greedy consumers....

[A]s soon as the war ended, I made absolutely sure that they were all rehabilitated, that their positions in Rivers State were promptly secured and that they could begin to make an Ogoni contribution to the development of the newly-created Rivers State. Their individual and collective achievement whatever its quality was a pride to me. I did not expect to be thanked for this service by any individuals. I was not. My reward was knowing that I had done my duty by my country and by my kith and kin.

Even in Rivers State, I remained conscious of the need for peace and justice among all the nine or so ethnic groups which comprise the state. I argued for fair treatment of all within the State and for Rivers State at the Federal level.

Every argument for rights in Nigeria lands in the deaf ear of rulers. Before long, my regular and consistent argument for equality and equity in Rivers State began to sound like a challenge to the authority of those who wielded power in the State. I was sacked from the Rivers State Government on March 21, 1973. In the four odd years I served as Commissioner, I became very conversant with the problems of the Ogoni people, I did what I could in that time to alleviate some of these problems. Education,

I realized, is basic for progress in the modern world; I did whatever was possible to encourage the Ogoni to acquire it. I cannot say that I was satisfied with my achievement. However, a beginning that could be built on had been made....

I did not fail, in the time I was in Government and thereafter to bring to the notice of all those who were in power or close to it, the angst of the Ogoni people. As a result of my role in the civil war, I developed close relationships with top army officers, including Generals Obasanjo and Danjuma who were to rise to power in 1975, two years after my service with the Rivers State Government ended. Both of them and the Nigerian public in general were fully briefed of the need to treat the Ogoni people fairly.

In something close to desperation, I initiated with other associates, the demand for a split of Rivers State in 1974. We were among the first to see that the twelve-state structure decided by the military in 1967 was not satisfactory, and that it could not satisfy the yearnings of various ethnic groups for development and dignity. I was encouraged in this view by the writings of Obafemi Awolwo and my brief meetings with the eminent philosopher.

I was to be greatly disappointed by those who used the argument which we proffered to take Nigeria down the row to disaster. Instead of state creation being used as an instrument for enhancing the status of the oppressed minority groups, it was used to bolster the power and authority of the majority ethnic groups who were split into a multiplicity of states in order to give them greater access to the oil wealth of the Ogoni and other minority groups in the Niger delta. By this action, the Ogoni and other such groups were being driven not just beyond the periphery of the Nigerian nation but to extinction. I decried this with all the energy at my disposal.

However, the more I cried, the worse the situation became. Were I given to violence, I would have considered using it to bring the argument home. Slavery, denigration, dehumanization are achieved by violence. Those who resort to the same methods to end these evils are only responding to the agenda set by the slave master. However, as a man of peace, I did not for once consider this alternative. I have always believed in the power of the intellect, the superior graces of dialogue as a means of conflict resolution.... In 1987, I found direction in the Directorate for Mass Mobilization, Social Justice, and Economic Recovery otherwise known as Mamser set up by the military dictator, Babangida and to which I was appointed as Executive Director in October 1987....

Here was a call to revolutionary change in Nigeria. Bearing in mind that these may merely be good intentions and realizing that the way to hell is paved with good intentions, I decided to give the Directorate a year of my time, in the first instance. It turned out to be an important year in my life, in the life of Ogoni people and, I dare say, in the life of ethnic minorities in Nigeria and the African continent. I found out, as Director in charge of Research, that the oppressed ethnic minorities of our land required just such mobilization, such ideas of social justice, just such economic recovery. This was the route to their salvation....

My lord, we all stand before history. I am a man of peace, of ideas. Appalled by the denigrating poverty of my people who live on a richly-endowed land, distressed by their political marginalization and economic strangulation, angered by the devastation of their land, their ultimate heritage, anxious to preserve their right to life and to a decent living, and determined to usher to this country as a whole a fair and just democratic system which protects everyone and every ethnic group and gives us all a valid claim to human civilization, I have devoted all my intellectual and material resources, my very life, to a cause in which I have total belief and from which I cannot be blackmailed or intimidated. I have no doubt at all about the ultimate success of my cause, no matter the trials and tribulations which I and those who believe with me may encounter on our journey. Nor imprisonment nor death can stop our ultimate victory.

I repeat that we all stand before history. I and my colleagues are not the only ones on trial. Shell is here on trial and it is well that it is represented by counsel said to be holding a watching brief. The company has, indeed, ducked this particular trial, but its day will surely come and the lessons learnt here may prove useful to it for there is no doubt in my mind that the ecological war the company has waged in the delta will be called to question sooner than later and the crimes of that war duly punished. The crime of the company's dirty wars against the Ogoni people will also be punished.

On trial also is the Nigerian nation, its present rulers and all those who assist them. Any nation which can do to the weak and disadvantaged what the Nigerian nation has done to the Ogoni, loses a claim to independence and to freedom from outside influence. I am not one of those who shy away from protesting injustice and oppression, arguing that they are expected from a military regime. The military do not act alone. They are supported by a gaggle of politicians, lawyers, judges, academics and businessmen, all of them hiding under the claim that they are only doing their duty, men and women too afraid to wash their pants of their urine. We all stand on trial, my lord, for by our actions we have denigrated our country and jeopardized the future of our children. As we subscribe to the sub-normal and accept double standards, as we lie and cheat openly, as we protect injustice and oppression, we empty our classrooms, degrade our hospitals, fill our stomachs with hunger and elect to make ourselves the slaves of those who subscribe to higher standards, pursue the truth, and honor justice, freedom and hard work.

I predict that the scene here will be played and replayed by generations yet unborn. Some have already cast themselves in the role of villains, some are tragic victims, some still have a chance to redeem themselves. The choice is for each individual.

I predict that a denouement of the riddle of the Niger delta will soon come. The agenda is being set at this trial. Whether the peaceful ways I have favored will prevail depends on what the oppressor decides, what signals it sends out to the waiting public.

In my innocence of the false charges I face here, in my utter conviction, I call upon the Ogoni people, the people of the Niger delta, and the oppressed ethnic minorities of

Nigeria to stand up now and fight fearlessly and peacefully, for their rights. History is on their side, God is on their side. For the Holy Quran says in Sura 42, verse 41: "All those who fight, when oppressed incur no guilt, but Allah shall punish the oppressor." Come the day.

[1] Ken Saro-Wiwa's statement to Ogoni Civil Disturbances Tribunal, September 21, 1995.

12.6 RAMACHANDRA GUHA ("RADICAL AMERICAN ENVIRONMENTALISM AND WILDERNESS PRESERVATION: A THIRD WORLD CRITIQUE," 1999)

Even God dare not appear to the poor man except in the form of bread.

Mahatma Gandhi

In this article I develop a critique of deep ecology....

My treatment of deep ecology is primarily historical and sociological, rather than philosophical, in nature. Specifically, I examine the cultural rootedness of a philosophy that likes to present itself in universalistic terms. I make two main arguments: first, that deep ecology is uniquely American, and despite superficial similarities in rhetorical style, the social and political goals of radical environmentalism in other cultural contexts (e.g., West Germany and India) are quite different; second, that the social consequences of putting deep ecology into practice on a worldwide basis (what its practitioners are aiming for) are very grave indeed.

The Tenets of Deep Ecology

While I am aware that the term deep ecology was coined by the Norwegian philosopher Arne Næss, this article refers specifically to the American variant.[1] Adherents of the deep ecological perspective in this country, while arguing intensely among themselves over its political and philosophical implications, share some fundamental premises about human-nature interactions. As I see it,

the defining characteristics of deep ecology are fourfold:

First, deep ecology argues that the environmental movement must shift from an "anthropocentric" to a "biocentric" perspective. In many respects, an acceptance of the primacy of this distinction constitutes the litmus test of deep ecology. A considerable effort is expended by deep ecologists in showing that the dominant motif in Western philosophy has been anthropocentric — i.e., the belief that man and his works are the center of the universe — and conversely, in identifying those lonely thinkers (Leopold, Thoreau, Muir, Aldous Huxley, Santayana, etc.) who, in assigning man a more humble place in the natural order, anticipated deep ecological thinking. In the political realm, meanwhile, establishment environmentalism (shallow ecology) is chided for casting its arguments in human-centered terms. Preserving nature, the deep ecologists say, has an intrinsic worth quite apart from any benefits preservation may convey to future human generations. The anthropocentric-biocentric distinction is accepted as axiomatic by deep ecologists, it structures their discourse, and much of the present discussion remains mired within it.

The second characteristic of deep ecology is its focus on the preservation of unspoiled wilderness — and the restoration of degraded areas to a more pristine condition — to the relative (and sometimes absolute) neglect of other issues on the environmental agenda. I later identify the cultural roots and portentous consequences of this obsession with wilderness. For the moment, let me indicate three distinct sources from which it springs. Historically, it represents a playing out of the preservationist (read radical) and utilitarian (read reformist) dichotomy that has plagued American environmentalism since the turn of the century. Morally, it is an imperative that follows from the biocentric perspective; other species of plants and animals, and nature itself, have an intrinsic right to exist. And finally, the preservation of wilderness also turns on a scientific argument — viz., the value of biological diversity in stabilizing ecological regimes and in retaining a gene pool for future generations. Truly radical policy proposals have been put forward by deep ecologists on the basis of these arguments. The influential poet Gary Snyder, for example, would like to see a 90 percent reduction in human populations to allow a restoration of pristine environments, while others have argued forcefully that a large portion of the globe must be immediately cordoned off from human beings.[2]

Third, there is a widespread invocation of Eastern spiritual traditions as forerunners of deep ecology. Deep ecology, it is suggested, was practiced both by major religious traditions and at a more popular level by "primal" peoples in non-Western settings. This complements the search for an authentic lineage in Western thought. At one level, the task is to recover those dissenting voices within the Judeo-Christian tradition; at another, to suggest that religious traditions in other cultures are, in contrast, dominantly if not exclusively "biocentric" in their orientation. This coupling of (ancient) Eastern and (modern) ecological wisdom seemingly helps consolidate the claim that deep ecology is a philosophy of universal significance.

Fourth, deep ecologists, whatever their internal differences, share the belief that they are the "leading edge" of the environmental movement. As the polarity of the shallow/deep and anthropocentric/biocentric distinctions makes clear, they see themselves as the spiritual, philosophical, and political vanguard of American and world environmentalism.

Toward a Critique

Although I analyze each of these tenets independently, it is important to recognize, as deep ecologists are fond of remarking in reference to nature, the inter-connectedness and unity of these individual themes.

Insofar as it has begun to act as a check on man's arrogance and ecological hubris,

the transition from an anthropocentric (human-centered) to a biocentric (humans as only one element in the ecosystem) view in both religious and scientific traditions is only to be welcomed.[3] What is unacceptable are the radical conclusions drawn by deep ecology, in particular, that intervention in nature should be guided primarily by the need to preserve biotic integrity rather than by the needs of humans. The latter for deep ecologists is anthropocentric, the former biocentric. This dichotomy is, however, of very little use in understanding the dynamics of environmental degradation. The two fundamental ecological problems facing the globe are (1) overconsumption by the industrialized world and by urban elites in the Third World and (2) growing militarization, both in a short-term sense (i.e., ongoing regional wars) and in a long-term sense (i.e., the arms race and the prospect of nuclear annihilation). Neither of these problems has any tangible connection to the anthropocentric-biocentric distinction. Indeed, the agents of these processes would barely comprehend this philosophical dichotomy. The proximate causes of the ecologically wasteful characteristics of industrial society and of militarization are far more mundane: at an aggregate level, the dialectic of economic and political structures, and at a micro-level, the lifestyle choices of individuals. These causes cannot be reduced, whatever the level of analysis, to a deeper anthropocentric attitude toward nature; on the contrary, by constituting a grave threat to human survival, the ecological degradation they cause does not even serve the best interests of human beings! If my identification of the major dangers to the integrity of the natural world is correct, invoking the bogey of anthropocentrism is at best irrelevant, and at worst a dangerous obfuscation.

If the above dichotomy is irrelevant, the emphasis on wilderness is positively harmful when applied to the Third World. If in the United States the preservationist/utilitarian division is seen as mirroring the conflict between "people" and "interests," in countries such as India the situation is very nearly the reverse. Because India is a long settled and densely populated country in which agrarian populations have a finely balanced relationship with nature, the setting aside of wilderness areas has resulted in a direct transfer of resources from the poor to the rich. Thus, Project Tiger, a network of parks hailed by the international conservation community as an outstanding success, sharply posits the interests of the tiger against those of poor peasants living in and around the reserve. The designation of tiger reserves was made possible only by the physical displacement of existing villages and their inhabitants; their management requires the continuing exclusion of peasants and livestock. The initial impetus for setting up parks for the tiger and other large mammals such as the rhinoceros and elephant came from two social groups, first, a class of ex-hunters turned conservationists belonging mostly to the declining Indian feudal elite, and second, representatives of international agencies, such as the World Wildlife Fund (WWF) and the International Union for the Conservation of Nature and Natural Resources (IUCN), seeking to transplant the American system of national parks onto Indian soil. In no case have the needs of the local population been taken into account, and as in many parts of Africa, the designated wild lands are managed primarily for the benefit of rich tourists. Until very recently, wild lands preservation has been identified with environmentalism by the state and the conservation elite; in consequence environmental problems that impinge far more directly on the lives of the poor — e.g., fuel, fodder, water shortages, soil erosion, and air and water pollution — have not been adequately addressed.[4]

Deep ecology provides, perhaps unwittingly, a justification for the continuation of such narrow and inequitable conservation practices under a newly acquired radical guise. Increasingly, the international conservation elite is using the philosophical, moral, and scientific arguments used by deep ecologists in advancing their wilderness crusade. A striking but by no means atypical example is the recent plea by a prominent American biologist for the take-over of large portions of the globe by the author and his scientific colleagues. Writing in a prestigious scientific forum, *The Annual Review of Ecol-*

ogy and Systematics, Daniel Janzen argues that only biologists have the competence to decide how the tropical landscape should be used. As "the representatives of the natural world," biologists are "in charge of the future of tropical ecology, and only they have the expertise and mandate to determine whether the tropical agroscape is to be populated only by humans, their mutualists, commensals, and parasites, or whether it will also contain some islands of the greater nature — the nature that spawned humans yet has been vanquished by them." Janzen exhorts his colleagues to advance their territorial claims on the tropical world more forcefully, warning that the very existence of these areas is at stake: "if biologists want a tropics in which to biologize, they are going to have to buy it with care, energy, effort, strategy, tactics, time, and cash."[5]

This frankly imperialist manifesto highlights the multiple dangers of the preoccupation with wilderness preservation that is characteristic of deep ecology. As I have suggested, it seriously compounds the neglect by the American movement of far more pressing environmental problems within the Third World. But perhaps more importantly, and in a more insidious fashion, it also provides an impetus to the imperialist yearning of Western biologists and their financial sponsors, organizations such as the WWF and IUCN. The wholesale transfer of a movement culturally rooted in American conservation history can only result in the social uprooting of human populations in other parts of the globe.

I come now to the persistent invocation of Eastern philosophies as antecedent in point of time but convergent in their structure with deep ecology. Complex and internally differentiated religious traditions — Hinduism, Buddhism, and Taoism — are lumped together as holding a view of nature believed to be quintessentially biocentric. Individual philosophers such as the Taoist Lao Tzu are identified as being forerunners of deep ecology. Even an intensely political, pragmatic, and Christian influenced thinker such as Gandhi has been accorded a wholly undeserved place in the deep ecological pantheon. Thus the Zen teacher Robert Aitken

Roshi makes the strange claim that Gandhi's thought was not human-centered and that he practiced an embryonic form of deep ecology which is "traditionally Eastern and is found with differing emphasis in Hinduism, Taoism and in Theravada and Mahayana Buddhism."[6]

Moving away from the realm of high philosophy and scriptural religion, deep ecologists make the further claim that at the level of material and spiritual practice "primal" peoples subordinated themselves to the integrity of the biotic universe they inhabited.

I have indicated that this appropriation of Eastern traditions is in part dictated by the need to construct an authentic lineage and in part a desire to present deep ecology as a universalistic philosophy. Indeed, in his substantial and quixotic biography of John Muir, Michael Cohen goes so far as to suggest that Muir was the "Taoist of the [American] West."[7] This reading of Eastern traditions is selective and does not bother to differentiate between alternate (and changing) religious and cultural traditions; as it stands, it does considerable violence to the historical record. Throughout most recorded history the characteristic form of human activity in the "East" has been a finely tuned but nonetheless conscious and dynamic manipulation of nature. Although mystics such as Lao Tzu did reflect on the spiritual essence of human relations with nature, it must be recognized that such ascetics and their reflections were supported by a society of cultivators whose relationship with nature was a far more active one. Many agricultural communities do have a sophisticated knowledge of the natural environment that may equal (and sometimes surpass) codified "scientific" knowledge. Yet the elaboration of such traditional ecological knowledge (in both material and spiritual contexts) can hardly be said to rest on a mystical affinity with nature of a deep ecological kind. Nor is such knowledge infallible; as the archaeological record powerfully suggests, modern Western man has no monopoly on ecological disasters.

In a brilliant article, the Chicago historian Ronald Inden points out that this romantic and essentially positive view of the East is a mirror image of the scientific and essentially pejorative view normally upheld by Western scholars of the Orient. In either case, the East constitutes the Other, a body wholly separate and alien from the West; it is defined by a uniquely spiritual and non-rational "essence," even if this essence is valorized quite differently by the two schools. Eastern man exhibits a spiritual dependence with respect to nature — on the one hand, this is symptomatic of his pre-scientific and backward self, on the other, of his ecological wisdom and deep ecological consciousness. Both views are monolithic, simplistic, and have the characteristic effect — intended in one case, perhaps unintended in the other — of denying agency and reason to the East and making it the privileged orbit of Western thinkers....

How radical, finally, are the deep ecologists? Notwithstanding their self image and strident rhetoric (in which the label "shallow ecology" has an opprobrium similar to that reserved for "social-democratic" by Marxist-Leninists), even within the American context their radicalism is limited and it manifests itself quite differently elsewhere....

Deep ecology runs parallel to the consumer society without seriously questioning its ecological and socio-political basis. In its celebration of American wilderness, it also displays an uncomfortable convergence with the prevailing climate of nationalism in the American frontier movement. For spokesmen such as the historian Roderick Nash, the national park system is America's distinctive cultural contribution to the world, reflective not merely of its economic but of its philosophical and ecological maturity as well. In what Walter Lippmann called the American century, the "American invention of national parks" must be exported worldwide. Betraying an economic determinism that would make even a Marxist shudder, Nash believes that environmental preservation is a "full stomach" phenomenon that is confined to the rich, urban, and sophisticated. Nonetheless, he hopes that "the less developed nations may eventually evolve economically and intellectually to the point where nature preservation is more than a business."[8]

The error which Nash makes (and which deep ecology in some respects encourages) is to equate environmental protection with the protection of wilderness. This is a distinctively American notion, born out of a unique social and environmental history. The archetypal concerns of radical environmentalists in other cultural contexts are in fact quite different. The German Greens, for example, have elaborated a devastating critique of industrial society which turns on the acceptance of environmental limits to growth. Pointing to the intimate links between industrialization, militarization, and conquest, the Greens argue that economic growth in the West has historically rested on the economic and ecological exploitation of the Third World. Rudolf Bahro is characteristically blunt:

> The working class here [in the West] is the richest lower class in the world. And if I look at the problem from the point of view of the whole of humanity, not just from that of Europe, then I must say that the metropolitan working class is the worst exploiting class in history.... What made poverty bearable in eighteenth or nineteenth-century Europe was the prospect of escaping it through exploitation of the periphery. But this is no longer a possibility, and continued industrialism in the Third World will mean poverty for whole generations and hunger for millions.[9]

Here the roots of global ecological problems lie in the disproportionate share of resources consumed by the industrialized countries as a whole and the urban elite within the Third World. Since it is impossible to reproduce an industrial monoculture worldwide, the ecological movement in the West must begin by cleaning up its own act. The Greens advocate the creation of a "no growth" economy, to be achieved by scaling down current (and clearly unsustainable) consumption levels.[10] This radical shift in consumption and production patterns requires the creation of alternate economic and political structures — smaller in scale and more amenable to social participation

— but it rests equally on a shift in cultural values. The expansionist character of modern Western man will have to give way to an ethic of renunciation and self-limitation, in which spiritual and communal values play an increasing role in sustaining social life. This revolution in cultural values, however, has as its point of departure an understanding of environmental processes quite different from deep ecology.

Many elements of the Green program find a strong resonance in countries such as India, where a history of Western colonialism and industrial development has benefited only a tiny elite while exacting tremendous social and environmental costs. The ecological battles presently being fought in India have as their epicenter the conflict over nature between the subsistence and largely rural sector and the vastly more powerful commercial-industrial sector. Perhaps the most celebrated of these battles concerns the Chipko (Hug the Tree) movement, a peasant movement against deforestation in the Himalayan foothills. Chipko is only one of several movements that have sharply questioned the non-sustainable demand being placed on the land and vegetative base by urban centers and industry. These include opposition to large dams by displaced peasants, the conflict between small artisan fishing and large-scale trawler fishing for export, the countrywide movements against commercial forest operations, and opposition to industrial pollution among downstream agricultural and fishing communities.[11]

Two features distinguish these environmental movements from their Western counterparts. First, for the sections of society most critically affected by environmental degradation — poor and landless peasants, women, and tribals — it is a question of sheer survival, not of enhancing the quality of life. Second, and as a consequence, the environmental solutions they articulate deeply involve questions of equity as well as economic and political redistribution. Highlighting these differences, a leading Indian environmentalist stresses that "environmental protection per se is of least concern to most of these groups. Their main concern is about the use of the environment and who should benefit from it."[12] They seek to wrest control of nature away from the state and the industrial sector and place it in the hands of rural communities who live within that environment but are increasingly denied access to it. These communities have far more basic needs, their demands on the environment are far less intense, and they can draw upon a reservoir of cooperative social institutions and local ecological knowledge in managing the "commons" — forests, grasslands, and the waters — on a sustainable basis. If colonial and capitalist expansion has both accentuated social inequalities and signaled a precipitous fall in ecological wisdom, an alternate ecology must rest on an alternate society and polity as well.

This brief overview of German and Indian environmentalism has some major implications for deep ecology. Both German and Indian environmental traditions allow for a greater integration of ecological concerns with livelihood and work. They also place a greater emphasis on equity and social justice (both within individual countries and on a global scale) on the grounds that in the absence of social regeneration environmental regeneration has very little chance of success. Finally, and perhaps most significantly, they have escaped the preoccupation with wilderness preservation so characteristic of American cultural and environmental history.[13]

A Homily

In 1958, the economist J. K. Galbraith referred to overconsumption as the unasked question of the American conservation movement. There is a marked selectivity, he wrote, "in the conservationist's approach to materials consumption. If we are concerned about our great appetite for materials, it is plausible to seek to increase the supply, to decrease waste, to make better use of the stocks available, and to develop substitutes. But what of the appetite itself? Surely this is the ultimate source of the problem. If it continues its geometric course, will it not one day have to be restrained? Yet in the literature of the resource problem this is the forbidden question. Over it hangs a nearly total silence."[14]

The consumer economy and society have expanded tremendously in the three decades since Galbraith penned these words, yet his criticisms are nearly as valid today. I have said "nearly," for there are some hopeful signs. Within the environmental movement several dispersed groups are working to develop ecologically benign technologies and to encourage less wasteful lifestyles. Moreover, outside the self-defined boundaries of American environmentalism, opposition to the permanent war economy is being carried on by a peace movement that has a distinguished history and impeccable moral and political credentials.

It is precisely these (to my mind, most hopeful) components of the American social scene that are missing from deep ecology. In their widely noticed book, Bill Devall and George Sessions make no mention of militarization or the movements for peace, while activists whose practical focus is on developing ecologically responsible lifestyles (e.g., Wendell Berry) are derided as "falling short of deep ecological awareness."[15] Truly radical ecology in the American context ought to work toward a synthesis of the appropriate technology, alternate lifestyle, and peace movements.[16] By making the (largely spurious) anthropocentric-biocentric distinction central to the debate, deep ecologists may have appropriated the moral high ground, but they are at the same time doing a serious disservice to American and global environmentalism.[17]

[1] Kirkpatrick Sale, "The Forest for the Trees: Can Today's Environmentalists Tell the Difference?" *Mother Jones* 11, no. 5 (November 1986): 26. One of the major criticisms I make in this essay concerns deep ecology's lack of concern with inequalities within human society. In the article in which he coined the term *deep ecology*, Naess himself expresses concerns about inequalities between and within nations. However, his concern with social cleavages and their impact on resource utilization patterns and ecological destruction is not very visible in the later writings of deep ecologists. See Arne Naess, "The Shallow and the Deep, Long-Range Ecology Movement: A Summary," *Inquiry* 16 (1973): 96 (I am grateful to Tom Birch for this reference).

[2] Gary Snyder, quoted in Sale, "The Forest for the Trees," 32. See also Dave Foreman, "A Modest Proposal for a Wilderness System," *Whole Earth Review* 53 (Winter 1987): 42–45.

3 See, for example, Donald Worster, *Nature's Economy: The Roots of Ecology* (San Francisco: Sierra Club Books, 1977).

4 See Center for Science and Environment, India, *The State of the Environment 1982: A Citizens Report* (New Delhi: Center for Science and Environment, 1982); R. Sukumar, "Elephant-Man Conflict in Karnataka," in *The State of Karnataka's Environment*, ed. Cecil Saldanha (Bangalore: Center for Taxonomic Studies, 1985). For Africa, see the brilliant analysis by Hedge Kjekshus, *Ecology Control and Economic Development in East African History* (Berkeley: University of California Press, 1977).

5 Daniel Janzen, "The Future of Tropical Ecology," *Annual Review of Ecology and Systematics* 17 (1986): 305–6 (emphasis added).

6 Robert Aitken Roshi, "Gandhi, Dogen, and Deep Ecology," reprinted as appendix C in Bill Devall and George Sessions, *Deep Ecology: Living as if Nature Mattered* (Salt Lake City: Peregrine Smith Books, 1985). For Gandhi's own views on social reconstruction, see the excellent three-volume collection, edited by Raghavan Iyer, *The Moral and Political Writings of Mahatma Gandhi* (Oxford: Clarendon Press, 1986–87).

7 Michael Cohen, *The Pathless Way* (Madison: University of Wisconsin Press, 1984), 120.

8 Roderick Nash, *Wilderness and the American Mind*, 3rd ed. (New Haven: Yale University Press, 1982).

9 Rudolf Bahro, *From Red to Green* (London: Verso Books, 1984).

10 From time to time, American scholars have themselves criticized these imbalances in consumption patterns. In the 1950s, William Vogt made the charge that the United States, with one-sixteenth of the world's population, was utilizing one-third of the globe's resources (Vogt, cited in E. F. Murphy, *Nature, Bureaucracy and the Rule of Property* [Amsterdam: North Holland, 1977], 29). More recently, Zero Population Growth has estimated that each American consumes thirty-nine times as many resources as an Indian. See *Christian Science Monitor*, March 2, 1987.

11 For an excellent review, see Anil Agarwal and Sunita Narain, eds., *India: The State of the Environment 1984–85: A Citizen's Report* (New Delhi: Center for Science and Environment, 1985). See also Ramachandra Guha, *The Unquiet Woods: Ecological Change and Peasant Resistance in the Indian Himalaya* (Berkeley: University of California Press)

12 Anil Agarwal, "Human-Nature Interactions in a Third World Country," *The Environmentalist* 6, no. 3 (1986): 167.

13 One strand in radical American environmentalism, the bioregional movement, by emphasizing a greater involvement with the bioregion people inhabit, does indirectly challenge consumerism. However, as yet bioregionalism has hardly raised the questions of equity and social justice (international, intranational, and intergenerational) which, I argue, must be a central plank of radical environmentalism. Moreover, its stress on (individual) experience as the key to involvement with nature is also somewhat at odds with the integration of nature with livelihood and work that I talk of in this paper. See Kirkpatrick Sale, *Dwellers in the Land: The Bioregional Vision* (San Francisco: Sierra Club Books, 1985).

14 John Kenneth Galbraith, "How Much Should a Country Consume?" in *Perspectives Conservation*, ed. Henry Janett (Baltimore: Johns Hopkins Press, 1958), 91–92.

15 Devall and Sessions, *Deep Ecology*, 122. For Wendel Berry's own assessment of deep ecology, see his "Applications: Preserving Wildness," *Wilderness* 50 (Spring 1987): 39–40, 50–54.

16 See the interesting recent contribution by one of the most influential spokesmen of appropriate technology, Barry Commoner, "A Reporter at Large: the Environment," *New Yorker*, June 15, 1987. While Commoner makes a forceful plea for the convergence of the environmental movement (viewed by him primarily as the opposition to air and water pollution and to the institutions that generate such pollution) and the peace movement, he significantly does not mention consumption patterns, implying that "limits to growth" do not exist.

17 In this sense, my critique of deep ecology, although that of an outsider, may facilitate the reassertion of those elements in the American environmental tradition for which there is a profound sympathy in other parts of the globe. A global perspective may also lead to a critical reassessment of figures such as Aldo Leopold and John Muir, the two patron saints of deep ecology. As Donald Worster has pointed out, the message of Muir (and, I would argue, of Leopold as well) makes sense only in an American context; he has very little to say to other cultures. See Worster's review of Stephen Fox's "John Muir and His Legacy," in *Environmental Ethics* 5 (1983): 277–81.

12.7 RIO DECLARATION ON ENVIRONMENT AND DEVELOPMENT (1992)[1]

Reaffirming the Declaration of the United Nations Conference on the Human Environment, adopted at Stockholm on 16 June 1972, and seeking to build upon it,

With the goal of establishing a new and equitable global partnership through the creation of new levels of cooperation among States, key sectors of societies and people,

Working towards international agreements which respect the interests of all and protect the integrity of the global environmental and developmental system,

Recognizing the integral and interdependent nature of the Earth, our home,

Proclaims that:

Principle 1

Human beings are at the center of concerns for sustainable development. They are entitled to a healthy and productive life in harmony with nature.

Principle 2

States have, in accordance with the Charter of the United Nations and the principles of international law, the sovereign right to exploit their own resources pursuant to their own environmental and developmental policies, and the responsibility to ensure that activities within their jurisdiction or control do not cause damage to the environment of other States or of areas beyond the limits of national jurisdiction.

Principle 3

The right to development must be fulfilled so as to equitably meet developmental and environmental needs of present and future generations.

Principle 4

In order to achieve sustainable development, environmental protection shall constitute an integral part of the development process and cannot be considered in isolation from it.

Principle 5

All States and all people shall cooperate in the essential task of eradicating poverty as an indispensable requirement for sustainable development, in order to decrease the disparities in standards of living and better meet the needs of the majority of the people of the world.

Principle 6

The special situation and needs of developing countries, particularly the least developed and those most environmentally vulnerable, shall be given special priority. International actions in the field of environment and development should also address the interests and needs of all countries.

Principle 7

States shall cooperate in a spirit of global partnership to conserve, protect and restore the health and integrity of the Earth's ecosystem. In view of the different contributions to global environmental degradation, States have common but differentiated responsibilities. The developed countries acknowledge the responsibility that they bear in the international pursuit of sustainable development in view of the pressures their societies place on the global environment and of the technologies and financial resources they command.

Principle 8

To achieve sustainable development and a higher quality of life for all people, States should reduce and eliminate unsustainable patterns of production and consumption and promote appropriate demographic policies.

Principle 9

States should cooperate to strengthen endogenous capacity-building for sustainable development by improving scientific understanding through exchanges of scientific and technological knowledge, and by enhancing the development, adaptation, diffusion and transfer of technologies, including new and innovative technologies.

Principle 10

Environmental issues are best handled with the participation of all concerned citizens, at the relevant level. At the national level, each individual shall have appropriate access to information concerning the environment that is held by public authorities, including information on hazardous materials and activities in their communities, and the opportunity to participate in decision-making processes. States shall facilitate and encourage public awareness and participation by making information widely available. Effective access to judicial and administrative proceedings, including redress and remedy, shall be provided.

Principle 11

States shall enact effective environmental legislation. Environmental standards, management objectives and priorities should reflect the environmental and developmental context to which they apply. Standards applied by some countries may be inappropriate and of unwarranted economic and social cost to other countries, in particular developing countries.

Principle 12

States should cooperate to promote a supportive and open international economic system that would lead to economic growth and sustainable development in all countries, to better address the problems of environmental degradation. Trade policy measures for environmental purposes should not constitute a means of arbitrary or unjustifiable discrimination or a disguised restriction on international trade.

Unilateral actions to deal with environmental challenges outside the jurisdiction of the importing country should be avoided. Environmental measures addressing transboundary or global environmental problems should, as far as possible, be based on an international consensus.

Principle 13

States shall develop national law regarding liability and compensation for the victims of pollution and other environmental damage. States shall also cooperate in an expeditious and more determined manner to develop further international law regarding liability and compensation for adverse effects of environmental damage caused by activities within their jurisdiction or control to areas beyond their jurisdiction.

Principle 14

States should effectively cooperate to discourage or prevent the relocation and transfer to other States of any activities and substances that cause severe environmental degradation or are found to be harmful to human health.

Principle 15

In order to protect the environment, the precautionary approach shall be widely applied by States according to their capabilities. Where there are threats of serious or irreversible damage, lack of full scientific certainty shall not be used as a reason for postponing cost-effective measures to prevent environmental degradation.

Principle 16

National authorities should endeavor to promote the internalization of environmental costs and the use of economic instruments, taking into account the approach that the polluter should, in principle, bear the cost of pollution, with due regard to the public interest and without distorting international trade and investment.

Principle 17

Environmental impact assessment, as a national instrument, shall be undertaken for proposed activities that are likely to have a significant adverse impact on the environment and are subject to a decision of a competent national authority.

Principle 18

States shall immediately notify other States of any natural disasters or other emergencies that are likely to produce sudden harmful effects on the environment of those States. Every effort shall be made by the international community to help States so afflicted.

Principle 19

States shall provide prior and timely notification and relevant information to potentially affected States on activities that may have a significant adverse transboundary environmental effect and shall consult with those States at an early stage and in good faith.

Principle 20

Women have a vital role in environmental management and development. Their full participation is therefore essential to achieve sustainable development.

Principle 21

The creativity, ideals and courage of the youth of the world should be mobilized to forge a global partnership in order to achieve sustainable development and ensure a better future for all.

Principle 22

Indigenous people and their communities and other local communities have a vital role in environmental management and development because of their knowledge and traditional practices. States should recognize and duly support their identity, culture and interests and enable their effective participation in the achievement of sustainable development.

Principle 23

The environment and natural resources of people under oppression, domination and occupation shall be protected.

Principle 24

Warfare is inherently destructive of sustainable development. States shall therefore respect international law providing protection for the environment in times of armed conflict and cooperate in its further development, as necessary.

Principle 25

Peace, development and environmental protection are interdependent and indivisible.

[1]Original publication details: United Nations Conference on Environment and Development, excerpt from "Rio Declaration on Environment and Development," June 14, 1992.

ON REFUGEES, IMMIGRANTS, AND SEXUAL TRAFFICKING

No one has described the subjection of refugees to severe human rights abuses more eloquently than the German political theorist Hanna Arendt (1906–1975). In her *Origins of Totalitarianism* (1951), she observed the great calamity of stateless people, deprived of life, liberty, and the pursuit of happiness, of equality before the law and freedom of opinion. Refugees are usually left without protection from either their own community or the state. "The danger," Arendt anticipated, "is that a global, universally interrelated civilization may produce barbarians from its own midst by forcing millions of people into conditions which, despite all appearances, are the conditions of savages" (see Section 12.9).

Her sentiments were echoed years later by Dutch sociologist Saskia Sassen, who depicted how war, economic despair, poor indebted governments, and unemployment have driven people across borders, shorn of legal protections. In our globalized age, Saskia Sassen argued, immigration rights policies and enforcement remain weak, contributing to the vulnerability of female migrants and the silence of abused illegal migrant women in their household or workplace. An extreme form of abuse of immigrants is the practice of sexual trafficking, in which women (and children of both sexes) suffer horrendous conditions of confinement and physical suffering. Reliant on remittances from their Diaspora migrant communities, poor governments have failed to change the fate of these migrant workers. "It is increasingly on the backs of women," Sassen commented, "that these forms of survival...operate" — i.e., criminal enterprises and government revenue enhancement — operate, making it very difficult to enhance legal protections for female migrant workers (see Section 12.10).

There has been an international legal response to the plight of refugees and migrants, in the form of numerous treaties and declarations against sexual trafficking and in support of the protection of female migrant workers and refugees. These include the U.N. Convention of the Rights of Children (1989; see Articles 34 to 35), the African Charter on the Rights and Welfare of the Child (1999; see Article 29), and the Beijing Declaration (paragraphs 224 and 226). Yet global economic forces, driven by the tourist trade and other industries, have so far overwhelmed such efforts to enforce the human rights of migrants and refugees.

12.8 HANNAH ARENDT: ON THE RIGHTS OF THE STATELESS (*THE ORIGINS OF TOTALITARIANISM*, 1951)[1]

... The calamity of the rightless is not that they are deprived of life, liberty, and the pursuit of happiness, or of equality before the law and freedom of opinion — formulas which were designed to solve problems *within* given communities — but that they no longer belong to any community whatsoever. Their plight is not that they are not equal before the law, but that no law exists for them; not that they are oppressed, but that nobody wants even to oppress them. Only in the last stage of a rather lengthy process is their right to live threatened; only if they remain perfectly "superfluous,"

if nobody can be found to "claim" them, may their lives be in danger. Even the Nazis started their extermination of Jews by first depriving them of all legal status (the status of second-class citizenship) and cutting them off from the world of the living by herding them into ghettos and concentration camps; and before they set the gas chambers into motion they had carefully tested the ground and found out to their satisfaction that no country would claim these people. The point is that a condition of complete rightlessness was created before the right to live was challenged.

The same is true even to an ironical extent with regard to the right of freedom which is sometimes considered to be the very essence of human rights. There is no question that those outside the pale of the law may have more freedom of movement than a lawfully imprisoned criminal or that they enjoy more freedom of opinion in the internment camps of democratic countries than they would in any ordinary despotism, not to mention in a totalitarian country.[2] But neither physical safety — being fed by some state or private welfare agency — nor freedom of opinion changes in the least their fundamental situation of rightlessness. The prolongation of their lives is due to charity and not to right, for no law exists which could force the nations to feed them; their freedom of movement if they have it at all gives them no right to residence which even the jailed criminal enjoys as a matter of course; and their freedom of opinion is a fool's freedom, for nothing they think matters anyhow.

These last points are crucial. The fundamental deprivation of human rights is manifested first and above all in the deprivation of a place in the world which makes opinions significant and actions effective. Something much more fundamental than freedom and justice, which are rights of citizens, is at stake when belonging to the community into which one is born is no longer a matter of course and not belonging no longer a matter of choice, or when one is placed in a situation where, unless he commits a crime, his treatment by others does not depend on what he does or does not do. This extremity, and nothing else, is the situation of people deprived of human rights. They are deprived, not of the right to freedom, but of the right to action; not of the right to think whatever they please, but of the right to opinion. Privileges in some cases, injustices in most, blessings and doom are meted out to them according to accident and without any relation whatsoever to what they do, did, or may do.

We became aware of the existence of a right to have rights (and that means to live in a framework where one is judged by one's actions and opinions) and a right to belong to some kind of organized community, only when millions of people emerged who had lost and could not regain these rights because of the new global political situation. The trouble is that this calamity arose not from any lack of civilization, backwardness, or mere tyranny, but, on the contrary, that it could not be repaired, because there was no longer any "uncivilized" spot on earth, because whether we like it or not we have really started to live in One World. Only with a completely organized humanity could the loss of home and political status become identical with expulsion from humanity altogether....

Not the loss of specific rights, then, but the loss of a community willing and able to guarantee any rights whatsoever, has been the calamity which has befallen ever-increasing numbers of people. Man, it turns out, can lose all so-called Rights of Man without losing his essential quality as man, his human dignity. Only the less of a polity itself expels him from humanity.

These facts offer what seems an ironical, bitter, and belated confirmation of the famous arguments with which Edmund Burke opposed the French Revolution's Declaration of the Rights of Man. They appear to buttress his assertion that human rights were an "abstraction," that it was much wiser to rely on an "entailed inheritance" of rights which one transmits to one's children like life itself, and to claim one's rights to be the "rights of an Englishman" rather than the inalienable rights of man.[3] According to Burke, the rights which we enjoy spring "from within the nation," so that neither natural law, nor divine command, nor any concept of mankind such as Robespierre's "human race," "the sovereign of the earth," are needed as a source of law.[4]

The pragmatic soundness of Burke's concept seems to be beyond doubt in the light of our manifold experiences. Not only did loss of national rights in all instances entail the loss of human rights; the restoration of human rights, as the recent example of the State of Israel proves, has been achieved so far only through the restoration or the establishment of national rights. The conception of human rights, based upon the assumed existence of a human being as such, broke down at the very moment when those who professed to believe in it were for the first time confronted with people who had indeed lost all other qualities and specific relationships — except that they were still human. The world found nothing sacred in the abstract nakedness of being human. And in view of objective political conditions, it is hard to say how the concepts of man upon which human rights are based — that he is created in the image of God (in the American formula), or that he is the representative of mankind, or that he harbors within himself the sacred demands of natural law (in the French formula) — could have helped to find a solution to the problem....

The more highly developed a civilization, the more accomplished the world it has produced, the more at home men feel within the human artifice — the more they will resent everything they have not produced, everything that is merely and mysteriously given them. The human being who has lost his place in a community, his political status in the struggle of his time, and the legal personality which makes his actions and part of his destiny a consistent whole, is left with those qualities which usually can become articulate only in the sphere of private life and must remain unqualified, mere existence in all matters of public concern. This mere existence, that is, all that which is mysteriously given us by birth and which includes the shape of our bodies and the talents of our minds, can be adequately dealt with only by the unpredictable hazards of friendship and sympathy, or by the great and incalculable grace of love, which says with Augustine, "*Volo ut sis* (I want you to be)," without being able to give any particular reason for such supreme and unsurpassable affirmation....

Our political life rests on the assumption that we can produce equality through organization, because man can act in and change and build a common world, together with his equals and only with his equals. The dark background of mere givenness, the background formed by our unchangeable and unique nature, breaks into the political scene as the alien which in its all too obvious difference reminds us of the limitations of human activity — which are identical with the limitations of human equality. The reason why highly developed political communities, such as the ancient city-states or modern nation-states, so often insist on ethnic homo-

geneity, is that they hope to eliminate as far as possible those natural and always present differences and differentiations which by themselves arouse dumb hatred, mistrust, and discrimination because they indicate all too clearly those spheres where men cannot act and change at will, i.e., the limitations of the human artifice. The "alien" is a frightening symbol of the fact of difference as such, of individuality as such, and indicates those realms in which man cannot change and cannot act and in which, therefore, he has a distinct tendency to destroy. If a Negro in a white community is considered a Negro and nothing else, he loses along with his right to equality that freedom of action which is specifically human; all his deeds are now explained as "necessary" consequences of some "Negro" qualities; he has become some specimen of an animal species, called man. Much the same thing happens to those who have lost all distinctive political qualities and have become human beings and nothing else. No doubt, wherever public life and its law of equality is completely victorious, wherever a civilization succeeds in eliminating or reducing a minimum the dark background of difference, it will end in complete petrifaction and be punished, so to speak, for having forgotten that man is only the master, not the creator of the world.

The great danger arising from the existence of people forced to live outside the common world is that they are thrown back, in the midst of civilization, on their natural givenness, on their mere differentiation. They lack that tremendous equalizing of differences which comes from being citizens of some commonwealth and yet, since they are no longer allowed to partake in the human artifice, they begin to belong to the human race in much the same way as animals belong to a specific animal species. The paradox involved in the loss of human rights is that such loss coincides with the instant when a person becomes a human being in general — without a profession, without a citizenship, without an opinion, without a deed by which to identify and specify himself — and different in general, representing nothing but his own absolutely unique individuality which, deprived of expression within and action upon a common world, loses all significance.

The danger in the existence of such people is twofold: first and more obviously, their ever-increasing numbers threaten our political life, our human artifice, the world which is the result of our common and coordinated effort in much the same, perhaps even more terrifying, way as the wild elements of nature once threatened the existence of man-made cities and country sides. Deadly danger to any civilization is no longer likely to come from without. Nature has been mastered and no barbarians threaten to destroy what they cannot understand, as the Mongolians threatened Europe for centuries. Even the emergence of totalitarian governments is a phenomenon within, not outside, our civilization. The danger is that a global, universally interrelated civilization may produce barbarians from its own midst by forcing millions of people into conditions which, despite all appearances, are the conditions of savages.[5]

[1] From the "End of Rights of Man."
[2] Even under the conditions of totalitarian terror, concentration camps sometimes have been the only place where certain remnants of freedom of thought and discussion still existed. See David Rousset, Les Jours de Notre Mort, Paris, 1947, passim, for freedom of discussion in Buchenwald, and Anton Ciliga, The Russian Enigma, London, 1940, p. 200, about "isles of liberty," "the freedom of mind" that reigned in some of the Soviet places of detention.
[3] Edmund Burke, "Reflections on the Revolution in France, 1790," edited by E. J. Payne, Everyman's Library.
[4] Robespierre, speeches, 1927 speech of April 24, 1793.
[5] This modern expulsion from humanity has much more radical consequences than the ancient and medieval custom of outlawry. Outlawry, certainly the "most fearful fate which primitive law could inflict," placing the life of the outlawed person at the mercy of anyone he met, disappeared with the establishment of an effective system of law enforcement and was finally replaced by extradition treaties between the nations. It had been primarily a substitute for a police force, designed to compel criminals to surrender.

The early Middle Ages seem to have been quite conscious of the danger involved in "civil death." Excommunication in the late Roman Empire meant ecclesiastical death but left a person who had lost his membership in the church full freedom in all other respects. Ecclesiastical and civil death became identical only in the Merovingian era, and there excommunication "in general practice [was] limited to temporary withdrawal or suspension of the rights of membership which might be regained." See the articles "Outlawry" and "Excommunication" in the Encyclopedia of Social Sciences. Also the article "Friedlosigkeit" in the Schweizer Lexikon.

12.9 SASKIA SASSEN ("WOMEN'S BURDEN: COUNTER-GEOGRAPHIES OF GLOBALIZATION AND THE FEMINIZATION OF SURVIVAL," 2000)

Government Debt

Debt and debt servicing problems have become a systemic feature of the developing world since the 1980s. In my estimation, they also induce the formation of new counter-geographies of globalization. They impact on women and on the feminization of survival through the particular features of this debt (rather than the fact of debt per se). It is with this logic in mind that this section examines various features of government debt in developing economies.

There is considerable research showing the detrimental effects of debt on government programs for women and children, notably education and health care, which clearly are investments necessary to ensure a better future. Further, the increased unemployment typically associated with the austerity and adjustment programs demanded by international agencies to address government debt have also been found to have adverse effects on women. Unemployment, both of women and of the men in their households, has added to the pressure on women to find ways to ensure household survival. Subsistence food production, informal work, emigration and prostitution have all gained prominence as survival options for women.[1]

Heavy government debt and high unemployment have heightened the need to search for survival alternatives. Shrinking economic opportunities have resulted in the increased use of illegal profit making by enterprises and organizations. In this regard, heavy debt burden plays an important role in the formation of counter-geographies of survival, profit-making and government revenue enhancement. Economic globalization has, to some extent, added to the rapid increase in certain components of this debt, and it has provided an institutional infrastructure for cross-border flows and global markets. We can see economic globalization as facilitating the operation of these counter-geographies on a global scale.[2]

Generally, most countries that became deeply indebted in the 1980s have not been able to solve their debt problem. And in the 1990s we have seen a new set of countries become deeply indebted. Over these two decades, the International Monetary Fund (IMF) and the World Bank through their SAPs and Structural Adjustment Loans launched many innovations. (The latter were tied to economic policy reform rather than the funding of a particular project.) The purpose of such programs is to make states more "competitive," which typically means sharp cuts in various social programs. By 1990 there were almost 200 such loans in place. (During the 1980s also, the Reagan administration put enormous pressure on many countries to implement neoliberal policies, which resembled the SAPs.)

Structural Adjustment Programs became a new norm for the World Bank and the IMF on the grounds that they were a promising way to secure long-term growth and sound government policy. Yet all of these countries have remained deeply indebted, with 41 of them now considered as being Highly Indebted Poor Countries (HIPCs). Furthermore, the actual structure of these debts, their servicing and how they fit into debtor-country economies, suggest that it is not likely that most of these countries will, under current conditions, be able to pay their debt in full.[3] SAPs seem to have made this even more likely by demanding economic reforms that have increased the rates

of unemployment and bankruptcy of many smaller, national market-oriented firms.

Even before the economic crisis of the 1990s, the debt of poor countries in the South had grown from US$507 billion in 1980 to US$1.4 trillion by 1992. Debt service payments alone had increased to US$1.6 trillion, more than the outstanding principal. Further, as is widely recognized now, the South has paid its debt several times over, and yet its debt grew by 250 percent. According to some estimates, from 1982 to 1998 indebted countries paid four times the original principal, yet at the same time their debt stocks went up by four times.[4] ...

It is these features of the current situation which suggest that most of these countries will not get out of their indebtedness through such current strategies as SAPs. Indeed it would seem that the latter have in many cases had the effect of raising the debt dependence of countries. Further, together with various other dynamics, SAPs have contributed to an increase in unemployment and in poverty....

Alternative Circuits for Survival

The economic situation described above sets the context for the emergence of alternative circuits of survival. This situation is marked by what I interpret as systemic high unemployment, poverty, bankruptcies of large numbers of firms and shrinking state resources to meet social needs. Here, I focus on some of the data on the trafficking of women for the sex industry and for work; the growing significance of this trafficking as a profit-making option; and the growing importance of emigrant remittances to the account balances of many of the sending states.

Trafficking in Women

Trafficking involves the forced recruitment and movement of people both within and across state boundaries for work or other services through a variety of forms, all involving coercion. Trafficking is a violation of distinct types of rights: human, civil and political. Trafficking in people appears to be related primarily to the sex market, to labor markets and to illegal migration. Legislation via international treaties and charters, UN resolutions and various bodies and commissions has sought to address the problem of trafficking.[5] Non-governmental organizations (NGOs) are also playing an increasingly important role.[6]

Trafficking in women for the sex industry is highly profitable for those running the trade. The United Nations estimates that 4 million people were trafficked in 1998, producing a profit of US$7 billion for criminal groups.[7] These funds include remittances from prostitutes' earnings and payments to organizers and facilitators. In Japan, profits in the sex industry have been approximately 4.2 trillion yen per year over the last few years. In Poland, police estimate that for each Polish woman delivered, traffickers receive about US$700. In Australia, the Federal Police estimate that the cash flow from 200 prostitutes is up to AUS$900,000 a week. Ukrainian and Russian women, highly prized in the sex market, earn the criminal gangs smuggling them about US$500 to US$1,000 per woman delivered. These women can be expected to service on average 15 clients a day, and each can be expected to make about US$215,000 per month for the gang controlling them.[8]

It is estimated that in recent years several million women and girls were trafficked within and out of Asia and the former Soviet Union, two major trafficking areas. Increases in trafficking in both these areas can be linked to women themselves being sold to brokers due to the poverty of their households or parents. High unemployment in the former Soviet republics has been one factor promoting growth of criminal gangs as well as trafficking in women. Upon implementation of market policies, unemployment rates among women in Armenia, Russia, Bulgaria and Croatia reached 70 percent and in Ukraine 80 percent. Some research indicates that economic need is fundamental for entry into prostitution.[10]

Trafficking in migrants is also a profitable business. According to a UN report, criminal organizations in the 1990s generated an estimated US$3.5 billion per year in profits from trafficking migrants gener-

ally (not only women).[11] Entry of organized crime into migrant trafficking is a recent development. In the past it was mostly petty criminals who engaged in this type of trafficking. There are reports that organized crime groups are creating global strategic alliances, often with co-ethnic groups across several countries. This facilitates transport, local contact and distribution and the provision of false documents. The Global Survival Network reported on these practices after a two-year investigation, which used a dummy company to enter the illegal trade.[12] Such networks also facilitate the organized circulation of trafficked women among third countries, not only from sending to receiving countries. Traffickers may move women from Burma, Laos, Vietnam and China to Thailand, while Thai women may be moved to Japan and the United States.[13]

Some of the features of immigration policy and enforcement may contribute to make women who are victims of trafficking even more vulnerable and give them little recourse in the law. If the women are undocumented, which is likely, they will not be treated as victims of abuse but as violators of the law insofar as they have violated entry, residence and work laws.[14] The attempt to address undocumented immigration and trafficking through greater border controls over entry raises the likelihood that women will use traffickers to cross the border, and some of these traffickers may turn out to belong to criminal organizations linked to the sex industry.

Further, in many countries prostitution is specifically forbidden for foreign women, which further enhances the role of criminal gangs in prostitution. It also diminishes one of the survival options for foreign women who may have limited access to jobs generally. Conversely, prostitution is tolerated for foreign women in many countries while regular labor market jobs are less so. This is the case for instance in the Netherlands and in Switzerland. According to the International Organization for Migration (IOM) data, the number of migrant women prostitutes in many EU countries is far higher than that for nationals (for example, 75 percent in Germany and 80 percent in the case of Milan, Italy).

While some women know that they are being trafficked for prostitution, for many the conditions of their recruitment and the extent of abuse and bondage only become evident after they arrive in the receiving country. The conditions of confinement are often extreme, and so are the conditions of abuse, including rape and other forms of sexual violence and physical punishments. They are severely underpaid, and wages are often withheld. They are prevented from using protection methods to prevent against HIV, and they typically have no right to medical treatment. If they seek police help they may be taken into detention because they are in violation of immigration laws; if they have been provided with false documents they are subject to criminal charges.[15]

As tourism has grown sharply over the last decade and become a major part of development strategy for cities, regions and countries, the entertainment sector has experienced parallel growth and recognition as a key development target.[16] In many places, the sex trade is part of the entertainment industry and has grown similarly.[17] At some point it becomes clear that the sex trade itself can become a development strategy in areas with high unemployment and poverty and where governments are desperate for revenue and foreign currency. When local manufacturing and agriculture can no longer function as sources of employment, profits and government revenue, what was once a marginal source of earnings, profits and revenues, now becomes a far more important one. The increased importance of these sectors in development generates greater tie-ins. For instance, if the IMF and the World Bank view tourism as a solution to some of the growth challenges in poor countries and proceed to provide loans for development, they may be contributing to development of a broader institutional setting for the expansion of the entertainment industry. This may also support indirectly the sex trade. This tie-in with development strategies suggests that trafficking in women may well see expansion.

Women in the sex industry become — in certain kinds of economies — a crucial link supporting the expansion of the entertainment industry and thereby of tourism as a development strategy. This in turn becomes a source of government revenue. These tie-ins are structural, not a function of conspiracies. Their weight in an economy will be raised by the absence or limited nature of other sources for securing a livelihood, profits and revenues for workers, businesspeople and governments.

The entry of organized crime in the sex trades, the formation of cross-border ethnic networks and the rising globalization of many aspects of tourism suggest that we are likely to see further development of a global sex industry. This could lead to further attempts to enter into more "markets" and a general expansion of the industry. It is a troubling possibility, especially in the context of growing numbers of women with few, if any, employment options. Such numbers are to be expected given high unemployment and poverty, the shrinking of work opportunities that were embedded in the more traditional sectors of these economies and the growing debt burden of governments rendering them incapable of providing social services and support to the poor.

Remittances

Women and migrants generally enter the macro-level of development strategies through yet another channel: sending of remittances, which in many countries represent a major source of foreign exchange for the government. While the flows of remittances may be minor compared to the massive daily capital flows in various financial markets, they are often very significant for developing or struggling economies.

In 1998 global remittances by immigrants to their home countries exceeded US$70 billion.[18] To understand the significance of this figure, it should be related to the GDP and foreign currency reserves of the specific countries involved, rather than to the global flow of capital. For instance, in the Philippines, a key sender of migrants generally and of women for the entertainment industry in several countries, remittances were the third largest source of foreign exchange over the last several years. In Bangladesh, a country with significant numbers of its workers in the Middle East, Japan and several European countries, remittances represent about a third of foreign exchange.

Exporting workers and securing an inflow of remittances are means for governments to cope with unemployment and foreign debt. There are two ways in which governments have secured benefits through these strategies. One of these is highly formalized and the other is simply a by-product of the migration process itself. Among the strongest examples of formal labor export programs are South Korea and the Philippines.[19] In the 1970s, South Korea developed specific programs to promote the export of construction workers, initially to the Middle Eastern OPEC countries and then worldwide. As South Korea entered its own economic boom, exporting workers became less of a necessity or attractive option. In contrast, the Philippine government expanded and diversified the export of its citizens as a means to deal with unemployment and to secure needed foreign exchange from their remittances. It is to this case that I turn now as it illuminates issues at the heart of this paper.

The Philippine government, through the Philippines Overseas Employment Administration (POEA), has played an important role in the emigration of Philippine women to the US, the Middle East and Japan. Established in 1982, it organized and oversaw the export of nurses and maids to high demand areas around the world. High foreign debt and unemployment combined to make this an attractive policy. Filipino overseas workers have sent home, on average, almost US$1 billion a year over the last few years. On the other side, the various labor-importing countries welcomed this policy for their own specific reasons. Oil producing countries in the Middle East saw the demand for domestic workers rise sharply after the 1973 oil boom. The United States, confronted with a sharp shortage of nurses, a profession that demands years of training yet at the time garnered low wages and little prestige, passed the Immigration Nursing Relief Act of 1989, which allowed for the importation of nurses.[20] And Japan, marked by rising expendable income and strong labor shortages, passed legislation that permitted the entry of "entertainment workers" into its booming economy in the 1980s.[21]

The Philippine government also passed regulations that permitted mail-order bride agencies to recruit young Filipinas for marriage to foreign men as a matter of contractual agreement. The rapid increase in this trade was primarily due to the organized efforts of the government. Among the major clients were the US and Japan. Japan's agricultural communities were a key destination for these brides. This was attributable to the booming economy where demand for labor in the large metropolitan areas was extremely high contributing to an enormous shortage of people and especially young women in the Japanese countryside. Consequently, municipal governments made it a policy to accept Filipina brides.

The largest numbers of Filipinas going through these channels work overseas as maids, particularly in other Asian countries.[22] The second largest group, and the fastest growing, are entertainers, mostly to Japan.[23] The rapid increase in the numbers of entertainer-migrants is largely due to the existence of over five hundred "entertainment brokers" in the Philippines operating outside the state umbrella even though the government may benefit from the remittances of these workers. These brokers work to provide women for the sex industry in Japan, which is basically supported or controlled by organized gangs rather than government-controlled programs for the entry of entertainers. These women are recruited for singing and entertaining, but frequently are forced into prostitution as well.[24]

There is growing evidence of significant violence among mail-order brides in several countries, regardless of nationality of origin. In the US, the Immigration and Naturalization Service (INS) has recently reported that domestic violence towards mail-order wives has become acute. Again, the law operates against these women seeking recourse, as they are liable to be detained if they do so prior to the first two years of marriage. In

Japan, the foreign mail-order wife is not granted full equal legal status to citizens and there is considerable evidence showing that many are subject to abuse not only by the husband but by his extended family as well. The Philippine government approved most mail-order bride organizations until 1989. But under the government of Corazon Aquino, the stories of abuse by foreign husbands led to the banning of the mail-order bride business. It is almost impossible to eliminate these organizations and they continue to operate in violation of the law.

The Philippines, while perhaps the country with the most developed program, is not the only one to have explored these strategies. Thailand started a campaign in 1998, after the financial crisis, to promote migration for work and recruitment of Thai workers by firms overseas. The government sought to export workers to the Middle East, the United States, Great Britain, Germany, Australia and Greece. Sri Lanka's government has tried to export 200,000 workers in addition to the one million it already has overseas. Sri Lankan women remitted US$880 million in 1998, mostly from their earnings as maids in the Middle East and East Asia. Bangladesh had already organized extensive labor export programs to the OPEC countries of the Middle East in the 1970s. This has continued along with individual migrations to these and other countries, notably the US and Great Britain, and it provides a significant source of foreign exchange for Bangladesh. Its workers remitted US$1.4 billion in each of the last few years.[25]

Conclusion

We are seeing the growth of a variety of alternative global circuits for making a living, earning a profit and securing government revenue. These circuits incorporate increasing numbers of women. Among the most important of these global circuits are the illegal trafficking in women for prostitution as well as for regular work, organized export of women as brides, nurses and domestic servants, and the remittances of an increasingly female emigrant work-

force. Some of these circuits operate partly or wholly in the shadow economy.

This article maps some of the main features of these circuits and argues that their emergence and strengthening are linked to major dynamics of economic globalization, which have had significant impacts on developing economies. Key indicators of such impacts are the heavy and rising burden of government debt, the growth in unemployment, sharp cuts in government social expenditures, the closure of a large number of firms in often fairly traditional sectors oriented to the local or national market and the promotion of export-oriented growth.

I call these circuits counter-geographies of globalization because they are: 1) directly or indirectly associated with some of the key programs and conditions that are at the heart of the global economy, but 2) are circuits not typically represented or seen as connected to globalization, and often actually operate outside and in violation of laws and treaties, yet are not exclusively embedded in criminal operations as is the case with the illegal drug trade. Further, the growth of a global economy has brought with it an institutional infrastructure that facilitates cross-border flows and represents, in that regard, an enabling environment for these alternative circuits.

It is increasingly on the backs of women that these forms of survival, profit making and government revenue enhancement operate. To this we can add the additional government savings attributed to severe cuts in health care and education. These cuts are often part of the effort to make the state more competitive, as demanded by Structural Adjustment Programs and other policies linked to the current phase of globalization. These types of cuts generally hit women particularly hard, as they are responsible for the health and education of household members.

These counter-geographies lay bare the systemic connections between, on the one hand, the mostly poor and low-wage women often considered a burden rather than a resource, and, on the other hand, what are emerging as significant sources for illegal profit-making and as important sources of convertible currency for governments. Linking these counter-geographies to programs and conditions at the heart of the global economy also helps us to understand how issues of gender enter into the information and viability.

[1] On these various issues see, for example, Diana Gonzalez-Alarcon and Terry McKinley, "The Adverse Effects of Structural Adjustment on Working Women in Mexico," *Latin American Perspectives* 26, no. 3 (1999): 103–17; Claudia Buchmann, "The Debt Crisis, Structural Adjustment and Women's Education," *International Journal of Comparative Studies* 37 (1996): ch. 1–2, pp. 5–30; Erika Jones, "The Gendered Toll of Global Debt Crisis," *Sojourner* 25, no. 3 (1999): 20–38; Nilufer Cagatay and Sule Ozler, "Feminization of the Labor Force: The Effects of Long-Term Development and Structural Adjustment," *World Development* 23, no. 11 (1995): 1883–94;

[2] This has been an important element in my research on globalization: the notion that once there is an institutional infrastructure for globalization, processes which have basically operated at the national level can scale up to the global level even when this is not necessary for their operation. This would contrast with processes that are by their very features global, such as the network of financial centers underlying the formation of a global capital market (for example, Saskia Sassen, "Global Financial Centers," *Foreign Affairs* 78, no. 1 (January/February 1999): 75–87.)

[3] In 1998, the debt was held as follows: multilateral institutions (IMF, World Bank and regional development banks: 45 percent of the debt; bilateral institutions, individual countries and the Paris group: 45 percent of the debt; and private commercial institutions: 10 percent). Thomas Ambrogi, "Jubilee 2000 and the Campaign for Debt Cancellation," *National Catholic Reporter*, July 1999.

[4] Eric Toussaint, "Poor Countries Pay More under a Debt Reduction Scheme?" at www.twnside.orq.sg/souths/twn/title/1921-cn.htm, July 1999, p. 1. According to Susan George, the South has paid back the equivalent of six Marshall plans to the north, Asoka Bandarage *Women, Population and Global Crisis: A Political-Economic Analysis.* (London: Zed Books, 1997).

[5] See, for example, Janie Chuang, "Redirecting the Debate over Trafficking in Women: Definitions, Paradigms, and Contexts," *Harvard Human Rights Journal* 10 (Winter 1998). Trafficking has become sufficiently recognized as an issue so that is was addressed in the G8 meeting in Birmingham in May 1998. The heads of the eight major industrialized countries stressed the importance of cooperation against international organized crime and trafficking in persons. The US President issued a set of directives to his administration in order to strengthen and increase efforts against trafficking in women and girls. This in turn generated the legislative initiative by Senator Paul Wellstone; bill S.600 was introduced in the senate in 1999. Dayan, "Policy Initiatives in the U.S. against the Illegal Trafficking of Women for the Sex Industry." (Department of Sociology: University of Chicago, 1999). On File with Author.

[6] The Coalition Against Trafficking in Women has centers and representatives in Australia, Bangladesh, Europe, Latin America, North America, Africa and Asia Pacific. The Women's Rights Advocacy Program has established the Initiative Against Trafficking in Persons to combat the global trade in persons. Other organizations are referenced throughout this article.

[7] See Foundation Against Trafficking in Women (STV) and the Global Alliance Against Traffic in Women (GAATW). For regularly updated sources of information on trafficking, see http://www.hrlawgroup.org/site/programs/traffic.html. See also, generally, Sietske Altink, *Stolen Lives: Trading Women into Sex and Slavery* (New York: Harrington Park Press, 1997); Kamala Kempadoo and Jo Doezema, *Global Sex Workers: Rights, Resistance, and Redefinition* (London: Routledge, 1998); Susan Shannon, "The Global Sex Trade: Humans as the Ultimate Commodity," *Crime and Justice International*99): 5–25; Lap-Chew Lin and Marian Wijers, *Trafficking in Women, Forced Labor and Slavery Like Practices in Marriage, Domestic Labor and Prostitution* (Utrecht: Foundation Against Trafficking in Women (STV), and Bangkok: Global Alliance Against Traffic in Women, 1997); Lin Lim, *The Sex Sector: The Economic and Social Bases of Prostitution in Southeast Asia* (Geneva: International Labor Office, 1998).

[8] For more detailed information on these various aspects, see the STV-GAATW reports: IOM (International Migration Office). (Annual Quarterly). "Trafficking in Migrants. (Quarterly Bulletin)." Geneva: IOM. (1996).

[9] There is also a growing trade in children for the sex industry. It has long existed in Thailand but is now also present in several other Asian countries, in Eastern Europe, and Latin America:.

[10] IOM (International Migration Office). (Annual Quarterly). "Trafficking in Migrants. (Quarterly Bulletin)." Geneva: IOM. (1996).

[11] See Global Survival Network. "Crime and Servitude: An Expose of the Traffic in Women for Prostitution from the Newly Independent States." www.globalsurvival.net/femaletrade.html (1997).

[12] There are various reports on the particular cross-border movements in trafficking. Malay brokers sell Malay women into prostitution in Australia. East European women from Albania and Kosovo have been trafficked by gangs into prostitution in London (Hamzic and Sheehan, "Kosovo Sex

Slaves Held in SoHo Flats," *London Times*. July 4,1999. European teens from Paris and other cities have been sold to Arab and African customers. See Susan Shannon. "The Global Sex Trade: Humans as the Ultimate Commodity." *Crime and Justice International*. May, 1999: 5-25; In the US the police broke up an international Asian ring that imported women from China, Thailand, Korea, Malaysia and Vietnam: William Booth, "Thirteen Charged in Gang Importing Prostitutes," *Washington Post*, August 21, 1999. The women were charged between US$30,000 and 40,000 in contracts to be paid through their work in the sex trade or needle trade. The women in the sex trade were shuttled around several states in the US to bring continuing variety to the clients.

[13] See, generally, Stephen Castles and Mark J. Miller, *The Age of Migration: International Population Movements in the Modern World*, 2nd ed. (New York: Guilford Press,1998); Sarah Mahler, *American Dreaming: Immigrant Life on the Margins* (Princeton, N.J.: Princeton University Press, 1995); Max Castro (ed). *Free Markets, Open Societies, Closed Borders?* (Berkeley, CA: University of California Press, 2000)

[14] A fact-sheet by the Coalition to Abolish Slavery and Trafficking reports that one survey of Asian sex workers found that rape often preceded sale into prostitution and that about one-third had been falsely led toward prostitution.

[15] Dennis Judd and Susan Fainstein, *The Tourist City* (New Haven, CT: Yale University Press, 1999).

[16] See, for example, Ryan Bishop and Lillian Robinson, *Night Market: Sexual Cultures and the Thai Economic Miracle* (New York: Routledge, 1998).

[17] See, generally, Castles and Miller (1998); Castro (2000).

[18] Saskia Sassen *The Mobility of Labor and Capital*. (Cambridge: Cambridge University Press, 1988).

[19] About 80 percent of the nurses brought in under the new act were from the Philippines.

[20] Japan passed a new immigration law (an amendment of an older law) which radically re-drew the conditions for entry of foreign workers. It allowed a series of professionals linked to the new service dominated economy-specialists in western-style finance, accounting, and law, but made the entry of what it termed "simple labor" illegal. The latter provision generated a rapid increase in undocumented entries of workers for low-wage jobs. This prohibition underlines the fact that the new law did make special provisions for the entry of "entertainers." See Chapter 6 in Saskia Sassen, *Globalization and its Discontents: Essays on the Mobility of People and Money*. (New York: New Press, 1998).

[21] Brenda Yeoh, Shirlena Huang, and Joaquin Gonzalez III, "Migrant Female Domestic Workers: Debating the Economic, Social and Political Impacts in Singapore," *International Migration Review* 33, no. 1 (1999): 114–36; Christine Chin, "Walls of Silence and Late 20th Century Representations of Foreign Female Domestic Workers: The Case of Filipina and Indonesian House Servants in Malaysia," *International Migration Review*, 31, no. 1 (1997): 353–85; Noeleen Heyzer. *The Trade in Domestic Workers*. (London: Zed, 1994).

[22] See Chapter 9 in Saskia Sessen. *Globalization and its Discontents: Essays on the Mobility of People and Money*. (New York: New Press, 2000).

[23] These women are recruited and brought in through both legal and illegal channels. Regardless, they have little power to resist. Even as they are paid below minimum wage, they produce significant profits for the brokers and employers involved. There has been an enormous increase in so-called entertainment businesses in Japan.

[24] Natacha David. "Migrants made the scapegoats of the crisis." ICFTU Online. International Confederation of Free Trade Unions:www.hartford-hwp.com/archives/50/012.html 1999).

12.10 UNITED NATIONS CONVENTION RELATING TO THE STATUS OF REFUGEES (1951)[1]

Chapter I: General Provisions

Article 1
Definition of the Term "Refugee"

A.   For the purposes of the present Convention, the term "refugee" shall apply to any person who:

(2)   As a result of events occurring before 1 January 1951 and owing to well-founded fear of being persecuted for reasons of race, religion, nationality, membership of a particular social group or political opinion, is outside the country of his nationality and is unable or, owing to such fear, is unwilling to avail himself of the protection of that country; or who, not having a nationality and being outside the country of his former habitual residence as a result of such events, is unable or, owing to such fear, is unwilling to return to it.

In the case of a person who has more than one nationality, the term "the country of his nationality" shall mean each of the countries of which he is a national, and a person shall not be deemed to be lacking the protection of the country of his nationality if, without any valid reason based on well-founded fear, he has not availed himself of the projection of one of the countries of which he is a national.

Article 18

Self-Employment

The Contracting States shall accord to a refugee lawfully in their territory treatment as favorable as possible and, in any event, not less favorable than that accorded to aliens generally in the same circumstances, as regards the right to engage on his own account in agriculture, industry, handicrafts and commerce and to establish commercial and industrial companies.

Article 23

Public Relief

The Contracting States shall accord to refugees lawfully staying in their territory the same treatment with respect to public relief and assistance as is accorded to their nationals.

Article 24

Labor Legislation and Social Security

1. The Contracting States shall accord to refugees lawfully staying in their territory the same treatment as is accorded to nationals in respect of the following matters:

(a) In so far as such matters are governed by laws or regulations or are subject to the control of administrative authorities: remuneration, including family allowances where these form part of remuneration, hours of work, overtime arrangements, holidays with pay, restrictions on home work, minimum age of employment, apprenticeship and training, women's work and the work of young persons, and the enjoyment of the benefits of collective bargaining;
(b) Social security (legal provisions in respect of employment injury, occupational diseases, maternity, sickness, disability, old age, death, unemployment, family responsibilities and any other contingency which, according to national laws or regulations, is covered by a social security scheme), subject to the following limitations:

Chapter V

Article 31

Refugees Unlawfully in the Country of Refuge

1. The Contracting States shall not impose penalties, on account of their illegal entry or presence, on refugees who, coming directly from a territory where their life or freedom was threatened in the sense of article 1, enter or are present in their territory without authorization, provided they present themselves without delay to the authorities and show good cause for their illegal entry or presence.

2. The Contracting States shall not apply to the movements of such refugees restrictions other than those which are necessary and such restrictions shall only be applied until their status in the country is regularized or they obtain admission into another country. The Contracting States shall allow such refugees a reasonable period and all the necessary facilities to obtain admission into another country.

Article 33

Prohibition of Expulsion or Return ("refoulement")

1. No Contracting State shall expel or return ("refouler") a refugee in any manner whatsoever to the frontiers of territories where his life or freedom would be threatened on account of his race, religion, nationality, membership of a particular social group or political opinion.

2. The benefit of the present provision may not, however, be claimed by a refugee whom there are reasonable grounds for regarding as a danger to the security of the country in which he is, or who having been convicted by a final judgment of a particularly serious crime, constitutes a danger to the community of that country.

[1] The convention was adopted on July 28, 1951, and entered into force on April 22, 1954.

12.11   UNITED NATIONS CONVENANT ON THE RIGHTS OF THE CHILD (1989)[1]

Article 22

1.   States Parties shall take appropriate measures to ensure that a child who is seeking refugee status or who is considered a refugee in accordance with applicable international or domestic law and procedures shall, whether unaccompanied or accompanied by his or her parents or by any other person, receive appropriate protection and humanitarian assistance in the enjoyment of applicable rights set forth in the present Convention and in other international human rights or humanitarian instruments to which the said States are Parties.

2.   For this purpose, States Parties shall provide, as they consider appropriate, co-operation in any efforts by the United Nations and other competent intergovernmental organizations or nongovernmental organizations co-operating with the United Nations to protect and assist such a child and to trace the parents or other members of the family of any refugee child in order to obtain information necessary for reunification with his or her family. In cases where no parents or other members of the family can be found, the child shall be accorded the same protection as any other child permanently or temporarily deprived of his or her family environment for any reason, as set forth in the present Convention.

[1] Adopted: November 20, 1989; entry into force: September 2, 1989. Editor: See also the African Charter on the Rights and Welfare of the Child, Article 23.

12.12   UNITED NATIONS GUIDELINES ON THE PROTECTION OF REFUGEE WOMAN (1991)[1]

Introduction

2.   Women share the protection problems experienced by all refugees. Along with all other refugees, women need protection against forced return to their countries of origin; security against armed attacks and other forms of violence; protection from unjustified and unduly prolonged detention; a legal status that accords adequate social and economic rights; and access to such basic items as food, shelter, clothing and medical care.

3.   In addition to these basic needs shared with all refugees, refugee women and girls have special protection needs that reflect their gender: they need, for example, protection against manipulation, sexual and physical abuse and exploitation, and protection against sexual discrimination in the delivery of goods and services.

Inequities in Granting of Status

62.   A further legal problem affecting refugee women is the actual status they are granted by a country of asylum. In most countries, family members who are accompanying or join a person who is granted refugee status are granted the same status. This practice is not followed in all places, however. Nor is recognition of refugee status automatic in some countries for spouses and children who follow a refugee to a country of asylum. Family reunification is not a right conferred on refugees by the 1951 Convention; it is a recommended practice that leaves much to the discretion of individual States. While many States allow family members to immigrate, a number of countries grant family members a residency status that provides less protection against deportation than does refugee status. Should the family

break up, the wife (who is more often the person to be joining the one granted refugee status) may find herself without any protection from forced return. Yet, her own claim to refugee status may be as strong as her husband's. She may, after some lapse in time since the events described by her husband or because she was not privy to some of the details, be unable to make the case convincingly for being granted her own refugee status.

[1] Prepared by the UN High Commissioner for Refugees, Geneva, July 1991.

12.13 UNITED NATIONS INTERNATIONAL CONVENTION ON THE PROTECTION OF THE RIGHTS OF ALL MIGRANT WORKERS AND MEMBERS OF THEIR FAMILIES (1990)[1]

Article 13

1. Migrant workers and members of their families shall have the right to hold opinions without interference.

2. Migrant workers and members of their families shall have the right to freedom of expression; this right shall include freedom to seek, receive and impart information and ideas of all kinds, regardless of frontiers, either orally, in writing or in print, in the form of art or through any other media of their choice.

3. The exercise of the right provided for in paragraph 2 of the present article carries with it special duties and responsibilities. It may therefore be subject to certain restrictions, but these shall only be such as are provided by law and are necessary:

(a) For respect of the rights or reputation of others;

(b) For the protection of the national security of the States concerned or of public order (ordre public) or of public health or morals;

(c) For the purpose of preventing any propaganda for war;

(d) For the purpose of preventing any advocacy of national, racial or religious hatred that constitutes incitement to discrimination, hostility or violence.

Article 17

1. Migrant workers and members of their families who are deprived of their liberty shall be treated with humanity and with respect for the inherent dignity of the human person and for their cultural identity.

2. Accused migrant workers and members of their families shall, save in exceptional circumstances, be separated from convicted persons and shall be subject to separate treatment appropriate to their status as unconvicted persons. Accused juvenile persons shall be separated from adults and brought as speedily as possible for adjudication.

3. Any migrant worker or member of his or her family who is detained in a State of transit or in a State of employment for violation of provisions relating to migration shall be held, in so far as practicable, separately from convicted persons or persons detained pending trial.

4. During any period of imprisonment in pursuance of a sentence imposed by a court of law, the essential aim of the treatment of a migrant worker or a member of his or her family shall be his or her reformation and social rehabilitation. Juvenile offenders shall be separated from adults and be accorded treatment appropriate to their age and legal status.

5. During detention or imprisonment, migrant workers and members of their families shall enjoy the same rights as nationals to visits by members of their families.

6. Whenever a migrant worker is deprived of his or her liberty, the competent authorities of the State concerned shall pay attention to the problems that may be posed for members of his or her family, in particular for spouses and minor children.

7. Migrant workers and members of their families who are subjected to any form

of detention or imprisonment in accordance with the law in force in the State of employment or in the State of transit shall enjoy the same rights as nationals of those States who are in the same situation.

8.   If a migrant worker or a member of his or her family is detained for the purpose of verifying any infraction of provisions related to migration, he or she shall not bear any costs arising therefrom.

Article 25

1.   Migrant workers shall enjoy treatment not less favorable than that which applies to nationals of the State of employment in respect of remuneration and:

(a)   Other conditions of work, that is to say, overtime, hours of work, weekly rest, holidays with pay, safety, health, termination of the employment relationship and any other conditions of work which, according to national law and practice, are covered by these terms;

(b)   Other terms of employment, that is to say, minimum age of employment, restriction on home work and any other matters which, according to national law and practice, are considered a term of employment.

2.   It shall not be lawful to derogate in private contracts of employment from the principle of equality of treatment referred to in paragraph 1 of the present article.

3.   States Parties shall take all appropriate measures to ensure that migrant workers are not deprived of any rights derived from this principle by reason of any irregularity in their stay or employment. In particular, employers shall not be relieved of any legal or contractual obligations, nor shall their obligations be limited in any manner by reason of such irregularity.

[1] The Convention was adopted on December 18, 1990, and entered into force on July 1, 2003.

12.14   ON SEXUAL TRAFFICKING: UNITED NATIONS CONVENTION ON THE RIGHTS OF THE CHILD (1989)[1]

Article 34

States Parties undertake to protect the child from all forms of sexual exploitation and sexual abuse. For these purposes, States Parties shall in particular take all appropriate national, bilateral and multilateral measures to prevent:

(a)   The inducement or coercion of a child to engage in any unlawful sexual activity;

(b)   The exploitative use of children in prostitution or other unlawful sexual practices;

(c)   The exploitative use of children in   pornographic   performances   and materials.

Article 35

States Parties shall take all appropriate national, bilateral and multilateral measures to prevent the abduction of, the sale of or traffic in children for any purpose or in any form.

[1] The Convention was adopted on November 20, 1989, and entered into force on September, 2, 1990. For similar UN instruments see also the UN Convention on the Elimination of All Forms of Discrimination against Women (CEDAW), Article 6, December, 10, 1979; CEDAW recommendation 19, adopted in January 1992; Conference on Human Rights, Declaration and Program of Action, Chapters II and III, adopted June 25, 1993; and UN Conference on Woman, the Platform of Action, Chapter D, paragraphs 123 and 131, adopted September 1995.

12.15   ON SEXUAL TRAFFICKING: THE BEIJING DECLARATION (1995)

224. Violence against women both violates and impairs or nullifies the enjoyment by women of human rights and fundamental freedoms. Taking into account the Declaration on the Elimination of Violence against Women and the work of Special Rapporteurs, gender-based violence, such as battering and other domestic violence, sexual abuse, sexual slavery and exploitation, and international trafficking in women and children, forced prostitution and sexual harassment, as well as violence against women, resulting from cultural prejudice, racism and racial discrimination, xenophobia, pornography, ethnic cleansing, armed conflict, foreign occupation, religious and anti-religious extremism and terrorism are incompatible with the dignity and the worth of the human person and must be combated and eliminated. Any harmful aspect of certain traditional, customary or modern practices that violates the rights of women should be prohibited and eliminated. Governments should take urgent action to combat and eliminate all forms of violence against women in private and public life, whether perpetrated or tolerated by the State or private persons.

226. The factors that cause the flight of refugee women, other displaced women in need of international protection and internally displaced women may be different from those affecting men. These women continue to be vulnerable to abuses of their human rights during and after their flight.

12.16   ON SEXUAL TRAFFICKING: AFRICAN CHARTER ON THE RIGHTS AND WELFARE OF THE CHILD (1999)

Article 29: Sale, Trafficking and Abduction

States Parties to the present Charter shall take appropriate measures to prevent:

(a)   the abduction, the sale of, or traffick in children for any purpose or in any form, by any person including parents or legal guardians of the child;

(b)   the use of children in all forms of begging.

CHAPTER 13

Human Rights for Whom? Cultural and Group Rights versus Universalism

Deepening globalization has both homogenized and sharpened national and cultural identities, creating controversies between universalist and cultural rights proponents. On one side of the debate, universalists — from either a liberal or a socialist persuasion — have criticized the cultural rights backlash against Western values as another rationale for repressing women and domestic minorities. On the other side, cultural rights advocates have argued that universalism remains another mechanism for the West to impose its (imperial) values regardless of indigenous patrimony. At the center of this debate remains the question: Whose group rights should be secured in our era of globalization?

Contending views in this debate can be traced to different theoretical approaches, which sociologist Stephen Lukes has described as Weberian ideal types ("Five Fables about Human Rights," 1993). The first approach, the utilitarian, originally defined human rights as the "greatest happiness for the greatest number," but more recently has measured these principles in terms of technological efficiency. The second, the communitarian, treats beliefs and practices of all subcommunities as equally valid, in effect maintaining that there are no universally valid principles of human rights. The third, the proletarian, views human rights from a social class perspective. Here, conflicts over rights reflect the division of labor as well as the unequal distribution of wealth among both individuals and nations. The fourth, the libertarian, appraises universal human rights in terms of their market value and cost-benefit analysis, and maintains a fundamental distrust toward the state. Rejecting all these perspectives, Lukes advocated a fifth approach, egalitarian, which defends basic liberties, the rule of law, toleration, and equality of opportunity. All of these should be constitutionally guaranteed, maintains Lukes, regardless of religion, class, ethnicity, or gender.

On the universalist (proletarian) side, British historian Eric Hobsbawm condemned socialist support for rights based on particular identities or cultural allegiance — whether gay, women, or ethnic. Promoters of "identity politics," he explained, "are about themselves, for themselves and nobody else." Human rights can never be realized by adding the sum total of minorities' interests. Particularlist positions often fail to emphasize the common ground that holds various identity groups together: a trend that leads to the fragmentation of the human rights agenda. Calling for the universalism of the Left, he asked, quoting the American sociologist Todd Gittlin: "What is Left if not … the voice of the whole people? If there is no people, but only peoples, there is no Left" (see Section 13.5).

Close to Hobsbawm, but from a liberal perspective of universalism, human rights scholars Rhoda Howard-Hassman and Jack Donnelly maintained that internationally recognized liberal and human rights, as laid out in the Universal Declaration of Human Rights and the international human rights covenants, are the only legitimate human rights standards (see Section 13.6). Defending a liberal view of individual rights against both the libertarian strand of liberalism and conservative communitarian rights, they argued, for example, that individuals' rights to property are constrained by individuals' rights to social justice. "When the full range of internationally recognized human rights is protected," they wrote, "when individuals are treated with equal concern, communities can and do thrive."

On the cultural relativist (or particularist) side stands the Malaysian political scientist scholar and human rights activist Chandra Muzaffar, a critic of Western values and imperialism based on civil and political rights (see Section 13.8). He condemned neoimperialist Western domination and its human rights double standards as cause for great skepticism about Western values in the developing world: "It is because many people in the non-Western world now know that dominance and control is the real motive of the West, that they become skeptical and critical of the West's posturing on human rights." In lieu of Western secular individualism, he offered a vision of God-guided human dignity drawn from religious and spiritual philosophies (see Section 13.8).

Also on the particularlist/relativist side, but from a pragmatist perspective, is philosopher Richard Rorty. In "Human Rights, Rationality, and Sentimentality" (1993) (see Section 13.7), Rorty characterized Western rationalist and foundationalist positions of universal rights (as defended by Plato, Kant, and others) as outmoded. Those views, in Rorty's opinion, are, despite their theoretical and universalist claims, *de facto* exclusive; for only rational individuals are regarded as fully human. According to this perspective, Rorty claimed, Muslims and women may be excluded from the rationalist equation of rights. He thus encouraged those who oppose oppression to concentrate their energies on promoting sentimental education, rather than following the so-called command of reason. This attitude would favor the possibility of "powerful people gradually ceasing to oppress others, or ceasing to countenance the oppression of others, out of mere niceness, rather than out of obedience to the moral law."

Somewhere in the middle of the universalist/particularlist spectrum is Canadian political philosopher Will Kymlicka, a leading advocate of multiculturalism. In the "Good, the Bad and the Intolerable: Minority and Group Rights" (1996), Kymlicka argued for group-specific rights consistent with liberalism. Distinguishing between external protection and internal restrictions, Kymlicka suggested that there are two types of group rights: one involves the claim of an indigenous group against its own members (internal restrictions); the other refers to the claim of an indigenous group against the larger society (external protection). While both are group rights claims, he observed, each has different implications. Drawing on the example of indigenous rights, he maintains that internal restrictions are almost always unjust (particularly when a group uses state power to restrict the liberty of its members), whereas external protections are more consistent with liberal democracy. External protection involves intergroup relations, specifically efforts to protect a vulnerable group against the decisions of the larger society. With this concern in mind, Kymlicka suggested that "reserving land for the exclusivity of indigenous peoples ensures that they are not outbid for this resource by the greater wealth of outsiders."

With respect to women, American political philosopher Martha Nussbaum argued against unqualified cultural rights positions, which she regards as a rationale for repressing women's rights. Drawing her position from a liberal universalist and Aristotelian approach, she maintained in "Women and Cultural Universals" (*Sex and Social Justice*, 1999) that is it absurd to treat one nation as a single culture. Conversely, it is absurd to treat women's rights, or any individual rights, without an understanding of an individual's capabilities to realize these rights (a concept she draws from Amartya Sen). "The capabilities approach," Nussbaum claimed, "insists that a woman's affiliation with a certain group or culture should not be taken as normative for her unless, on due consideration, with all the capabilities at her disposal, she makes that norm her own."

The conflict between universalism and cultural rights has been also evoked in the struggle for gay rights. In "Same-Sex Sexuality and the Globalization of Human Rights Discourse" (2004), legal and social theory scholar Carl F. Stychin observed that despite significant legal achievements for the international gay movement, non-Western gay activists have traveled between the universalizing and essentializing discourse of sexual identity. Because homosexuality is often seen in the developing world as a legacy of colonialism or as an "abhorrent Western import," gay activists often turn to local traditions and history to question the idea of heterosexuality. It is by reclaiming their culture's homoerotic history that indigenous gay activists have challenged the idea that homosexuality has polluted the purity of their culture, explained Stychin. Yet because non-Western activists have also benefited from the achievements of the international gay movement, Styching concludes by calling for the establishment of a bridge between cosmopolitan gay rights and culturally oriented same-sex struggle activists.

13.1   UNITED NATIONS UNIVERSAL DECLARATION OF HUMAN RIGHTS (1948): ARTICLES 1–2 AND 29

The General Assembly,

Proclaims this Universal Declaration of Human Rights as a common standard of achievement for all peoples and all nations, to the end that every individual and every organ of society, keeping this Declaration constantly in mind, shall strive by teaching and education to respect for these rights and freedoms and by progressive measures, national and international, to secure their universal and effective recognition and observance, both among the peoples of Member States themselves and among the peoples of territories under jurisdiction.

Article 1

All human beings are born free and equal in dignity and rights. They are endowed with reason and conscience and should act toward one another in a spirit of brotherhood.

Article 2

Everyone is entitled to all the rights and freedoms set forth in this Declaration, without distinction of any kind, such as race, color, sex, language, religion, political or other opinion, national or social origin, property, birth or other status.

Furthermore, no distinction shall be made on the basis of political, jurisdictional or international status of the country or territory to which a person belongs, whether it be independent, non-self-governing or under any other limitation of sovereignty.

Article 29

1.   Everyone has duties to the community in which alone the free and full development of his personality is possible.

2.   In the exercise of his rights and freedoms, everyone shall be subject only to such limitations as are determined by law solely for the purpose of securing due recognition and respect for the rights and freedoms of others and of meeting the just requirements of morality, public order and the general welfare in a democratic society.

3.   These rights and freedoms may in no case be exercised contrary to the purposes and principles of the United Nations.

13.2   UNITED NATIONS INTERNATIONAL COVENANT ON ECONOMIC, SOCIAL, AND CULTURAL RIGHTS (1966)

Article 15

1.   The States Parties to the present Covenant recognize the right of everyone:

a.   To take part in cultural life;

b.   To enjoy the benefits of scientific progress and its applications;

c.   To benefit from the protection of the moral and material interests resulting from any scientific, literary or artistic production of which he is the author.

2.   The steps to be taken by the States Parties to the present Covenant to achieve the full realization of this right shall include those necessary for the conservation, the development and the diffusion of science and culture.

3.   The States Parties to the present Covenant undertake to respect the freedom indispensable for scientific research and creative activity.

4.   The States Parties to the present Covenant recognize the benefits to be derived from the encouragement and development of international contracts and cooperation in the scientific and cultural fields.

13.3   UNITED NATIONS INTERNATIONAL COVENANT ON CIVIL AND POLITICAL RIGHTS (1966)

Article 27

In those States in which ethnic, religious or linguistic minorities exist, persons belonging to such minorities shall not be denied the right, in community with the other members of their group, to enjoy their own culture, to profess and practice their own religion, or to use their own language.

13.4   STEVEN LUKES ("FIVE FABLES ABOUT HUMAN RIGHTS," 1993)

I propose here to discuss the topic of human rights as seen from the standpoint of five doctrines or outlooks that are dominant in our time. I don't propose to be fair to these outlooks. Rather, I shall treat them in the form of Weberian "ideal types" or caricatures — a caricature being an exaggerated and simplified representation which, when it succeeds, captures the essentials of what is represented.

The principle that human rights must be defended has become one of the commonplaces of our age. Sometimes the universality of human rights has been challenged: those historically proclaimed are said to be Eurocentric and to be inappropriate, or only partly appropriate, to other cultures and circumstances.[1] So alternative, or partly alternative, lists are proposed. Sometimes the historic lists are said to be too short, and so further human rights are proposed, from the second unto the third and fourth generation.[2] Sometimes the appeal to human rights, or the language in which it is couched, is said to be unhelpful or even counterproductive in particular campaigns or struggles — in advancing the condition and position of women,[3] say, or in promoting third-world development,[4] but virtually no one actually *rejects* the principle of defending human rights.

So, in some sense, it is accepted virtually everywhere. It is also violated virtually everywhere, though much more in some places than in others. Hence the pressing need for organizations such as Amnesty International and Helsinki Watch. But its virtually universal acceptance, even when hypocritical, is very important, for this is what gives such organizations such political leverage as they have in otherwise unpromising situations. In this essay I want to focus

on the significance of that acceptance by asking: what way of thinking does accepting the principle of defending human rights deny and what way of thinking does it entail? I want to proceed in two stages: first by asking: what would it be like *not* to accept the principle? And second: what would it be like to take it seriously?

First, then, let us ask: what would a world without the principle of human rights look like? I would like to invite you to join me in a series of thought experiments. Let us imagine a series of places in which the principle in question is unknown — places that are neither utopian nor dystopian but rather places that are in other respects as attractive as you like, yet which simply lack this particular feature, whose distinctiveness we may thereby hope to understand better.

First, let us imagine a society called *Utilitaria*. Utilitarians are public-spirited people who display a strong sense of collective purpose: their single and exclusive goal, overriding all others, is to maximize the overall utility of all of them. Traditionally this has meant "the Greatest Happiness of the Greatest Number" (which is the national motto) but in more recent times there have been disputes about what "utility" is. Some say that it is the same as "welfare," as measured by objective indicators such as income, access to medical facilities, housing, and so on. Others, of a more mystical cast of mind, see it as a kind of inner glow, an indefinable subjective state that everyone aims at. Others say that it is just the satisfaction of whatever desires anyone happens to have. Others say that it is the satisfaction of the desires people ought to have or of those they would have if they were fully informed and sensible. Yet others, gloomier in disposition, say that it is just the avoidance of suffering: for them the "greatest happiness" just means the "least unhappiness." Utilitarians are distinctly philistine people, who are disinclined to see utility in High Culture and never tire of citing the proverb that "pushpin is as good as poetry," though there is a minority tradition of trying to enrich the idea of "utility" to include the more imaginative sides of life. But despite all these differences, all Utilitarians seem to be agreed on one principle: that what counts is what can be counted. The priced possession of every Utilitarian is a pocket calculator. When faced with the question "What is to be done?" he or she invariably translates it into the question "Which option will produce the greatest sum of utility?" Calculating is the national obsession.

Technocrats, bureaucrats, and judges are the most powerful people in Utilitaria and are much admired. They are particularly adept at calculating, using state-of-the-art computers of ever-increasing power. There are two political parties that vie for power — the Act party and the Rule party. What divides them is that the Act party (the "Actors") encourages everyone to use their calculators on all possible occasions, while the Rule party (the "Rulers") discourages ordinary people from using them in everyday life. According to the Rule Utilitarians, people should live by conventions or rules of thumb that are devised and interpreted by the technocrats, bureaucrats, and judges according to their superior methods of calculation.

Life in Utilitaria has its hazards. Another national proverb is *"Utilitas populi suprema lex est."* The problem is that no one can ever know for sure what sacrifices he or she may be called on to make for the greater benefit of all. The Rule party's rules of thumb are some protection, since they tend to restrain people from doing one another in, but they can, of course, always be overridden if a technocrat or a bureaucrat or a judge makes a calculation that overrides them. Everyone remembers the famous case at the turn of the last century of an army captain from a despised minority group who was tried on a charge of treason and found guilty of passing documents to an Enemy Power. The captain was innocent of the charge but the judges and the generals all agreed that the doctrine of *"Utilitas populi"* must prevail. Some intellectuals tried to make a fuss, but they got nowhere. And recently, six people were found guilty of exploding a bomb at a time of troubles for Utilitaria caused by fanatical terrorists from a neighboring island. It turned out that the six were innocent, but *"Utilitas populi"* prevailed and the six stayed in jail.

These hazards might seem troubling to an outsider, but Utilitarians put up with them.

For their public spiritedness is so highly developed that they are ready to sacrifice themselves, and indeed one another, whenever calculations show this to be necessary.

Let us now visit a very different kind of country called *Communitaria*. Communitarians are much more friendly people, at least to one another, than are the Utilitarians, but they are like them in their very high degree of public spiritedness and collective purpose. Actually, "friendliness" is too superficial a word to describe the way they relate to one another. Their mutual bonds constitute their very being. They cannot imagine themselves "unencumbered" and apart from them; they call such a nightmarish vision "atomism" and recoil with horror from it. Their selves are, as they say, "embedded" or "situated." They identify with one another and identify themselves as so identifying. Indeed, you could say that the Communitarians' national obsession is identity.

Communitaria used to be a very *gemütlich* place, much given to agricultural metaphors. Communitarians were attached to the *soil*, they cultivated their *roots* and they felt a truly *organic* connection with one another. They particularly despised the Utilitarians' calculative way of life, relying instead on "shared understandings" and living according to slowly evolving traditions and customs with which they would identify and by which they would be identified.

Since then Communitaria has undergone great changes. Waves of immigration and movements of people and modern communications have unsettled the old *gemütlich* ways and created a far more heterogeneous and "pluralistic" society. New Communitaria is a true "Community of Communities" — a patchwork quilt of subcommunities, each claiming recognition for the peculiar value of its own specific way of life. New Communitarians believe in "multiculturalism" and practice what they call the "politics of recognition," recognizing each subcommunity's identity with scrupulous fairness in the country's institutions. Positive discrimination is used to encourage those that are disadvantaged or in danger of extinction; quotas ensure that all are fairly represented in representative institutions and in the professions. The schools and colleges teach curricula that exactly reflect the exactly equal value of those communities' cultures and none (and certainly not the old *gemütlich* one) is allowed to predominate.

The new Communitarians feel "at home" in their subcommunities but further take pride in being Communitarians who recognize one another's subcommunitarian identities. But there are problems. One is the "inclusion-exclusion problem": how to decide which subcommunities are included in the overall framework and which are not. Some groups get very angry at being included in subcommunities that recognize them but that they don't recognize; others get angry because they recognize themselves as a subcommunity but are not recognized by others. Recently, for example, a province of Communitaria in which one subcommunity forms a majority passed a law prohibiting *both* members of their subcommunity *and* all immigrants from attending schools that teach the language that prevails in the rest of Communitaria and in which most of its business and trade are conducted. The immigrants in particular are none too pleased. A related problem is the "vested interests problem": once on the official list, subcommunities want to stay there for ever and keep others out. Moreover, to get on the list, you have to be, or claim to be, an indigenous people or the victims of colonialism, and preferably both.

Then there is the "relativism problem." It is obligatory in Communitaria to treat the beliefs and practices of all recognized subcommunities as equally valid, or rather, none is to be treated as more or less valid than any other. But different subcommunities have incompatible beliefs and some engage in very nasty practices, mistreating, degrading, and persecuting groups and individuals, including their own members. Typically, the definers of subcommunitarian identities are men; and their women are sometimes oppressed, marginalized, and badly abused. Some require their womenfolk to conceal *their* identities in hooded black shrouds. Some practice female circumcision. Unfortunately, Communitaria's official relativism must allow such practices to continue

unmolested. Recently, a famous writer from one subcommunity wrote a satirical novel that was partly about the life of another subcommunity's holy religious Prophet and Founder. Hotheads from the latter subcommunity became wildly incensed at what they took to be an insult to their faith and publicly burned the book in question, while their fanatical and fiery leader, in the home community from which they came, ordered the famous writer to be killed. Other writers from other subcommunities all over the world signed petitions and manifestoes in the famous writer's defense. Communitaria's government dealt with this tricky situation in a suitably relativistic way, declaring that the practice of writing satirical novels was no more but also no less valid than the practice of protecting one's faith against insults.

And finally there is the "deviant problem." Not all Communitarians fit well into the subcommunitarian categories. Recalcitrant individuals have been known to reject the category by which they are identified or to pretend that they don't belong to it. Some cross or refuse to acknowledge the identifying boundaries, and some even reject the very idea of such boundaries. Non-, ex-, trans-, and anti-identifiers are not the happiest people in Communitaria. They feel uneasy because they tend to be seen as "not true Communitarians," as disloyal, even as "rootless cosmopolitans." Fortunately, however, they are few and unorganized. Least of all are they likely to form another subcommunity.

Now I propose to take you to another place which is called *Proletaria*, so called, nostalgically, after the social class that brought it into being but that has long since withered away, along with all other social classes. Proletaria has no state: that too has withered away. Indeed, it is not a particular country, but embraces the entire world. Human and other rights existed in prehistoric times, but these too have withered away. The Proletariat in its struggle sometimes used to appeal to them for tactical reasons, but they are no longer needed in Proletaria's "truly human" communist society.

Proletarians lead extremely varied and fulfilling lives. They hunt in the morning, fish in the afternoon and criticize after dinner; they develop an enormous range of skills; and no one has to endure a one-sided, crippled development, to fit into a given job-description or role or an exclusive sphere of activity from which one cannot escape. The division of labor has also withered away: people are no longer identified with the work they do or the functions they fulfill. No one is a "such-and-such": as the prophet Gramsci put it, no one is even "an intellectual," because everyone is (among all the other things he or she is). They organize their factories like orchestras and watch over automated machinery, they organize production as associated producers, rationally regulating their interchange with Nature, bringing it under their common control, under conditions most favorable to, and worthy of, human nature, and they elect representatives to Communes on an annual basis. As the prophet Engels foretold, the government of persons has been replaced by the administration of things and by the conduct of processes of production. The distinction between work and leisure has withered away; so also has that between the private and the public spheres of life. Money, according to the prophet Marx, "abases all the gods of mankind and changes them into commodities" and has "deprived the whole world, both the human world and nature, of their own proper value,"[5] but now the whole "cash nexus" too has withered away. Now at last, as foretold, "love can only be exchanged for love, trust for trust, etc."; influence can only be through stimulation and encouragement; and all relations to man and to nature express one's "real individual life."[6] An arcadian abundance exists in which all produce what they are able to and get what they need. People identify with one another not, as among the Communitarians, because they belong to this or that community or subcommunity, but rather because they are equally and fully human. Relations between the sexes are fully reciprocal, and prostitution is unknown. In Proletaria there is no single dominating obsession or way of living; everyone develops their rich individuality, which is as all-sided in its production as in its consumption, free of external impediments. There is no longer any contradiction between the interest of the separate individual or the individual family and the interest of all individuals who have intercourse with one another.

The only problem with Proletarian life is that there are no problems. For with communism, as Marx prophesied, we see the *definitive* resolution of the antagonism between man and nature and between man and man. It is the true solution of the conflict between existence and essence, between objectification and self-affirmation, between freedom and necessity, between individual and species. It is the solution of the riddle of history and knows itself to be this solution.[7]

Yet visitors to Proletaria (from other planets) are sometimes disbelieving of what they behold, for they find it hard to credit that such perfection could be attained and, moreover, maintained without friction. How, they wonder, can the planning of production run so smoothly without markets to provide information through prices about demand? Why are there no conflicts over allocating resources? Don't differing styles of living get in each other's way? Aren't there personal conflicts, between fathers and sons, say, or lovers? Do Proletarians suffer inner turmoil? No sign of any such problems is visible: Proletarians seem able to combine their rich individuality, developing their gifts in all directions, with fully communal social relations. Only sometimes does it occur to such extraterrestrial visitors that they may have lost their way and landed somewhere else than Earth and that these are not human beings after all.

Human rights are unknown in all the three places we have visited, but for different reasons. Utilitarians have no use for them because those who believe in them are, by definition, disposed to question that Utilitarian calculations should be used in all circumstances. As the Utilitarian State's founder Jeremy Bentham famously remarked, the very idea of such rights is not only nonsense but "nonsense on stilts," for "there is no right which, when the abolition of it is advantageous to society, should not be abolished."[8] The Communitarians, by contrast, have always rejected such rights because of their *abstractness* from real, living, concrete, local ways of life. As that eloquent Old Communitarian speechifier Edmund Burke put it, their "abstract perfection" is their "practical defect," for "the liberties and the restrictions vary with times and circumstances, and admit of infinite modifications, that cannot be settled upon any abstract rule."[9] A no less eloquent New Communitarian, Alasdair MacIntyre broadens the attack: "natural or human rights," he says, "are fictions — just as is utility." They are like "witches and unicorns" for "every attempt to give good reasons for believing that there are such rights has failed." According to MacIntyre, forms of behavior that presuppose such rights "always have a highly specific and socially local character, and ... the existence of particular types of social institution or practice is a necessary condition for the notion of a claim to the possession of a right being an intelligible type of human performance."[10] As for Proletarians, their rejection of human rights goes back to the Prophet of their Revolution, Karl Marx, who described talk of them as "ideological nonsense" and "obsolete verbal rubbish,"[11] for two reasons. First, they tended to soften hearts in the heat of the class struggle; the point was to win, not feel sympathy for class enemies. It was, as Trotsky used to say, a matter of "our morals" versus "theirs,"[12] and Lenin observed that "our morality is entirely subordinated to the interests of the proletariat's class struggle.... To a communist all morality lies in this united discipline and conscious mass struggle against the exploiters. We do not believe in an eternal morality, and we expose the falseness of all the fables about morality."[13] And second, Marx regarded human rights as anachronistic because they had been necessary only in that prehistoric era when individuals needed protection from injuries and dangers generated out of an imperfect, conflictual, class-ridden world. Once that world was transformed and a new world born, emancipated human beings would flourish free from the need for rights, in abundance, communal relations, and real freedom to develop their manifold human powers.

What, then, does our draft experiment so far suggest we are accepting when we accept the principle of defending human rights? First, that they are *restraints* upon the pursuit of what is held to be "advantageous to society," however enlightened or benevolent that pursuit may be. Second, that they invoke a certain kind of *abstraction* from "specific and socially local" practices: they involve seeing persons behind their identifying (even their self-identifying) labels and securing them a protected space within which to live their lives from the inside, whether this be in conformity with or in deviation from the life their community requires of or seeks to impose on them. And third, that they *presuppose a set* of permanent existential facts about the human condition: that human beings will always face the malevolence and cruelty of others, that there will always be scarcity of resources, that human beings will always give priority to the interests of themselves and those close to them, that there will always be imperfect rationality in the pursuit of individual and collective aims, and that there will never be an unforced convergence in ways of life and conceptions of what makes it valuable. In the face of these facts, if all individuals are to be equally respected, they will need public protection from injury and degradation, and from unfairness and arbitrariness in the allocation of basic resources and in the operation of the laws and rules of social life. You will not be able to rely on others' altruism or benevolence or paternalism. Even if the values of those others are your own, they can do you in countless ways, by sheer miscalculation or mistake or misjudgment. Limited rationality puts you in danger from the well-meaning no less than from the malevolent and the selfish.

But often the values of others will not be your own: you will need protection to live your own life from the inside, pursuing your own conception of what is valuable, rather than a life imposed upon you. To do so, social and cultural preconditions must exist; thus Kurds in Turkey must not be treated as "Mountain Turks" but have their own institutions, education, and language. Now we can see the sense in which human rights are *individualistic* and the sense in which they are not. To defend them is to protect individuals from utilitarian sacrifices, communitarian impositions, and from injury, degradation and arbitrariness, but doing so cannot be viewed independently of economic, legal, political, and cultural conditions, and may well involve the protection and even fostering of collective goods, such as the Kurdish language and culture. For to defend human rights is not merely to protect individuals. It is also to protect the activities and relations that make their lives more valuable, activities and relations that cannot be conceived reductively as merely individual goods. Thus, the right to free expression and communication protects artistic expression and the communication of information; the right to a fair trial protects a well-functioning legal system; the right to free association protects democratic trade unions, social movements and political demonstrations, and so on.

I turn now to the second stage of my inquiry. What would it be like to take human rights, thus understood, seriously? To approach this question, let me propose a further thought experiment. Let us now imagine worlds *with* human rights, where they are widely recognized and systematically put into practice.

One place where some people think rights flourish is *Libertaria*. Libertarian life runs exclusively and entirely on market principles. It is located somewhere in Eastern Europe or maybe in China in the near future. Everything there can be bought and sold; everything of value has a price and is subject to Libertarians' national obsession: cost-benefit analysis. The most basic and prized of all their rights is the right to property, beginning with each Libertarian's ownership of himself or herself and extending (as Libertarians like to say) to whatever they "mix their labor with." They own their talents and abilities and, in developing and deploying these, Libertarians claim the right to whatever rewards the market will bring. They love to tell the story of Wilt Chamberlain, the famous basketball player whom thousands are willing to pay to watch. Would it be just, they ask, to deprive him of these freely given rewards in order to benefit others?

They also attach great importance to the right of engaging in voluntary transfers of what they rightly own — transactions of giving, receiving, and exchanging, which they use to the advantage of their families, through private education and the inheritance of wealth. There is a very low level of regressive taxation, which is used only to maintain Libertaria's system of free exchange — the infrastructure of the economy, the army and the police, and the justice system to enforce free contracts. Compulsory redistribution is prohibited, since it would violate people's unlimited rights to whatever they can earn. Inequalities are great and growing, based on social class, as well as on differential talents and efforts. There is no public education, no public health system, no public support for the arts or recreation, no public libraries, no public transport, roads, parks or beaches. Water, gas, electricity, nuclear power, garbage disposal, postal and telecommunications are all in private hands, as are the prisons. The poor, the ill, the handicapped, the unlucky, and the untalented are given some sympathy and a measure of charity, but Libertarians do not regard their worsening plight as any kind of injustice, since they do not result from anyone's rights being infringed.

No one is tortured in Libertaria. All have the right to vote, the rule of law prevails, there is freedom of expression (in media controlled by the rich) and of association (though trade unions cannot have closed shops or call strikes, since that would violate others' rights). There is equal opportunity in the sense that active discrimination against individuals and groups is prohibited, but there is an unequal start to the race for jobs and rewards; the socially privileged have a considerable advantage stemming from their social backgrounds. All can enter the race, but losers fall by the wayside: the successful are fond of quoting the national motto: "The Devil take the hindmost."[14] The homeless sleeping under bridges and the unemployed are, however, consoled by the thought that they have the same rights as every other Libertarian.

Are human rights taken seriously enough in Libertaria? I believe the answer is no, for two reasons. First, as I said, the basic civil rights are respected there — there is no torture, there is universal franchise, the rule of law, freedom of expression and association and formal equality of opportunity. Yet the possessors of these rights are not equally respected; not all Libertarians are treated as equally human. To adapt a phrase of Anatole France, those who sleep under the bridges have the same rights as those who don't. Though all Libertarians have the right to vote, the worst off, the marginalized and the excluded, do not have equal power to organize and influence political decisions, or equal access to legal processes, or an equal chance to articulate and communicate their points of view, or an equal representation in Libertarian public and institutional life, or an equal chance in the race for qualifications, positions, and rewards.

The second reason for thinking that Libertaria fails to take human rights seriously enough relates to the distinctively Libertarian rights. Libertarians believe that they have an unlimited right to whatever rewards their abilities and efforts can bring in the marketplace and the unlimited right to make voluntary choices that benefit themselves and their families. No Libertarians ever take a step outside the narrowly self-interested point of view of advancing their own, or at most their family's, interests. They are impervious to the thought that others might have more urgent claims on resources, or that some of their and their family's advantages are gained at the expense of others' disadvantage, or that the structure of Libertarian life is a structure of injustice.

Are human rights in better shape elsewhere? Where is the principle of defending them more securely defended? Where, in other words, are all human beings more securely treated as equally human? Where are they protected against Utilitarian sacrifices for the advantage of society and against Communitarian imposition of a particular way of life, against the Communist illusion that a world beyond rights can be attained and against the Libertarian illusion that a world run entirely on market principles is a world that recognizes them fully?

Is *Egalitaria* such a place? Egalitaria is a one-status society in the sense that all Egalitarians are treated as being of equal *worth*: one person's well-being and freedom are regarded as just as valuable as any other's. The basic liberties, the rule of law, toleration, equality of opportunity are all constitutionally guaranteed. But they are also made real by Egalitarians' commitment to rendering everyone's conditions of life such that these equal rights are of equal worth to their possessors. They differ about how to do this but one currently influential view is that a basic economic and political structure can be created that can make everyone better off while giving priority to bettering the condition of the worst off: on this view no inequality is justified unless it results in making the worst off better off than they would otherwise, be. All agree that progressive taxation and extensive welfare provision should ensure a decent minimum standard of life for all. But there is also within Egalitarian culture a momentum toward raising that minimum through policies that gradually eliminate involuntary disadvantage. That momentum is fueled by a sense of injustice that perpetually tracks further instances of illegitimate inequality or involuntary disadvantage — whether these result from religion or class or ethnicity or gender, and so on, and seeks policies that will render Egalitarians more equal in their conditions of life.

Could there be such a place as Egalitaria? More precisely, is Egalitaria *feasible*? Could it be *attained* from anywhere in the present world? And is it *viable*? Could it be *maintained* stably over time? Some doubt that it is feasible. Some say that, even if feasible, it is not viable. Some say that it might be viable, if it were feasible, but it is not. Others say that it is neither feasible nor viable. I fear that there are good reasons for all these doubts. I shall suggest two major reasons for doubting the attainability and the maintainability of Egalitaria and conclude by suggesting what they imply about how we should view the principle of defending human rights.

The first reason for thinking that Egalitaria may, after all, be a mirage is what we may call the *libertarian constraint*. This is found, above all, in the economic sphere. Egalitarians are (or should be) extremely concerned to achieve maximal economic growth. For them "equality" is not to be traded off against "efficiency." Rather, they seek most efficiently to achieve an economy that will attain the highest level of equality of condition at the highest feasible economic level. The worst off (and everyone else) under a more equal system should, they hope, be at least as well off as the worst off (and everyone else) under a less equal system. If the cost of more equality is lesser prospects of prosperity for everyone or most people, their hopes of attaining, let alone maintaining, Egalitaria, at least under conditions of freedom, are correspondingly dimmed.

Egalitarians these days are (or should be) keen students of Libertarian economics. For one thing, they know what markets can and cannot do. On the one hand, they know when and how markets can fail. Markets reproduce existing inequalities of endowments, resources, and power; they can generate external diseconomies, such as pollution, which they cannot deal with; they can, when unchecked, lead to oligopolies and monopolies; they can ravage the environment, through deforestation and in other ways; they can produce destabilizing crises of confidence with ramifying effects; they can encourage greed, consumerism, commercialism, opportunism, political passivity, indifference and anonymity, a world of alienated strangers. They cannot fairly allocate public goods, or foster social accountability in the use of resources or democracy at the workplace, or meet social and individual needs that cannot be expressed in the form of purchasing power, or balance the needs of present and future generations. On the other hand, they are indispensable and cannot be simulated. There is no alternative to them, as a signaling device for transmitting in a decentralized process information about tastes, productive techniques, resources and so on; as a discovery procedure through which restless individuals, in pursuit of entrepreneurial profit, seek new ways of satisfying needs; and even, as the Prophet Marx himself acknowledged, as an arena of freedom and choice. Egalitarians

know that command economies can only fail in comparison with market economies, and they know that, even if the market can in various ways be socialized, "market socialism" is, at best, an as yet ill-defined hope.

They also know that no economy can function on altruism and moral incentives alone, and that material incentives, and notably the profit motive, are indispensable to a well-functioning economy. Most work that needs to be done, and, in particular, entrepreneurial functions, must draw on motives that derive from individuals' pursuit of material advantage for themselves and for their families. They know, in short, that *any* feasible and viable economy must be based on market processes and material incentives, however controlled and supplemented in order to render them socially accountable,[15] thereby creating and reinforcing the very inequalities they earnestly seek to reduce.

The second major reason for skepticism that Egalitaria can be attained and, if so, maintained we may call the *communitarian constraint*. This is to be found, primarily, in the cultural sphere. Egalitarians hope that people can, at least when considering public and political issues, achieve a certain kind of abstraction from their own point of view and circumstances. Egalitarians hope that they can view anyone, including themselves, impartially, seeing everyone's life as of equal worth and everyone's well-being and freedom as equally valuable. John Rawls has modeled such a standpoint in his image of an "Original Position" where individuals reason behind a "veil of ignorance"; others have tried to capture it in other ways.

Yet Egalitarians must admit that this is not a natural attitude in the world in which we live and that it seems in increasingly many places to be becoming less and less so. Former Yugoslavs turn almost overnight into Serbs and Croats. It matters urgently to some Czechoslovaks that they are Slovaks and to some Canadians that they are Quebecois. Even African Americans or Hispanic or Asian Americans are insisting on seeing themselves in politically correct ways. It seems that belonging to certain kinds of "encompassing groups" with cultures of self-recognition, and identifying and being identified as so belonging, is increasingly essential to many people's well-being,[16] but, to the extent that this is so, the "politics of equal dignity" that would treat individuals equally, irrespective of their group affiliations, is put in jeopardy.[17]

Consider the idea of "fraternity." Unlike "liberty" and "equality," which are conditions to be *achieved*, who your brothers are is determined by the past. You and they form a collectivity in contradistinction to the rest of humankind, and in particular to that portion of it that you and they see as sources of danger or objects of envy or resentment. The history of "fraternity" during the course of the French Revolution is instructive.[18] It began with a promise of universal brotherhood; soon it came to mean patriotism; and eventually the idea was used to justify militancy against external enemies and purges of enemies within. The revolutionary slogan *la fraternité ou la mort* thus acquired a new and ominous meaning, promising violence first against non-brothers and then against false brothers. For collective or communal identity always requires, as they say, an "other," every affirmation of belonging includes an explicit or implicit exclusion clause. The Egalitarians' problem is to render such exclusions harmless.

The problem is to attain a general acceptance of multiple identities that do not conflict. But how many situations in the present world are favorable to such an outcome? The least promising, and most explosive, seems to be that of formerly communist federal states containing peoples with historical enmities at different levels of economic development. The least unpromising, perhaps, are polyethnic societies composed mainly of various immigrant groups who demand the right freely to express their particularity within the economic and political institutions of the dominant culture. But there too, wherever that right is interpreted as a *collective* right to equal recognition, a threat to egalitarian outcomes is raised: that of treating individuals only or mainly as the bearers of their collective identities[19] and thus of building not Egalitaria but Communitaria.

Here, then, are two major reasons for doubting that Egalitaria can be realized anywhere in this world (let alone across it as a whole). They very naturally lead those impressed by them to take up anti-egalitarian political positions. Indeed, they constitute the two main sources of right-wing thinking today — libertarian and communitarian. Both point to severe limitations on the capacity of human beings to achieve that abstraction or impartial regard that could lead them to view all lives as equally valuable.[20] Both are sufficiently powerful and persuasive to convince reasonable people to reject egalitarian politics.

How, in the light of this last fact, should we view human rights? I think it follows that the *list* of human rights should be kept both reasonably short and reasonably abstract. It should include the basic civil and political rights, the rule of law, freedom of expression and association, equality of opportunity, and the right to some basic level of material well-being, but probably no more. For only these have a prospect of securing agreement across the broad spectrum of contemporary political life, even though disagreement breaks out again once you ask how these abstract rights are to be made concrete: how the formal is to become real.

Who are the possessors of civil and political rights? Nationals? Citizens? Guest workers? Refugees? All who are residents within a given territory? Exactly what does the rule of law require? Does it involve equalizing access to legal advice and representation? Public defenders? The jury system? Equal representation of minorities on juries? The right to challenge jurors without cause? When are freedom of expression and association truly free? Does the former have implications for the distribution and forms of ownership of mass media and the modes and principles of their public regulation? Does the latter entail some form of industrial democracy that goes beyond what currently obtains? What must be equal for opportunities to be equal? Is the issue one of non-discrimination against an existing background of economic, social and cultural inequalities or is that background itself the field within which opportunities can be made more equal? What is the basic minimum? Should it be set low to avoid negative incentive effects? If so, how low? Or should there be a basic income for all, and, if so, should that include those who could but don't work, or don't accept work that is on offer? And how is a basic minimum level of material well-being to be conceived and measured — in terms of welfare, or income, or resources, or "level of living," or "basic capabilities," or in *some* other way?

To defend these human rights is to defend a kind of "egalitarian plateau" upon which such political conflicts and arguments can take place.[21] On the plateau, human rights are taken seriously on all sides, though there are wide and deep disagreements about what defending and protecting them involves. There are powerful reasons against abandoning it for any of the first four countries we have visited.

Yet the plateau is under siege from their armies. One of those armies flies a communitarian flag and practices "ethnic cleansing." It has already destroyed Mostar and many other places, and is currently threatening Kosovo and Macedonia. Right now it is laying siege to Sarajevo, slaughtering and starving men, women, and children, and raping women, only because they have the wrong collective identity. We are complicitly allowing this to go on, within the very walls of modern, civilized Europe. The barbarians are within the gates.

I believe that the principle of defending human rights requires an end to our complicity and appeasement: that we raise the siege of Sarajevo and defeat them by force. Only then can we resume the journey to Egalitaria, which, if it can indeed be reached at all, can only be reached from the plateau of human rights.

[1]See "*La Conception occidentale des droits de l'homme reforce le malentendu avec l'Islam*', interview with Mohamed Arkoun, *Le Monde*, March 15, 1989, p. 2; and the essays in Adamantia Pollis and Peter Schwab, eds., *Human Rights: Cultural and Ideological Perspectives* (New York: Praeger, 1979), esp. Ch. I, pp. 14 sqq.

[2] See D.D. Raphael, ed., *Political Theory and the Rights of Man* (London: MacMillan, 1967).

[3] See Elizabeth Kingdom, *What's Wrong with Rights? Problems for Feminist Politics of Law* (Edinburgh: Edinburgh University Press, 1991).

[4] Reginald Herbold Green, *Human Rights, Human Conditions and Law: Some Explorations Towards Interaction* (Brighton: IDS, 1989), Discussion Paper no. 267.

[5] Karl Marx, "Bruno Bauer, Die Fahigkeit der Heutigen Juden und Christen, frei zu werden," translated in T.B. Bottomore, ed., *Karl Marx: Early Writings* (London: Watts, 1963), p. 37.

[6] Karl Marx, "Money," translated in Bottomore, op. cit., pp. 193—94.

[7] Karl Marx, "Private Property and Communism," translated in Bottomore, op. cit., p. 155.

[8] Jeremy Bentham, *Anarchical Fallacies*, reproduced in Jeremy Waldron, ed., *Nonsense on Stilts: Bentham, Burke and Marx on the Rights of Man* (London: Methuen, 1987), p. 53.

[9] Edmund Burke, *Reflections on the Revolution in France*, reproduced in Waldron, op. cit., pp. 105–6.

[10]Alasdair MacIntyre, *After Virtue: A Study in Moral Theory* (London: Duckworth, 1981), pp. 65–67.

[11]Karl Marx, *Critique of the Gotha Programme*, in Karl Marx and Friedrich Engels, *Selected Works*, 2 vols. (Moscow: Foreign Languages Publishing House, 1962), vol. 2, p. 25.

[12]Leon Trotsky, "Their Morals and Ours," *The New International*, June 1938, reproduced in *Their Morals and Ours: Marxist versus Liberal Views on Morality* (four essays by Leon Trotsky, John Dewey, and George Novack), 4th ed. (New York, Pathfinder Press, 1969).

[13]V. I. Lenin, "Speech at Third Komsomol Congress, 2 October 1920," in V. I. Lenin, *Collected Works*, 45 vols. (Moscow: Foreign Languages Publishing House), vol. 31, pp. 291, 294.

[14]See Samuel Bowles, "What Markets Can — and Cannot — Do," *Challenge, The Magazine of Economic Affairs*, July–August 1991, pp. 11-16.

[15] See Diane Elson, "The Economics of a Socialized Market," in Robin Blackburn, ed., *After the Fall: The Failure of Communism and the Future of Socialism* (London: Verso, 1991).

[16]See Avishai Margalit and Joseph Raz, "National Self-Determination," *Journal of Philosophy* 87, no. 9 (1990): 441–61.

[17]See *Multiculturalism and "The Politics of Recognition,"* an essay by Charles Taylor, with commentary by Amy Gutmann (ed.), Steven C. Rockerfeller, Michael Walzer, and Susan Wolf (Princeton, Princeton University Press, 1992).

[18]See the entry on "*Fratemitc*" (by Mona Ozouf) in Francois Furet and Mona Ozouf, eds., *Dictionnain critique de la Révolution française* (Paris, Flammarion, 1988), pp. 731–40.

[19] See Stephen L. Carter, *Reflections of an Affirmative Action Baby* (New York: Basic Books, 1991) and Will Kymlicka, "Liberalism and the Politization of Ethnicity," *Canadian Journal of Law and Jurisprudence* 4, no. 2 (1991): 239–56. Kymlicka makes an interesting distinction between two kinds of cultural pluralism: one associated with multination states, the other with polyethnic immigrant societies.

[20] See Thomas Nagel, *Equality and Partiality* (New York: Oxford University Press, 1991).

[21] The idea of the egalitarian plateau is Ronald Dworkin's. See his "What Is Equality? Part I: Equality of Welfare; Part 2: Equality of Resources," *Philosophy and Public Affairs* 10, no. 3–4 (1981): 185–246, 283–345; "What Is Equality? Part 3: The Place of Liberty," *Iowa Law Review* 73, no. 1 (1987): 1–54; "What Is Equality? Part 4: Political Equality," *University of San Francisco Law Review* 22, no. I (1988): 1–30; and *A Matter of Principle* (Cambridge, Mass.: Harvard University Press, 1985). See also the discussion in Will Kymlica, *Contemporary Political Philosophy: An Introduction* (Oxford: Clarendon, 1990).

13.5 ERIC HOBSBAWM ("THE UNIVERSALISM OF THE LEFT," 1996)

The Universalism of the Left

What has all this to do with the Left? Identity groups were certainly not central to the Left. Basically, the mass social and political movements of the Left, that is, those inspired by the American and French revolutions and socialism, were indeed coalitions or group alliances, but held together not by aims that were specific to the group, but by great, universal causes through which each group believed its particular aims could be realized: democracy, the Republic, socialism, communism or whatever. Our own Labor Party in its great days was both the party of a class and, among other things, of the minority nations and immigrant communities of mainland Britainians. It was all this, because it was a party of equality and social justice.

Let us not misunderstand its claim to be essentially class-based. The political labor and socialist movements were not, ever, anywhere, movements essentially confined to the proletariat in the strict Marxist sense. Except perhaps in Britain, they could not have become such vast movements as they did, because in the 1880s and 1890s, when mass labor and socialist parties suddenly appeared on the scene, like fields of bluebells in spring, the industrial working class in most countries was a fairly small minority, and in any case a lot of it remained outside socialist labor organization. Remember that by the time of World War I the social-democrats polled between 30 and 47 per cent of the electorate in countries like Denmark, Sweden and Finland, which were hardly industrialized, as well as in Germany. (The highest percentage of votes ever achieved by the Labor Party in this country, in 1951, was 48 per cent....

So what does identity politics have to do with the Left? Let me state firmly what should not need restating. The political project of the Left is universalist: it is for *all* human beings. However we interpret the words, it isn't liberty for shareholders or blacks, but for everybody. It isn't equality for all members of the Garrick Club or the handicapped, but for everybody. It is not fraternity only for old Etonians or gays, but for everybody. And identity politics is essentially not for everybody but for the members of a specific group only. This is perfectly evident in the case of ethnic or nationalist movements. Zionist Jewish nationalism, whether we sympathize with it or not, is exclusively about Jews, and hang — or rather bomb — the rest. All nationalisms are. The nationalist claim that they are for *everyone's* right to self-determination is bogus.

That is why the Left cannot *base* itself on identity politics. It has a wider agenda. For the Left, Ireland was, historically, one, but only one, out of the many exploited, oppressed and victimized sets of human beings for which it fought. For the IRA kind of nationalism, the Left was, and is, only one possible ally in the fight for its objectives in certain situations. In others it was ready to bid for the support of Hitler as some of its leaders did during World War II. And this applies to every group which makes identity politics its foundation, ethnic or otherwise.

Now the wider agenda of the Left does, of course, mean it supports many identity groups, at least some of the time, and they in turn look to the Left. Indeed, some of these alliances are so old and so close that the Left is surprised they come to an end, as people are surprised when marriages break up after a lifetime. In the USA it almost seems against nature that the "ethnics" — that is, the groups of poor mass immigrants and their descendants — no longer vote almost automatically for the Democratic Party. It seems almost incredible that a black American could even consider standing for the Presidency of the USA as a Republican (I am thinking of Colin Powell). And yet, the common interest of Irish, Italian, Jewish and black Americans in the Democratic Party did not derive from respects to these. What united them was the hunger for equality and social justice, and a program believed capable of advancing both.

The Common Interest

But this is just what so many on the Left have forgotten, as they dive head first into the deep waters of identity politics. Since the 1970s there has been a tendency — an increasing tendency — to see the Left essentially as a coalition of minority groups and interests: of race, gender, sexual or other cultural preferences and lifestyles, even of economic minorities such as the old getting-your-hands-dirty, industrial working class have now become. This is understandable enough, but it is dangerous, not least because winning majorities is not the same as adding up minorities.

First, let me repeat: identity groups are about themselves, for themselves, and nobody else. A coalition of such groups that is not held together by a single common set of aims or values, has only an ad hoc unity, rather like states temporarily allied in war against a common enemy. They break up when they are no longer so held together. In any case, as identity groups, they are not committed to the Left as such, but only to get support for their aims wherever they can. We think of women's emancipation as a cause closely associated with the Left, as it has certainly been since the beginnings of socialism, even before Marx and Engels. And yet, historically, the British suffragist movement before 1914 was a movement of

all three parties, and the first woman MP, as we know, was actually a Tory.[1]

Secondly, whatever their rhetoric, the actual *movements* and *organizations* of identity politics mobilize only minorities, at any rate before they acquire the power of coercion and law. National feeling may be universal, but, to the best of my knowledge, no secessionist nationalist party in democratic states has so far ever got the votes of the majority of its constituency (though the Québecois last autumn came close — but then their nationalists were careful not actually to demand complete secession in so many words). I do not say it cannot or will not happen — only that the safest way to get national independence by secession so far has been not to ask populations to vote for it until you already have it first by other means.

That, by the way, makes two pragmatic reasons to be against identity politics. Without such outside compulsion or pressure, under normal circumstances it hardly ever mobilizes more than a minority — even of the target group. Hence, attempts to form separate political women's parties have not been very effective ways of mobilizing the women's vote. The other reason is that forcing people to take on one, and only one, identity divides them from each other. It therefore isolates these minorities.

Consequently to commit a general movement to the specific demands of minority pressure groups, which are not necessarily even those of their constituencies, is to ask for trouble. This is much more obvious in the USA, where the backlash against positive discrimination in favor of particular minorities, and the excesses of multiculturalism, is now very powerful; but the problem exists here also.

Today both the Right and the Left are saddled with identity politics. Unfortunately, the danger of disintegrating into a pure alliance of minorities is unusually great on the Left because the decline of the great universalist slogans of the Enlightenment, which were essentially slogans of the Left, leaves it without any obvious way of formulating a common interest across sectional boundaries. The only one of the so-called "new social movements" which crosses all such boundaries is that of the ecologists. But, alas, its political appeal is limited and likely to remain so.

However, there is one form of identity politics which is actually comprehensive, inasmuch as it is based on a common appeal, at least within the confines of a single state: citizen nationalism. Seen in the global perspective this may be the opposite of a universal appeal, but seen in the perspective of the national state, which is where most of us still live, and are likely to go on living, it provides a common identity, or in Benedict Anderson's phrase, [an imagined community" not the less real for being imagined. The Right, especially the Right in government, has always claimed to monopolize this and can usually still manipulate it.

Even Thatcherism, the grave-digger of "one-nation Totyism," did it. Even its ghostly and dying successor, Major's government, hopes to avoid electoral defeat by damning its opponents as unpatriotic.

Why then has it been so difficult for the Left, certainly for the Left in English-speaking countries, *to see itself* as the representative *of the entire nation*? (I am, of course, speaking of the nation as the community of all people in a country, not as an ethnic entity.) Why have they found it so difficult even to try? After all, the European Left began when a class, or a class alliance, the Third Estate in the French Estates General of 1789, decided to declare itself the nation as against the minority of the ruling class, thus creating the very concept of the political "nation." After all, even Marx envisaged such a transformation in *The Communist Manifesto*.[2] Indeed, one might go further. Todd Gitlin, one of the best observers of the American Left, has put it dramatically in his new book. *The Twilight of Common Dreams*: "What is a Left if it is not, plausibly at least, the voice of the whole people? ... If there is no people, but *only* peoples, there *is no left*."[3]

[1] Libang Park, "The British Suffrage Activists of 1913," *Past & Present*, no. 120 (1988), 156–157.

[2] "Since the proletariat must first of all acquire political supremacy, must raise itself to be the national class, must constitute itself the nation, it is so far, itself national, though not in the bourgeois sense." Karl Marx and Fredrich Engels, *The Communist Manifesto*, 1848, part II. The original (German) edition has "the national class"; the English translation of 1888 gives this as "the leading class of the nation."

[3] Gitlin, *The Twilight of Common Dreams* (New York: Henry Holt & Co., 1995), 165.

13.6 RHODA HOWARD-HASSMAN AND JACK DONNELLY ("LIBERALISM AND HUMAN RIGHTS: A NECESSARY CONNECTION," 1996)[1]

If human rights are the rights one has simply as a human being, as they usually are thought to be, then they are held "universally" by all human beings. Furthermore, as paramount moral rights they (ought to) govern the basic structures and practices of political life, and in ordinary circumstances (ought to) take priority over competing moral, legal, and political claims. These dimensions reflect what we can call the *moral* universality of human rights.

In the contemporary world, human rights are also almost universally endorsed by governments and peoples, at least in word, as normative standards. As the 1993 Vienna World Conference on Human Rights indicated, whatever the disputes over details and over the politics of implementation, virtually all states accept as authoritative the international human rights standards laid out in the Universal Declaration of Human Rights and the International Human Rights Covenants. We can call this the *international normative* universality of human rights.

Human rights, however, are not universal, even as ideals, in a broad, cross-cultural and historical perspective. As we have argued elsewhere,[2] pre-modern societies *in both the western and non-western worlds* lacked the very idea of equal and inalienable rights held by all individuals simply because they are human. All societies embody conceptions of personal dignity, worth, well-being, and flourishing. There may even be considerable cross-cultural consensus on social values such as equity and fairness. But human rights represent a distinctive approach to realizing a particular conception of human dignity or flourishing. The practice of seeking social justice and human dignity through the mechanism of rights held equally by every citizen, and which can be exercised even against society, first originated in the modern west.

This historical fact, however, should not lead us to commit the genetic fallacy of judging an argument or practice by its origins. Quite the contrary, we argue that the historical particularity of human rights is fully compatible with their moral and international normative universality. In fact, we contend that internationally recognized human rights, which are based on a liberal conception of justice and human dignity, represent the only standard of political legitimacy that has both wide popular appeal (in the North, South, East, and West alike) and a concrete record of delivering a life of dignity in modern social and political conditions....

We argue that the current international normative hegemony of human rights rests on the fact that it represents the only plausible vision of human dignity that has been able to establish itself widely in practice in the conditions of life that have been created in most corners of the globe by modern markets and states.

A. Liberalism, Equality, and Personal Autonomy

Following Ronald Dworkin, we contend that the heart of liberalism is expressed in the basic political right to equal concern and respect:

> Government must treat those whom it governs with concern, that is, as human beings who are capable of suffering and frustration, and with respect, that is, as human beings who are capable of forming and acting on intelligent conceptions of how their lives should be lived. Government must not only treat people with concern and respect, but with equal concern and respect. It must not distribute goods or opportunities unequally on the ground that some citizens are entitled to more because they are wor-

thy of more concern. It must not constrain liberty on the ground that one citizen's conception of the good life ... is nobler or superior to another's.[3]

The state must treat each person as a moral and political equal; it need not assure each person an equal share of social resources, but it must treat all with equal concern and respect. Inequalities in goods or opportunities that arise directly or indirectly from political decisions (and many such inequalities are easily justified within a liberal regime) must be compatible with the right to equal concern and respect.

Personal liberty, especially the liberty to choose and pursue one's own life, clearly is entailed in the principle of equal respect. If the state were to interfere in matters of personal morality, it would be treating the life plans and values of some as superior to others. A certain amount of economic liberty is also required, at least to the extent that decisions concerning consumption, investment, and risk reflect free decisions based on personal values that arise from autonomously chosen conceptions of the good life. But liberty alone cannot serve as the overriding value of social life, nor can it be the sole end of political association. Unless checked by a fairly expansive, positive conception of the persons in relation to whom it is exercised, individual liberty readily degenerates into license and social atomization. If liberty is to foster dignity, it must be exercised within the constraints of the principle of equal concern and respect.

In fact, autonomy and equality are less a pair of guiding principles than different manifestations of the central liberal commitment to the equal worth and dignity of each and every person. Each human being has an equal, irreducible moral worth, whatever his or her social utility. Regardless of who they are or where they stand, individuals have an inherent dignity and worth for which the state must demonstrate an active concern. Furthermore, everyone is *entitled* to this equal concern and respect. Minimum standards of political treatment are embodied in human rights; they are not merely desirable goals of social policy.

This implies a particular conception of the relation of the individual to the community and the state. Man is a social animal. Human potential, and even personal individuality, can be developed and expressed only in a social context. Society requires the discharge of certain political functions, and large-scale political organization requires the state. The state, however, also can present serious threats to human dignity and equal concern and respect if it seeks to enforce a particular vision of the good life or to entrench privileged inequality. Therefore, human rights have a special reference to the state in order to keep it an instrument to realize rather than undermine equal concern and respect.

In the inevitable conflicts between the individual and the state, the liberal gives prima facie priority, in the areas protected by human rights, to the individual. For the liberal, the individual is not merely separable from the community and social roles, but especially valued precisely as a distinctive, discrete individual — which is why each person must be treated with equal concern and respect. The state and society are conceived, in more or less contractarian terms, as associations for the fuller unfolding of human potential, through the exercise and enjoyments of human rights. Human dignity, for the liberal, is largely encompassed in the vision of a life in which each person is an equal and autonomous member of society enjoying the full range of human rights.

This view of man is rooted in structural changes that began to emerge in late medieval and early modern Europe, gained force in the eighteenth and nineteenth centuries, and today are increasingly the norm throughout the world. The "creation" of the private individual separate from society is closely linked to the rise of a new and more complex division of labor, the resulting changes in class structure (particularly the rise and then dominance of the bourgeoisie), and a new vision of the individual's relationship to God, society, and the state.

These developments are well known and need not be recounted here. The social changes of modernization — especially migration, urbanization, and technological development, in the context of capitalist market economies — replaced the all-encompassing moral role of traditional or feudal society with a much more segmented social order. Politics was separated from religion, the economy, and law (which were likewise separated from one another). Individuals too were separated from society as a whole; no longer could they be reduced to their roles, to parts of the community. With the recognition of separate individuals possessing special worth and dignity precisely as individuals, the basis for human rights was established.

Occurring parallel to these changes in society was the equally well known development of the modern state. The newly rising bourgeois class was initially a principal backer of the newly ascendant princes and kings, who also wanted to free themselves from the constraints of the old feudal order. As the state's power grew, however, it increasingly threatened the individual citizen. Bourgeois "freemen" thus began to demand that they indeed be free.

Such demands eventually took the form of arguments for the Universal natural rights and equality of all people. In this new and socially mobile society in which entrance to and exit from the bourgeois class was relatively unpredictable, a new set of privileges could not readily be reserved for a new elite defined by birth or some similar characteristic. Therefore, in order for some (the bourgeoisie) to be able to enjoy these new rights, they had to be demanded and at least formally guaranteed for all. Thus human rights came to be articulated primarily as claims of any individual against the state. Human rights lay down the basic form of the relationship between the (new, modern) individual and the (new, modern) state, a relationship based on the prima facie priority of the individual over the state in those areas protected by human rights.

Human rights are morally prior to and superior to society and the state, and under the control of individuals, who hold them and may exercise them against the state in extreme cases. This reflects not only the equality of all individuals but also their autonomy, their right to have and pursue interests and goals different from those of the state or its rulers. In the areas and endeavors protected by human rights, the individual is "king" — or rather as equal and autonomous person entitled to equal concern and respect.

In practice, these values and structural changes remain incompletely realized even today, and for most of the modern era they have been restricted to a small segment of the population. Nevertheless, the ideal was established and its implementation begun. And even if the demand for human rights began as a tactic of the bourgeoisie to protect its own class interests, the logic of universal and inalienable personal rights has long since broken free of these origins.

Furthermore, although these processes of sociopolitical individuation and state-building were first played out in Europe, they are increasingly the rule throughout the world. The structural basis for a society of equal and autonomous individuals is thus being universalized despite its historically particular and contingent origin. Social structure today increasingly parallels the near universal diffusion of the idea of human rights and the philosophical claim that human rights are universal. Individual human rights therefore increasingly appear not merely as moral ideals but as both objectively and subjectively necessary to protect and realize human dignity.

B.   Liberalism and International Human Rights

The standard list of human rights in the Universal Declaration of Human Rights can be easily derived from the liberal conception of the individual and the state. Other lists have been and may be derived from these principles, but we contend that the near-perfect fit between liberalism and the Universal Declaration reflects a deep and essential theoretical connection.

In order to treat an individual with concern and respect, the individual must first be recognized as a moral and legal person. This in turn requires certain basic personal rights. Rights to recognition before the law and to nationality (Universal Declaration,

Articles 6, 15) are prerequisites to political treatment as a person. In a different vein, the right to life, as well as rights to protection against slavery, torture, and other inhuman or degrading treatment (Articles 3, 4, 5), are essential to recognition and respect as a person.

Such rights as freedom of speech, conscience, religion, and association (Articles 18, 19) protect a sphere of personal autonomy. The right to privacy (Article 12) even more explicitly aims to guarantee the capacity to realize personal visions of a life worthy of a human being. Personal autonomy also requires economic and social rights, such as the right to education (Article 26), which makes available the intellectual resources for informed autonomous choices and the skills needed to act on them, and the right to participate in the cultural life of the community (Article 27), which recognizes the social and cultural dimensions of personal development. In its political dimension, equal respect also implies democratic control of the state and therefore rights to political participation and to freedoms of (political) speech, press, assembly, and association (Articles 19, 20, 21).

The principle of equal concern and respect also requires that the government intervene to reduce social and economic inequalities that deny equal personal worth. The state must protect those who, as a result of natural or voluntary membership in an unpopular group, are subject to social, political, or economic discrimination that limits their access to a fair share of social resources or opportunities. Such rights as equal protection of the laws and protection against discrimination on such bases as race, color, sex, language, religion, opinion, origin, property, birth, or status (Articles 2, 7) are essential to assure that all people are treated as fully and equally human.

In the economic sphere, the traditional liberal attachment to the market is not accidental. Quite aside from its economic efficiency, the market places minimal restraints on economic liberty and thus maximizes personal autonomy. Market distribution, however, tends to be grossly unequal. Inequality per se is not objectionable to the liberal, but the principle of equal concern and respect does imply a floor of basic economic welfare; degrading inequalities cannot be permitted.[4] The state also has an appropriate interest in redressing market-generated inequalities, because a "free market" system of distributing resources is a creature of social and political action, actively backed by the state, which protects and enforces property rights. Differential market rewards are not neutral; they reward morally equal individuals unequally. Market distributions may be substantially affected by such morally irrelevant factors as race, sex, class, or religion. Furthermore, many of the "talents" which are rewarded by the market are of dubious moral significance. Even "achieved" inequalities, should they threaten the (moral) equality or autonomy of other citizens, present at least a prima facie case for state intervention. The principle of equal concern and respect requires the state to act positively to cancel unjustifiable market inequalities, at least to the point that all are assured a minimum share of resources through the implementation of social and economic rights. In human rights terms this implies, for example, rights to food, health care, and social insurance (Articles 22, 25).

Efforts to alleviate degrading or disrespectful misery and deprivation do not exhaust the scope of the economic demands of the principle of equal concern and respect. The right to work (Article 23), which is essentially a right to economic participation, is of special importance. It has considerable intrinsic value (work is typically held to be essential to a life of dignity) as well as great instrumental value, both for the satisfaction of basic material needs and for providing a secure and dignified economic foundation from which to pursue personal values and objectives. A (limited) right to property (Article 17) can be justified in similar terms. Finally, the special threat to personal autonomy and equality presented by the modern state requires a set of legal rights, such as the presumption of innocence and rights to due process, fair and public hearings before an independent tribunal, and protection from arbitrary arrest, detention, or exile (Articles 8–11). More broadly, the special threat to

dignity posed by the state is reflected in the fact that all human rights are held particularly against the state. Moreover, they hold against all types of states, democratic as much as any other: if one's government treats one as less than fully human, it matters little how that government came to power. The individual does have social duties (Article 29), but the discharge of social obligations is not a precondition for having or exercising human rights.

We have thus moved from the liberal principle of equal concern and respect to the full list of human rights in the Universal Declaration. These rights, in turn, demand a liberal society and the ideal person envisioned by it, and if implemented these rights would play a crucial role in creating that society. This intimate, almost circular, relationship between internationally recognized human rights and the liberal ideal of equal concern and respect given by the state to equal and autonomous individuals is, we contend, essential, not coincidental.

We are well aware that the conception of liberalism we have adopted here is controversial. Many critics and defenders alike use the term to refer instead to a "minimal" or "night-watchman" state that protects only "negative" civil and political rights and restricts economic, social, and cultural rights to the right to private property.[5] This "libertarian" strand does have a strong liberal pedigree. But no less strong is the pedigree of the more radical or "social democratic" liberalism we have relied on, which runs from Locke, through Paine, to contemporary liberals such as Rawls and Dworkin.[6]

Furthermore, and for our purposes even more importantly, this strand of liberalism is not merely a theoretical ideal. It is embodied in the practice of twentieth century liberal democratic welfare states, most notably in Northern Europe over the past four decades. Whether we are concerned with civil and political rights or economic, social, and cultural rights — and above all if we are genuinely concerned with the often repeated interdependence and indivisibility of all human rights — it is in the liberal democratic regimes of Western Europe that internationally recognized human rights have been most fully realized in practice. In (the social democratic strand of) liberalism we thus have a long tradition of theory *and practice* that suggests it is not only the source of contemporary human rights ideas but also the type of political system that is best able to realize those rights.

We do not want to become tangled in disputes over labels. Call a regime that rests on a vision of equal and autonomous individuals and draws its legitimacy from its contribution to the realization of the equal and inalienable rights of its citizens "x." Only "x" reflects a plausible, realizable political model for a world dominated by modern markets and modern states. And only such a regime is compatible with authoritative international human rights standards. Not in spite of, but rather precisely because of, its historical particularly, the liberal democratic welfare state demanded by internationally recognized human rights represents a universal political project for the end of the twentieth century.

Critiques of both the left and the communitarian (or religious) right have attacked the excessive, even corrosive, individualism of the liberal model of human rights. We would contend, however, that such criticisms apply largely to the libertarian theory we have rejected. The practice of rights-protective liberal democratic regimes in the past half century provides little support for such claims. The isolated, atomized, possessive individual is a far cry from the reality of even the United States, probably the worlds most individualistic and rights-obsessed country. And to the extent that this picture is accurate, it is largely a result of disregard of, rather than excessive respect for, individual human rights.

Autonomy does not necessarily mean alienation from the community. Autonomous individuals in liberal western societies usually are embedded in their communities through multiple associations based on, for example, families, churches, work, schools, citizenship, ethnicity, gender, charities, NGOs, political parties, the arts, sports, hobbies, personal interests, and friendships. To the (considerable) extent that individuals define themselves and live their lives as

part of such groups, they will exercise their human rights less as separate individuals than as group members. The liberal vision embodied in international human rights standards is one of autonomous individuals treated with equal concern and respect by the state, participating in a strong and active civil society, and enmeshed in multiple and diverse social groups and communities.

Far from being hostile to the rights of groups, many internationally recognized human rights, especially family rights and rights to nondiscrimination, protect individuals as group members. Many human rights even have as a principal use the protection of groups. Consider, for example, the ways in which freedoms of speech, association, and religion have protected religious sects and institutions, political parties, trade unions, farmers' organizations, and a raft of other formal and informal groups based on countless affiliations. In fact, a vibrant civil society, the heart of political community in urban industrial societies, is inextricably tied to human rights that allow individuals to participate in social, economic, and political life not only separately but collectively.

Conflicts between individuals and communities rarely arise because of an excess of individual human rights. Take the familiar complaint of violent crime in American cities. Which human rights are hoodlums exercising to excess? And wouldn't greater respect for individual rights to personal security be the solution? In any case, lawless violence in the United States is deeply rooted in the American failure to take economic and social rights seriously and the persistence of pervasive social discrimination based on race, ethnicity, and wealth.

The principal destroyer of community in modern societies is the elevation of the individual pursuit of wealth to a paramount social value, systematically disregarding the poor and disadvantaged. The unbridled individualism typical of some sectors of the North American population is less a sign of individual rights running out of control than of human rights not being protected. Ideological celebrations of material achievement, which allow societal disregard for those who haven't "made it," are attacks on, rather than embodiments of, liberal human rights values. Far from demanding equal concern and respect from the state, the social vision popularized by the Reagan and Thatcher "revolutions" of the 1980s base dignity and respect on acquired wealth. They are indeed destructive of community — because they flagrantly disregard international human rights standards and their underlying (liberal) values. Unbridled materialistic individualism is an argument not for less emphasis on human rights but rather for taking seriously the full range of internationally recognized human rights, especially economic rights and rights that guarantee full and equal participation in society. Social disorder and decay are usually the result of systematic violations of individual human rights by the state or some other organized segment of society. When the full range of internationally recognized human rights is protected, when individuals are treated with equal concern and respect, communities can and do thrive.

For all the talk of excessive individualism, the problem in the world today is not too many individual rights, but that individual human rights are not sufficiently respected. States and societies have multiple claims on individuals. Modern states have awesome powers to bring individuals to their knees; if necessary, to break their bodies and minds. Capitalist markets treat persons as commodities and undermine family ties. Changes in the international division of labor destroy local communities. And we should never forget the hostility of many communities to difference, and the repressive social roles associated with "traditional family values."

Human rights are among the few resources available to individuals faced with these powerful threats to their dignity and autonomy. The balance is already (always?) tilted against individuals — and, we might add, families and most other groups that give meaning and value to their lives. If anything, what we need today is not fewer individual human rights but more. The result would be not only more secure individuals with greater opportunities to flourish, but stronger communities with a powerful claim to our respect, even admiration.

[1] The heart of this selection is taken from Rhoda E. Howard and Jack Donnelly, "Human Rights, Human Dignity, and Political Regimes," *American Political Science Review* 80 (September 1986): Additional material has been drawn, with considerable revision, from Rhoda E. Howard, "Cultural Absolutism and the Nostalgia for Community," *Human Rights Quarterly* 15 (May 1993): 332–37, and Jack Donnelly, *Universal Human Rights in Theory and Practice* (Ithaca: Cornell University Press, 1989), 1, 106, 149–52.

[2] See, for example, Rhoda E. Howard, *Human Rights in Commonwealth Africa* (Totowa: Rowman and Littlefield, 1986), ch. 2, and Jack Donnelly, *Universal Human Rights in Theory and Practice* (Ithaca: Cornell University Press, 1989), ch. 3.

[3] Ronald Dworkin, *Taking Rights Seriously* (Cambridge, Mass.: Harvard University Press, 1977), 272–73.

[4] Henry Schue, *Basic Rights: Subsistence, Affluence, and U.S. Foreign Policy* (Princeton: Princeton University Press, 1980), 119–23.

[5] See, for example, C. B. Macpherson, *The Political Theory of Possessive Individualism* (Oxford: Oxford University Press, 1962); Isaiah Berlin, "Two Concepts of Liberty," in *Four Essays on Liberty* (London: Oxford University Press, 1969); and Ian Shapiro, *The Evolution of Rights in Liberal Theory* (Cambridge: Cambridge University Press, 1986), 276. In the literature explicitly addressed to human rights, see Maurice Cranston, *What Are Human Rights?* (New York: Basic Books, 1964); Adamantia Pollis, "Liberal, Socialist and Third World Perspectives on Human Rights," in Peter Schwab and Adamantia Pollis, eds., *Toward a Human Rights Framework* (New York: Praeger Publishers, 1982); Tom Farer, "Human Rights and Human Wrongs: Is the Liberal Model Sufficient?" *Human Rights Quarterly* 7 (May 1985): 189–204; and Josiah A. M. Cobbah, "African Values and the Human Rights Debate: An African Perspective," *Human Rights Quarterly* 9 (May 1987): 311ff. Donnelly, *Universal Human Rights*, chapter 5, elaborates this claim.

[6] See the sources cited in note 2 above.

13.7 RICHARD RORTY ("HUMAN RIGHTS, RATIONALITY, AND SENTIMENTALITY," 1993)

... To overcome this idea of a *sui generis* sense of moral obligation, it would help to stop answering the question "What makes us different from the other animals?" by saying "We can know, and they can merely feel." We should substitute "We can feel for *each other* to a much greater extent than they can." This substitution would let us disentangle Christ's suggestion that love matters more than knowledge from the neo-Platonic suggestion that knowledge of the truth will make us free. For as long as we think that there is an ahistorical power which makes for righteousness — a power called truth, or rationality — we shall not be able to put foundationalism behind us.

The best, and probably the only, argument for putting foudationalism behind us is the one I have already suggested: It would be more efficient to do so, because it would let us concentrate our energies on manipulating sentiments, on sentimental education. That sort of education sufficiently acquaints people of different kinds with one another so that they are less tempted to think of those different from themselves as only quasi-human. The goal of this manipulation of sentiment is to expand the reference of the terms "our kind of people" and "people like us." ...

Plato thought that the way to get people to be nicer to each other was to point out what they all had in common — rationality. But it does little good to point out, to the people I have just described, that many Muslims and women are good at mathematics or engineering or jurisprudence. Resentful young Nazi toughs were quite aware that many Jews were clever and learned, but this only added to the pleasure they took in beating them up. Nor does it do much good to get such people to read Kant, and agree that one should not treat rational agents simply as means. For everything turns on who counts as a fellow human being, as a rational agent in the only relevant sense — the sense in which rational agency is synonomous with membership in our moral community.

For most white people, until very recently, most Black people did not so count. For most Christians, up until the seventeenth century or so, most heathen did not so count. For the Nazis, Jews did not so count. For most males in countries in which the average annual income is under four thousand dollars, most females still do not so count. Whenever tribal and national rivalries become important, members of rival tribes and nations will not so count. Kant's account of the respect due to rational agents tells you that you should extend the respect you feel for people like yourself to all featherless bipeds. This is an excellent suggestion, a good formula for secularizing the Christian doctrine of the brotherhood of man. But it has never been backed up by an argument based on neutral premises, and it never will be outside the circle of post-Enlightenment European culture, the circle of relatively safe and secure people who have been manipulating each others' sentiments for two hundred years, most people are simply unable to understand why membership in a biological species is supposed to suffice for membership in a moral community. This is not because they are insufficiently rational. It is, typically, because they live in a world in which it would be just too risky — indeed, would often be insanely dangerous — to let one's sense of moral community stretch beyond one's family, clan, or tribe.

To get whites to be nicer to Blacks, males to females, Serbs to Muslims, or straights to gays, to help our species link up into what Rabossi calls a "planetary community" dominated by a culture of human rights, it is of no use whatever to say, with Kant: Notice that what you have in common, your humanity, is more important than these trivial differences. For the people we are trying to convince will rejoin that they notice nothing of the sort. Such people are *morally* offended by the suggestion that they should treat someone who *is not* kin as if he were a brother, or a nigger as if he were white, or a queer as if he were normal, or an infidel as if she were a believer. They are offended by the suggestion that they treat people whom they do not think of as human as if they were human. When utilitarians tell them that all pleasures and pains felt by members of our biological species are equally relevant to moral deliberation, or when Kantians tell them that the ability to engage in such deliberation is sufficient for membership in the moral community, they are incredulous. They rejoin that these philosophers seem oblivious to blatantly obvious moral distinctions, distinctions any decent person will draw.

This rejoinder is not just a rhetorical device, nor is it in any way irrational. It is heartfelt. The identity of these people, the people whom we should like to convince to join our Eurocentric human rights culture, is bound up with their sense of who they are not. Most people — especially people relatively untouched by the European Enlightenment — simply do not think of themselves as, first and foremost, a human being. Instead, they think of themselves as being a certain *good* sort of human being — a sort defined by explicit opposition to a particularly bad sort. It is crucial for their sense of who they are that they are not an infidel, not a queer, not a woman, not an untouchable. Just insofar as they are impoverished, and as their lives are perpetually at risk, they have little else than pride in not being what they are not to sustain their self-respect. Starting with the days when the term "human being" was synonomous with "member of our tribe," we have always thought of human beings in terms of paradigm members of the species. We have contrasted us, the *real* humans, with rudimentary, or perverted, or deformed examples of humanity.

We Eurocentric intellectuals like to suggest that we, the paradigm humans, have overcome this primitive parochialism by using that paradigmatic human faculty, reason. So we say that failure to concur with us is due to "prejudice." Our use of these terms in this way may make us nod in agreement when Colin McGinn tells us, in the introduction to his recent book,[1] that learning to tell right from wrong is not as hard as learning French. The only obstacles to agreeing with his moral views, McGinn explains, are "prejudice, vested interest and laziness."

One can see what McGinn means: If, like many of us, you teach students who have been brought up in the shadow of the Holocaust, brought up believing that prejudice against racial or religious groups is a terrible thing, it is not very hard to convert them to standard liberal views about abortion, gay rights, and the like. You may even get them to stop eating animals. All you have to do is convince them that all the arguments on the other side appeal to "morally irrelevant" considerations. You do this by manipulating their sentiments in such a way that they imagine themselves in the shoes of the despised and oppressed. Such students are already so nice that they are eager to define their identity in nonexclusionary terms. The only people they have trouble being nice to are the ones they consider irrational — the religious fundamentalist, the smirking rapist, or the swaggering skinhead.

Producing generations of nice, tolerant, well-off, secure, other-respecting students of this sort in all parts of the world is just what is needed — indeed *all* that is needed — to achieve an Enlightenment utopia. The more youngsters like this we can raise, the stronger and more global our human rights culture will become. But it is not a good idea to encourage these students to label "irrational" the intolerant people they have trouble tolerating. For that Platonic-Kantian epithet suggests that, with only a little more effort, the good and rational part of these other people's souls could have triumphed over the bad and irrational part. It suggests that we good people know something these bad people do not know, and that it is probably their own silly fault that they do not know it. All they have to do, after all, is to think a little harder, be a little more self-conscious, a little more rational.

But the bad people's beliefs are not more or less "irrational" than the belief that race, religion, gender, and sexual preference are all morally irrelevant — that these are all trumped by membership in the biological species. As used by moral philosophers like McGinn, the term "irrational behavior" means no more than "behavior of which we disapprove so strongly that our spade is turned when asked *why* we disapprove of it." It would be better to teach our students that these bad people are no less rational, no less clearheaded, no more prejudiced, than we good people who respect otherness. The bad people's problem is that they were not so lucky in the circumstances of their upbringing as we were. Instead of treating as irrational all those people out there who are trying to find and kill Salman Rushdie, we should treat them as deprived.

Foundationalists think of these people as deprived of truth, of moral knowledge. But it would be better — more specific, more suggestive of possible remedies — to think of them as deprived of two more concrete things: security and sympathy. By "security" I mean conditions of life sufficiently risk-free as to make one's difference from others inessential to one's self-respect, one's sense of worth. These conditions have been enjoyed by Americans and Europeans — the people who dreamed up the human fights culture — much more than they have been enjoyed by anyone else. By "sympathy" I mean the sort of reaction that the Athenian had more of after seeing Aeschylus' *The Persians* than before, the sort that white Americans had more of after reading *Uncle Tom's Cabin* than before, the sort that we have more of after watching TV programs about the genocide in Bosnia. Security and sympathy go together, for the same reasons that peace and economic productivity go together. The tougher things are, the more you have to be afraid of, the more dangerous your situation, the less you can afford the time or effort to think about what things might be like for people with whom you do not immediately identify. Sentimental education only works on people who can relax long enough to listen.

If Rabossi and I are right in thinking human rights foundationalism outmoded, then Hume is a better advisor than Kant about how we intellectuals can hasten the coming of the Enlightenment Utopia for which both men yearned. Among contemporary philosophers, the best advisor seems to me to be Annette Baier. Baier describes Hume as "the woman's moral philosopher" because Hume held that "corrected (sometimes rule-corrected) sympathy, not law-discerning reason, is the fundamental moral capacity."[2] Baier would like us to get rid of both the Platonic idea that we have a true self, and the Kantian idea that it is rational to be moral. In aid of this project, she suggests that we think of "trust" rather than "obligation" as the fundamental moral notion. This substitution would mean thinking of the spread of the human rights culture not as a matter of our becoming more aware of the requirements of the moral law, but rather as what Baier calls "a progress of sentiments."[3]

This progress consists in an increasing ability to see the similarities between ourselves and people very unlike us as outweighing the differences. It is the result of what I have been calling "sentimental education." The relevant similarities are not a matter of sharing a deep true self which instantiates true humanity, but are such little, superficial, similarities as cherishing our parents and our children — similarities that do not interestingly distinguish us from many non-human animals.

To accept Baier's suggestions, however, we should have to overcome our sense that sentiment is too weak a force, and that something stronger is required. This idea that reason is "stronger" than sentiment, that only an insistence on the unconditionality of moral obligation has the power to change human beings for the better, is very persistent. I think that this persistence is due mainly to a semiconscious realization that, if we hand our hopes for moral progress over to sentiment, we are in effect handing them over to *condescension*. For we shall be relying on those who have the power to change things — people like the rich New England abolitionists, or rich bleeding hearts like Robert Owen and Friedrich Engels — rather than on something that has power over them. We shall have to accept the fact that the fate of the women of Bosnia depends on whether TV journalists manage to do for them what Harriet Beecher Stowe did for black slaves, whether these journalists can make us, the audience back in the safe countries, feel that these women are more like us, more like real human beings, than we had realized.

To rely on the suggestions of sentiment rather than on the commands of reason is to think of powerful people gradually ceasing to oppress others, or ceasing to countenance the oppression of others, out of mere niceness, rather than out of obedience to the moral law. But it is revolting to think that our only hope for a decent society consists in softening the self-satisfied hearts of a leisure class. We want moral progress to burst up from below, rather than waiting patiently upon condescension from the top. The residual popularity of Kantian ideas of "unconditional moral obligation" — obligation imposed by deep ahistorical noncontingent forces — seems to me almost entirely due to our abhorrence for the idea that the people on top hold the future in their hands, that everything depends on them, that there is nothing more powerful to which we can appeal against them.

Like everyone else, I too should prefer a bottom-up way of achieving utopia, a quick reversal of fortune which will make the last first. But I do not think this is how utopia will in fact come into being. Nor do I think that our preference for this way lends any support to the idea that the Enlightenment project lies in the depths of every human soul. So why does this preference make us resist the thought that sentimentality may be the best weapon we have? I think Nietzsche gave the right answer to this question: We resist out of resentment. We *resent* the idea that we shall have to wait for the strong to turn their piggy little *eyes* to the suffering of the weak. We desperately hope that there is something stronger and more powerful that will *hurt* the strong if they do *not* — if not a vengeful God, then a vengeful aroused proletariat, or, at least, a vengeful superego, or, at the very least, the offended majesty of Kant's tribunal of pure practical reason. The desperate hope for a noncontingent and powerful ally is, according to Nietzsche, the common core of Platonism, of religious insistence on divine omnipotence, and of Kantian moral philosophy.[4] ...

[1] Colin McGinn, *Moral Literacy; or, How to Do the Right Thing* (London: Duckworth, 1992), 16.
[2] Baier, "Hume, the Women's Moral Theorist?" in Eva Kittay and Diana Meyers, eds., *Women and Moral Theory* (Totowa, N.J.: Rowman and Littlefield, 1987), 40.
[3] Baier's book on Hume is entitled *A Progress of Sentiments: Reflections on Hume's Treatise* (Cambridge, Mass.: Harvard University Press, 1991). Baier's view of the inadequacy of most attempts by contemporary moral philosophers to break with Kant comes out most clearly when she characterizes Allan Gibbard (in his book *Wise Choices, Apt Feelings*) as focusing "on the feelings that a patriarchal religion has bequeathed to us," and says that "Hume would judge Gibbard to be, as a moral philosopher, basically a divine disguised as a fellow expressivist" (p. 312).
[4] Nietzsche's diagnosis is reinforced by Elizabeth Anscombe's famous argument that atheists are not entitled to the term "moral obligation."

13.8 CHANDRA MUZAFFAR: ON WESTERN IMPERIALISM AND HUMAN RIGHTS ("FROM HUMAN RIGHTS TO HUMAN DIGNITY," 1999)

It is important, at the very outset, to explain what has come to be accepted as the conventional meaning of human rights. Though the human rights contained in the multitude of UN human rights declarations, covenants, and conventions cover a whole range of rights, including an economic right such as the right to food, and a collective right such as the people's right to self-determination, the term "human rights" as used by most human rights activists today carries a more restricted meaning. Human rights are often equated with individual rights — specifically individual civil and political rights. This equation has a genealogy, a history behind it.

The equation of human rights with individual civil and political rights is a product of the European Enlightenment and the secularization of thought and society of the last 150 years. Whatever the weaknesses of this conception of human rights, there is no doubt at all that it has contributed significantly to human civilization.

First, it has helped to empower the individual. By endowing the individual with rights, such as the right of expression, the right of association, the right of assembly, the right to vote, the right to a fair trial, and so on, it has strengthened the position of the individual as never before in history. These are rights that inhere in the individual as a human being. They are his/her rights: he/she does not owe these rights to a benevolent government or a magnanimous monarch.

Second, by empowering the individual, this particular human rights tradition has contributed towards the transformation of what were once authoritarian political systems into democratic political structures. For the empowerment of the individual — as demonstrated by the history of European democracies — helped to create the political space which resulted in the entrenchment of civil society. It was the growth of civil society in the West which strengthened the sinews of democratic political culture.

Third, the empowerment of the individual and the evolution of civil society played a big part in checking the arbitrary exercise of power of those in authority. In Europe, as in other parts of the world, right through human history, the arbitrariness of the wielders of power and authority has been one of the greatest banes upon the well-being of both individual and community. Human rights ideas born out of the Enlightenment and the secularization of society — more than perhaps any other set of ideas from any other epoch —challenged this blight upon humanity.

Fourth, by curbing their arbitrariness, by regulating their activities, the wielders of power in Europe were compelled to become more accountable to the people. Public accountability developed into a norm of democratic governance. The empowerment and the enhancement of the individual have, in other words, brought governments within the control of the governed through institutions established to ensure public accountability.

But what is sad is that while Europe built the edifice of the individual within its own borders, it destroyed the human person on other shores. As human rights expanded among white people, European empires inflicted horrendous human wrongs upon the colored inhabitants of the planet. The elimination of the native populations of the Americas and Australasia and the enslavement of millions of Africans during the European slave trade were two of the greatest human rights tragedies of the colonial epoch. Of course, the suppression of millions of Asians in almost every part of the continent during the long centuries of colonial domination was also another colossal human rights calamity. Western colonialism in Asia, Australasia, Africa, and Latin America represents the most massive, systematic violation of human rights ever known in history.

Though formal colonial rule has ended, Western domination and control continues to impact upon the human rights of the vast majority of the people of the non-Western world in ways which are more subtle and sophisticated but no less destructive and dev-

astating. The dominant West, for instance, controls global politics through the United Nations Security Council (UNSC). If certain Western powers so desire, they can get the UNSC to impose sanctions, however unjust they may be, upon any state which, in their view, needs to be coerced to submit to their will. This ability to force others to submit to their will is backed by the West's — particularly the United States' — global military dominance. It is a dominance which bestows upon the West effective control over high-grade weapons technology and most weapons of mass destruction. The dominant West also controls global economics through the IMF, the World Bank, the World Trade Organization (WTO), and the G7. The self-serving economic policies of powerful states have cost the poor in the non-Western world billions of dollars in terms of revenue — money which, translated into basic needs, could have saved some 15 million lives in the non-Western world every year. The dominant West controls global news and information through Reuters, AP, UPI, AFP, and most of all CNN. Likewise, Western music, Western films, Western fashions, and Western foods are creating a global culture which is not only Western in character and content but also incapable of accommodating non-Western cultures on a just and equitable basis. Underlying this Western-dominated global culture and information system is an array of ideas, values, and even worldviews pertaining to the position of the individual, inter-gender relations, inter-generational ties, the family, the community, the environment, and the cosmos which have evolved from a particular tradition — namely the Western secular tradition. These ideas, values, and worldviews are marginalizing other ideas about the human being, about human relations and about societal ties embodied in older and richer civilizations. It is a process of marginalization which could, in the long run, result in the moral degradation and spiritual impoverishment of the human being.

Though the consequences of domination are enormous for the dominated, the major centers of power in the West — the US, Britain, and France, the Western military establishment, Western multinational corporations (MNCs), the mainstream Western media, a segment of Western academia, some Western NGOs — are determined to perpetuate their global power. They are determined to do this even if it leads to the violation of the very principles of democracy and human rights which they espouse. This is why a superpower like the US has, since 1945, in spite of its professed commitment to human rights and democracy, aided and abetted many more dictatorships than democracies in the non-Western world.

Even today, after the end of the Cold War, the US and its allies continue to suppress genuine human rights and pro-democracy movements in various parts of the world. The US's continued support for Israel against the Palestinian struggle for nationhood is one such example. The US and its Western allies, notably France, have also failed to support the Algerian movement for human rights and social justice expressed through Islam. There are similar movements for freedom and justice in Egypt and Saudi Arabia which Western governments see as a threat to their interests in the region. Long-standing movements for self-determination in East Timor, Tibet, and Kashmir also have little support from major Western governments. Perhaps, more than anything else, it is the West's lack of commitment to the human rights of the people of Bosnia and Herzegovina in initial phases which reveals that in the ultimate analysis it is not human rights which count but the preservation of self-interest and the perpetuation of dominant power.

It is because many people in the non-Western world now know that dominance and control is the real motive and goal of the West that they have become skeptical and critical of the West's posturing on human rights. This skepticism has increased as a result of the deterioration and degeneration in human rights standards within Western society itself, which is occurring in at least five areas:

1. White racism in Europe and North America is making a mockery of the Western claim that it is a champion of human rights. The rights and dignity of non-White minorities are challenged almost every day in the West by the arrogance of racist sentiments among segments of the white population.

2. The economic malaise in the West is eroding fundamental economic rights such as the right to work. Can the West protect the economic rights of its people in the midst of rising unemployment and continuing economic stagnation?

3. As violence, and the fear it generates, increases in Western societies, one wonders whether Western societies are capable any longer of protecting the basic right of the people to live without fear. After all, isn't freedom from fear a fundamental human right?

4. Since the right to found a family is a fundamental human right in the Universal Declaration of Human Rights, isn't the disintegration of the family as the basic unit of society in many Western countries today a negation of a fundamental human right?

5. Confronted by the reality of family disintegration, violence, economic stagnation, and racism, one senses that the Western political system — emphasis upon human rights and democracy notwithstanding — no longer possesses the will and the wherewithal to bring about fundamental changes to society. What is the meaning of individual rights and liberties if they are utterly incapable of affecting meaningful transformations in values, attitudes, and structures which are imperative if the West is to lift itself out of its spiritual and psychological morass?

The dominant West's violations of human rights in the non-Western world, coupled with its inability to uphold some of the fundamental rights of its own citizens, has raised some important questions about the very nature and character of Western human rights:

1. Has the creative individuality of an earlier phase in Western history given way to gross, vulgar individualism which today threatens the very fabric of Western society? Isn't individualism of this sort a negation of the community?

2. Has the glorification and adulation of individual freedom as an end in itself reached a point where individual freedom has become the be-all and end-all of human existence? Isn't freedom in the ultimate analysis a means towards a greater good rather than an end in itself?

3. Isn't this notion of freedom in the West linked to an idea of rights which is often divorced from responsibilities? Can rights be separated from responsibilities in real life?

4. Isn't the dominant Western concept of rights itself particularistic and sectional since it emphasizes only civil and political rights and downplays economic, social, and cultural rights?

5. How can a concept of rights confined to the nation-state respond to the challenges posed by an increasingly global economic, political, and cultural system? Isn't it true that the dominant Western approach to human rights fails to recognize the role of global actors — like the UNSC, IMF and MNCs — in the violation of human rights?

6. Whether one articulates rights or upholds responsibilities, shouldn't they be guided by universal moral and spiritual values which would determine the sort of rights we pursue and the type of responsibilities we fulfill? Without a larger spiritual and moral framework, which endows human endeavor with meaning and purpose, with coherence and unity, wouldn't the emphasis on rights *per se* lead to moral chaos and confusion?

7. What are human rights if they are not related to more fundamental questions about the human being? Who is the human being? Why is the human being here? Where does the human being go from here? How can one talk of the rights of the human being without a more profound understanding of the human being him- or herself?

It is because of these and other flaws in the very character of the Western approach to human rights that there is an urgent need to try to evolve a vision of human dignity which is more just, more holistic, and more universal. In Islam, Hinduism, Sikhism, Taoism, Christianity, Judaism and even in the theistic strains within Confucianism and Buddhism there are elements of such a vision of the human being, of human rights and of human dignity. The idea that human being is vice-regent or trustee of God whose primary role is to fulfill God's trust is lucidly articulated in various religions. As God's trustee, the human being lives life according to clearly established spiritual and moral values and principles. The rights one possesses, like the responsibilities one undertakes, must be guided by these values and principles. What this means is that human rights and human freedoms are part of a larger spiritual and moral worldview. This also means that individual freedom is not the be-all and end-all of human existence. Neither is the individual the ultimate arbiter of right and wrong, of good and evil. The individual and community must both submit to spiritual and moral values which transcend both individual and community. It is the supremacy of these values and, in the end, of the Divine which distinguishes our God-guided concept of human dignity from the present individual-centered notion of human rights.

The great challenge before us is to develop this vision of human dignity culled from our religious and spiritual philosophies into a comprehensive charter of values and principles, responsibilities and rights, roles and relationships acceptable to human beings everywhere. To do this we should first distinguish what is universal and eternal within our respective traditions from what is particularistic and contextual. On that basis we should conduct a dialogue with people of all religions on the question of human dignity. Even those of secular persuasion should be invited to dialogue with people of faith. Indeed, as we have indicated, there is a great deal in the secular human rights tradition that we should absorb and imbibe in the process of developing our vision of human dignity.

To develop our vision into a vision which has relevance to the realities which human beings have to grapple with, our dialogue should focus upon concrete contemporary issues that challenge human dignity everywhere — issues of global domination and global control of poverty and disease, of political oppression and cultural chauvinism, of moneyism and materialism, of corruption and greed, of the disintegration of the community and the alienation of the individual. It would, in other words, be a dialogue on life and living. This is perhaps the best time to initiate such a dialogue since Asian societies are now beginning to ask some searching questions about the nexus between moral values and human rights.

Of course, not all sections of Asian societies are asking the same questions about the link between morality and rights. Some Asian governments, for instance, have chosen to focus solely upon the adverse consequences of crass individualism upon the moral fabric of Western societies. As an antidote, they emphasize the importance of strengthening existing family and community ties in Asian cultures. For us who seek inspiration and guidance from our spiritual and moral philosophies in a non-selective manner, it is not just family and community that are important. We know that the individual expressing himself or herself through the community also has a crucial place in most of our philosophies. After all, in all religions, the Divine message is, in the ultimate analysis, addressed to the individual. For it is the individual, and the individual alone, who is capable of moral and spiritual transformation. Similarly, it is not just the moral crisis of Western society that we lament; we are no less sensitive to the moral decadence within our own societies — especially within our elite strata. If we adhere to a universal spiritual and moral ethic that applies to all human beings, we should not hesitate to condemn the suppression of human rights and the oppression of dissident groups that occur from time to time in

a number of our countries. Our commitment to spiritual and moral values, drawn from our religions, should never serve as a camouflage for authoritarian elites who seek to shield their sins from scrutiny. Indeed, any attempt to do so would be tantamount to a travesty of the eternal truth embodied in all our religions. And what is that truth? That religion's primary concern is the dignity of all human beings.

This, then, is the road that we must travel; the journey we must undertake. From Western human rights, which has been so selective and sectarian, to a genuinely universal human dignity — which remains the human being's yet unfulfilled promise to God.

13.9 WILL KYMLICKA ("THE GOOD, THE BAD, AND THE INTOLERABLE: MINORITY GROUP RIGHTS," 1996)

Ethnocultural minorities around the world are demanding various forms of recognition and protection, often in the language of "group rights." Many commentators see this as a new and dangerous trend that threatens the fragile international consensus on the importance of individual rights. Traditional human rights doctrines are based on the idea of the inherent dignity and equality of all individuals. The emphasis on group rights, by contrast, seems to treat individuals as the mere carriers of group identities and objectives, rather than as autonomous personalities capable of defining their own identity and goals in life. Hence it tends to subordinate the individual's freedom to the group's claim to protect its historical traditions or cultural purity.

I believe that this view is overstated. In many cases, group rights supplement and strengthen human rights, by responding to potential injustices that traditional rights doctrine cannot address. These are the "good" group rights. There are cases, to be sure, where illiberal groups seek the right to restrict the basic liberties of their members. These are the "bad" group rights. In some cases, these illiberal practices are not only bad, but intolerable, and the larger society has a right to intervene to stop them. But in other cases, liberal states must tolerate unjust practices within a minority group. Drawing the line between the bad and the intolerable is one of the thorniest issues liberal democracies face.

I want to look at the relationship between group and individual rights in the context of the claims of indigenous peoples in North America. In both the United States and Canada, these peoples have various group rights. For example, they have rights of self-government, under which they exercise control over health, education, family law, policing, criminal justice, and resource development. They also have legally recognized land claims, which reserve certain lands for their exclusive use and provide guaranteed representation on certain regulatory bodies. And in some cases, they have rights relating to the use of their own language.

The situation of indigenous peoples is a useful example, I think, for several reasons. For one thing, they have been at the forefront of the movement toward recognizing group rights at the international level — reflected in the Draft Universal Declaration on Indigenous Rights at the United Nations. The case of indigenous peoples also shows that group rights are not a new issue. From the very beginning of European colonization, the "natives" fought for rights relating to their land, languages, and self-government. What has changed in recent years is not that indigenous peoples have altered their demands, but rather that these demands have become more visible, and that the larger society has started to listen to them.

Reflecting on this long history should warn us against the facile assumption that the demand for group rights is somehow a byproduct of current intellectual fashions, such as postmodernism, or of ethnic entrepreneurs pushing affirmative action programs beyond their original intention. On the contrary, the consistent historical demands of indigenous peoples suggests that the issue of group rights is an enduring and endemic one for liberal democracies.

Group rights, as I will use the term, refer to claims to something more than, or other than, the common rights of citizenship. The

category is obviously very large and can be subdivided into any number of more refined categories, reflecting the different sorts of rights sought by different sorts of groups.

Two Kinds of Group Rights

For my purposes, however, the most important distinction is between two kinds of group rights: one involves the claim of an indigenous group against its own members; the other involves the claim of an indigenous group against the larger society. Both of these can be seen as protecting the stability of indigenous communities, but they respond to different sources of instability. The first is intended to protect a group from the destabilizing impact of internal dissent (that is, the decision of individual members not to follow traditional practices or customs), whereas the second is intended to protect the group from the impact of external decisions (that is, the economic or political policies of the larger society). I will call the first "internal restrictions" and the second "external protections."

Both are "group rights," but they raise very different issues. Internal restrictions involve intra-group relations. An indigenous group may seek the use of state power to restrict the liberty of its own members in the name of group solidarity. For example, a tribal government might discriminate against those members who do not share the traditional religion. This sort of internal restriction raises the danger of individual oppression. Group rights in this sense can be invoked by patriarchal and theocratic cultures to justify the oppression of women and the legal enforcement of religious orthodoxy.

Of course, all forms of government involve restricting the liberty of those subject to their authority. In all countries, no matter how liberal and democratic, people are required to pay taxes to support public goods. Most democracies also require people to undertake jury duty or to perform some amount of military or community service, and a few countries require people to vote. All governments expect and sometimes require a minimal level of civic responsibility and participation from their citizens.

But some groups seek to impose much greater restrictions on the liberty of their members. It is one thing to require people to do jury duty or to vote, and quite another to compel people to attend a particular church or to follow traditional gender roles. The former are intended to uphold liberal rights and democratic institutions, the latter restrict these rights in the name of orthodoxy or cultural tradition. It is these latter cases that I have in mind when talking about internal restrictions.

Obviously, groups are free to require respect for traditional norms and authorities as terms of membership in private, voluntary associations. A Catholic organization can insist that its members be Catholics in good standing, and the same applies to voluntary religious organizations within indigenous communities. The problem arises when a group seeks to use *governmental* power, or the distribution of public benefits, to restrict the liberty of members.

On my view, such legally imposed internal restrictions are almost always unjust. It is a basic tenet of liberal democracy that whoever exercises political power within a community must respect the civil and political rights of its members, and any attempt to impose internal restrictions that violate this condition is unjust.

External protections, by contrast, involve *inter-group* relations. In these cases, the indigenous group seeks to protect its distinct existence and identity by limiting its vulnerability to the decisions of the larger society. For example, reserving land for the exclusive use of indigenous peoples ensures that they are not outbid for this resource by the greater wealth of outsiders. Similarly, guaranteeing representation for indigenous peoples on various public regulatory bodies reduces the chance that they will be outvoted on decisions that affect their community. And allowing indigenous peoples to control their own health care system ensures that critical decisions are not made by people who are ignorant of their distinctive health needs or their traditional medicines.

On my view, these sorts of external protections are often consistent with liberal democracy, and may indeed be necessary for democratic justice. They can be seen as putting indigenous peoples and the larger society on a more equal footing, by reducing the extent to which the former is vulnerable to the latter.

Of course, one can imagine circumstances where the sorts of external protections demanded by a minority group are unfair. Under the apartheid system in South Africa, for example, whites, who constituted less than 20 percent of the population, demanded 87 percent of the land mass of the country, monopolized all the political power, and imposed Afrikaans and English throughout the entire school system. They defended this in the name of reducing their vulnerability to the decisions of other larger groups, although the real aim was to dominate and exploit these groups.

However, the sorts of external protections sought by indigenous peoples hardly put them in a position to dominate others. The land claims, representation rights, and self-government powers sought by indigenous peoples do not deprive other groups of their fair share of economic resources or political power, nor of their language rights. Rather, indigenous peoples simply seek to ensure that the majority cannot use its superior numbers or wealth to deprive them of the resources and institutions vital to the reproduction of their communities. And that, I believe, is fully justified. So, whereas internal restrictions are almost inherently in conflict with liberal democratic norms, external protections are not — so long as they promote equality between groups rather than allowing one group to oppress another....

The Limits of Toleration

How should liberal states respond in such cases? It is right and proper, I think, for liberals to criticize oppressive practices within indigenous communities, just as we should criticize foreign countries that oppress their citizens. These oppressive practices may be traditional (although many aren't), but tradition is not self-validating. Indeed, that an oppressive practice is traditional may just show how deep the injustice goes.

But should we intervene and impose a liberal regime on the Pueblo, forcing them to respect the religious liberty of Protestants and the sexual equality of women? Should we insist that indigenous governments be subject to the Bill of Rights, and that their decisions be reviewable by federal courts?

It's important here to distinguish two questions: (1) Are internal restrictions consistent with liberal principles? and (2) Should liberals impose their views on minorities that do not accept some or all of these principles? The first is the question of *identifying* a defensible liberal theory of group rights; the second is the question of *imposing* that theory.

The first question is easy: internal restrictions are illiberal and unjust. But the answer to the second question is less clear. That liberals cannot automatically impose their principles on groups that do not share them is obvious enough, I think, if the illiberal group is another country. The Saudi Arabian government unjustly denies political rights to women or non-Muslims. But it doesn't follow that liberals outside Saudi Arabia should forcibly intervene to compel the Saudis to give everyone the vote. Similarly, the German government unjustly denies political rights to the children and grandchildren of Turkish "guest-workers," born and raised on German soil. But it doesn't follow that liberals outside Germany should use force to compel Germany to change its citizenship.

What isn't clear is the proper remedy for rights violations. What third party (if any) has the authority to intervene in order to force the government to respect those rights? The same question arises when the illiberal group is a self-governing indigenous community within a single country. The Pueblo tribal council violates the rights of its members by limiting freedom of conscience and by employing sexually discriminatory membership rules. But what third party (if any) has the authority to compel the Pueblo council to respect those rights?

Liberal principles tell us that individuals have certain claims that their government must respect, such as individual freedom of conscience. But having identified those claims, we now face the very different question of imposing liberalism. If a particular government fails to respect those claims, who can legitimately step in and force compliance?

In short, contemporary liberals have become more reluctant to impose liberalism on foreign countries, but more willing to impose liberalism on indigenous minorities. This, I think, is inconsistent. Both foreign states and indigenous minorities form distinct political communities, with their own claims to self-government. Attempts to impose liberal principles by force are often perceived, in both cases, as a form of aggression or paternalistic colonialism. And, as a result, these attempts often backfire. The plight of many former colonies in Africa shows that liberal institutions are likely to be unstable when they are the products of external imposition rather than internal reform. In the end, liberal institutions can work only if liberal beliefs have been internalized by the members of the self-governing society, be it an independent country or an indigenous minority.

There are, of course, important differences between foreign states and indigenous minorities. Yet, in both cases, there is relatively little scope for legitimate coercive interference. Relations between the majority society and indigenous peoples should be determined by peaceful negotiation, not force. This means searching for some basis of agreement. The most secure basis would be agreement on fundamental principles. But if the two groups do not share basic principles, and cannot be persuaded to adopt the other's principles, they will have to rely on some more minimalist modus vivendi.

The resulting agreement may well exempt the indigenous minority from the Bill of Rights and judicial review. Indeed, such exemptions are often implicit in the historical treaties by which the minority entered the larger state. This means that the majority will sometimes be unable to prevent the violation of individual rights within the minority community. Liberals have to learn to live with this, just as they must live with illiberal laws in other countries.

13.10 MARTHA NUSSBUM ("WOMEN AND CULTURAL UNIVERSALS," *SEX AND SOCIAL JUSTICE*, 1999)

...Unlike the type of liberal approach that focuses only on the distribution of resources, the capability approach maintains that resources have no value in themselves, apart from their role in promoting human functioning. It therefore directs the planner to inquire into the varying needs individuals have for resources and their varying abilities to convert resources into functioning. In this way, it strongly invites a scrutiny of tradition as one of the primary sources of such unequal abilities.[1]

But the capabilities approach raises the question of cultural universalism, or, as it is often pejoratively called, "essentialism." Once we begin asking how people are actually functioning, we cannot avoid focusing on some components of lives and not others, some abilities to act and not others, seeing some capabilities and functions as more central, more at the core of human life, than others. We cannot avoid having an account, even if a partial and highly general account, of what functions of the human being are most worth the care and attention of public planning the world over. Such an account is bound to be controversial.

II. Anti-Universalist Conversations

The primary opponents of such an account of capability and functioning will be "anti-essentialists" of various types, thinkers who urge us to begin not with sameness but with difference — both between women and men and across groups of women — and to seek norms defined relatively to a local context and locally held beliefs. This opposition takes many forms, and I shall be responding to several distinct objections. But I can begin to motivate the enterprise by telling several true stories of conversations that have taken place at the World Institute for Development Economics Research (WIDER), in which the anti-universalist position seemed to have alarming implications for women's lives.[2]

At a conference on "Value and Technology," an American economist who has long been a leftwing critic of neoclassical economics delivers a paper urging the preservation of traditional ways of life in a rural area of Orissa, India, now under threat of contamination from Western development projects. As evidence of the excellence of this rural way of life, he points to the fact that whereas we Westerners experience a sharp split between the values that prevail in the workplace and the values that prevail in the home, here, by contrast, exists what the economist calls "the embedded way of life," the same values obtaining in both places. His example: Just as in the home a menstruating woman is thought to pollute the kitchen and therefore may not enter it, so too in the workplace a menstruating woman is taken to pollute the loom and may not enter the room where looms are kept. Some feminists object that this example is repellant rather than admirable; for surely such practices both degrade the women in question and inhibit their freedom. The first economist's collaborator, an elegant French anthropologist (who would, I suspect, object violently to a purity check at the seminar room door), replies: Don't we realize that there is, in these matters, no privileged place to stand? This, after all, has been shown by both Derrida and Foucault. Doesn't he know that he is neglecting the otherness of Indian ideas by bringing his Western essentialist values into the picture?[3]

The same French anthropologist now delivers her paper. She expresses regret that the introduction of smallpox vaccination to India by the British eradicated the cult of Sittala Devi, the goddess to whom one used to pray to avert smallpox. Here, she says, is another example of Western neglect of difference. Someone (it might have been me) objects that it is surely better to be healthy rather than ill, to live rather than to die. The answer comes back; Western essentialist medicine conceives of things in terms of binary oppositions: life is opposed to death, health to disease.[4] But if we cast away this binary way of thinking, we will begin to comprehend the otherness of Indian traditions.

At this point Eric Hobsbawm, who has been listening to the proceedings in increasingly uneasy silence, rises to deliver a blistering indictment of the traditionalism and relativism that prevail in this group. He lists historical examples of ways in which appeals to tradition have been politically engineered to support oppression and violence.[5] His final example is that of National Socialism in Germany. In the confusion that ensues, most of the relativist social scientists — above all those from far away, who do not know who Hobsbawm is — demand that Hobsbawm be asked to leave the room. The radical American economist, disconcerted by this apparent tension between his relativism and his affiliation with the left, convinces them, with difficulty, to let Hobsbawm remain.

We shift now to another conference two years later, a philosophical conference on the quality of life.[6] Members of the quality-of-life project are speaking of choice as a basic good, and of the importance of expanding women's sphere of choices. We are challenged by the radical economist of my first story, who insists that contemporary anthropology has shown that non-Western people are not especially attached to freedom of choice. His example: A book on Japan has shown that Japanese males, when they get home from work, do not wish to choose what to eat for dinner, what to wear, and so on. They wish all these choices to be taken out of their hands by their wives. A heated exchange follows about what this example really shows. I leave it to your imaginations to reconstruct it. In the end, the confidence of the radical economist is unshaken: We are victims of bad universalist thinking, who fail to respect "difference."[7]

The phenomenon is an odd one. For we see here highly intelligent people, people deeply committed to the good of women and men in developing countries, people who think of themselves as progressive and feminist and antiracist, people who correctly argue that the concept of development is an evaluative concept requiring normative argument[8] — effectively eschewing normative argument and taking up positions that converge, as Hobsbawm correctly saw, with the positions of reaction, oppression, and sexism. Under the banner of their fashionable opposition to universalism march ancient religious taboos,

the luxury of the pampered husband, educational deprivation, unequal health care, and premature death.

Nor do these anti-universalists appear to have a very sophisticated conception of their own core notions, such as "culture," "custom," and "tradition." It verges on the absurd to treat India as a single culture, and a single visit to a single Orissan village as sufficient to reveal its traditions. India, like all extant societies, is a complex mixture of elements.[9] Hindu, Muslim, Parsi, Christian, Jewish, atheist; urban, suburban, rural; rich, poor, and middle class; high caste, low caste, and aspiring middle caste; female and male; rationalist and mystical. It is renowned for mystical religion but also for achievements in mathematics and for the invention of chess. It contains intense, often violent sectarianism, but it also contains Rabindranath Tagore's cosmopolitan humanism and Mahatma Gandhi's interpretation of Hinduism as a religion of universal nonviolence. Its traditions contain views of female whorishness and childishness that derive from the Laws of Manu.[10] But it also contains the sexual agency of Draupadi in the *Mahabharata*, who solved the problem of choice among Pandava husbands by taking all five, and the enlightened sensualism and female agency of the *Kama Sutra*, a sacred text that foreign readers wrongly interpret as pornographic. It contains women like Metha Bai, who are confined to the home; it also contains women like Amita Sen (mother of Amartya Sen), who fifty years ago was among the first middle-class Bengali women to dance in public, in Rabindranath Tagore's musical extravaganzas in Santiniketan. It contains artists who disdain the foreign, preferring, with the Marglins, the "embedded" way of life, and it also contains Satyajit Ray, that great Bengali artist and lover of local traditions, who could also write, "I never ceased to regret that while I had stood in the scorching summer sun in the wilds of Santiniketan sketching *simul* and *palash* in full bloom, *Citizen Kane* had come and gone, playing for just three days in the newest and biggest cinema in Calcutta.[11]

What, then, is "the culture" of a woman like Metha Bai? Is it bound to be that determined by the most prevalent customs in Rajasthan, the region of her marital home? Or, might she be permitted to consider with what traditions or groups she wishes to align herself, perhaps forming a community of solidarity with other widows and women, in pursuit of a better quality of life? What is "the culture" of Chinese working women who have recently been victims of the government's "women go home" policy, which appeals to Confucian traditions about woman's "nature"?[12] Must it be the one advocated by Confucius, or may they be permitted to form new alliances — with one another, and with other defenders of women's human rights? What is "the culture" of General Motors employee Mary Carr? Must it be the one that says women should be demure and polite, even in the face of gross insults, and that an "unladylike" woman deserves the harassment she gets? Or might she be allowed to consider what norms are appropriate to the situation of a woman working in a heavy metal shop, and to act accordingly? Real cultures contain plurality and conflict, tradition, and subversion. They borrow good things from wherever they find them, none too worried about purity. We would never tolerate a claim that women in our own society must embrace traditions that arose thousands of years ago — indeed, we are proud that we have no such traditions. Isn't it condescending, then, to treat Indian and Chinese women as bound by the past in ways that we are not?

Indeed, as Hobsbawm suggested, the vision of "culture" propounded by the Marglins, by stressing uniformity and homogeneity, may lie closer to artificial constructions by reactionary political forces than to any organic historical entity. Even to the extent to which it is historical, one might ask, exactly how does that contribute to make it worth preserving? Cultures are not museum pieces, to be preserved intact at all costs. There would appear, indeed, to be something condescending in preserving for contemplation a way of life that causes real pain to real people.

Let me now, nonetheless, describe the most cogent objections that might be raised by a relativist against a normative universalist project.

III.   The Attack on Universalism

Many attacks on universalism suppose that any universalist project must rely on truths eternally fixed in the nature of things, outside human action and human history. Because some people believe in such truths and some do not, the objector holds that a normative view so grounded is bound to be biased in favor of some religious/metaphysical conceptions and against others.[13] *But universalism does not require such metaphysical support.*[14] For universal ideas of the human do arise within history and from human experience, and they can ground themselves in experience. Indeed, those who take all human norms to be the result of human interpretation can hardly deny that universal conceptions of the human are prominent and pervasive among such interpretations, hardly to be relegated to the dustbin of metaphysical history along with recondite theoretical entities such as phlogiston. As Aristotle so simply puts it, "One may observe in one's travels to distant countries the feelings of recognition and affiliation that link every human being to every other human being."[15] ...

Neglect of Historical and Cultural Differences

The opponent charges that any attempt to pick out some elements of human life as more fundamental than others, even without appeal to a transhistorical reality, is bound to be insufficiently respectful of actual historical and cultural differences. People, it is claimed, understand human life and humanness in widely different ways, and any attempt to produce a list of the most fundamental properties and functions of human beings is bound to enshrine certain understandings of the human and to demote others. Usually, the objector continues, this takes the form of enshrining the understanding of a dominant group at the expense of minority understandings. This type of objection, frequently made by feminists, can claim support from many historical examples in which the human has indeed been defined by focusing on actual characteristics of males.

It is far from clear what this objection shows. In particular it is far from clear that it supports the idea that we ought to base our ethical norms, instead, on the current preferences and the self-conceptions of people who are living what the objector herself claims to be lives of deprivation and oppression. But it does show at least that the project of choosing one picture of the human over another is fraught with difficulty, political as well as philosophical.

Neglect of Autonomy

A different objection is presented by liberal opponents of universalism. The objection is that by determining in advance what elements of human life have most importance, the universalist project fails to respect the right of people to choose a plan of life according to their own lights, determining what is central and what is not.[16] This way of proceeding is "imperialistic." Such evaluative choices must be left to each citizen. For this reason, politics must refuse itself a determinate theory of the human being and the human good....

IV.   A Conception of the Human Being: The Central Human Capabilities

The list of basic capabilities is generated by asking a question that from the start is evaluative: What activities[17] characteristically performed by human beings are so central that they seem definitive of a life that is truly human? In other words, what are the functions without which (meaning, without the availability of which) we would regard a life as not, or not fully, human?[18]

The other question is a question about kind inclusion. We recognize other humans as human across many differences of time and place, of custom and appearance. We often tell ourselves stories, on the other hand, about anthropomorphic creatures who do not get classified as human, on account of some feature of their form of life and functioning. On what do we base these inclusions and exclusions? In short, what do we be believe must be there, if we are going to acknowledge that a given life is human?[19] The answer to these questions points us to a subset of common or characteristic human functions, informing us that these are likely to have a special importance for everything else we choose and do....

I introduce this as a list of capabilities rather than of actual functionings, because I shall argue that capability, not actual functioning, should be the goal of public policy.

Central Human Functional Capabilities

1. *Life.* Being able to live to the end of a human life of normal length,[20] not dying prematurely or before one's life is so reduced as to be not worth living.

2. *Bodily health and integrity.* Being able to have good health, including reproductive health; being adequately nourished;[21] being able to have adequate shelter.[22]

3. *Bodily integrity.* Being able to move freely from place to place; being able to be secure against violent assault, including sexual assault, marital rape, and domestic violence; having opportunities for sexual satisfaction and for choice in matters of reproduction.

4. *Senses, imagination, thought.* Being able to use the senses; being able to imagine, to think, and to reason — and to do these things in a "truly human" way, a way informed and cultivated by an adequate education, including, but by no means limited to, literacy and basic mathematical and scientific training; being able to use imagination and thought in connection with experiencing and producing expressive works and events of one's own choice (religious, literary, musical, etc.); being able to use one's mind in ways protected by guarantees of freedom of expression with respect to both political and artistic speech and freedom of religious exercise; being able to have pleasurable experiences and to avoid no beneficial pain.

5. *Emotions.* Being able to have attachments to things and persons outside ourselves; being able to love those who love and care for us; being able to grieve at

their absence; in general, being able to love, to grieve, to experience longing, gratitude, and justified anger; not having one's emotional developing blighted by fear or anxiety. (Supporting this capability means supporting forms of human association that can be shown to be crucial in their development.[23])

6. *Practical reason*. Being able to form a conception of the good and to engage in critical reflection about the planning of one's own life. (This entails protection for the liberty of conscience.)

7. *Affiliation*. (a) Being able to live for and in relation to others, to recognize and show concern for other human beings, to engage in various forms of social interaction; being able to imagine the situation of another and to have compassion for that situation; having the capability for both justice and friendship. (Protecting this capability means, once again, protecting institutions that constitute such forms of affiliation, and also protecting the freedoms of assembly and political speech.) (b) Having the social bases of self-respect and no humiliation; being able to be treated as a dignified being whose worth is equal to that of others. (This entails provisions of nondiscrimination.)

8. *Other species*. Being able to live with concern for and in relation to animals, plants, and the world of nature.[24]

9. *Play*. Being able to laugh, to play, to enjoy recreational activities.

10. *Control over one's environment*. (a) *Political*: being able to participate effectively in political choices that govern one's life; having the rights of political participation, free speech, and freedom of association. (b) *Material*: being able to hold property (both land and movable goods); having the right to seek employment on an equal basis with others; having the freedom from unwarranted search and seizure.[25] In work, being able to work as a human being, exercising practical reason and entering into meaningful relationships of mutual recognition with other workers.

The "capabilities approach," as I conceive it,[26] claims that a life that lacks any one of these capabilities, no matter what else it has, will fall short of being a good human life. Thus it would be reasonable to take these things as a focus for concern, in assessing the quality of life in a country and asking about the role of public policy in meeting human needs. The list is certainly general — and this is deliberate, to leave room for plural specification and also for further negotiation. But like (and as a reasonable basis for) a set of constitutional guarantees, it offers real guidance to policymakers, and far more accurate guidance than that offered by the focus on utility, or even on resources.[27]

The list is, emphatically, a list of separate components. We cannot satisfy the need for one of them by giving a larger amount of another one. All are of central importance and all are distinct in quality. This limits the trade-offs that it will be reasonable to make and thus limits the applicability of quantitative cost-benefit analysis. At the same time, the items on the list are related to one another in many complex ways. Employment rights, for example, support health, and also freedom from domestic violence, by giving women a better bargaining position in the family. The liberties of speech and association turn up at several distinct points on the list, showing their fundamental role with respect to several distinct areas of human functioning ... strenuous fasting. Whether for religious or for other reasons, a person may prefer a celibate life to one containing sexual expression. A person may prefer to work with an intense dedication that precludes recreation and play. Am I saying that these are not fully human or flourishing lives? Does the approach instruct governments to nudge or push people into functioning of the requisite sort, no matter what they prefer?

Here we must answer: No, capability, not functioning, is the political goal. This is so because of the very great importance the approach attaches to practical reason, as a good that both suffuses all the other functions, making them human rather than animal,[28] and figures, itself, as a central function on the list. It is perfectly true that functionings, not simply capabilities, are what render a life fully human: If there were no functioning of any kind in a life, we could hardly applaud it, no matter what opportunities it contained. Nonetheless, for political purposes it is appropriate for us to shoot for capabilities, and those alone. Citizens must be left free to determine their course after that. The person with plenty of food may always choose to fast, but there is a great difference between fasting and starving, and it is this difference we wish to capture. Again, the person who has normal opportunities for sexual satisfaction can always choose a life of celibacy, and we say nothing against this. What we do speak against, for example, is the practice of female genital mutilation, which deprives individuals of the opportunity to choose sexual functioning (and indeed, the opportunity to choose celibacy as well).[29] A person who has opportunities for play can always choose a workaholic life; again, there is a great difference between that chosen life and a life constrained by insufficient maximum-hour protections and/or the "double day" that makes women in many parts of the world unable to play....

The aim of public policy is production of *combined capabilities*. This means promoting the states of the person by providing the necessary education and care; it also means preparing the environment so that it is favorable for the exercise of practical reason and the other major functions.[30]

This clarifies the position. The approach does not say that public policy should rest content with *internal capabilities* but remain indifferent to the struggles of individuals who have to try to exercise these in a hostile environment. In that sense, it is highly attentive to the goal of functioning, and instructs governments to keep it always in view. On the other hand, we are not pushing individuals into the function: Once the stage is fully set, the choice is up to them....

A preference-based approach that gives priority to the preferences of dominant males in a traditional culture is likely to be especially subversive of the quality of life of women, who have been on the whole badly treated by prevailing traditional norms. And one can see this clearly in the Marglins' own examples. For menstruation taboos, even if endorsed by habit and custom, impose severe restrictions on women's power to form a plan of life and to execute the plan they have chosen.[31] They are members of the same family of traditional attitudes that make it difficult for women like Metha Bai to sustain the basic functions of life. Vulnerability to smallpox, even if someone other than an anthropologist should actually defend it as a good thing, is even more evidently a threat to human functioning. And the Japanese husband who allegedly renounces freedom of choice actually shows considerable attachment to it, in the ways that matter, by asking the woman to look after the boring details of life. What should concern us is whether the woman has a similar degree of freedom to plan her life and to execute her plan.

As for Metha Bai, the absence of freedom to choose employment outside the home is linked to other capability failures, in the areas of health, nutrition, mobility, education, and political voice. Unlike the type of liberal view that focuses on resources alone, my view enables us to focus directly on the obstacles to self-realization imposed by traditional norms and values and thus to justify special political action to remedy the unequal situation. No male of Metha Bai's caste would have to overcome threats of physical violence in order to go out of the house to work for life-sustaining food.

The capabilities approach insists that a woman's affiliation with a certain group or culture should not be taken as normative for her unless, on due consideration, with all the capabilities at her disposal, she makes that norm her own. We should take care to extend to each individual full capabilities to pursue the items on the list — and then see whether they want to avail themselves of those opportunities.

Women belong to cultures. But they do not choose to be born into any particular culture, and they do not really choose to endorse its norms as good for themselves, unless they do so in possession of further options and opportunities — including the opportunity to form communities of affiliation and empowerment with other women. The contingencies of where one is born, whose power one is afraid of, and what habits shape one's daily thought are chance events that should not be permitted to play the role they now play in pervasively shaping women's life chances. Beneath all these chance events are human powers, powers of choice and intelligent self-formation. Women in much of the world lack support for the most central human functions, and this denial of support is frequently caused by their being women. But women, unlike rocks and plants and even horses, have the potential to become capable of these human functions, given sufficient nutrition, education, and other support. That is why their unequal failure in capability is a problem of justice. It is up to all human beings to solve this problem. I claim that a conception of human functioning gives us valuable assistance as we undertake this task.

[1] See Amartya Sen, "Equality of What?" in *Choice, Welfare, and Measurement* (Oxford: Basil Blackwell, 1982), 353–72; and M. Nussbaum, "Aristotelian Social Democracy," in *Liberalism and the Good,* Bruce Douglass, Gerald M. Mara and Henry S. Richardson eds., (New York & London: Routledge, 1990), pp. 203-252.

[2] Much of the material described in these examples is now published in *Dominating Knowledge: Development, Culture, and Resistance,* ed. Frédérique Apffel Marglin and Stephen A. Marglin (Oxford: Clarendon Press, 1990). The issue of "embeddedness" and menstruation taboos is discussed in S. A. Marglin, "Losing Touch: The Cultural Conditions of Worker Accommodation and Resistance," 217–82, and related issues are discussed in S. A.Marglin, "Toward the Decolonization of the Mind," 1–28. On Sittala Devi, see F. A. Marglin, "Smallpox in Two Systems of Knowledge," 102–44; and for related arguments, see Ashis Nandy and Shiv Visvanathan, "Modern Medicine and Its Non-Modern Critics," 144–84. I have in some cases combined two conversations into one; otherwise things happened as I describe them.

[3] For Sen's account of the plurality and internal diversity of Indian values, one that strongly emphasizes the presence of a rationalist and critical strand in Indian traditions, see M. Nussbaum and A. Sen, "Internal Criticism and Indian Relativist Traditions," in *Relativism: Interpretation and Confrontation,* ed. M. Krausz (Notre Dame: Notre Dame University Press, 1989), 299–325 (an essay originally presented at the same WIDER conference and refused publication by the Marglins in its proceedings); and A. Sen, "India and the West," *The New Republic,* June 7, 1993. See also Bimal K. Matilal, *Perception* (Oxford: Clarendon Press, 1995) (a fundamental study of Indian traditions regarding knowledge and logic); and B. K. Matilal, "Ethical Relativism and the Confrontation of Cultures," in Krausz, ed., *Relativism,* 339–62.

[4] S. A. Marglin, "Toward the Decolonization," 22–23, suggests that binary thinking is peculiarly Western. But such oppositions are pervasive in Indian, Chinese, and African traditions (see M. Nussbaum, "Human Capabilities, Female Human Beings," in *Women Culture, and Development: A Study of Human Capabilities,* M. Nussbaum and Jonathan Glover, eds., (Oxford: Clarendon Press; New York: Oxford University Press, 1995). To deny them to a culture is condescending; for how can one utter a definite idea without bounding off one thing against another?

[5] See Eric Hobsbawm and Terence Ranger, eds., *The Invention of Tradition* (Cambridge: Cambridge University Press, 1983). In his *New Republic* piece, Sen makes a similar argument about contemporary India: The Western construction of India as mystical and "other" serves the purposes of the fundamentalist Bharatiya Janata Party (BJP), who are busy refashioning history to serve the ends of their own political power. An eloquent critique of the whole notion of the "other" and of the associated "nativism," where Africa is concerned, can be found in Kwame Anthony Appiah, *In My Father's House: Africa in the Philosophy of Cultures* (New York: Oxford University Press, 1991).

[6] The proceedings of this conference are now published as M. Nussbaum and A. Sen, eds., *The Quality of Life* (Oxford: Clarendon Press, 1993).

[7] Marglin has since published this point in "Toward the Decolonization." His reference is to Takeo Doi, *The Anatomy of Dependence* (Tokyo: Kodansha, 1971).

[8] See S. A.Marglin, "Toward the Decolonization."

[9] See Nussbaum and Sen, "Internal Criticism," and A. Sen, "Human Rights and Asian Values," *The New Republic,* July 10/17, 1997, pp. 33–34.

[10] See Roop Rekha Verma, "Femininity, Equality, and Personhood," in *Women, Culture, and Development: A Study of Human Capabilities,* M. Nussbaum, ed., (New York: Oxford University Press, 1995).

[11] Satyajit Ray, "Introduction," in *Our Films, Their Films* (Bombay: Orient Longman, 1976; reprinted, New York: Hyperion, 1994), 5.

[12] Personal communication, scholars in women's studies at the Chinese Academy Social Sciences, June 1995.

[13] Note that this objection itself seems to rely on some universal values such as fairness and freedom from bias.

[14] See HF for a longer version of this discussion.

[15] Aristotle, *Nicomachean Ethics* VIII. I discuss this passage in M. Nussbaum, "Aristotle on Human Nature and the Foundation of Ethics, in *World, Mind, and Ethics, Essays on the Ethical Philosophy of Bernard Williams* (Cambridge & New York: Cambridge University Press, 1995), pp. 86-131, and *Non-relative Virtues: An Aristotelian Approach,* (Helsinki, World Institute for Development Economics Research, 1987).

[16] This point is made by the Marglins, as well as by liberal thinkers, but can they consistently make it while holding that freedom of choice is just a parochial Western value? It would appear not; on the other hand, F. A. Marglin (here differing, I believe, from S. A.Marglin) also held in oral remarks delivered at the 1986 conference that logical consistency is simply a parochial Western value.

[17] The use of this term does not imply that the functions all involved doing something especially "active." See here A. Sen, "Capability and Well-Being," in *The Quality of Life*, 30–53. In Aristotelian terms, and in mine, being healthy, reflecting, and being pleased are all "activities."

[18] For further discussion of this point, and for examples, see HN.

[19] See HN for a more extended account of this procedure and how it justifies.

[20] Although "normal length" is clearly relative to current human possibilities and may need, for practical purposes, to be to some extent relativized to local conditions, it seems important to think of it — at least at a given time in history — in universal and comparative terms, as the *Human Development Report* does, to give rise to complaint in a country that has done well with some indicators of life quality but badly on life expectancy. And although some degree of relativity may be put down to the differential genetic possibilities of different groups (the "missing women" statistics, for example, allow that on the average women live somewhat longer than men), it is also important not to conclude prematurely that inequalities between groups — for example, the growing inequalities in life expectancy between blacks and whites in the United States — are simply genetic variation, not connected with social injustice.

[21] The precise specification of these health rights is not easy, but the work currently being done on them in drafting new constitutions in South Africa and Eastern Europe gives reasons for hope that the combination of a general specification of such a right with a tradition of judicial interpretation will yield something practicable. It should be noticed that I speak of health, not just health care; and health itself interacts in complex ways with housing, with education, with dignity. Both health and nutrition are controversial as to whether the relevant level should be specified universally, or relatively to the local community and its traditions. For example, is low height associated with nutritional practices to be thought of as "stunting" or as felicitous adaptation to circumstances of scarcity? For an excellent summary of this debate, see S. R. Osmani, ed., *Nutrition and Poverty* (Oxford: Clarendon Press, WIDER Series, 1990), especially the following papers: on the relativist side, T. N. Srinivasan, "Undernutrition: Concepts, Measurements, and Policy Implications," 97–120; on the universalist side, C. Gopalan, "Undernutrition: Measurement and Implications," 17–48; for a compelling adjudication of the debate, coming out on the universalist side, see Osmani, "On Some Controversies in the Measurement of Undernutrition," 121–61.

[22] There is a growing literature on the importance of shelter for health; for example, that the provision of adequate housing is the single largest determinant of health status for HIV-infected persons. Housing rights are increasingly coming to be constitutionalized, at least in a negative form — giving squatters grounds for appeal, for example, against a landlord who would bulldoze their shanties. On this as a constitutional right, see proposed Articles 11, 12, and 17 of the South African Constitution, in a draft put forward by the African National Congress (ANC) committee adviser Albie Sachs, where this is given as an example of a justiciable housing right.

[23] Some form of intimate family love is central to child development, but this need not be the traditional Western nuclear family. In the development of citizens it is crucial that the family be an institution characterized by justice as well as love. See Susan Moller Okin, *Justice, Gender, and the Family* (New York: Basic Books, 1989).

[24] In terms of cross-cultural discussion, this item has proven the most controversial and elusive on the list. It also properly raises the question whether the list ought to be anthropocentric at all, or whether we should seek to promote appropriate capabilities for all living things. I leave further argument on these questions for another occasion.

[25] ASD argues that property rights are distinct from, for example, speech rights, in the sense that property is a tool of human functioning and not an end in itself. See also M. Nussbaum, "Capabilities and Human Rights," *Fordham Law Review* 66(2): 273-300 (1997).

[26] Sen has not endorsed any such specific list of the capabilities.

[27] See Sen, "Gender Inequality and Theories of Justice," in WCD, 259–73; Becker, "The Economic Way of Looking at Behavior."

[28] See HN. This is the core of Marx's reading of Aristotle.

[29] See Chapter 4.

[30]This distinction is related to Rawls's distinction between social and natural primary goods. Whereas he holds that only the social primary goods should be on the list, and not the natural (such as health, imagination), we say that the social basis of the natural primary goods should most emphatically be on the list.

[31]Chapter 3 argues that religious norms should not be imposed without choice on individuals who may not have opted for that religious tradition. In that sense, any religiously based employment restriction is questionable.

13.11 CARL F. STYCHIN ("SAME-SEX SEXUALITIES AND THE GLOBALIZATION OF HUMAN RIGHTS DISCOURSE," 2004)

Introduction

Only a few years ago, it was sometimes queried whether "sexual orientation" raised any human rights issues.[1] Today, those questions have largely ceased to be asked, as sexuality has permeated human rights consciousness. For that, an enormous collective debt is owed to those many courageous activists around the world who have struggled in difficult and dangerous circumstances to articulate their claims openly in a discourse of human rights in order to better people's lives. That is, they have used "human rights" as a way to connect with others in and out of struggle and to make a collective difference.

These human rights claims have also connected to the academic and judicial interpretations of human rights. In the past decade, we have witnessed a far more receptive attitude from courts and legislatures in a range of different ways. Same-sex sexuality cases have come to receive a more positive response from many national courts through the interpretation of domestic constitutional rights documents;[2] through the development of the common law;[3] through transnational legal regimes, such as the European Union[4] and through the discourse of international law and international human rights.[5] Moreover, these different levels and frames through which the language of rights can be mobilized often intersect and interact.[6] As a consequence, rights proponents can claim

that the strategy of deploying human rights in the sexuality arena has met with considerable success (but setbacks as well), and believers in liberal legal progress will argue that there is nowhere to go but forward in the making of human rights arguments.

I. A Double Movement of Globalization

This story of success and progress can be explained, I argue, through a double movement of globalization. First, we have witnessed a globalization of human rights, whereby human rights become, as Peter Fitzpatrick has argued, the "pervasive criteria" by which nations approach a universal standard of civilization, progress, and modernity.[7] Rights transcend the particular (despite the fact that human rights discourse presumably must come from a particular place) and become the marker and measure of a global civil society embracing all "humans" (itself a historically contested concept).

But there is another globalization move that has occurred: the universalizing of same-sex sexualities as identities.[8] There are many examples that demonstrate the export of an Anglo-American, "Stonewall" model of sexuality, identity, and liberation.[9] In the Stonewall model, same-sex sexuality marks an identity category that comes to be labeled as gay, lesbian, or both (and the two are often problematically conflated). Put crudely, who (in terms of gender) one has sexual relations with is the key to who you are, and the "coming out" is the central moment of identity formation.[10] The sexual relations model has increasingly transcended its own cultural and historical roots to become universalized as the paradigm of sexual identity. This paradigm, however, is a dramatic oversimplification of the dynamics of sexual identity outside of a Western (or, more specifically, Anglo-American) frame.

Despite this globalization movement, activists in many non-Western countries travel between the universalizing and essentializing discourse of sexual identity ("we are everywhere"), to a local, historically and culturally-specific reading of sexuality that resists the bluntness of the Stonewall model.[11] Nevertheless, as gays come to appropriate a sexual identity, the universalizing language of human rights neatly fits the globalizing movement of sexual identity that seems to be occuring (most obviously in urban spaces around the globe). Furthermore, this fusion of the two movements of globalization has been advanced by human rights law and international human rights experts, who have assisted activists in many parts of the world and have brought to the attention of the world the abuses of human dignity that have been experienced.[12] Claims to privacy, equality, and dignity for those who have been constructed as less than human because of their same-sex sexual practices and desires, clearly lend themselves to these universalizing and globalizing currents. In this way, they become cosmopolitan claims to justice, which transcend the particularities of time and place through the powerful argument that flows from the desire to be "who we are."[13]

Although the ways in which these human rights claims are made are important, what is no less interesting are the ways in which they have been *resisted* in a number of different cultural locations:[14] we consistently find opposition to *cosmopolitan* claims to human justice firmly grounded in a *communitarian* language that speaks to the preservation of a particular community's "way of life," tradition, and often, national or local culture.[15] Of course, "nation" (like sexuality and human rights) is a socially constructed, historically specific identity, which has come to be universalized.[16] To use Benedict Anderson's famous phrase, nations are "imagined communities,"[17] and it is this imagining that provocatively has been deployed to resist claims for universal human rights through a reverse discourse that employs the language of difference, specificity, history, community, and ultimately, the language of rights itself.

None of this should be surprising. It is well documented how the construction of the imagined community of "nation" has frequently been realized through the deployment of gender, race, and sexuality.[18] Women have been constructed as "mothers to the nation," a discursive device by which procreation becomes central to national sur-

vival.[19] Race has also been part of the constitutive formation of the nation, summed up memorably by Paul Gilroy's phrase "there ain't no black in the Union Jack."[20] Less widely known are cases that demonstrate how, when the nation state perceives a threat to its existence, that danger is frequently translated into homosexualized terms. Male same-sex sexuality, for example, has been deployed as the alien "other," linked to conspiracy, recruitment, the "third column," and ultimately, constructed as a threat to Western civilization itself.[21]

Interesting inversions of this discourse of civilization can be documented within a post-colonial context. The southern African region provides perhaps the best known example, particularly as demonstrated by the discourses employed by Robert Mugabe in Zimbabwe, most famously around the Zimbabwean International Book Fair in 1995 — for which the theme was "human rights" and which was to feature a presence by the organization Gays and Lesbians of Zimbabwe ("GALZ"). On the eve of the opening, a letter from the state director of information advised the book fair trustees that the government strongly objected to the presence of GALZ. The trustees, claiming that they had been placed in an impossible position, cancelled GALZ's registration. A storm of protest ensued, much of it emanating from South Africa. In this example, Mugabe skillfully used a discourse of colonial contamination to shore up the post-colonial state, wherein homosexuality is attributed to the white colonizer, and homosexual relations were the means he used to exploit and contaminate the colonized sexually.[22] Homosexuality becomes an abhorrent Western import.

This discourse is also an important means to strengthen the identity of the beleaguered nation state and the masculine subject, under threat in the current conditions of post-colonial globalization. The expulsion of homosexuals from the imagery of the nation state becomes metaphorically equated with the erasure of the white colonizer and, with him, his degenerate influence on a mythologized, pre-colonial, "pure" African (hetero) sexuality. Condemnations of sexual perversion thus are made in the name of an Afrocentric and specifically Zimbabwean national tradition. In this trope, the defense of heterosexuality becomes essential to securing the group right of self-determination of a people protecting its cultural heritage, pre-colonial way of life, and very survival. This is a communitarian claim in defense of a people against threats from globalization and (neo) colonial powers, and it also lends itself to the language of international human rights (i.e., the right of a community to preserve its way of life).

One can find parallel movements in the West, for example, in the campaign in the mid-1990s over the decriminalization of same-sex sexual acts in the state of Tasmania, Australia.[23] The goal of this struggle was explicitly achieved through the deployment of a discourse of international human rights (cosmopolitan claim), which, it was successfully argued, had been incorporated into a set of Australian cultural values (a communitarian argument) that trumped the particular claim to a uniquely Tasmanian, heterosexual way of life. Australia has long entered into a range of treaty obligations and has sought to abide by their terms domestically, such as the *International Covenant of Civil and Political Rights*, which proved relevant in the case of same-sex sexuality in Tasmania through its protection of the right to privacy.[24] The explanation for the Tasmanian laws — an anomalous legal situation in Australia — was, as Australians will readily explain, the cultural "peculiarity" of Tasmania, an island state removed from an island continent. Gays, like other "outsiders" such as environmentalists, have been consistently constructed as those who had arrived in Tasmania to undermine the traditional values of "the people."

The implicit, and sometimes explicit, argument of opponents of decriminalization thus was that to be an authentic Tasmanian was to be heterosexual. This was a somewhat more complex and nuanced battle over communitarian and cosmopolitan claims, but the language of rights — states' rights — was often deployed in defense of the anti-gay laws.[25] In this resistance to gay rights claims, the community itself is constructed as under siege from powerful, metropolitan interests seeking to undermine the rights of a disadvantaged and disenfranchised, "politically incorrect" community.[26] Moreover, it was argued that the federal system of Australia was intended to protect states from these majoritarian impulses.[27]

Thus, theoretically, we can often find ourselves in a cul-de-sac of rights claims spawned by the globalization of human rights and sexual identities. Resistance to gay rights is grounded in communitarian claims to difference, specificity, cultural authenticity, and history, which are also, in turn, grounded in the language of rights of self-determination of a people. The question is then about which self, which group, and which right to protect. What "trumps" what?

Although this may seem to be a theoretical dead end, a closer examination of social movement struggles reveals that activists have had relatively little difficulty rhetorically maneuvering through the cul-de-sac. Gay rights activists, in an array of cultural contexts, have become highly skilled in answering claims to cultural difference and cultural authenticity.[28] Specifically, I refer here to local activists engaged in social struggle resisting nationalist, heterosexist discourses, rather than international lobby groups, which may themselves fall into the trap of a highly cosmopolitan discourse that gives away too much of the communitarian ground to their opponents.[29] Moreover, international gay rights activism, particularly in some forms that emanate from the United States, is sometimes itself in danger of forms of neo-colonialism in relation to local contexts through its adoption of a discourse "in which a premodern, pre-political non-Euro-American queerness must consciously assume the burdens of representing itself to itself and others as 'gay' in order to attain political consciousness, subjectivity, and global modernity."[30]

By contrast, local activists have adopted a number of effective strategies in making claims to human rights, chief among which is a redeployment of the very communitarian arguments that have been used against them.[31] Rather than speaking solely in cosmopolitan terms, we find gay activists first turning to local history and the cultural past to question the idea of an authentic, opposite-sex sexuality and tradition. In other words, they retell the story of nation, but with some new characters introduced (or they redefine well-known characters in terms of sexual desire). It is a reclaiming of a same-sex sexual history that challenges the idea that homosexuality has polluted a sexually pure culture.[32] This, of course, is closely tied to discourses of colonialism....[This strategy] rewrites the history of community, allowing for its reimagination in more inclusive terms.

A second strategy that again tackles communitarian claims on their own terrain has also proven powerful. Gay activists have skillfully devised a rhetoric that adopts the theoretical idea of multiple and intersecting identities, which often provides an effective response to the idea of a homogeneous, one-dimensional identity. For example, placards at demonstrations in Tasmania that read "GAY and TASMANIAN" provided an important counter to claims that these identities are mutually exclusive.[33] This is often an important dimension of strategy. It forces opponents to concede that, in their construction of the imagined community, indigenous gays *do* exist, and that they have been expelled from the bounds of community, rather than saying they never existed within it....

[The third strategy] may involve the attempt to universalize and essentialize the concept of human rights, as activists claim a history of human rights in a non-Western context. In other words, human rights, like homosexuals, existed prior to the imperialist mission that devastated both — as part of a history of a community — and, therefore, are culturally *authentic* today.[34] Once again, this is undoubtedly anthropologically problematic, for both "human rights" and "homosexuality" are historically and culturally contingent.[35] They are a product of a time and place. Nevertheless, it may be a rhetorically and politically useful strategy.

In sum, we find activists operate at different registers simultaneously: from local, communitarian discourses through to cosmopolitan global claims. They argue from the local level on behalf of grassroots social movements to the transnational level, through organizations such as the International Lesbian and Gay Association.[36] It is this seamless movement between the local and the global that best describes human rights activism around same-sex sexualities today....

IV. From Rights to Politics

It is tempting to end the story there, to conclude that rights are politically indeterminate, socially constructed (as are sexuality and nationhood), and open to both cosmopolitan and communitarian claims. But if that is the conclusion, then we are left — perhaps particularly *because of* the language of rights — with a tendency toward polarization and irreconcilable political demands. Ultimately, though, I expect gay rights arguments will win the day because of their easy articulation as part of globalization discourse. They represent the triumph of the global and of modernity itself. The language of rights cannot, however, apolitically provide resolutions to these moments. Legal claims *have* led to results, but a turn to law does not mask the political character of the dispute and its outcome. If anything, it exacerbates both....

From the struggles of human rights organizations mobilized on the ground around sexuality, we can find operating within activism a response to the theoretical difficulties in the use of the globalizing cosmopolitanism of rights discourse when it meets rights claims made by communities of difference. The key may be to see the deployment of human rights as a "calling card" to enter into political and civil society; indeed, a calling card to enter what was constructed as a community of difference (or, to put it differently, to heterogenize a community). Activist strategies in practice move between cosmopolitan and communitarian discourses, and this is an important moment in bridging this divide. It allows for claims, not to abstract cosmopolitan rights, but to participation as full members of a wider community, and to have specific grievances emanating from same-sex sexualities recognized and heard as legitimate citizenship claims made by full members of that community.

Concluding Thoughts

In conclusion, the implications of this analysis are multi-faceted. While we will, I predict, increasingly see lesbians and gay men achieving human rights victories and successfully making claims to full citizenship, with these rights to participate within wider society come responsibilities to engage in struggles for political transformation. In my view, it is easy for gay politics to become politically conservative in an era of gay marriage and same-sex partnership benefits. These arguably assimilationist political moves also lead to the construction of some "queers" as rights undeserving — the dangerous and the uncivilizable. It becomes far too tempting for "citizen gay" to consume human rights and then withdraw from any kind of progressive politics, especially when those who have bestowed the rights are also pursuing policies that are eviscerating the human rights of others on issues from migration to counterterrorism....

The critique of rights is that lesbian and gay human rights struggles have become disconnected from politics and, moreover, that we have become depoliticized consumers through the fetishization of rights. But, to the extent that rights may provide a key that opens the political realm on the basis of full citizenship, the language of human rights does remain a valuable discourse in today's political tool box.

[1] I was asked this very question by a law professor in 1994 at an academic conference on human rights.

[2] See, e.g., *Egan v. Canada*, [1995] 2 S.C.R. 513, 124 D.L.R. (4th) 609; *M. v. H.*, [1999] 2 S.C.R. 3, 171 D.L.R. (4th) 577; *Little Sisters Book and Art Emporium v. Canada (Minister of Justice)*, [2000] 2 S.C.R. 1120, 193 D.L.R. (4th) 193.

[3] See, e.g., *Fitzpatrick v. Sterling Housing Association*, [2001] 1 A.C. 27, [1999] 4 All E.R. 705.

[4] For example, the adoption by the Council of the European Union of a general framework directive on equal treatment in employment that includes "sexual orientation" among the prohibited grounds of discrimination, which all Member States of the EU have been required to implement:

EU, *Council Directive 2000/78/EC of 27 November 2000 Establishing a General Framework for Equal Treatment in Employment and Occupation*, [2000] O.J.L. 303/16.

[5] See, e.g., *Toonen v. Australia*, 1994, CCPR/C/50/D/488/1992, online: Office of the High Commissioner for Human Rights, http://www.unhchr.ch.tbs.doc.nsf/(Symbol)/d22a00bcdl320c9c802 56724005e60d5?Opendocument, holding that anti-gay sex laws violate a right to privacy.

[6] For example, the development of domestic law may be informed by emerging international legal standards.

[7] Peter Fitzpatrick, *Modernism and the Grounds of Law* (Cambridge: Cambridge University Press, 2001), 120.

[8] Pennis Altman, *Global Sex* (Chicago: University of Chicago Press, 2002); Martin F. Manalansan IV, "(Re) Locating the Gay Filipino: Resistance, Post-colonialism, and Identity," *Journal of Homosexuality* 26 (1993): 53.

[9] In using the term "Stonewall," I am referring to the birth of contemporary American lesbian and gay identity politics at the Stonewall riots in New York City in 1969.

[10] On the centrality of "coming out" to a same-sex sexual identity, see Mark Blasius, "An Ethos of Lesbian and Gay Existence," in Mark Blasius, ed., *Sexual Identities, Queer Politics* (Princeton: Princeton University Press, 2001), 143. Note that I am passing over the interesting cultural question of what constitutes the "sexual." See, e.g., Gilbert Herdt, *Same Sex, Different Culture: Exploring Gay and Lesbian Lives* (Boulder: Westview Press, 1997).

[11] See Amaldo Cruz-Malave and Martin F. Manalansan IV, eds., *Queer Globalizations: Citizenship and the Afterlife of Colonialism* (New York: New York University Press, 2002).

[12] See, e.g., *Public Scandals: Sexual Orientation and Criminal Law in Romania* (New York: Human Rights Watch and the International Gay and Lesbian Human Rights Commission, 1998), online: Human Rights Watch, http://www.hrw.org/reports97/romania; Baden Offord, *Homosexual Rights as Human Rights: Activism in Indonesia, Singapore and Australia* (Oxford: Peter Lang, 2003).

[13] On cosmopolitanism, see, e.g., Kimberly Hutchings and Roland Dannreuther, eds., *Cosmopolitan Citizenship* (Basingstoke: Macmillan, 1999); Gerard Delanty, *Citizenship in a Global Age: Society, Culture, Politics* (Buckingham: Open University Press, 2000).

[14] See, e.g., Carl F. Stychin, *A Nation by Rights: National Cultures, Sexual Identity Politics, and the Discourse of Rights* (Philadelphia: Temple University Press, 1998).

[15] On communitarianism, see, e.g., Elizabeth Frazer and Nicola Lacey, *The Politics of Community: A Feminist Critique of the Liberal Communitarian Debate* (Toronto: University of Toronto Press, 1993).

[16] See, e.g., Peter Jackson and Jan Penrose, eds., *Constructions of Race, Place and Nation* (Minneapolis: University of Minnesota Press, 1994).

[17] Benedict Anderson, *Imagined Communities: Reflections on the Origin and Spread of Nationalism*, rev. ed. (London: Verso, 1991).

[18] See Stychin, *Nation by Rights*, supra note 14, c. 1.

[19] See NiraYuval-Davis, *Gender and Nation* (London: Sage Publications, 1997).

[20] Paul Gilroy, *There Ain't No Black in the Union Jack: The Cultural Politics of Race and Nation* (London: Routledge, 1992).

[21] See L. J. Moran, "The Uses of Homosexuality: Homosexuality for National Security," *International Journal of the Sociology of Law*, 19 (1991): 149; Lee Edelman, *Homographesis: Essays in Gay Literary and Cultural Theory* (New York: Routledge, 1994).

[22] See Stychin, *Nation by Rights*, supra note 14 at 89–114; Oliver Phillips, "Zimbabwean Law and the Production of a White Man's Disease," *Social and Legal Studies* 6 (1997): 471; Matthew Engelke, "'We Wondered What Human Rights He Was Talking About': Human Rights, Homosexuality and the Zimbabwe International Book Fair," *Critique of Anthropology* 19 (1999): 289.

[23] See, e.g., Stychin, *Nation by Rights*, supra note 14 at 145–93; Wayne Morgan, "Identifying Evil for What It Is: Tasmania, Sexual Perversity and the United Nations," *Melbourne University Legal Review* 19 (1994): 740; Miranda Morris, *The Pink Triangle: The Gay Law Reform Debate in Tasmania* (Sydney: New South Wales University Press, 1995).

[24] The UN Human Rights Committee found the Tasmanian law in violation of privacy rights in *Toonen*, supra note 5; *International Covenant on Civil and Political Rights*, December 19, 1966, 999 U.N.T.S. 171.

[25] See Tim Tenbensel, "International Human Rights Conventions and Australian Political Debates: Issues Raised by the 'Toonen Case,'" *Australian Journal of Political Science* 31 (1996): 7.

[26] I explore this point in detail in Stychin, *Nation by Rights*, supra note 14, c. 6.

[27] See Tenbensel, supra note 25.

[28] See generally the case studies in Stychin, *Nation by Rights*, supra note 14; Carl Stychin, *Governing Sexuality: The Changing Politics of Citizenship and Law Reform* (Oxford: Hart Publishing, 2003).

[29] My point being that in adopting a highly universalist discourse, international lobby groups leave themselves open to claims grounded in the language of cultural relativism.

[30] Arnaldo Cruz-Malavé and Martin F. Manalansan IV, "Introduction: Dissident Sexualities/Alternative Globalisms," in Cruz-Malavé and Manalansan IV, eds., supra note 11, 1 at 5–6.

[31] See, generally, Stychin, *Nation by Rights*, supra note 14; Stychin, *Governing Sexuality*, supra note 28; Nicole LaViolette and Sandra Whitworth, "No Safe Haven: Sexuality as a Universal Human Right and Gay and Lesbian Activism in International Politics," *Millennium Journal of International Studies* 23 (1994): 563.

[32] See e.g. Stephen O. Murray and Will Roscoe, *Boy-Wives and Female Husbands: Studies of African Homosexualities* (New York: St. Martin's Press, 1998).

[33] See Morris, supra note 23.

[34] For a fuller discussion in the South African context, see Mark Gevisser, "A Different Fight for Freedom: A History of South African Lesbian and Gay Organization from the 1950s to the 1990s," in Mark Gevisser and Edwin Cameron, eds., *Defiant Desire: Gay and Lesbian Lives in South Africa* (New York: Routledge, 1995), 14.

[35] See LaViolette and Whitworth, supra note 31; Marie-Bénédicte Dembour, "Human Rights Talk and Anthropological Ambivalence: The Particular Context of Universal Claims," in Olivia Harris, ed., *Inside and Outside the Law: Anthropological Studies of Authority and Ambiguity* (London: Routledge, 1996), 19.

[36] The International Lesbian and Gay Association is an international federation of national and local groups dedicated to achieving equal rights for lesbians, gay men, bisexuals, and transgendered people. It was founded in 1978 and now has more than 350 member organizations, representing approximately 80 countries. See online: ILGA Home, http://www.ilsa.org/.

[37] See also Richard Bellamy, *Liberalism and Pluralism: Towards a Politics of Compromise* (London: Routledge, 1999).

CHAPTER 14

How to Promote Human Rights

CIVIL LIBERTIES, SECURITY, AND WAR

The clash between cultural rights activists and universalists has heightened as a result of military interventions by the United States and other Western powers since the end of the cold war. The tragedy of September 11 unleashed an effort to establish an international security regime — under the tutelage of American power — and as a result, the divide within the human rights community has widened. This section considers this human rights schism, focusing first on the tension between civil liberties and security, and then on the debate over humanitarian intervention.

Yale Law School Professor David Cole addressed the security versus civil liberties issue in "Let's Fight Terrorism, Not the Constitution" (2003). The Patriot Act, passed soon after September 11, he maintained, violated three principles: "It imposes guilt by association on immigrants, resurrecting a long-abandoned philosophy of the McCarthy era; it authorizes executive detention on mere suspicion that an immigrant has at some point engaged in violent crime or provided humanitarian aid to a proscribed organization; and it resurrects ideological exclusion, denying admission to aliens for pure speech." Cole, in raising serious constitutional concerns regarding the bartering of American freedom for security, calls for a more measured and balanced response to the need to combat terror (see Section 14.1).

Pepperdine Law School Professor Douglass W. Kmiec charged Cole with underappreciating the requirements of the war against terrorism. The American founders' conception of freedom, he maintained, was not a freedom to do anything, but a freedom that must be evaluated in terms of the common good. In this respect, he insisted, *"Congress can no longer afford, if it ever could, to confuse freedom and license because doing so licenses terrorism, not freedom"* (author's italic). In Kmiec's rebuttal to opponents of the Patriotic Act, he defended the suspension of some civil liberties for illegal residents associated with criminal acts or terrorist activities as necessary to secure the United States against imminent terrorist dangers (see Section 14.2).

The debate over what constitutes an infringement of rights in the face of terrorism has also focused on when, and to what extent, it is permissible to use torture as a technique of interrogation. These questions were on the front burner of political debate in Israel, where for years the Israeli government had argued that given the special circumstances faced by Israelis — many of whom have been victims of terrorist attacks — it was necessary to employ what was referred to as "moderate physical pressure" when interrogating terrorist suspects. The U.N. Committee Against Torture has long vociferously condemned such techniques, including shaking and hooding, as forms of torture. Under increasing pressure from the international community, the Israeli Supreme Court, in September 1999, unanimously banned the Israeli General Security Service's use of interrogation techniques involving physical pressure against a suspect. While an investigator accused of torture is allowed to claim special circumstances (i.e., the ticking bomb argument) in hopes of reducing his or her sentence, these forms of interrogations are now illegal (see Section 14.3).

After September 11, these techniques, banned in Israel, were deemed acceptable by the U.S. Department of Justice, which concluded in a "Memorandum for Alberto Gonzales" (2002) that "acts [of interrogation] may be cruel, inhuman or degrading, but still not produce pain and suffering of the requisite intensity to fall within Section 2340 A's proscription against torture." Section 2340 refers to extreme forms of torture, whereby inflicted pain is difficult to endure and may result in organ failure, impairment of bodily function, or death (U.S. Department of Justice, Memorandum, On Torture, 2002). Following the scandal over abusive techniques used by U.S. guards against Iraqi prisoners at Abu Ghraib prison in Iraq, the U.S. Department of Justice amended its 2002 memorandum and pronounced the illegality of such interrogation techniques (see Section 14.4).

American legal scholar and judge Richard Posner has been a consistent voice against all forms of torture. In "Torture, Terrorism and Interrogation" (2004), Posner challenged Harvard legal scholar Alan Dershowitz's defense of requiring judicial warrants for coercive interrogations, even in the extreme circumstance of "the ticking bomb." If legal rules permit torture in defined circumstances, Posner maintained, officials would inevitably explore the outer bounds of the rules. In this respect, Posner agreed with other civil libertarians, who have long maintained that sacrifice of civil liberties in the name of national security may represent a slippery slope toward the loss of fundamental human rights.

Defending himself from Posner's attack, Dershowitz asked, in "Tortured Reasoning" (2004), if torture was used in an actual ticking bomb terrorist case, "would it be normatively better or worse to have such torture regulated by some kind of warrant, with accountability, recordkeeping, standards and limitations?" While praising Amnesty International for taking the high road, namely, condemning torture in any form, Dershowitz noted that Amnesty is never in the position to make hard judgments between evils. Once one accepts the premise that torture is certain to occur, Dershowitz argued, the worse abuse is bound to happen when "a don't ask, don't tell" policy is in place — as evidenced by the disclosure of the abuses at Abu Ghraib.

In addition to questions regarding the relationship between human rights and security, the legitimacy of humanitarian intervention as an acceptable means to promote human rights was also widely debated after the cold war, a debate that was reignited in light of the human rights rationale for the 2003 invasion of Iraq offered by the Bush administration. The need for intervention was strongly endorsed by Harvard journalist and scholar Samantha Power in "Raising the Cost of Genocide" (2002). Having analyzed Western inaction in the face of genocide since the Turkish massacre of the Armenians in 1915, she questioned why, more than half a century after the passing of the Genocide Convention, the U.S. administration stood aside as mass atrocities were committed in Bosnia and Rwanda. "Although U.S. officials have sometimes expressed remorse after genocide, none fear professional accountability for their sins of omission," Power pointed out. While acknowledging growing concerns over the costs of U.S. interventionism since September 11 and despite appeals for more isolationism, Power maintains that American leadership is essential for mobilizing local, regional, and international responses to genocide. "Citizens victimized by genocide or abandoned by the international community," she observed, "do not make good neighbors."

Canadian scholar Michael Ignatieff, Power's former colleague at Harvard and now Liberal member of parliament in the Canadian House of Commons, shares Power's concerns. In his *New York Times* article, "The Burden" (2003), Ignatieff acknowledged the imperial dimension of the United States' willingness to contemplate "regime change" in various countries. Yet to those who reject all such interventions in moral terms, he asked rhetorically: "What moral authority rests with a sovereign who murders and ethnically cleanses his own people?" Overthrowing a tyrannical regime may well be the politics of the lesser evil if the outcome of intervention means the freedom of Kosovars, Afghans, and Iraqis, Ignatieff maintained against the arguments for inaction of both liberals and right-wing isolationists. Regardless of the inevitably mixed motives of the intervening states in these cases, they were right to act against murderous regimes.

Writing in *The Guardian* on June 14, 2003, British historian Eric Hobsbawm rejected such a human rights rationale for what he characterized as a dangerous U.S. foreign policy. Instead, he insisted that supporting intervention on the ground that "it will eliminate some local and regional injustice ... may be called the imperialism of human rights." In "Spreading Democracy" (2004), Hobsbawm rebuffed the views of liberals like Ignatieff, labeling the American "humanitarian" ambition as quixotic and dangerous. It is dangerous, Hobsbawm claimed, because it presupposes that "the rhetoric surrounding this crusade implies that the system is applicable in a standardized (Western) form." Moreover, even if the tactics of great powers may have morally or politically desirable consequences, their methods produce barbarism, thereby threatening the integrity of universal rights. Finally, it is dangerous because such actions convey to those who do not enjoy freedom that electoral democracy necessarily ensures effective freedom of the press, citizen rights, and an independent judiciary.

Part V concludes with Micheline Ishay's effort to point out ways to move beyond the current human rights debate over globalization and intervention. In "Debating Globalization and Intervention: Spartacists versus Caesarists" (2006), she draws on two ideal worldviews. Spartacists are those who share an anti-authoritarian, anti-imperialist, and often isolationist view. Most Spartacists are highly critical of unfettered economic globalization, sanctioned by U.S. hegemonic influence in cultural, political, and military realms. The Caesarist worldview, by contrast, maintains that in a world of terrorism, rampant nationalism, civil wars, and proliferating mass destruction weapons, the United States is the only power able to counter international dangers driven by fundamentalist groups or authoritarian regimes. For weaker states, the only alternative, Caesarists believe, is to gravitate within the orbit of U.S. influence, an outcome that will ultimately deliver economic and human rights benefits. Ishay proposes that it is possible to reconcile the best arguments from each camp, paving the way toward a more integrated and effective human rights approach position with respect to globalization, humanitarian intervention, and nation building.

CIVIL LIBERTIES VERSUS SECURITY

14.1   DAVID COLE ("LET'S FIGHT TERRORISM, NOT THE CONSTITUTION," 2003)[1]

The terrorist attacks of September 11 have shocked and stunned us all and have quite properly spurred renewed consideration of our capability to forestall future attacks. Yet in doing so, we must not rashly trample on the very freedoms that we are fighting for. Nothing tests our commitment to principle like fear and terror. But precisely because the terrorists violated every principle of civilized society and human dignity, we must remain true to our principles as we fashion a response.

Three principles in particular should guide our response to the threat of terrorism. First, we should not overreact in a time of fear, a mistake we have made all too often in the past. Second, we should not sacrifice the bedrock foundations of our constitutional democracy — political freedom and equal treatment — absent a compelling showing of need and adoption of narrowly tailored means. And third, in balancing liberty and security, we should not succumb to the temptation to trade a vulnerable minority's liberties, namely, the liberties of immigrants in general or Arab and Muslim immigrants in particular, for the security of the rest of us.

Unfortunately, the USA Patriot Act, our government's first legislative attempt to respond to the threats posed by September 11, violates all three of these principles. It overreacts in just the way that we have so often overreacted in the past: by substituting guilt by association for targeted measures directed at guilty conduct. It violates core constitutional principles, rendering immigrants deportable for their political associations, excludable for pure speech, and detainable on the attorney general's say-so. And by reserving its harshest measures for immigrants — in the immediately foreseeable future, Arab and Muslim immigrants — it sacrifices commitments to equality by trading a minority group's liberty for the majority's security. In addition to being unprincipled, our response will in all likelihood be ineffective. Painting with a broad brush is not a good law enforcement tool. It wastes resources on innocents, alienates the very communities we need to be working with, and makes it all the more difficult to distinguish the true threat from the innocent bystander.

The Patriot Act's principal flaws are as follows: (1) It imposes guilt by association on immigrants, resurrecting a long-abandoned philosophy of the McCarthy era; (2) it authorizes executive detention on mere suspicion that an immigrant has at some point engaged in a violent crime or provided humanitarian aid to a proscribed organization; and (3) it resurrects ideological exclusion, denying admission to aliens for pure speech, resurrecting yet another long-interred relic of the McCarthy era.

A History of Mistakes

Before turning to the specifics of the Patriot Act, it is worth reviewing a little history and assessing what powers government already had in the fight against terrorism before September 11. Both assessments are critical to asking whether our immediate reactions to the events of September 11 were measured and likely to be effective.

This is not the first time we have responded to fear by targeting immigrants and treating them as suspect because of their group identities rather than their individual conduct. In World War I, we imprisoned "enemy aliens" for their national identity and dissidents for merely speaking out against the war. In the winter of 1919–1920, the federal government responded to a series of politically motivated bombings, including one of Attorney General A. Mitchell Palmer's home in Washington, D.C., by rounding up 6,000 to 10,000 suspected immigrants in thirty-three cities across the country — not for their part in the bombings but for their political affiliations. They were detained in overcrowded "bull pens" and coerced into signing confessions. Many of those arrested turned out to be citizens. In the end, 556 were deported, but for their political affiliations, not for their part in the bombings.

In World War II, we interned 110,000 persons, over two-thirds of whom were citizens of the United States, not because of individualized determinations that they posed a threat to national security or the war effort but solely for their Japanese ancestry. And in the fight against Communism, which reached its height in the McCarthy era, we made it a crime even to be a member of the Communist Party and passed the McCarran-Walter Act, which authorized the government to keep out and expel noncitizens who advocated Communism or other proscribed ideas or who belonged to groups advocating those ideas. Under the McCarran-Walter Act, which remained a part of our law until 1990, the United States denied visas to, among others, writers Gabriel Garcia Marquez and Carlos Fuentes and to Nino Pasti, former deputy commander of NATO, because he was going to speak against the deployment of nuclear cruise missiles.

All these past responses are now seen as mistakes. Yet while today's response does not yet match these historical overreactions, it is characterized by many of the same mistakes of principle — namely, targeting vulnerable groups not for illegal conduct but because of their group identity or political affiliation.

In considering whether the new laws directed at immigrants are necessary, it is also important to know what authority the government had prior to September 11 to deny admission to, detain, and deport aliens engaged in terrorist activity. Before the Patriot Act, the government could detain without bond any alien with any visa violation if it had reason to believe that he posed a threat to national security or a risk of flight. It could deny admission to mere members of terrorist groups, and it could deport any alien who had in any way engaged in, furthered, supported, or facilitated terrorist activity, expansively defined to include virtually any use or threat to use a firearm with intent to endanger person or property. Moreover, the Immigration and Naturalization Service (INS) maintained that it had the power to expel, detain, and deport aliens using secret evidence that the alien had no chance to confront or rebut.

The extent of these preexisting powers is illustrated by the unprecedented incarceration of between 1,500 and 2,000 persons in connection with the investigation of the September 11 attacks. As of December 2002, the identity of the vast majority of these detainees was still a secret, as was even the total number detained. (The government stopped issuing a daily tally in early November 2001, when the number was 1,182.) The bulk of the detainees were held on immigration charges, and all the immigration detainees were tried in proceedings entirely closed to the public, a practice that three federal courts have declared unconstitutional. In October 2002, one court upheld the constitutionality of the closed hearings, and the matter is likely to be resolved in the Supreme Court. As of October 2002, not one person arrested since September 11 had been charged with any involvement in the attacks under investigation. The only person so charged was Zaccarias Moussaoui, and he was arrested before September 11. Most of the detainees have been affirmatively "cleared" by the FBI of any involvement in terrorism. And most important for purposes of assessing the need for new powers, the government carried out this unprecedented program of secret mass detentions without even relying on the Patriot Act.

Guilt by Association

The single most problematic feature of the Patriot Act is its adoption of the philosophy of guilt by association, which the Supreme Court has condemned as "alien to the traditions of a free society and the First Amendment itself." Under prior law, aliens were deportable for engaging in or supporting terrorist *activity*. The Patriot Act makes aliens deportable for wholly innocent *associations* with a "terrorist organization," regardless of any nexus between the alien's support and any act of violence, much less terrorism. And because the Patriot Act defines "terrorist activity" to include virtually any use or

threat to use violence and defines a "terrorist organization" as any group that has used or threatened to use violence, the proscription on political association potentially encompasses every organization that has ever been involved in a civil war or a crime of violence, from a pro-life group that once threatened workers at an abortion clinic to the African National Congress (ANC), the Irish Republican Army (IRA), or the Northern Alliance in Afghanistan.

The law contains no requirement that the alien's support have any connection whatsoever to a designated organization's terrorist activity. Thus, an alien who sent coloring books to a day care center run by an organization that was ever involved in armed struggle would be deportable as a terrorist, even if she could show that the coloring books were used only by three-year-olds. Indeed, the law apparently extends even to those who seek to support a group in the interest of *countering* terrorism. Thus, an immigrant who offered his services in peace negotiating to the Real IRA in the hope of furthering the peace process in Great Britain and forestalling further violence could be deported as a terrorist.

Guilt by association, the Supreme Court has ruled, violates the First and the Fifth Amendments. It violates the First Amendment because people have a right to associate with groups that have lawful and unlawful ends, so long as they do not further the groups' illegal ends. And it violates the Fifth Amendment because "in our jurisprudence guilt is personal." To hold an alien responsible for the military acts of the ANC, for example, because he offered a donation to the ANC's peaceful anti-apartheid efforts, or for providing peace-negotiating training to the Real IRA, violates that principle. Without some connection between the alien's support and terrorist activity, the Constitution is violated.

Some suggest that the threat from terrorist organizations abroad requires some compromise on the principle prohibiting guilt by association. But this principle was developed in connection with measures directed at the Communist Party, an organization that Congress found to be, and the Supreme Court accepted as, a foreign-dominated organization that used sabotage and terrorism for the purpose of overthrowing the United States by force and violence. Others argue that because money is fungible, even support of lawful activities may free up resources that can then be devoted to terrorism. But, of course, the same argument could have been made of the Communist Party or indeed any organization that engages in legal as well as illegal activity. Yet surely it cannot be the case that Congress could have simply reenacted all the anti-Communist laws struck down on guilt by association grounds simply by rewriting them to hinge their penalties on the payment of dues to the Communist Party instead of membership in that party.

Detention versus Due Process

The Patriot Act also authorizes the INS to detain, potentially indefinitely, any alien certified by the attorney general as a "suspected terrorist." While "suspected terrorists" sounds like a class that ought to be locked up, the law defines the class so broadly that it includes virtually every immigrant who has been involved in a barroom brawl or domestic dispute, as well as aliens who have never committed an act of violence in their life, and whose only "crime" is to have provided humanitarian aid to an organization disfavored by the government. And the act provides that such persons may be detained indefinitely even if they are *granted* relief from removal — and therefore have a legal right to remain here.

This provision raises several constitutional concerns. First, it mandates preventive detention of persons *who pose no threat to national security or risk of flight*. The Supreme Court has upheld preventive detention of accused criminals and aliens in deportation proceedings, but only where the government demonstrates a specific need for the detention — by showing that the individual poses a danger to others or a risk of flight. In doing away with that minimal requirement, the legislation vests the attorney general with unprecedented and unconstitutional authority.

Second, the law allows the INS to detain aliens *indefinitely, even where they have prevailed in their removal proceedings*. This, too, is patently unconstitutional. Once an alien has prevailed in his removal proceeding and has been granted relief from removal, he has a legal right to remain here. There is no longer a legitimate immigration reason to detain such a person because immigration detention is permissible only as an aid to removing a person from the country. Yet the act provides that even aliens *granted* relief from removal may still be detained. This is akin to detaining a prisoner even after he has received a pardon. Once an alien has prevailed in his immigration proceeding, the INS has no legitimate basis for detaining the individual.

Third, and most important, it is critical to the constitutionality of any executive detention provision that the person detained have a meaningful opportunity to contest his detention both administratively and in court. The bill affords an alien no opportunity to make a case that he should not be detained within the administrative process. It relegates him to the filing of a habeas corpus petition. But due process requires that the agency depriving a person of his liberty afford him a meaningful opportunity to be heard, and the fact that one can sue the agency afterward is not generally sufficient.

Finally, the Patriot Act permits detention of certified aliens for up to seven days without the filing of any charges. The Supreme Court has ruled that individuals arrested in the criminal setting must be brought before a judge for a probable cause hearing within forty-eight hours except in the most extraordinary circumstances. This law extends blanket authority to detain an alien for seven days on mere certification that he or she was at one time involved in a barroom brawl. Such overbroad authority clearly does not meet the Supreme Court's requirement that any preventive detention authority be accompanied by heightened procedural protections and narrowly drawn laws.

Ideological Exclusion

The Patriot Act also revives ideological exclusion, denying entry to aliens for pure speech. It excludes aliens who "endorse or espouse terrorist activity" or who "persuade others to support terrorist activity or a terrorist organization" in ways that the secretary of state determines undermine U.S. efforts to combat terrorism. It also excludes aliens who are representatives of groups that "endorse acts of terrorist activity" in ways that similarly undermine U.S. efforts to combat terrorism.

Excluding people for their ideas and associations is flatly contrary to the spirit of freedom for which the United States stands. Moreover, such exclusions have a negative impact on free debate within the United States by denying those who live here access to those who might dissent from government policies. It was for that reason that Congress repealed all such "ideological exclusion" grounds in 1990 after years of embarrassing visa denials for political reasons. We are a strong enough country, and our resolve against terrorism is strong enough, to make such censorship wholly unnecessary.

Conclusion

We must respond to terrorism, but we must also ensure that our responses are measured and balanced. Is it measured to make deportable anyone who provides humanitarian aid to any organization engaged in a civil war? Is it measured to label domestic disputes or barroom fights with weapons acts of terrorism? Is it measured to subject anyone who might engage in such activity to mandatory detention without any procedural protections and without any showing that he poses any current danger? Is it measured to restore exclusion for pure ideas?

The overbreadth of the Patriot Act reflects the overreaction that we have often indulged in when threatened and raises serious constitutional concerns even if it were shown that such measures would make us more secure. But there is also reason to doubt that the expansive authorities that the act grants will in fact make us safer. By penalizing even

wholly lawful, nonviolent, and counterterrorist associational activity, we are likely to waste valuable resources tracking innocent political activity, drive other activity underground, encourage extremists, and make the communities that will inevitably be targeted by such broad-brush measures far less likely to cooperate with law enforcement. As Justice Louis Brandeis wrote nearly seventy-five years ago, the framers of our Constitution knew "that fear breeds repression; that repression breeds hate; and that hate menaces stable government."[2] In other words, freedom and security need not necessarily be traded off against one another; maintaining our freedoms is itself critical to maintaining our security.

The immigration provisions of the Patriot Act fail to live up to the very commitments to freedom that the president has said that we are fighting for. As the Supreme Court wrote in 1967, declaring invalid an anti-Communist law, "It would indeed be ironic if, in the name of national defense, we would sanction the subversion of one of those liberties — the freedom of association — which makes the defense of the Nation worthwhile."[3]

[1] An earlier version of this chapter appeared in *The Responsive Community* 12, no. 1 (Winter 2001–2): 48–55.
[2] *Whitney v. California*, 274 U.S. 357 (1927).
[3] *United States v. Rubel*, 389 U.S. 258 (1967).

14.2 DOUGLAS W. KMIEC ("CONFUSING FREEDOM WITH LICENSE — LICENSES TERRORISM, NOT FREEDOM," 2003)[1]

The events of September 11 remain ever present in the minds of American citizens. For thousands of families, a husband or wife or child will never return home because of what happened that day. The diabolical events of that morning will be forever etched in our consciousness. And yet, along with those mental pictures, it is important to grasp fully what happened: It wasn't a political rally, it wasn't a nonviolent speech protest, it wasn't an example of urban street crime, it wasn't even an attack by another sovereign state or nation. It was the deliberate murder of innocent men and women, not for a high political purpose or cause — or even a base one — but simply the random manifestation of hate intended to spread panic and fracture the civil order and continuation of American society.

As grievously wounded as we may be, American society and its principled understanding of freedom with responsibility does not fracture or panic that easily. But it does expect that justice will be done. It earnestly desires, along with our president, to see those who so mercilessly took sacred human life to be held accountable — not in a local criminal court but by the able men and women of the military and our law enforcement communities, working together either to eliminate on a field of battle these "enemies of mankind," as Blackstone called them, or to apprehend and punish them — presumably before the bar of a properly convened military tribunal, like those employed against Nazi saboteurs in World War II.

In considering the USA Patriot Act, it is useful to remember that our founders' conception of freedom was not a freedom to do anything or associate for any purpose but to do those things that do not harm others and that, it was hoped, would advance the common good. Freedom separated from this truth is not freedom at all but license. *Congress can no longer afford, if it ever could, to confuse freedom and license because doing so licenses terrorism, not freedom.* Those who have voiced opposition to the Patriot Act seem to have either a more extreme view of freedom, a less sober view of the threats we face, or both.

With due respect, such unrefined autonomy or complacency hides a basic confusion or underappreciation for the war against terrorism that now must be fought. The objectors think of the mass destruction of the World Trade Center and the Pentagon as the equivalent of murder, kidnapping, or bank robbery. They think the point is a criminal trial; it is not — it is the elimination of terrorism.

The primary authority for dealing with the terrorist threat resides both in the president, as commander in chief, and in Congress, as the architect of various specific legal authorities under the Constitution, to meet that threat. The president has courageously told the nations of the world that all are either for the United States in this or with the terrorists. There is no middle ground. Similarly, Congress, by joint resolution, has given President Bush authority to act against not only those wealthy and bloody hands that orchestrated the events of September 11 but also all cooperators in those cowardly actions or "any future act" of international terrorism. However, to ensure successful application of our military might, Congress needed to equip our law enforcement and intelligence communities with adequate and constitutional legal authority to address a war crime on a scale that previously was not seen in this generation or seen ever in peacetime.

The Patriot Act supplied the necessary authority and direction. The act gives due regard to the necessary balance between the civil liberties enjoyed by our citizens under the Constitution and the law enforcement authority needed. In particular, the act advances two fundamental purposes: to subject terrorism to at least the same rigorous treatment as organized crime and prosecution of the drug trade and to supply up-to-date law enforcement capabilities that address the technology of the day, which no longer observes some of the lines previously drawn under existing law. Terrorists don't stay in one place using only land-line telephones and postcards, and it is folly to have a legal investigation authority that still assumes that.

While the Patriot Act's provisions are a bit arcane and complex, they incorporate the recommendations of virtually every commission in the last decade to study terrorism. Specifically, with respect to conducting intelligence gathering against a foreign power or their agents, the act ensures that the insights of the specialized foreign intelligence court are available to superintend the investigative process. There is no reason to deny the Justice Department this authority even if a given investigation has a significant criminal purpose as well. So, too, information gathered on the criminal justice side of an investigation or through a grand jury should be made available to those tasked with the difficult worldwide manhunt of shadowy and elusive terrorist cells. Such are matters of prudent legal reform and just plain common sense.

Widening the Net

Turning to the immigration provisions, the broadened definition of "terrorist" is necessary to meet the current dangers we now face. Under past law, an alien was inadmissible and deportable for, among other reasons, engaging in a terrorist activity employing "explosives or firearms." The Patriot Act adds the words "or other weapon or dangerous device" to the applicable section of the U.S. Code.

Professor David Cole objects, arguing that expanding the term to include a residual category of other weapons trivializes terrorism. With due respect, this is not constitutional law but opinion — and not likely one shared by the families of the innocent men and women who were killed with a "box cutter" en route to crashing into the World Trade Center or the Pentagon or in rural Pennsylvania. Perhaps, prior to September 11, we could be lulled into the notion that not even terrorists would conceive of using innocent human beings as a weapon against other innocent human beings on our own soil, but sadly that is no longer our reality. Hypothetical objections that the statute might be contorted to apply to a barroom brawl or a domestic dispute are, in my judgment and the present context, too facetious to be credited as a legal objection.

Similarly, opponents of the new law expressed a concern that aliens who associate with terrorist organizations may be deported even when they supposedly kept their association to the non-terrorist functions of the organization. Yet this objection, too, seems overstated. The Patriot Act does not punish those who innocently may support a front organization. Moreover, the act even allows for giving support to an individual who had previously committed a terrorist act if the alien establishes that the individual had renounced his terrorist activity before the alien provided support.

Reality tells us that terrorists unfortunately gain financial and other support hiding behind the facade of charity. Those opposing this new immigration authority seem undisturbed by this. That is again a policy choice; it is not a constitutional one. A statute like the present one, aimed at supplying a general prohibition against an alien contributing funds or other material support to a terrorist organization (as designated under current law by the secretary of state) or to any non-designated organization that the alien "knows or reasonably should know" furthers terrorist activity, does not violate the Constitution. Some civil libertarians have supported their opposition to this provision by loosely referencing older cases that wrongfully assigned criminal guilt to U.S. citizens for associating with the domestic cause of civil rights in the 1950s and 1960s; such analogies are simply inappropriate. Surely it is possible to draw distinction between nonviolent associations of American citizens, which are entitled to full First Amendment protection, and the fanatical planning of widespread mass destruction against innocents by non-citizens, which clearly is not.

Considering Intent

Still unpersuaded and want the fine print? Well, here it is: "Engaging in terrorist activity" means committing a terrorist act or otherwise committing an act that "the actor knows, or reasonably should know, affords material support ... [to any organization that the actor knows, or reasonably should know, is a terrorist organization, or] to any individual whom the actor knows, or reasonably should know, has committed or plans to commit any terrorist activity."[2] The specific intent requirements are not only explicit but multiple. This is not, as the objectors claim, guilt by association, but rather guilt for associating with terrorists for terrorism purposes.

Critics of the Patriot Act have claimed that the First and Fifth Amendments apply without distinction to citizens and aliens residing in the United States. However, this cannot be said without qualification. American citizens enjoy certain privileges and immunities within our Constitutional structure that non-citizens do not. Americans, for example, travel freely in and out of our sovereign borders. That same freedom is obviously not afforded non-citizens. With regard to exclusion of immigrants, U.S. authority is plenary, and such authority may be exercised by Congress to prohibit entry altogether. The Court has long held that "whatever the procedure authorized by Congress is, it is due process as far as an alien denied entry is concerned."

Terrorists or those seeking association with them clearly can be excluded from our nation without offending the First Amendment or any other provision of the Constitution. While additional rights do attend an immigrant granted admission, such rights are not necessarily on par with those of citizens. In *U.S. v. Verdugo-Urquidez*, for example, the Court opined that "[our] cases ... establish only that aliens receive constitutional protections when they have come within the territory of the United States and developed substantial connections with this country."[3] Lower courts have thus upheld the deportation of an alien who associated with groups assisting Nazi persecution, even without proof that the alien himself engaged in the act of persecution.

More problematic is the question of how long those aliens subject to removal who also pose a terrorist threat can be detained by the attorney general. The detention provision was the subject of much debate. The Patriot Act ultimately provided that "the Attorney General *may* certify [for detention] an alien he has reason to believe may commit, further, or facilitate [terrorist] acts ... or engage in any other activity that endangers the national security of the United States"[4] (emphasis added). This is authority that is reminiscent of that exercised by the United Kingdom against the Irish Republican Army (IRA). In that context in the 1970s, the British secretary of state could issue a detention order against those attempting or carrying out or organizing for the purpose of terrorist activity. In *the Republic of Ireland v. the United Kingdom*, the European Court of Human Rights found this similar — indeed,

more sweeping — detention authority, applicable to those who were not always suspected of a crime but were sought to be interrogated for intelligence purposes, to be compatible with the European Convention on Human Rights. The individual right against deprivation of liberty, held the unanimous court, was subordinate to the emergency presented by the terrorist activity found at that point in Northern Ireland.

Is the less expansive detention authority given to the U.S. attorney general under the Patriot Act unconstitutional? Not even the opponents claim this; instead, they merely opine that it raises "constitutional concerns." They say, for example, that the Constitution would be transgressed if the detention power were used to detain those giving "peace training to the IRA." Any statute can be made to raise constitutional concerns if it is manipulated to apply against something other than its constitutional object. Congress is not tasked with drafting against the absurd. It is tasked with addressing the very real dangers of those who wish to kill us for no reason other than that we are American. The attorney general can be given authority to address such hatred. He can also be given the authority to address the risks posed by enemy aliens who may flee or who may seek to thwart our security by exchanging information or launching an additional attack.

But, claim the objectors, the attorney general cannot be given authority to detain persons he cannot deport. Perhaps, but that is not the question that needs to be answered. The attorney general did not ask for that authority. He sought and was given the power to detain those who have been found to be removable. An alien is removable principally when the alien has entered the nation illegally, is in present violation of a previously granted immigration status, or has been engaged in other criminal activity. But for various reasons — mostly related to international obligations that prevent deportation and repatriation to a country where torture is inevitable — being removable is not always the same as being capable of being removed immediately.

So, then, for how long can a removable alien be detained? Under the law prior to the Patriot Act, removable aliens could be detained when "determined by the Attorney General to be a risk to the community or unlikely to comply with the order of removal." This pre-Patriot Act postremoval detention authority was construed by the Supreme Court in *Zadvydas v. Davis*, and the Court suggested six months as a reasonable postremoval detention period.

Yet *Zadvydas*, as a case of statutory interpretation, did not rule out more indefinite detention where risk to community or flight risk is accompanied by special circumstance. The Court explicitly noted that in establishing a presumptive six-month period for detention, it was not denying the government detention beyond this point under unique circumstances. Wrote Justice Brayer for the Court, "Neither do we consider terrorism or other special circumstances where special arguments might be made for forms of preventive detention and for heightened deference to the judgments of the political branches with respect to matters of national security."[5]

The detention by attorney general certification under the Patriot Act should thus not be seen as anomalous or beyond constitutional limit. The attorney general is required to review his certification every six months. Moreover, even the opponents of this highly debated aspect of the act concede that it explicitly provides for judicial review of the attorney general's determination — "Judicial review of any action or decision relating to [detention] (including judicial review of the merits of a determination [by the attorney general that an alien presents a danger to national security]) is available by habeas corpus."[6]

In addition to detention following a removal decision, the Patriot Act provides for short-term detention of a suspected terrorist for up to seven days *before* charging an alien with a crime or a basis for removal. If no charges are filed, the alien is released. Prior to the act, the Immigration and Naturalization Service could detain an alien for forty-eight hours before charging a crime or removable offense. Extending this time of detention without charge does present some legal questions that cannot be fully answered apart from the facts of individual cases. In

this respect, whether a constitutional problem is presented by the act likely depends on the extent of due process protection the courts decide must be afforded an individual alien in light of the degree of his or her substantial connection with this country.

Conclusion

Raising civil libertarian objections to new law enforcement provisions is a healthy sign of a vibrant democracy committed to human rights. America should be justly proud of its temperate actions in response to September 11, including its ongoing debate over the proper protection of civil liberties. But no significant constitutional objections have been raised to the USA Patriot Act, either before or after its passage by Congress. Moreover, Congress should be commended for providing a sunset of some of the law enforcement and intelligence authorities that this legislation granted. As Congress has recognized, the possibility of abuse should not obscure the present need and the supposition of trust that one must have if our democratic order is to be safeguarded from those outside our borders who wish to subvert it.

[1] An earlier version of this chapter appeared in *The Responsive Community* 12, no. 1 (Winter 2001–2): 56–63.
[2] Uniting and Strengthening America by Providing Appropriate Tools Required to Intercept and Obstruct Terrorism Act (USA Patriot Act), H.R. 3162, 107th Cong., 1st sess., October 24, 2001, Sec. 411.
[3] *U.S. v. Verdugo-Urquidez*, 494 U.S. 259 (1990).
[4] USA Patriot Act, Sec. 412.
[5] *Zadvydas v. Davis*, 533 U.S. 678 (2001).
[6] USA Patriot Act, Sec. 412.

14.3   ISRAEL SUPREME COURT JUDGMENT ON TORTURE (1999)[1]

38. Our conclusion is therefore the following: According to the existing state of the law, neither the government nor the heads of security services possess the authority to establish directives and bestow authorization regarding the use of liberty infringing physical means during the interrogation of

suspects suspected of hostile terrorist activities, beyond the general directives which can be inferred from the very concept of an interrogation. Similarly, the individual GSS[2] investigator — like any police officer — does not possess the authority to employ physical means which infringe upon a suspect's liberty during the interrogation, unless these means are inherently accessory to the very essence of an interrogation and are both fair and reasonable.

An investigator who insists on employing these methods, or does so routinely, is exceeding his authority. His responsibility shall be fixed according to law. His potential criminal liability shall be examined in the context of the "necessity" defense and according to our assumptions the investigator may find refuge under the "necessity" defense's wings (so to speak), provided this defense's conditions are met by the circumstances of the case. Just as the existence of the "necessity" defense does not bestow authority, so too the lack of authority does not negate the applicability of the necessity defense or that of other defenses from criminal liability. The Attorney General can instruct himself regarding the circumstances in which investigators shall not stand trial, if they claim to have acted from a feeling of "necessity." Clearly a legal statutory provision is necessary for the purpose of authorizing the government to instruct in the use of physical means during the course of an interrogation, beyond what is permitted by the ordinary "law of investigation," and in order to provide the individual GSS investigator with the authority to employ these methods. The "necessity" defense cannot serve as a basis for this authority....

[I]t is decided that the order *nisi* be made absolute, as we declare that the GSS does not have the authority to "shake" a man, hold him in the "Shabach" position,[3] ... force him into a "frog crouch" position and deprive him of sleep in a manner other than that which is inherently required by the interrogation. Likewise, we declare that the "necessity" defense, found in the Penal Law, cannot serve as a basis of authority for the use of these interrogation practices, or for the existence of directives pertaining to

GSS investigators, allowing them to employ interrogation practices of this kind. Our decision does not negate the possibility that the "necessity" defense be available to GSS investigators, be within the discretion of the Attorney General, if he decides to prosecute, or if criminal charges are brought against them, as per the Court's discretion.

[1] September 6, 1999.
[2] Editor: GSS stands for General Security Service.
[3] Editor's insertion of clause 26: The "Shabach" method is composed of a number of cumulative components: the cuffing of the suspect, seating him on a low chair, covering his head with an opaque sack (head covering) and playing powerfully loud music in the area.

14.4 U.S. DEPARTMENT OF JUSTICE MEMORANDUM, ON TORTURE (2002)[1]

Re: Standards of Conduct for Interrogation under 18 U.S.C. §§ 2340-2340A

You have asked for our Office's views regarding the standards of conduct under the Convention Against Torture and Other Cruel, Inhuman and Degrading Treatment or Punishment as implemented by Sections 2340–2340A of title 18 of the United States Code. As we understand it, this question has arisen in the context of the conduct of interrogations outside of the United States. We conclude below that Section 2340A proscribes acts inflicting, and that are specifically intended to inflict, severe pain or suffering, whether mental or physical. Those acts must be of an extreme nature to rise to the level of torture within the meaning of Section 2340A and the Convention. We further conclude that certain acts may be cruel, inhuman, or degrading, but still not produce pain and suffering of the requisite intensity to fall within Section 2340A's proscription against torture. We conclude by examining possible defenses that would negate any claim that certain interrogation methods violate the statute.

In Part I, we examine the criminal statute's text and history. We conclude that for an act to constitute torture as defined in Section 2340, it must inflict pain that is difficult to endure. Physical pain amounting to torture must be equivalent in intensity to the pain accompanying serious physical injury, such as organ failure, impairment of bodily function, or even death. For purely mental pain or suffering to amount to torture under Section 2340, it must result in significant psychological harm of significant duration, e.g., lasting for months or even years. We conclude that the mental harm also must result from one of the predicate acts listed in the statute, namely: threats of imminent death; threats of infliction of the kind of pain that would amount to physical torture; infliction of such physical pain as a means of psychological torture; use of drugs or other procedures designed to deeply disrupt the senses, or fundamentally alter an individual's personality; or threatening to do any of these things to a third party. The legislative history simply reveals that Congress intended for the statute's definition to track the Convention's definition of torture and the reservations, understandings, and declarations that the United States submitted with its ratification. We conclude that the statute, taken as a whole, makes plain that it prohibits only extreme acts.

In Part II, we examine the text, ratification history, and negotiating history of the Torture Convention. We conclude that the treaty's text prohibits only the most extreme acts by reserving criminal penalties solely for torture and declining to require such penalties for "cruel, inhuman, or degrading treatment or punishment." This confirms our view that the criminal statute penalizes only the most egregious conduct. Executive branch interpretations and representations to the Senate at the time of ratification further confirm that the treaty was intended to reach only the most extreme conduct.

In Part III, we analyze the jurisprudence of the Torture Victims Protection Act, 28 U.S.C. § 1350 note (2000), which provides civil remedies for torture victims, to predict the standards that courts might follow in determining what actions reach the threshold of torture in the criminal context. We conclude from these cases that courts are likely to take a totality-of-the-circumstances

approach, and will look to an entire course of conduct, to determine whether certain acts will violate Section 2340A. Moreover, these cases demonstrate that most often torture involves cruel and extreme physical pain. In Part IV, we examine international decisions regarding the use of sensory deprivation techniques. These cases make clear that while many of these techniques may amount to cruel, inhuman or degrading treatment, they do not produce pain or suffering of the necessary intensity to meet the definition of torture. From these decisions, we conclude that there is a wide range of such techniques that will not rise to the level of torture.

In Part V, we discuss whether Section 2340A may be unconstitutional if applied to interrogations undertaken of enemy combatants pursuant to the President's Commander-in-Chief powers. We find that in the circumstances of the current war against al Qaeda and its allies, prosecution under Section 2340A may be barred because enforcement of the statute would represent an unconstitutional infringement of the President's authority to conduct war. In Part VI, we discuss defenses to an allegation that an interrogation method might violate the statute. We conclude that, under the current circumstances, necessity or self-defense may justify interrogation methods that might violate Section 2340A.

[1] Memorandum by Jay Bybee for Alberto R. Gonzales, counsel to the president, Washington, D.C., August 2002.

14.5   U.S. DEPARTMENT OF JUSTICE MEMORANDUM, ON TORTURE (2004)[1]

Torture is abhorrent both to American law and values and to international norms. This universal repudiation of torture is reflected in our criminal law, for example, 18 U.S.C. §§ 2340–2340A; intentional agreements, exemplified by the United Nations Convention Against Torture (the "CAT")[2]; customary international law[3]; centuries of Anglo-American law[4]; and the longstanding policy of the United States, repeatedly and recently reaffirmed by the President.[5]

This Office interpreted the federal criminal prohibition against torture — codified at 18 U.S.C. §§ 2340–2340A — in *Standards of Conduct for Interrogation under 18 U.S.C. 2340–2340A* (Aug. 1, 2002) ("August 2002 Memorandum"). The August 2002 Memorandum also addressed a number of issues beyond interpretation of those statutory provisions, including the President's Commander-in-Chief power, and various defenses that might be asserted to avoid potential liability under sections 2340–2340A. See *id.* at 31–46.

Questions have since been raised, both by this Office and by others, about the appropriateness and relevance of the non-statutory discussion in the August 2002 Memorandum, and also about various aspects of the statutory analysis, in particular the statement that "severe" pain under the statute was limited to pain "equivalent in intensity to the pain accompanying serious physical injury, such as organ failure, impairment of bodily function, or even death." *id.* at 1.[6] We decided to withdraw the August 2002 Memorandum, a decision you announced in June 2004. At that time, you directed this Office to prepare a replacement memorandum. Because of the importance of — and public interest in — these issues, you asked that this memorandum be prepared in a form that could be released to the public so that interested parties could understand our analysis of the statute.

This memorandum supersedes the August 2002 Memorandum in its entirety.[7] Because the discussion in that memorandum concerning the President's Commander-in-Chief power and the potential defenses to liability was — and remains — unnecessary, it has been eliminated from the analysis that follows. Consideration of the bounds of any such authority would be inconsistent with the President's unequivocal directive that United States personnel not engage in torture.[8]

We have also modified in some important respects our analysis of the legal standards applicable under 18 U.S.C. §§ 2340–2340A. For example, we disagree with statements in the August 2002 Memorandum limiting "severe" pain under the statute to "excruciating and agonizing" pain, *id.* at 19, or to pain "equivalent in intensity to the pain accompanying serious physical injury, such as organ failure, impairment of bodily function, or even death," *id.* at 1. There are additional areas where we disagree with or modify the analysis in the August 2002 Memorandum, as identified in the discussion below.[9]

Section 2340A provides that "[w]hoever outside the United States commits or attempts to commit torture shall be fined under this title or imprisoned not more than 20 years, or both, and if death results to any person from conduct prohibited by this subsection, shall be punished by death or imprisoned for any term of years or for life."[10] Section 2340(1) defines "torture" as "an act committed by a person acting under the color of law specifically intended to inflict severe physical or mental pain or suffering (other than pain or suffering incidental to lawful sanctions) upon another person within his custody or physical control."

[1] Memorandum by Daniel Levin for James B. Comey, Deputy Attorney General, December 30, 2004.
[2] Convention Against Torture and Other Cruel, Inhuman or Degrading Treatment or Punishment, Dec. 10, 1984, S. Treaty Doc. No. 100-20, 1465 U.N.T.S. 85. See also, e.g., International Covenant on Civil and Political Rights, Dec. 16, 1966, 999 U.N.T.S. 171.
[3] It has been suggested that the prohibition against torture has achieved the status of *jus cogens* (i.e., a peremptory norm) under international law. See, e.g., *Siderman de Blake v. Republic of Argentina*, 965 F.2d 699, 714 (9th Cir. 1992); *Regina v. Bow Street Metro. Stipendiary Magistrate Ex Porte Pinochet Ugarte* (No. 3), [2000] 1 AC 147, 198; see also Restatement (Third) of Foreign Relations Law of the United States § 702 reporters' note 5.
[4] See generally John H. Langbein, *Torture and the Law of Proof: Europe and England in the Ancient Regime* (1977).
[5] See, e.g., Statement on United Nations International Day in Support of Victims of Torture, 40 Weekly Comp. Pres. Doc. 1167 (July 5, 2004) ("Freedom from torture is an inalienable human right...."); Statement on United Nations International Day in Support of Victims of Torture, 39 Weekly Comp. Pres. Doc. 824 (June 30, 2003) ("Torture anywhere is an affront to human dignity everywhere."); see also Letter of Transmittal from President Ronald Reagan to the Senate (May 20, 1988), in Message from the President of the United States Transmitting the Convention Against Torture and Other Cruel, Inhuman or Degrading Treatment or Punishment, S. Treaty

Doc. No. 100-20, at iii (1988) ("Ratification of the Convention by the United Slates will clearly express United States opposition to torture, an abhorrent practice unfortunately still prevalent in the world today").

6 See, e.g., Anthony Lewis, Making Torture Legal, *N.Y. Rev. of Books*, July 15, 2004; R. Jeffrey Smith, "Slim Legal Grounds for Torture Memos," *Wash. Post*, July 4, 2004, at A12; Kathleen Clark & Julie Mertus, "Torturing the Law; the Justice Department's Legal Contortions on Interrogation," *Wash. Post*, June 20, 2004, at B3; Derek Jinks & David Sloss, "Is the President Bound by the Geneva Conventions?" 90 *Cornell L. Rev.* 97 (2004).

7 This memorandum necessarily discusses the prohibition against torture in sections 2340–2340A in somewhat abstract and general terms. In applying this criminal prohibition to particular circumstances, great care must be taken to avoid approving as lawful any conduct that might constitute torture. In addition, this memorandum does not address the many other sources of law that may apply, depending on the circumstances, to the detention or interrogation of detainees (for example, the Geneva Conventions; the Uniform Code of Military Justice, 10 U.S.C. § 801 et seq.; the Military Extraterritorial Jurisdiction Act, 18 U.S.C. §§ 3261–3267; and the War Crimes Act, 18 U.S.C. § 2441, among others). Any analysis of particular facts must, of course, ensure that the United States complies with all applicable legal obligations.

8 See, e.g., Statement on United Nations International Day in Support of Victims of Torture, 40 Weekly Comp. Pres. Doc. 1167–68 (July 5, 2004). ("America stands against and will not tolerate torture. We will investigate and prosecute all acts of torture ... in all territory under our jurisdiction. Torture is wrong no matter where it occurs, and the United States will continue to lead the fight to eliminate it everywhere.")

9 While we have identified various disagreements with the August 2002 Memorandum, we have reviewed this Office's prior opinions addressing issues involving treatment of detainees and do not believe that any of their conclusions would be different under the standards set forth in this memorandum.

10 Section 2340A provides in full:
(a)   Offense. — Whoever outside the United States commits or attempts to commit torture shall be fined under this title or imprisoned not more than 20 years, or both, and if death results to any person from conduct prohibited by this subsection, shall be punished by death or imprisoned for any term of years or for life....

14.6   RICHARD A. POSNER ("TORTURE, TERRORISM AND INTERROGATION," 2004)

...Dershowitz believes that the occasions for the use of torture should be regularized by requiring a judicial warrant for the needle treatment. Which brings me to the third question I said I would discuss. I think, to begin with, that he exaggerates the significance of the warrant as a check on executive discretion. A warrant is issued in an ex parte proceeding, and usually the officer seeking the warrant has a choice of judges or magistrates from whom to seek it. So there isn't much actual screening, in most cases. And it is probably inevitable that in national security cases the judicial officers authorized to issue such warrants will be chosen in part for their sensitivity to security concerns. Moreover, the warrants and the affidavits supporting them, as well as the judges' reasons for granting the warrants, would be likely to remain secret. The requirement of a warrant would no doubt make the officers seeking them a little more careful, but perhaps not much more truthful or candid. Dershowitz's argument for a judicial screen is particularly surprising given his well-known distrust of judges' competence and probity. I should think he would worry that requiring a warrant in cases of coercive interrogation would operate merely to whitewash questionable practices by persuading the naive that there was firm judicial control over such interrogations.

There is a more interesting argument for leaving the decision whether to employ highly coercive means of interrogation that violate conventional constitutional norms to executive discretion, rather than dragging in courts and the rest of the apparatus of formal law. If legal rules are promulgated permitting torture in defined circumstances, officials are bound to want to explore the outer bounds of the rules; and the practice, once it were thus regularized, would be likely to become regular. Better, I think, to leave in place the customary legal prohibitions, but with the understanding that of course they will not be enforced in extreme circumstances. Abraham Lincoln suspended habeas corpus during the early months of the Civil War. The Constitution almost certainly does not authorize the president to suspend habeas corpus.[1] Lincoln did it anyway and was probably right to do so — the Union was in desperate straits, and its survival was more important than complying with every provision of the Constitution, since, had the rebellion succeeded, the Constitution would have gone by the boards. It does not follow that the Constitution should be amended to authorize the president to suspend habeas corpus; for he might be inclined to test the scope of that authority. The fact that Lincoln was acting illegally must have given him pause, and must also have reduced the danger of what civil libertarians profess to fear (though there is no support for the fear in U.S. history), which is a ratchet effect by which restrictions of civil liberties in times of national emergency would persist when the emergency ended and become a platform for further restrictions the next time there was an emergency.

Likewise it is unnecessary and probably, from the civil liberties standpoint, counterproductive to enact a statute authorizing torture — a statute that, as Dershowitz argues, might well be deemed constitutional, provided that no effort was made to introduce a confession obtained by torture in judicial proceedings against the person tortured. After all, if there is no use of a confession in a judicial proceeding, there is not even an attenuated sense in which an out-of-court declaration makes the declarant a "witness" against himself or herself within the meaning of the Fifth Amendment's self-incrimination clause, though it could still be argued that highly coercive interrogation is a deprivation of a form of liberty (liberty as physical and perhaps psychological integrity), and that if the deprivation is extreme enough to "shock the [judicial] conscience," then there is a denial of due process of law within the meaning of the Fifth and Fourteenth Amendments.

Regularizing the use of extreme measures against terrorists would, moreover, amplify a valid concern of civil libertarians that I have not yet mentioned — that once one starts down the balancing path, the protection of civil liberties quickly erodes. One starts with the extreme case, the terrorist with plague germs or a nuclear bomb in his traveling case, or the kidnapper who alone can save his victim. Well, if torture is legally justifiable if the lives of thousands are threatened, what about when the lives of hundreds are threatened, or tens? And the kidnap victim is only one. By such a chain of reflections we might be moved to endorse a rule that torture is justified if, all things considered, the benefits, which will often be tangible (lives, or a life, saved), exceed the costs, which will often be nebulous. It is better I think to stick with our perhaps overly strict rules, trusting executive officials to break them when the stakes are high enough to enable the officials to obtain political absolution for their illegal conduct.

[1] Posner, *Law, Pragmatism, and Democracy*, (Cambridge, MA: Harvard University Press, 2003) p. 273.

14.7   ALAN DERSHOWITZ ("TORTURED REASONING," 2004)

... Let me once again present my actual views on torture, so that no one can any longer feign confusion about where I stand, though I'm certain the "confusion" will persist among some who are determined to argue that I am a disciple of Torquemada.[1]

I am against torture as a *normative* matter, and I would like to see its use minimized. I believe that at least moderate forms of non-lethal torture are *in fact* being used by the United States and some of its allies today. I think that if we ever confronted an actual case of imminent mass terrorism that could be prevented by the infliction of torture, we would use torture (even lethal torture) and the public would favor its use. Whenever I speak about this subject, I ask my audience for a show of hands on the empirical question "How many of you think that nonlethal torture *would* be used if we were ever confronted with a ticking bomb terrorist case?" Almost no one dissents from the view that torture *would in fact* be used, though there is widespread disagreement about whether it *should* be used. That is also my empirical conclusion. It is either true or false, and time will probably tell. I then present my *conditional normative* position, which is the central point of my chapter on torture.

I pose the issue as follows. If torture is, in fact, being used and/or would, in fact, be used in an actual ticking bomb terrorist case, would it be *normatively* better or worse to have such torture regulated by some kind of warrant, with accountability, recordkeeping, standards and limitations?[2] This is an important debate, and *a different one* from the old, abstract Benthamite debate over whether torture can ever be justified. It is not so much about the substantive issue of torture as it is about accountability, visibility, and candor in a democracy that is confronting a choice of evils. For example, William Schulz, the executive director of Amnesty International USA, asks whether I would favor "brutality warrants," "testilying warrants,"[3] and "prisoner rape warrants."[4] Although I strongly oppose brutality, testilying, and prisoner rape, I answered [William] Schulz with "a heuristic yes, if requiring a warrant would subject these horribly brutal activities to judicial control and accountability." In explaining my preference for a warrant, I wrote the following:

The purpose of requiring judicial supervision, as the framers of our Fourth Amendment understood better than Schulz does, is to assure accountability and neutrality. There is another purpose as well: it forces a democratic country to confront the choice of evils in an open way. My question back to Schulz is do you prefer the current situation in which brutality, testilying, and prisoner rape are rampant, but we close our eyes to these evils?

There is, of course, a downside: legitimating a horrible practice that we all want to see ended or minimized. Thus we have a triangular conflict unique to democratic societies: If these horrible practices continue to operate below the radar screen of accountability, there is no legitimation, but there is continuing and ever expanding *sub rosa* employment of the practice. If we try to control the practice by demanding some kind of accountability, then we add

a degree of legitimation to it while perhaps reducing its frequency and severity. If we do nothing, and a preventable act of nuclear terrorism occurs, then the public will demand that we constrain liberty even more. There is no easy answer.

I praise Amnesty for taking the high road —that is its job, because it is not responsible for making hard judgments about choices of evil. Responsible government officials are in a somewhat different position. Professors have yet a different responsibility: to provoke debate about issues before they occur and to challenge absolutes.

That is my position. I cannot say it any more clearly.

The strongest argument against my preference for candor and accountability is the claim that it is better for torture — or any other evil practice deemed necessary during emergencies — to be left to the low-visibility discretion of low-level functionaries than to be legitimated by high-level, accountable decision-makers. Posner makes this argument:

Dershowitz believes that the occasions for the use of torture should be regularized — by requiring a judicial warrant for the needle treatment, for example. But he overlooks an argument for leaving such things to executive discretion. If rules are promulgated permitting torture in defined circumstances, some officials are bound to want to explore the outer bounds of the rules. Having been regularized, the practice will become regular. Better to leave in place the formal and customary prohibitions, but with the understanding that they will not be enforced in extreme circumstances....

Experience has not necessarily proved Posner's prediction to be well founded....

The *Wall Street Journal* reported that "a U.S. intelligence official" told them that detainees with important information could be treated roughly:

Among the techniques: making captives wear black hoods, forcing them to stand in painful "stress positions" for a long time and subjecting them to interrogation sessions lasting as long as 20 hours.

U.S. officials overseeing interrogations of captured al-Qaeda forces at Bagram and Guantanamo Bay Naval Base in Cuba can even authorize "a little bit of smacky-face," a U.S. intelligence official says. "Some al-Qaeda just need some extra encouragement," the official says.

"There's a reason why [Mr. Mohammed] isn't going to be near a place where he has Miranda rights or the equivalent of them," the senior federal law-enforcer says. "He won't be someplace like Spain or Germany or France. We're not using this to prosecute him. This is for intelligence. God only knows what they're going to do with him. You go to some other country that'll let us pistol whip this guy." ...

U.S. authorities have an additional inducement to make Mr. Mohammed talk, even if he shares the suicidal commitment of the Sept. 11 hijackers: The Americans have access to two of his elementary-school-age children, the top law enforcement official says. The children were captured in a September raid that netted one of Mr. Mohammed's top comrades, Ramzi Binalshibh.[5]

There is no doubt that these tactics would be prohibited by the Israeli Supreme Court's decision described earlier, but the U.S. Court of Appeals for the District of Columbia recently ruled that American courts have no power even to review the conditions imposed on detainees in Guantanamo or other interrogation centers outside the United States.[6] That issue is now before the U.S. Supreme Court, despite efforts by the administration to preclude review.

This, then, is the virtue of explicitness. The Supreme Court of Israel was able to confront the issue of torture precisely because it had been openly addressed by the Landau Commission in 1987. This open discussion led to Israel being condemned — including by countries that were doing worse but without acknowledging it. It also led to a judicial decision outlawing the practice. As I demonstrated in *Why Terrorism Works*, it is generally more possible to end a questionable practice when it is done openly rather than covertly.[7]

My own belief is that a warrant requirement, if properly enforced, would probably reduce the frequency, severity, and duration of torture. I cannot see how it could possibly increase it, since a warrant requirement simply imposes an additional level of prior review. As I discussed in *Why Terrorism Works*, here are two examples to demonstrate why I think there would be less torture with a warrant requirement than without one. Recall the case of the alleged national security wiretap being placed on the phones of Martin Luther King by the Kennedy administration in the early 1960s. This was in the days when the attorney general could authorize a national security wiretap without a warrant. Today no judge would issue a warrant in a case as flimsy as that one. When Zaccarias Moussaui was detained after trying to learn how to fly an airplane, without wanting to know much about landing it, the government did not even seek a national security wiretap because its lawyers believed that a judge would not have granted one. If Moussaui's computer could have been searched without a warrant, it almost certainly would have been.

It should be recalled that in the context of searches, the framers of our Fourth Amendment opted for a judicial check on the discretion of the police, by requiring a search warrant in most cases. The Court has explained the reason for the warrant requirement as follows. "The informed and deliberate determinations of magistrates ... are to be preferred over the hurried actions of officers."[8] Justice Jackson elaborated:

> The point of the Fourth Amendment, which often is not grasped by zealous officers, is not that it denies law enforcement the support of the usual inferences, which reasonable men draw from evidence. Its protection consists in requiring that those inferences be drawn by a neutral and detached magistrate instead of being judged by the officer engaged in the often-competitive enterprise of ferreting out crime. Any assumption that evidence sufficient to support a magistrate's disinterested determination to issue a search warrant will justify the officers in making a search without a warrant would reduce the Amendment to nullify

and leave the people's homes secure only in the discretion of police officers.[9]

Although torture is very different from a search, the policies underlying the warrant requirement are relevant to whether there is likely to be more torture or less if the decision were left entirely to field officers, or if a judicial officer had to approve a request for a torture warrant. As Mark Twain once observed, "To a man with a hammer, everything looks like a nail." If the man with the hammer must get judicial approval before he can use it, he will probably use it less often and more carefully.

The major downside of any warrant procedure would be its legitimization of a horrible practice, but in my view it is better to legitimate and control a *specific* practice that will occur than to legitimate a *general* practice of tolerating extralegal actions so long as they operate under the table of scrutiny and beneath the radar screen of accountability. Judge Posner's "pragmatic" approach would be an invitation to widespread (and officially — if surreptitiously — approved) lawlessness in "extreme circumstances." Moreover, the very concept of "extreme circumstances" is subjective and infinitely expandable.

We know that Jordan, which denies that it ever uses torture, has, in fact, tortured the innocent relatives of suspect terrorists. We also know that when we captured Mohammed, we also took into custody his two elementary-school-age children — and let him know that we had them.

There is a difference in principle, as Bentham noted more than two hundred years ago, between torturing the guilty to save the lives of the innocent and torturing innocent people. A system that requires an articulated justification for the use of nonlethal torture and approval by a judge is more likely to honor that principle than a system that relegates these decisions to low-visibility law enforcement agents whose only job is to protect the public from terrorism....

The recent disclosure of significant abuses by military intelligence and military police officers in the Abu Ghraib prison outside of Baghdad demonstrates what happens when high-ranking officials have a "don't ask, don't tell policy" toward the use of extraordinary pressures in interrogation. While our leaders in Washington and our commanders in the field adamantly denied the use of any form of torture — light or otherwise — a subtle message was being conveyed down the chain of command that intelligence and police officials on the ground could do what they had to do to obtain important information. If this had not been perceived by the soldiers as the message from above, there is no way the photographs they took would have been so openly distributed.

When the message is sent in this way — by a wink and nod — no lines are drawn, no guidelines issued, and no accountability accepted. The result was massive abuses by those on the ground, coupled with deniability by those at the top.

How much better it would have been if we required that any resort to extraordinary means — means other than routine interrogation — be authorized in advance by someone in authority and with accountability. If a warrant requirement of some kind had been in place, the low-ranking officers on the ground could not plausibly claim that they had been subtly (or secretly) authorized to do what they did, since the only acceptable form of authorization would be in writing. Nor could the high-ranking officials hide behind plausible deniability, since they would have been required to give the explicit authorization. Moreover, since authorization would have to go through the chain of command, limitations would have been imposed on allowable methods. These would not have included the kind of gratuitous humiliation apparently inflicted on these prisoners.

There are of course no guarantees that individual officers would not engage in abuses on their own, even with a warrant requirement. But the current excuse being offered — we had to do what we did to get information — would no longer be available, since there would be an authorized method of securing information in extraordinary cases by the use of extraordinary means. Finally, the requirement of securing advanced written approval would reduce the incidence of abuses, since it would be a rare case in which a high-ranking official, knowing that the record will eventually be made public, would authorize extraordinary methods — and never methods of the kind shown in the Abu Ghraib photographs.

1 Editor: Tomas de Torquemada (1420–1498) was prosecutor general during the Spanish Inquisition.
2 Although my specific proposal is for a judicial warrant, my general point relates to visibility and accountability. Accordingly, an executive warrant or an explicit executive approval would also serve these democratic values. A judicial warrant has the added virtue of a decision-maker who — at least in theory — is supposed to balance liberty and security concerns (see the Fourth Amendment). A legislative warrant for specific cases would be both cumbersome and violative of the spirit of the bill of attainder clause, though a general legislative enactment requiring judicial or executive approval would be desirable.

3 "Testilying" is a term coined by New York City police to describe systematic perjury regarding the circumstances that led to a search, seizure, or interrogation.
4 William F. Schulz, "The Torturer's Apprentice: Civil Liberties in a Turbulent Age," *Nation*, May 13, 2002. Editor: William Schulz is the director of Amnesty International.
5 Jess Bravin and Gary Fields, "How Do Interrogators Make Terrorists Talk?" *Wall Street Journal*, March 3, 2003.
6 *Al Odah v. United States*, 321 F.3d 1134 (2003).
7 *Dershowitz, Why Terrorism Works*, (New Haven, CT: Yale University Press, 2002) 155–160.
8 *U.S. v. Lefkowitz*, 285 U.S. 452, 464 (1932).
9 *Johnson v. U.S.*, 333 U.S. 10, 13–14 (1948).

HUMANITARIAN INTERVENTIONS

14.8   SAMANTHA POWER ("RAISING THE COST OF GENOCIDE," 2002)

RAPHAEL LEMKIN, a Polish jurist who lost forty-nine members of his family in the Holocaust, invented the word "genocide" in 1944 because he believed that, in the aftermath of the Turkish "race murder" of the Armenians and of Hitler's extermination campaign against the Jews, the world's "civilized" powers needed to band together to outlaw crimes that were said to "shock the conscience." Prior to Lemkin's coinage, the systematic targeting of national, ethnic, or religious groups was known as "barbarity," a word that Lemkin believed failed to convey the unique horror of the crime. "Genocide," he hoped, would send shudders down the spines of those who heard it and oblige them to prevent, punish, and even suppress the carnage.

An amateur historian of mass slaughter from medieval times to the twentieth century, Lemkin knew that genocide would continue to occur with "biological regularity." Moreover, he knew from reviewing the recent past that if it were left to political leaders to decide how to respond, they

would inevitably privilege their short-term interests over both the moral imperative of stopping genocide and the long-term consequences of ignoring it.

In 1948, largely on Lemkin's prodding, the UN General Assembly unanimously passed the United Nations' first-ever human rights treaty, the Genocide Convention, which required signatories "to undertake to prevent and punish" genocide. The Convention's language was vague on precisely how the UN member states would meet their obligations, making no mention of military intervention and trusting that domestic prosecution of future "genocidists" would deter massacres. Still, the lively debates over ratification that occurred in national legislatures testified to the seriousness with which delegates believed they were committing their country's resources and prestige to banning targeted slaughter.

More than a half century has passed since the Genocide Convention came into effect, and genocide has proceeded virtually unabated. Press coverage of the atrocities has generated outrage, but it has generally been insufficient to prompt Western action. As the 1990s showed, particularly in the reactions of the United States and Europe to carnage in Yugoslavia and Rwanda (the scene, in 1994, of the fastest and most efficient genocidal campaign of the twentieth century), Western countries replicated the pattern established in their earlier responses to the rise and domination of Hitler — long after they had supposedly internalized the "lessons of the Holocaust." ...

With the end of the cold war and the apparent rebirth of the UN (aided by the obsolescence of the superpower veto), one might have expected a greater readiness to prevent genocide. But the pattern of nonintervention established in 1915 proved durable....

NEARLY A CENTURY after the "race murder" of the Armenians and more than a half century after the liberation of the Nazi death camps, the crucial question is, why do decent men and women who firmly believe genocide should "never again" be permitted allow it to happen? The most typical response throughout the twentieth century was, "We didn't know." But this is simply untrue. To be sure, the information emanating from countries victimized by genocide was imperfect. Embassy personnel were withdrawn, intelligence assets on the ground were scarce, editors were typically reluctant to assign their reporters to places where neither Western interests nor Western readers were engaged, and journalists who attempted to report the atrocities were limited in their mobility. As a result, refugee claims were difficult to confirm and body counts notoriously hard to establish. Because genocide is usually veiled beneath the cover of war, when the killing began, some Western officials had genuine difficulty initially distinguishing genocide from conventional conflict.

But although Western governments did not know all there was to know about the nature and scale of the violence, they knew plenty. Well-connected ambassadors and junior intelligence analysts pumped a steady stream of information up the chain to senior decision makers — both early warnings ahead of genocide and vivid documentation during it. Much of the best intelligence appeared in the morning papers. Back in 1915, when communications were far more primitive, the New York Times managed

145 stories about the Turkish massacre of Armenians. During the Holocaust, though stories on the extermination of the Jews were not given anywhere near the prominence they warranted, they did regularly appear. In 1994, the Times reported just four days after the beginning of the Rwanda genocide that "tens of thousands" of Rwandans had already been murdered. It devoted more column inches to the horrors of Bosnia between 1992 and 1995 than it did to any other single foreign story....

THE SECOND consoling response usually offered to the question of why the major powers did so little to stop genocide is that any intervention would have been futile. Each time states began slaughtering and deporting their citizens, Western officials claimed that the proposed measures would do little to stem the horrors, or that they would do more harm than good. Usually they cited this lack of capacity to ameliorate suffering as a central reason for staying uninvolved. If the hatreds were "age-old" and "two-sided," as was usually claimed, and if the "parties" had in fact been killing one another "for centuries," the implication was that they would kill one another for centuries more. Thus, there was little a wellmeaning band of foreign do-gooders could achieve by meddling.

It is difficult, in retrospect, to ascertain what a determined diplomatic, economic, legal, or military intervention could have achieved or what it would have cost. All we do know is that the perpetrators of genocide were quick studies who were remarkably attuned both to the tactics of their predecessors and to the world's response. From their brutal forerunners, they picked up lessons in everything from dehumanizing their victims and deploying euphemisms to constructing concentration camps and covering their tracks. And from the outside world, they learned the lesson of impunity. The Turkish minister of the interior, Talaat Pasha, was aware that Sultan Abdul Hamid II had gotten away with murdering Armenians in 1895. In 1939 Hitler was emboldened by the fact that absolutely nobody "remembered the Armenians." Saddam Hussein noted the international community's relaxed response to his chemical weapons attacks against Iran and his bulldozing of Kurdish villages....But because the killers told themselves they were doing the world a favor by "cleansing" the "undesirables," some surely interpreted silence as consent or even support....

The real reason the United States and the European states did not do what they could and should have done to stop genocide was not a lack of knowledge or a lack of capacity, but a lack of will. Simply put, Western leaders did not act because they did not want to...

To understand why the United States did not do more to stem genocide, of course, it is not enough to focus on the actions of American presidents or their foreign-policy teams. In a democracy, even an administration disinclined to act can be pressured into doing so. This pressure can come from inside and outside. Bureaucrats within the system who grasp the stakes can patiently lobby or brazenly agitate in the hope of forcing their bosses to entertain a full range of options. Unfortunately, while every genocide generated some activism within the U.S. foreign-policy establishment, U.S. civil and foreign servants typically heeded what they took to be presidential indifference and public apathy. They assumed U.S. policy was immutable, that their concerns were already understood by their bosses, and that speaking (or walking) out would only reduce their capacity to improve the policy.

But the main reason American leaders can persist in turning away is that genocide in distant lands has not captivated American Senators, congressional caucuses, Washington lobbyists, elite opinion shapers, grassroots groups, and individual constituents. The battle to stop genocide has thus been repeatedly lost in the realm of domestic politics. Although isolated voices have protested the atrocities, Americans outside the executive branch were largely mute when it mattered. As a result of this society-wide silence, officials at all levels of government calculated that the political costs of getting involved in genocide prevention far exceeded the costs of remaining uninvolved.

Here, the exception that proved the rule was the NATO air campaign in Bosnia. Bos-nia was the only genocide of the twentieth century that generated a wave of resignations from the U.S. government. It is probably not coincidental that this was the one case where the protests of American officials in the foreign service were legitimated daily by sustained public and press activism outside Foggy Bottom. NATO intervened with a heavy barrage of bombing in August 1995, when its assessment of the costs of intervening was lowered by the Croatian Army's rout of Serb forces, and when its assessment of the costs of *not* intervening was raised by the U.S. Congress's vote to unilaterally lift the arms embargo against the Bosnian Muslims. The lifting of the embargo embarrassed Clinton at home because foreign policy was being made on Capitol Hill by a future presidential challenger, Senate Majority Leader Bob Dole. It also made it likely that European governments were going to pull their peacekeepers out of the Balkans, which would have required U.S. troop participation in a potentially bloody and certainly humiliating rescue mission. This scenario was one that President Clinton wanted to avoid on the eve of his bid for reelection.

With foreign policy crises all over the world implicating more traditional U.S. interests, the slaughter of civilians will rarely secure top-level attention on its own merits....

Although U.S. officials have sometimes expressed remorse after genocide, none fear professional accountability for their sins of omission....

Other countries and institutions whose personnel were actually present when genocide was committed have been forced to be more introspective. The Netherlands, France, and the UN have each staged inquiries into their responsibility for the fall of Srebrenica and the massacres that followed. The inquiries did not lead to any notable political reforms, but they at least "named names," which might affect the behavior of bureaucrats the next time around. The United States has not looked back. When the UN's Srebrenica investigators approached the U.S. mission in New York for assistance, their phone calls were not returned. In the end, the UN team was forbidden from making any independent contact with U.S. government employees. The investigators were granted access to a group of hand-picked junior and mid-level officials who knew or revealed next to nothing about what the United States knew during the Srebrenica slaughter.

The French, the Belgians, the UN, and the Organization for African Unity have undertaken investigations on the Rwanda genocide. But in the United States, when Cynthia McKinney and Donald Payne, two disgruntled members of the Congressional Black Caucus (which was itself quiet during the 1994 massacres), attempted to stage hearings on the U.S. role, they were rebuffed. Two officials in the Clinton administration, one at the National Security Council, the other at the State Department, conducted internal studies on the administration's response to the Rwanda genocide. But they examined only the paper trail and did not publicly disclose their findings. What is needed are congressional inquiries with the power to subpoena documents and U.S. officials of all ranks and roles in the executive and legislative branches. Without meaningful disclosure, public awareness, and official shame, it is hard to imagine the U.S. response improving the next time around.

The September 11, 2001, attacks on the United States may have permanently altered U.S. foreign policy. The hope is that the attacks will make Americans inside and outside government more capable of imagining evil committed against innocent civilians. The fanatics targeting America resemble the perpetrators of genocide in their espousal of collective responsibility of the most savage kind. They attack civilians not because of anything the unwitting targets do personally, but because of who they are. To earn a death sentence, it was enough in the last century to be an Armenian, a Jew, or a Tutsi. On September 11, it was enough to be an American. Instead of causing Americans to retreat from global humanitarian engagement, the terrorist attacks could cause us to empathize with peoples victimized by genocide. In 1994, Rwanda, a country of eight million, experienced the equivalent of more than two World Trade Center attacks every single day for a hundred days. This was the proportional equivalent of two hundred and thirty thousand Americans killed each day, or twenty-three million Americans murdered in three months. When, on September 12, 2001, the United States turned for help to America's allies around the world, Americans were gratified by the overwhelming response. When the Tutsi cried out, by contrast, every country in the world turned away.

The fear, after September 11, is that the United States will view genocide prevention as a luxury it cannot afford as it sets out to better protect Americans. Some are now arguing, understandably, that fighting terrorism requires husbanding America's resources and avoiding "social work" such as humanitarian intervention, which is said to harm U.S. "readiness." Many believe that NATO's 1999 intervention in Kosovo and the current trial of Serbian president Slobodan Milosevic, which were once thought to mark important precedents, will in fact represent high-water marks for genocide prevention and punishment.

Without U.S. leadership, the last century showed, others will be unwilling to step forward to act, and genocide will continue. If the United States treats the war on terrorism as a war that can be prosecuted in a vacuum, with no regard for *genocidal* terror, it will be making a colossal mistake. There are two main reasons that the United States and its European allies should stop genocide. The first and most convincing reason is moral. When innocent life is being taken on such a scale and the United States and its allies have the power to stop the killing at reasonable risk, they have a duty to act. It is this belief that motivates most of those who seek intervention. But foreign policy is not driven by morality; it is driven by interests, narrowly defined. And history has shown that the suffering of victims has rarely been sufficient to spark a Western intervention.

The second reason for acting is the threat genocide in fact does pose to Western interests. Allowing genocide undermines regional and international stability, creates militarized refugees, and signals dictators that hate and murder are permissible tools of statecraft. Because these dangers to national interests are long-term dangers and not immediately apparent, however, they have rarely convinced top Western policy makers. Genocide has undermined regional stability, but the regions the conflicts destabilized tended also to lie outside the U.S. and European spheres of concern. Refugees have been militarized, but they tended not to wash up on America's shores. A key reason European leaders were more engaged in the Balkans in the 1990s than their American counterparts was that Bosnian refugees did land in Britain, France, and Germany. But generally dictators recognized that, provided the spillover costs were contained locally, their treatment of their own citizens would have little impact on Western leaders' perception of their country's military or economic security. Thus intervention only came about on the rare occasions when the shorter-term political interests of Western policy makers were triggered.

American leadership remains essential for mobilizing local, regional, and international responses to genocide. But if it was difficult before September 11 to get U.S decision makers to see the long-term costs of allowing genocide, it will be even harder today when U.S. security needs are so acute....

Citizens victimized by genocide or abandoned by the international community do not make good neighbors, as their thirst for vengeance, their irredentism, and their acceptance of violence as a means of generating change can turn them into future threats. In Bosnia, where the United States and Europe maintained an arms embargo against the Muslims, extremist Islamic fighters and proselytizers eventually turned up to offer succor. Some secular Muslim citizens became radicalized by the partnership, and the failed state of Bosnia became a haven for Islamic terrorists shunned elsewhere in the world. It appears that one of the organizations that infiltrated Bosnia in its hour of need and used it as a training base was Osama bin Laden's al-Qaeda. And however high the number of Islamic radicals that were imported during or created by the Serb slaughter of Bosnia's Muslims, the figure would have been exponentially higher if the United States and its allies had allowed the killing to continue past 1995. The current Bosnian government, one legacy of the U.S.-brokered Dayton Peace Agreement, is far from perfect, but it is at least a strategic partner in the war against terrorism. Without NATO bombing and U.S. diplomatic leadership, that same Bosnian government might today be an American foe....

Instead of regarding intervention as an all-or-nothing proposition, the United States and its allies should respond to genocide by publicly identifying and threatening its perpetrators with prosecution, demanding the expulsion of representatives of genocidal regimes from international institutions such as the United Nations, closing the perpetrators' embassies in Western capitals, and calling upon countries aligned with the perpetrators to ask them to use their influence. Depending on the circumstances, Western powers might establish economic sanctions or freeze foreign assets, impose an arms embargo, or, if warranted, lift an arms embargo. They might use their technical resources to jam inflammatory radio or television broadcasts that are essential to propaganda, panic, and hate. They might set up safe areas to house refugees and civilians, and enforce them with well-armed and robustly mandated peacekeepers, air power, or both.

Genocide prevention is an immense burden and one that must be shared. But even if U.S. troops stay home, American leadership will be indispensable in assembling "coalitions of the willing" to deploy ground troops, in encouraging U.S. allies to step up their capacities, and in strengthening regional and international institutions that might eventually carry more of the weight.

For most of the second half of the twentieth century, the existence of the Genocide Convention appeared to achieve little. The United States did not ratify the Convention for forty years. Those countries that did ratify it never invoked it to stop or punish genocide. And instead of making Western policy makers more inclined to stop genocide, ratification seemed only to make them more reluctant to use the "g-word." Still, Lemkin's coinage has done more good than harm. It is unlikely that the international tribunals for the former Yugoslavia and Rwanda or the future International Criminal Court would have come into existence without the Convention's passage. The punishment that takes place at these courts will help deter genocide in the long term. But more fundamentally, without the existence of the Convention, or Lemkin's proselytizing around it, the word genocide would not carry the moral stigma it has acquired. Hope for enforcement of the Genocide Convention lies in the stigma associated with committing *and allowing* the crime of genocide — and paradoxically in the lengths to which Western policy makers have gone to vow never again to allow genocide and the comparable lengths to which they have gone, while allowing it, to deny its occurrence.

Because it is unlikely that Western leaders will have the vision to recognize that they endanger their countries' long-term vital national interests by allowing genocide, the most realistic hope for combating it lies in the rest of us creating short-term political costs for those who do nothing.

14.9 MICHAEL IGNATIEFF ("THE BURDEN," 2003)

II

Even at this late date, it is still possible to ask: Why should a republic take on the risks of empire? Won't it run a chance of endangering its identity as a free people? The problem is that this implies innocent options that in the case of Iraq may no longer exist. Iraq is not just about whether the United States can retain its republican virtue in a wicked world. Virtuous disengagement is no longer a possibility. Since Sept. 11, it has been about whether the republic can survive in safety at home without imperial policing abroad. Face to face with "evil empires" of the past, the republic reluctantly accepted a division of the world based on mutually assured destruction. But now it faces much less stable and reliable opponents — rogue states like Iraq and North Korea with the potential to supply weapons of mass destruction to a ter-

rorist internationale. Iraq represents the first in a series of struggles to contain the proliferation of weapons of mass destruction, the first attempt to shut off the potential supply of lethal technologies to a global terrorist network.

Containment rather than war would be the better course, but the Bush administration seems to have concluded that containment has reached its limits — and the conclusion is not unreasonable. Containment is not designed to stop production of sarin, VX nerve gas, anthrax and nuclear weapons. Threatened retaliation might deter Saddam from using these weapons, but his continued development of them increases his capacity to intimidate and deter others, including the United States. Already his weapons have sharply raised the cost of any invasion, and as time goes by this could become prohibitive. The possibility that North Korea might quickly develop weapons of mass destruction makes regime change on the Korean peninsula all but unthinkable. Weapons of mass destruction would render Saddam the master of a region that, because it has so much of the world's proven oil reserves, makes it what a military strategist would call the empire's center of gravity.

Iraq may claim to have ceased manufacturing these weapons after 1991, but these claims remain unconvincing, because inspectors found evidence of activity after that date. So what to do? Efforts to embargo and sanction the regime have hurt only the Iraqi people. What is left? An inspections program, even a permanent one, might slow the dictator's weapons programs down, but inspections are easily evaded. That leaves us, but only as a reluctant last resort, with regime change.

Regime change is an imperial task par excellence, since it assumes that the empire's interest has a right to trump the sovereignty of a state. The Bush administration would ask, What moral authority rests with a sovereign who murders and ethnically cleanses his own people, has twice invaded neighboring countries and usurps his people's wealth in order to build palaces and lethal weapons? And the administration is not alone. Not even Kofi Annan, the secretary general, charged with defending the United Nations Charter, says that sovereignty confers impunity for such crimes, though he has made it clear he would prefer to leave a disarmed Saddam in power rather than risk the conflagration of war to unseat him.

Regime change also raises the difficult question for Americans of whether their own freedom entails a duty to defend the freedom of others beyond their borders. The precedents here are inconclusive. Just because Wilson and Roosevelt sent Americans to fight and die for freedom in Europe and Asia doesn't mean their successors are committed to this duty everywhere and forever. The war in Vietnam was sold to a skeptical American public as another battle for freedom, and it led the republic into defeat and disgrace.

Yet it remains a fact — as disagreeable to those left wingers who regard American imperialism as the root of all evil as it is to the right-wing isolationists, who believe that the world beyond our shores is none of our business — that there are many peoples who owe their freedom to an exercise of American military power. It's not just the Japanese and the Germans, who became democrats under the watchful eye of Generals MacArthur and Clay. There are the Bosnians, whose nation survived because American air power and diplomacy forced an end to a war the Europeans couldn't stop. There are the Kosovars, who would still be imprisoned in Serbia if not for Gen. Wesley Clark and the Air Force. The list of people whose freedom depends on American air and ground power also includes the Afghans and, most inconveniently of all, the Iraqis.

The moral evaluation of empire gets complicated when one of its benefits might be freedom for the oppressed. Iraqi exiles are adamant: even if the Iraqi people might be the immediate victims of an American attack, they would also be its ultimate beneficiaries. It would make the case for military intervention easier, of course, if the Iraqi exiles cut a more impressive figure. They feud and squabble and hate one another nearly as much as they hate Saddam. But what else is to be expected from a political culture pulverized by 40 years of state terror?

If only invasion, and not containment, can build democracy in Iraq, then the question becomes whether the Bush administration actually has any real intention of doing so. The exiles fear that a mere change of regime, a coup in which one Baathist thug replaces another, would suit American interests just as well, provided the thug complied with the interests of the Pentagon and American oil companies. Whenever it has exerted power overseas, America has never been sure whether it values stability — which means not only political stability but also the steady, profitable flow of goods and raw materials — more than it values its own rhetoric about democracy. Where the two values have collided, American power has come down heavily on the side of stability, for example, toppling democratically elected leaders from Mossadegh in Iran to Allende in Chile. Iraq is yet another test of this choice. Next door in Iran, from the 1950's to the 1970's, America backed stability over democracy, propping up the autocratic rule of the shah, only to reap the whirlwind of an Islamic fundamentalist revolution in 1979 that delivered neither stability nor real democracy. Does the same fate await an American operation in Iraq?

International human rights groups, like Amnesty International, are dismayed at the way both the British government of Tony Blair and the Bush administration are citing the human rights abuses of Saddam to defend the idea of regime change. Certainly the British and the American governments maintained a complicit and dishonorable silence when Saddam gassed the Kurds in 1988. Yet now that the two governments are taking decisive action, human rights groups seem more outraged by the prospect of action than they are by the abuses they once denounced. The fact that states are both late and hypocritical in their adoption of human rights does not deprive them of the right to use force to defend them.

The disagreeable reality for those who believe in human rights is that there are some occasions — and Iraq may be one of them — when war is the only real remedy for regimes that live by terror. This does not mean the choice is morally unproblematic. The choice is one between two evils, between containing and leaving a tyrant in place and the targeted use of force, which will kill people but free a nation from the tyrant's grip.

VI

...For 50 years, Europe rebuilt itself economically while passing on the costs of its defense to the United States. This was a matter of more than just reducing its armed forces and the proportion of national income spent on the military. All Western European countries reduced the martial elements in their national identities. In the process, European identity (with the possible exception of Britain) became postmilitary and postnational. This opened a widening gap with the United States. It remained a nation in which flag, sacrifice and martial honor are central to national identity. Europeans who had once invented the idea of the martial nation-state now looked at American patriotism, the last example of the form, and no longer recognized it as anything but flag-waving extremism. The world's only empire was isolated, not just because it was the biggest power but also because it was the West's last military nation-state.

Sept. 11 rubbed in the lesson that global power is still measured by military capability. The Europeans discovered that they lacked the military instruments to be taken seriously and that their erstwhile defenders, the Americans, regarded them, in a moment of crisis, with suspicious contempt.

Yet the Americans cannot afford to create a global order all on their own. European participation in peacekeeping, nation-building and humanitarian reconstruction is so important that the Americans are required, even when they are unwilling to do so, to include Europeans in the governance of their evolving imperial project. The Americans essentially dictate Europe's place in this new grand design. The United States is multilateral when it wants to be, unilateral when it must be; and it enforces a new division of labor in which America does the fighting, the French, British and Germans do the police patrols in the border zones and the Dutch, Swiss and Scandinavians provide the humanitarian aid.

This is a very different picture of the world than the one entertained by liberal international lawyers and human rights activists who had hoped to see American power integrated into a transnational legal and economic order organized around the United Nations, the World Trade Organization, the International Criminal Court and other international human rights and environmental institutions and mechanisms. Successive American administrations have signed on to those pieces of the transnational legal order that suit their purposes (the World Trade Organization, for example) while ignoring or even sabotaging those parts (the International Criminal Court or the Kyoto Protocol) that do not. A new international order is emerging, but it is designed to suit American imperial objectives. America's allies want a multilateral order that will essentially constrain American power. But the empire will not be tied down like Gulliver with a thousand legal strings.

14.10 ERIC HOBSBAWM ("SPREADING DEMOCRACY," 2004)

We are at present engaged in what purports to be a planned reordering of the world by the powerful states. The wars in Iraq and Afghanistan are but one part of a supposedly universal effort to create world order by "spreading democracy." This idea is not merely quixotic — it is dangerous. The rhetoric surrounding this crusade implies that the system is applicable in a standardized (Western) form, that it can succeed everywhere, that it can remedy today's transnational dilemmas, and that it can bring peace, rather than sow disorder. It cannot.

Democracy is rightly popular. In 1647, the English Levellers broadcast the powerful idea that "all government is in the free consent of the people." They meant votes for all. Of course, universal suffrage does not guarantee any particular political result, and elections cannot even ensure their own perpetuation — witness the Weimar Republic. Electoral democracy is also unlikely to produce outcomes convenient to hegemonic or imperial powers. (If the Iraq war had depended on the freely expressed consent of "the world community," it would not have happened.) But these uncertainties do not diminish the appeal of electoral democracy.

Several other factors besides democracy's popularity explain the dangerous and illusory belief that its propagation by foreign armies might actually be feasible. Globalization suggests that human affairs are evolving toward a universal pattern. If gas stations, iPods, and computer geeks are the same worldwide, why not political institutions? This view underrates the world's complexity. The relapse into bloodshed and anarchy that has occurred so visibly in much of the world has also made the idea of spreading a new order more attractive. The Balkans seemed to show that areas of turmoil and humanitarian catastrophe required the intervention, military if need be, of strong and stable states. In the absence of effective international governance, some humanitarians are still ready to support a world order imposed by U.S. power. But one should always be suspicious when military powers claim to be doing favors for their victims and the world by defeating and occupying weaker states.

Yet another factor may be the most important: The United States has been ready with the necessary combination of megalomania and messianism, derived from its revolutionary origins. Today's United States is unchallengeable in its techno-military supremacy, convinced of the superiority of its social system, and, since 1989, no longer reminded — as even the greatest conquering empires always had been — that its material power has limits. Like President Woodrow Wilson (a spectacular international failure in his day), today's ideologues see a model society already at work in the United States: a combination of law, liberal freedoms, competitive private enterprise, and regular, contested elections with universal suffrage. All that remains is to remake the world in the image of this "free society."

This idea is dangerous whistling in the dark. Although great power action may have morally or politically desirable consequences, identifying with it is perilous because the logic and methods of state action are not those of universal rights. All established states put their own interests first. If they have the power, and the end is considered sufficiently vital, states justify the means of achieving it (though rarely in public) — particularly when they think God is on their side. Both good and evil empires have produced the barbarization of our era, to which the "war against terror" has now contributed.

While threatening the integrity of universal values, the campaign to spread democracy will not succeed. The 20th century demonstrated that states could not simply remake the world or abbreviate historical transformations. Nor can they easily effect social change by transferring institutions across borders. Even within the ranks of territorial nation-states, the conditions for effective democratic government are rare: an existing state enjoying legitimacy, consent, and the ability to mediate conflicts between domestic groups. Without such consensus, there is no single sovereign people and therefore no legitimacy for arithmetical majorities. When this consensus — be it religious, ethnic, or both — is absent, democracy has been suspended (as is the case with democratic institutions in Northern Ireland), the state has split (as in Czechoslovakia), or society has descended into permanent civil war (as in Sri Lanka). "Spreading democracy" aggravated ethnic conflict and produced the disintegration of states in multinational and multicommunal regions after both 1918 and 1989, a bleak prospect.

Beyond its scant chance of success, the effort to spread standardized Western democracy also suffers from a fundamental paradox. In no small part, it is conceived of as a solution to the dangerous transnational problems of our day. A growing part of human life now occurs beyond the influence of voters — in transnational public and private entities that have no electorates, or at least no democratic ones. And electoral democracy cannot function effectively outside political units such as nation-states. The powerful states are therefore trying to spread a system that even they find inadequate to meet today's challenges.

Europe proves the point. A body like the European Union (EU) could develop into a powerful and effective structure precisely because it has no electorate other than a small number (albeit growing) of member governments. The EU would be nowhere without its "democratic deficit," and there can be no future for its parliament, for there is no "European people," only a collection of "member peoples," less than half of whom bothered to vote in the 2004 EU parliamentary elections. "Europe" is now a functioning entity, but unlike the member states it enjoys no popular legitimacy or electoral authority. Unsurprisingly, problems arose as soon as the EU moved beyond negotiations between governments and became the subject of democratic campaigning in the member states.

The effort to spread democracy is also dangerous in a more indirect way: It conveys to those who do not enjoy this form of government the illusion that it actually governs those who do. But does it? We now know something about how the actual decisions to go to war in Iraq were taken in at least two states of unquestionable democratic bonafides: the United States and the United Kingdom. Other than creating complex problems of deceit and concealment, electoral democracy and representative assemblies had little to do with that process. Decisions were taken among small groups of people in private, not very different from the way they would have been taken in non-democratic countries. Fortunately, media independence could not be so easily circumvented in the United Kingdom. But it is not electoral democracy that necessarily ensures effective freedom of the press, citizen rights, and an independent judiciary.

14.11 MICHELINE R. ISHAY ("DEBATING GLOBALIZATION AND INTERVENTION: SPARTACISTS VERSUS CAESARISTS," 2006)

There was a time, not so long ago, when international politics witnessed a more unified universal human rights worldview. From the Dumbarton Oaks meeting to the San Francisco conference near the end of World War II, political leaders and activists across the globe conceived of a new international order, guided by the principles of the Universal Declaration of Human Rights, dedicated to global economic reconstruction and development, and enforced by a new international organization (the United Nations) under the leadership of the major victorious powers. Unfortunately, that vision has been challenged ever since, first by the events of the cold war, then by globalization, and now by the war on terror.

While the human rights community has hardly abandoned its myriad concerns, its pre-September 11 preoccupations have now been overshadowed by a searing divide over a central question: the human rights implications of America's global military campaign. For many on both sides of this debate, America is viewed in Manichean terms — either as a crucial entity for the worldwide advance of human rights or as an empire disposed to quash human rights in the pursuit of unlimited power.

Great power has always engendered resistance, and it may thus be appropriate to draw on the era of imperial Rome to shed light on the current schism. In that spirit, one side in the current debate might be labeled "Ceasarists," after the emperor who not only spread Greco-Roman civilization with ruthless force, but who also implemented new constitutions in conquered territories while extending the Roman vision of republican citizenship. I will call the other side in the debate "Sparticists," after the Thracian gladiator Spartacus, leader of the famous rebellion of slaves against the rule of Caesar's Rome.

Today's Spartacists share an anti-authoritarian, anti-imperialist and often isolationist view. Most Spartacists are highly critical of unfettered economic globalization, sanctioned by US hegemonic influence in the cultural, political and military realms. When this influence is imperiled in places of critical geopolitical or economic importance, according to Spartacists, force is used to repress the "empire's" perceived "outlaws." In these circumstances, Spartacists argue, the message and institutional mechanisms of human rights are invoked as mere subterfuges to hide imperial self-interests, which often require replacing rogue regimes with more docile governments.

The Caesarist worldview, on the other hand, maintains that in a world of terrorism, rampant nationalism, civil wars and proliferating mass destruction weapons, the US is the only power able to counter international dangers driven by fundamentalist groups or authoritarian regimes. For weaker states, Caesarists argue, there is no alternative but to gravitate within the orbit of US influence, an outcome that will ultimately deliver economic and human rights benefits. As the US wages war against anti-democratic forces, it is accepted that trampling on civil rights and international conventions may be necessary means to achieve victory.

These two human rights worldviews crystallized as the Bush administration shed longstanding US commitments — at least in principle — to act within the constraints of international laws, norms and institutions. In that context, it is not surprising that debate increasingly centered on an assessment of the means and ends of American power rather than on impersonal forces like "globalization," or on bypassed international organizations like the UN or NATO. As the Bush administration increasingly made human rights promotion the central rationale for its global agenda, the connection between rhetoric and reality became the focus of intense debate.

It is worth noting at the outset that the dispute over the human rights implications of American power transcends the ideological cleavage between "left" and "right" — as both groups experience bitter internal divisions over the means and ends of US foreign and "homeland security" policies. The following discussion treats "Caesarism" and "Spartacism" as Weberian "ideal types," representing starkly opposed positions on the merits of globalization, humanitarian intervention and nation-building. Viewing consequential policy issues through these two different prisms can pave the way for a critical assessment of both, a necessary step toward a more integrated position on human rights.

Dueling over Globalization

Spartacists and Caesarists voice the position of two camps increasingly at odds with each other, each believing themselves to be the representative of the more authentic human rights position. On the issue of globalization, the Caesarists (exemplified by journalist and author Thomas Friedman) maintain that it is the absence — rather than the deepening — of free trade that accounts for pervasive poverty, and arguing that the benefits of trade require societies committed to accountable and transparent institutions. This position has been advanced by mainstream US politicians of both major political parties, who have supported free trade agreements (i.e., NAFTA and the WTO, etc.) without insisting on serious labor standards, professing along with other leaders like British Prime Minister Tony Blair and former advisor on German Economic Affairs, Hans Gerhard Petersmann, that expanded trade will ineluctably help universalize liberal notions of human rights.

By contrast, for the Spartacist grassroot activists of the world social forums, globalization has shaped a new imperial economic regime, one in which the IMF, WTO, and G-8 and other international institutions continue to reflect the self-interest of the wealthiest states. If anything, for Spartacists, globalization has produced a sinister reality: one in which labor rights have been undercut and welfare policies scrapped; one in which bait and switch immigration policies shaped by elites in the privileged world have intensified the hardships suffered by refugees and immigrants fleeing from poverty, repression or war; one in which the poorest countries are getting poorer both in relative and absolute terms; and one in which environmental degradations driven by pollution and deforestation have endangered the livelihood of indigenous peoples. After September 11, these conflicting human rights positions over globalization intensified, turning into a broader debate over the legitimacy of American economic and military power.

Dueling over Humanitarian Interventions: The Sharpening of the Spartacist and Caesarist Positions

With the September 11 attack against America, humanitarian agencies, NGOs, academics and grassroots activists found themselves more intensely split than ever over the role of military intervention. Needless to say, international legal documents have hardly provided clear guidelines to human rights sympathizers. For instance, while the UN Charter had decreed the inviolability of sovereign states, the Convention Against Genocide permitted the indictment of individuals charged with crimes against humanity, thereby circumventing state authority. Further, over the years, the members of the UN Security Council failed to show the level of commitment to human rights envisioned by the founders of the UN and the international body consequently attracted the criticisms of human right supporters.

In the absence of consistent legal criteria and wavering UN policy regarding human rights, activists oscillated between Spartacist and Ceasarist impulses. As Spartacists, they criticized the unchallenged economic and military hegemony of the US, even as local acts of barbarism provoked thoughts of Caesarist solutions, including condemnations of the inaction of states in the face of human rights violations. Over time, however, these mixed sentiments over humanitarian interventions gradually gave way to a more dichotomized worldview, as early concerns over US inaction engendered the post–September 11 reality of global interventionism. These conflicted views were heightened by the invasions of Afghanistan and Iraq, and confrontational rhetoric aimed primarily at Iran and North Korea. To illuminate the role of humanitarian intervention in intensifying the Caesarist/Spartacist divide, it is worth briefly reviewing the background of post–Cold War intervention.

At first, it may well have been the specter of the Vietnam War that initially prevented the US and NATO from sending troops to prevent mass killings and genocide in Bosnia (1992–1995). In a sense, the Somali fiasco of 1993 had reignited the paralyzing "Vietnam syndrome," seemingly laid to rest in Desert Storm, as attacks on UN troops inspired visions of new quagmires. American and European indifference toward mass suffering in Rwanda (1994) and Bosnia reignited interventionist sentiments among human rights sympathizers. With graphic coverage of rape camps and evidence of mass graves, the US, NATO and UN were now condemned for their insufficient political will. Amnesty International and Human Rights Watch, among other NGOs, Nobel Peace Prize laureate Elie Wiesel and the writer Susan Sontag, among many other public personalities, demanded action.[1] For many representatives of the human rights community, NATO intervention in Bosnia in 1995, which quickly halted the ongoing massacre, came far too late.

By the time of the Rambouillet Conference, held in France in February 1999, to resolve the crisis in the Serb-controlled province of Kosovo, the human rights community was clearly divided over the prospect of another US-led NATO air campaign against the actions of Serb leader Slobodan Milosovic. Intervening on behalf of the Kosovars was a US and NATO "liberal imperialist adventure," proclaimed British scholar Tariq Ali in *The Guardian*, giving voice to the Spartacist standpoint. Others reacted similarly, condemning the intervention as an aggressive action overriding international law and the sacrosanctity of sovereignty stipulated by the UN Charter.[2] For many human rights critics, air strikes in civilian areas were seen as barbarous acts, comparable to similar tactics used in Vietnam and World War II.[3] Whether the Kosovars would have faced genocide had Milosovic not been stopped, was a question that only a handful of prominent voices in the human rights community were prepared to ask.[4]

The Caesarist camp won the day when force was used to prevent genocide. Their view was forcefully articulated by leaders like Clinton, who drew on the appeasement of Adolf Hitler in the 1930s to illustrate the need to intervene in Kosovo: "Just imagine if leaders back then had acted wisely and early enough, how many lives could have been saved, how many Americans would not have had to die?"[5] 11,334 Albanians, murdered by Serbian forces, were later found buried in 529 sites in Kosovo alone, and despite the bombing of civilian sites, the campaign, one could well argue, had stopped the ethnic cleansing and prevented thousands, if not hundreds of thousands, of civilian deaths.[6] Strangely, it was American and European leaders — and not the Spartacist-dominated human rights community — who now appeared united behind an interventionist human rights stance. As US Secretary of State Madeleine Albright explained during the Kosovo intervention, the US was determined "never [to] fall back to complacency, or [to] presume that totalitarianism is forever dead, or retreat in the face of aggression."[7]

Such views were merely a means to camouflage the consolidation of US hegemony in military and economic affairs, claimed Spartacist protesters during repeated demonstrations throughout Europe against the military intervention in Kosovo, and in other mass protests at G-8 and IMF meetings. Yet the burgeoning anti-globalization and anti-intervention movement was soon silenced by the September 11, 2001, attacks on America. For a short time, given the horrendous acts committed by Al Qaeda, President Bush's declaration that one must simply choose the American side in a global war had resonated broadly within the human rights community.

With the Afghan war well on its way, and building on the legacy of the Clinton administration, Bush struck a Caesarist human rights tone in a speech to West Point cadets: "In our development aid, in our diplomatic efforts, in our international broadcasting, and in our educational assistance, the United States will promote moderation and tolerance and human rights. And we will defend the peace that makes all progress possible."[8] Unsurprisingly, Bush's invocation of the right to self-defense as stipulated by international law to justify the US intervention in Afghanistan did not get the unqualified support of the human rights community. Indeed this view was rebuffed by some Spartacists who, like Dietmar Henning, claimed that "the continuous bombardment of an impoverished and defenseless country by the world's most powerful military nation has clearly demonstrated that what is at stake is not a police action against a few terrorists. It has, rather, the makings of a classical colonial war, which has as its aim the military suppression of an entire region and the establishment of regimes that are willing to places themselves at the beck and call of the USA."[9]

When weapons of mass destruction were not found in occupied Iraq, casting doubt on the main original rationale for the US-led invasion, Bush, along with Blair and other leaders of the US-led coalition against Iraq, reiterated even more forcefully the human rights dimension of their Caesarist mission. "A democratic government in Iraq that truly cares for the welfare of its people would benefit not only Iraqis but the region and the whole world," asserted US Deputy Secretary of Defense Paul Wolfowitz.[10] While the human rights justification for the intervention in Iraq became the lynchpin of the neo-conservative foreign policy platform, it was also supported by many liberal and leftist human rights activists, journalists and scholars (associated in the past with the Spartacist position), like Christopher Hitchens, Thomas Friedman, Niall Ferguson, and Michael Ignatieff, who regarded the approaching war in Iraq as an opportunity — whatever the role of American geopolitical interests — to eradicate an oppressive and genocidal regime, which had, among other large-scale atrocities, executed approximately 100,000 Kurds, according to Human Rights Watch, in the months of February to September 1988 alone.[11]

Yet most on the liberal to the left side of the Spartacist political spectrum did not agree with the conclusions of Hitchens and Ignatieff. The escalating confrontation between the Caesarists and Spartacists, reaching a zenith as the US prepared to attack Iraq, dramatized the extent to which the division over the US global role had supplanted old ideological differences over human rights. From US Governor Howard Dean, to many leftist European politicians, to scholars such as Chalmers Johnson and Noam Chomsky, the Spartacists were enraged by US policy toward Iraq. In the words of British historian

Eric Hobsbawm, the question was "How is the world to confront — contain — the US? Some people, believing that they have not the power to confront the US, prefer to join it. More dangerous are those who hate the ideology behind the Pentagon, but support the US project on the grounds that it will eliminate some local and regional injustices. This may be called an imperialism of human rights."[12] Just as the conservative Caesarists have attracted odd leftist bedfellows, Spartacist anti-war demonstrations were ironically joined by the nationalist right, including US politician and commentator Pat Buchanan, French leader of Le Front National Jean-Marie Le Pen, and Austrian political leader Georg Haider, who viewed the war in Iraq as "America's war against civilization."

Dueling over Nation-Building

If war is an expected source of division, the issue of how to build a democratic culture in conflict-ridden civil societies also continues to confuse the human rights community. To what extent (if any) should the United States (and its Western allies) take the lead in directing nation-building?

For Caesarists, like best-selling author Niall Ferguson, the United States has been too long in denial of its imperial role, and must learn to take seriously its formidable responsibilities in the world. It is the only power, Ferguson maintains (with other like-minded Ceasarists), that has the capacity to bring prosperity, peace and human rights to divided societies in an increasingly hostile world environment. The real problem is that the US, unlike its British predecessor, has lacked the will to make a long-term commitment to nation-building.[13]

To leave only several thousand American troops centered around Kabul, as the US did after toppling the Taliban regime in Afghanistan, or to fail to halt gross human rights violations in Liberia, Sudan and other trouble spots of limited geopolitical importance to the US, argue Caesarists, will only plant the seeds of demise of the new American empire. The British Empire sent legions of career civil servants abroad to permanent posts, and the American empire will be short-lived if it fails

to emulate that model. In that regard, it is a dangerous sign that the US has failed to send thousands of Arabic-speaking envoys to the Middle East, well equipped to help in the process of democratization. While institutional efforts, such as truth commissions, are steps in the right direction, it is time, Caesarists argue, for the US to reclaim its moral authority by fully committing itself to the full spectrum of nation-building activities.

That US track record of alleged detachment has, however, been intensely challenged by Spartacists. For Chalmers Johnson, the fact that the US has spread hundreds of its military bases in geopolitically and economically strategic areas of the world is sufficient evidence of its long-standing imperialist nature.[14] That the United States denies rights under the Geneva Convention to Guantanamo prisoners, and conducts torture of alleged insurgents in Abu Ghraib prison and elsewhere, demonstrates the emptiness of its claim to represent an "empire of liberty." Spartacists add that the United States has used the war on terror to create an elaborate system of surveillance, which has enabled authorities to violate privacy rights, to harass domestic dissidents and to deport peaceful immigrants as criminals — thereby denying fundamental rights of hospitality to foreigners.

These abuses cumulatively reveal the Janus face of the American empire's purported "good intentions." The Spartacists predict that the US will suffer other cases of blowback like the one experienced on September 11, arguing that such attacks are due not to US neglect of global problems — but to the excessive and repressive nature of US global commitments, as the US supports authoritarian regimes in places like Saudi Arabia or Pakistan whenever it appears to serve its economic or geopolitical interests. That long history of support of "friendly" dictators throughout the cold war, from its current refusal to submit to international institutions such as the International Criminal Court, preferring to withhold evidence that could implicate its own officials during truth commission investigations (in Haiti, El Salvador, Guatemala, Chile, and Chad among other post-authoritarian countries which the US supported),[15] shows all too well that the United States remains above justice while promoting democracy and human rights for the rest of the world. Even for those more inclined to acknowledge some measure of good intentions on the part of the US, it is daunting to recognize that out of sixteen cases of US military occupation going back to 1945, only four countries (Japan, Germany, Panama and Grenada) emerged as democracies.[16]

While the Caesarist and Spartacist discourses have been sharply opposed on questions of US foreign policy, both perspectives have supported reconciliatory efforts consistent with human rights. From South Africa and Chad, to Ecuador and Chile, to East Timor and Nepal, to Palestine and Iraq, human rights activists are struggling to forge new paths toward reconciliation shaped by one or the other worldview. The spread of truth commissions, among other efforts, has rekindled a new sense of justice and human rights across the globe, helping to heal deeply aggrieved societies. While truth commissions inevitably involve hard trade-offs between collective healing and justice for victims, these commissions provide an important institutional mechanism to correct wrongdoing and build the judicial apparatus in weak or failed states. Without the help of the international community in synergy with grassroots and local organizations, most agree that reconciliation and nation-building efforts will not succeed.

What really separates Spartacists from Caesarists with respect to nation-building is neither the merits of truth commissions, nor the broader goal of reconstructing civil society as an anchor for progress in democratization — most adherents from all sides are in principle supportive of these means and ends in conflict-ridden regions. The disagreement, which divides the two camps, is over the prospect of US leadership in the process of promoting reconciliation, human rights and nation-building. While Caesarists prefer to seize the unique opportunities offered by US military might, Spartacists, fearing that unilateral US intervention will create backlashes and power abuses, insist on multilateral involvement supported by

international organizations' efforts as essential to the advancement of human rights in war-torn societies.

Transcending Spartacism and Caesarism

Can the Spartacist and Caesarist worldviews be reconciled? A vital first step in that process will be for human rights adherents to recall and reclaim the integrative and universal vision of human rights, encapsulated in the UN Universal Declaration of Human Rights, after World War II. Before making reflexive generalizations regarding United States policies or purposes, advocates of human rights should reacquaint themselves with the indivisible and inalienable legacy of human rights founded on civil, political, social, economic, cultural and security rights. Knowledge of that tradition is critical to avoiding the pitting of one set of fundamental human rights against another (e.g., civil rights versus the right to security). It is a tradition that provides tools for critical assessments and constructive proposals, rather than automatic rejection or embracing of humanitarian intervention.

In applying that tradition to current challenges, how can the human rights community carve a strategic position between charges of indifference to human rights abuses, to which Spartacists are vulnerable, and accusations of imperialism associated with Caesarist support for wars against tyrannical regimes? Can one be both a Spartacist and a Caesarist? The following addresses this question and offers guidelines toward a realist approach to human rights, drawing from both camps, while briefly reviewing the salient issues of globalization, humanitarian intervention and nation-building.

The claim by Spartacists that globalization, with the United States in the driver's seat, is antithetical to the advancement of human rights is simply excessive. One should recognize that there are aspects of capitalism that represent dramatic improvement when compared to the feudal arrangements that prevail in much of the global South: its progressive capacity, its formidable power to develop the forces of production, to overcome scarcity, and to kindle humankind's unlimited potential. That hardly entails an unqualified endorsement of neo-liberal ideology, which is accountable for unfair rules imposed on developing countries by the institutions controlling globalization (e.g., the IMF).

While a new human rights realism should always condemn the harsh conditions of workers in sweatshops, it should also acknowledge that the often-romanticized alternative of self-sufficient agrarian feudalism might be even worse. The Spartacists should confront what it means, for example, when millions of young women are left beyond the reach of globalization, with no choice but to be subjugated under patriarchal domination, or under the arbitrary tyranny of local mullahs in one or another remote corner of the world like Sudan and Nigeria. Such conditions are not only unacceptable from a universal human rights standpoint; they are hardly conducive to domestic or international peace. For women and other destitute people within the most impoverished and conflict-prone regions of the world, opportunities for change offered by market-driven economic growth should be welcomed when synchronized with redistributive policies to ensure sustained economic welfare and democratization. While market development should be included in reconstruction efforts, it should also be carefully monitored as not to create new forms of inequity. Caesarists who place all their faith in markets, and who ignore the needs of workers and the poor in areas like Iraq, will likely see their dreams of liberty come to ruin. The indivisibility of political and economic human rights objectives should always be kept in sight.

With respect to intervention, it is important to distinguish a human rights position *ad bellum* (before the war), *in bello* (during the war), and *post bellum* (post-war reconciliation and reconstruction efforts).

Spartacists are correct to insist to draw attention to grave human rights abuses that are on no one's active political agenda, such as in Rwanda and Sudan. Yet human rights advocates should not shrink, as Spartacists often do, from actively opposing oppressive regimes, like that of Saddam Hussein, simply because they have become the *bête noire* of British and US leaders.

One can add, perhaps with a Caeasarist impulse, that human rights activists should condemn repressive regimes with equal fervor regardless of whether they are seen as friends or foes by the US or other powers. With this in mind, one cannot disparage the impact of power politics or the CNN effect, which draws human rights interest in one area of the world while overlooking others. Because great powers are less likely to intervene in countries which possess nuclear arsenals and because great powers are not likely to work beneath their geopolitical or economic radars, human rights sympathizers should not shy away from working within the ambit of realpolitik, making the political rhetoricians of human rights accountable for their deeds and promised missions. In this respect, one could argue that the war against the Taliban, while hardly undertaken to liberate women from feudal slavery, had considerable (though not sufficient) positive consequence for women's rights, just as NATO's intervention in Kosovo may well have averted a repetition of Serbia's genocidal war against Muslims in Bosnia. In these circumstances, one can support the plausibility of the Caeasarist case for humanitarian intervention.

Even if a convincing human rights case for intervention is made, Spartacists are right to insist on maintaining the balance between means and ends during a war. Multilateral actions, guided by international laws, are more legitimate in the eyes of the intervened. Further failing to respect accepted civil and international human rights (such as at Guantanamo or Abu Ghraib) may preclude the ultimate achievement of human rights goals, sending a message of hypocrisy to the rest of the world. Spartacists are also correct to consider the possible negative consequences of military action, such as the prospects that the invasion of Iraq, undertaken in the name of democracy and human rights, may result in widening violence within the Arab world, destabilizing the Middle East and spawning more terrorism against the United States and its allies.

At the same time, Caesarists are correct to point out that international legal documents have hardly provided clear guidelines to human rights sympathizers. Indeed, over the years, the members of the UN Security Council failed to show the level of commitment to human rights envisioned by the founders of the UN, and as such the international body has attracted the criticisms of human right supporters, strengthening thereby rationale for intervention outside the aegis of the UN or NATO.

To overcome the limitations of either approach, one can deplore the long record of human rights abuses in the foreign or domestic policies of all five permanent members of the Security Council or within NATO; support with Caesarists those instances when military action, even if unilateral, advances the cause of human rights, while accepting the general Spartacist principle that the UN, multilateral efforts and local human rights–motivated NGOs are preferable mechanisms for resolving humanitarian crises.

Post bellum, the problem for some Caesarists leaning toward support for Bush's human rights efforts is that from Egypt to the Palestinian territories to Iraq, and now Lebanon, the neo-conservatives have privileged political rights over social and economic rights, hence strengthening fundamentalist groups, which have gained grassroots support thanks to their social welfare organizations. A successful nation-building effort, based on human rights, still requires commitment to the encompassing principles, adopted by the Universal Declaration adopted in 1948. In other words, privileging selected clusters of rights as the Bush administration did (namely security or political rights) over other families of rights (such as economic rights) created narrow right-specific policy, which has paved the road to resentment and reaction, as evidenced by the inability to counter the popularity of Hizbollah in Lebanon.

At the same time, rejecting the hawkish quick-fix predisposition of some Caesarists, as Spartacists have correctly done, does not absolve the human rights community from providing viable alternatives. Rage and ridicule directed at the Bush administration and the impulse to simply withdraw from unstable countries and regions do not amount to an alternative approach to the linked problems of terrorism, human rights violations and poverty. That alternative needs to draw lessons from the "global New Deal" approach to foreign policy envisioned at the end of World War II, and within that tradition, I will offer guidelines for future foreign policy, some broad and long term in scope, others more immediate.

Franklin Roosevelt's approach succeeded in overcoming the domestic crisis caused by the Great Depression, crushed the global threat of fascism and set in motion the integration of the European continent, long plagued by wars. Prior to Franklin Roosevelt, assistance to the poor and the unemployed had hitherto depended upon the discretion of whichever leadership happened to be in power. Under Roosevelt, welfare programs would be systematically grounded on legal, social, and economic rights, institutionalized with the development of the welfare state, and strengthened by the need to sustain societal cohesion during World War II and the cold war, while spreading throughout the Western world. A key problem was that Bretton Woods and the Marshall Plan (the latter, implemented two years after the death of Roosevelt, was certainly consistent with his vision) was limited to Europe and did not extend to the colonies and the developing world. September 11, 2001, should have awakened us to the need to extend that vision globally.

While the US and other powerful states may lack the will and resources to address human rights violations in territories that become the hotbed of terrorist activities, a sustained investment of political and economic resources in selected places may well create new outposts of democracy that could in turn stimulate further regional economic growth, democratization and human rights. How would this start? It could take the form of New Deal–style public works projects aimed at relieving unemployment by putting money in the hands of ordinary workers. These projects would be designed to build infrastructure for future economic development, such as ports, power plants and desalinization plants, that would then simulate public and private investment. Such outposts (in Palestine or even the Sudan, for example) could represent magnets that would then stimulate further regional economic growth, democratization and human rights. (There is unlikely to be a better way of delegitimizing or deradicalizing extremism than to outbid their popular and grassroots support where it counts, namely by investing more heavily and effectively in the same domains Islamists have sought to dominate: public health, education and economic welfare.)

Empowering women in destabilized and deeply ingrained authoritarian societies can also be part of long-term non-violent policies designed to democratize the Middle East as well as other regions of less geopolitical interest to the US and its friends. For instance, empowering women (with microlending, literacy efforts, vocational training, etc.) even within the world's poorest and most repressive states can galvanize democratic forces, just as suffragette efforts stimulated democratic impulses in Western civil societies during the late nineteenth century. One needs to free women, and men will be freer to join them in challenging political oppression.

Envisioning non-violent long-term strategies will also require tackling pressing problems. How do we reduce violent conflicts in a region of the world where Sunnis and Shiites, Israelis and Palestinians, Americans and Iranians are at each other throats? Agreeing with the Caesarists on the laudable democratic goals articulated by the Bush administration, and deploring with the Spartacists the means employed by US foreign policy, one can easily conclude that bringing democracy and human rights to the Middle East should have taken place first in Palestine. Why Palestine? Palestine is relatively tiny: it has only a small fraction of the population of Iraq. Unlike Iraq, Palestinians are animated by a shared national identity. Addressing Palestinian aspirations would have responded to the Arab world's most resonant source of grievance against the US — rather than feeding the darkest Arab fears about American designs. After the "shock and awe" of the Iraq invasion and its aftermath, never has the hatred against Americans in the Arab world (and elsewhere) been so visceral, never was the idea of a US double standard for Jews and Arabs so entrenched. Creating a viable Palestine would be a far more difficult undertaking today than it would have been just a few years ago. Given the massive US resource commitment to Iraq, few will be eager to fund a new nation-building project in the Middle East, a prospect made even more daunting by the post-Iraq invasion radicalization of the region, including the ascension of Hamas and Hizbollah. Yet it would be tragic if a disastrous misallocation of resources in Iraq provides yet another excuse for ignoring the problem that most needs attention. In short, enduring peace in the Middle East and elsewhere cannot be achieved without recognizing the indivisibility of universal human rights: security, political, economic welfare and cultural rights.

Conflict prevention strategies such as these could well prove far less costly than President Bush's campaign to "hunt terrorism wherever it is harbored," a campaign that could well spawn more terrorism then it stops. A serious search for alternatives to the current US drift toward endless and expanding war are missing both from Spartacist and Caesarist worldviews. Devising non-violent strategies for reconciliation, democratization and human rights should be the place where human rights advocates — whatever the lean toward Spartacist or the Caesarist approach toward US intervention — can unite in building a viable future for universal human rights.

SEPTEMBER 6, 2006

ENDNOTES

1 "The Fall of Srebrenica and the Failure of UN Peacekeeping," *Human Rights Watch* 7, no. 13 (October 1995), http://www.hrw. org/summaries/s.bosnia9510.html (consulted November 8, 2006); Amnesty International, Carl Bildt, Opening Remarks by Mr. Carl Bildt, the High Representative, at the first meeting of the Human Rights Task Force, Brussels, January 29, 1996, http://web.amnesty.org/library/Index/

ENGEUR630141996?open&of=ENG-332 (consulted March 31, 2004); Susan Sontag, "Why Are We in Kosovo?" *New York Times Magazine*, May 2, 1999; Elie Wiesel, in "Interview with Elie Wiesel," *Tikkun*, July/August 1999, p. 33.

2 Editorial Comments, "NATO's Kosovo Intervention," *American Journal of International Law* 93, no. 4 (October 1999); Eqbal Ahmed, "The Controversy over Kosovo," *Al-Ahram Weekly*, April 15–21, 1999; N. F. Bradshaw, "The Legality of NATO's Attack on Serbia," *Conflict Studies Research Centre* (Royal Military Academy, Sandhurst), 174 (1999), http://www.mpr.co.uk/scripts/sweb.dll/li_archive_item?method=GET&object=CSRC_174 (consulted November 8, 2006).

3 J. Bryan Hehir, "Kosovo: A War of Values and the Values of War," *America* 180 (May 15, 1999): 7–12.

4 Samantha Power, *A Problem from Hell* (New York: Basic Books, 2002).

5 Quoted in ibid. p, 449.

6 Ibid., 450.

7 Madeleine K. Albright, "Speech on the Occasion of the Accession of the Czech Republic, Hungary and Poland to the North Atlantic Treaty Organization at the Truman Presidential Library," March 12, 1999, http://www.mbk.org/php/index.php?name=News&file=article&sid=235 (consulted November 8, 2006).

8 President Bush delivers graduate speech at West Point, June 2002, The White House Papers, http://www.whitehouse.gov/news/releases/2002/06/20020601-3.html (con-sulted November 8, 2006); see also Paul Wolfowitz, "U.S. Dedicated to Liberation of Afghanistan," speech delivered June 26, 2002, American Embassy, http://www.globalsecurity.org/military/library/news/2002/06/mil-020626-usia04.htm (consulted November 8, 2006)

9 Dietmar Henning, "German Green Party Supports War against Afghanistan," October 19, 2001, World Socialist Web Site, http://www.wsws.org/articles/2001/oct2001/gree-o19.shtml (consulted November 8, 2006).

10 "Wolfowitz Says Democracy in Iraq Would Benefit Whole World," July 17, 2002, http://www.usembassy.it/file2002_07/alia/a2071801.htm (consulted November 8, 2006).

11 Samantha Power, op.cit., 244.

12 Eric Hobsbawm, "America's Imperial Delusion," *The Guardian*, June 15, 2003.

13 Niall Ferguson, *Colossus: The Price of America's Empire* (New York: Penguin Press, 2004).

14 Chalmers Johnson, *The Sorrows of Empire, Militarism, Secrecy and the End of the Republic* (New York: Metropolitan Books, Henry Holt and Company, 2004).

15 Priscilla B. Hayner, *Unspeakable Truth: Confronting State Terror and Atrocity* (New York: Routledge, 2001), 242–243.

16 Mixin Pei, "Lessons from the Past: The American Record of Nation-Building," Carnegie Endowment Policy Paper 24, April 2003.

PART VI

Human Rights and Legal Documents: A Brief Historical Narrative

INTRODUCTION

The modern history of human rights legal documents was shaped by critical social events, beginning with the Enlightenment's popular and legislative struggle to create representative governments, and followed by late nineteenth and twentieth-century efforts to establish an international human rights regime. While the modern edifices of the nation-state were justified in universal human rights terms, the tension between allegiance to one's state and a cosmopolitan commitment to human rights remains a continuous source of discord within human rights. The legal journey of human rights can be divided into five historical phases, following an organizational trajectory similar to that adopted in Parts I to V of this reader.

The first historical phase coincides with the Enlightenment's efforts to curtail the power of the king and strengthen the role of parliament. The second covers the nineteenth century's struggle to broaden the legitimacy of the state, as a growing class of industrial workers began to demand political and economic rights. The third phase encompasses twentieth-century efforts to construct an international legal regime that would prevent interstate wars and acts of genocide. The fourth comprises the development of legal human rights documents shaped by the demands of former colonies, as they joined the international community. The fifth phase focuses on the development of rights-specific documents (for women, immigrants, refugees, etc.) shaped by globalization.

Phase I: The Enlightenment Project

Efforts to limit the power of the king began well before the Enlightenment, in Medieval Europe, with the promulgation of the Magna Charta (1215). Ironically, the Christian Crusades against Muslims had contributed inadvertently to human rights victories in England. The need for heavy taxation to finance the Third Crusade and for the ransom of Richard I after his capture by Holy Emperor Henry VI increased the financial demands on the English kingdom. The resulting tax burden on the landowning aristocracy provoked opposition, and feudal barons began to demand more power and rights. The Magna Charta of 1215, also known as the Articles of Barons, is the product of this struggle. It subsequently became a battle cry against oppression, as each succeeding generation invoked it to protect its own threatened liberties.

In England, the Petition of Right (1628) and the Habeas Corpus Act (1679) referred directly to the clause of the Charter of 1215 that stated that "no freeman shall be arrested, or detained in prison or deprived of this freehold ... except by the lawful judgment of his peers or by the law of his land." In the United States, both the national and state constitutions contain ideas and even phrases directly traceable to the Magna Charta. In that sense, it is the Magna Charta that is invoked whenever people oppose government efforts to suspend civil liberties in the name of raison d'état.

The English Bill of Rights (1689) codified the rights and liberties of subjects and provided rules for succession of the British crown. It also granted the rights foundation on which the British government based its legitimacy after the 1688 Glorious Revolution. The product of a century-long struggle between the kings and the parliament, this bill subordinated the monarchy to parliament and provided the English people freedom from arbitrary government. It also forbade the monarch to dispense with the law. Among its most important stipulations were that elections must be free and that members of parliament must have complete freedom of speech.

Building on the English Bill of Rights, the U.S. Declaration of Independence (1776) announced the secession of the thirteen American colonies from England. Largely written by Thomas Jefferson, and influenced by liberal thinkers like Locke and Paine, the declaration advanced a conception of the social contract based on a doctrine of fundamental natural rights. The notion that "all men are created equal, that they are endowed by their Creator with inalienable rights, that among these are life, liberty, and the pursuit of happiness," had an electrifying effect far beyond the thirteen colonies. The conception of a people's right to a government of their choice helped inspire Antonio de Nariño and Francisco de Miranda to launch rebellions against the Spanish Empire in South America and French revolutionaries like Maximilien Robespierre to challenge feudal absolutism in France.

In the spirit of the U.S. Declaration of Independence, the French Declaration of the Rights of Man and Citizen (1789) represented another milestone in the Enlightenment's human rights journey. It derived its doctrine of natural rights from John Locke and the *Encyclopédie*, its theory of the general will and popular sovereignty from Jean-Jacques Rousseau, the notion of individual safeguards against arbitrary police or judicial action from Beccaria and Voltaire, and the inviolability of property rights from the physiocrats. It specified rights fundamental to individuals and was therefore, in the view of the French Jacobins, universally applicable. The declaration extended the liberties recognized during the American Revolution and became, in the words of nineteenth-century French historian Michelet, "the credo of a new age."

Phase II: From Social Reforms to the International Geneva Convention

If the Enlightenment introduced into world politics the notion that the state, with its separation of powers, existed only to secure the rights of its inhabitants and ultimately to extend those rights to humankind, the universality of that liberal vision would be severely challenged during the industrial revolution. Could the envisioned republican state secure the rights of all people, or even the rights of its own citizens? One should note that the American Constitution and the French Declaration of the Rights of Man and the Citizen both restricted voting rights and simply omitted social and economic rights.

During the nineteenth century, as the industrial revolution and economic globalization progressed, those limitations on universal rights would contribute to domestic and international conflict. As the prevailing elite understanding of the national interest proved too exclusive, the labor movement of the nineteenth century injected politics with a new democratic impulse. From the nineteenth century, radical and reformist socialists alike called for redefining the Enlightenment vision of the state to include increased economic equity at home and abroad. England led the way in adopting manhood suffrage and welfare reforms that would be later implemented by other industrialized states. For example, suffrage was advanced by the Chartist Petition of 1837 and the Second Reform Act of 1867; workers' health and safety by the Factory Health and Morals Acts of 1802 and the Factory Act of 1833; and limits on work by the Ten Hours Act of 1847. Other legislation advanced the right to education and other social welfare rights.[1]

Beyond domestic legal reforms, two critical international documents deserve our attention. One is the General Act of the Berlin Conference (1884), whose stipulation that "trading slaves is forbidden in compatibility with principles of international law" represented the success of the antislavery movement in making its cause a global norm. The other significant legal document grew out of the campaign launched by Henry Dunant to ensure the provision of medical treatment for wounded soldiers (see Section 10.7). Dunant's efforts culminated in the ratification of the Geneva Convention in 1864, a document later amended to include broader concerns with the wartime protection of human rights (see the "Geneva Convention Relative to the Treatment of Prisoners of War of 1949," Section 15.9).

Phase III: The Search for an International Legal Regime

The growing struggle over economic inequity within and between nations, colonial rivalries, and finally the descent into World War I prompted the search for additional humanitarian and peace efforts buttressed by international institutions. After World War I, liberal internationalists, led by American President Woodrow Wilson (1856–1924), sought to implement their conviction that human rights, commerce, and security needed to be integrated and safeguarded by international organizations. Building on the nineteenth-century Socialist Internationals, one of the two organizations that emerged at the Treaty of Versailles (1919) was the International Labor Organization (ILO). The ILO grafted internationalist socialist convictions onto liberal thought, insisting that world peace could be preserved only if workers' rights and basic standards of economic welfare were respected in all countries.

The other overarching organization, the League of Nations, placed the concept of collective security against aggression at the center of the effort to preserve international peace, and guaranteed the right to self-determination, though mainly to European nationalities. With the formation of new independent nations, the League of Nations also tried to guarantee the protection of minority rights (see the Covenant of the League of Nations and the Polish Minority Treaty, both adopted in 1919; see selections in Part IV). However, those efforts would prove ineffective and short-lived, weakened initially by the refusal of the United States to join the league and ultimately overtaken by the rise of fascism in Europe.

Phase IV: The Road to the U.N. Charter and the U.N. Universal Declaration of Human Rights

It would take another World War, leaving fifty million dead, to unleash new efforts to establish a new international regime to promote trade, human rights, and peace. In President Franklin Roosevelt's (1882–1945) message to Congress on the State of the

Union (1941), he defined "The Four Freedoms," which all Americans should defend in the face of Hitler's bid for unlimited power. The four essential human freedoms that must be secured worldwide, he proclaimed, were freedom of speech and expression, freedom of every person to worship God, freedom from want, and freedom from fear. With these principles, Roosevelt proceeded by pledging to the Europeans "our energies, our resources, and our organizing powers to give you the strength to regain and maintain a free world."

After Franklin Roosevelt's death in 1945 and the end of World War II, his wife, Eleanor Roosevelt (1884–1962), struggled to realize her husband's vision. Leading the American delegation at the San Francisco Conference, Eleanor Roosevelt helped plan the establishment of the United Nations (1945). The United Nations Charter (1945) reaffirmed the principle of nonintervention in the domestic affairs of other states (i.e., national sovereignty), thus initially appearing to preclude international intervention on behalf of human rights. Nevertheless, the Charter contained human rights clauses, including the affirmation of the "dignity and worth of the human person" and the equality of rights of men and women.

The first critical international human rights convention adopted after World War II was the United Nations Convention on the Prevention and Punishment of the Crime of Genocide (1948), which emerged in response to the attempt by Nazi Germany to exterminate the Jewish population of Europe. At the Nuremberg trials (1945–1946) and the Tokyo trial (1946), former Nazi and Japanese leaders were indicted and tried as war criminals by an international military tribunal. These trials established a new principle in international law, namely, that no one, whether a ruler, a public official, or a private individual, was immune from punishment for war crimes.

The Convention on the Prevention and Punishment of the Crime of Genocide reflected these principles, and they were unanimously adopted by the General Assembly on December 9, 1948. One day later, the General Assembly proceeded to adopt the Universal Declaration of Human Rights. When this historic document was put to a vote, the U.N. counted only fifty-eight members. Fifty states ratified the declaration, while Byeklorussia, Czchesolovakia, Poland, Saudi Arabia, South Africa, Ukraine, the Soviet Union, and Yugoslavia abstained. While nonbinding, the Universal Declaration became a touchstone of human rights law, recognizing the indivisibility and inalienability of security, civil, political, economic, social, and cultural rights, regardless of sex, nationality, and race.

Phase V: The Cold War, Anticolonial Struggle, and Division of Human Rights

If the two superpowers had briefly seemed united in support of a vision of a U.N. strong enough to enforce international peace, the onset of the Cold War quickly defeated that hope. One manifestation of the ideological conflict dividing the superpowers was their opposed conception of the domestic and economic systems to be adopted by the new states emerging from colonial rule. Two separate U.N. covenants were shaped by that dispute: the International Covenant on Civil and Political Rights (ICCPR) and the International Covenant on Economic, Social, and Cultural Rights (ICESCR). Drafted in 1966 and ratified ten years later, the ICCPR and ICESCR pitted the values of the leading capitalist states against a socialist conception of rights. Thus, the ICCPR emphasizes a Western liberal perspective on human rights, while the ICESCR stresses solidarity rights rooted in socialism. Moreover, the ICCPR requires immediate attention to the protection of rights, while the ICESCR contains a proviso that encourages states to recognize the rights contained in the covenant and to implement them over time.

Additional treaties and conventions often reflect that divide. For instance, the European Convention for the Protection of Human Rights and Fundamental Freedoms (1950) sought to provide citizens with a mechanism to redress violations of their civil and political rights. The European Social Charter (1961), by contrast, addressed the protection of economic and social rights. The American

Convention on Human Rights of 1969 was modeled on the European Convention and, like its European counterpart, is concerned mainly with civil and political rights, though a list of economic, social, and cultural rights was later added.

Phase VI: The Development of a Rights-Specific Legal Regime

If the 1948 U.N. Declaration on Human Rights had epitomized a vision of a unified human rights movement, human rights activists over subsequent decades increasingly divided their energies, promoting the rights of particular groups or causes. One outcome of that division was a plethora of specific, sometimes conflicting international human rights documents. These include, among a long list of treaties, declarations, and conventions, the United Nations Declaration of the Rights of the Disabled (1975; see Section 15.15), the United Nations Convention on the Elimination of All Forms of Discrimination against Women (1979; see selection in 15.16), the United Nations Rio Declaration on Environment and Development (1992; see selection in 12.7), United Nations documents on refugee and migrant rights (see selections in Part V), United Nations documents on sexual trafficking (see selections in Part V), and the Convention on the Rights of Children (see selections in Part VI).

Despite their diverse objectives, the abundance of international human rights legal documents and the unparalleled expansion of human rights organizations suggest a historic opportunity to build a stronger international human rights regime. That aspiration continues to be opposed by some adherents of the realist school of international relations, who maintain that the national interest takes precedence over, and often conflicts with, efforts to strengthen international regimes — including treaties and laws aimed at guaranteeing universal human rights. After September 11, this realist perspective has been used to justify both the narrowing of long-established civil liberties within the United States and the repudiation of international agreements protecting prisoner's rights (including the prohibition against torture).

Yet while particular conceptions of national or group interests will no doubt continue to threaten efforts to advance universal human rights, such setbacks should be seen in light of the enormous historical progress represented in the selections of this reader and depicted at length in this reader's companion volume *The History of Human Rights: From Ancient Times to the Era of Globalization (2004)*. The arrival and advance of the industrial age, along with a succession of wars and social revolutions, eventually gave rise to representative government and at least minimal domestic guarantees of social welfare within the developed world. While the events of September 11 and their aftermath have reminded us of the potential for violence associated with globalization, one may hope that current dangers will yield to rekindled efforts to secure human rights and welfare on the world stage.

VI.1 FRANKLIN DELANO ROOSEVELT ("THE FOUR FREEDOMS," 1941)

Message to Congress

January 6, 1941

I address you, the Members of the Seventy-seventh Congress, at a moment unprecedented in the history of the Union. I use the word "unprecedented" because at no previous time has American security been as seriously threatened from without as it is today.

Since the permanent formation of our government under the Constitution, in 1789, most of the periods of crisis in our history have related to our domestic affairs. Fortunately, only one of these — the four-year War Between the States — ever threatened our national unity. Today, thank God, one hundred and thirty million Americans, in forty-eight states, have forgotten points of the compass in our national unity.

It is true that prior to 1914 the United States often had been disturbed by events in other continents. We had even engaged in two wars with European nations and in a number of undeclared wars in the West Indies, in the Mediterranean, and in the Pacific for the maintenance of American rights and for the principles of peaceful commerce. But in no case had a serious threat been raised against our national safety or our continued independence.

What I seek to convey is the historic truth that the United States as a nation has at all times maintained clear, definite opposition to any attempt to lock us in behind an ancient Chinese wall while the procession of civilization went past. Today, thinking of our children and of their children, we oppose enforced isolation for ourselves or for any other part of the Americas. ...

Every realist knows that the democratic way of life is at this moment being directly assailed in every part of the world — assailed either by arms, or by secret spreading of poisonous propaganda by those who seek to destroy unity and promote discord in nations that are still at peace.

During sixteen long months this assault has blotted out the whole pattern of democratic life in an appalling number of independent nations, great and small. The assailants are still on the march, threatening other nations, great and small.

Therefore, as your President, performing my constitutional duty to "give to the Congress information of the state of the Union," I find it, unhappily, necessary to report that the future and the safety of our country and of our democracy are overwhelmingly involved in events far beyond our borders.

Armed defense of democratic existence is now being gallantly waged in four continents. If that defense fails, all the population and all the resources of Europe, Asia, Africa, and Australasia will be dominated by the conquerors. Let us remember that the total of those populations and their resources in those four continents greatly exceeds the sum total of the population and the resources of the whole of the western hemisphere — many times over. ... Just as our national policy in internal affairs has been based upon a decent respect for the rights and the dignity of all our fellow-men within our gates, so our national policy in foreign affairs has been based on a decent respect for the rights and dignity of all nations, large and small. And the justice of morality must and will win in the end. ...

Certainly this is no time for any of us to stop thinking about the social and economic problems which are the root cause of the social revolution which is today a supreme factor in the world.

For there is nothing mysterious about the foundations of a healthy and strong democracy. The basic things expected by our people of their political and economic systems are simple. They are:

Equality of opportunity for youth and for others.
Jobs for those who can work.
Security for those *who need it.*
The ending of special privilege for the few.
The preservation of *civil* liberties for all.
The enjoyment of the fruits of scientific progress
in a wider and constantly rising standard of living.

These are the simple, basic things that must never be lost sight of in the turmoil and unbelievable complexity of our modern world. The inner and abiding strength of our economic and political systems is dependent upon the degree to which they fulfill these expectations.

Many subjects connected with our social economy call for immediate improvement.

As examples:

We should bring more *citizens* under the coverage of old-age pensions and unemployment insurance.
We should widen the opportunities for adequate medical care.
We should plan a better system by which persons deserving or needing gainful employment may obtain it.

I have called for personal sacrifice. I am assured of the willingness of almost all Americans to respond to that call.

A part of the sacrifice means the payment of more money in taxes. In my budget message I shall recommend that a greater portion of this great defense program be paid for from taxation than we are paying today. No person should try, or be allowed, to get rich out of this program; and the principle of tax payments in accordance with ability to pay should be constantly before our eyes to guide our legislation.

If the Congress maintains these principles, the voters, putting patriotism ahead of pocketbooks, will give you their applause.

In the future days, which we seek to make secure, we look forward to a world founded upon four essential human freedoms.

The first is freedom of speech and expression — everywhere in the world.

The second is freedom of every person to worship God in his own way — everywhere in the world.

The third is freedom from want — which, translated into world terms, means economic understandings which will secure to every nation a healthy peacetime life for its inhabitants — everywhere in the world.

The fourth is freedom from fear — which, translated into world terms, means a world-wide reduction of armaments to such a point and in such a thorough fashion that no nation will be in a position to commit an act of physical aggression against any neighbor — anywhere in the world.

That is no vision of a distant millennium. It is a definite basis for a kind of world attainable in our own time and generation. That kind of world is the very antithesis of the so-called new order of tyranny which the dictators seek to create with the crash of a bomb.

To that new order we oppose the greater conception — the moral order. A good society is able to face schemes of world domination and foreign revolutions alike without fear.

Since the beginnings of our American history, we have been engaged in change — in a perpetual peaceful revolution — a revolution which goes on steadily, quietly adjusting itself to changing conditions — without the concentration camp or the quicklime in the ditch. The world order which we seek is the co-operation of free countries, working together in a friendly, civilized society.

This nation has placed its destiny in the hands and heads and hearts of its millions of free men and women; and its faith in freedom under the guidance of God. Freedom means the supremacy of human rights everywhere. Our support goes to those who struggle to gain those rights or keep them. Our strength is our unity of purpose.

To that high concept there can be no end Save Victory.

ENDNOTES

[1] For more details on these documents, see Micheline Ishay, *The History of Human Rights: From Ancient Times to the Era of Globalization* (Berkeley, Calif.: University of California Press, 2004), ch. 3.

CHAPTER 15

Documents

15.1   THE MAGNA CHARTA (1215)

1.   We have in the first place granted to God and by this our present charter have confirmed, for us and our heirs forever, that the English Church shall be free and shall have her rights entire and her liberties inviolate.... We have also granted to all freemen of our kingdom, for us and our heirs forever, all the liberties herein under written, to be had and held by them and their heirs of us and our heirs....

17.   Common pleas shall not follow our Court, but shall be held in some fixed place.

20.   A freeman shall be punished[1] a small offense only according to the degree of the offense; and for a grave offense he shall be punished according to the gravity of the offense saving his contenement. And a merchant shall be punished in the same way, saving his merchandise; and a villein the same way, saving his wainage — should they fall into our mercy. And none of the aforesaid punished shall be imposed except by the oaths of good men from the neighborhood.

21.   Earls and barons shall not be punished expect through their peers, and only in accordance with the degree of the offense.

22.   No clergyman shall be punished with respect to his lay holding, except in the manner of the other foregoing persons, and not according to the value of his church benefice.

23.   No community or individual shall be compelled to make bridges at river banks, except those who from of old were legally bound to do so....

28.   No constable or other bailiff of ours shall take grain or other chattels of any one without immediately paying therefor in money (denarios), unless by the will of the seller he may secure postponement of that payment.

30.   No sheriff or bailiff of ours, or any other person, shall take the horses or carts of any freeman for carrying service, except by the will of that freeman.

31.   Neither we nor our bailiffs will take some one else's wood for [repairing] castles or for doing any other work of ours, except by the will of him to whom the wood belongs.

32.   We will hold the lands of those convicted of felony only for a year and a day, and the lands shall then be given to the lords of the fiefs concerned....

38.   No bailiff for the future shall put any man to his "law" upon his own mere words of mouth, without credible witnesses brought for this purpose.
     No freeman shall be arrested, or detained in prison, or deprived of his freehold, or outlawed, or banished, or in any way molested; and we will not set forth against him nor send against him, unless by the lawful judgment of his peers and by the law of the land....

40.   To no one will we sell, to no one will we deny or delay right or justice.

41.   All merchants may safely and securely go away from England, come to England, stay in and go through England, by land or by water, for buying and selling under right and ancient customs and without any evil exactions, except in time of war if they are from the land at war with us. And if such persons are found in our land at the beginning of a war, they shall be arrested without

injury to their bodies or goods until we or our chief justice can ascertain how the merchants of our land who may then be found in the land at war with us are to be treated. And if our men are to be safe, the others shall be safe in our land.

42. It shall be lawful in future for any one (excepting always those imprisoned or outlawed in accordance with the law of the kingdom, and natives of any country at war with us, and merchants, who shall be treated as is above provided) to leave our kingdom and to return, safe and secure by land and water, except for a short period in time of war, on grounds of pulic policy — reserving always the allegiance due to us....

44. Men dwelling outside the forest shall no longer, in consequence of a general summons, come before our justices of the forest, unless they are [involved] in a plea [of the forest] or are sureties of some person or persons who have been arrested for offenses against the forest.

45. We will appoint as justiciars, constables, sheriffs, or bailiffs only such men as know the law of the kingdom and well desire to observe it....

54. No one shall be arrested or imprisoned upon the appeal of a woman, for the death of any other than her husband....

60. Moreover, all the aforesaid customs and liberties, the observance of which we have granted in our kingdom as far as pertains to us towards our men, shall be observed by all of our kingdom, by clergy as well as by laymen, as far as pertains to them towards their men....

63. Wherefore it is our will, and we firmly enjoin, that the English Church be free, and that the men in our kingdom have and hold all the aforesaid liberties, rights, and concessions, well and peaceably, freely and quietly, fully and wholly, for themselves and their heirs, of us and our heirs, in all respects and in all places for ever, as is aforesaid. An oath, moreover, has been taken, as well on our part as on the part of the barons, that all these conditions aforesaid shall be kept in good faith and without evil intent....

¹Editor: amerced changed to punished.

15.2   THE HABEAS CORPUS ACT (1679)

An act for the better securing the liberty of the subject, and for prevention of imprisonments beyond the seas.

WHEREAS *great delays have been used by sheriffs, golfers and other officers, to whose custody, any of the King's subjects have been committed for criminal or supposed criminal matters, in making returns of writs of habeas corpus to them directed, by standing out an alias and pluries habeas corpus, and sometimes more, and by other shifts to avoid their yielding obedience to such writs, contrary to their duty and the known laws of the land, whereby many of the King's subjects have been and hereafter may be long detained in prison, in such cases when by law they are bailable, to their great charges and vexation.*

II.   For the prevention whereof, and the more speedy relief of all persons imprisoned for any such criminal or supposed criminal matters; (2) be it enacted by the King's most excellent majesty, by and with the advice and consent of the lords spiritual and temporal, and commons, in this present parliament assembled, and by the authority thereof. That when so ever any person or persons shall bring any *habeas corpus* directed unto any sheriff or sheriffs, jailer, minister or other person whatsoever, for any person in his or their custody, and the said writ shall be served upon the said officer, or left at the jail or prison with any of the under-officers, under-keepers or deputy of the said officers or keepers, that the said officer or officers, his or their under-officers, under-keepers or deputies, shall within three days after the service thereof as aforesaid (unless the commitment aforesaid were for treason or felony, plainly and specially expressed in the warrant of commitment) upon payment or tender of the charges of bringing the said prisoner, to be ascertained by the judge or court that awarded the same, and endorsed upon the said writ, not exceeding twelve pence per mile, and upon security given by his own bond to pay the charges of carrying back the prisoner, if he shall be remanded by the court or judge to which he shall be brought according to the true intent of this present act, and that he will not make any escape by the way, make return of such writ; (3) and bring or cause to be brought the body of the party so committed or restrained, unto or before the lord chancellor, or lord keeper of the great seal of England for the time being, or the judges or barons of the said court from whence the said writ shall issue, or unto and before such other person or persons before whom the said writ is made returnable, according to the command thereof; (4) and shall then likewise certify the true causes of his retainer or imprisonment, unless the commitment of the said party be in any place beyond the distance of twenty miles from the place or places where such court or person is or shall be residing; and if beyond the distance of twenty miles, and not above one hundred miles, then within the space of ten days, and if beyond the distance of one hundred miles, then within the space of twenty days, after such delivery aforesaid, and not longer.

III. And to the intent that no sheriff, jailer or other officer may pretend ignorance of the import of any such writ; (2) be it enacted by the authority aforesaid, that all such writs shall be marked in this manner, *Per statutum tricesimo primo Caroli secundi Regis*, and shall be signed by the person that awards the same; (3) and if any person or persons shall be or stand committed or detained as aforesaid, for any crime, unless for felony or treason plainly expressed in the warrant of commitment, in the vacation-time, and out of term, it shall and may be lawful to and for the person

or persons so committed or detained (other than persons convict or in execution by legal process) or any one on his or their behalf, to appeal or complain to the lord chancellor or lord keeper, or any one of his Majesty's justices, either of the one bench or of the other, or the barons of the exchequer of the degree of the coif; (4) and the said lord chancellor, lord keeper, justices or barons or any of them, upon view of the copy or copies of the warrant or warrants of commitment and retainer, or otherwise upon oath made that such copy or copies were denied to be given by such person or persons in whose custody the prisoner or prisoners is or are detained, are hereby authorized and required, upon request made in writing by such person or persons, or any on his, her or their behalf, attested and subscribed by two witnesses who were present at the delivery of the same, to award and grant an *habeas corpus* under the seal of such court whereof he shall then be one of the judges, (5) to be directed to the officer or officers in whose custody the party so committed or detained shall be, returnable *immediate* before the said lord chancellor or lord keeper or such justice, baron or any other justice or baron of the degree of the coif of any of the said courts; (6) and upon service thereof as aforesaid, the officer or officers, his or their under-officer or under-officers, under-keeper or under-keepers, or their deputy in whose custody the party is so committed or detained, shall within the times respectively before limited, bring such prisoner or prisoners before the said lord chancellor or lord keeper, or such justices, barons or one of them, before whom the said writ is made returnable, and in case of his absence before any other of them, with the return of such writ, and the true causes of the commitment and retainer; (7) and thereupon within two days after the party shall be brought before them, the said lord chancellor or lord keeper, or such justice or baron before whom the prisoner shall be brought as aforesaid, shall discharge the said prisoner from his imprisonment, taking his or their recognizance, with one or more surety or sureties, in any sum according to their discretions, having regard to the quality of the prisoner and nature of the offense, for his or their appearance in the court of King's bench the term following, or at the next assizes, sessions or general jail-delivery of and for such county, city or place where the commitment was, or where the offense was committed, or in such other court where the said offense is properly cognizable, as the case shall require, and then shall certify the said writ with the return thereof, and the said recognizance or recognizances unto the said court where such appearance is to be made; (8) unless it shall appear unto the said lord chancellor or lord keeper or justice or justices, or baron or barons, that the party so committed is detained upon a legal process, order or warrant, out of some court that hath jurisdiction of criminal matters, or by some warrant signed and scaled with the hand and seal of any of the said justices or barons, or some justice or justices of the peace, for such matters or offenses for which by the law the prisoner is not bailable....

15.3   THE ENGLISH BILL OF RIGHTS (1689)

Whereas the late King James the Second, by the assistance of divers evil counselors, judges, and ministers employed by him, did endeavor to subvert and extirpate the protestant religion, and the laws and liberties of this kingdom.

1. By assuming and exercising a power of dispensing with and suspending of laws, and the execution of laws, without consent of parliament.
2. By committing and prosecuting divers worthy prelates, for humbly petitioning to be excused from concurring to the said assumed power.
3. By issuing and causing to be executed a commission under the great seal for erecting court called, the court of commissioners for ecclesiastical causes.
4. By levying money for and to the use of the crown, by pretence of prerogative, for another time, and in other manner, than the same was granted by parliament.
5. By raising and keeping a standing army within this kingdom in time of peace, without consent of parliament, and quartering soldiers contrary to law.
6. By causing several good subjects, being protestants, to be disarmed, at the same time when papists were both armed and employed, contrary to law.
7. By violating the freedom of election of members to serve in parliament.
8. By prosecutions in the court of King's bench, for matters and causes cognizable only in parliament; and by divers other arbitrary and illegal courses.
9. And whereas of late years, partial, corrupt, and unqualified persons have been returned and served on juries in trials, and particularly divers jurors in trials for high treason, which were not freeholders.
10. And excessive bail hath been required of persons committed in criminal cases, to elude the benefit of the laws made for the liberty of the subjects.
11. And excessive fines have been imposed; and illegal and cruel punishments inflicted.
12. And several grants and promises made of fines and forfeitures, before any conviction or judgment against the persons, upon whom the same were to be levied.

All which are utterly and directly contrary to the known laws and statutes, and freedom of this realm.

And whereas the said late King James the Second having abdicated the government, and the throne being thereby vacant, his highness the prince of Orange (whom it hath pleased Almighty God to make the glorious instrument of delivering this kingdom from popery and arbitrary power) did (by the advice of the lords spiritual and temporal, and divers principal persons of the commons) cause letters to be written to the lords spiritual and temporal, being protestants; and other letters to the several counties, cities, universities, boroughs, and cinque-ports, for the choosing of such persons to represent them, as were of right to be sent to parliament, to meet and sit at Westminster upon the two and twentieth day of January, in this year one thousand six hundred eighty and eight, in order to such an establishment, as that their religion, laws, and liberties might not again be in danger of being subverted: upon which letters, elections have been accordingly made.

And thereupon the said lords spiritual and temporal, and commons, pursuant to their respective letters and elections, being now assembled in a full and free representative of this nation, taking into their most serious consideration the best means for attaining the ends aforesaid; do in the first place (as their ancestors in like case have usually done) for the vindicating and asserting their ancient rights and liberties, declare:

1. That the pretended power of suspending of laws, or the execution of laws, by regal authority, without consent of parliament, is illegal.
2. That the pretended power of dispensing with laws, or the execution of laws, by regal authority, as it hath been assumed and exercised of late, is illegal.
3. That the commission for erecting the late court of commissioners for ecclesiastical causes, and all other commissions and courts of like nature are illegal and pernicious.
4. That levying money for or to the use of the crown, by pretence of prerogative, without grant of parliament, for longer time, or in other manner than the same is or shall be granted, is illegal.
5. That it is the right of the subjects to petition the King, and all commitments and prosecutions for such petitioning are illegal.
6. That the raising or keeping a standing army within the kingdom in time of peace, unless it be with consent of parliament, is against law.
7. That the subjects which are Protestants may have arms for their defense suitable to their conditions, and as allowed by law.
8. That election of members of parliament ought to be free.
9. That the freedom of speech, and debates or proceedings in parliament, ought not to be impeached or questioned in any court or place out of parliament.
10. That excessive bail ought not to be required, nor excessive fines imposed; nor cruel and unusual punishments inflicted.
11. That jurors ought to be duly impaneled and returned, and jurors which pass upon men in trials for high treason ought to be freeholders.
12. That all grants and promises of fines and forfeitures of particular persons before conviction are illegal and void.
13. And that for redress of all grievances, and for the amending, strengthening, and preserving of the laws, parliaments ought to be held frequently.

And they do claim, demand, and insist upon all and singular the premises as their undoubted rights and liberties; and that no declarations, judgments, doings or proceedings, to the prejudice of the people in any of the said premises, ought in any wise to be drawn hereafter into consequence or example.

To which demand of their rights they are particularly encouraged by the declaration of his highness the prince of Orange, as being the only means for obtaining a full redress and remedy therein.

Having therefore an entire confidence, that his said highness the prince of Orange will perfect the deliverance so far advanced by him, and will still preserve them from the violation of their rights, which they have here asserted, and from all other attempts upon their religion, rights, and liberties ...

15.4 THE UNITED STATES DECLARATION OF INDEPENDENCE (1776)

When in the course of human events it becomes necessary for one people to dissolve the political bands which have connected them with another and to assume, among the powers of the earth, the separate and equal station to which the laws of nature and of nature's God entitle them, a decent respect to the opinions of mankind requires that they should declare the causes which impel them to the separation.

We hold these truths to be self-evident, that all men are created equal; that they are endowed by their Creator with certain unalienable rights; that among these are life, liberty, and the pursuit of happiness. That, to secure these rights, governments are instituted among men, deriving their just powers from the consent of the governed; that, whenever any form of government becomes destructive of these ends, it is the right of the people to alter or to abolish it, and to institute a new government, laying its foundation on such principles, and organizing its powers in such form, as to them shall seem most likely to effect their safety and happiness. Prudence, indeed, will dictate that governments long established should not be changed for light and transient causes; and, accordingly, all experience hath shown that mankind are more disposed to suffer, while evils are sufferable, than to right themselves by abolishing the forms to which they are accustomed. But when a long train of abuses and usurpations, pursuing invariably the same object, evinces a design to reduce them under absolute despotism, it is their right, it is their duty, to throw off such government and to provide new guards for their future security. Such has been the patient sufferance of these colonies, and such is now the necessity which constrains them to alter their former systems of government. The history of the present King of Great Britain is a history of repeated injuries and usurpations, all having, in direct object, the establishment of an absolute tyranny over these States. To prove this, let facts be submitted to a candid world:

He has refused his assent to laws the most wholesome and necessary for the public good. He has forbidden his governors to pass laws of immediate and pressing importance, unless suspended in their operation for his assent should be obtained; and, when so suspended, he has utterly neglected to attend to them.

He has refused to pass other laws for the accommodation of large districts of people, unless those people would relinquish the right of representation in the legislature; a right inestimable to them and formidable to tyrants only.

He has called together legislative bodies at places unusual, uncomfortable, and distant from the depository of their public records, for the sole purpose of fatiguing them into compliance with his measures.

He has dissolved representative houses, repeatedly for opposing with manly firmness, his invasions on the rights of the people.

He has refused, for a long time after such dissolutions, to cause others to be elected; whereby the legislative powers, incapable of annihilation, have returned to the people at large for their exercise; the state remaining, in the meantime, exposed to all the danger of invasion from without and convulsions within.

He has endeavored to prevent the population of these States; for that purpose, obstructing the laws for naturalization of foreigners, refusing to pass others to encourage their migration hither, and raising the conditions of new appropriations of lands.

He has obstructed the administration of justice by refusing his assent to laws for establishing judiciary powers.

He has made judges dependent on his will alone for the tenure of their offices and the amount and payment of their salaries.

He has erected a multitude of new offices and sent hither swarms of officers to harass our people and eat out their substance.

He has kept among us, in time of peace, standing armies, without the consent of our legislatures.

He has affected to render the military independent of, and superior to, the civil power.

He has combined with others to subject us to a jurisdiction foreign to our Constitution and unacknowledged by our laws, giving his assent to their acts of pretended legislation:

For quartering large bodies of armed troops among us;

For protecting them by a mock trial from punishment for any murders which they should commit on the inhabitants of these States;

For cutting off our trade with all parts of the world;

For imposing taxes on us without our consent;

For depriving us, in many cases, of the benefit of trial by jury;

For transporting us beyond seas to be tried for pretended offenses;

For abolishing the free system of English laws in a neighboring province, establishing therein an arbitrary government, and enlarging its boundaries, so as to render it at once an example and fit instrument for introducing the same absolute rule into these colonies;

For taking away our charters, abolishing our most valuable laws and altering, fundamentally, the powers of our governments;

For suspending our own legislatures and declaring themselves invested with power to legislate for us in all cases whatsoever.

He has abdicated government here by declaring us out of his protection and waging war against us.

He has plundered our seas, ravaged our coasts, burnt our towns, and destroyed the lives of our people.

He is, at this time, transporting large armies of foreign mercenaries to complete the works of death, desolation, and tyranny already begun with circumstances of cruelty and perfidy scarcely paralleled in the most barbarous ages, and totally unworthy the head of a civilized nation.

He has constrained our fellow citizens, taken captive on the high seas, to bear arms against their country, to become the executioners of their friends and brethren, or to fall themselves by their hands.

He has excited domestic insurrections amongst us and has endeavored to bring on the inhabitants of our frontiers, the merciless Indian savages, whose known rule of warfare is an undistinguished destruction of all ages, sexes, and conditions.

In every stage of these oppressions, we have petitioned for redress in the most humble terms; our repeated petitions have been answered only by repeated injury. A prince whose character is thus marked by every act which may define a tyrant is unfit to be the ruler of a free people.

Nor have we been wanting in attention to our British brethren. We have warned them, from time to time, of attempts made by their legislature to extend an unwarrantable jurisdiction over us. We have reminded them of the circumstances of our emigration and settlement here. We have appealed to their native justice and magnanimity, and we have conjured them, by the ties of our common kindred, to disavow these usurpations, which would inevitably interrupt our connections and correspondence. They, too, have been deaf to the voice of justice and consanguinity. We must, therefore, acquiesce in the necessity which denounces our separation, and hold them, as we hold the rest of mankind, enemies in war, in peace, friends.

We, therefore, the representatives of the United States of America, in general Congress assembled, appealing to the Supreme Judge of the world for the rectitude of our intentions, do, in the name and by the authority of the good people of these colonies, solemnly publish and declare, that these united colonies are, and of right ought to be, free and independent states: that they are absolved from all allegiance to the British Crown, and that all political connection between them and the state of Great Britain is, and ought to be, totally dissolved; and that, as free and independent states, they have full power to levy war, conclude peace, contract alliances, establish commerce, and to do all other acts and things which independent states may of right do. And, for the support of this declaration, with a firm reliance on the protection of Divine Providence, we mutually pledge to each other our lives, our fortunes, and our sacred honor.

15.5 THE FRENCH DECLARATION OF THE RIGHTS OF MAN AND CITIZEN (1789)

The representatives of the French people, organized in National Assembly, considering that ignorance, forgetfulness, or contempt of the rights of man are the sole causes of public misfortunes and of the corruption of governments, have resolved to set forth in a solemn declaration the natural, inalienable, and sacred rights of man, in order that such declaration, continually before all members of the social body, may be a perpetual reminder of their rights and duties; in order that the acts of the legislative power and those of the executive power may constantly be compared with the aim of every political institution and may accordingly be more respected; in order that the demands of the citizens, founded henceforth upon simple and incontestable principles, may always be directed towards the maintenance of the Constitution and the welfare of all.

Accordingly, the National Assembly recognizes and proclaims, in the presence and under the auspices of the Supreme Being, the following rights of man and citizen:

1. Men are born and remain free and equal in rights; social distinctions may be based only upon general usefulness.
2. The aim of every political association is the preservation of the natural and inalienable rights of man; these rights are liberty, property, security, and resistance to oppression.
3. The source of all sovereignty resides essentially in the nation; no group, no individual may exercise authority not emanating expressly therefrom.
4. Liberty consists of the power to do whatever is not injurious to others; thus the enjoyment of the natural rights of every man has for its limits only those that assure other members of society the enjoyment of those same rights; such limits may be determined only by law.
5. The law has the right to forbid only actions which are injurious to society. Whatever is not forbidden by law may not be prevented, and no one may be constrained to do what it does not prescribe.
6. Law is the expression of the general will; all citizens have the right to concur personally, or through their representatives, in its formation; it must be the same for all, whether it protects or punishes. All citizens, being equal before it, are equally admissible to all public offices, positions, and employments, according to their capacity, and without other distinction than that of virtues and talents.
7. No man may be accused, arrested, or detained except in the cases determined by law, and according to the forms prescribed thereby. Whoever solicit, expedite, or execute arbitrary orders, or have them executed, must be punished; but every citizen summoned or apprehended in pursuance of the law must obey immediately; he renders himself culpable by resistance.
8. The law is to establish only penalties that are absolutely and obviously necessary; and no one may be punished except by virtue of a law established and promulgated prior to the offense and legally applied.
9. Since every man is presumed innocent until declared guilty, if arrest be deemed indispensable, all unnecessary severity for securing the person of the accused must be severely repressed by law.
10. No one is to be disquieted because of his opinions, even religious, provided their manifestation does not disturb the public order established by law.
11. Free communication of ideas and opinions is one of the most precious of the rights of man. Consequently, every citizen may speak, write, and print freely, subject to responsibility for the abuse of such liberty in the cases determined by law.

12. The guarantee of the rights of man and citizen necessitates a public force; such a force, therefore, is instituted for the advantage of all and not for the particular benefit of those to whom it is entrusted.

13. For the maintenance of the public force and for the expenses of administration a common tax is indispensable; it must be assessed equally on all citizens in proportion to their means.

14. Citizens have the right to ascertain, by themselves or through their representatives, the necessity of the public tax, to consent to it freely, to supervise its use, and to determine its quota, assessment, payment, and duration.

15. Society has the right to require of every public agent an accounting of his administration.

16. Every society in which the guarantee of rights is not assured or separation of powers not determined has no constitution at all.

17. Since property is a sacred and inviolable right, no one may be deprived thereof unless a legally established public necessity obviously requires it, and upon condition of a just and previous indemnity.

15.6 UNITED NATIONS CHARTER (ADOPTED, 1945; ENTRY INTO FORCE, 1945)[1]

We the peoples of the United Nations determined

to save succeeding generations from the scourge of war, which twice in our lifetime has brought untold sorrow to mankind, and to reaffirm faith in fundamental human rights, in the dignity and worth of the human person, in the equal rights of men and women and of nations large and small, and to establish conditions under which justice and respect for the obligations arising from treaties and other sources of international law can be maintained, and to promote social progress and better standards of life in larger freedom,

and for the ends to practice tolerance and live together in peace with one another as good neighbors, and to unite our strength to maintain international peace and security, and to ensure, by the acceptance of principles and the institution of methods, that armed force shall not be used, save in the common interest, and to employ international machinery for the promotion of the economic and social advancement of all peoples,

have resolved to combine our efforts to accomplish these aims.

Accordingly, our respective Governments, through representatives assembled in the city of San Francisco, who have exhibited their full powers found to be in good and due form, have agreed to the present Charter of the United Nations and do hereby establish an international organization to be known as the United Nations.

Chapter I: Purposes and Principles

Article 1

The Purposes of the United Nations are:

1. To maintain international peace and security, and to that end: to take effective collective measures for the prevention and removal of threats to the peace, and for the suppression of acts of aggression or other breaches of the peace, and to bring about by peaceful means, and in conformity with the principles of justice and international law, adjustment or settlement of international disputes or situations which might lead to a breach of the peace;

2. To develop friendly relations among nations based on respect for the principle of equal rights and self-determination of peoples, and to take other appropriate measures to strengthen universal peace;

3. To achieve international cooperation in solving international problems of an economic, social, cultural, or humanitarian character, and in promoting and encouraging respect for human rights and for fundamental freedoms for all without distinction as to race, sex, language, or religion; and

4. To be a center for harmonizing the actions of nations in the attainment of these common ends.

Article 2

7. Nothing contained in the present Charter shall authorize the United Nations to intervene in matters which are essentially within the domestic jurisdiction of any state or shall require the Members to submit such matters to settlement under the present Charter; but this principle shall not prejudice the application of enforcement measures under Chapter VII.

[1]Adopted on June 26, 1945; entry into force, October 24, 1945.

15.7   UNITED NATIONS CONVENTION ON THE PREVENTION AND PUNISHMENT OF THE CRIME OF GENOCIDE (ADOPTED, 1948; ENTRY INTO FORCE, 1951)[1]

The Contracting Parties,

Having considered declaration made by the General Assembly of the United Nations in its resolution 96 (I) dated 11 December 1946 that genocide is a crime under international law, contrary to the spirit and aims of the United Nations and condemned by the civilized world;

Recognizing that at all periods of history genocide has inflicted great losses on humanity; and

Being convinced that, in order to liberate mankind from such an odious scourge, international cooperation is required,

Hereby agree as hereinafter provided:

Article I

The Contracting Parties confirm that genocide, whether committed in time of peace or in time of war, is a crime under international law which they undertake to prevent and to punish.

Article II

In the present Convention, genocide means any of the following acts committed with intent to destroy, in whole or in part, a national, ethnical, racial or religious group as such:

a. Killing members of the group;

b. Causing serious bodily or mental harm to members of the group;

c. Deliberately inflicting on the group conditions of life calculated to bring about its physical destruction in whole or in part;

d. Imposing measures intended to prevent births within the group;

e. Forcibly transferring children of the group to another group.

Article III

The following acts shall be punishable:

a. Genocide;

b. Conspiring to commit genocide;

c. Direct and public incitement to commit genocide;

d. Attempt to commit genocide;

e. Complicity in genocide.

Article IV

Persons committing genocide or any of the other acts enumerated in article III shall be punished, whether they are constitutionally responsible rulers, public officials or private individuals.

Article V

The Contracting Parties undertake to enact, in accordance with their respective Constitutions, the necessary legislation to give effect to the provisions of the present Convention and, in particular, to provide effective penalties for persons guilty of genocide or any other acts enumerated in article III.

Article VI

Persons charged with genocide or any of the other acts enumerated in article III shall be tried by a competent tribunal of the State in territory of which the act was committed, or by such international penal tribunal as may have jurisdiction with respect to those Contracting Parties which shall have accepted its jurisdiction.

Article VII

Genocide and the other acts enumerated in article III shall not be considered as political crimes for the purpose of extradition.

The Contracting Parties pledge themselves in such cases to grant extradition in accordance with their laws and treaties in force.

Article VIII

Any Contracting Party may call upon the competent organs of the United Nations to take such actions under the Charter of the Nations as they consider appropriate for the prevention and suppression of acts of genocide or any of the other acts enumerated in article III.

Article IX

Disputes between the Contracting Parties relating to the interpretation, application, or fulfillment of the present Convention, including those relating to the responsibility of a State for genocide or any of the other acts enumerated in article III, shall be submitted to the International Court of Justice at the request of any of the parties to the dispute.

Article X

The present Convention of which the Chinese, English, French, Russian and Spanish texts are equally authentic, shall bear the date of 9 December 1948.

[1]Adopted on December 9, 1948; entry into force January 12, 1951.

15.8   UNITED NATIONS UNIVERSAL DECLARATION OF HUMAN RIGHTS (1948)[1]

Whereas recognition of the inherent dignity and of the equal and inalienable rights of all members of the human family is the foundation of freedom, justice and peace in the world,

Whereas disregard and contempt for human rights have resulted in barbarous acts which have outraged the conscience of mankind, and the advent of a world in which human beings shall enjoy freedom of speech and belief and freedom from fear and want has been proclaimed as the highest aspiration of the common people,

Whereas it is essential, if man is not to be compelled to have recourse, as a last resort, to rebellion against tyranny and oppression, that human rights should be protected by the rule of law,

Whereas it is essential to promote the development of friendly relations between nations,

Whereas the peoples of the United Nations have in the Charter reaffirmed their faith in fundamental human rights, in the dignity and worth of the human person and in the equal rights of men and women and have determined to promote social progress and better standards of life in larger freedom,

Whereas Member States have pledged themselves to achieve, in cooperation with the United Nations, the promotion of universal respect for and observance of human rights and fundamental freedoms,

Whereas a common understanding of these rights and freedoms is of the greatest importance for the full realization of this pledge,

Now, therefore,

The General Assembly,
Proclaims this Universal Declaration of Human Rights as a common standard of achievement for all peoples and all nations, to the end that every individual and every

organ of society, keeping this Declaration constantly in mind, shall strive by teaching and education to promote respect for these rights and freedoms and by progressive measures, national and international, to secure their universal and effective recognition and observance, both among the peoples of Member States themselves and among the peoples of territories under jurisdiction.

Article 1

All human beings are born free and equal in dignity and rights. They are endowed with reason and conscience and should act toward one another in a spirit of brotherhood.

Article 2

Everyone is entitled to all the rights and freedoms set forth in this Declaration, without distinction of any kind, such as race, color, sex, language, religion, political or other opinion, national or social origin, property, birth or other status.

Furthermore, no distinction shall be made on the basis of political, jurisdictional or international status of the country or territory to which a person belongs, whether it be independent, non-self-governing or under any other limitation of sovereignty.

Article 3

Everyone has the right to life, liberty and the security of person.

Article 4

No one shall be held in slavery or servitude; slavery and the slave trade shall be prohibited in all their forms.

Article 5

No one shall be subjected to torture or to cruel, inhuman or degrading treatment or punishment.

Article 6

Everyone has the right to recognition everywhere as a person before the law.

Article 7

All are equal before the law and are entitled without any discrimination to equal protection of the law. All are entitled to equal protection against any discrimination in violation of this Declaration and against any incitement to such discrimination.

Article 8

Everyone has the right to an effective remedy by the competent national tribunals for acts violating the fundamental rights granted him by the constitution or by law.

Article 9

No one shall be subjected to arbitrary arrest, detention or exile.

Article 10

Everyone is entitled to full equality to a fair and public hearing by an independent and impartial tribunal, in the determination of his rights and obligations and of any criminal charge against him.

Article 11

1. Everyone charged with a penal offense has the right to be presumed innocent until proved guilty according to law in a public trial at which he has had all the guarantees necessary for his defense.

2. No one shall be held guilty of any penal offense on account of any act or omission which did not constitute a penal offense, under national or international law, at the time when it was committed. Nor shall a heavier penalty be imposed than the one that was applicable at the time the penal offense was committed.

Article 12

No one shall be subjected to arbitrary interference with his privacy, family, home or correspondence, nor to attacks upon his honor and reputation. Everyone has the right to the protection of the law against such interference or attacks.

Article 13

1. Everyone has the right to freedom of movement and residence within the borders of each state.

2. Everyone has the right to leave any country, including his own, and to return to his country.

Article 14

1. Everyone has the right to seek and to enjoy in other countries asylum from persecution.

2. This right may not be invoked in the case of prosecutions genuinely arising from non-political crimes or from acts contrary to the purposes and principles of the United Nations.

Article 15

1. Everyone has the right to a nationality.

2. No one shall be arbitrarily deprived of his nationality nor denied the right to change his nationality.

Article 16

1. Men and women of full age, without any limitation due to race, nationality, or religion, have the right to marry and to found a family. They are entitled to equal rights as to marriage, during marriage and at its dissolution.

2. Marriage shall be entered into only with the free and full consent of the intending spouses.

3. The family is the natural and fundamental group unit of society and is entitled to protection by society and the State.

Article 17

1. Everyone has the right to own property alone as well as in association with others.

2. No one shall be arbitrarily deprived of his property.

Article 18

Everyone has the right to freedom of thought, conscience and religion; this right includes freedom to change his religion or belief, and freedom, either alone or in community with others and in public or private, to manifest his religion or belief in teaching, practice, worship and observance.

Article 19

Everyone has the right to freedom of opinion and expression; this right includes freedom to hold opinions without interference and to seek, receive and impart information and ideas through any media and regardless of frontiers.

Article 20

1. Everyone has the right to freedom of peaceful assembly and association.

2. No one may be compelled to belong to an association.

Article 21

1. Everyone has the right to take part in the Government of his country, directly or through freely chosen representatives.

2. Everyone has the right of equal access to public service in his country.

3. The will of the people shall be the basis of the authority of government; this will shall be expressed in periodic and genuine elections which shall be by universal and equal suffrage and shall be held by secret vote or by equivalent free voting procedures.

Article 22

Everyone, as a member of society, has the right to social security and is entitled to realization, through national effort and international cooperation and in accordance with the organization and resources of each State, of the economic, social and cultural rights indispensable for his dignity and the free development of his personality.

Article 23

1. Everyone has the right to work, to free choice of employment, to just and favorable conditions of work and to protection against unemployment.

2. Everyone, without any discrimination, has the right to equal pay for equal work.

3. Everyone who works has the right to just and favorable remuneration insuring for himself and his family an existence worthy of human dignity, and supplemented, if necessary, by other means of social protection.

4. Everyone has the right to form and to join trade unions for the protection of his interests.

Article 24

Everyone has the right to rest and leisure, including reasonable limitation of working hours and periodic holidays with pay.

Article 25

1. Everyone has the right to a standard of living adequate for the health and well-being of himself and of his family, including food, clothing, housing and medical care and necessary social services, and the right to security in the event of unemployment, sickness, disability, widowhood, old age or other lack of livelihood in circumstances beyond his control.

2. Motherhood and childhood are entitled to special care and assistance. All children, whether born in or out of wedlock, shall enjoy the same social protection.

Article 26

1. Everyone has the right to education. Education shall be free, at least in the elementary and fundamental stages. Elementary education shall be compulsory. Technical and professional education shall be made generally available and higher education shall be equally accessible to all on the basis of merit.

2. Education shall be directed to the full development of the human personality and to the strengthening of respect for human rights and fundamental freedoms. It shall promote understanding, tolerance and friendship among all nations, racial or religious groups, and shall further the activities of the United Nations for the maintenance of peace.

3. Parents have a prior right to choose the kind of education that shall be given to their children.

Article 27

1. Everyone has the right freely to participate in the cultural life of the community, to enjoy the arts and to share in scientific advancement and its benefits.

2. Everyone has the right to the protection of the moral and material interests resulting from any scientific, literary or artistic production of which he is the author.

Article 28

Everyone is entitled to a social and international order in which the rights and freedoms set forth in this Declaration can be fully realized.

Article 29

1. Everyone has duties to the community in which alone the free and full development of his personality is possible.

2. In the exercise of his rights and freedoms, everyone shall be subject only to such limitations as are determined by law solely for the purpose of securing due recognition and respect for the rights and freedoms of others and of meeting the just requirements of morality, public order and the general welfare in a democratic society.

3. These rights and freedoms may in no case be exercised contrary to the purposes and principles of the United Nations.

Article 30

Nothing in this Declaration may be interpreted as implying for any State, group or person any right to engage in any activity or to perform any act aimed at the destruction of any of the rights and freedoms set forth herein.

[1]Adopted and Proclaimed by General Assembly resolution 217A (III) of December 10, 1948.

15.9   GENEVA CONVENTION RELATIVE TO THE TREATMENT OF PRISONERS OF WAR (ADOPTED, 1949; ENTRY INTO FORCE, 1950)[1]

General Provisions

Article 1

The High Contracting Parties undertake to respect and to ensure respect for the present Convention in all circumstances.

Article 2

In addition to the provisions which shall be implemented in peace time, the present Convention shall apply to all cases of declared war or of any other armed conflict which may arise between two or more of the High Contracting Parties, even if the state of war is not recognized by one of them.

The Convention shall also apply to all cases of partial or total occupation of the territory of a High Contracting Party, even if the said occupation meets with no armed resistance.

Although one of the Powers in conflict may not be a party to the present Convention, the Powers who are parties thereto shall remain bound by it in their mutual relations. They shall furthermore be bound by the Convention in relation to the said Power, if the latter accepts and applies the provisions thereof.

Article 3

In the case of armed conflict not of an international character occurring in the territory of one of the High Contracting Parties, each party to the conflict shall be bound to apply, as a minimum, the following provisions:

1. Persons taking no active part in the hostilities, including members of armed forces who have laid down their arms and those placed hors de combat by sickness, wounds, detention, or any other cause, shall in all circumstances be treated humanely, without any adverse distinction founded on race, color, religion or faith, sex, birth or wealth, or any other similar criteria.

To this end the following acts are and shall remain prohibited at any time and in any place whatsoever with respect to the above-mentioned persons:

(a) Violence to life and person, in particular murder of all kinds, mutilation, cruel treatment and torture;

(b) Taking of hostages;

(c) Outrages upon personal dignity, in particular, humiliating and degrading treatment;

(d) The passing of sentences and the carrying out of executions without previous judgment pronounced by a regularly constituted court affording all the judicial guarantees which are recognized as indispensable by civilized peoples.

2. The wounded and sick shall be collected and cared for.

An impartial humanitarian body, such as the International Committee of the Red Cross, may offer its services to the Parties to the conflict.

The Parties to the conflict should further endeavor to bring into force, by means of special agreements, all or part of the other provisions of the present Convention.

The application of the preceding provisions shall not affect the legal status of the Parties to the conflict.

Article 4

A. Prisoners of war, in the sense of the present Convention, are persons belonging to one of the following categories, who have fallen into the power of the enemy:

1. Members of the armed forces of a Party to the conflict as well as members of militias or volunteer corps forming part of such armed forces.

2. Members of other militias and members of other volunteer corps, including those of organized resistance movements, belonging to a Party to the conflict and operating in or outside their own territory, even if this territory is occupied, provided that such militias or volunteer corps, including such organized resistance movements, fulfill the following conditions:

(a) That of being commanded by a person responsible for his subordinates;

(b) That of having a fixed distinctive sign recognizable at a distance;

(c) That of carrying arms openly;

(d) That of conducting their operations in accordance with the laws and customs of war.

3. Members of regular armed forces who profess allegiance to a government or an authority not recognized by the Detaining Power.

4. Persons who accompany the armed forces without actually being members thereof, such as civilian members of military aircraft crews, war correspondents, supply contractors, members of labor units or of services responsible for the welfare of the armed forces, provided that they have received authorization from the armed forces which they accompany, who shall provide them for that purpose with an identity card similar to the annexed model....

Article 5

The present Convention shall apply to the persons referred to in Article 4 from the time they fall into the power of the enemy and until their final release and repatriation.

Should any doubt arise as to whether persons, having committed a belligerent act and having fallen into the hands of the enemy, belong to any of the categories enumerated in Article 4, such persons shall enjoy the protection of the present Convention until such time as their status has been determined by a competent tribunal.

Article 6

In addition to the agreements expressly provided for in Articles 10, 23, 28, 33, 60, 65, 66, 67, 72, 73, 75, 109, 110, 118, 119, 122 and 132, the High Contracting Parties may conclude other special agreements for all matters concerning which they may deem it suitable to make separate provision. No special agreement shall adversely affect the situation of prisoners of war, as defined by the present Convention, nor restrict the rights which it confers upon them.

Prisoners of war shall continue to have the benefit of such agreements as long as the Convention is applicable to them, except where express provisions to the contrary are contained in the aforesaid or in subsequent agreements, or where more favorable measures have been taken with regard to them by one or other of the Parties to the conflict.

Article 7

Prisoners of war may in no circumstances renounce in part or in entirety the rights secured to them by the present Convention, and by the special agreements referred to in the foregoing Article, if such there be.

Article 15

The Power detaining prisoners of war shall be bound to provide free of charge for their maintenance and for the medical attention required by their state of health.

Article 16

Taking into consideration the provisions of the present Convention relating to rank and sex, and subject to any privileged treatment which may be accorded to them by reason of their state of health, age or professional qualifications, all prisoners of war shall be treated alike by the Detaining Power, without any adverse distinction based on race, nationality, religious belief or political opinions, or any other distinction founded on similar criteria.

Article 30

Every camp shall have an adequate infirmary where prisoners of war may have the attention they require, as well as appropriate diet. Isolation wards shall, if necessary, be set aside for cases of contagious or mental disease.

Prisoners of war suffering from serious disease, or whose condition necessitates special treatment, a surgical operation or hospital care, must be admitted to any military or civilian medical unit where such treatment can be given, even if their repatriation is contemplated in the near future. Special facilities shall be afforded for the care to be given to the disabled, in particular to the blind, and for their rehabilitation, pending repatriation.

Prisoners of war shall have the attention, preferably, of medical personnel of the Power on which they depend and, if possible, of their nationality.

Article 33

Members of the medical personnel and chaplains while retained by the Detaining Power with a view to assisting prisoners of war, shall not be considered as prisoners of war. They shall, however, receive as a minimum the benefits and protection of the present Convention, and shall also be granted all facilities necessary to provide for the medical care of, and religious ministration to, prisoners of war.

Article 81

Prisoners' representatives shall not be required to perform any other work, if the accomplishment of their duties is thereby made more difficult.

Prisoners' representatives may appoint from amongst the prisoners such assistants as they may require. All material facilities shall be granted them, particularly a certain freedom of movement necessary for the accomplishment of their duties (inspec-

tion of labor detachments, receipt of supplies, etc.).

Prisoners' representatives shall be permitted to visit premises where prisoners of war are detained, and every prisoner of war shall have the right to consult freely his prisoners' representative.

Direct Repatriation and Accommodation in Neutral Countries

Article 109

Subject to the provisions of the third paragraph of this Article, Parties to the conflict are bound to send back to their own country, regardless of number or rank, seriously wounded and seriously sick prisoners of war, after having cared for them until they are fit to travel, in accordance with the first paragraph of the following Article.

Throughout the duration of hostilities, Parties to the conflict shall endeavor, with the cooperation of the neutral Powers concerned, to make arrangements for the accommodation in neutral countries of the sick and wounded prisoners of war referred to in the second paragraph of the following Article. They may, in addition, conclude agreements with a view to the direct repatriation or internment in a neutral country of able-bodied prisoners of war who have undergone a long period of captivity.

[1]Adopted on August 12, 1949; entry into force, October 21, 1950.

15.10 PROTOCOL ADDITIONAL TO THE GENEVA CONVENTIONS OF 1949 (ADOPTED 1977; ENTRY INTO FORCE, 1979)[1]

Article 45: Protection of Persons Who Have Taken Part in Hostilities

1. A person who takes part in hostilities and falls into the power of an adverse Party shall be presumed to be a prisoner of war, and therefore shall be protected by the Third Convention, if he claims the status of prisoner of war, or if he appears to be entitled to such status, or if the Party on which he depends claims such status on his behalf by notification to the detaining Power or to the Protecting Power. Should

any doubt arise as to whether any such person is entitled to the status of prisoner of war, he shall continue to have such status and, therefore, to be protected by the Third Convention and this Protocol until such time as his status has been determined by a competent tribunal.

2. If a person who has fallen into the power of an adverse Party is not held as a prisoner of war and is to be tried by that Party for an offense arising out of the hostilities, he shall have the right to assert his entitlement to prisoner-of-war status before a judicial tribunal and to have that question adjudicated. Whenever possible under the applicable procedure, this adjudication shall occur before the trial for the offense. The representatives of the Protecting Power shall be entitled to attend the proceedings in which that question is adjudicated, unless, exceptionally, the proceedings are held in camera in the interest of State security. In such a case the detaining Power shall advise the Protecting Power accordingly.

3. Any person who has taken part in hostilities, who is not entitled to prisoner-of-war status and who does not benefit from more favorable treatment in accordance with the Fourth Convention shall have the right at all times to the protection of Article 75 of this Protocol. In occupied territory, any such person, unless he is held as a spy, shall also be entitled, notwithstanding Article 5 of the Fourth Convention, to his rights of communication under that Convention.

[1] Adopted on June 8, 1977; entry into force, December 7, 1979.

15.11 EUROPEAN CONVENTION FOR THE PROTECTION OF HUMAN RIGHTS AND FUNDAMENTAL FREEDOMS (ADOPTED, 1977; ENTRY INTO FORCE, 1979)[1]

The Governments signatory hereto, being Members of the Council of Europe,

Considering the Universal Declaration of Human Rights proclaimed by the General Assembly of the United Nations on 10th December 1948;

Considering that this Declaration aims at securing the universal and effective recognition and observance of the Rights therein declared;

Considering that the aim of the Council of Europe is the achievement of greater unity between its Members and that one of the methods by which that aim is to be pursued is the maintenance and further realization of Human Rights and Fundamental Freedoms;

Reaffirming their profound belief in those Fundamental Freedoms which are the foundation of justice and peace in the world and are best maintained on the one hand by an effective political democracy and on the other by a common understanding and observance of the Human Rights upon which they depend;

Being resolved, as the Governments of European countries which are like minded and have a common heritage of political traditions, ideals, freedom and the rule of law to take the first steps for the collective enforcement of certain of the Rights stated in the Universal Declaration,

Have agreed as follows:

Article 1

The High Contracting Parties shall secure to everyone within their jurisdiction the rights and freedoms defined in Section I of this convention.

Section I

Article 2

1. Everyone's right to life shall be protected by law. No one shall be deprived of his life intentionally save in the execution of a sentence of a court following his conviction of a crime for which this penalty is provided by law.

2. Deprivation of life shall not be regarded as inflicted in contravention of this Article when it results from the use of force which is no more than absolutely necessary:

(a) in defense of any person from unlawful violence;

(b) in order to effect a lawful arrest or to prevent the escape of a person lawfully detained;

(c) in action lawfully taken for the purpose of quelling a riot or insurrection.

Article 3

No one shall be subjected to torture or to inhuman or degrading treatment or punishment.

Article 4

1. No one shall be held in slavery or servitude.

2. No one shall be required to perform forced or compulsory labor.

3. For the purpose of this Article the term "forced or compulsory labor" shall not include:

(a) any work required to be done in the ordinary course of detention imposed according to the provisions of Article 5 of this Convention or during conditional release from such detention;

(b) any service of a military character or, in case of conscientious objectors in countries where they are recognized, service exacted instead of compulsory military service;

(c) any service exacted in case of an emergency or calamity threatening the life or well-being of the community;

(d) any work or service which forms part of normal civic obligations.

Article 5

1. Everyone has the right to liberty and security of person. No one shall be deprived of his liberty save in the following cases and in accordance with a procedure prescribed by law:

(a) the lawful detention of a person after conviction by a competent court;

(b) the lawful arrest or detention of a person effected for non-compliance with the lawful order of a court or in order to secure the fulfillment of any obligation prescribed by law;

(c) the lawful arrest or detention of a person effected for the purpose of bringing him before the competent legal authority on reasonable suspicion of having committed an offense or when it is reasonably considered necessary to prevent his committing an offense or fleeing after having done so;

(d) the detention of a minor by lawful order for the purpose of educational supervision or his lawful detention for the purpose of bringing him before the competent legal authority;

(e) the lawful detention of persons for the prevention of the spreading of infectious diseases, of persons of unsound mind, alcoholics or drug addicts or vagrants;

(f) the unlawful arrest or detention of a person to prevent his effecting an unauthorized entry into the country or of a person against whom action is being taken with a view to deportation or extradition.

2. Everyone who is arrested shall be informed promptly, in a language which he understands, of the reasons for his arrest and of any charge against him.

3. Everyone arrested or detained in accordance with the provisions of paragraph 1(c) of this Article shall be brought promptly before a judge or other officer authorized by law to exercise judicial power and shall be entitled to trial within a reasonable time or to release pending trial. Release may be conditioned by guarantees to appear for trial.

4. Everyone who is deprived of his liberty by arrest or detention shall be entitled to take proceedings by which the lawfulness of his detention shall be decided speedily by a court and his release ordered if the detention is not lawful.

5. Everyone who has been the victim of arrest or detention in contravention of

the provisions of this Article shall have an enforceable right to compensation.

Article 6

1. In the determination of his civil rights and obligations or of any criminal charge against him, everyone is entitled to a fair and public hearing within a reasonable time by an independent and impartial tribunal established by law. Judgment shall be pronounced publicly but the press and public may be excluded from all or part of the trial in the interests of morals, public order or national security in a democratic society, where the interests of juveniles or the protection of the private life of the parties so require, or to the extent strictly necessary in the opinion of the court in special circumstances where publicity would prejudice the interests of justice.

2. Everyone charged with a criminal offense shall be presumed innocent until proved guilty according to law.

3. Everyone charged with a criminal offense has the following minimum rights:

(a) to be informed promptly, in a language which he understands and in detail, of the nature and cause of the accusation against him;

(b) to have adequate time and facilities for the preparation of his defense;

(c) to defend himself in person or through legal assistance of his own choosing or, if he has not sufficient means to pay for legal assistance, to be given it free when the interests of justice so require;

(d) to examine or have examined witnesses against him and to obtain the attendance and examination of witnesses on his behalf under the same conditions as witnesses against him;

(e) to have the free assistance of an interpreter if he cannot understand or speak the language used in court.

Article 7

1. No one shall be held guilty of any criminal offense on account of any act or omission which did not constitute a criminal offense under national or international law at the time when it was committed. Nor shall a heavier penalty be imposed than the one that was applicable at the time the criminal offense was committed.

2. This Article shall not prejudice the trial and punishment of any person for any act or omission which, at the time when it was committed, was criminal according to the general principles of law recognized by civilized nations.

Article 8

1. Everyone has the right to respect for his private and family life, his home and his correspondence.

2. There shall be no interference by a public authority with the exercise of this right except such as is in accordance with the law and is necessary in a democratic society in the interests of national security, public safety or the economic well-being of the country, for the prevention of disorder or crime, for the protection of health or morals, or for the protection of the rights and freedoms of others.

Article 9

1. Everyone has the right to freedom of thought, conscience and religion; this right includes freedom to change his religion or belief and freedom, either alone or in community with others and in public or private, to manifest his religion or belief, in worship, teaching, practice and observance.

2. Freedom to manifest one's religion or beliefs shall be subject only to such limitations as are prescribed by law and are necessary in a democratic society in the interests of public safety, for the protection of public order, health or morals, or for the protection of the rights and freedoms of others.

Article 10

1. Everyone has the right to freedom of expression. This right shall include freedom

to hold opinions and to receive and impart information and ideas without interference by public authority and regardless of frontiers. This Article shall not prevent States from requiring the licensing of broadcasting, television or cinema enterprises.

2. The exercise of these freedoms, since it carries with it duties and responsibilities, may be subject to such formalities, conditions, restrictions or penalties as are prescribed by law and are necessary in a democratic society, in the interests of national security, territorial integrity of public safety, for the prevention of disorder or crime, for the protection of health or morals, for the protection of the reputation or rights of others, for preventing the disclosure of information received in confidence, or for maintaining the authority and impartiality of the judiciary.

Article 11

1. Everyone has the right to freedom of peaceful assembly and to freedom of association with others, including the right to form and to join trade unions for the protection of his interests.

2. No restrictions shall be placed on the exercise of these rights other than such as are prescribed by law and are necessary in a democratic society in the interests of national security or public safety, for the prevention of disorder or crime, for the protection of health or morals or for the protection of the rights and freedoms of others. This Article shall not prevent the imposition of lawful restrictions on the exercise of these rights by members of the armed forces, of the police or of the administration of the State.

Article 12

Men and women of marriageable age have the right to marry and to found a family, according to the national laws governing the exercise of this right.

Article 13

Everyone whose rights and freedoms as set forth in this Convention are violated shall have an effective remedy before a national authority notwithstanding that the viola-

tion has been committed by persons acting in an official capacity.

Article 14

The enjoyment of the rights and freedoms set forth in this Convention shall be secured without discrimination on any ground such as sex, race, color, language, religion, political or other opinion, national or social origin, association with a national minority, property, birth or other status.

Article 15

1. In time of war or other public emergency threatening the life of the nation any High Contracting Party may take measures derogating from its obligations under this Convention to the extent strictly required by the exigencies of the situation, provided that such measures are not inconsistent with its other obligations under international law.

2. No derogation from Article 2, except in respect of deaths resulting from lawful acts of war, or from Articles 3, 4 (paragraph 1) and 7 shall be made under this provision.

3. Any High Contracting Party availing itself of this right of derogation shall keep the Secretary-General of the Council of Europe fully informed of the measures which it has taken and the reasons therefor. It shall also inform the Secretary-General of the Council of Europe when such measures have ceased to operate and the provisions of the Convention are again being fully executed.

Article 16

Nothing in Articles 10, 11 and 14 shall be regarded as preventing the High Contracting Parties from imposing restrictions on the political activity of aliens.

Article 17

Nothing in this Convention may be interpreted as implying for any State, group or person any right to engage in any activity or perform any act aimed at the destruction of any of the rights and freedoms set forth herein or at their limitation to a greater extent than is provided for in the Convention.

Article 18

The restrictions permitted under this Convention to the said rights and freedoms shall not be applied for any purpose other than those for which they have been prescribed.

Section II

Article 19

To ensure the observance of the engagements undertaken by the High Contracting Parties in the present Convention, there shall be set up:

(1) A European Commission of Human Rights hereinafter referred to as "the Commission;"

(2) A European Court of Human Rights, hereinafter referred to as "the Court."

Section III

Article 20

The Commission shall consist of a number of members equal to that of the High Contracting Parties. No two members of the Commission may be nationals of the same State....

Article 25

1. The Commission may receive petitions addressed to the Secretary-General of the Council of Europe from any person, non-governmental organization or group of individuals claiming to be the victim of a violation by one of the High Contracting Parties of the rights set forth in this Convention, provided that the High Contracting Party against which the complaint has been lodged has declared that it recognizes the competence of the Commission to receive such petitions. Those of the High Contracting Parties who have made such a declaration undertake not to hinder in any way the effective exercise of this right.

2. Such declarations may be made for a specific period.

3. The Declarations shall be deposited with the Secretary-General of the Council of Europe who shall transmit copies thereof to the High Contracting Parties and publish them.

4. The Commission shall only exercise the powers provided for in this Article when at least six High Contracting Parties are bound by declarations made in accordance with the preceding paragraphs....

[1] Adopted on November 4, 1950; entry into force, September 3, 1953.

First Protocol to the Convention for the Protection of Human Rights and Fundamental Freedoms (Paris, 1952)

The Governments signatory hereto, being Members of the Council of Europe,

Being resolved to take steps to ensure the collective enforcement of certain rights and freedoms other than those already included in Section I of the Convention for the Protection of Human Rights and Fundamental Freedoms signed at Rome on 4th November, 1950 (hereinafter referred to as '"the Convention"),

Have agreed as follows:

Article 1

Every natural or legal person is entitled to the peaceful enjoyment of his possessions. No one shall be deprived of his possessions except in the public interest and subject to the conditions provided for by law and by the general principles of international law.

The preceding provisions shall not, however, in any way impair the right of a State to enforce such laws as it deems necessary to control the use of property in accordance with the general interest or to secure the payment of taxes or other contributions or penalties.

Article 2

No person shall be denied the right to education. In the exercise of any functions which it assumes in relation to education and to teaching, the State shall respect the right of parents to ensure such education and teaching in conformity with their own religious and philosophical convictions.

Article 3

The High Contracting Parties undertake to hold free elections at reasonable intervals by secret ballot, under conditions which will ensure the free expression of the opinion of the people in the choice of the legislature.

Article 4

Any High Contracting Party may at the time of signature or ratification or at any time thereafter communicate to the Secretary-General of the Council of Europe a declaration stating the extent to which it undertakes that the provisions of the present Protocol shall apply to such of the territories for the international relations of which it is responsible as are named therein. Any High Contracting Party which has communicated a declaration in virtue of the preceding paragraph may from time to time communicate a further declaration modifying the terms of any former declaration or terminating the application of the provisions of this Protocol in respect of any territory.

A declaration made in accordance with this Article shall be deemed to have been made in accordance with Paragraph 1 of Article 63 of the Convention.

Article 5

As between the High Contracting Parties the provisions of Articles 1, 2, 3 and 4 of this Protocol shall be regarded as additional Articles to the Convention and all the provisions of the Convention shall apply accordingly.

Article 6

This Protocol shall be open for signature by the Members of the Council of Europe, who are the signatories of the Convention;

it shall be ratified at the same time as or after the ratification of the Convention. It shall enter into force after the deposit of ten instruments of ratification. As regards any signatory ratifying subsequently, the Protocol shall enter into force at the date of the deposit of ten instruments of ratification....

The instruments of ratification shall be deposited with the Secretary-General of the Council of Europe, who will notify all Members of the names of those who have ratified....

Fourth Protocol to the Convention for the Protection of Human Rights and Fundamental Freedoms, Securing Certain Rights and Freedoms Other Than Those Already Included in the Convention and in the Protocol Thereto (Strasbourg, 1963)

The Governments signatory hereto, being Members of the Council of Europe;

Being resolved to take steps to ensure the collective enforcement of certain rights and freedoms other than those already included in Section I of the Convention for the Protection of Human Rights and Fundamental Freedoms signed at Rome on 4 November 1950 (hereinafter referred to as "the Convention") and in Articles 1 to 3 of the First Protocol to the Convention, signed at Paris on 20 March 1952,

Have agreed as follows:

Article 1

No one shall be deprived of his liberty merely on the ground of inability to fulfill a contractual obligation.

Article 2

1. Everyone lawfully within the territory of a State shall, within that territory, have the right to liberty of movement and freedom to choose his residence.

2. Everyone shall be free to leave any country, including his own.

3. No restrictions shall be placed on the exercise of these rights other than such as are in accordance with law and are necessary in a democratic society in the interests of national security or public safety, for the maintenance of *ordre public*, for the prevention of crime, for the protection of health or morals, or for the protection of the rights and freedoms of others.

4. The rights set forth in paragraph 1 may also be subject, in particular areas, to restrictions imposed in accordance with law and justified by the public interest in a democratic society.

Article 3

1. No one shall be expelled, by means either of an individual or of a collective measure, from the territory of the State of which he is a national.

2. No one shall be deprived of the right to enter the territory of the State of which he is a national.

Article 4

Collective expulsion of aliens is prohibited.

Article 5

1. Any High Contracting Party may, at the time of signature or ratification of this Protocol, or at any time thereafter, communicate to the Secretary-General of the Council of Europe a declaration stating the extent to which it undertakes that the provisions of this Protocol shall apply to such of the territories for the international relations of which it is responsible as are named therein.

2. Any High Contracting Party which has communicated a declaration in virtue of the preceding paragraph may, from time to time, communicate a further declaration modifying the terms of any former declaration or terminating the application of the provisions of this Protocol in respect of any territory.

3. A declaration made in accordance with this Article shall be deemed to have been made in accordance with paragraph 1 of Article 63 of the Convention.

4. The territory of any State to which this Protocol applies by virtue of ratification or acceptance by that State, and each territory to which this Protocol is applied by virtue of a declaration by that State under this Article, shall be treated as separate territories for the purpose of the references in Articles 2 and 3 to the territory of a State.

Article 6

1. As between the High Contracting Parties the provisions of Articles 1 to 5 of this Protocol shall be regarded as additional Articles to the Convention, and all the provisions of the Convention shall apply accordingly.

2. Nevertheless, the right of individual recourse recognized by a declaration made under Article 25 of the Convention, or the acceptance of the compulsory jurisdiction of the Court by a declaration made under Article 46 of the Convention, shall not be effective in relation to this Protocol unless the High Contracting Party concerned has made a statement recognizing such right, or accepting such jurisdiction, in respect of all or any of Articles 1 to 4 of the Protocol....

Sixth Protocol to the Convention for the Protection of Human Rights and Fundamental Freedoms Concerning the Abolition of the Death Penalty (Strasbourg, 1983)

The member States of the Council of Europe, signatory to this Protocol to the Convention for the Protection of Human Rights and Fundamental Freedoms, signed at Rome on 4 November 1950 (hereinafter referred to as "the Convention"),

Considering that the evolution that has occurred in several member States of the Council of Europe expresses a general tendency in favor of abolition of the death penalty,

Have agreed as follows:

Article 1

The death penalty shall be abolished. No one shall be condemned to such penalty or executed.

Article 2

A State may make provision in its law for the death penalty in respect of acts committed in time of war or of imminent threat of war; such penalty shall be applied only in the instances laid down in the law and in accordance with its provisions. The State shall communicate to the Secretary-General of the Council of Europe the relevant provisions of that law....

[1] Adopted 1977; entry into force, 1979.

15.12 UNITED NATIONS INTERNATIONAL COVENANT ON CIVIL AND POLITICAL RIGHTS (ADOPTED, 1966; ENTRY INTO FORCE, 1976)[1]

Preamble

The States Parties to the present Covenant,

Considering that, in accordance with the principles proclaimed in the Charter of the United Nations, recognition of the inherent dignity and of the equal and unalienable rights of all members of the human family is the foundation of freedom, justice and peace in the world,

Recognizing that these rights derive from the inherent dignity of the human person,

Recognizing that, in accordance with the Universal Declaration of Human Rights, the ideal of free human beings enjoying civil and political freedom and freedom from fear and want can only be achieved if conditions are created whereby everyone may enjoy his civil and political rights, as well as his economic, social and cultural rights,

Considering the obligation of States under the Charter of the United Nations to promote universal respect for, and observance of, human rights and freedoms.

Realizing that the individual, having duties to other individuals and to the community to which he belongs, is under a responsibility to strive for the promotion and observance of the rights recognized in the present Covenant,

Agree upon the following articles:

Part I

Article 1

1. All peoples have the right of self-determination. By virtue of the right they freely determine their political status and freely pursue their economic, social and cultural development.

2. All peoples, may, for their own ends, freely dispose of their natural wealth and resources without prejudice to any obligations arising out of international economic cooperation, based upon the principle of mutual benefit, and international law. In no case may a people be deprived of its own means of subsistence.

3. The States Parties to the present Covenant, including those having responsibility for the administration of Non-Self-Governing and Trust Territories, shall promote the realization of the right of self-determination, and shall respect that right, in conformity with the provisions of the United Nations Charter.

Part II

Article 2

1. Each State Party to the present Covenant undertakes to respect and to ensure to all individuals within its territory and subject to its jurisdiction the rights recognized in the present Covenant, without distinction of any kind, such as race, color, sex, language, religion, political or other opinion, national or social origin, property, birth or other status.

2. Where not already provided for by existing legislative or other measures, each State Party to the present Covenant undertakes to take the necessary steps, in accordance with its constitutional processes and with the provisions of the present Covenant, to

adopt such legislative or other measures as may be necessary to give effect to the rights recognized in the present Covenant.

3. Each State Party to the present Covenant undertakes:

(a) To ensure that any person whose rights or freedoms as herein recognized are violated shall have an effective remedy notwithstanding that the violation has been committed by persons acting in an official capacity;

(b) To ensure that any person claiming such a remedy shall have his right thereto determined by competent judicial, administrative or legislative authorities, or by any other competent authority provided for by the legal system of the State, and to develop the possibilities of judicial remedy;

(c) To ensure that the competent authorities shall enforce such remedies when granted.

Article 3

The States Parties to the present Covenant undertake to ensure the equal right of men and women to the enjoyment of all civil and political rights set forth in the present Covenant.

Article 4

1. In time of public emergency which threatens the life of the nation and the existence of which is officially proclaimed, the States Parties to the present Covenant may take measures derogating from their obligations under the present Covenant to the extent strictly required by the exigencies of the situation, provided that such measures are not inconsistent with their other obligations under international law and do not involve discrimination solely on the ground of race, color, sex, language, religion or social origin.

2. No derogation from articles 6, 7, 8 (paragraphs 1 and 2), 11, 15, 16 and 18 may be made under this provision.

3. Any State Party to the present Covenant availing itself of the right of derogation

shall inform immediately the other States Parties to the present Covenant, through the intermediary of the Secretary-General of the United Nations of the provisions from which it has derogated and of the reasons by which it was actuated. A further communication shall be made, through the same intermediary, on the date on which it terminates such derogation.

Article 5

1. Nothing in the present Covenant may be interpreted as implying for any State, group or person any right to engage in any activity or perform any act aimed at the destruction of any of the rights and freedoms recognized herein or at their limitation to a greater extent than is provided for in the present Covenant.

2. There shall be no restriction upon or derogation from any of the fundamental human rights recognized or existing in any State Party to the present Covenant pursuant to law, conventions, regulations or custom on the pretext that the present Covenant does not recognize such rights or that it recognizes them to a lesser extent.

Part III

Article 6

1. Every human being has the inherent right to life. This right shall be protected by law. No one shall be arbitrarily deprived of his life.

2. In countries which have not abolished the death penalty, sentence of death may be imposed only for the most serious crimes in accordance with law in force at the time of the commission of the crime and not contrary to the provisions of the present Covenant and to the Convention on the Prevention and Punishment of the Crime of Genocide. This penalty can only be carried out pursuant to a final judgment rendered by a competent court.

3. When deprivation of life constitutes the crime of genocide, it is understood that nothing in this article shall authorize any State Party to the present Covenant to derogate in any way from any obligation assumed under the provisions of the Con-

vention on the Prevention and Punishment of the Crime of Genocide.

4. Anyone sentenced to death shall have the right to seek pardon or commutation of the sentence. Amnesty, pardon or commutation of the sentence of death may be granted in all cases.

5. Sentence of death shall not be imposed for crimes committed by persons below eighteen years of age and shall not be carried out on pregnant women.

6. Nothing in this article shall be invoked to delay or to prevent the abolition of capital punishment by any State Party to the present Covenant.

Article 7

No one shall be subjected to torture or to cruel, inhuman or degrading treatment or punishment. In particular, no one shall be subjected without his free consent to medical or scientific experimentation.

Article 8

1. No one shall be held in slavery; slavery and the slave trade in all their forms shall be prohibited.

2. No one shall be held in servitude.

3. (a) No one shall be required to perform forced or compulsory labor;

(b) The preceding subparagraph shall not be held to preclude in countries where imprisonment with hard labor may be imposed as a punishment for a crime, the performance of hard labor in pursuance of a sentence to such punishment by a competent court;

(c) For the purpose of this paragraph the term "forced or compulsory labor" shall not include:

i. Any work or service, not referred to in subparagraph (b), normally required of a person who is under detention in consequence of a lawful order of a court, or of a person during conditional release from such detention;

ii. Any service of a military character and, in countries where conscientious objection is recognized, any national service required by law of conscientious objectors;

iii. Any service exacted in cases of emergency or calamity threatening the life or well-being of the community;

iv. Any work or service which forms part of normal civil obligations.

Article 9

1. Everyone has the right to liberty and security of person. No one shall be subjected to arbitrary arrest or detention. No one shall be deprived of his liberty except on such grounds and in accordance with such procedures as are established by law.

2. Anyone who is arrested shall be informed, at the time of arrest, of the reasons for his arrest and shall be promptly informed of any charges against him.

3. Anyone arrested or detained on a criminal charge shall be brought promptly before a judge or other officer authorized by law to exercise judicial power and shall be entitled to trial within a reasonable time or to release. It shall not be the general rule that persons awaiting trial shall be detained in custody, but release may be subject to guarantees to appear for trial, at any other stage of the judicial proceedings, and, should occasion arise, for execution of the judgment.

4. Anyone who is deprived of his liberty by arrest or detention shall be entitled to take proceedings before a court, in order that such court may decide without delay on the lawfulness of his detention and order his release if the detention is not lawful.

5. Anyone who has been the victim of unlawful arrest or detention shall have an enforceable right to compensation.

Article 10

1. All persons deprived of their liberty shall be treated with humanity and with

respect for the inherent dignity of the human person.

2. (a) Accused persons shall, save in exceptional circumstances, be segregated from convicted persons, and shall be subject to separate treatment appropriate to their status as unconvicted persons;

(b) Accused juvenile persons shall be separated from adults and brought as speedily as possible for adjudication.

3. The penitentiary system shall comprise treatment of prisoners the essential aim of which shall be their reformation and social rehabilitation. Juvenile offenders shall be segregated from adults and be accorded treatment appropriate to their age and legal status.

Article 11

No one shall be imprisoned merely on the ground of inability to fulfill a contractual obligation.

Article 12

1. Everyone lawfully within the territory of a State shall, within that territory, have the right to liberty of movement and freedom to choose his residence.

2. Everyone shall be free to leave any country, including his own.

3. The above-mentioned rights shall not be subject to any restrictions except those which are provided by law, are necessary to protect national security, public order ("*ordre public*"), health or morals or the rights and freedoms of others, and are consistent with the other rights recognized in the present Covenant.

4. No one shall be arbitrarily deprived of the right to enter his own country.

Article 13

An alien lawfully in the territory of a State Party to the present Covenant may be expelled therefrom only in pursuance of a decision reached in accordance with law and shall, except where compelling reasons of national security otherwise require, be allowed to submit the reasons against his expulsion and to have his case reviewed by, and be represented for the purpose before, the competent authority or a person or persons especially designated by the competent authority.

Article 14

1. All persons shall be equal before the courts and tribunals. In the determination of any criminal charge against him, or of his rights and obligations in a suit at law, everyone shall be entitled to a fair and public hearing by a competent, independent and impartial tribunal established by law. The Press and the public may be excluded from all or part of a trial for reasons of morals, public order ("*ordre public*") or national security in a democratic society, or when the interest of the private lives of the parties so requires, or to the extent strictly necessary in the opinion of the court in special circumstances where publicity would prejudice the interests of justice; but any judgment rendered in a criminal case or in a suit at law shall be made public except where the interest of juveniles otherwise requires or the proceedings concern matrimonial disputes or the guardianship of children.

2. Everyone charged with a criminal offense shall have the right to be presumed innocent until proved guilty according to law.

3. In the determination of any criminal charge against him, everyone shall be entitled to the following minimum guarantees, in full equality:

(a) To be informed promptly and in detail in a language which he understands of the nature and cause of the charge against him;

(b) To have adequate time and facilities for the preparation of his defense and to communicate with counsel of his own choosing;

(c) To be tried without undue delay.

(d) To be tried in his presence, and to defend himself in person or through legal assistance of his own choosing; to be informed, if he does not have legal assistance, of this right; and to have legal assistance assigned to him, in any case where the interests of justice so require, and without payment by him in any such case if he does not have sufficient means to pay for it;

(e) To examine, or have examined, the witnesses against him and to obtain the attendance and examination of witnesses on his behalf under the same conditions as witnesses against him;

(f) To have the free assistance of an interpreter if he cannot understand or speak the language used in court;

(g) Not to be compelled to testify against himself, or to confess guilt.

4. In the case of juveniles, the procedure shall be such as will take account of their age and the desirability of promoting their rehabilitation.

5. Everyone convicted of a crime shall have the right to his conviction and sentence being reviewed by a higher tribunal according to law.

6. When a person has by a final decision been convicted of a criminal offense and when subsequently his conviction has been reversed or he has been pardoned on the ground that a new or newly discovered fact shows conclusively that there has been a miscarriage of justice, the person who has suffered punishment as a result of such conviction shall be compensated according to law, unless it is proved that the non-disclosure of the unknown fact in time is wholly or partly attributable to him.

7. No one shall be liable to be tried or punished again for an offense for which he has already been finally convicted or acquitted in accordance with the law and penal procedure of each country.

Article 15

1. No one shall be held guilty of any criminal offense on account of any act or omission which did not constitute a criminal offense, under national or international law, at the time when it was committed. Nor shall a heavier penalty be imposed than the one that was applicable at the time when the criminal offense was committed. If, subsequently to the commission of the offense, provision is made by law for the imposition of a lighter penalty, the offender shall benefit thereby.

2. Nothing in this article shall prejudice the trial and punishment of any person for any act or omission which, at the time when it was committed, was criminal according to the general principles of law recognized by the community of nations.

Article 16

Everyone shall have the right to recognition everywhere as a person before the law.

Article 17

1. No one shall be subjected to arbitrary or unlawful interference with his privacy, family, home or correspondence, nor to unlawful attacks on his honor and reputation.

2. Everyone has the right to the protection of the law against such interference or attacks.

Article 18

1. Everyone shall have the right to freedom of thought, conscience and religion. This right shall include freedom to have or to adopt a religion or belief of his choice, and freedom either individually or in community with others and in public or private, to manifest this religion or belief in worship, observance, practice and teaching.

2. No one shall be subject to coercion which would impair his freedom to have or to adopt a religion or belief of his choice.

3. Freedom to manifest one's religion or beliefs may be subject only to such limitations as are prescribed by law and are necessary to protect public safety, order, health, or morals or the fundamental rights and freedoms of others.

4. The States Parties to the present Covenant undertake to have respect for the liberty of parents and, when applicable, legal guardians, to ensure the religious and moral education of their children in conformity with their own convictions.

Article 19

1. Everyone shall have the right to hold opinions without interference.

2. Everyone shall have the right to freedom of expression; this right shall include freedom to seek, receive and impart information and ideas of all kinds, regardless of frontiers, either orally, in writing or in print, in the form of art, or through any other media of his choice.

3. The exercise of the rights provided for in the foregoing paragraph carries with it special duties and responsibilities. It may therefore be subject to certain restrictions, but these shall be such only as are provided by law and are necessary, (1) for respect of the rights or reputations of others, (2) for the protection of national security or of public order (*"ordre public"*), or of public health or morals.

Article 20

1. Any propaganda for war shall be prohibited by law.

2. Any advocacy of national, racial, or religious hatred that constitutes incitement to discrimination, hostility or violence shall be prohibited by law.

Article 21

The right of peaceful assembly shall be recognized. No restrictions may be placed on the exercise of this right other than those imposed in conformity with the law and which are necessary in a democratic society in the interests of national security or public safety, public order (*"ordre public"*), the protection of public health or morals or the protection of the rights and freedoms of others.

Article 22

1. Everyone shall have the right to freedom of association with others, including the right to form and join trade unions for the protection of his interests.

2. No restrictions may be placed on the exercise of this right other than those prescribed by law and which are necessary in a democratic society in the interests of national security or public safety, public order (*"ordre public"*), the protection of public health or morals or the protection of the rights and freedoms of others. This article shall not prevent the imposition of lawful restrictions on members of the armed forces and of the police in their exercise of this right.

3. Nothing in this article shall authorize States Parties to the International Labor Convention of 1948 on Freedom of Association and Protection of the Right to Organize to take legislative measures which would prejudice, or to apply the law in such a manner as to prejudice, the guarantees provided for in the Convention.

Article 23

1. The family is the natural and fundamental group unit of society and is entitled to protection by society and the State.

2. The right of men and women of marriageable age to marry and to found a family shall be recognized.

3. No marriage shall be entered into without the free and full consent of the intending spouses.

4. States Parties to the present Covenant shall take appropriate steps to ensure equality of rights and responsibilities of spouses as to marriage, during marriage and at its dissolution. In the case of a dissolution, provision shall be made for the necessary protection of any children.

Article 24

1. Every child shall have, without any discrimination as to race, color, sex, language, religion, national or social origin, property or birth, the right to such measures of pro-

tection as required by his status as a minor, on the part of his family, the society and the State.

2. Every child shall be registered immediately after birth and shall have a name.

3. Every child has the right to acquire a nationality.

Article 25

Every citizen shall have the right and the opportunity, without any of the distinctions mentioned in Article 2 and without unreasonable restrictions:

(a) To take part in the conduct of public affairs, directly or through freely chosen representatives;

(b) To vote and to be elected at genuine periodic elections which shall be by universal and equal suffrage and shall be held by secret ballot, guaranteeing the free expression of the will of the electors;

(c) To have access, on general terms of equality, to public service in his country.

Article 26

All persons are equal before the law and are entitled without any discrimination to equal protection of the law. In this respect the law shall prohibit any discrimination and guarantee to all persons equal and effective protection against discrimination on any ground such as race, color, sex, language, religion, political or other opinion, national or social origin, property, birth or other status.

Article 27

In those States in which ethnic, religious or linguistic minorities exist, persons belonging to such minorities shall not be denied the right, in community with the other members of their group, to enjoy their own culture, to profess and practice their own religion, or to use their own language.

[1] Adopted on December 16, 1966; entry into force, March 23, 1976.

15.13 UNITED NATIONS INTERNATIONAL COVENANT ON ECONOMIC, SOCIAL, AND CULTURAL RIGHTS (ADOPTED, 1966; ENTRY INTO FORCE, 1976)[1]

Preamble

The States Parties to the present Covenant,

Considering that, in accordance with the principles proclaimed in the Charter of the United Nations, recognition of the inherent dignity and of the equal and inalienable rights of all members of the human family is the foundation of freedom, justice and peace in the world,

Recognizing that these rights derive from the inherent dignity of the human person,

Recognizing that, in accordance with the Universal Declaration of Human Rights, the ideal of free human beings enjoying freedom from fear and want can only be achieved if conditions are created whereby everyone may enjoy his economic, social and cultural rights, as well as his civil and political rights,

Considering the obligation of States under the Charter of the United Nations to promote universal respect for, and observance of, human rights and freedoms,

Realizing that the individual, having duties to other individuals and to the community to which he belongs, is under a responsibility to strive for the promotion and observance of the rights recognized in the present Covenant,

Agree upon the following articles:

Part I

Article 1

1. All peoples have the right of self-determination. By virtue of that right they freely determine their political status and freely pursue their economic, social and cultural development.

2. All peoples may, for their own ends, freely dispose of their natural wealth and resources without prejudice to any obliga-

tions arising out of international economic co-operation, based upon the principle of mutual benefit, and international law. In no case may a people be deprived of its own means of subsistence.

3. The States Parties to the present Covenant, including those having responsibility for the administration of Non-Self-Governing and Trust Territories, shall promote the realization of the right of self-determination, and shall respect that right, in conformity with the provisions of the Charter of the United Nations.

Part II

Article 2

1. Each State Party to the present Covenant undertakes to take steps, individually and through international assistance and co-operation, especially economic and technical, to the maximum of its available resources, with a view to achieving progressively the full realization of the rights recognized in the present Covenant by all appropriate means, including particularly the adoption of legislative measures.

2. The States Parties to the present Covenant undertake to guarantee that the rights enunciated in the present Covenant will be exercised without discrimination of any kind as to race, color, sex, language, religion, political or other opinion, national or social origin, property, birth or other status.

3. Developing countries, with due regard to human rights and their national economy, may determine to what extent they would guarantee the economic rights recognized in the present Covenant to non-nationals.

Article 3

The States Parties to the present Covenant undertake to ensure the equal right of men and women to the enjoyment of all economic, social and cultural rights set forth in the present Covenant.

Article 4

The States Parties to the present Covenant recognize that, in the enjoyment of those rights provided by the State in conformity with the present Covenant, the State may subject such rights only to such limitations as are determined by law only in so far as this may be compatible with the nature of these rights and solely for the purpose of promoting the general welfare in a democratic society.

Article 5

1. Nothing in the present Covenant may be interpreted as implying for any State, group or person any right to engage in any activity or to perform any act aimed at the destruction of any of the rights or freedoms recognized herein, or at their limitation to a greater extent than is provided for in the present Covenant.

2. No restriction upon or derogation from any of the fundamental human rights recognized or existing in any country in virtue of law, conventions, regulations or custom shall be admitted on the pretext that the present Covenant does not recognize such rights or that it recognizes them to a lesser extent.

Part III

Article 6

1. The States Parties to the present Covenant recognize the right to work, which includes the right of everyone to the opportunity to gain his living by work which he freely chooses or accepts, and will take appropriate steps to safeguard this right.

2. The steps to be taken by a State Party to the present Covenant to achieve the full realization of this right shall include technical and vocational guidance and training programs, policies and techniques to achieve steady economic, social and cultural development and full and productive employment under conditions safeguarding fundamental political and economic freedoms to the individual.

Article 7

The States Parties to the present Covenant recognize the right of everyone to the enjoyment of just and favorable conditions of work which ensure, in particular:

a. Remuneration which provides all workers, as a minimum, with:

(i) Fair wages and equal remuneration for work of equal value without distinction of any kind, in particular women being guaranteed conditions of work not inferior to those enjoyed by men, with equal pay for equal work;

(ii) A decent living for themselves and their families in accordance with the provisions of the present Covenant;

b. Safe and healthy working conditions;

c. Equal opportunity for everyone to be promoted in his employment to an appropriate higher level, subject to no considerations other than those of seniority and competence;

d. Rest, leisure and reasonable limitation of working hours and periodic holidays with pay, as well as remuneration for public holidays.

Article 8

1. The States Parties to the present Covenant undertake to ensure:

(a) The right of everyone to form trade unions and join the trade union of his choice, subject only to the rules of the organization concerned, for the promotion and protection of his economic and social interests. No restrictions may be placed on the exercise of this right other than those prescribed by law and which are necessary in a democratic society in the interests of national security or public order or for the protection of the rights and freedoms of others;

(b) The right of trade unions to establish national federations or confederations and the right of the latter to form or join international trade-union organizations;

(c) The right of trade unions to function freely subject to no limitations other than those prescribed by law and which are necessary in a democratic society in the interests of national security or public

order or for the protection of the rights and freedoms of others;

(d) The right to strike, provided that it is exercised in conformity with the laws of the particular country.

2. This article shall not prevent the imposition of lawful restrictions on the exercise of these rights by members of the armed forces or of the police or of the administration of the State.

3. Nothing in this article shall authorize States Parties to the International Labor Organization Convention of 1948 concerning Freedom of Association and Protection of the Right to Organize to take legislative measures which would prejudice, or apply the law in such a manner as would prejudice, the guarantees provided for in that Convention.

Article 9

The States Parties to the present Covenant recognize the right of everyone to social security, including social insurance.

Article 10

The States Parties to the present Covenant recognize that:

1. The widest possible protection and assistance should be accorded to the family, which is the natural and fundamental group unit of society, particularly for its establishment and while it is responsible for the care and education of dependent children. Marriage must be entered into with the free consent of the intending spouses.

2. Special protection should be accorded to mothers during a reasonable period before and after childbirth. During such period working mothers should be accorded paid leave or leave with adequate social security benefits.

3. Special measures of protection and assistance should be taken on behalf of all children and young persons without any discrimination for reasons of parentage or other conditions. Children and young per-

sons should be protected from economic and social exploitation. Their employment in work harmful to their morals or health or dangerous to life or likely to hamper their normal development should be punishable by law. States should also set age limits below which the paid employment of child labor should be prohibited and punishable by law.

Article 11

1. The States Parties to the present Covenant recognize the right of everyone to an adequate standard of living for himself and his family, including adequate food, clothing and housing, and to the continuous improvement of living conditions. The States Parties will take appropriate steps to ensure the realization of this right, recognizing to this effect the essential importance of international co-operation based on free consent.

2. The States Parties to the present Covenant, recognizing the fundamental right of everyone to be free from hunger, shall take, individually and through international co-operation, the measures, including specific programs, which are needed:

(a) To improve methods of production, conservation and distribution of food by making full use of technical and scientific knowledge, by disseminating knowledge of the principles of nutrition and by developing or reforming agrarian systems in such a way as to achieve the most efficient development and utilization of natural resources;

(b) Taking into account the problems of both food-importing and food-exporting countries, to ensure an equitable distribution of world food supplies in relation to need.

Article 12

1. The States Parties to the present Covenant recognize the right of everyone to the enjoyment of the highest attainable standard of physical and mental health.

2. The steps to be taken by the States Parties to the present Covenant to achieve the full realization of this right shall include those necessary for:

(a) The provision for the reduction of the stillbirth-rate and of infant mortality and for the healthy development of the child;

(b) The improvement of all aspects of environmental and industrial hygiene;

(c) The prevention, treatment and control of epidemic, endemic, occupational and other diseases;

(d) The creation of conditions which would assure to all medical service and medical attention in the event of sickness.

Article 13

1. The States Parties to the present Covenant recognize the right of everyone to education. They agree that education shall be directed to the full development of the human personality and the sense of its dignity, and shall strengthen the respect for human rights and fundamental freedoms. They further agree that education shall enable all persons to participate effectively in a free society, promote understanding, tolerance and friendship among all nations and all racial, ethnic or religious groups, and further the activities of the United Nations for the maintenance of peace.

2. The States Parties to the present Covenant recognize that, with a view to achieving the full realization of this right:

(a) Primary education shall be compulsory and available free to all;

(b) Secondary education in its different forms, including technical and vocational secondary education, shall be made generally available and accessible to all by every appropriate means, and in particular by the progressive introduction of free education;

(c) Higher education shall be made equally accessible to all, on the basis of capacity, by every appropriate means, and in particular by the progressive introduction of free education;

(d) Fundamental education shall be encouraged or intensified as far as possible for those persons who have not received or completed the whole period of their primary education;

(e) The development of a system of schools at all levels shall be actively pursued, an adequate fellowship system shall be established, and the material conditions of teaching staff shall be continuously improved.

3. The States Parties to the present Covenant undertake to have respect for the liberty of parents and, when applicable, legal guardians to choose for their children schools, other than those established by the public authorities, which conform to such minimum educational standards as may be laid down or approved by the State and to ensure the religious and moral education of their children in conformity with their own convictions.

4. No part of this article shall be construed so as to interfere with the liberty of individuals and bodies to establish and direct educational institutions, subject always to the observance of the principles set forth in paragraph 1 of this article and to the requirement that the education given in such institutions shall conform to such minimum standards as may be laid down by the State.

Article 14

Each State Party to the present Covenant which, at the time of becoming a Party, has not been able to secure in its metropolitan territory or other territories under its jurisdiction compulsory primary education, free of charge, undertakes, within two years, to work out and adopt a detailed plan of action for the progressive implementation, within a reasonable number of years, to be fixed in the plan, of the principle of compulsory education free of charge for all.

Article 15

1. The States Parties to the present Covenant recognize the right of everyone:

(a) To take part in cultural life;

(b) To enjoy the benefits of scientific progress and its applications;

(c) To benefit from the protection of the moral and material interests resulting from any scientific, literary or artistic production of which he is the author.

2. The steps to be taken by the States Parties to the present Covenant to achieve the full realization of this right shall include those necessary for the conservation, the development and the diffusion of science and culture.

3. The States Parties to the present Covenant undertake to respect the freedom indispensable for scientific research and creative activity.

4. The States Parties to the present Covenant recognize the benefits to be derived from the encouragement and development of international contacts and co-operation in the scientific and cultural fields.

Part IV

Article 16

1. The States Parties to the present Covenant undertake to submit in conformity with this part of the Covenant reports on the measures which they have adopted and the progress made in achieving the observance of the rights recognized herein.

2. (a) All reports shall be submitted to the Secretary-General of the United Nations, who shall transmit copies to the Economic and Social Council for consideration in accordance with the provisions of the present Covenant;

(b) The Secretary-General of the United Nations shall also transmit to the specialized agencies copies of the reports, or any relevant parts therefrom, from States Parties to the present Covenant which are also members of these specialized agencies in so far as these reports, or parts therefrom, relate to any matters which fall within the responsibilities of the said agencies in accordance with their constitutional instruments.

Article 17

1. The States Parties to the present Covenant shall furnish their reports in stages, in accordance with a program to be established by the Economic and Social Council within one year of the entry into force of the present Covenant after consultation with the States Parties and the specialized agencies concerned.

2. Reports may indicate factors and difficulties affecting the degree of fulfillment of obligations under the present Covenant.

3. Where relevant information has previously been furnished to the United Nations or to any specialized agency by any State Party to the present Covenant, it will not be necessary to reproduce that information, but a precise reference to the information so furnished will suffice.

Article 18

Pursuant to its responsibilities under the Charter of the United Nations in the field of human rights and fundamental freedoms, the Economic and Social Council may make arrangements with the specialized agencies in respect of their reporting to it on the progress made in achieving the observance of the provisions of the present Covenant falling within the scope of their activities. These reports may include particulars of decisions and recommendations on such implementation adopted by their competent organs.

Article 19

The Economic and Social Council may transmit to the Commission on Human Rights for study and general recommendation or, as appropriate, for information the reports concerning human rights submitted by States in accordance with articles 16 and 17, and those concerning human rights submitted by the specialized agencies in accordance with article 18.

Article 20

The States Parties to the present Covenant and the specialized agencies concerned may submit comments to the Economic and Social Council on any general recommendation under article 19 or reference to such general recommendation in any report of the Commission on Human Rights or any documentation referred to therein.

Article 21

The Economic and Social Council may submit from time to time to the General Assembly reports with recommendations of a general nature and a summary of the information received from the States Parties to the present Covenant and the specialized agencies on the measures taken and the progress made in achieving general observance of the rights recognized in the present Covenant.

Article 22

The Economic and Social Council may bring to the attention of other organs of the United Nations, their subsidiary organs and specialized agencies concerned with furnishing technical assistance any matters arising out of the reports referred to in this part of the present Covenant which may assist such bodies in deciding, each within its field of competence, on the advisability of international measures likely to contribute to the effective progressive implementation of the present Covenant.

Article 23

The States Parties to the present Covenant agree that international action for the achievement of the rights recognized in the present Covenant includes such methods as the conclusion of conventions, the adoption of recommendations, the furnishing of technical assistance and the holding of regional meetings and technical meetings for the purpose of consultation and study organized in conjunction with the Governments concerned.

Article 24

Nothing in the present Covenant shall be interpreted as impairing the provisions of the Charter of the United Nations and of the constitutions of the specialized agencies which define the respective responsibilities of the various organs of the United Nations and of the specialized agencies in regard to the matters dealt with in the present Covenant.

Article 25

Nothing in the present Covenant shall be interpreted as impairing the inherent right of all peoples to enjoy and utilize fully and freely their natural wealth and resources.

[1] Adopted on December 16, 1966; entry into force, January 3, 1976.

15.14   AMERICAN CONVENTION ON HUMAN RIGHTS (ADOPTED, 1969; ENTRY INTO FORCE, 1978)[1]

Preamble

The American states signatory to the present Convention,

Reaffirming their intention to consolidate in this hemisphere, within the framework of democratic institutions, a system of personal liberty and social justice based on respect for the essential rights of man;

Recognizing that the essential rights of man are not derived from one's being a national of a certain state, but are based upon attributes of the human personality, and that they therefore justify international protection in the form of a convention reinforcing or complementing the protection provided by the domestic law of the American states;

Considering that these principles have been set forth in the Charter of the Organization of American States, in the American Declaration of the Rights and Duties of Man, and in the Universal Declaration of Human Rights, and that they have been reaffirmed and refined in other international instruments, worldwide as well as regional in scope;

Reiterating that, in accordance with the Universal Declaration of Human Rights, the ideal of free men enjoying freedom from fear and want can be achieved only if conditions are created whereby everyone may enjoy his economic, social, and cultural rights, as well as his civil and political rights; and

Considering that the Third Special Inter-American Conference (Buenos Aires, 1967) approved the incorporation into the Charter of the Organization itself broader standards with respect to economic, social, and educational rights and resolved that an inter-American convention on human rights should determine the structure, competence, and procedure of the organs responsible for these matters,

Have agreed upon the following:

Part I: State Obligations and Rights Protected

Chapter I: General Obligations

Article 1: Obligation to Respect Rights

1. The States Parties to this Convention undertake to respect the rights and freedoms recognized herein and to ensure to all persons subject to their jurisdiction the free and full exercise of those rights and freedoms, without any discrimination for reasons of race, color, sex, language, religion, political or other opinion, national or social origin, economic status, birth, or any other social condition.

2. For the purposes of this Convention, "person" means every human being.

Article 2: Domestic Legal Effects

Where the exercise of any of the rights or freedoms referred to in Article 1 is not already ensured by legislative or other provisions, the States Parties undertake to adopt, in accordance with their constitutional processes and the provisions of this Convention, such legislative or other measures as may be necessary to give effect to those rights or freedoms.

Chapter II: Civil and Political Rights

Article 3: Right to Juridical Personality

Every person has the right to recognition as a person before the law.

Article 4: Right to Life

1. Every person has the right to have his life respected. This right shall be protected by law and, in general, from the moment of conception. No one shall be arbitrarily deprived of his life.

2. In countries that have not abolished the death penalty, it may be imposed only for the most serious crimes and pursuant to a final judgment rendered by a competent court and in accordance with a law establishing such punishment, enacted prior to the commission of the crime. The application of such punishment shall not be extended to crimes to which it does not presently apply.

3. The death penalty shall not be reestablished in states that have abolished it.

4. In no case shall capital punishment be inflicted for political offenses or related common crimes.

5. Capital punishment shall not be imposed upon persons who, at the time the crime was committed, were under 18 years of age or over 70 years of age; nor shall it be applied to pregnant women.

6. Every person condemned to death shall have the right to apply for amnesty, pardon, or commutation of sentence, which may be granted in all cases. Capital punishment shall not be imposed while such a petition is pending decision by the competent authority.

Article 5: Right to Humane Treatment

1. Every person has the right to have his physical, mental, and moral integrity respected.

2. No one shall be subjected to torture or to cruel, inhuman, or degrading punishment or treatment. All persons deprived of their liberty shall be treated with respect for the inherent dignity of the human person.

3. Punishment shall not be extended to any person other than the criminal.

4. Accused persons shall, save in exceptional circumstances, be segregated from convicted persons, and shall be subject to separate treatment appropriate to their status as unconvicted persons.

5. Minors while subject to criminal proceedings shall be separated from adults and brought before specialized tribunals, as speedily as possible, so that they may be treated in accordance with their status as minors.

6. Punishments consisting of deprivation of liberty shall have as an essential aim the reform and social readaptation of the prisoners.

Article 6: Freedom from Slavery

1. No one shall be subject to slavery or to involuntary servitude, which are prohibited in all their forms, as are the slave trade and traffic in women.

2. No one shall be required to perform forced or compulsory labor. This provision shall not be interpreted to mean that, in those countries in which the penalty established for certain crimes is deprivation of liberty at forced labor, the carrying out of such a sentence imposed by a competent court is prohibited. Forced labor shall not adversely affect the dignity or the physical or intellectual capacity of the prisoner.

3. For the purposes of this article, the following do not constitute forced or compulsory labor:

(a) work or service normally required of a person imprisoned in execution of a sentence or formal decision passed by the competent judicial authority. Such work or service shall be carried out under the supervision and control of public authorities, and any persons performing such work or service shall not be placed at the disposal of any private party, company, or juridical person;

(b) military service and, in countries in which conscientious objectors are recognized, national service that the law may provide for in lieu of military service;

(c) service exacted in time of danger or calamity that threatens the existence or the well-being of the community; or

(d) work or service that forms part of normal civic obligations.

Article 7: Right to Personal Liberty

1. Every person has the right to personal liberty and security.

2. No one shall be deprived of his physical liberty except for the reasons and under the conditions established beforehand by the constitution of the State Party concerned or by a law established pursuant thereto.

3. No one shall be subject to arbitrary arrest or imprisonment.

4. Anyone who is detained shall be informed of the reasons for his detention and shall be promptly notified of the charge or charges against him.

5. Any person detained shall be brought promptly before a judge or other officer authorized by law to exercise judicial power and shall be entitled to trial within a reasonable time or to be released without prejudice to the continuation of the proceedings. His release may be subject to guarantees to assure his appearance for trial.

6. Anyone who is deprived of his liberty shall be entitled to recourse to a competent court, in order that the court may decide without delay on the lawfulness of his arrest or detention and order his release if the arrest or detention is unlawful. In States Parties whose laws provide that anyone who believes himself to be threatened with deprivation of his liberty is entitled to recourse to a competent court in order that it may decide on the lawfulness of such threat, this remedy may not be restricted or abolished. The interested party or another person on his behalf is entitled to seek these remedies.

7. No one shall be detained for debt. This principle shall not limit the orders of a competent judicial authority issued for no fulfillment of duties of support.

Article 8: Right to a Fair Trial

1. Every person has the right to a hearing, with due guarantees and within a reasonable time, by a competent, independent and impartial tribunal, previously established by law, in the substantiation of any accusation of a criminal nature made against him or for the determination of his rights and obligations of a civil, labor, fiscal, or any other nature.

2. Every person accused of a criminal offense has the right to be presumed innocent so long as his guilt has not been proven according to law. During the proceedings, every person is entitled, with full equality, to the following minimum guarantees:

(a) the right of the accused to be assisted without charge by a translator or interpreter, if he does not understand or does not speak the language of the tribunal or court;

(b) prior notification in detail to the accused of the charges against him;

(c) adequate time and means for the preparation of his defense;

(d) the right of the accused to defend himself personally or to be assisted by legal counsel of his own choosing, and to communicate freely and privately with his counsel;

(e) the inalienable right to be assisted by counsel provided by the state, paid or not as the domestic law provides, if the accused does not defend himself personally or engage his own counsel within the time period established by law;

(f) the right of the defense to examine witnesses present in the court and to obtain the appearance, as witnesses, of experts or other persons who may throw light on the facts;

(g) the right not to be compelled to be a witness against himself or to plead guilty; and

(h) the right to appeal the judgment to a higher court.

3. A confession of guilt by the accused shall be valid only if it is made without coercion of any kind.

4. An accused person acquitted by a non-appealable judgment shall not be subjected to a new trial for the same cause.

5. Criminal proceedings shall be public, except insofar as may be necessary to protect the interests of justice.

Article 9: Freedom from *Ex Post Facto* Laws

No one shall be convicted of any act or omission that did not constitute a criminal offense, under the applicable law, at the time it was committed. A heavier penalty shall not be imposed than the one that was applicable at the time the criminal offense was committed. If subsequent to the commission of the offense the law provides for the imposition of a lighter punishment, the guilty person shall benefit therefrom.

Article 10: Right to Compensation

Every person has the right to be compensated in accordance with the law in the event he has been sentenced by a final judgment through a miscarriage of justice.

Article 11: Right to Privacy

1. Everyone has the right to have his honor respected and his dignity recognized.

2. No one may be the object of arbitrary or abusive interference with his private life, his family, his home, or his correspondence, or of unlawful attacks on his honor or reputation.

3. Everyone has the right to the protection of the law against such interference or attacks.

Article 12: Freedom of Conscience and Religion

1. Everyone has the right to freedom of conscience and of religion. This right includes freedom to maintain or to change one's religion or beliefs, and freedom to profess or disseminate one's religion or beliefs, either individually or together with others, in public or in private.

2. No one shall be subject to restrictions that might impair his freedom to maintain or to change his religion or beliefs.

3. Freedom to manifest one's religion and beliefs may be subject only to the limitations prescribed by law that are necessary to protect public safety, order, health, or morals, or the rights or freedoms of others.

4. Parents or guardians, as the case may be, have the right to provide for the religious and moral education of their children or wards that is in accord with their own convictions.

Article 13: Freedom of Thought and Expression

1. Everyone has the right to freedom of thought and expression. This right includes freedom to seek, receive, and impart information and ideas of all kinds, regardless of frontiers, either orally, in writing, in print, in the form of art, or through any other medium of one's choice.

2. The exercise of the right provided for in the foregoing paragraph shall not be subject to prior censorship but shall be subject to subsequent imposition of liability, which shall be expressly established by law to the extent necessary to ensure:

(a) Respect for the rights or reputations of others; or

(b) The protection of national security, public order, or public health or morals.

3. The right of expression may not be restricted by indirect methods or means, such as the abuse of government or private controls over newsprint, radio broadcasting frequencies, or equipment used in the dissemination of information, or by any other means tending to impede the communication and circulation of ideas and opinions.

4. Notwithstanding the provisions of paragraph 2 above, public entertainments may be subject by law to prior censorship for the sole purpose of regulating access to them for the moral protection of childhood and adolescence.

5. Any propaganda for war and any advocacy of national, racial, or religious hatred that constitute incitements to lawless violence or to any other similar illegal action against any person or group of persons on any grounds including those of race, color, religion, language, or national origin shall be considered as offenses punishable by law.

Article 14: Right of Reply

1. Anyone injured by inaccurate or offensive statements or ideas disseminated to the public in general by a legally regulated medium of communication has the right to reply or to make a correction using the same communications outlet, under such conditions as the law may establish.

2. The correction or reply shall not in any case remit other legal liabilities that may have been incurred.

3. For the effective protection of honor and reputation, every publisher, and every newspaper, motion picture, radio, and Television Company, shall have a person responsible who is not protected by immunities or special privileges.

Article 15: Right of Assembly

The right of peaceful assembly, without arms, is recognized. No restrictions may be placed on the exercise of this right other than those imposed in conformity with the law and necessary in a democratic society in the interest of national security, public safety or public order, or to protect public health or morals or the rights or freedoms of others.

Article 16: Freedom of Association

1. Everyone has the right to associate freely for ideological, religious, political, economic, labor, social, cultural, sports, or other purposes.

2. The exercise of this right shall be subject only to such restrictions established by law as may be necessary in a democratic society, in the interest of national security, public safety or public order, or to protect public health or morals or the rights and freedoms of others.

3. The provisions of this article do not bar the imposition of legal restrictions, including even deprivation of the exercise of the right of association, on members of the armed forces and the police.

Article 17: Rights of the Family

1. The family is the natural and fundamental group unit of society and is entitled to protection by society and the state.

2. The right of men and women of marriageable age to marry and to raise a family shall be recognized, if they meet the conditions required by domestic laws, insofar as such conditions do not affect the principle of nondiscrimination established in this Convention.

3. No marriage shall be entered into without the free and full consent of the intending spouses.

4. The States Parties shall take appropriate steps to ensure the equality of rights and the adequate balancing of responsibilities of the spouses as to marriage, during marriage, and in the event of its dissolution. In case of dissolution, provision shall be made for the necessary protection of any children solely on the basis of their own best interests.

5. The law shall recognize equal rights for children born out of wedlock and those born in wedlock.

Article 18: Right to a Name

Every person has the right to a given name and to the surnames of his parents or that of one of them. The law shall regulate the manner in which this right shall be ensured for all, by the use of assumed names if necessary.

Article 19: Rights of the Child

Every minor child has the right to the measures of protection required by his condition as a minor on the part of his family, society, and the state.

Article 20: Right to Nationality

1. Every person has the right to a nationality.

2. Every person has the right to the nationality of the state in whose territory he was born if he does not have the right to any other nationality.

3. No one shall be arbitrarily deprived of his nationality or of the right to change it.

Article 21: Right to Property

1. Everyone has the right to the use and enjoyment of his property. The law may subordinate such use and enjoyment in the interest of society.

2. No one shall be deprived of his property except upon payment of just compensation, for reasons of public utility or social interest, and in the cases and according to the forms established by law.

3. Usury and any other form of exploitation of man by man shall be prohibited by law.

Article 22: Freedom of Movement and Residence

1. Every person lawfully in the territory of a State Party has the right to move about in it, and to reside in it subject to the provisions of the law.

2. Every person has the right to leave any country freely, including his own.

3. The exercise of the foregoing rights may be restricted only pursuant to a law to the extent necessary in a democratic society to prevent crime or to protect national security, public safety, public order, public morals, public health, or the rights or freedoms of others.

4. The exercise of the rights recognized in paragraph 1 may also be restricted by law in designated zones for reasons of public interest.

5. No one can be expelled from the territory of the state of which he is a national or be deprived of the right to enter it.

6. An alien lawfully in the territory of a State Party to this Convention may be expelled from it only pursuant to a decision reached in accordance with law.

7. Every person has the right to seek and be granted asylum in a foreign territory, in accordance with the legislation of the state and international conventions, in the event he is being pursued for political offenses or related common crimes.

8. In no case may an alien be deported or returned to a country, regardless of whether or not it is his country of origin, if in that country his right to life or personal freedom is in danger of being violated because of his race, nationality, religion, social status, or political opinions.

9. The collective expulsion of aliens is prohibited.

Article 23: Right to Participate in Government

1. Every citizen shall enjoy the following rights and opportunities:

(a) to take part in the conduct of public affairs, directly or through freely chosen representatives;

(b) to vote and to be elected in genuine periodic elections, which shall be by universal and equal suffrage and by secret ballot that guarantees the free expression of the will of the voters; and

(c) to have access, under general conditions of equality, to the public service of his country.

2. The law may regulate the exercise of the rights and opportunities referred to in the preceding paragraph only on the basis of age, nationality, residence, language, edu-

cation, civil and mental capacity, or sentencing by a competent court in criminal proceedings.

Article 24: Right to Equal Protection

All persons are equal before the law. Consequently, they are entitled, without discrimination, to equal protection of the law.

Article 25: Right to Judicial Protection

1. Everyone has the right to simple and prompt recourse, or any other effective recourse, to a competent court or tribunal for protection against acts that violate his fundamental rights recognized by the constitution or laws of the state concerned or by this Convention, even though such violation may have been committed by persons acting in the course of their official duties.

2. The States Parties undertake:

(a) to ensure that any person claiming such remedy shall have his rights determined by the competent authority provided for by the legal system of the state;

(b) to develop the possibilities of judicial remedy; and

(c) to ensure that the competent authorities shall enforce such remedies when granted.

Chapter III: Economic, Social, and Cultural Rights

Article 26: Progressive Development

The States Parties undertake to adopt measures, both internally and through international cooperation, especially those of an economic and technical nature, with a view to achieving progressively, by legislation or other appropriate means, the full realization of the rights implicit in the economic, social, educational, scientific, and cultural standards set forth in the Charter of the Organization of American States as amended by the Protocol of Buenos Aires.

Chapter IV: Suspension of Guarantees, Interpretation, and Application

Article 27: Suspension of Guarantees

1. In time of war, public danger, or other emergency that threatens the independence or security of a State Party, it may take measures derogating from its obligations under the present Convention to the extent and for the period of time strictly required by the exigencies of the situation, provided that such measures are not inconsistent with its other obligations under international law and do not involve discrimination on the ground of race, color, sex, language, religion, or social origin.

2. The foregoing provision does not authorize any suspension of the following articles: Article 3 (Right to Juridical Personality), Article 4 (Right to Life), Article 5 (Right to Humane Treatment), Article 6 (Freedom from Slavery), Article 9 (Freedom from *Ex Post Facto* Laws), Article 12 (Freedom of Conscience and Religion), Article 17 (Rights of the Family), Article 18 (Right to a Name), Article 19 (Rights of the Child), Article 20 (Right to Nationality), and Article 23 (Right to Participate in Government), or of the judicial guarantees essential for the protection of such rights.

3. Any State Party availing itself of the right of suspension shall immediately inform the other States Parties, through the Secretary-General of the Organization of American States, of the provisions the application of which it has suspended, the reasons that gave rise to the suspension, and the date set for the termination of such suspension.

Article 28: Federal Clause

1. Where a State Party is constituted as a federal state, the national government of such State Party shall implement all the provisions of the Convention over whose subject matter it exercises legislative and judicial jurisdiction.

2. With respect to the provisions over whose subject matter the constituent units of the federal state have jurisdiction, the national government shall immediately take suitable measures, in accordance with its constitution and its laws, to the end that

the competent authorities of the constituent units may adopt appropriate provisions for the fulfillment of this Convention.

3. Whenever two of more States Parties agree to form a federation or other type of association, they shall take care that the resulting federal or other compact contains the provisions necessary for continuing and rendering effective the standards of this Convention in the new state that is organized.

Article 29: Restrictions Regarding Interpretation

No provision of this Convention shall be interpreted as:

(a) permitting any State Party, group, or person to suppress the enjoyment or exercise of the rights and freedoms recognized in this Convention or to restrict them to a greater extent than is provided for herein;

(b) restricting the enjoyment or exercise of any right or freedom recognized by virtue of the laws of any State Party or by virtue of another convention to which one of the said states is a party;

(c) precluding other rights or guarantees that are inherent in the human personality or derived from representative democracy as a form of government; or

(d) excluding or limiting the effect that the American Declaration of the Rights and Duties of Man and other international acts of the same nature may have.

Article 30: Scope of Restrictions

The restrictions that, pursuant to this Convention, may be placed on the enjoyment or exercise of the rights or freedoms recognized herein may not be applied except in accordance with laws enacted for reasons of general interest and in accordance with the purpose for which such restrictions have been established.

Article 31: Recognition of Other Rights

Other rights and freedoms recognized in accordance with the procedures established in Articles 76 and 77 may be included in the system of protection of this Convention.

Chapter V: Personal Responsibilities
Article 32: Relationship between Duties and Rights

1. Every person has responsibilities to his family, his community, and mankind.

2. The rights of each person are limited by the rights of others, by the security of all, and by the just demands of the general welfare, in a democratic society.

Part II: Means of Protection

Chapter VI: Competent Organs
Article 33

The following organs shall have competence with respect to matters relating to the fulfillment of the commitments made by the States Parties to this Convention:

(a) The Inter-American Commission on Human Rights, referred to as "The Commission"; and

(b) The Inter-American Court of Human Rights, referred to as "The Court."

[1]Adopted on November 22, 1969; entry into force, July 18, 1978.

15.15 UNITED NATIONS DECLARATION ON THE RIGHTS OF DISABLED PERSONS (1975)[1]

1. The term "disabled person" means any person unable to ensure by himself or herself, wholly or partly, the necessities of a normal individual and/or social life, as a result of deficiency, either congenital or not, in his or her physical or mental capabilities.

2. Disabled persons shall enjoy all the rights set forth in this Declaration. These rights shall be granted to all disabled persons without any exception whatsoever and without distinction or discrimination on the basis of race, color, sex, language, religion, political or other opinions, national or social origin, state of wealth,

birth or any other situation applying either to the disabled person himself or herself or to his or her family.

3. Disabled persons have the inherent right to respect for their human dignity. Disabled persons, whatever the origin, nature and seriousness of their handicaps and disabilities, have the same fundamental rights as their fellow-citizens of the same age, which implies first and foremost the right to enjoy a decent life, as normal and full as possible.

4. Disabled persons have the same civil and political rights as other human beings; paragraph 7 of the Declaration on the Rights of Mentally Retarded Persons applies to any possible limitation or suppression of those rights for mentally disabled persons.

5. Disabled persons are entitled to the measures designed to enable them to become as self-reliant as possible.

6. Disabled persons have the right to medical, psychological and functional treatment, including prosthetic and orthetic appliances, to medical and social rehabilitation, education, vocational training and rehabilitation, aid, counseling, placement services and other services which will enable them to develop their capabilities and skills to the maximum and will hasten the processes of their social integration or reintegration.

7. Disabled persons have the right to economic and social security and to a decent level of living. They have the right, according to their capabilities, to secure and retain employment or to engage in a useful, productive and remunerative occupation and to join trade unions.

8. Disabled persons are entitled to have their special needs taken into consideration at all stages of economic and social planning.

9. Disabled persons have the right to live with their families or with foster parents and to participate in all social, creative or recreational activities. No disabled person shall be subjected, as far as his or her resi-

dence is concerned, to differential treatment other than that required by his or her condition or by the improvement which he or she may derive therefrom. If the stay of a disabled person in a specialized establishment is indispensable, the environment and living conditions therein shall be as close as possible to those of the normal life of a person of his or her age.

10. Disabled persons shall be protected against all exploitation, all regulations and all treatment of a discriminatory, abusive or degrading nature.

11. Disabled persons shall be able to avail themselves of qualified legal aid when such aid proves indispensable for the protection of their persons and property. If judicial proceedings are instituted against them, the legal procedure applied shall take their physical and mental condition fully into account.

12. Organizations of disabled persons may be usefully consulted in all matters regarding the rights of disabled persons.

13. Disabled persons, their families and communities shall be fully informed, by all appropriate means, of the rights contained in this Declaration.

[1] Proclaimed by General Assembly Resolution 3447 of December 9, 1975.

15.16 CONVENTION ON THE ELIMINATION OF ALL FORMS OF DISCRIMINATION AGAINST WOMEN (ADOPTED, 1979; ENTRY INTO FORCE, 1981)[1]

The states parties to the present Convention,

Noting that the Charter of the United Nations reaffirms faith in fundamental human rights, in the dignity and worth of the human person and in the equal rights of men and women,

Noting that the Universal Declaration of Human Rights affirms the principle of the inadmissibility of discrimination and proclaims that all human beings are born free and equal in dignity and rights and that everyone is entitled to all the rights and freedoms set forth therein, without distinction of any kind including distinction based on sex,

Noting that States Parties to the International Covenant on Human Rights have the obligation to secure the equal rights of men and women to enjoy all economic, social, cultural, civil and political rights,

Considering the international conventions concluded under the auspices of the United Nations and the specialized agencies promoting equality of rights of men and women,

Noting also the resolutions, declarations and recommendations adopted by the United Nations and the specialized agencies promoting equality of rights of men and women,

Concerned, however, that despite these various instruments extensive discrimination against women continues to exist,

Recalling that discrimination against women violates the principles of equality of rights and respect for human dignity, is an obstacle to the participation of women, on equal terms with men, in the political, social, economic and cultural life of their countries, hampers the growth of the prosperity of society and the family, and makes more difficult the full development of the potentialities of women in the service of their countries and of humanity,

Concerned that in situations of poverty women have the least access to food, health, education, training and opportunities for employment and other needs,

Concerned that the establishment of the new international economic order based on equity and justice will contribute significantly towards the promotion of equality between men and women,

Emphasizing that the eradication of apartheid, of all forms of racism, racial discrimination, colonialism, neocolonialism, aggression, foreign occupation and domination and interference in the internal affairs of States is essential to the full enjoyment of the rights of men and women,

Affirming that the strengthening of international peace and security, relaxation of international tension, mutual cooperation among all States irrespective of their social and economic systems, general and complete disarmament and in particular nuclear disarmament under strict and effective international control, the affirmation of the principles of justice, equality and mutual benefit in relations among countries, and the realization of the right of peoples under alien and colonial domination and foreign occupation to self-determination and independence as well as respect for national sovereignty and territorial integrity will promote social progress and development and as a consequence will contribute to the attainment of full equality between men and women,

Convinced that the full and complete development of a country, the welfare of the world and the cause of peace require the maximum participation of women on equal terms with men in all fields,

Bearing in mind the great contribution of women to the welfare of the family and to the development of society, so far not fully recognized, the social significance of maternity and the role of both parents in the family and in the upbringing of children, and aware that the role of women in procreation should not be a basis for discrimination but that the upbringing of children requires a sharing of responsibility between men and women and society as a whole.

Aware that a change in the traditional role of men as well as the role of women in society and in the family is needed to achieve full equality between men and women,

Determined to implement the principles set forth in the Declaration on the Elimination of Discrimination against Women and, for that purpose, to adopt the measures required for the elimination of such discrimination in all its forms and manifestations,

Have agreed on the following:

Part 1

Article 1

For the purposes of the present Convention, the term "discrimination against women" shall mean any distinction, exclusion or restriction made on the basis of sex which has the effect or purpose of impairing or nullifying the recognition, enjoyment or exercise by women, irrespective of their marital status, on a basis of equality of men and women, of human rights and fundamental freedoms in the political, economic, social, cultural, civil or any other field.

Article 2

States parties condemn discrimination against women in all its forms, agree to pursue, by all appropriate means and without delay, a policy of eliminating discrimination against women and, to this end, undertake:

a. To embody the principle of the equality of men and women in national Constitutions or other appropriate legislation if not yet incorporated therein, and to ensure, through law and other appropriate means, the practical realization of this principle;

b. To adopt appropriate legislative and other measures, including sanctions where appropriate, prohibiting all discrimination against women;

c. To establish legal protection of the rights of women on an equal basis with men and to ensure through competent national tribunals and other public institutions the effective protection of women against any act of discrimination;

d. To refrain from engaging in any act or practice of discrimination against women and to ensure that public authorities and institutions shall act in conformity with this obligation;

e. To take all appropriate measures to eliminate discrimination against women by any person, organization or enterprise;

f. To take all appropriate measures, including legislation, to modify or abolish existing laws, regulations, customs and practices which constitute discrimination against women;

g. To repeal all national penal provisions which constitute discrimination against women.

Article 3

States Parties shall take in all fields, in particular in the political, social, economic and cultural fields, all appropriate measures, including legislation, to ensure the full development and advancement of women, for the purpose of guaranteeing them the exercise and enjoyment of human rights and fundamental freedoms on a basis of equality with men.

Article 4

1. Adoption by States Parties of temporary special measures aimed at accelerating *de facto* equality between men and women shall not be considered discrimination as defined in this Convention, but shall in no way entail, as a consequence, the maintenance of unequal or separate standards; these measures shall be discontinued when the objectives of equality of opportunity and treatment have been achieved.

2. Adoption by States Parties of special measures, including those measures contained in the present Convention, aimed at protecting maternity, shall not be considered discriminatory.

Article 5

States Parties shall take all appropriate measures:

a. To modify the social and cultural patterns of conduct of men and women, with a view to achieving the elimination of prejudices and customary and all other practices which are based on the idea of the inferiority or the superiority of either of the sexes or on stereotyped roles for men and women;

b. To ensure that family education includes a proper understanding of maternity as a social function and the recognition of the common responsibility of men and women in the upbringing and development of their children, it being understood that the interest of the children is the primordial consideration in all cases.

Article 6

States Parties shall take all appropriate measures, including legislation, to suppress all forms of traffic in women and exploitation of prostitution of women.

Part II

Article 7

States Parties shall take all appropriate measures to eliminate discrimination against women in the political and public life of the country and, in particular, shall ensure, on equal terms with men, the right:

a. To vote in all elections and public referenda and to be eligible for election to all publicly elected bodies;

b. To participate in the formulation of government policy and the implementation thereof and to hold public office and perform all public functions at all levels of government;

c. To participate in non-governmental organizations and associations concerned with the public and political life of the country.

Article 8

States Parties shall take all appropriate measures to ensure to women on equal terms with men, and without any discrimination, the opportunity to represent their Governments at the international level and to participate in the work of international organizations.

Article 9

1. States Parties shall grant women equal rights with men to acquire, change or retain their nationality. They shall ensure in particular that neither marriage to an alien nor change of nationality by the husband during marriage shall automatically change the nationality of the wife, render her stateless or force upon her the nationality of the husband.

2. States Parties shall grant women equal rights with men with respect to the nationality of their children.

Part III

Article 10

States Parties shall take all appropriate measures to eliminate discrimination against women in order to ensure to them equal rights with men in the field of education and in particular to ensure, on a basis of equality of men and women:

a. The same conditions for career and vocational guidance, for access to studies and for the achievement of diplomas in educational establishments of all categories in rural as well as in urban areas; this equality shall be ensured in pre-school, general, technical, professional and higher technical education, as well as in all types of vocational training;

b. Access to the same curricula, the same examinations, teaching staff with qualifications of the same standard and school premises and equipment of the same quality;

c. The elimination of any stereotyped concept of the roles of men and women at all levels and in all forms of education by encouraging coeducation and other types of education which will help to achieve this aim and, in particular, by the revision of textbooks and school programs and the adaptation of teaching methods;

d. The same opportunities to benefit from scholarships and other study grants;

e. The same opportunities for access to programs of continuing education, including adult and functional literacy programs, particularly those aimed at reducing, at the earliest possible time, any gap in education existing between men and women;

f. The reduction of female student dropout rates and the organization of programs for girls and women who have left school prematurely;

g. The same opportunities to participate actively in sports and physical education;

h. Access to specific educational information to help to ensure the health and well-being of families, including information and advice on family planning.

Article 11

1. States Parties shall take all appropriate measures to eliminate discrimination against women in the field of employment in order to ensure, on a basis of equality of men and women, the same rights, in particular:

(a) The right to work as an inalienable right of all human beings;

(b) The right to the same employment opportunities, including the application of the same criteria for selection in matters of employment;

(c) The right to free choice of profession and employment, the right to promotion, job security and all benefits and conditions of service and the right to receive vocational training and retraining, including apprenticeships, advanced vocational training and recurrent training;

(d) The right to equal remuneration, including benefits, and to equal treatment in respect of work of equal value, as well as equality of treatment in the evaluation of the quality of work;

(e) The right to social security, particularly in cases of retirement, unemployment, sickness, invalidity and old age and other incapacity to work, as well as the right to paid leave;

(f) The right to protection of health and to safety in working conditions, including the safeguarding of the function of reproduction.

2. In order to prevent discrimination against women on the grounds of marriage or maternity and to ensure their effective right to work, States Parties shall take appropriate measures:

(a) To prohibit, subject to the imposition of sanctions, dismissal on the grounds of pregnancy or of maternity leave and discrimination in dismissals on the basis of marital status;

(b) To introduce maternity leave with pay or with comparable social benefits without loss of former employment, seniority or social allowances;

(c) To encourage the provision of the necessary supporting social services to enable parents to combine family obligations with work responsibilities and participation in public life, in particular through promoting the establishment and development of a network of child-care facilities;

(d) To provide special protection to women during pregnancy in types of work proved to be harmful to them.

3. Protective legislation relating to matters covered in this article shall be reviewed periodically in the light of scientific and technological knowledge and shall be revised, repealed or extended as necessary.

Article 12

1. States Parties shall take all appropriate measures to eliminate discrimination against women in the field of health care in order to ensure, on a basis of equality of men and women, access to health care services, including those related to family planning.

2. Notwithstanding the provisions of paragraph 1 above, States Parties shall ensure to women appropriate services in connection with pregnancy, confinement and the post-natal period, granting free services where necessary, as well as adequate nutrition during pregnancy and lactation.

Article 13

States Parties shall take all appropriate measures to eliminate discrimination against women in other areas of economic and social life in order to ensure, on a basis of equality of men and women, the same rights, in particular:

a. The right to family benefits;

b. The right to bank loans, mortgages and other forms of financial credit;

c. The right to participate in recreational activities, sports and in all aspects of cultural life.

Article 14

1. States Parties shall take into account the particular problems faced by rural women and the significant roles which they play in the economic survival of their families, including their work in the non-monetized sectors of the economy, and shall take all appropriate measures to ensure the to women in rural areas.

2. States Parties shall take all appropriate measures to eliminate discrimination against women in rural areas in order to ensure, on a basis of equality of men and women, that they participate in and benefit from rural development and, in particular, shall ensure to such women the right:

(a) To participate in the elaboration and implementation of development planning at all levels;

(b) To have access to adequate health care facilities, including information, counseling and services in family planning;

(c) To benefit directly from social security programs;

(d) To obtain all types of training and education, formal and non-formal, including that relating to functional literacy, as well the benefit of all community and extension services, *inter alia*, in order to increase their technical proficiency;

(e) To organize self-help groups and cooperatives in order to obtain equal access to economic opportunities through employment or self-employment;

(f) To participate in all community activities;

(g) To have access to agricultural credit and loans, marketing facilities, appropriate technology and equal treatment in land and agrarian reform as well as in land resettlement schemes;

(h) To enjoy adequate living conditions, particularly in relation to housing, sanitation, electricity and water supply, transport and communications.

Part IV

Article 15

1. States Parties shall accord to women equality with men before the law.

2. States Parties shall accord to women, in civil matters, a legal capacity identical to that of men and the same opportunities to exercise that capacity. They shall in particular give women equal rights to conclude contracts and to administer property and treat them equally in all stages of procedure in courts and tribunals.

3. States Parties agree that all contracts and all other private instruments of any kind with a legal effect which is directed at restricting the legal capacity of women shall be deemed null and void.

4. States Parties shall accord to men and women the same rights with regard to the law relating to the movement of persons and the freedom to choose their residence and domicile.

Article 16

1. States Parties shall take all appropriate measures to eliminate discrimination against women in all matters relating to marriage and family relations and in particular shall ensure, on a basis of equality of men and women:

(a) The same right to enter into marriage;

(b) The same right freely to choose a spouse and to enter into marriage only with their free and full consent;

(c) The same rights and responsibilities during marriage and at its dissolution;

(d) The same rights and responsibilities as parents, irrespective of their marital status, in matters relating to their children. In all cases the interests of the children shall be paramount;

(e) The same rights to decide freely and responsibly on the number and spacing of their children and to have access to the information, education and means to enable them to exercise these rights;

(f) The same rights and responsibilities with regard to guardianships, wardship, trusteeship and adoption of children, or similar institutions where these concepts exist in national legislation. In all cases the interest of the children shall be paramount;

(g) The same personal rights as husband and wife, including the right to choose a family name, a profession and an occupation;

(h) The same rights for both spouses in respect of the ownership, acquisition, management, administration, enjoyment and disposition of property, whether free of charge or for a valuable consideration.

2. The betrothal and the marriage of a child shall have no legal effect and all necessary action, including legislation, shall be taken to specify a minimum age for marriage and to make the registration of marriages in an official registry compulsory....

[1] Adopted on December 18, 1979; entry into force, September 3, 1981.

15.17   AFRICAN [BANJUL] CHARTER ON HUMAN AND PEOPLES' RIGHTS (ADOPTED, 1981; ENTRY INTO FORCE, 1986)[1]

Preamble

The African States members of the Organization of African Unity, parties to the present convention entitled "African Charter on Human and Peoples' Rights";

Recalling Decision 115 (XVI) of the Assembly of Heads of State and Government at its Sixteenth Ordinary Session held in Monrovia, Liberia, from 17 to 20 July 1979 on the preparation of a "preliminary draft on an African Charter on Human and Peoples' Rights providing *inter alia* for the establishment of bodies to promote and protect human and peoples' rights";

Considering the Charter of the Organization, of African Unity, which stipulates that "freedom, equality, justice and dignity are essential objectives for the achievement of the legitimate aspirations of the African peoples";

Reaffirming the pledge they solemnly made in Article 2 of the said Charter to eradicate all forms of colonialism from Africa, to co-ordinate and intensify their co-operation and efforts to achieve a better life for the peoples of Africa and to promote international co-operation having due regard to the Charter of the United Nations and the Universal Declaration of Human Rights;

Taking into consideration the virtues of their historical tradition and the values of African civilization which should inspire and characterize their reflection on the concept of human and peoples' rights;

Recognizing on the one hand, that fundamental human rights stem from the attributes of human beings, which justifies their national and international protection and on the other hand that the reality and respect of peoples' rights should necessarily guarantee human rights;

Considering that the enjoyment of rights and freedoms also implies the performance of duties on the part of everyone;

Convinced that it is henceforth essential to pay a particular attention to the right to development and that civil and political rights cannot be dissociated from economic, social and cultural rights in their conception as well as universality and that the satisfaction of economic, social and cultural rights is a guarantee for the enjoyment of civil and political rights;

Conscious of their duty to achieve the total liberation of Africa, the peoples of which are still struggling for their dignity and genuine independence, and undertaking to eliminate colonialism, neo-colonialism, apartheid, Zionism and to dismantle aggressive foreign military bases and all forms of discrimination, particularly those based on race, ethnic group, color, sex, language, religion or political opinions;

Reaffirming their adherence to the principles of human and peoples' rights and freedoms contained in the declarations, conventions and other instruments adopted by the Organization of African Unity, the Movement of Non-Aligned Countries and the United Nations;

Firmly convinced of their duty to promote and protect human and peoples' rights and freedoms taking into account the importance traditionally attached to these rights and freedoms in Africa;

Have agreed as follows:

Part I: Rights and Duties

Chapter I: Human and Peoples' Rights
Article 1

The Member States of the Organization of African Unity parties to the present Charter shall recognize the rights, duties and freedoms enshrined in this Charter and shall undertake to adopt legislative or other measures to give effect to them.

Article 2

Every individual shall be entitled to the enjoyment of the rights and freedoms recognized and guaranteed in the present Charter without distinction of any kind such as race, ethnic group, color, sex, language, religion, political or any other opinion, national and social origin, fortune, birth or other status.

Article 3

1. Every individual shall be equal before the law.

2. Every individual shall be entitled to equal protection of the law.

Article 4

Human beings are inviolable. Every human being shall be entitled to respect for his life

and the integrity of his person. No one may be arbitrarily deprived of this right.

Article 5

Every individual shall have the right to the respect of the dignity inherent in a human being and to the recognition of his legal status. All forms of exploitation and degradation of man particularly slavery, slave trade, torture, cruel, inhuman or degrading punishment and treatment shall be prohibited.

Article 6

Every individual shall have the right to liberty and to the security of his person. No one may be deprived of his freedom except for reasons and conditions previously laid down by law. In particular, no one may be arbitrarily arrested or detained.

Article 7

1. Every individual shall have the right to have his cause heard.

This comprises:

(a) the right to an appeal to competent national organs against acts of violating his fundamental rights as recognized and guaranteed by conventions, laws, regulations and customs in force;

(b) the right to be presumed innocent until proved guilty by a competent court or tribunal;

(c) the right to defense, including the right to be defended by counsel of his choice;

(d) The right to be tried within a reasonable time by an impartial court or tribunal.

2. No one may be condemned for an act or omission which did not constitute a legally punishable offense at the time it was committed. No penalty may be inflicted for an offense for which no provision was made at the time it was committed. Punishment is personal and can be imposed only on the offender.

Article 8

Freedom of conscience, the profession and free practice of religion shall be guaranteed. No one may, subject to law and order, be submitted to measures restricting the exercise of these freedoms.

Article 9

1. Every individual shall have the right to receive information.

2. Every individual shall have the right to express and disseminate his opinions within the law.

Article 10

1. Every individual shall have the right to free association provided that he abides by the law.

2. Subject to the obligation of solidarity provided for in Article 29 no one may be compelled to join an association.

Article 11

Every individual shall have the right to assemble freely with others. The exercise of this right shall be subject only to necessary restrictions provided for by law in particular those enacted in the interest of national security, the safety, health, ethics and rights and freedoms of others.

Article 12

1. Every individual shall have the right to freedom of movement and residence within the borders of a State provided he abides by the law.

2. Every individual shall have the right to leave any country including his own, and to return to his country. This right may only be subject to restrictions, provided for by law for the protection of national security, law and order, public health or morality.

3. Every individual shall have the right, when persecuted, to seek and obtain asylum in other countries in accordance with laws of those countries and international conventions.

4. A non-national legally admitted in a territory of a State party to the present Charter, may only be expelled from it by virtue of a decision taken in accordance with the law.

5. The mass expulsion of non-nationals shall be prohibited. Mass expulsion shall be that which is aimed at national, racial, ethnic or religious groups.

Article 13

1. Every citizen shall have the right to participate freely in the government of his country, either directly or through freely chosen representatives in accordance with the provisions of the law.

2. Every citizen shall have the right of equal access to the public service of his country.

3. Every individual shall have the right of access to public property and services in strict equality of all persons before the law.

Article 14

The right to property shall be guaranteed. It may only be encroached upon in the interest of public need or in the general interest of the community and in accordance with the provisions of appropriate laws.

Article 15

Every individual shall have the right to work under equitable and satisfactory conditions, and shall receive equal pay for equal work.

Article 16

1. Every individual shall have the right to enjoy the best attainable state of physical and mental health.

2. States parties to the present Charter shall take the necessary measures to protect the health of their people and to ensure that they receive medical attention when they are sick.

Article 17

1. Every individual shall have the right to education.

2. Every individual may freely take part in the cultural life of his community.

3. The promotion and protection of morals and traditional values recognized by the community shall be the duty of the State.

Article 18

1. The family shall be the natural unit and basis of society. It shall be protected by the State which shall take care of its physical and moral health.

2. The State shall have the duty to assist the family which is the custodian of morals and traditional values recognized by the community.

3. The State shall ensure the elimination of every discrimination against women and also censure the protection of the rights of the woman and the child as stipulated in international declarations and conventions.

4. The aged and the disabled shall also have the right to special measures of protection in keeping with their physical or moral needs.

Article 19

All peoples shall be equal; they shall enjoy the same respect and shall have the same rights. Nothing shall justify the domination of a people by another.

Article 20

1. All peoples shall have right to existence. They shall have the unquestionable and inalienable right to self-determination. They shall freely determine their political status and shall pursue their economic and social development according to the policy they have freely chosen.

2. Colonized or oppressed peoples shall have the right to free themselves from the bonds of domination by resorting to any means recognized by the international community.

3. All peoples shall have the right to the assistance of the States parties to the present Charter in their liberation struggle against foreign domination, be it political, economic or cultural.

Article 21

1. All peoples shall freely dispose of their wealth and natural resources. This right shall be exercised in the exclusive interest of the people. In no case shall a people be deprived of it.

2. In case of spoliation the dispossessed people shall have the right to the lawful recovery of its property as well as to an adequate compensation.

3. The free disposal of wealth and natural resources shall be exercised without prejudice to the obligation of promoting international economic cooperation based on mutual respect, equitable exchange and the principles of international law.

4. States parties to the present Charter shall individually and collectively exercise the right to free disposal of their wealth and natural resources with a view to strengthening African unity and solidarity.

5. States parties to the present Charter shall undertake to eliminate all forms of foreign economic exploitation particularly that practiced by international monopolies so as to enable their peoples to fully benefit from the advantages derived from their national resources.

Article 22

1. All peoples shall have the right to their economic, social and cultural development with due regard to their freedom and identity and in the equal enjoyment of the common heritage of mankind.

2. States shall have the duty, individually or collectively, to ensure the exercise of the right to development.

Article 23

1. All peoples shall have the right to national and international peace and security. The principles of solidarity and friendly relations implicitly affirmed by the Charter of the United Nations and reaffirmed by that of the Organization of African Unity shall govern relations between States.

2. For the purpose of strengthening peace, solidarity and friendly relations, States parties to the present Charter shall ensure that:

(a) any individual enjoying the right of asylum under Article 12 of the present Charter shall not engage in subversive activities against his country of origin or any other State party to the present Charter;

(b) their territories shall not be used as bases for subversive or terrorist activities against the people of any other State party to the present Charter.

Article 24

All peoples shall have the right to a general satisfactory environment favorable to their development.

Article 25

States parties to the present Charter shall have the duty to promote and ensure through teaching, education and publication, the respect of the rights and freedoms contained in the present Charter and to see to it that these freedoms and rights as well as corresponding obligations and duties are understood.

Article 26

States parties to the present Charter shall have the duty to guarantee the independence of the Courts and shall allow the establishment and improvement of appropriate national institutions entrusted with the promotion and protection of the rights and freedoms guaranteed by the present Charter.

Chapter II: Duties

Article 27

1. Every individual shall have duties towards his family and society, the State and other legally recognized communities and the international community.

2. The rights and freedoms of each individual shall be exercised with due regard to the rights of others, collective security, morality and common interest.

Article 28

Every individual shall have the duty to respect and consider his fellow beings without discrimination, and to maintain relations aimed at promoting, safeguarding and reinforcing mutual respect and tolerance.

Article 29

The individual shall also have the duty:

1. To preserve the harmonious development of the family and to work for the cohesion and respect of the family; to respect his parents at all times, to maintain them in case of need;

2. To serve his national community by placing his physical and intellectual abilities at its service;

3. Not to compromise the security of the State whose national or resident he is;

4. To preserve and strengthen social and national solidarity, particularly when the latter is threatened;

5. To preserve and strengthen the national independence and the territorial integrity of his country and to contribute to its defense in accordance with the law;

6. To work to the best of his abilities and competence, and to pay taxes imposed by law in the interest of the society;

7. To preserve and strengthen positive African cultural values in his relations with other members of the society, in the spirit of tolerance, dialogue and consultation

and, in general, to contribute to the promotion of the moral well-being of society;

8. To contribute to the best of his abilities, at all times and at all levels, to the promotion and achievement of African unity....

[1] Adopted on June 27, 1981; entry into force, October 21, 1986.

15.18   UNITED NATIONS CONVENTION ON THE RIGHTS OF THE CHILD (ADOPTED, 1989; ENTRY INTO FORCE, 1990)[1]

Part I

Article 1

For the purposes of the present Convention, a child means every human being below the age of eighteen years unless under the law applicable to the child, majority is attained earlier.

Article 2

1. States Parties shall respect and ensure the rights set forth in the present Convention to each child within their jurisdiction without discrimination of any kind, irrespective of the child's or his or her parent's or legal guardian's race, color, sex, language, religion, political or other opinion, national, ethnic or social origin, property, disability, birth or other status.

2. States Parties shall take all appropriate measures to ensure that the child is protected against all forms of discrimination or punishment on the basis of the status, activities, expressed opinions, or beliefs of the child's parents, legal guardians, or family members.

Article 4

States Parties shall undertake all appropriate legislative, administrative, and other measures for the implementation of the rights recognized in the present Convention. With regard to economic, social and cultural rights, States Parties shall undertake such measures to the maximum extent of their available resources and, where needed, within the framework of international co-operation.

Article 5

States Parties shall respect the responsibilities, rights and duties of parents or, where applicable, the members of the extended family or community as provided for by local custom, legal guardians or other persons legally responsible for the child, to provide, in a manner consistent with the evolving capacities of the child, appropriate direction and guidance in the exercise by the child of the rights recognized in the present Convention.

Article 6

1. States Parties recognize that every child has the inherent right to life.

2. States Parties shall ensure to the maximum extent possible the survival and development of the child.

Article 7

1. The child shall be registered immediately after birth and shall have the right from birth to a name, the right to acquire a nationality and as far as possible, the right to know and be cared for by his or her parents.

2. States Parties shall ensure the implementation of these rights in accordance with their national law and their obligations under the relevant international instruments in this field, in particular where the child would otherwise be stateless.

Article 8

1. States Parties undertake to respect the right of the child to preserve his or her identity, including nationality, name and family relations as recognized by law without unlawful interference.

Article 9

1. States Parties shall ensure that a child shall not be separated from his or her parents against their will, except when competent authorities subject to judicial review determine, in accordance with applicable law and procedures, that such separation is necessary for the best interests of the child. Such determination may be necessary in a

particular case such as one involving abuse or neglect of the child by the parents, or one where the parents are living separately and a decision must be made as to the child's place of residence.

Article 11

1. States Parties shall take measures to combat the illicit transfer and non-return of children abroad.

Article 13

1. The child shall have the right to freedom of expression; this right shall include freedom to seek, receive and impart information and ideas of all kinds, regardless of frontiers, either orally, in writing or in print, in the form of art, or through any other media of the child's choice.

2. The exercise of this right may be subject to certain restrictions, but these shall only be such as are provided by law and are necessary:

(a) For respect of the rights or reputations of others; or

(b) For the protection of national security or of public order (*ordre public*), or of public health or morals.

Article 15

1. States Parties recognize the rights of the child for freedom of association and to freedom of peaceful assembly.

Article 17

States Parties recognize the important function performed by the mass media and shall ensure that the child has access to information and material from a diversity of national and international sources, especially those aimed at the promotion of his or her social, spiritual and moral well-being and physical and mental health....

Article 18

1. States Parties shall use their best efforts to ensure recognition of the principle that both parents have common responsibilities for the upbringing and development of the child. Parents or, as the case may be, legal guardians, have the primary responsibility for the upbringing and development of the child. The best interests of the child will be their basic concern.

2. For the purpose of guaranteeing and promoting the rights set forth in the present Convention, States Parties shall render appropriate assistance to parents and legal guardians in the performance of their child-rearing responsibilities and shall ensure the development of institutions, facilities and services for the care of children.

3. States Parties shall take all appropriate measures to ensure that children of working parents have the right to benefit from child-care services and facilities for which they are eligible.

Article 19

1. States Parties shall take all appropriate legislative, administrative, social and educational measures to protect the child from all forms of physical or mental violence, injury or abuse, neglect or negligent treatment, maltreatment or exploitation, including sexual abuse, while in the care of parent(s), legal guardian(s) or any other person who has the care of the child.

2. Such protective measures should, as appropriate, include effective procedures for the establishment of social programs to provide necessary support for the child and for those who have the care of the child, as well as for other forms of prevention and for identification, reporting, referral, investigation, treatment and follow-up of instances of child maltreatment described heretofore, and, as appropriate, for judicial involvement.

Article 20

1. A child temporarily or permanently deprived of his or her family environment, or in whose own best interests cannot be allowed to remain in that environment, shall be entitled to special protection and assistance provided by the State.

Article 22

States Parties shall take appropriate measures to ensure that a child who is seeking refugee status or who is considered a refugee in accordance with applicable international or domestic law and procedures shall, whether unaccompanied or accompanied by his or her parents or by any other person, receive appropriate protection and humanitarian assistance in the enjoyment of applicable rights set forth in the present Convention and in other international human rights or humanitarian instruments to which the said States are Parties.

Article 23

2. States Parties recognize the right of the disabled child to special care and shall encourage and ensure the extension, subject to available resources, to the eligible child and those responsible for his or her care, of assistance for which application is made and which is appropriate to the child's condition and to the circumstances of the parents or others caring for the child.

3. Recognizing the special needs of a disabled child, assistance extended in accordance with paragraph 2 of the present article shall be provided free of charge, whenever possible, taking into account the financial resources of the parents or others caring for the child, and shall be designed to ensure that the disabled child has effective access to and receives education, training, health care services, rehabilitation services, preparation for employment and recreation opportunities in a manner conducive to the child's achieving the fullest possible social integration and individual development, including his or her cultural and spiritual development.

Article 24

1. States Parties recognize the right of the child to the enjoyment of the highest attainable standard of health and to facilities for the treatment of illness and rehabilitation of health. States Parties shall strive to ensure that no child is deprived of his or her right of access to such health care services.

Article 26

1. States Parties shall recognize for every child the right to benefit from social security, including social insurance, and shall take the necessary measures to achieve the full realization of this right in accordance with their national law.

2. The benefits should, where appropriate, be granted, taking into account the resources and the circumstances of the child and persons having responsibility for the maintenance of the child, as well as any other consideration relevant to an application for benefits made by or on behalf of the child.

Article 27

1. States Parties recognize the right of every child to a standard of living adequate for the child's physical, mental, spiritual, moral and social development.

2. The parent(s) or others responsible for the child have the primary responsibility to secure, within their abilities and financial capacities, the conditions of living necessary for the child's development.

Article 28

1. States Parties recognize the right of the child to education, and with a view to achieving this right progressively and on the basis of equal opportunity....

3. States Parties shall promote and encourage international cooperation in matters relating to education, in particular with a view to contributing to the elimination of ignorance and illiteracy throughout the world and facilitating access to scientific and technical knowledge and modern teaching methods. In this regard, particular account shall be taken of the needs of developing countries.

Article 29

1. States Parties agree that the education of the child shall be directed to:

(a) The development of the child's personality, talents and mental and physical abilities to their fullest potential;

(b) The development of respect for human rights and fundamental freedoms, and for the principles enshrined in the Charter of the United Nations;

(c) The development of respect for the child's parents, his or her own cultural identity, language and values, for the national values of the country in which the child is living, the country from which he or she may originate, and for civilizations different from his or her own.

Article 31

1. States Parties recognize the right of the child to rest and leisure, to engage in play and recreational activities appropriate to the age of the child and to participate freely in cultural life and the arts.

Article 32

1. States Parties recognize the right of the child to be protected from economic exploitation and from performing any work that is likely to be hazardous or to interfere with the child's education, or to be harmful to the child's health or physical, mental, spiritual, moral or social development.

2. States Parties shall take legislative, administrative, social and educational measures to ensure the implementation of the present article. To this end, and having regard to the relevant provisions of other international instruments, States Parties shall in particular:

(a) Provide for a minimum age or minimum ages for admission to employment;

(b) Provide for appropriate regulation of the hours and conditions of employment;

(c) Provide for appropriate penalties or other sanctions to ensure the effective enforcement of the present article.

Article 33

States Parties shall take all appropriate measures, including legislative, administrative, social and educational measures, to protect children from the illicit use of narcotic drugs and psychotropic substances as defined in the relevant international trea-

ties, and to prevent the use of children in the illicit production and trafficking of such substances.

Article 35

States Parties shall take all appropriate national, bilateral and multilateral measures to prevent the abduction of, the sale of or traffic in children for any purpose or in any form.

Article 36

States Parties shall protect the child against all other forms of exploitation prejudicial to any aspects of the child's welfare.

Article 37

States Parties shall ensure that:

(a) No child shall be subjected to torture or other cruel, inhuman or degrading treatment or punishment. Neither capital punishment nor life imprisonment without possibility of release shall be imposed for offenses committed by persons below eighteen years of age;

(b) No child shall be deprived of his or her liberty unlawfully or arbitrarily. The arrest, detention or imprisonment of a child shall be in conformity with the law and shall be used only as a measure of last resort and for the shortest appropriate period of time;

(c) Every child deprived of liberty shall be treated with humanity and respect for the inherent dignity of the human person, and in a manner which takes into account the needs of persons of his or her age. In particular, every child deprived of liberty shall be separated from adults unless it is considered in the child's best interest not to do so and shall have the right to maintain contact with his or her family through correspondence and visits, save in exceptional circumstances;

(d) Every child deprived of his or her liberty shall have the right to prompt access to legal and other appropriate assistance, as well as the right to challenge the legality of the deprivation of his or her liberty before a court or other competent, independent and impartial authority, and to prompt decision on any such action.

Article 38

1. States Parties undertake to respect and to ensure respect for rules of international humanitarian law applicable to them in armed conflicts which are relevant to the child.

2. States Parties shall take all feasible measures to ensure that persons who have not attained the age of fifteen years do not take a direct part in hostilities.

3. States Parties shall refrain from recruiting any person who has not attained the age of fifteen years into their armed forces. In recruiting among those persons who have at the age of fifteen years but who have not attained the age of eighteen years, States Parties shall endeavor to give priority to those who are oldest.

4. In accordance with their obligations under international humanitarian law to protect the civilian population in armed conflicts, States Parties shall take all feasible measures to ensure protection and care of children who are affected by an armed conflict.

Article 39

States Parties shall take all appropriate measures to promote physical and psychological recovery and social reintegration of a child victim of: any form of neglect, exploitation, or abuse; torture or any other form of cruel, inhuman or degrading treatment or punishment; or armed conflicts. Such recovery and reintegration shall take place in an environment which fosters the health, self-respect and dignity of the child.

Article 40

1. States Parties recognize the right of every child alleged as, accused of, or recognized as having infringed the penal law to be treated in a manner consistent with the promotion of the child's sense of dignity and worth, which reinforces the child's respect for the human rights and fundamental freedoms of others and which

takes into account the child's age and the desirability of promoting the child's reintegration and the child's assuming a constructive role in society.

2. (b) Every child alleged as or accused of having infringed the penal law has at least the following guarantees:

(i) To be presumed innocent until proven guilty according to law;

(ii) To be informed promptly and directly of the charges against him or her, and, if appropriate, through his or her parents or legal guardians, and to have legal or other appropriate assistance in the preparation and presentation of his or her defense;

(iii)To have the matter determined without delay by a competent, independent and impartial authority or judicial body in a fair hearing according to law, in the presence of legal or other appropriate assistance and, unless it is considered not to be in the best interest of the child, in particular, taking into account his or her age or situation, his or her parents or legal guardians;

(iv) Not to be compelled to give testimony or to confess guilt; to examine or have examined adverse witnesses and to obtain the participation and examination of witnesses on his or her behalf under conditions of equality;

(v) If considered to have infringed the penal law, to have this decision and any measures imposed in consequence thereof reviewed by a higher competent, independent and impartial authority or judicial body according to law;

(vi) To have the free assistance of an interpreter if the child cannot understand or speak the language used;

(vii) To have his or her privacy fully respected at all stages of the proceedings.

3. States Parties shall seek to promote the establishment of laws, procedures, authorities and institutions specifically applicable to children alleged as, accused of, or rec-

ognized as having infringed the penal law, and, in particular:

(a) The establishment of a minimum age below which children shall be presumed not to have the capacity to infringe the penal law;

(b) Whenever appropriate and desirable, measures for dealing with such children without resorting to judicial proceedings, providing that human rights and legal safeguards are fully respected.

4. A variety of dispositions, such as care, guidance and supervision orders; counseling; probation; foster care; education and vocational training programs and other alternatives to institutional care shall be available to ensure that children are dealt with in a manner appropriate to their well-being and proportionate both to their circumstances and the offense.

[1] Adopted on November 20, 1989; entry into force, September 2, 1990.

PERMISSION ACKNOWLEDGMENTS

al-Husri, Sati. "Muslim Unity and Arab Unity." In *Arab Nationalism: An Anthology* translated by Sylvia G. Haim (pp. 147-53). Rev. ed. Berkeley: University of California Press, 1962. Reprinted by the permission of Sylvia G. Haim.

Amnesty International, "Amnesty International on Human Rights and Labour Rights," 1998, courtesy of Amnesty International.

Arendt, Hannah. Excerpts from *The Origins of Totalitarianism*, copyright © 1976, 1973, 1968, 1966, 1958, 1951, 1948 by Hannah Arendt and renewed 2001, 1996, 1994, 1986 by Lotte Kohler, renewed 1979 by Mary McCarthy West, reprinted by permission of Harcourt, Inc.

Aristotle. "Politics." In *Aristotle*, translated by E. Barker, Oxford: Oxford University Press, 1998. Reprinted by permission of Oxford University Press.

Aquinas, Thomas. *Summa Theologica*. Edited by Fathers of the English Dominican Province. Hamphsire, UK: Eyre & Spottiswoode, 1947.

Asoka. *The Edicts of Asoka*, edited by Nikam & McKeon, pp. 27-28, 53-54. Reprinted by permission of The University of Chicago Press.

Beccaria, Cesare. *On Crimes and Punishments and Other Writings*, edited by Richard Bellamy. ©1955. Excerpts from pp. 10-11, 39-44, 66-71. Reprinted by permission of Cambridge University Press.

Blanc, Louis. "Organization of Labor," in *Socialist Thought: A Documentary History, Revised Edition*. Edited by Albert Fried and Ronald Sanders. New York: Columbia University Press, 1992. Reprinted by permission of the publisher.

Cicero. *De Republica and De Legibus* Volume XVI, Loeb Classical Library® Volume 213, translated Clinton W. Keyes, Cambridge, Mass.: Harvard University Press, 1928. Reprinted by permission of Harvard University Press and The Loeb Classical Library.

Cole, David. "Let's Fight Terrorism, Not the Constitution." In *Rights vs. Public Safety after 9/11: America in the Age of Terror-ism*, edited by Amitai Etzioni and Jason H. Marsh. Lanham, MD: Rowman & Littlefield, 2003. Reprinted by permission of David Cole.

Confucius. *The Analects*, translated by D.C. Lau. London: Penguin Classics, 1979. Copyright © by D.C. Lau, 1979. Reprinted by Permission of Penguin Classics, Ltd.

Dershowittz, Alan. "Tortured Reasoning," from *Torture: A Collection*, ed. Sanford Levinson, 2004. Reprinted by permission of Oxford University Press, Inc.

Engels, Fredrich. "Herr Eugen Duhring's Revolution." *The Anti-Duhring* ©1939. Reprinted by permission of International Publishers.

Epictectus. *Discourses*, translated by Thomas Wentworth Higginson. New York: Walter J. Black, 1944.

Fanon, Frantz. *The Wretched of the Earth*, translated by Constance Farring. © 1963 by Frantz Fanon. Reprinted by permission of Grove / Atlantic, Inc.

Friedman, Milton. "Economic Freedom, Human Freedom, Political Freedom." Speech delivered November 1, 1991, Hayward California: The Smith Center for Private Enterprise Studies. Reprinted by permission of Milton Friedman.

Friedman, Thomas L. and Ignacio Ramonet, "Dueling Globalization." *Foreign Policy* pp. 40-41. Reprinted by permission of *Foreign Policy*.

Gandhi, Mahatma. *The Writings of M.K. Gandhi*, edited by Raghavan Nlyer. ©1990. Reprinted by permission of Navajivan trust, Ahmedabad, India.

Gouge, Olympe de. "The Declaration on the Rights of Women" in *Women in Revolutionary Paris 1789-1795*, edited by D.G Levy, et al. ©1977 by the Board of Trustees of the University of Illinois Press. Reprinted by permission of the editors and University of Illinois Press.

Grotius, Hugo. *The Laws of War and Peace* translated by Francis W. Kelsely, edited by James Brown Scott, ed. Reprinted by permission of Oxford University Press, Inc.

Guha, Ramachandra. "Radical Environmentalism and Wilderness Preservation: A Third World Critique." Originally appeared in *Environment Ethics*, Vol. 11. Reprinted by permission of the author.

"Hammurabi Code" in *Babylonian Law,* edited by G.R. Driver & J.C. Miles, 1955. Reprinted by permission of Oxford University Press, Inc.

Hobsbawm, Eric. "Spreading Democracy." *Foreign Policy* 144 (Sept/Oct 2004): 40-41. Reprinted by permission of *Foreign Policy.*

Hobsbawm, Eric. "The Universalism of the Left." *The New Left Review* 21 (May/June 1996). Reprinted by permission of the author.

Howard Hassmann, Rhoda and Jack Donnelly. "Liberalism and Human Rights: A Necessary Connection" 1996. Reprinted by permission of the authors.

Ignatieff, Michael. "The Burden." *New York Times Magazine,* January 5, 2003.

Kant, Immanuel. *Perpetual Peace* and *The Metaphysics of Morals.* In *Political Writings,* translated by H.B. Nisbet, edited by H.S. Reiss. ©1970. Reprinted by permission of Cambridge University Press.

Kautilya. The excerpts from *The Arthashastra* by Kautyilya; translated into English by L.N. Rangarajan is reproduced courtesy of the Publishers (Penguin Books India) and the translator.

Kautsky, Karl. *Dictatorship of the Proletariat.* In *Karl Kautsky: Selected Political Writings* edited by Patrick Goode, ©Patrick Goode. Reprinted by permission of St. Martin's Press, Inc. and Palgrave Mcmillan.

Kmiec, Douglas W. "Confusing Freedom with License—Licenses Terrorism, Not Freedom." In *Rights vs. Public Safety after 9/11: America in the Age of Terrorism,* edited by Amitai Etzioni and Jason H. Marsh. Lanham, MD: Rowman & Littlefield, 2003. Reprinted by permission of The Institute for Communitarian Policy Studies.

Kymlicka, Will. "The Good, the Bad, and the Intolerable: Minority Group Rights." *Dissent.* Summer 1996. Reprinted by permission of Foundation for the Study of Independent Social Ideas.

Lasalle, Ferdinand. "The Working Class Program." In *Socialist Thought: A Documentary History, Revised Edition,* edited by Albert Fried and Ronald Sanders. New York: Columbia University Press, 1992.

Las Casas, Bartolomé de. *In Defense of the Indians,* translated by Stefford Poole. Copyright ©1974 by Northern Illinois University Press. Reprinted by permission of Northern Illinois University Press.

Lenin, Vladimir. *The Right of Nations to Self-Determination.* New York: International Publishers, 1970.

Lenin, Vladimir. *Women and Society.* New York: International Publishers, 1970.

Lukes, Steven. "Five Fables about Human Rights." In *On Human Rights: Oxford Amnesty Lectures,* edited by Stephen Shute. ©1993 by Basic Books. Reprinted by permission of BasicBooks, a member of Perseus Books, LLC.

Luxemburg, Rosa. "The Junius Pamphlet." In *Rosa Luxemburg Speaks,* edited with an introduction by Mary-Alice Waters. New York: Pathfinder Press, 1970.

Manu. *The Laws of Manu,* translated with an introduction and notes by Wendy Doniger with Brian K. Smith. London: Penguin Classics, 1991. Copyright © Wendy Doniger and Brian K. Smith, 1991.

Maritain, Jacques, "Introduction," from *Human Rights: Comments and Interpretations* edited by UNESCO. Copyright by Columbia University Press. Reprinted by permission of the publisher.

Marx, Karl. *The Class Struggles in France.* In *Karl Marx and Frederick Engels' Collected Works* ©1978. Reprinted by the permission of International Publishers.

———. *The Communist Manifesto.* In *Birth of the Communist Manifesto,* edited by Dirk J. Struik. New York: International Publishers, 1971. Reprinted by the permission of International Publishers.

———. *Critique of the Gotha Program.* New York: International Publishers, 1938. Reprinted by the permission of International Publishers.

———. "The Inaugural Address." In *Karl Marx and Frederick Engels' Collected Works* vol. 20, New York: International Publishers, 1984. Reprinted by the permission of International Publishers.

———. "The Jewish Question." In *Karl Marx and Frederick Engels' Collected Works* vol. 3, New York: International Publishers, 1975. Reprinted by the permission of International Publishers.

———. "Letter to Abraham Lincoln on the Abolition of Slavery." In *Dynamics of Social Change: A Reader in Marxist Social Science*, edited by H. Selsam, D. Goldway, and H. Martel. New York: International Publishers. Reprinted by the permission of International Publishers.

———. "The Possibility of a Non-Violent Revolution." In *Collected Works* vol. 23, New York: International Publishers, 1984. Reprinted by the permission of International Publishers.

———. Selections in *Karl Marx and Frederick Engels' Collected Works* vols. 6, 20-21 New York: International Publishers, 1976, 1985. Reprinted by the permission of International Publishers.

———. "Universal Suffrage." *Karl Marx Selected Writings*, edited by David McLellan. Oxford: Oxford UP, 1977. Reprinted by the permission of International Publishers.

Mencius. *Mencius*, translated by D.C. Lau. London: Penguin Classics, 1970. Copyright © D.C. Lau, 1970. Reprinted by permission of Penguin Books Ltd.

Minh, Ho Chi. "Declaration of Independence of the Democratic Republic of Vietnam." In *Ho Chi Minh On Revolution: Selected Writings, 1920-66.* Edited and with an introduction by Bernard Fall. New York: Frederick A. Praeger, 1967. Reprinted by the permission of Dorothy Fall.

Muzattar, Chandra. Excerpt from "From Human Rights to Human Dignity." In *Debating Human Rights: Critical Essays from the United States and Asia*, edited by Peter Van Ness. Routledge: London, 1999. Reprinted by permission of the author.

New English Bible. © Oxford University Press and Cambridge University Press, Cambridge, UK 1961, 1970.

Nkrumah, Kwame. Speech on Decolonization at the United Nations. In *I Speak Freedom.* New York: Frederick A. Praeger, 1961.

Nussbaum, Martha. "Women and Cultural Universals." In *Sex and Social Justice.* Oxford: Oxford University Press: 1999. Reprinted by permission of Oxford University Press.

Owen, Robert. "An Address to the Inhabitants of Lanark." In *Socialist Thought: A Documentary History, Revised Edition.* Edited by Albert Fried and Ronald Sanders. New York: Columbia University Press, 1992.

Plato. *The Republic*, translated by Benjamin Jowett ©1942. Reprinted by permission of Modern Library, a division of Random House.

———. *The Symposium*, translated with an introduction and notes by Christopher Gill. London: Penguin Classics, 1991. Copyright © Christopher Gill, 1999. Reprinted by permission of Penguin Classics, Ltd.

Posner, Richard. "Torture, Terrorism and Interrogation," from *Torture: A Collection*, ed. Sanford Levinson, 2004. Reprinted by permission of Oxford University Press, Inc.

Power, Samantha. "Raising the Cost of Genocide." *Dissent*, Spring 2002. Reprinted by permission of Foundation for the Study of Independent Social Ideas.

Proudhon, Pierre-Joseph. *What is Property? An Inquiry Into the Principle of Right and Government*, translated by Benjamin R. Tucker. New York: Humboldt Library of Science, 1902 ©1994 by Cambridge University Press.

Proudhon, Pierre-Joseph. *The Principle of Federalism*, translated by Richard Vernon ©1979. Reprinted by permission of University of Toronto Press.

Robespierre, Maximilien de. Excerpts from *Robespierre*, edited by George Rude, reprinted by the permission of Simon & Schuster Adult Publishing Group. Copyright © 1967 by Prentice-Hall, Inc.; copyright renewed © 1995 by George Rude.

Rorty, Richard. "Human Rights, Rationality and Sentimentality." *On Human Rights: Oxford Amnesty Lectures*, edited by Stephen Shute ©1993 by Basic Books. Reprinted by permission of BasicBooks, a member of Perseus Books, LLC.

Rousseau, Jean-Jacques. *The Government of Poland*, translated by Willmoore Kendall. Cambridge, MA: Hackett, 1985. Excerpts from pp. 68-70. Reprinted by permission of Hackett Publishing Company, Inc. All rights reserved.

———. Excerpt from "Geneva Manuscript." In *Social Contract, Discourse on the Virtue Most Necessary for a Hero, Political Fragments, and Geneva Manuscript*, edited by Roger D. Masters and Christopher Kelly.

© 1994 by the Trustees of Dartmouth College. Reprinted by permission of University Press of New England, Hanover NH.

————."The State of War and Fragments on War": Extracts taken from *The Theory of International Relations: Selected Texts from Gentili to Trietschke* by Forsyth, Keens-Soper, and Savigear; reproduced by kind permission of Unwin Hyman Limited. Copyright © Unwin Hyman Limited, London, 1970.

Saint Augustine. *City of God*, translated by Marcus Dods. New York: Modern Library, 1994.

Sen, Amartya. *Development as Freedom*. New York: Knopf, 1999. Excerpts from pp.35-41 and 301-302. Reprinted by permission of author.

Stychin, Carl F. "Same-Sexualities and the Globalization of Human Rights Discourses." *McGill Law Journal*, 49(2004): 951. Reprinted by permission of *McGill Law Journal*.

Sassen, Saskia. "Women's Burden: Counter-Geographies of Globalization and the Feminization of Survival." *Journal of International Relations*, 53.2 (Spring 2000). Reprinted courtesy of *The Journal of International Affairs*.

Tilly, Charles, "Globalization Threatens Labor's Rights" in *International Labor and Working-Class History*, 1995. No. 47, Spring 1995, pp. 1-23. Reprinted by the permission of Cambridge University Press.

Trotsky, Leon. *Their Morals and Ours*. ©1969, 1973 by Pathfinder Press. Reprinted by permission of the publisher.

Zetkin, Clara. Selection from *The Socialist Register 1976*. Edited by Ralph Miliband and John Saville. London: The Merlin Press, 1976. Reprinted by permission of the publisher.

INDEX